THE OFFICIAL® PRICE GUIDE TO
BOTTLES

D1417803

THE OFFICIAL® PRICE GUIDE TO

BOTTLES

TWELFTH EDITION

JIM MEGURA

HOUSE OF COLLECTIBLES

The Ballantine Publishing Group • New York

Copyright © 1998 by Jim Megura

 This is a registered trademark of Random House, Inc.

All rights reserved under International and Pan-American Copyright Conventions.

Published by: House of Collectibles
The Ballantine Publishing Group
201 East 50th Street
New York, New York 10022

Distributed by The Ballantine Publishing Group, a division of Random House, Inc., New York, and simultaneously in Canada by Random House of Canada Limited, Toronto.

Text design by Holly Johnson
Cover design by Kristine V. Mills-Noble
Cover photo © George Kerrigan

Manufactured in the United States of America

ISSN: 0747-8747

ISBN: 0-676-60009-3

Twelfth Edition: January 1998

10 9 8 7 6 5 4 3 2 1

This book is dedicated to my late mother, Julia Bukoch Megura, who instilled in me an interest in antiques; to Nathanial James Megura, who at an early age has already caught the collecting bug; and to my wife, Lynda, for supporting me through all those late nights of writing and the 5:00 A.M. alarms to go bottle digging.

CONTENTS

NEW BOTTLES

ACKNOWLEDGMENTS

Sincere thanks are given to those who provided help, expertise, and support in the writing of this book, including, but not limited to (in alphabetical order):

Duff Allen, Phil Bernard, Stan Block, Phil Cortina, Tom Croley, Jeff Fisher, Glassworks, Julian Gottlieb, Harold Krevolin, Lynda Megura, Tom Megura, Charles Moore Americana, Ken Previtali, Noel Tomas.

INTRODUCTION

ABOUT THIS BOOK

The intention in writing this book was to develop a good, basic reference guide which could be of value to beginning and advanced collectors, as well as those in the antiques field desirous of a better understanding of early bottles and glass. As this is meant to be merely a general reference source, throughout the book the reader will be referred to recommended reference books and articles which will delve much more deeply into specific areas.

Besides being a reference guide, however, this book is also mainly a price guide to bottles, and determining the value of old and new bottles is a difficult undertaking. The various pricing sources available, such as auction results, dealers' price lists, bottle show prices, and nationally advertised prices, often point to major valuation discrepancies. For example, those of you who attend bottle shows would probably agree that it is not unusual to find both very overpriced, as well as bargain-priced, bottles for sale. Also, factors such as economic conditions, the type of bottles that are currently "hot," and supply and demand all play a major role in the daily fluctuations in price. The value estimates contained within this book were determined by observing price trends for a specific bottle at auction, at bottle shows, and in shops, tempered with an average value estimate. For example, just because a bottle sold for $500 at auction does not mean it is worth that amount. Sometimes bargains can be found at auction, so that particular $500 bottle might sell consistently at shows for $800. On the other hand, a bottle selling for $500 at auction might only be worth $300 and may have sold for an inflated price simply because two people really wanted the bottle and bid accordingly. The values in this book are estimates and may or may not be consistent with the fair market value of a bottle today or in the future.

MARKET REVIEW

Blown three-mold has fallen off substantially. Historical flasks have actually dropped off a bit, except for the great rarities, which are at all-time highs. Bitters are doing quite well, again with rare and unusual colored examples doing quite well, and with the middle-market items in the $500–$1000 range also growing in value. Inks are a mixed bag, with the Watt White sale of a few months ago pointing to very strong, almost phenomenal, prices for the rarities, with common, aqua items and teakettles down from a few years ago. Medicines have held their value or increased a bit, with rare and colored examples selling very well, and simply not often available, even at auction. Target balls are doing better than a few years ago, with fire grenades down a bit. Pitkin flasks and inks are much higher. Pickles, fruit jars, and whiskeys are doing better, with sodas unchanged, and with mineral waters off a bit. Pyroglazed dairy bottles are doing very well, with the earlier tin-topped items dropping and hard to sell. Figurals are not doing very well. Blown glass is doing well among the small group of die-hard collectors, but the scarcity and expense of genuine items coupled with the abundance of reproductions is keeping a lot of would-be collectors from venturing into the field. Pressed glass is limping along, with clear items very hard to sell and the colored pieces enjoying popularity. Lacy glass has dropped right off. Marbles have come full circle with the money chasing the 20th-century machine-made and transitional, with sulphides, end of day, and swirls falling off substantially. Modern bottles have dropped dramatically across the board—Are there any new collectors coming into this field?

I am writing this section in March 1997 and some value trends are going the opposite way from five years ago. Maybe there is something to be said about buying the best examples in a category that is not popular, and waiting for it to come back into vogue. Even though the economy is supposedly doing well, what with the stock market at an all-time high, there seems to be an undercurrent of unrest or uncertainty within the average person, or collector, and it is translating into a smaller demand for the low-end bottles. The high end continues to do well, however. Keep in mind the old adage about buying the single five-hundred-dollar piece instead of ten fifty-dollar items; you will have an easier time getting your money out of a good piece than from a bunch of low-end stuff.

What follows is a listing which shows how certain bottles have appreciated, or depreciated, over the years, going back as far as 1945.

Bottle Type	1945	1971	1978	1986	1990	1996
BININGER						
Bininger handled urn	$425			$900	$700–1000	$1250–1650
Bininger's Travelers Guide, ¹/₂ pt., amber	$140				$200–300	$250–325
BITTERS						
Drake's Plantation	$45				$65	$50–70
Fish Bitters, amber	$140		$100		$140–180	$160–230
Fish Bitters, colorless	$380				$500–700	$900–1250
Greeley's, aqua			$950		$1200–1500	$1400–2000
HP Herb Wild Cherry	$140				$250–400	$250–350
Kelly's Old Cabin	$300				$400–600	$1300–1750
Kimball's Jaundice			$210		$250–350	$375–500
National Bitters, amber	$170				$225–325	$350–450
Pineapple-shaped, olive yellow			$600		$2000–3000	$2000–3000
Pocahontas, aqua	$570				$1000–1200	$1500–2000
Simon's Centennial, aqua	$300		$500		$800–1200	$500–625
Suffolk Pig Bitters			$400		$400–600	$650–825
BLOWN THREE-MOLD DECANTERS						
GII-6, light green	$85				$4000–6000	$3000–4500
GIII-2, olive green	$60				$5000–8000	$1500–2500
GIII-5, colorless	$35			$130	$150–225	$125–185
GIII-16, olive amber			$200	$210	$450–550	$350–425
GV-8, colorless	$55				$300–450	$150–250
COLOGNE						
Wickered demijohn figural, aqua	$10				$20–30	$20–30
Monument, black, 12″	$50				$800–1200	$750–1150
FIGURAL						
Atterbury Duck, milk glass				$220	$300–400	$250–350
John Bull, amber	$85			$170	$200–250	$195–245
Kummel Bear, black	$25				$40–60	$25–35
Eye opener, milk glass	$45				$200–275	$150–175
Pretzel, ceramic	$7				$40–60	$40–60

Bottle Type	1945	1971	1978	1986	1990	1996
FIRE GRENADE						
Harden's, cobalt				$160	$200–250	$175–245
FLASKS						
GI-14, aqua				$150	$125–175	$130–180
GI-16, aqua		$70			$100–150	$130–190
GI-17, aqua	$12				$50–75	$55–75
GI-28, pale blue green				$150	$400–550	$500–625
GI-34, olive amber				$180	$125–175	$135–185
GI-35, cobalt				$5100	$4000–5500	$4000–5000
GI-109, light green	$50				$1200–1500	$1000–1350
GI-117, aqua				$250	$300–500	$350–440
GII-24, sapphire blue	$90				$1800–2600	$2000–2400
GIII-16, deep aqua				$180	$125–150	$150–180
GV-5, olive green				$135	$150–250	$190–225
GV-9, olive amber				$130	$150–250	$160–190
GV-8, olive amber		$190			$150–250	$140–190
GII-60, light amber		$500			$800–1200	$800–1200
GVIII-2, green		$325			$300–500	$375–450
GX-25, olive amber	$385				$15,000+	$40,000+
GVII-3, amber		$130			$800–1200	$1200–1800
FOOD						
Peppersauce, ridged sides, aqua		$10			$15–25	$15–25
FRUIT JARS						
Belle, qt., aqua				$500	$400–475	$750–1000
Moore's Patent, qt., aqua		$20			$70–90	$70–85
INK						
Farley's, olive amber, 1³/₄″				$235	$300–350	$600–900
Blown three-mold, green			$70		$125–175	$125–185
Cabin-shaped, colorless			$110		$350–400	$300–450
LABEL-UNDER-GLASS						
Flask, woman's portrait, ¹/₂ pt.		$5			$250–400	$300–450
MEDICINE						
Clemen's Indian Tonic, labeled, pontiled				$310	$250–350	$200–300
Schenck's Pulmonic Balsam		$15			$10–20	$10–15
Jelly of Pomegranate, pontiled		$110			$80–120	$60–90

Bottle Type	1945	1971	1978	1986	1990	1996
MINERAL WATER						
Clark & White, emerald green		$25			$60–90	$60–90
Syracuse Springs, yellow amber				$40	$100–150	$200–300
Avon, qt., red amber				$260	$300–400	$300–500
PICKLE						
Cathedral, aqua, pontiled		$45			$200–300	$125–175
WHISKEY						
Star Whiskey, handled, amber, pontiled	$210				$200–300	$350–500
Casper's, cobalt				$230	$250–350	$375–475

HISTORY OF BOTTLES

It is unclear just when glass was first made and used, but it *is* known that glass has been around for at least the last 5000 years. The earliest known glass vessels were made by the core form method, whereby a molten string of glass was wrapped around and around a clay body which resembled the shape of the vessel which the craftsman meant to make from glass. Once the entire object was coated with glass, it was cooled, or annealed, which is a gradual cooling process taking 12 or more hours. The clay was then chipped out and a glass bottle was born. Early glassmakers also used molds into which they poured molten glass.

Around the 1st century B.C. the blow pipe was invented. The blow pipe is a long hollow metal rod, the tip of which is dipped into molten glass. The glass blower then blows into the rod and is able to manipulate the molten glass into any number of desired forms. Though the basic glass recipe of sand and wood ash will generally result in a greenish-colored glass (though the actual coloring is based on the minerals in the sand used), man discovered early on how to use various substances, mainly metallic oxides, in order to make an endless and varied range of colors.

The first attempt to make glass in America was believed to have been at the Jamestown settlement in Virginia in 1608, and it is interesting to note that the main purpose of the glasshouse was not to supply the early American settlers with bottles, window glass or drinking vessels. Rather, the great majority of any glass produced at the Jamestown settlement was intended to be shipped back to England, where there were virtually no forests left to fuel the glasshouse furnaces and to supply the ash for the glass mixture. As far as is known, the Jamestown glass-blowing venture was a total misadventure, and it is doubtful that any glass was ever made there. Later in the 17th century, several glasshouses were started in America to partially satisfy the colonists' need for bottles and window glass. Glasshouses were erected in Salem, Massachusetts, New York City, and Philadelphia, Pennsylvania. Although it is unclear what products were produced at these houses, the fact that a few were in existence for several decades points to their prosperity.

The first truly successful American glasshouse was started in 1739 in southern New Jersey by Caspar Wistar, a Philadelphia brass button manufacturer who had emigrated from Germany. It is known that the main commercial output of his glasshouse was window glass and bottles. The next major glass enterprise was formed by Henry William Stiegel, who operated several glasshouses out of the Manheim, Pennsylvania, area from 1763 to 1774. More is known about the Stiegel line of products than of all previous American glass enterprises combined, and two particular pattern flasks, the diamond daisy and the daisy hexagon, can be attributed exclusively to Stiegel. Pattern molds, which were used to a very limited degree in earlier American glasshouses, were widely used in the Stiegel enterprise.

During the late 18th century, American glassmakers attempted to take full advantage of the strong anti-British sentiments prevalent at the time. Advertisements were taken in local newspapers attempting to convince Americans to buy American-made products, and these ads touted the fact that domestic wares were of the same quality and style as imported wares. Because the vast majority of American glasshouses attempted to copy imported tableware until the 19th century, it is generally very difficult, if not impossible, to specifically attribute any early glasswork as being made in America.

Despite the early attempts to establish glass blowing in America, the output of glass factories at that time was minimal at best, and right up through the first quarter of the 19th century the vast majority of all glass used in America was imported. The early American government was greatly in favor of developing the American glass industry, however, and a lottery system was developed to help finance prospective glass factories. In the lottery, citizens could purchase "lottery tickets," the proceeds of which were used to finance the glassworks. Also, it was common practice in Colonial days for the government to grant a license to a specific glassworks which restricted other enterprising glasshouses from opening and competing in the same geographical area. As a result of this, more and more glassworks began to appear late in the 18th and early 19th centuries.

The locations of the glasshouses were generally based on several factors. These included the presence of a sufficient supply of raw materials such as sand and wood, the possibility of securing competent glass blowers, and close proximity to thoroughfares or navigable rivers to transport raw materials and finished products to the major markets in Boston, Philadelphia, and New York City.

The Pitkin Glassworks of East Hartford, Connecticut, was opened in 1783 and has the distinction of probably being the first American glasshouse to have produced historical flasks. Around 1810, Mr. J. P. Foster became manager of the Pitkin Glassworks, and it is believed that those flasks bearing the initials "JPF" were indeed made at the Pitkin Glassworks. Pitkin flasks were also named for the Pitkin Glassworks, since for many years it was believed that they were the exclusive products of the Pitkin Glassworks. However, it is now believed that no Pitkin-type flasks were ever produced there. In addition to producing all types of bottles and early glassware, the Pitkin Glassworks also was known to have produced window glass in the early days as well as "clock glasses," which is the glass covering a clock face. The Pitkin Glassworks was quite successful until it closed around 1830 due to the cost of wood for fuel. Pitkin's necessity to discontinue operations due to the lack of wood was not uncommon. Other reasons for early glasshouses shutting down were often the loss of skilled glass blowers, who had a tendency to migrate from one glass factory to another, and accidental fires, which leveled many a glasshouse building.

By the early 19th century, the use of bottle molds was becoming more and more widespread, with ribbed-type molds being the most common. In addition, we have seen where some 18th-century glasshouses such as Stiegel used molds extensively, and we also know that the first molded figured flasks were probably made in Connecticut around 1815. Nothing, however, could compare to the skyrocketing usage of molds that started around 1820. Around that time in America, "blown three-mold" products began to appear, which were intricate geometric-type patterns meant to inexpensively copy the fashionable imported Irish and English blown glass which had real cut designs. Though the major output in blown three-mold was decanters, a few rare flasks were patterned as well as a vast array of pitchers, dishes, bowls, and other tableware. Much of this blown three-mold glass was made at the Sandwich Glassworks in Sandwich, Massachusetts, though factories in Connecticut, New Hampshire, and Ohio also played a major role. Blown three-mold began to lose its appeal around 1840, and the advances in fine lacy and patterned pressed glass helped mark its demise.

Also around 1820, historical flasks exploded in popularity, and dozens of glass factories produced literally thousands of these fine flasks in a wide variety of designs and colors. Though America was still dependent on imported glassware, it was soon able to fill its own glass needs with less of a dependence on imported wares, through the domestic production of blown three-mold, figured flasks, spirits, and medicine bottles.

Throughout the 19th century, glasshouses continued to come and go, opening and closing due to changes in demand and technological improvements. In the early 20th century, the invention of the automatic bottle-making machine marked the end of the handblown bottle.

HOW BOTTLES ARE MADE

Glass is basically a mixture of sand and ash, heated to the desired temperature of approximately 1800°–2200° F. Though these two ingredients would ordinarily result in a greenish-colored glass, the minerals present in the sand and the varying proportion of ash to the mixture might result in a range of coloring from almost colorless to a dark green or black glass. There are also a wide assortment of chemicals and metallic oxides which one could use to make artificial colors, which run the entire color spectrum.

Right up until the late 19th and into the 20th century, the vast majority of collectible bottles were blown. This was accomplished by the glass blower "gathering" glass on the tip of his 3- or 4-foot metal blow pipe, which was done by dipping the pipe end into a molten tank of glass. After insuring that the gather was symmetrical, the glass blower would forcibly blow into the hollow blow pipe to expand the molten glass into a variety of shapes. The making of molded bottles involved the same steps, except the glass blower would insert the molten glass into a mold, usually made of metal, and impress the mold shape onto the molten glass by blowing. Once the bottle had been blown, it needed to be removed from the blow pipe in order to finish the lip. On pre-Civil War bottles, this was accomplished through the use of a 3- or 4-foot metal pontil rod, which was dipped into the tank of molten glass and then applied to the bottom of the bottle. The neck of the bottle was then touched with a wet stick, which separated it from the blow pipe. Now the lip could be evened off, or a lip could be attached. The earliest lip treatments were often uneven, since they resulted from the bottle being pontiled and removed from the blow pipe, and then reheated to melt down the jagged areas only. In later years, shears were used to evenly trim the molten lip. The shears were very similar to tin snips available in hardware stores today. In the second quarter of the 19th century, several lipping techniques were developed which allowed the use of a wide range of lip styles.

Around the mid-19th century, the snap case became popular. This was a springlike metal cage which fit around the base of the bottle and held it while the lip was finished. The snap case was used extensively throughout the 19th century and into the 20th, until the invention of the automatic bottle-making machine virtually eliminated the handmade bottle in America.

For most of the 20th century, the art of handblown glass had all but been forgotten in America, except for a few small factories such as Blenko and Clevenger Brothers. Beginning in the 1960s, a revival in the interest of handblown glassware led to the Studio Movement whereby individual glass artisans were able to establish small glass-blowing studios. Today these studios are flourishing, and thousands of glass blowers, plus numerous universities and craft schools, continue to practice the time-honored art of handblown glass. It is strongly recommended that all serious glass and bottle collectors and dealers have a good working knowledge of how glass and bottles are blown, and every attempt should be made to visit a local glass studio or public facility—such as the Corning Museum of Glass in Corning, New York, or Wheaton Village in Millville, New Jersey—in order to watch firsthand how glass is fashioned. I cannot overemphasize the importance of a good working knowledge of glass techniques, as it can prove to be invaluable when watching for fakes and reproductions. Those interested in watching a local glass blower might find one by contacting a local crafts gallery or by attending one of the many nationwide crafts shows.

STARTING A COLLECTION

If one were to interview each and every bottle collector and inquire as to why they became interested in the hobby, one might be surprised at the wide range of responses. One of the main reasons would be that bottle collecting is such a social hobby, where groups of friends or relatives quite naturally spread their enthusiasm for collecting to everyone around them. Many of us began our pursuit of bottles as teenagers, or perhaps even children, when in our adventures in the woods we stumbled upon an old dump. No matter how we began in the hobby, however, there are many things which continue to attract us throughout the years. Some are drawn to the historic aspect, and wonder what life may have been like 150 years ago when a given bottle may have been made. And how many of us have fantasized over which famous personality may have drank from our bottle in years past? The wide range of beautiful colors and shapes also attracts many, and the economic and investment aspects surely attract some.

The choice of which type of bottles to collect is also influenced by a wide range of factors. Personal finances are an important consideration, since certain areas of bottle collecting, such as flasks, can be quite expensive. The amount of space for display and storage can also be an important consideration, as can the amount of free time that an individual has to pursue the hobby. Some pursue a given type of bottle because it relates to their profession, such as a barber collecting hair bottles, whereas others search for the bottles that have their last name on them. No matter how the choices are made, the fact is that most collectors eventually tend to specialize in a given field of bottle collecting. Specialization has its advantages over the general collecting of bottles since the specialist, who may well be an expert in his given area of bottle collecting, is usually more knowledgeable on market trends and pricing in his given area, and is thus more likely to find a bargain. The general bottle collector has a much wider range of knowledge of many different bottle categories, which is advantageous since he may be able to spot a rare or underpriced bottle that a specialist may pass by. The general bottle collector, however, may not know a rarity or its price range in a specialized field.

Regardless of where your interests lie, a good collection in almost any bottle category can be easily started with a minimum investment. Many bottle collectors are avid bottle diggers, and it is quite common for a digger to find a rare bottle which may not be in his area of collecting, which opens up the possibilities of selling the item or trading it to someone who may have something that he wants for his collection.

There are several basic guidelines which any beginning collector should seriously consider. Join a local bottle club where you will meet others with similar interests and have the opportunity to handle more and more bottles. If you do not know where your local bottle club is, consult Appendix B at the end of this book and contact the nearest one in your area and inquire about local club activities. In order to become familiar with bottle shapes, colors, rarity, and reproductions, all collectors should try to handle as much glass as they possibly can. Though it is of great help to study the reference books mentioned in this guide and to visit museum collections, there is no substitute for the actual handling of both old and new bottles. By handling the items, one will begin to get a feel for the weight and texture of glass, as well as gain a better understanding of what ordinary exterior wear on a bottle is, as opposed to a mint bottle with no exterior wear or a heavily worn bottle. Again, I must emphasize that when going to bottle shows, just walking up and down the aisles and looking at the bottles is not enough; ask the dealers questions and get their permission to handle the glass! The collector should attempt to learn as much as he possibly can about bottles in general or about his field of specialization. This will usually require studying many of the specialized glass books, many of which are listed in this book, as well as joining one of the speciality clubs operating throughout the country.

Collect what you like, and try to be as knowledgeable in your area as you can be. *Try to obtain the finest possible examples* of a given bottle, and remember that chipped, cracked, and badly stained pieces will always be worth a fraction of the values contained within this book. Consider having one $200 bottle instead of ten $20 bottles. If the time ever comes when you want to sell your bottles, you will have a much easier time of it if they are rare and desirable; the poor examples and common types usually are much more difficult to sell. The flea markets, group shops and, to a lesser extent, the bottle shows, are loaded with low-end and common bottles, but remember that mixed in with the junk might be a few treasures.

DETERMINING VALUES

As previously discussed, there are many factors which determine the value of any given bottle. The laws of supply and demand come fully into play when a highly sought-after bottle is pursued by many collectors, with a corresponding increase in sales price. Factors such as economic conditions, the number of known bottles in a given color or form, and the "what's in and what's out" syndrome, among other things, all have an effect. No matter what the area of bottle specialization, collectors of both old and new bottles must be able to spot the rarities, and there are certain characteristics that the astute collector should note on his mental checklist when looking at a bottle. Some of these characteristics are:

UNUSUAL COLOR
In the area of old bottles, color is the major ingredient in determining rarity and price. Generally speaking, aqua and colorless bottles are the most common and are thus less pursued and lower in price; however, there are many categories of bottles where aqua and colorless are rarities, and the knowledgeable collector would realize that the National Bitters bottle in the shape of an ear of corn is a $400 bottle in amber, whereas in aqua it is priced at around $2500 to $3500. The serious collector must become familiar with the rare colors by studying the auction catalogs, going to bottle shows, and reading the speciality reference books.

UNUSUAL SIZE
Bottles come in a wide assortment of sizes, from as small as 1 inch to well over 5 gallons. Generally speaking, the extremities in size, both large and small, are generally rarer than the "normal size" of a given bottle. The collector must become familiar with what is "normal" for a given bottle. Be on the lookout for those rare miniature blown bottles, such as chestnuts, globulars, and early spirits bottles.

UNUSUAL METHOD OF MANUFACTURE
Most bottles made after the Civil War have smooth bases since they were

made by the use of a snap case. The snap case fit over the bottle while the lip was being finished. This is in contrast to a rough pontil, which is a jagged scar on the bottom of a bottle and is generally found on pre-Civil War bottles; it involved the use of a pontil rod with a bit of glass on the end which was attached to the base of the bottle so that the lip could be finished. Be on the lookout for those common bottles which have a rough pontil. For example, the Drake's Plantation, cabin-shaped Bitters bottle is quite common with a smooth base; however, a variant with the rough pontil scar is an extreme rarity. The collector should also become familiar with the common lip treatments used for bottles. For example, the average Pitkin-type flask exhibits a straight sheared lip. However, a few very rare examples show a flaring lip. Also, many flasks were made with a wide variety of lip treatments, and collectors should become familiar as to which ones are the rarer variants.

STRIATIONS

Striations are strands of color running through a bottle which are a different shading than the bottle itself. For example, an aqua bottle may have stringlike lines of amber or dark green running through it, which can often greatly enhance the collectivity and rarity of a given bottle.

BUBBLES

In the natural melting process of making glass, the glass goes through what is called a "fining out" process. This is where air bubbles, trapped between the layers of raw materials, slowly rise through the viscous glass mixture to the surface, where they pop. If a tank of glass is given adequate time at the proper temperature, the fining out will result in glass which is relatively free of bubbles. However, some batches were never given the opportunity to fine out, thus resulting in bottles that are full of tiny bubbles or seeds. Sometimes the presence of very seedy glass can either make the bottle more attractive or reduce its desirability.

LABELS AND ORIGINAL CONTENTS

Many collectors pursue those bottles which have their original labels, boxes, and contents. Obviously, old bottles such as these are rare and bring a premium. The collector should be on the lookout for labeled bottles which do not have the original label or have reproduction labels.

HISTORIC IMPORT

Bottles which were once part of a famous collection have generally commanded a premium, and for such bottles it is not uncommon for a relatively common item to sell for considerably more than its fair market value. Collections put together by such bottle and glass experts as Charles Gardner and George McKearin, among others, have historically brought strong prices. Usually when bottles from a noted collection are sold, they have some type of identification to help authenticate which collection they came from.

QUANTITY KNOWN

The quantity of bottles of a given type on the market can dramatically impact the fair market value of a given bottle. For example, the so-called "Dutch Squat" spirits bottle, manufactured in the early 18th century, was at one point considered to be quite rare and was valued at around $200. In the past several years, literally thousands of these bottles have been discovered in the freshwater lakes and bays of South America where they had been imported in the 18th century. The recovery of massive quantities of these bottles by divers has resulted in a flooding of the market, thus driving the average price down on these to $50–100 each. Another example was when a major medicine bottle collection was sold several years ago, which negatively impacted the values of many other pontiled medicines which, up to that point, had been considered very rare.

FAKES AND REPRODUCTIONS

A reproduction is a copy of an earlier style which is sold and advertised as a reproduction. Many museums sell reproduction bottles and glassware, since certain styles, popular in the 18th and 19th centuries, appear to be timeless in their form and beauty. Fakes, on the other hand, are attempts by unscrupulous individuals to fool and deceive. It is recommended that all collectors become familiar with fakes and reproductions, and there are several books on the market that cover this subject such as *American Bottles and Flasks and Their Ancestry* by McKearin and Wilson, *Antique Fakes and Reproductions* by Ruth Webb Lee, and *Fake, Fraud or Genuine* by Kaye, just to mention a few. The experienced collector should have minimal problems in identifying fake- and reproduction-mold blown bottles, but the early pattern-molded pieces and free-blown items can be quite deceiving. The collector should always deal with reputable dealers and auction houses who are willing to stand behind what they sell.

CONTENTS

As mentioned earlier, many collectors seek bottles which contain the original labels and contents. However, all collectors should be *extremely careful* of the contents of early bottles, such as poisons, fire grenades, medicines, chemical bottles, etc., since the contents may still be toxic, perhaps even fatal. It is very important that bottles with contents be kept out of reach of children, and that proper measures be taken to prevent the bottles from falling over, since the contents may leak through the corks.

WEAR, STAINS, CHIPS AND CRACKS

The closer a bottle is to mint condition—that is, relatively free of wear, chips, cracks or stains—the greater the value. Considerable damage on any piece can have a major impact on its value, and value reductions of 50%–70% or more are not uncommon. Even if a piece is free of chips, cracks or stains, heavy exterior wear is a detriment. Collectors must handle enough glass to know what is ordinary wear and what is heavy wear. The collector should be very careful to look for "potstones"; these are small stones, usually about $1/8$–$1/4$ inch in diameter, that are generally white in color and are frequently found embedded in a bottle. It is not unusual for tiny cracks to radiate from the potstone, which can have a major impact on the collectibility of the bottle.

HOW DO YOU TELL IF YOUR BOTTLE IS OLD?

Determining the age of a bottle, and knowing how to spot a fake or reproduction, is a necessity for those willing to invest time and money on a bottle collection. A bottle or piece of glass that has been used for many years, or one which has been buried in the ground for a long time, develops certain wear patterns on the high points of the bottle. Look for wear on the bottom and on the sides. Legitimate wear will usually appear very fine and feel almost silky smooth when a fingernail is rubbed against it. Artificially induced wear often feels rough, with large uneven scratches often extending beyond those areas which would have actually touched the surface, table, or ground. The most reliable wear indicator is usually the bottom of the bottle. If you are suspicious of the wear pattern, place the standing bottle on a sheet of paper and, with a sharp pencil, trace the outline of the base, and then see where the base touches the surface. If the wear pattern on the base matches the outline that shows where the base actually touches the table, then you are more comfortable as to the bottle being genuine.

Often, scratches on the sides, small chips or flakes on the lip, and a light inner haze may lend support to the bottle's age. But the astute collector realizes that many things can be done to make a bottle look old. As in everything else in life, nothing can compensate for hands-on experience and study. Go to a bottle club or show and *handle* as much glass as possible. Study the books that can tell you which items have been reproduced. Buying from reliable dealers who stand behind their merchandise is also a good idea.

DIGGING FOR BOTTLES

There are many ways to hunt for bottles, and one favorite way is through digging. For both the beginning and advanced collector, digging for bottles is both an exciting and economical way to add to any collection. Prospecting for old bottles has become one of the favorite pastimes for collectors, and there is certainly no shortage of bottles waiting to be uncovered by the enterprising explorer. Though the thrill of finding a rare and valuable bottle is paramount in every bottle collector's dreams, exploring for the bottles is half the fun. It's like a treasure hunt! One of the great things about digging for bottles is that it allows the young collector, who may be unable to afford the more valuable bottles, to prospect for his own bottles and build a stock from which he can sell and trade for better bottles. Though some American cities had refuse removal services as far back as the 18th century, most early American families handled their refuse themselves. Oftentimes the garbage was thrown over a stone wall at the back end of the property or dumped into the privy hole in the outhouse. Other times trash was thrown into the ocean or down a river bank. All of these places are potential bonanzas for bottle collectors, and one often has to research to find which areas of which cities were thriving in the 18th and 19th centuries.

Before we go any further in prospecting for bottles, however, it is of paramount importance that we discuss some of the safety hazards associated with bottle digging. Unless you are one of the lucky people who discovers a dump in their own backyard, odds are you will be looking for bottles on someone else's private property. Always get permission to dig for bottles on someone's property. Since you may find yourself prospecting in the woods, be aware of bees, poison ivy, ticks, snakes, barbed wire fences, dogs, etc., and it might not hurt to have a good supply of Band-Aids and hydrogen peroxide on hand. As far as the actual digging goes, it is highly recommended that you never do it alone, since cave-ins are not uncommon. Twenty-five years ago a cousin of mine returned to an excavated foundation, which we had together explored the day before, to dig for bottles on his own. During his tunneling a large rock fell free and knocked him unconscious. This can happen to you!

WHERE TO DIG

Though taking a leisurely walk in the woods in search of a bottle dump on a summer's day is pleasurable even if nothing is found, there are ways in which the bottle archeologist can improve his chances for success. As mentioned earlier, behind stone walls in back of old houses are often good places to look, and some of the best prospects, if you are able to locate them, are where old outhouses or privys stood.

The problems with outhouse digging are numerous, since they are probably no longer standing and are difficult to locate. The very early privys had stone linings; in the 19th century wood liners were used. The lucky prospector may find the privy lining visible at ground level, though this is doubtful. Occasionally one may be able to find the privy location through an unexpected clump of small trees or brush, since vegetation may be drawn to the well-fertilized grounds. Finding the outhouse location at a rural or country home is very difficult, whereas 19th-century urban home locations may be more accessible. Often in large cities very specific property plans were drawn up which specifically stated where on the property an outhouse must be situated. Once you have a guestimate as to where the outhouse may have been, one method of finding it is by the use of a "probe." This is a long narrow metal rod which, when pushed into the earth, will often meet very little resistance when pushed into a privy location, as opposed to being pushed into the rocky soil which surrounds it.

Now that you have found your outhouse, it is probably located in the middle of the lawn of the backyard of the house. Surprisingly, it is not uncommon for homeowners to allow bottle diggers access to their yards, and arrangements can be made with homeowners to split up the bottles when found. When digging up the lawn, you can use a garden tool to cut an even perimeter in the lawn area which you expect to excavate, and then gently roll up the grass, removing it in small squares which should be put on a plastic sheet alongside the hole. After the excavation is completed, you will often need to use some type of filler in order to even out the ground. Before you go digging up a stranger's lawn, however, it is recommended that you experiment in your own backyard to learn the methods of grass removal and transplantation. It is not uncommon to dig down six or eight or more feet in a privy, and you must be *extremely* cautious to the possibility of a cave-in. This cave-in possibility also exists when digging at street excavations and new house foundations. Another reason not to go digging alone!

Looking for bottles behind walls in the woods is often difficult because the bottles you are seeking were thrown there 100 or 200 years ago, and they are ordinarily covered with leaves and years of sediment. Often, however, the same dumping area was used for a long period of time, and it is often possible to discover an early dump through finding early 20th-century cans and bottles on the surface, and then just digging deeper.

Construction excavations are a great place to look for bottles. Once again, getting permission is imperative. Street and sewer excavations are other good sites for bottle hunters, and a few years back a bottle was found in a Massachusetts street excavation which sold for $9000. Probably one of the largest untapped sources of bottles is in our streams, lakes, and oceans. Obviously, this presents major problems in locating the bottles, but river banks and stream beds continue to be major sources of bottle finds for many prospectors.

Apart from actually digging for bottles, many good finds can be also found in attics, basements, crawl spaces, and barns. Over the years I have heard many stories of people finding bottles and early glass dating to the early 19th century, with original contents, in the corners of attics in old homes. Those of you in the construction business should also be on the lookout for early American bottles and antiques which may have been placed inside walls, which are often uncovered during renovations.

DIGGING TOOLS

There are several tools which the bottle hunter should consider bringing. A shovel will be required, and for all tall bottle collectors out there, such as myself, be sure the shovel has a long handle, which will do wonders for your back. A pitchfork is good in rocky areas, and a thin metal probe, which can be purchased at bottle shows or through bottle magazines, can often come in handy when searching for privys or in swamps. A clam rake or potato rake is excellent for scratching through the ground. As for small hand tools, small scratchers and shovels are good, and some people prefer trowels, which is a favorite tool of professional archeologists. Extreme caution should be taken, however, to dig a site gently so as not to break any of the precious bottles that may lie underneath. (Many of us have put a pitchfork through a rare medicine or historical flask over the years.) Also, work boots, gloves, and eye protection, along with durable clothing, are recommended. Make sure to bring a heavy-duty canvas or other bag, along with newspaper, to wrap your newfound treasures!

BUYING, SELLING, AND TRADING

Though many bottles are dug up or found, most of the items in any collection are acquired through buying or trading. Since many bottle collectors tend to specialize in a given type of bottle, a rare bottle found in a dump site may be of little interest except for its potential monetary or trade value.

There are many places to buy and trade bottles, the largest being bottle shows and clubs. Virtually every weekend of the year, bottle shows and club meetings take place where all sorts of dealings are made. Those actively involved in the bottle business know who collects what, and often the major collector will be given a phone call before a given bottle is made available to the general public. Often at bottle shows some of the best merchandise is not to be found on the tables, but rather under the tables, where dealers and collectors attempt to make their own private sales and trades. Though the bottle shows will display the wares of many dealers to thousands of collectors, it is often difficult to find bargain merchandise. More people are knowledgeable as to bottle rarity and value now than at any other time, and one may have to look for bargains in unusual areas of bottle collecting, where there may be less interest and subsequently less knowledgeable dealers and collectors. Also, it is becoming harder and harder to find top-quality bottles for sale at bottle shows, since the rarer bottles are being sold more and more frequently through the bottle auction houses, where many believe higher prices can be obtained than would be received at a bottle show. Probably the best way to find out about bottle shows is to subscribe to the *Antique Bottle and Glass Collector* monthly magazine, which lists bottle shows for the entire country. To get this magazine call (215) 679-5849.

Other sources of buying bottles are antique shops, flea markets, antique shows, pawn shops, Salvation Army thrift shops, and tag sales. In many instances, the astute collector may be able to find an incredible bargain since he is often probably purchasing the bottle from someone who knows nothing about bottle value.

Bottles are also available through nationwide bottle magazines and specialty collectors' newsletters, as well as through local newspapers and antiques publi-

22

cations. Of course, when one deals through the mail it is difficult to be certain of what one is receiving. Care should be taken that the bottles are properly wrapped and insured, and a seven- or ten-day return privilege should always be asked for.

Bottle and early glass auction houses have increased in number over the last ten years and represent probably the major methods of disposing of, and acquiring, major bottles for a collection. Several of the auction houses have on-site auctions whereby prospective buyers can actively bid while the piece is on the block; mail bids and phone bids are also encouraged. Other auction houses are of the absentee type, whereby buyers bid over the phone and through the mail. All of the auction houses publish impressive sale catalogs, which generally cost $10 to $20 each. These are filled with descriptive information, including bottle condition, along with photographs. The catalogs themselves are important reference tools, and serious collectors should obtain them whenever possible. The auction houses charge a commission to sell the bottles, which generally ranges from 10% to 20% of the gross selling price; in addition, a buyer's premium is often added to the sales price, which is usually a 10% charge added onto the purchase price and assessed against the successful bidder.

Should you decide to sell or purchase bottles through auction, you may wish to contact one or all of the following:

OLD
Glass Works Auctions
P.O. Box 187
East Greenville, PA 18041
(215) 679-5849

BLOWN AND PRESSED GLASS
Skinners Inc.
Rt. 117
Bolton, MA 01740
(508) 779-6241

Norman Heckler
Bradford Corner Road
Woodstock Valley, CT 06282
(203) 974-1634

MARBLES, PAPERWEIGHTS
Blocks Box
P.O. Box 51
Trumbull, CT 06611
(203) 261-0057

MODERN
Homestead Collectibles
P.O. Box 173
Mill Hall, PA 17751–0173
(717) 726-3597

BOTTLE CARE

Compared to many other types of collector items, bottles require very little care and maintenance. Once the hobbiest has learned to display his bottles properly and safely, he will have few maintenance problems.

When a freshly dug bottle has been brought in from the field, the surface condition is likely to be so miserable that it offers very little encouragement of ever being successfully cleaned. However, most bottles will clean up well with a bit of patience and hard work. The first step is to remove loose surface particles (sand, small stones, etc.) with a soft, bristled brush. Care should be taken not to exert any pressure while removing loose debris as it may scratch the bottle. Surface dirt can be removed by soaking the bottle, but caution should be exercised to avoid any scratching. To soften and break down the tough impacted grime, the bottle must soak in something stronger than plain water. There are several cleaners which are used to successfully remove any dirt and stains. The combination of ammonia and water is a good cleaner, assuming adequate ventilation is present. Some may wish to use dish detergent, while other collectors use a few tablespoons of bleach in a gallon of lukewarm water. The water should never be too hot nor too cold, as this may shock the bottle and result in breakage. Depending on the amount of dirt and stain on a given bottle, it may require soaking for over a week. In addition, some bottles may be cleaned with steel wool or a stiff brush, but be wary of this method since it may result in scratching the surface.

Quite frequently a collector will purchase a bottle which has an interior stain, which is often difficult to clean. Some collectors use an ammonia solution. Another popular way of cleaning interiors is to fill the bottle with approximately $1/2$ inch of water and add ordinary beach sand; when shaken vigorously, it may help to loosen some of the staining.

In addition to the above-mentioned ways of cleaning, there are professional bottle cleaners who use a variety of methods to rid even the harshest of stains. One of the methods employed by professionals is called the "tumbler," whereby copper pellets, water, and possibly a polishing agent are added to the inside of the bottle. The bottle is then put into a tumbling machine which rapidly vibrates the bottle, causing the copper pellets to scrub the inner bottle. The professional also may use cerium oxide, which is a very fine powder used in glass polishing, to help rid the bottle of any scratches or stains. Still others employ strong chemicals and acids, which actually may eat away the surface of the glass. Exterior stains may also be removed by the use of a buffing wheel, which can often obscure the sharpness of the lettering of a bottle or make an impression slightly fuzzy. Others often oil bottles both inside and out, which will often hide any stains and small scratches. Some of these cleaning methods are used to deceive prospective purchasers into believing that a damaged bottle is in perfect condition. Care should be taken to be aware of any acid or oil polishing, or repairs, as such treatments may actually lower the value of the bottle.

Now that your bottles are clean, you will wish to display them. The chief consideration in display is to prevent breakage while allowing the specimens to be viewed and handled. The collector may wish to keep his bottles in a cabinet, on wall shelving, or distributed at random about the house to provide decorative touches. While certainly appealing, this last approach tends to be riskier. When a collection is not grouped together in one place or one part of the house, it becomes more difficult to guard against an accident. This is especially true if pets or small children are around. When a collection is within a cabinet or on shelves, it is less likely to be broken. What some collectors do is hang a $1/8$-inch sheet of Plexiglas from two hooks along the top of their cabinet, which helps to minimize accidental breakage but still allows easy access to bottles. Almost any type of cabinet is suitable for a bottle collection; the choice will depend on personal taste, room decor, size of the collection, and the cost of the unit. An ordinary bookcase with glass doors or grill work will do if it has adjustable shelves and is not too small, whereas a case with wooden sides will not provide much visibility or light penetration to the inside. However, with very little expense or trouble a lighting fixture can be installed inside. Cabinets with glass sides are ideal for displaying bottles and can often be picked up at antique shops or from used furniture dealers.

No matter how you decide to display your bottle collection, care should be taken to avoid any rapid changes in temperature, which can crack a bottle. Many people display their bottles in windows, but I have heard stories of bottles breaking due to temperature changes evident at a window.

As for the storage of bottles, the collector may wish to obtain empty liquor boxes with cardboard dividers, which, along with each bottle being individually wrapped with newspaper, should provide the necessary protection for long-term storage. Once again, care should be taken to ensure that the bottles are not going to be subject to extreme temperatures, and be careful when moving the boxes, since any floor dampness may weaken the box bottoms.

FAKES, REPRODUCTIONS, AND REPAIRS

As bottle values continue to escalate, often into the thousands of dollars, the importance of being able to spot a fake, reproduction or repaired bottle is paramount. There is a major difference between a fake and a reproduction; the reproduction is a legitimately produced item, meant to copy the timeless beauty of items from the past. Generally, reproductions are marked in some way, such as on the blown three-mold decanters made for the Metropolitan Museum of Art which are engraved "MMA" on or around the pontil mark. A fake, on the other hand, is a copy whose main purpose is to deceive the purchaser into believing it is a genuine article.

The purpose of this section is by no means to provide a master listing of fakes and reproductions, but rather to alert the collector and dealer to certain more commonly seen bottles and to suggest ways to help identify copies. The reader is strongly advised to obtain a copy of *American Bottles and Flasks and Their Ancestry* by McKearin and Wilson, which gives the most detailed information on fakes available anywhere. Some of the reproduction flasks tend to have a pebbly or granularlike surface which is the result of using inferior or plaster molds. Note that there are several genuine flasks that also exhibit this grainy type of surface, and the astute collector must know which flasks were made in that fashion. Sometimes the pontil scars on reproductions are unusual, with unusual indentations in the base of the bottle meant to simulate pontil scars. On bitters and medicines, the collector must watch for an unusual mold seam; the mold seam will come to within 1/4 inch of the lip and stop, and then continue to the lip, but the mold seams are not aligned. I have seen this on a reproduced Suffolk Pig Bitters. Sometimes a copy is discovered because it simply does not "feel right," such as if the glass is too transparent or too light in weight, or there is simply not enough wear on the item.

As mentioned before, both beginning and advanced bottle enthusiasts should attempt to handle as much glass as possible, rather than relying on pictures in books or pieces behind glass showcases in museums. Visit your local bottle dealer, go to bottle shows or club meets, and physically pick up as many bottles as you possibly can to get a feel for what is right and what is not right. Tell the dealer that you are interested in learning about fakes and reproductions, and he may be able to show you some or alert you to a new copy he has just found. A few years ago my bottle club, the Southern Connecticut Antique Bottle Collectors Association, devoted one of its monthly meetings to reproductions, and approximately 50 reproduced items were on display for all to see and handle. Why not do it with your club?

COMMON REPRODUCTIONS AND FAKES

Here is a selective listing of certain categories of bottles that have been faked or reproduced.

BITTERS BOTTLES

Simmons Centennial Bitters: Reproduced in green, blue, and amber. The embossing on the reproduced item is virtually impossible to read, and unlike the original, the copy has a pontil scar.

Suffolk Pig Bitters: This bottle of greenish amber has an unusual mold seam, which is discussed above.

BLOWN BOTTLES

There is a reproduction chestnut flask going around which has a flared lip. Chestnut bottles were never made with a flared lip, and generally have a crude applied string lip. The reproduction is also heavier in weight than the original. The collector should be wary when purchasing any blown bottle, and be aware that it is very easy for a glass blower of today to closely copy an 18th-century bottle form.

BLOWN THREE-MOLD

There have been blown three-mold copies on the market since as far back as the 1920s. Usually the copies are of unusual coloration, such as blue, purple or amber, but numerous clear fakes are also known. An example of a copied pattern is the GIII-5. One of the telltale signs of this copy is that the diamond pattern does not run straight across, but goes up at an angle. Also, there are several blown three-mold items being reproduced for the Museum of Metropolitan Art, similar to McKearin pattern GV-9, which often have the initials "MMA" engraved on the pontil mark.

ENAMELED BOTTLES

Enameled bottles made in the last half-post method in the Germany/Switzerland area in the 18th century are popular, and very good reproductions are made today. Oftentimes the enameling on the modern pieces is much brighter and sharper, and the designs may differ from the earlier pieces. Also, look for lack of wear and be suspicious if an item is of especially bubbly glass. Reproductions of this type often tend to be heavier than the original.

FRUIT JARS

There are both free-blown and patterned fruit jars which have been reproduced. The free-blown jars are often difficult to identify, and collectors should check to see if wear on the item is legitimate or induced, and if the form and color are consistent with an early jar. Many of the reproduced molded jars, such as Mason jars, have a number impressed on the base which will help to identify it as a reproduction. Interested parties should refer to the *Red Book of Fruit Jars* by Creswick for more detailed information on reproduced fruit jars.

INK BOTTLES

There are several funnel-shaped ink bottles which are free-blown and unpatterned, and these are elaborated on in Covill's book on inks. Be wary of any free-blown ink bottles, and check for legitimate wear.

MEDICINE BOTTLES

There are several reproduced medicines on the market, and the collector should watch for unusual mold seams and termination, as mentioned previously for Suffolk Pig Bitters.

NAILSEA-TYPE BOTTLES

These free-blown bottles, which have multicolored loopings, are easily reproduced. Check for legitimate wear and unusual form or colors.

PATTERN-MOLDED BOTTLES

I have seen several midwestern-type globular bottles in amber which are reproductions, and these differ from the originals in that they have flaring lips and do not have the grace and fluidity of the originals. There are some straight-sides, cylindrical jarlike pieces on the market, some having swirled ribs and some unribbed, which are reproductions. These items have folded rims and I have seen them in amber and amethyst. The Stiegel diamond and daisy flask has also been copied, with the distinguishing feature on the copy being six diamonds, whereas the original only has five. Be wary of any ribbed flasks and bottles since many continue to be made in Mexico and are easily confused with the original American pieces. Emil Larsen was a prolific glass blower who worked in the New Jersey area in the early part of this century. He made some beautifully patterned flasks, such as those in a 12-diamond pattern, and the pieces can often be confused with Stiegel by the untrained eye. However, once you have had the opportunity to handle the Larsen pieces, you will notice a slight difference in form and uses of color from the 18th-century pieces.

HISTORICAL FLASKS

Fakes and reproductions among historical flasks are the most numerous and often the most difficult to detect. In the "Historical Flasks" section in this book, I have put an asterisk next to those flasks which are known to be copied. Here I will discuss some of the better copies and how to identify them.

GI-26, Washington—Eagle: This well-reproduced quart flask is similar to the original in most ways except the mold seam goes almost all the way to the top of the lip on the copy.

GI-107A, Jenny Lind—Fislerville: This is a well-made copy and is difficult to distinguish from the original. However, the copy holds exactly one quart of liquid and the skirting at the neck and shoulder differs on the copy from the original.

GII-76, Concentric Ring—Eagle: This is one of the most difficult reproductions to distinguish from the original, with the reproductions each having a serial number engraved in the base of the bottle. Be mindful that the serial number can be scratched or polished off.

GIV-1, Masonic—Eagle: This is a fairly good reproduction pint flask, and the main way to distinguish it from the original is by the letters "JP" that are enclosed within the oval, as opposed to "IP" which was on the original bottle.

GV-5, Success to the Railroad: This pint flask is one of the finest reproductions you will ever see, with the main difference being that the mane on the horse's neck stands straight out.

GVIII-2: This is a very well-made reproduction, distinguishable only from the original because it is much lighter in weight.

GVII-3, EG Boozs Old Cabin Bottle: This is a well-made reproduction, made in New Jersey beginning in the 1930s. On the originals, a period can be found after the word whiskey. Also, on the reproduction a mold seam is evident on the base, whereas the original does not have a mold seam. If the Boozs bottle does not have a period after whiskey, this does not necessarily make it a fake, as a cold mold may have resulted in the period not being filled in.

GVII-4, EG Boozs Old Cabin Bottle: This reproduction is distinguishable from the original since the corner edges extend below the first row of shingles, whereas on the original they do not.

REPAIRS

There are two major types of bottle repairs that must be watched for: 1) the epoxy type wherein epoxy or some other type of hardener is used to create a new lip or to fill in a chip; and 2) polishing repairs, which ordinarily involve felt or cork belts to remove any traces of a chip or jagged edge. The epoxy-type repairs are often extremely well done, and it is not uncommon for an entire neck to be replaced right down to a bottle's shoulder, for a hole in the side of a piece to be filled, or for a rough area to have a surface coating of resin.

There are several ways to help spot a repair. Sometimes a repair will show an odd color when exposed to black light, and the epoxy will have a different, slippery type of feel than the glass. Some people apply acetone to a suspected repaired area, which will frost the resin. Sometimes the repair just does not look right, and a noticeable line can be seen where the epoxy begins and the bottle ends. However, some repairs are very difficult to spot. This is not to say that epoxy-type repairs are all bad, as major bottles are often repaired to enhance their display quality.

As to polish-type repairs, these are often the most difficult to detect. In fact, if a lip has been properly polished to hide a chip, it is very possible that even the most experienced bottle collector will not be able to tell with certainty that the item has been polished. What can you look for to determine if a bottle has been polished? If the lip is suspected, there may be a "file mark" that runs completely around the lip perimeter. If the file mark suddenly stops and there is a small indentation, with a sheen or luster that is unlike the rest of the lip, then you may have a polishing job. Sometimes polishing may be used to rid scratches from the side of a bottle; look for an unusual indentation on one area of the bottle that may be overly shiny or dull, and look for embossing that may seem dull, both of which may indicate that a light buffing may have been done. As stated before, the best practice is to handle as much glass as possible and to ask other bottle collectors if they can show you any repaired items or suspected repairs.

BOTTLE AGE AND BOTTLE SHAPES

BOTTLE AGE

Free-Blown Bottles: B.C.–1860; some are still free blown today.

Pontil: 1618–1866; also some modern handblown bottles.

Raised Letters: 1790 to date.

Three-Part Mold: 1806–1889.

Amethyst or Sun-Colored Glass: 1800 to date.

Sheared Lip: 1800–1830 (the top has been sheared off).

Machine-Made Bottles: 1903 to date (mold line runs from base through the top).

Black or Dark Olive Green Glass: 1700–1800 approx.

Blob Top: Thick rounded lip; on most soda and mineral water bottles.

Crown Cap or Top: 1895 to date.

AGE AS DETERMINED BY MOLD LINE

-1800+   -1880+   -1890+   -1903+   1910 to Date

BOTTLE SHAPES

Cone Ink

Glue

Umbrella

Conical

Cylindrical

Old Beer

New Beer

Hutchinson-type Soda

New Soda

Shoe Polish

Hutchinson-type stopper

Tear Drop or Torpedo

Round Bottom

Old Whiskey

New Whiskey

Broken
Pontil

Sheared Lip
(1800s)

18 "Seal"

Graphite Pontil

Two-part Mold   Three-part Mold   Side Mold   Lady Leg Neck

Medicine or
Bitters, label

Old Medicine

New Medicine

Free Blown

Ten Pin

Fire Extinguisher

Squat or Onion

Scroll Flask

*Wide Mouth Case
Bottle*

OTHER BOTTLE FORMS

Note that all of the following photos are courtesy of Glass Works Auctions.

Target Ball

Teakettle Ink

*Blown Three-mold, or
Geometric, Ink*

Barrel-shaped Bottle, usually a bitters or whiskey

Cabin-shaped Bottle, usually a bitters, whiskey or flask

Case Gin, square with slightly tapering sides

Chestnut Bottle (see Blown Bottles Section)

Shaft and Globe Form, made 1660–1680, rare (see Blown Bottles)

Blown Three-mold, or Geometric, Decanter

Blown Three-mold Toilet Water Bottle

Fire Grenade

Midwestern Globular Swirled Rib Bottle (see Pattern Molded)

Mineral Water Bottle

*Pineapple-shaped
Bottle, usually a bitters
or whiskey*

Sunburst Flask

*Peppersauce, Cathedral
(see Food Bottles)*

*Pickle, Cathedral (see
Pickle Bottles)*

*Indian Queen Figure,
usually a bitters
or whiskey*

Baby-faced Milk Bottle

*Medicine,
rectangular-shaped,
sloping collared lip*

Wax Sealer Fruit Jar   *Pitkin Flask*

PONTIL MARKS

Note that all of the following photos are courtesy of Glass Works Auctions.

Open pontil mark. This type of pontil mark shows itself as either a round or jagged scar on the bottom of a piece, and can be either very pronounced, such as when a huge crater has been gouged out of the bottom, or with a very faint ring or circular impression. Some pontil marks actually show a broken off piece of glass attached to the bottom, sometimes so pronounced that the piece cannot even stand up. Pontils are almost always very sharp, so sharp that you can often cut your finger when touching one. The pontil shown in this photo is called a "ring" or "donut" pontil, since it is circular in nature and hollow in the center. This type of pontil is often encountered on blown glass, as well as bottles.

Left: *Another pontil, though much more faint than the previous huge open pontil.* Right: *This pontil has been made on a molded base and is slightly recessed into the bottom. It is sharp enough to cut your finger.*

Left: *An iron pontil, also called a "graphite pontil," because its color is very much like that in the lead of a pencil. It usually shows itself as a wide and circular depression in the center bottom, and is almost completely covered with the graphitelike grayish coating. Some iron pontil marks are tan or orange colored, and some are rectangular or square in form, but look for the relatively even and thin coating within the circular depression. Some people confuse an iron pontil with an open pontil which has traces of iron from the end of the pontil rod. This is not an iron pontil!* Right: *A polished pontil, which you would usually find on fancy decanters and blown and pressed glass. Look for a circular polished bevel within the bottom center.*

HOW TO USE THIS BOOK

This book is divided into Old and New bottle sections. The "Old Bottles" section is categorized by bottle type such as beer, flasks or inks. The listings are organized alphabetically by trade name or subject. The listings include the written material exactly as it appears on each bottle along with a bottle description.

The "New Bottles" section is arranged alphabetically by manufacturer. Some of the most popular modern bottle companies in the collector market are listed including Avon, Jim Beam, Ezra Brooks, Ski Country, and Old Commonwealth. The listings are organized alphabetically by trade name or subject. The bottle's description is given in each listing.

Read the printed descriptions carefully in both sections. The prices given are for the specific bottles listed. Assume that the prices given are for bottles in perfect condition unless otherwise stated within the listing. Understand that damage such as chips, cracks, stains, and heavy wear can *greatly* impact the value of a bottle. For example, the ST Drake's Plantation Bitters cabin-shaped amber bottle in mint condition is worth about $60. A $1/4$-inch lip chip will reduce the value to maybe $20–25. A $1/2$-inch crack in the side will reduce the mint bottles value to $20–30. A bad inner stain might devalue the piece to $30–35, since someone might be able to clean it. Exterior stains are more of a problem because to clean them may require polishing or disfiguring the exterior surface, so that may reduce the value to $20–30. Heavy wear may reduce the value to $30–40.

Throughout the Old Bottles categories you will see the following: OP means an open, pontiled bottle; SB means a smooth base and bottle; and IP refers to iron pontiled.

QUESTIONS, ANYONE?

Readers should feel free to write the author directly with any questions, comments, or suggestions on how to improve the next book. If writing about a bottle or piece of glass, it's strongly recommended that you send a good photo or photos, and list any embossing, markings, color, and whether the item is pontiled or not. *You must include a self-addressed, stamped envelope in order to get a response.* I will try to respond within two weeks of receiving your query. Please do *not* send in any actual glass pieces. Please write to: Jim Megura, P.O. Box 9357, Bridgeport, CT 06601.

OLD BOTTLES

APOTHECARY BOTTLES

Apothecary bottles were used to store drugs and chemicals. They almost always have ground and air-tight stoppers, since exposure to air would tend to weaken, dilute or contaminate the product. Some of the bottles have a label under a glass panel (label-under-glass) and it is important that the glass panel be intact and that the label be in good condition. Other bottles may have gilt and painted chemical names across the face of the bottle, with faded and chipped colors detracting from the values. Also see Label-Under-Glass Bottles, and Medicine Bottles.

Apothecary Bottle, ribbed, "Tinct Cannab Ind Poison" label under glass, 5⅞", green .... $60–$85

Apothecary Bottle, "Aconito," milk glass with floral pattern, decorated stopper, 8"... .... $90–$135

Apothecary Bottle, "AQ: Auran" on gilt label, 11", deep olive amber, SB . $125–$150

Apothecary Bottle, "Chloruret: Ferric" on label under glass, original tin lid, 8½", sapphire .... $80–$120

Apothecary Bottle, round, "Creta C Camph" red, black, gold label, stopper, 11⅝", pink amethyst .... $500–$750

Apothecary Bottle, ribbed, "Lotto Calamin" on label under glass, 8", green.. $70–$95

Apothecary Bottle, "Morph Ac" on red, black, and gilt label, original stopper, 4⅛", cobalt.. $150–$200

Apothecary Bottle, "P Ipecac C" on gold and black painted label, stopper, 8½", cobalt .... $200–$260

Apothecary Bottle, "P Myrist" on gold, red, and black label, original stopper, 8½", cobalt.. $175–$250

Apothecary Bottle, "P Myrist" on red, black, and gold label, stopper, 8½", cobalt.... .... $200–$300

Apothecary Bottle, "Syr Scillae" on red, black and gold label, stopper, round, 6⅞", cobalt.. $125–$165

Apothecary Bottle, "Tablettes Menthe A" on gold and black label, tin cap, rect., 7½", cobalt.. $130–$190

Apothecary Bottle, enameled "Tinct Cathario," horizonal ribs, stopper, 5⅝", cobalt .... $150–$200

Apothecary Bottle, "Tinct Ipecac," black and gold label, footed, stopper, 9⅞", clear .... $100–$135

Left: *Apothecary with gilded painted label.* Right: *Apothecary with label-under-glass panel.* PHOTOS COURTESY OF GLASS WORKS AUCTIONS.

Apothecary Bottle, horizontal rings, enameled "Tinct Opii Poison," stopper, $5^5/_8$", cobalt. . . . . $200–$300

Apothecary Bottle, enameled "Tinct Opii Poison," stopper, $5^5/_8$", cobalt . . $200–$300

Apothecary Bottle, "TR Mirra," black, white, and gold label, stopper, $9^1/_8$", cobalt . . . . $90–$135

Apothecary Bottle, no label or embossing, globular, long neck, stopper, 13", amethyst . . . . $275–$375

Apothecary Bottle, "Ant Sulph" on gold and black label, stopper, $6^3/_4$", cobalt . . . . $150–$210

Apothecary Bottle, "Calx Sulphurata" on paper label, stopper, $4^1/_4$", opal powder blue . . . . $150–$200

Apothecary Bottle, "Dentifrice" on gold, white, and black label, original stopper, $8^5/_8$", clear. . . . . $60–$80

Apothecary Bottle, "Dentrifice" on white, black and gold label, stopper, $8^5/_8$", clear . . . . $50–$70

Apothecary Bottle, "EF Bellard" label under glass, stopper, label panel crack, $5^3/_8$", cobalt. . . . . $75–$100

Apothecary Bottle, "Etr Cocae Fluid" on white and black label, original tin lid, $6^3/_4$", blue . . . . $60–$80

Apothecary Bottle, "Lin Belladon" on label under glass, original stopper, $6^3/_4$", yellow green . . . . $70–$90

Apothecary Bottle, "Ol Tereb," red, white, and gold label under glass, stopper, $5^7/_8$", clear. . . . . $20–$25

Apothecary Bottle, "Oxym Scill" on gold, red, and black painted label, stopper, $7^1/_4$", cobalt. . . . . $160–$210

Apothecary Bottle, "Pulv G Trgaca" on gold and black painted label, stopper, $7^5/_8$", clear. . . . . $765–$90

Apothecary Bottle, "Pulv Sacch Alb" on gold and black painted label, stopper, $6^3/_4$", clear. . . . . $55–$70

Apothecary Bottle, "Rose Water" on printed paper label, stopper, $6^3/_4$", cobalt . . . . $90–$135

Apothecary Bottle, "Sulphurata" on paper label, original stopper, $4^1/_4$", opal powder blue . . . . $175–$250

Apothecary Bottle, "Syr Auran" on gold, red, and black label, stopper, 7⅝", purple . . . . $150–$200

Apothecary Bottle, "Syr Mori" on gold and black label, stopper, 7", cobalt . . . . $140–$190

Apothecary Bottle, "Syr Papava" on red, black and gold label, original stopper, 8½", cobalt . . . . $150–$225

Apothecary Bottle, "Syr Rhoead" on gold and black painted label, stopper, 7¾", cobalt . . . . $145–$195

Apothecary Bottle, "Syr Scillae" on gold and black painted label, stopper, 6⅞", cobalt . . . . $125–$175

Apothecary Bottle, "Syr Tolu" on gilt label, 7¾", cobalt, OP . . . . $90–$135

Apothecary Bottle, "Tinct Canthario," enameled, horizontal ribs, stopper, 5⅝", cobalt . . . . $150–$200

Apothecary Bottle, "Tinct Opii Poison," colorful enameling, cobalt stopper, 5⅝" . . . . $150–$225

Apothecary Bottle, "Tinct Stramon Poison," red, white, and gold label, 5⅞", yellow green . . . . $100–$150

Apothecary Bottle, "TR Assaf" red, white and gold label under glass, stopper, 6⅞", clear. . . . . $20–$25

Apothecary Bottle, "Vin Opii" on gold and black label, stopper, 5", clear . . . $70–$90

Apothecary Bottle, "XYM Scillae" on gold and black painted label, stopper, 6⅝", cobalt. . . . . $125–$175

Apothecary Jar, "Ex Cannab Ind," colorful enameled label, 2⅜", white pottery, brown wrap. . . . . $125–$175

Apothecary Jar, "Ex Cannab Ind," colorful enameled label, 2⅜", white pottery, brown wrap. . . . . $75–$125

Apothecary Jar, cobalt wrap, "Pil Opii" on black, red, gold, and white label, 2⅜", white pottery . . . . $150–$200

Apothecary Jar, "Pil Opii" on white, red, gold, and black label, 2⅜", white pottery . . . . $150–$250

Apothecary Jar, "Tartrate Borico Potascio" on paper label, 4½", white pottery. . . . . $75–$95

Apothecary Jar, pottery, forest green wrap, "Ung Opii" paper label, lid, 4¼" $50–$70

Apothecary Jar, OP with painted floral decoration, original stopper, 7⅝", fiery opal. . . . . $80–$120

BARBER BOTTLES

An area of bottle collecting which offers one of the widest ranges of colors and bottle styles and decorations is the barber bottle area. As early as the 1860s, and continuing right through until about 1920, barbers used very colorful and highly decorated bottles which they often filled with their own tonics and colognes. Though the usage of barber bottles peaked around the turn of the century, the Pure Food and Drug Act of 1906, which restricted the usage of alcohol-based substances and unlabeled and refillable containers, marked the slow demise of these beautiful and distinctive bottles. During this time period, many of the bottles were made in the United States, with many others being imported from Europe. It is generally difficult to differentiate between an American-made bottle and its European counterpart. The earlier bottles often had rough pontil scars. The popular types of ornamentation included fancy pressed designs, cutting, enameling, painting, and labels under glass. The bottles were generally fit with cork and metal or porcelain-type closures. The reader is referred to *Collecting Barber Bottles* by Richard Holiner, which the letter "H" denotes in the following listing.

Please keep in mind the following when buying and collection barber bottles:

- Much of the barber bottle value comes from the painted or enameled decoration; worn, chipped or faded decoration can greatly affect the value of a bottle.
- Some barber bottles have been reproduced, including hobnail types, Mary Gregory types, and cranberry and white banded bottles. Check for wear!

Art Nouveau Floral Pattern, H-32, 8", clear frosted, OP . . . . $300–$500
Art Nouveau Design, ring/wreath pattern, H-118 bottom, 8", ruby, OP. . . $800–$1200
Bay Rum, well-painted pansies, floral, opal milk glass, 9", OP . . . . $300–$400
Bay Rum, with enameled floral, tapering cylinder, milk glass, 9", OP . . . . . . $90–$150
Bay Rum, ruby flashing cut to clear, 7", PP. . . . . $100–$140
Beaded Design, enameled, bulbous base, 8", cobalt, OP. . . . . $125–$175
Brilliantine, round, paneled upper portion, silver neck overlay, 4", ruby . . . $100–$145
Brilliantine, double thumbprint pattern, H-47, 4", deep ruby . . . . $125–$200
Cherub With Floral Decor, bell form, milk glass, OP, 7³/₄" . . . . $100–$150
Clambroth Colored, paneled neck, worn enameled lettering, 7" . . . . $5–$10
Coin Spot Design, bulbous body, 8³/₈", teal blue (all one color). . . . . $70–$90
Coin Spot Design, SB, white opalescent over turquoise, 7" . . . . $125–$175
Dog Chasing Deer, enameled design, cylinder, milk glass, 11", OP . . . . . . $250–$350
Dot Pattern, bulbous form, 7¹/₂", amethyst. . . . . $65–$95
Dot Pattern, bulbous form, 7¹/₂", cobalt, OP. . . . . $65–$95
Dot Pattern, bulbous form, 7¹/₂", light green . . . . $75–$125
Dot Pattern, hourglass shaped, 7¹/₂", amethyst. . . . . $80–$120
Floral Pattern, Art Nouveau style, bulbous, turquoise blue, OP . . . . $300–$400
Floral Pattern, Art Nouveau style, H-7, bulbous, 7³/₄", yellow green, OP. . $300–$375
Floral Pattern, milk glass, H-44, 8", multicolored floral . . . . $90–$135
Floral Pattern, squat form, H-84, yellow green . . . . $75–$100
Floral Pattern, squat form, H-84, 6³/₄", cobalt . . . . $60–$80
Floral Sprigs, bell form, OP, 7¹/₂", cobalt. . . . . $100–$135
Floral Sprigs, enameled design, bulbous body, 8¹/₈", amethyst, OP. . . . . $75–$125
Footed, bulbous base, white floral enameling, 7", cobalt, OP . . . . $400–$600

Fox and Hound Scene, milk glass, 7¹/₂", opalescent, OP . . . . $75–$100
Gilt Bird on Branch Design, bulbous base, 8", cobalt, SB. . . . . $125–$175
Girl's Head, milk glass, with floral design, 8", OP . . . . $650–$900
Hobnail Patterned, H-64, 7", purple amethyst, SB . . . . $125–$185
Hobnail Patterned, H-68, white opalescent hobnail, label under glass with "Tonic" and pretty girl, clear, 7¹/₂", cranberry body . . . . $350–$450
Hobnail Patterned, LeVarn's Rose Hair Tonic Dandruff Cure, 7¹/₂", clear. . $70–$100
Mary Gregory, boy with flowers, bulbous, 8", emerald green (rare color) . $250–$350
Mary Gregory, boy with flowers, bulbous, 8", green, OP . . . . $225–$275
Mary Gregory, boy with flying birds, bulbous, 7³/₄", amethyst, OP. . . . . . . $200–$250
Mary Gregory, girl tennis player, bulbous form, 8", cobalt, OP . . . . $225–$275
Mary Gregory, grist mill, "Bay Rum," bulbous form, 8", amethyst, OP . . . $300–$365
Mary Gregory, seated girl, bulbous, 7³/₄", amethyst, OP . . . . $300–$350
Mary Gregory, standing girl, bell form (rare form), 8", green, OP . . . . $250–$325
Mary Gregory, standing girl, bulbous, 8", cobalt, OP . . . . $225–$275
Mary Gregory, standing girl, cylinder (rare form), 8", cobalt, OP . . . . $400–$600
Paneled Clear, H-109, ABM with stopper, 6¹/₂". . . . . $10–$15
Paneled Clear, H-109, ABM with stopper, 8³/₄". . . . . $10–$15
Personalized, tall cylinder, "Bay Rum," floral decor, metal stopper, 10³/₄", cobalt . . . .
. . . . $400–$600
Personalized, tapering cylinder, "Tonic," painted on cabin scene, metal stopper, milk glass, 9¹/₂". . . . . $400–$450
Personalized, tapering cylinder, "Tonic," floral painted motif, milk glass, metal stopper, 8". . . . . $350–$450
Ribbed, semi-bowling pin shaped, SB, 8¹/₂", turquoise blue. . . . . $100–$150
Round, stepped sides, cranberry with white splotches, 8¹/₄. . . . . $100–$135
Sea Foam, with floral decor, cylinder, opal milk glass, 9", OP . . . . $300–$400
Segmented, round with petal-like lobes, opalized cranberry coin spot, 7" . . $100–$125
Segmented, round with petal-like lobes, opalized daisy and fern, 7", cranberry, OP . . .
. . . . $90–$125
Shampoo, opal floral sprigs, milk glass, 7", OP. . . . . $150–$200

Left: *Mary Gregory–type bottle.* Center: *Hobnail bottle.* Right: *Enamel decorated bottle.* PHOTOS COURTESY OF GLASS WORKS AUCTIONS.

Silver Overlay Floral Pattern, 7³/₄", emerald green, OP . . . . $500–$700
Spanish Lace Pattern, H-27, square, white opalescent over turquoise, PP, 8" . . . .
. . . . $275–$360
Spanish Lace Pattern, H-27, white opalescent over cranberry, square, PP, 8" . . . .
. . . . $250–$350
Spanish Lace Pattern, H-82, bulbous, white opalescent over cranberry, PP, 7" . . . . . .
. . . . $250–$350
Square Irregular Line Pattern, surface iridescence, 7³/₄", cranberry . . . . . $100–$145
Starburst Patterned, pressed clear, 6¹/₂" . . . . $75–$110
Stars and Stripes Pattern, white opalescent over cranberry, PP, 7" . . . . . . $250–$350
Stripe Pattern, multicolored vertical stripes, H-30, PP, 8⁵/₈", frosted clear . $200–$300
Stripe Pattern, red and white vertical stripes, H-59, PP, 8¹/₂", frosted clear $200–$300
Stripe Pattern, bulbous, white opalescent over cranberry, SB, H-95, 7" . . . $150–$200
Swirled Rib Pattern, white opalescent over turquoise, PP, H-77, 7" . . . . . . $250–$325
T. Noonan & Co. Barber Supplies Boston Mass (on base), 6³/₄", frosted green . . . . .
. . . . $60–$80
T. Noonan & Co. Barber Supplies Boston Mass (on base), 7", frosted light pink . . .
. . . . $50–$65
Thumbprint Patterned, opalescent highlights, PP, 8³/₄" . . . . $200–$300
Tiffany-Type Iridescent Stretch Glass, H-31, SB, 8", blue . . . . $400–$600
Toilet Water, floral decor, OP, 8³/₄", opal milk glass . . . . $135–$185
Toilet Water, ruby flashing cut to clear, metal stopper, PP, 7" . . . . $100–$140
Vegederma, enameled with woman's head and hair, bulbous, 8¹/₈", amethyst, OP . . . .
. . . . $300–$400
Vegederma, enameled with woman's head and hair, bulbous, 8", light green, OP . . . . .
. . . . $400–$500
Vegederma, enameled with woman's head and hair, heavy scratching to enameling, 8",
light green . . . . $90–$120
Water, silver overlay lettering, clambroth body, fluted neck, stopper, 7" . . . . . $40–$55
Witch Hazel, deer jumping log, shouldered cylinder, milk glass, 9", OP . . . $250–$350
Witch Hazel, floral design, square, stopper, milk glass, 9" . . . . $80–$120
Witch Hazel, silver overlay lettering, clambroth body, fluted neck, stopper, 7" . . $40–$55

BEER BOTTLES

Beer has long been a staple of American life, and it is believed that as early as
1587 a brewery was established in Roanoke, Virginia. This early beer was sold
and transported in wooden barrels, and it was not until the mid-18th century that
advertising references were made to bottled beer. Though it is unclear as to
which type of bottle was used in the early days, it is quite possible that free-
blown globular and chestnut-type bottles were used, as well as early wine bottles.

As to where these early bottles were made, it must be remembered that up until the first quarter of the 19th century most of the bottles used in the beer and spirits industries were imported. Up until around the mid-19th century the standard beer bottle was the familiar black glass pontiled bottle, often made in a three-piece mold and rarely embossed. Around 1850, embossed bottles began to appear and were usually marked "ale" or "porter." Later in the 1860s, beer and ale bottles began to be embossed with breweries' names, a practice which has continued into the 20th century.

During the late 19th century, there were many different shapes, colors, and closure styles used, including "torpedo"-shaped bottles and beer bottles in shades of cobalt blue and green. Around this time, the lightning stopper was developed, which was a convenient way of sealing and resealing blob top bottles. The reader is referred to *American Bottles and Flasks and Their Ancestry* by McKearin and Wilson, pgs. 229–232.

Adam Bez, Louisville, Ky, 9", amber . . . . $30–$40
Anheuser-Busch, amber crown top . . . . $5–$8
Anheuser-Busch Brewing Co., San Francisco, 8", amber . . . . $100–$150
Audubon Bottling Co., crown top, clear . . . . $1–$2
Bay Bottling Company, San Francisco, Ca, pint . . . . $50–$65
Binders, Renovo, Pa, amber crown top . . . . $1–$3
Boardman, IP, cobalt . . . . $60–$90
Breckenfelder & Jochem, Oakland, Ca, pint . . . . $20–$30
Budweiser, miniature, amber crown top, label . . . . $3–$5
Buffalo Brewing Co, SF Agency, BBCo monogram, pint . . . . $150–$250
Buffalo Brewing Co, SF Agency, BBCo monogram, quart . . . . $250–$350
Burr & Waters Celebrated Ale, deep yellow amber, IP . . . . $250–$350
Cal Bottling Company, John Wieland Export Beer, SF, half pint . . . . $75–$100
Cal Bottling Company, John Wieland Export Beer, SF, pint . . . . $60–$80
California Bottling Works, T Blauth, quart . . . . $35–$55
Carling's Red Cap Ale, Cleveland, Ohio, 12oz., green . . . . $1–$2
Cascade Bottling Company, Pereira Bros, Santa Clara, Cal, pint . . . . $30–$40
Champion P&C Scotch Ale, 6⅞", root beer amber, SB . . . . $250–$350

Beer, ca. 1860, three-piece mold. PHOTO
COURTESY OF NEIL GROSSMAN.

CJ Vath Co, San Jose, pint . . . . $8–$12
CJ Vath Co, San Jose, quart . . . . $10–$14
Cooper & Conger St. Louis Ale Brewery, 9¹/₂", yellow olive . . . . $300–$400
Cowley Company, Flemington, NJ, aqua blob top . . . . $9–$13
Cream Ale A Templeton, Louisville, 9", amber . . . . $60–$75
D Davis, 12 sided, 10", cobalt . . . . $1000–$1500
D Meinke, San Francisco, quart . . . . $30–$45
DH Evans No. 211 Main Street, St. Louis, 3-piece mold, 9¹/₂", black, OP. . $75–$100
Dotterweich Beer Co, Olean, NY, clear blob top. . . . . $5–$8
Dotterweich, Bottling Co, Olean NY, 9¹/₂", light amber . . . . $4–$6
Dr Brown's Lemon Beer, stoneware, blue lettering, 9³/₄" . . . . $125–$175
Dr Brown, stoneware, blue colored lip, 10" . . . . $90–$125
Dr Cronk, 7¹/₂" stoneware, gray glaze, 7¹/₂" . . . . $60–$80
Dr Cronk, 9³/₈", yellow olive . . . . $20–$30
Dr Cronk Gibbons & Co Superior Ale, deep green, IP . . . . $400–$600
Dr Cronk Gibbons & Co Superior Ale, green, IP. . . . . $200–$250
Dr Cronk RMC C, 12 sided, 10", cobalt, IP. . . . . $2000–$3000
DuBois DB (on base), crown top, light green . . . . $1–$2
Duhme & Meyer, 115 Christopher St. New York, quart . . . . $50–$75
Dukehart & Co, Maryland Brewery, Baltimore, 8", amber, SB . . . . $60–$90
Elkins brewing Co, WV, crown top, amber . . . . $3–$5
EM Keane XXX Ale, 9", deep blue. . . . . $450–$700
Enterprise Brewing Co, EBCo, quart. . . . . $7–$10
Enterprise Brewing Co, EBCo monogram, quart. . . . . $8–$12
Erie Bottling Co, Erie Pa, blob top lady's leg, amber . . . . $20–$30
Etna Brewery, Etna Mills, half pint, amber . . . . $6–$9
Eugene Klemt, Phila, clear blob top . . . . $4–$6
Excelsior Bottled Lager, Brooklyn, NY, pint . . . . $12–$16
Excelsior Bottling Works, Dayton, Ohio, quart, yellow amber . . . . $20–$25
Excelsior Lager, blob top, aqua. . . . . $12–$15
F Hinckel Sparkling Lager Beer, Albany, NY, amber pint . . . . $28–$35
F McKinney's Mead, stoneware quart . . . . $30–$40
Fairbanks and Beard, stoneware quart. . . . . $30–$50
Fishkill Wine & Liquor Store, Fishkill, NY, aqua blob top . . . . $25–$35
Florida Brewing Co, Tampa, Fla. . . . . $20–$22
FO Brandt, Healdsburg, quart . . . . $20–$25
Fredricksburg Bottling Co, San Francisco, Ca, FBCo monogram, pint . . $80–$120
Fredricksburg Brewing, Property of, 11¹/₄", red amber . . . . $10–$15
Fredricksburg Brewing, Property of, miniature . . . . $80–$125
G Woburn, Oak Hill NY, amber blob top . . . . $4–$6
Gambrinus Bottling Co, San Fran, Ca, GBCo monogram, pint . . . . $40–$50
Geo Burrell, squat cylinder, half pint, IP, dark amber. . . . . $350–$550
Geo Schlegel & Co, Columbus, O, 9¹/₂", olive amber, OP . . . . $300–$400
George Otto, Phila, Pa, blob top, aqua . . . . $10–$15
Gold Edge Bottling Works, JF Deininger, Vallejo, pint . . . . $30–$40
Grace Bros Brewing Co, Santa Rosa, Ca, GBCo monogram, pint . . . . $35–$45
Grace Bros Brewing Co, Santa Rosa, Ca, GBCo mongram, quart . . . . $40–$55
H Denhalter & Son, Salt Lake City, Hutchinson, aqua. . . . . $40–$50
Hansen & Kahler, Oakland, Ca, quart . . . . $10–$15
Henry C Meyer, San Francisco, Ca, pint . . . . $20–$30
J Smith & Co, Neshannock, Pa, quart, aqua, SB . . . . $60–$90

JBG, 12 sided, 10", cobalt blue, IP .... $1500+
JF Zimmer, Gloucester City, NJ, clear blob top, lightning-type stopper .... $15–$25
Johann Hoff, 7^1/$_2$", black.. $5–$6
John Kuhlmann Brewing Co, Ellenville, NY, aqua blob top .... $15–$20
John Rapp & Son, SF, Ca, pint .... $7–$12
John Rapp & Son, SF, Ca, quart .... $12–$17
John Ryan Porter & Ale Philada, 7" cobalt, IP...................... $80–$120
John Ryan, Philada XX Porter & Ale, cobalt blue, IP .... $75–$125
John Tons Stockton, Ca, JT monogram, quart...................... $60–$80
John Ulrich, Brooklyn, NY, clear blob top .... $5–$7
JSP (monogram), teal blue green .... $10–$14
Koch's, 12 ounce, crown top, clear .... $1–$2
L Block's Bottles St Louis, 3-piece mold, 9^1/$_2$", deep olive green .... $50–$80
L Potter & Co Compound, pottery, 9^1/$_4$".......................... $45–$65
LJ Miday & Co, Canton, Ohio, quart, lightning stopper, aqua .... $60–$90
M Keeley Chicago Ill, W McCully, 10", amber........................ $55–$75
Marusville Bottling Works, Ca, pint .... $50–$65
McClure, Peekskill, NY, aqua blob top .... $15–$20
Moerlein's Old Jug Lager Beer, pottery, pint .... $30–$40
Moerlein's Old Jug Lager Beer, pottery, quart .... $35–$45
Morgan's Brewery Co. Ltd, screw top, 9^1/$_2$", green .... $1–$2
National Lager Beer, HR monogram, half pint....................... $15–$20
North Star Bottling Works, Trade Mark (star), quart................. $38–$48
Ohio Bottling Works, 122 N Main St, La, quart .... $80–$100
Pabst, embossed on circle at shoulder, clear pint, crown top............... $2–$3
Pacific Bottling Co, San Francisco, JW monogram, quart............. $80–$120
Pearl Brewing Co, San Antonio, Texas, crown top..................... $1–$2
Perkins, Tannerville, NY, sun-colored amethyst blob top .... $15–$20
Rapp, quart, amber... $4–$6
Rizzuto Bros, Forest Glen, NY, blob top, clear .... $10–$14
Robert Portner Brewing Co, medium olive green...................... $40–$48
Robinson, Wilson & Legaree, 102 Sudbury St, Boston, 7", blue green, SB . $35–$45
Robinson, Wison & Legaree, 102 Sudbury St, Boston, 7", yellow green, SB.......
.... $40–$60
Rocco Di Nubile, Phila Registered, paneled, blob top................. $9–$14
Rock Island Brewing Co, Rock Island, Ill, amber picnic flask............ $30–$50
Ruhstaller's Gilt Edge, quart, crown top .... $2–$3
Salinas Bottling Co, Salinas, Ca, half pint........................ $35–$50
San Jose Bottling Co, C Maurer, quart .... $20–$30
San Jose Bottling Co, C Maurer, pint .... $20–$30
Scheidt, Norristown, Pa, crown top, aqua .... $1–$3
Schlitz, ruby red quart .... $40–$50
Schwarzenbach Brewing Co, 7^1/$_2$", clear.......................... $2–$3
Sebastopol Brewing Co, pint....................................... $20–$30
SH Boughton Root Porter, cobalt, IP............................... $300–$500
Standard SF Bottling Co, pint .... $25–$35
Standard SF Bottling Co, quart .... $35–$45
Swan Brewing Co, half pint, amber .... $500–$700
Swan Brewing Co, half pint, olive green............................ $550–$750
T & R Bottling Co, Camden, NJ, blob top .... $15–$25
T Balkely, Knapps Creek, NY, aqua blob top .... $10–$15

Terre Haute Brewing Co, Terre Haute, Ind, pint, amber................. $6–$9
Thos Maher, Dyottville Glass Works, Philada, 7", deep teal green, IP..... $60–$90
TJ Baker, Oneonta, NY, aqua blob top .... $15–$20
Unembossed, crown top, aqua.. $1–$2
Unembossed, three-piece mold, black, OP .... $10–$15
Unembossed, three-piece mold, smooth base, black...................... $3–$5
Van Merritt, Burlington Brewing Co, Burlington, Wis .... $2–$3
Vath, San Jose, Ca, quart, amber .... $5–$8

BININGER BOTTLES

Bininger and Co. ran a grocery business in New York City prior to 1830, and for over 50 years operated a thriving spirits business. The earliest spirits bottles used by Bininger and Co. were imported from England. Over the years some of the finest figural whiskey bottles ever made were used by Bininger's, with shapes such as barrels, cannons, and urns. One can often determine the approximate date during which a particular bottle was used by checking the address imprinted on the label or embossed on the bottle. For example, the 329 Greenwich Street address was used for the period from 1852 through 1857; 17 Broad Street was used from 1859 to 1861; and 19 Broad Street was used from 1861 through 1864.

AM Bininger No. 19 Broad Street New York, handled, 7³/₄", medium amber.......
.... $250–$350
Am Bininger & Co 19 Broad St NY, Old Kentucky 1849 Reserve, yellow barrel, double collar, 9¹/₂" .... $225–$275
AM Bininger & Co 19 Broad St NY, medium amber cannon, full labels, 12".......
.... $1400–$1800
AM Bininger & Co 338 Broadway NY, Old Kentucky 1849 Reserve, amber barrel, double collar, 9¹/₂" .... $175–$250
AM Bininger & Co 338 Broadway NY, Old Kentucky 1849 Reserve, amber barrel, rare applied lip, 9¹/₂".. $350–$475
AM Bininger & Co Heidelberg Branntwein, 9⁵/₈", yellow olive, SB..... $700–$950
AM Bininger & Co New York, square, 9⁷/₈", amber .... $75–$110
AM Bininger & Co No 19 Broad St New York, handled, medium amber urn, 9"....
.... $1800–$2500
AM Bininger & Co No 19 Broad St New York, yellow amber urn, 10" $1250–$1650
AM Bininger & Co, No 338 Broad St NY Old London Dry Dock Gin, square, medium yellow with strong olive coloration, 9¹/₂".................... $150–$200
AM Bininger & Co, Old London Dock Gin, No 19 Broad St, square, 8", medium amber.. $175–$225

Left: *Handled Bininger bottle.* Center: *Bininger barrel.* Right: *Bininger cannon.* PHOTOS COURTESY OF GLASS WORKS AUCTIONS.

AM Bininger & Co, Old London Dock Gin, No 19 Broad St, square, $9^1/2$", deep orange amber. . . . . $150–$200

AM Bininger & Co, Old London Dock Gin, No 19 Broad St, square, $9^3/4$", emerald green . . . . $200–$260

AM Bininger & Co, Old London Dock Gin, No 19 Broad St, square, $9^5/8$", yellow olive amber . . . . $125–$175

AM Bininger Co No 375 Broadway NY, square, $9^5/8$", medium pink puce . . . . $400–$550

AM Bininger, No 338 Broadway NY, full labels, $9^3/4$, olive green . . . . . . $750–$1000

Bininger New York, flower (on seal), $11^1/4$", olive amber, OP . . . . $1000–$1250

Bininger New York, grapes on seal, Ricketts on base, IP, $11^1/4$", deep olive amber, OP . . . . $1250–$1750

Bininger's Knickerbocker, handle attachment crack, $6^1/2$", yellow amber, OP. . . . . $400–$600

Bininger's Knickerbocker, handled, $6^1/2$", medium golden amber, OP. . $1200–$1500

Bininger's Night Cap No 19 Broad St NY, amber flask, inner screw threads, 8". . . . . $350–$450

Bininger's Old Dominion Wheat Tonic, No 19 Broad Street, NY, 10", deep olive green . . . . $200–$250

Bininger's Old Kentucky Bourbon 1849 Reserve No 19 Broad St NY, $9^5/8$", medium amber. . . . . $85–$110

Bininger's Old Times Family Rye No 338 Broadway AM Bininger & Co., square, $9^3/4$", olive green . . . . $250–$350

Bininger's Peep O Day No 19 Broad Street, medium amber flask, $7^3/4$" . . $325–$450

Bininger's Regulator, clock form, 6", amber, OP . . . . $350–$325

Bininger's Regulator, clock form, 6", aqua, OP. $700–$950

Bininger's Traveler's Guide, yellow amber tear drop, $6^5/8$" . . . . $250–$325

BITTERS BOTTLES

One of the most highly collectible and sought-after types of bottles are the bitters bottles, of which an amazing variety of shapes, sizes, and colors were made. The term "bitters" comes from a type of medicine made from roots and herbs having a bitter and disagreeable taste, and many 17th- and 18th- century books on medicine, cooking, and drugs contain recipes for homemade bitters. In the 18th century, bitters were generally added to spring water, ale or spirits and were intended to cure a wide assortment of maladies.

Beginning in the 1830s, embossed bitters bottles with brand names began to appear. With the growing Temperance Movement, most bitters were becoming alcoholic beverages under the guise of medicine through the addition of bitter herbs, roots, and barks. Also around this time a wide variety of figural bitters bottles in an incredible variety of colors unequaled in any other bottle collecting category began to appear. Collectors should become familiar with the common and unusual colors of the figural bitters, since an unusual coloration may result in one bottle being worth 50 to 100 times more than its more commonly colored twin. The reader is referred to *For Bitters Only* by Carlyn Ring, which the letters refer to below. OP refers to open pontil, SB means smooth based, and IP means iron pontil.

Please keep in mind the following when buying and collecting Bitters bottles.

- Color is extremely important when valuing Bitters bottles. Even seemingly common colors such as aqua or amber may be extremely rare if that particular bottle was usually made in another color. For example, the most frequently found bitters, the ST Drake's Cabin is worth about $50 to $60 in amber, but over $3000 in green. The Brown's Indian Queen is worth about $400 to $500 in amber, but over $7500 in aqua. Learn the common colors for the common bottles, and then watch for the rare colors.
- Labeled bitters can often be valued up to five or more times the value of similar non-labeled bottles.
- There are a few bitters reproductions out there, with one of the better made being the Suffolk Pig Bitters. On the reproduction, the mold seam extends right up to the top of the lip. Check for wear!!

A Guckenheimer Bros German Stomach Bitters, G-27, 9^1/$_2$", dark amber . . . . $600–$800
A Hoffeld's Liver Bitters, H-132, 9^3/$_4$", yellow amber. . . . . $1000–$2000
A Lambert Bitters, Philada, unlisted, 11", olive green, IP . . . . $2750–$3500

African Stomach Bitters, A-15, 9$^1/_2$", amber . . . . $75–$95

Ageno Nerve & Stomach Bitters (on label), A-19, full label, 9", amber . . $160–$210

Aimars Sarracenia Bitters, A-21, 7", aqua . . . . $120–$170

American Celebrated Stomach Bitters, A-46, 8$^5/_8$", medium amber . . . . . $125–$175

American Life Bitters, A-49, 9", yellow amber cabin . . . . $3200–$4300

American Stomach Bitters, Buffalo, NY, A-55, full labels, 10$^1/_2$", amber . $200–$250

American Stomach Bitters, Rochester, NY, A-54, 8", amber . . . . $140–$180

Andrew Lee Compound Cathartic Bitters, C-208, 7$^7/_8$", aqua. . . . . $80–$120

Andrew's, David, Vegetable Jaundice Bitters, A-57, 8", aqua . . . . $1300–$1800

Angostura Bark Bitters, A-68, 7", amber . . . . $45–$55

Angostura Bark Bitters, A-69, 7", amber . . . . $50–$60

Angostura Bitters (on base), ABM, screw cap, green amber. . . . . $1–$2

Appentine Bitters, Geo Benz & Sons, A-78, 7$^7/_8$", red amber. . . . . $325–$425

AR Thayer's Iron Bitters, T-15, 7", aqua . . . . $500–$800

Arabian Bitters, A-80, 9$^3/_8$", golden amber . . . . $160–$230

Argyle Bitters, A-83, 9$^1/_8$", yellow olive. . . . . $150–$195

Aromatic Orange Stomach Bitters, A-90, 10", medium amber . . . . $600–$800

Atwood's Jaundice Bitters, ABM, 12 sided, aqua. . . . . $4–$7

Atwood's Jaundice Bitters, aqua, OP, 12 sided . . . . $20–$30

Atwood's Jaundice Bitters, SB, BIMAL, 12 sided . . . . $7–$11

Atwood's Jaundice Bitters, sample, A-113, 4", aqua. . . . . $25–$35

Atwood's Quinine Tonic Bitters, A-129, 8$^1/_2$", aqua. . . . . $75–$85

Atwood's Vegetable Dyspeptic Bitters, 6$^1/_2$", OP, aqua . . . . $175–$250

Atwood's Vegetable Dyspeptic Bitters, A-130, SB, full label, 6$^1/_2$" . . . . $80–$100

Atwood's Vegetable Jaundice Bitters, A-131, 5$^3/_8$", aqua, OP . . . . $50–$60

Augauer Bitters, A-134, full labels, 8", yellow green. . . . . $60–$75

Austen's Oswego Bitters, A-139, 7", amber. . . . . $30–$45

Baker's Orange Grove Bitters, B-9, full label, 9$^1/_2$", gold amber . . . . $350–$450

Baker's Orange Grove Bitters, B-9, 9$^1/_4$", apricot puce . . . . $350–$450

Baker's Orange Grove Bitters, B-9, light pinkish gasoline puce, 9$^3/_8$". . . . $600–$900

Baker's Orange Grove Bitters, B-9, 9$^1/_2$", deep golden yellow . . . . $275–$400

Baker's Orange Grove Bitters, B-9, 9$^3/_8$", strawberry puce . . . . $600–$800

Baker's Orange Grove Bitters, B-9, 9$^1/_2$", yellow amber, olive tint . . . . . . $475–$575

E Baker's Premium Bitters, B-10.2, 6$^1/_2$", aqua, OP. . . . . $500–$700

Bancroft's Bitters DW Bancroft Marshfield VT, B-16, 8$^7/_8$", aqua. . . . . . $100–$150

Barley Malt Bitters Co Cincinatti Ohio, B-22, 10", red amber . . . . $550–$750

Barrel-shaped Bottle, unembossed, 9$^1/_2$", amber . . . . $100–$175

Barrel-shaped Bottle, unembossed, 9$^1/_2$", cobalt . . . . $1000–$1350

Barrel-shaped Bottle, unembossed, lip chip, small bruises, 9$^7/_8$", cobalt. . . $450–$650

Barrel-shaped Bottle, unembossed, 9$^1/_2$", olive amber. . . . . $125–$200

Barto's Great Gun Bitters, B-32, medium apricot cannon figural, 10$^3/_4$" . . . .
. . . . $6000–$9000

Bavarian Bitters Hoffheimer Brothers, B-34, 9$^3/_8$", amber . . . . $150–$200

Begg's Dandelion Bitters, B-53, 9", deep golden amber . . . . $100–$145

Bell's Cocktail Bitters, B-58, amber lady's leg, 10$^1/_2$". . . . . $275–$375

Bell's Dr, Golden Tonic Bitters, B-60, 9", amber . . . . $175–$275

Ben Hur Bitters, B-69, 9", amber . . . . $75–$95

Ben Hur Celebrated Stomach Bitters, B-70, 8$^7/_8$", reddish amber . . . . $100–$135

Bender's Bitters, B-67, 10$^1/_4$", medium amber. $4500–$5500

Bennet's Celebrated Stomach Bitters, B-73, 8$^7/_8$", light yellow amber . . . $225–$325

Berkshire Bitters, B-81, 4, 10$^3/_8$", golden amber . . . . $1500–$2000

Berkshire Bitters, B-81.2, 9¹/₂", golden amber..................... $1400–$1900
Berkshire Bitters, Amann & Co, B-81, 9³/₄", amber pig.............. $700–$900
Berliner Bitter, B-84, 10", amber .... $40–$60
Berliner Magen Bitters Co, B-86, 9", amber .... $50–$70
Best Bitters in America, B-92, 9¹/₂", golden amber .... $1000–$1500
Big Bill's Best Bitters, decanter, 11¹/₂", amber...................... $375–$450
Big Bill's Best Bitters, B-95, full labels, 12", amber .... $250–$350
Bischoff's Bitters Charleston SC, SB, 9³/₈", medium amber.......... $1000–$1450
Bischoff's Stomach Bitters, B-102, 6", yellow amber .... $750–$1000
Bismark Bitters, B-107, 6¹/₄", amber .... $45–$60
GC Blake's Anti Dyspeptic Bitters, B-119, IP, 7", aqua.............. $750–$950
Blake's Tonic & Diuretic Bitters, B-122, 9³/₄", aqua .... $50–$65
Blue Mountain Bitters, B-128, 7³/₄", aqua............................ $50–$60
Blue Mountain Bitters, B-128, 8", amber.............................. $80–$110
Bodeker's Constitution Bitters, B-131, 7⁷/₈", medium amber.......... $700–$950
Bodekers Constitution Bitters, B-132, amber strap flask, 6¹/₂"......... $800–$1200
Botanic Stomach Bitters, B-168, 9³/₈", amber......................... $150–$200
Botanical Society Hierapirca Bitters, H-116, 9¹/₂", deep bluish aqua .... $250–$300
Bourbon Whiskey Bitters, B-171, barrel, 9¹/₄", strawberry puce......... $375–$475
Bourbon Whiskey Bitters, B-171, barrel, 9¹/₄", light pinkish puce ..... $3800–$4600
Bowe's Bitters, Waterbury, Conn., B-174, 9¹/₂", clear................. $80–$120
Brady's Family Bitters, B-193, 9¹/₂", amber .... $90–$125
Brand Bros Co., B-201, sample bottle, 10³/₈", amber................... $30–$40
Brand Bros Co., B-201, sample bottle, 4⁷/₈", amber.................... $30–$45
Brobst & Rentschler WC Bitters, W-57, yellow amber barrel, 10³/₄" .... $400–$550
Brown & Lyons Blood Bitters, B-218, 9⁷/₈", amber .... $175–$250
Brown's Celebrated Indian Herb Bitters, B-223, 12¹/₈", medium gold amber ......
.... $475–$600
Brown's Celebrated Indian Herb Bitters, B-224, traces of gilding, 12", yellow amber
.... $700–$900
Brown's Celebrated Indian Herb Bitters, B-225, 12", golden yellow... $800–$1200
Brown's Celebrated Indian Herb Bitters, B-225, 12", light yellow green..........
.... $5000–$6250
Brown's Celebrated Indian Herb Bitters, B-225 epoxy repair to head, 12", gold amber... $150–$200
Brown's Celebrated Indian Herb Bitters, B-226, 12¹/₄", greenish aqua ....
.... $8000–$12000
Brown's Celebrated Indian Herb Bitters, B-226, ground lip, 12", medium amber...
.... $450–$500
Brown's Herb Bitters, Philada, B-230, 9¹/₂", medium yellow lime green ....
.... $3500–$4500
Brown's Iron Bitters, B-231, 8⁵/₈", amber .... $40–$55
Bryant's Stomach Bitters, B-243, deep yellow olive lady's leg, 12¹/₄".. $1400–$2000
Buhrer's Gentian Bitters, B-251, 8³/₈", yellow, amber tone .... $150–$200
Burdock's Blood Bitters, aqua.. $15–$20
Burdock's Blood Bitters, clear....................................... $15–$20
Burton's Stomach Bitters, B-275, 8⁷/₈", amber .... $100–$145
By LA Lacraix Patd October 1st 1870, P-101, bluish aqua pineapple, 8⁷/₈" ....
.... $1200–$1500
C & C Bitters, PR Delany & Co, C-1, 10", aqua..................... $200–$290
C Gautier's Native Wine Bitters, G-8, 9³/₄", olive green, olive tone ..... $250–$375

C Moller Catawba Bitters, unlisted, 8¹/₈", medium amber . . . . $140–$190
Cabin Shaped, unembossed, similar to ST Drake's, 9⁷/₈", yellow amber. . . $100–$150
Caldwell's Wine & Iron Bitters, C-10, full labels, 9⁷/₈", medium amber . . . .
. . . . $900–$1100
Canton Bitters, C-35, 12¹/₄", medium amber lady's leg . . . . $250–$325
Carey's Grecian Bend Bitters, C-46, 9³/₄", strawberry puce . . . . $17,500–$22,500
Carlsbader Bitters, C-50, ¹/₂" base edge chip, 9⁷/₈", clear . . . . $90–$120
Carmeltier Stomach Bitters, C-53, 10", amber . . . . $70–$90
Carmeltier Stomach Bitters, C-54, 10", deep yellow olive green . . . . $300–$425
Carmeltier Stomach Bitters, C-54, 10", golden amber . . . . $80–$100
Carpathian Herb Bitters, C-62, 9", amber. . . . . $60–$80
Carter's Liver Bitters, C-67, 8¹/₂", amber . . . . $60–$75
Castilian Bitters, C-80, yellow amber cannon, 10". . . . . $275–$375
Catawba Wine Bitters, C-85, 9¹/₄", olive green . . . . $1000–$1400
Celebrated Berlin Stomach Bitters, C-90, 9¹/₈", amber . . . . $60–$75
Cerndenin's Golden Tonic Bitters, handled stoneware jug, 15" . . . . $375–$475
CH Swain's Bourbon Bitters, S-227, 9¹/₄", yellow amber . . . . $150–$200
CH Swain's Bourbon Bitters, S-228, 9", amber . . . . $150–$200
CH Swain's Bourbon Bitters, S-227, 9¹/₈", deep olive yellow . . . . $450–$700
CH Swain's Bourbon Bitters, S-228, 9¹/₈", medium orange amber. . . . . . . $150–$225
Chartreuse Damiana Bitters, C-132, 8³/₄", amber. $50–$65
Cider Wine Bitters DR AM Higgins, C-149, 9¹/₈", aqua. . . . . $100–$150
Clarke's Sherry Wine Bitters, C-165, full back label, 7⁷/₈", aqua. . . . . $145–$185
Clarke's Sherry Wine Bitters, Only 25c, C-164, 9", aqua, OP. . . . . $40–$55
Clarke's Sherry Wine Bitters, Rockland Me, C-162, 9", aqua . . . . $50–$80
Clarke's Sherry Wine Bitters, Sharon Mass, C-161, 10", aqua, OP . . . . . $475–$600
Clarke's Sherry Wine Bitters, Sharon Mass, C-163, 9", aqua, OP . . . . $40–$60
Clarke's Vegetable Sherry Wine Bitters, C-155, 14", aqua, OP . . . . $650–$800
Clarke's Vegetable Sherry Wine Bitters, C-155, 14", aqua . . . . $375–$500
Clarke's Vegetable Sherry Wine Bitters, C-156, 12¹/₂" . . . . $400–$550
Clarke's Vegetable Sherry Wine Bitters, C-157, label, 11³/₄", aqua, OP. . $450–$600
Cliff's Aromatic Bitters, R-173.9, 10", yellow amber . . . . $125–$200
Clifford's & Fernald's Original Indian Vegetable Bitters, C-174, 8", aqua, OP . . . .
. . . . $650–$800

Indian Queen-shaped Bitters. PHOTO COURTESY OF GLASS WORKS
AUCTIONS.

Climax Bitters San Francisco Ca, C-175, 9¹/₂", yellow amber . . . . $200–$300
Clotworthy's Oriental Tonic Bitters, C-176, 9¹/₂", yellow amber . . . . $90–$125
Coca Bitters, C-178, 8¹/₂", amber . . . . $80–$120
Coca Bitters The Best Tonic, C-180, full label, 9¹/₈", medium amber. . . $1400–$1850
Cocamoke Bitter Co Hartford, Conn, C-182, 9⁵/₈", amber . . . . $200–$260
Cognac Bitters S Steinfeld Sole Agents, C-187, 11¹/₈", olive green . . . . . $400–$500
Colburg Stomach Bitters, C-188, full label, 10", medium amber . . . . $150–$225
Cole Bros Vegetable Bitters, C-189, 7³/₄", amber . . . . $100–$145
Cole Bros Vegetable Bitters, C-189, 7³/₄", aqua . . . . $50–$80
Colleton Bitters, C-195, 6¹/₄", aqua, OP . . . . $150–$200
Columbo Peptic Bitters, square, 9", amber . . . . $20–$30
Commander Aromatic Bitters, C-205, 11", amber . . . . $225–$325
Compound Hepatica Bitters, C-210, 8³/₈", aqua . . . . $175–$250
Congress Bitters, C-217, 10", light yellow green . . . . $500–$750
Constitution Bitters, C-222, 9¹/₄", golden amber . . . . $1100–$1500
Constitution Bitters, C-223, 9", yellow olive, amber tone . . . . $3000–$3400
Constitution Bitters, AMS 2 1864, C-223, full label, 9", yellow, olive tone . . . .
. . . . $3500–$4500
Constitution Bitters, Bodeker Bros Proprietors Richmond Va, C-221, 7", yellow
amber. . . . . $600–$850
Constitution Bitters, Put Up By BM & EAW, C-220, aqua gazebo, OP, 8¹/₄" . . . . . .
. . . . $7500–$12,000
Corn Juice Bitters, pint, aqua flask. . . . . $250–$400
Covert's Modoc Stomach Bitters, C-241, 8³/₄", medium amber . . . . $125–$175
Creole Bitters, 10³/₈", aqua . . . . $175–$250
Cribb's Davidson & Co Cocktail Bitters, C-183, 9", yellow amber. . . . . . $450–$650
Crittenden's Dyspepsia Bitters St Louis, C-251, 9¹/₈", medium amber . . . $200–$250
Crow's Celebrated Tonic Bitters, unlisted, medium amber barrel, 9⁷/₈" . . . .
. . . . $16,000–$22,000
Cumberland Bitters, C-256, 9¹/₂", medium amber. . . . . $1500–$2000
Curran's Herb Bitters, C-258, 8", yellow green . . . . $140–$190
Curtis & Perkins Wild Cherry Bitters, C-262, 6⁷/₈", aqua, OP . . . . $90–$125
Curtis Cordial Calisaya Great Stomach Bitters, C-261, 11⁵/₈", yellow olive . . . .'.
. . . . $1500–$2500
Damiana Bitters, D-4, 11⁵/₈", aqua . . . . $150–$200
Dandelion Bitters, D-8, 7¹/₄", amber. . . . . $800–$1200
Davis's Kidney and Liver Bitters, D-28, 10", amber . . . . $75–$95
Demuth's Stomach Bitters, D-51, 9³/₈", yellow amber . . . . $150–$200
Der Wahre Jakob Bitters, D-51, 10³/₈", clear . . . . $80–$120
Deutenhoff's Swiss Bitters, D-55, 9¹/₄", dark amber . . . . $750–$950
DeWitt's Stomach Bitters, D-64, full labels, 8¹/₄", amber . . . . $75–$100
Diamond Stomach Bitters, D-69, 9³/₄", medium amber. . . . . $275–$375
Diamond's Blood Bitters, D-70, 7⁵/₈", yellow amber, olive tone . . . . $200–$245
Didier's Bitters, D-72, full labels, 7⁷/₈", amber. $150–$200
Dimmitt's 50 Cts Bitters Saint Louis, D-75, flask form, full label, 6¹/₂" . . . .
. . . . $375–$475
Dimock's, Dr. Tally Ho Bitters, D-76, 8¹/₂", golden amber. . . . . $250–$325
Dingen's Brothers Napoleon Bitters, N-2, 10", light yellow olive . . . . . . $800–$1200
Dingen's Napoleon Cocktail Bitters, N-3, gray case, IP, 10", clear . . . . $2500–$3250
Dingen's Napoleon Cocktail Bitters, N-4, yellowish green. . . . . $7000–$9000
Dingen's Napoleon Cocktail Bitters, N-4, olive amber banjo, 9³/₈" . . . . $4000–$5000

Dingen's Napoleon Cocktail Bitters, N-4, olive amber banjo, large crack, $9^3/_8$" . . . . .
. . . . $800–$1100
Doyle's Hop Bitters, D-93, $9^7/_8$", olive yellow . . . . $300–$500
Doyle's Hop Bitters, D-93, 9", amber. . . . . $30–$50
Dr AH Smith's Celebrated Old Style Bitters, unlisted, 9", amber. . . . . $60–$80
Dr AS Hopkin's Bitters Hartford Conn, H-177, yellow amber lady's leg, partial
label, $12^1/_4$". . . . . $2500–$3250
Dr AS Hopkin's Union Stomach Bitters, H-180, full labels, 10", medium yellow olive
. . . . $800–$1100
Dr AS Hopkin's Union Stomach Bitters, H-182, $9^5/_8$", amber . . . . $40–$50
Dr AW Coleman's Antidyspeptic, C-194, IP, $9^1/_8$", medium green . . . . $3500–$4500
Dr Allen's Stomach Bitters, A-31, $12^1/_8$", aqua . . . . $300–$375
Dr Anthony's Angostura Improved Bitters, medium amber lady's leg, $8^1/_2$" . . . .
. . . . $125–$175
Dr Atherton's Dew Drop Bitters, A-106, $9^3/_4$", yellow, olive tone. . . . . $3500–$4500
Dr BF Shermans Compound Prickley Ash Bitters, unlisted, $9^1/_4$", yellow olive . . . .
. . . . $325–$450
Dr Ball's Vegetable Stomachic Bitters, B-14, $6^3/_4$", aqua, OP . . . . $90–$125
Dr Beard's Alternative Tonic & Laxative Bitters, B-41, $8^5/_8$", aqua. . . . . . . $60–$75
Dr Bell's Blood Purifying Bitters, B-56, $9^3/_4$", amber. . . . . $40–$50
Dr Bergelt's Magen Bitters, B-79, $9^7/_8$", olive green. . . . . $65–$90
Dr Bergmanns Magen Bitters, B-80, $6^1/_4$", clear. . . . . $65–$85
Dr Bishop's Wahoo Bitters, B-103, 10", medium amber. . . . . $500–$700
Dr Blake's Aromatic Bitters, B-120, 7", aqua, OP . . . . $80–$100
Dr Boerhaave's Stomach Bitters, B-133, $8^5/_8$", yellow olive . . . . $200–$250
Dr Boyce's Tonic Bitters, B-176, 7", aqua. . . . . $60–$85
Dr Brown's Berry Bitters Houts Mfg Co St Louis, B-221, clear. . . . . $75–$95
Dr CG Garrison's Bitters, G-6.5, 8", aqua . . . . $150–$250
Dr CH Smith's American Stomach Bitters, S-121, $7^3/_4$", clear . . . . $125–$175
Dr CW Roback's Stomach Bitters, R-73, $9^5/_8$", dark olive green. . . . . . $1200–$1600
Dr CW Roback's Stomach Bitters, R-73, amber barrel, $10^1/_8$". . . . . $275–$350
Dr CW Roback's Stomach Bitters, R-73, amber barrel, lip flake, $9^3/_4$" . . . $175–$250
Dr CW Roback's Stomach Bitters, R-73, medium amber barrel, IP, crack, $9^3/_4$". . . . .
. . . . $125–$150
Dr CW Roback's Stomach Bitters, R-74, amber barrel, heavy wear, $9^1/_4$". . . . .
. . . . $125–$150
Dr CW Roback's Stomach Bitters, R-74, amber barrel, lightly cleaned, $9^1/_8$". . . . . . .
. . . . $150–$190
Dr CW Roback's Stomach Bitters, R-74, medium olive green barrel, $9^3/_4$". . . . .
. . . . $4000–$6000
Dr CW Roback's Stomach Bitters, R-75, medium amber barrel, $9^3/_8$". . . . $200–$260
Dr CW Roback's Stomach Bitters, R-75, strong olive tone barrel, $9^1/_4$", yellow. . . . .
. . . . $900–$1250
Dr Caldwell's Herb Bitters, $12^1/_2$", yellowish amber. . . . . $175–$225
Dr Campbell's Scotch Bitters, C-31, 6", medium amber. . . . . $50–$70
Dr Carey's Original Mandrake Bitters, Elmira, NY, C-48, $6^3/_8$", aqua . . . . $50–$65
Dr Carey's Original Mandrake Bitters, Waverly, NY, C-49, $6^3/_8$", aqua. . . $50–$65
Dr Carson's Stomach Bitters, C-64, $7^1/_4$", aqua . . . . $50–$65
Dr Chandler's Jamaica Ginger Root Bitters, C-127, $9^5/_8$", golden yellow . . . .
. . . . $5000–$6000
Dr Corbett's Renovating Shaker Bitters, C-234, $9^1/_2$", aqua, OP . . . . . $2000–$2750

Dr De Andre's Sarsaparilla Bitters, D-35, 9⁷/₈", red amber . . . . $300–$450
Dr EP Eastman's Yellow Dock Bitters, E-14, IP, 7³/₄", aqua . . . . $600–$850
Dr FA Mitchell's San Gento Bitters, M-105, 8⁷/₈", yellow amber . . . . $240–$320
Doctor Fisch's Bitters, F-44, 11¹/₂", amber . . . . $125–$185
Doctor Fisch's Bitters, F-44, 11³/₄", light golden yellow . . . . $400–$500
Dr FFW Hogguers Bitters, H-141, 9", reddish amber . . . . $400–$500
Dr F Hibbard's Wild Cherry Bitters, H-110, 7", aqua . . . . $75–$90
Dr F Hibbard's Wild Cherry Bitters, H-111, 8¹/₄", aqua . . . . $75–$90
Dr Fisch's Bitters, F-44, fish figural, 11¹/₂", golden yellow amber . . . . $350–$450
Dr Fleschhut's Celebrated Stomach Bitters, F-54, 8³/₄", deep blue aqua . $300–$375
Dr Flint's Quaker Bitters, F-60, 9¹/₂", aqua . . . . $30–$40
Dr Flint's Quaker Bitters Providence RI, F-58, 9¹/₂", aqua . . . . $30–$40
Dr Flint's Quaker Bitters, Q-1, fully labeled, 9¹/₂", aqua . . . . $600–$900
Dr Flint's Stomach Bitters, F-60.3, 8", aqua . . . . $30–$40
Dr Forest's Tonic Bitters, F-68, 9¹/₂", amber . . . . $350–$450
Dr Geo Pierce's Indian Restorative Bitters, P-95, 8¹/₂", aqua . . . . $80–$110
Dr George W Bonds Vegetable Strengthening Bitters, B-140, 8", aqua . . $400–$525
Dr Gilmore's Laxative Kidney & Liver Bitters, G-43, 10", medium amber . . . .
. . . . $75–$125
Dr Goddin's Comp Gentian Bitters, G-51, 9³/₄", aqua . . . . $1000–$1500
Dr Goddin's Compound Gentian Bitters, G-52, 9⁷/₈", aqua . . . . $200–$280
Dr Green's Poleish Bitters, G-107, IP, 10³/₄", deep peach puce . . . . $600–$850
Dr HA Jackson's Bitters, J-5, 7³/₈", aqua, OP . . . . $90–$125
Dr Harter's Cherry Bitters, St Louis Mo, H-42, 9¹/₄", aqua . . . . $150–$250
Dr Harter's Wild Cherry Bitters, H-44, 4³/₄", amber . . . . $25–$35
Dr Harter's Wild Cherry Bitters, H-51, 7¹/₄", amber . . . . $125–$150
Dr Hartshorn's Family Medicines, H-62, 9¹/₂", aqua . . . . $30–$50
Dr Henley's California IXL Bitters, 10¹/₄", aqua . . . . $300–$400
Dr Henley's Wild Grape Root IXL Bitters, H-84, 12¹/₈", deep blue aqua . . $80–$100
Dr Henley's Wild Grape Root IXL Bitters, H-85, 12", bright green, olive tone . . . . .
. . . . $2500–$3500
Dr Herbert Johns Indian Bitters, J-43, 8¹/₂", amber . . . . $250–$300
Dr Herbert Johns Indian Bitters, J-43, heavy external stain, 8¹/₂", amber . . $80–$110
Dr Hoff's German Stomach Bitters, H-138, 8⁷/₈", yellow amber . . . . $300–$450
Dr Hoofland's German Bitters, Liver Complaint, H-168, 7¹/₂", aqua . . . . . $40–$60
Dr Hostetter's Stomach Bitters, H-194, 9⁷/₈", deep olive green . . . . $150–$225
Dr Hostetter's Stomach Bitters, citron . . . . $400–$550
Dr Hostetter's Stomach Bitters, H-195, 8⁷/₈", golden yellow amber . . . . . . $90–$125
Dr Hostetter's Stomach Bitters, H-195, 8⁷/₈", yellow with olive tone . . . . $150–$250
Dr Hostetter's Stomach Bitters, H-195, 9", amber . . . . $40–$50
Dr Hostetter's Stomach Bitters, H-195, dark amber . . . . $40–$55
Dr Hostetter's Stomach Bitters, H-195, medium amber, very bubbly, 9" . . . .
. . . . $110–$145
Dr Hostetter's Stomach Bitters, H-196, full labels, 8³/₄", amber . . . . $100–$150
Dr Hostetter's Stomach Bitters, H-199, 10", yellow with olive tone . . . . . $125–$175
Dr RT Hylton's 1867 Wild Cherry Tonic Bitters, H-224, milk glass, 8³/₄" . . . .
. . . . $1500–$2000
Dr Jacob's Bitters SA Spencer New Haven, Conn, J-11, 8³/₈", aqua, OP . $140–$180
Dr JC Chesley's Golden Bitters, C-149, 9¹/₈", aqua . . . . $100–$150
Dr John Bull's Cedron Bitters, unlisted, 9⁷/₈", olive amber . . . . $1100–$1400
Dr John Bull's Compound Cedron Bitters, B-254, 9¹/₂", amber . . . . $300–$380

Dr LaFontain's Imperial Tonic Bitters, L-4, full label, 9$1/4$", amber . . . . $40–$60
Dr LG Bertarm's Long Life Aromatic Stomach Bitters, B-91, 9$1/2$", amber . . . .
. . . . $100–$150
Dr Langley's Root & Herb Bitters, L-20, 6$1/8$", aqua . . . . $125–$165
Dr Langley's Root & Herb Bitters, L-21, 8$1/2$", amber . . . . $200–$240
Dr Langley's Root & Herb Bitters, L-22, 6$1/2$", yellowish olive green . . . .
. . . . $2000–$2750
Dr Langley's Root & Herb Bitters, L-22, 7$1/8$", aqua . . . . $50–$75
Dr Langley's Root & Herb Bitters, L-22, 7", yellow amber . . . . $175–$225
Dr Langley's Root & Herb Bitters, L-24, 6$7/8$", light green . . . . $200–$275
Dr Langley's Root & Herb Bitters, L-26, 6$3/4$", deep aqua . . . . $75–$95
Dr Lawrence's Wild Cherry Family Bitters, L-51, large size, 8$1/2$", yellow amber . .
. . . . $110–$150
Dr Lawrence's Wild Cherry Family Bitters, L-51, large size, 9", amber . . . .
. . . . $100–$140
Dr Lawrence's Wild Cherry Family Bitters, L-51, sample, 5$5/8$", medium amber . . .
. . . . $250–$325
Dr Linwood's Cabinet Bitters, L-94.5, 8$3/4$", amber . . . . $25–$35
Dr LN Hostater Stomach Bitters, brilliant green, yellow striations, 9$1/2$". . . . .
. . . . $1900–$2250
Dr Loew's Celebrated Stomach Bitters, L-111, 9$1/4$", bright yellowish green . . . .
. . . . $325–$450
Dr Loew's Celebrated Stomach Bitters, L-112, sample, 3$7/8$", aqua . . . . . $400–$550
Dr Loew's Celebrated Stomach Bitters, L-112, sample, 3$7/8$", yellowish green . . . . .
. . . . $175–$245
Dr Loew's Stomach Bitters, L-116, 75% labels, 9$1/8$", deep yellowish green . . . .
. . . . $400–$500
Dr Lovegood's Family Bitters, L-124, golden amber building, 10$1/4$" . . $2500–$3500
Dr Lovegood's Family Bitters, L-125, 9$1/8$", amber . . . . $3500–$4500
Dr Lovegood's Family Bitters, L-125, very large crack, 9$1/4$", gold amber . . . .
. . . . $500–$800
Dr Lowerre & Lyon's Restorative Bitters, L-129, 8$5/8$", aqua, OP . . . . . . $500–$650
Dr Lyford's Bitters, L-136, 9$5/8$", aqua . . . . $150–$190
Dr MM Fenner's Capital Bitters, F-11, 10$1/4$", aqua . . . . $25–$35
Dr Mackenzie's Wild Cherry Bitters, M-5, 8$3/4$", clear . . . . $90–$135
Dr Mampe's Herb Stomach Bitters, M-26, 6$3/4$", aqua . . . . $30–$35
Dr Manly Hardy's Genuine Jaundice Bitters, H-34, 6$1/4$", deep blue aqua, op . . . . . .
. . . . $200–$250
Dr Manly Hardy's Genuine Jaundice Bitters, H-35, 7$1/8$", aqua, OP . . . . $125–$175
Dr Manly Hardy's Jaundice Bitters, H-36, 7$1/2$", aqua . . . . $40–$50
Dr Marcus Universal Bitters, M-35, 7$7/8$", bluish aqua, OP . . . . $550–$750
Dr Mavor's Stomach Bitters, M-51, 9$7/8$", olive amber . . . . $3200–$4000
Dr M McHenry Stomach Bitters, 7$7/8$", aqua . . . . $50–$65
Dr Med Koch's Universal Magen Bitters, unlisted, 8$1/4$", medium olive green, OP . .
. . . . $350–$450
Dr Med Koch's Universal Magen Bitters, unlisted, 7$7/8$", olive green . . . . $175–$225
Dr Mowe's Vegetable Bitters, M-154, 10", aqua . . . . $125–$175
Dr Mowe's Vegetable Bitters, M-155, 10", aqua . . . . $150–$200
Dr Owen's European Life Bitters, O-98, 7", bluish aqua, OP . . . . $400–$500
Dr M Perl & Co Peruvian Bark Bitters, P-70, 8$1/2$", bluish aqua . . . . $275–$350
Dr Perley's Leptandrin Bitters, P-58, 8$1/4$", aqua . . . . $150–$200

Dr Petzold's Genuine German Bitters, P-74, 10⁵/₈", reddish amber ..... $200–$250
Dr Petzold's Genuine German Bitters, P-74, full labels, 10¹/₂", medium amber .....
.... $600–$900
Dr Petzold's Genuine German Bitters, P-74, potstone bruise, 10³/₈", amber........
.... $65–$90
Dr Petzold's Genuine German Bitters, P-77, 7", medium amber........ $125–$175
Dr Petzold's Genuine German Bitters, P-78, 10¹/₈", medium amber...... $90–$120
Dr Petzold's Genuine German Bitters, P-78, full label, 10¹/₂", medium amber......
.... $600–$900
Dr Planet's Bitters, P-107, 9³/₄", aqua, IP.......................... $750–$950
Dr Rattinger's Herb & Root Bitters, R-12, 8³/₄", amber .... $40–$50
Dr J Henry Salisbury, Hinsdale, NY, Mountain Herb, M-150, 9", gold amber .....
.... $600–$900
Dr MC Ayer Restorative Bitters, A-144, 8¹/₄", aqua................... $40–$55
Dr S Beltzhoover's Dyspeptic Bitters, unlisted, 9¹/₄", amber .... $350–$425
Dr SD Warner's German Hop Bitters, W-32, 9³/₄", amber .... $300–$375
Dr S Grigg's, G-117, full labels, 10⁷/₈", yellow amber.............. $1000–$1400
Dr Setewar's Tonic Bitters Col O, S-1957, ³/₄", amber................. $75–$90
Dr Shepard's Compound Wahoo Bitters, S-99, 7¹/₂", aqua............. $75–$100
Dr Sim's Anti Constipation Bitters, S-108, amber sample, 7" .... $300–$350
Dr Skinner's Celebrated 25 Cent Bitters, S-115, 8¹/₂", aqua, OP .... $225–$300
Dr Soule's Hop Bitters, S-145, 10", yellow, oilve tone .... $160–$220
Dr Soule's Hop Bitters, S-145, 9¹/₄", amber........................ $75–$100
Dr Soule's Hop Bitters, S-145, 9³/₄", medium yellow, amber tint .... $150–$200
Dr Soule's Hop Bitters, S-145, 9⁵/₈", medium gasoline puce........... $125–$175
Dr Soule's Hop Bitters, S-145, base edge chip, 9¹/₂", medium apricot puce ....
.... $80–$95
Dr Soule's Hop Bitters, S-147, 7³/₄", light golden amber.............. $150–$200
Dr Stanley's South American Indian Bitters, S-174, 8⁷/₈", dark amber.... $80–$120
Dr Stanley's South American Indian Bitters, S-174, 9", golden yellow amber......
.... $240–$310
Dr Stephen Jewett's Celebrated Health Restoring Bitters, J-37, 7³/₈", aqua, OP....
.... $125–$175
Dr Stewart's Tonic Bitters (on base), S-194, labeled, 7³/₄", amber .... $80–$100
Dr Stiebel's Stomach Bitters, S-196, 8³/₄", amber.................... $175–$250
Dr Stoever's Bitters, S-199, full labels, 9¹/₂", medium amber.......... $800–$1100
Dr Stoughton's National Bitters, S-208, 10", golden amber.......... $1500–$2250
Dr Thos Hall's California Pepsin Hall Bitters, H-11, 8¹/₂", yellow amber ....
.... $150–$200
Dr Tompkins Vegetable Bitters, 8⁷/₈", teal blue .... $1000–$1500
Dr Van Dyke, V-7, full labels, 9⁵/₈", clear.......................... $100–$130
Dr Varena's Japan Bitters, V-12, 8⁷/₈", amber .... $100–$175
Dr Von Hopf's Curacao Bitters, V-27, 9¹/₄", amber................... $40–$60
Dr WH Black's Rocky Mountain Bitters, B-116, 8³/₄", yellow amber.... $400–$500
Dr Walkinshaw's Curative Bitters, W-14, full labels, contents, 10", amber ....
.... $475–$600
Dr Warren's Universal Tonic Bitters, W-50, 8¹/₄", light yellow amber... $500–$650
Dr Washington's American Life Bitters, W-53, 9¹/₈", medium amber ... $175–$240
Dr Wheeler's Sherry Wine Bitters, painted label, 8¹/₈", clear .... $150–$225
Dr Wheeler's Tonic Sherry Wine Bitters, W-87, 9⁵/₈", deep aqua...... $900–$1100
Dr Wise's Olive Bitters, W-143, clear bell form, 10¹/₂"................ $325–$475

Dr Wood's Sarsaparilla & Wild Cherry Bitters, W-151, 8⁷/₈", aqua, OP . . . .
. . . . $325–$425
Dr Wosner's Bitters, W-145, 8⁷/₈", deep aqua . . . . $500–$600
Dr Wright's Rocky Mountain Bitters, W-164, 8⁷/₈", medium amber . . . . . $350–$475
Dr Young's Wild Cherry Bitters, Y-11, 8¹/₄", medium amber . . . . $125–$175
Dunbar's Wild Cherry Bitters, D-116.5, 7¹/₂", golden amber . . . . $50–$100
E Bull's Luxury Bitters, unlisted, 9¹/₄", amber . . . . $375–$475
E Dexter Loveridge Wahoo Bitters, L-126, full labels, 10", yellow olive . . . .
. . . . $10,000–$13,500
E Dexter Loveridge Wahoo Bitters, L-126, 10", yellow, green overtones . . . .
. . . . $6000–$7500
E Long's Indian Herb Bitters, L-119, 12", yellow amber . . . . $2500–$3500
E Long's Indian Herb Bitters, L-119, Indian queen figural, 12", light amber . . . .
. . . . $7000–$9000
E Mishler's Wild Cherry Tonic Bitters (on label under glass), 12", amber . . . .
. . . . $800–$1100
ER Clarke's Sarsaparilla Bitters, C-154, 7¹/₄", deep aqua, OP . . . . $250–$350
ER Clarke's Sarsaparilla Bitters, C-154, inner stain, 7³/₈", aqua, OP . . . . $175–$250
Eagle Angostura Bark Bitters, E-2, full labels, 7", amber . . . . $95–$135
Eagle Angostura Bark Bitters, E-3, full labels, sample, 3⁷/₈", amber . . . . . $300–$360
Eagle Angostura Bark Bitters, E-3, sample, 3⁷/₈", amber . . . . $120–$150
Eclipse Bitters Stewart & Kiel, 8³/₄", amber . . . . $250–$350
Edwards Bitters Prepared by Steven's & Co, E-21, 8", aqua . . . . $500–$700
Edwards Bitters Prepared by Steven's & Co, 8", aqua . . . . $500–$700
Electric Bitters, E-29, full label, contents, 9¹/₂", amber . . . . $30–$50
Electric Bitters, E-32, full label, 8³/₄", amber . . . . $25–$40
Elias's Effectual Elixir Bitters, E-35, 8", clear . . . . $100–$140
English Female Bitters, E-45, 8", clear . . . . $30–$40
Excelsior Aromatic Bitters, E-64, 10¹/₄", reddish amber . . . . $750–$950
Excelsior Herb Bitters, E-65, 10", golden amber . . . . $500–$750
F Brown Boston Sarsaparilla & Tomato Bitters, S-36, label, 9³/₈", aqua . . . .
. . . . $375–$500
Faith Whitcomb's Bitters, W-90, 9¹/₈", aqua . . . . $40–$50
Favorite Bitters, Powell & Stutenroth, F-6, amber barrel, 9" . . . . $8000–$11,000
Ferro Quina Bitters DP Rossi, F-41, sample, 3³/₄", yellow amber . . . . $150–$200
Fish Bitters, The, WH Ware, F-45, 11³/₄", yellow root beer amber . . . . . $200–$250
Fish Bitters, The WH Ware, F-46, 11³/₄", yellowish green . . . . $3500–$5000
Fish Bitters, The WH Ware, F-46, 11³/₄", yellowish green . . . . $3500–$5000
Fish Bitters, The WH Ware, F-46, aqua . . . . $6500–$8000
Fish Bitters, The WH Ware, F-46, aqua . . . . $6500–$8000
Fish Bitters, The WH Ware, F-46, lip flake, edge bruise, 11¹/₂", light yellow green . .
. . . . $2000–$3000
Fish Bitters, The WH Ware, F-46, 11⁵/₈", amber . . . . $160–$230
Fish Bitters, The, WH Ware, F-45, 11⁵/₈", amber . . . . $160–$230
Fish Bitters, The, WH Ware, F-46, potstone crack, 11⁵/₈", amber . . . . $100–$125
Fitzpatrick's CE 50 NT Stomach Bitters, clear flask, 8¹/₈" . . . . $120–$170
4 in 1 Bitters Co, F-74, 10¹/₄", amber . . . . $30–$40
Fowler's Stomach Bitters, F-76, label, 9⁷/₈", medium yellowish amber . . $750–$1250
Frazier's Root Bitters, F-83, 7³/₄", aqua . . . . $75–$110
French Bitters, Morse & Williams, F-87, 9⁷/₈", amber . . . . $200–$250
French Tonic Bitters, unlisted, 12³/₈", aqua . . . . $1500–$2500

Frisco Hop Bitters, F-91, 9", aqua .... $200–$250

Fritz Reuter Bitters, R- 40, milk glass, 10" .... $200–$240

Fulton M McRae Yazoo Valley Bitters, Y-2, 8⅝", yellow amber .... $125–$175

Garry Owen Strengthening Bitters, C-97, 9", amber .... $80–$100

Gen'l Frank Cheatam's Bitters, C-136, 10", reddish amber .... $5000–$6500

Genuine Black Walnut Bitters, G-140, 7¾", clear .... $120–$150

Genuine Bull Wild Cherry Bitters, G-15, 8¼", clear .... $50–$75

Geo C Hubbel 7 Co Golden Bitters, G-63, 10", aqua .... $300–$425

German Hop Bitters, G-24, 9⅜", amber .... $125–$195

German Hop Bitters, G-24, 9⅜", medium yellow amber .... $190–$260

German Hop Bitters, DR CD Warner, W-32, 10", amber .... $400–$550

German Hop Bitters, Warner, G-25, almost full labels, 9¾", yellow amber........
.... $400–$550

German Tonic Bitters, G-28, 9⅝", aqua, IP .... $450–$625

German Wine Bitters, G-32, 10", golden amber .... $500–$800

Germania Bitters, G-331, seated lady, milk glass, full labels, 8½".... $1750–$2250

Germania Bitters Wm C Oesting, G-34, 9", yellow amber............. $125–$165

Gilbert's Sarsaparilla Bitters, G-42, 8⅞", yellow amber.............. $375–$475

Gipp's Land Hop Bitters, G-45, 9½", aqua........................ $200–$250

Globe Bitters, G-47, 10½", light yellow amber .... $750–$900

Globe Stomach Bitters (on label only), golden amber barrel, 9⅜"....... $250–$350

Globe Tonic Bitters, G-49, 9¾", medium amber.................... $80–$120

GM Bayly & Pond Crescent Bitters, C-248, 9⅝", yellow amber...... $2500–$3500

Golden Gate Medicine Co Pepsin Bitters, P-46, 8¾", yellow amber..... $100–$200

Golden Seal Bitters, G-64, 9", golden yellow...................... $300–$400

Gordon's Kidney & Liver Bitters, G-77, 9¾", amber .... $40–$50

Grave's & Son Louisville Ky Tonic Bitters, G-96, 9¾", deep aqua .... $350–$500

Great Tonic, The, Caldwell's Herb Bitters, C-8, 12", amber, IP .... $100–$200

Great Universal Compound Stomach Bitters, B-280, 10½", clear .... $4500–$5500

Greeley's Bourbon Bitters, G-101, puce tone barrel, 9", copper........ $275–$375

Greeley's Bourbon Bitters, G-101, smoky copper barrel, 9¼".......... $275–$375

Greeley's Bourbon Bitters, G-101, smoky olive barrel, lip chip, 9" ...... $550–$700

Greeley's Bourbon Bitters, G-101, smoky topaz green barrel, 9"........ $700–$950

Greeley's Bourbon Bitters, G-102, 9", medium smoky grape puce....... $700–$900

Greeley's Bourbon Bitters, G-102, medium strawberry puce barrel, 9" ... $400–$500

Greeley's Bourbon Bitters, G-102, aqua barrel, 9" .... $1400–$2000

Bitters, Greeley's, barrel shaped. PHOTO COURTESY OF NEIL
GROSSMAN.

Greeley's Bourbon Bitters, G-102, deep pink amethyst barrel, 9" .... $400–$500
Green Mountain Cider Bitters, 8³/₄", aqua .... $110–$160
Greenhut's Bitters, G-109, 11", amber............................ $140–$190
Greer's Eclipse Bitters, G-112, 8³/₄", amber .... $100–$200
Griffith's Opera Bitters, G-116, 8⁷/₈", golden amber.................. $180–$260
GW Day's Stomach Bitters, 9¹/₂", aqua........................... $100–$150
H & K Stomach Tonic Bitters, unlisted, 8³/₄", amber .... $125–$175
Hagan's Bitters, H-5, 9³/₄", yellow amber .... $175–$225
Hall's Bitters, H-9, puce amber barrel, 9¹/₄" .... $2250–$3250
Hall's Bitters, EE Hall, New Haven, H-10, amber barrel, 9¹/₈".......... $200–$300
Hall's Bitters, EE Hall, New Haven, H-10, 9¹/₄", yellow, amber tone .... $240–$300
Hall's Bitters, EE Hall, New Haven, H-10, labels, 9¹/₄", yellow amber ... $300–$380
Hart's Star Bitters, H-58, 9¹/₈", aqua............................. $275–$350
Hart's Star Bitters, H-58, 9¹/₈", aqua............................. $275–$350
Hartwig Kantorowicz Berlin, unlisted, rear label, 6⁷/₈", deep olive green ....
.... $150–$200
Hartwig Kantorowicz, sloping collar, 8¹/₂", deep red amber .... $600–$850
Hartwig's Celebrated Alpine Bitters, H-64, 8⁷/₈", amber.............. $400–$500
Harvey's Prairie Bitters, H-67, 9³/₈", gold amber cabin .... $1500–$2500
Harzer Krauter Bitters, H-68, 9³/₈", amber......................... $30–$50
Jno Hauvert's German Bitters, 9³/₄", yellow amber.................. $250–$350
HB, H-75, milk glass, case gin form, 9"........................... $125–$175
HB Matthew's Stomach Bitters, H-210, 9", golden amber.............. $90–$120
HM Crooke's Stomach Bitters, C-253, olive green................... $475–$600
Heilbron's Aromatic Bitters, unlisted, aqua lady's leg, 9³/₈" .... $120–$160
Hentz's Curative Bitters, H-88, 9⁵/₈", aqua .... $30–$50
Hentz's Curative Bitters, H-89, aqua sample, 4¹/₄" .... $40–$55
Hepatic Bitters Dr AS Russell & Co, H-90, 8¹/₂", amber .... $125–$175
Herb Bitters, Estd 1834 Telliers, unlisted, 9³/₄", yellow amber......... $150–$200
Hercule's Bitter Ca, H-98, 7¹/₈", rich yellow green .... $450–$650
Hercule's Bitter Ca, H-98, 7", emerald green..................... $1400–$1800
Hertrich's Bitter Einzinger Fabikant, H-104, 9¹/₄", olive green .... $400–$550
Hertrich's Bitter, unlisted, 5¹/₄", yellow green.................... $175–$225
Herzberg Bros Botanic Bitters New York, H-165, 9⁵/₈", yellow amber............
.... $1200–$1500
Herzberg's Bitters, 11¹/₂", yellow, olive tint .... $190–$240
Hi Hi Bitters, H-118, 9¹/₂", amber................................ $35–$45
Highland Bitters & Scotch Tonic, deep golden yellow barrel, 9¹/₂" ..... $750–$1250
HN Winfree's Aromatic Stomach Bitters, W-135, 6¹/₂", greenish aqua .. $200–$300
Hoffheimer Brothers Bavarian Bitters, B-34, 9¹/₈", golden amber ..... $150–$200
Holtzermann's Patent Stomach Bitters, H-153, amber cabin full label, 4¹/₈" ....
.... $225–$300
Holtzermann's Patent Stomach Bitters, H-154, amber cabin, 9⁷/₈" ...... $225–$350
Holtzermann's Patent Stomach Bitters, H-154, amber cabin, full labels, 9" ....
.... $500–$650
Holtzermann's Patent Stomach Bitters, H-154, full label, 9⁵/₈", medium amber ....
.... $400–$600
Holtzermann's Patent Stomach Bitters, H-154, golden amber cabin, 9³/₄" ....
.... $225–$325
Holtzermann's Patent Stomach Bitters, H-155, light yellow amber cabin, 9¹/₂" .....
.... $1750–$2250

Holtzermann's Patent Stomach Bitters, H-155, medium amber cabin, 9¹/₂" . . . .
. . . . $1250–$1650
Holtzermann's Patent Stomach Bitters, H-154, 9³/₄", reddish amber . . . . $225–$300
Home Bitters Jas A Jackson & Co, H-157, 9¹/₈", yellow amber. . . . . $125–$175
Home Bitters, Jackson Prouts & Douglas, H-159, 9", amber. . . . . $75–$100
Home Stomach Bitters, H-162, 9¹/₄", amber . . . . $65–$90
Hop & Iron Bitters, full labels, contents, 8¹/₂", amber. . . . . $175–$275
Hops & Malt Bitters, H-186, full labels, 9⁷/₈", amber . . . . $750–$1100
Horse Shoe Bitters (horse), H-189, 8⁵/₈", red amber . . . . $4000–$5000
HP Herb Wild Cherry Bitters, H-93, yellow amber cabin, 9⁷/₈". . . . . $250–$350
HP Herb Wild Cherry Bitters, H-94, 8³/₄", Seven-up green . . . . $4000–$5000
Hutchings Dyspepsia Bitters New York, H-217, 9¹/₂", aqua, IP. . . . . $70–$90
Hutchings Dyspepsia Bitters New York, H-218, 8¹/₂", aqua, IP. . . . . $150–$210
Hygeia Bitters, Fox & Co, H-223, 9¹/₄", golden amber . . . . $110–$150
I Newton's Jaundice Bitters, N-25, 6³/₄", aqua, OP. . . . . $300–$375
Imhoff & Glass Bitters, (on label under glass), 11³/₄", yellow amber . . . . $800–$1100
Imperial Kidney, Liver, Nerve, Blood, Stomach Bitters, R-15, 9¹/₂", orange amber
. . . . $100–$200
Indian Blood Bitters, I-14, 9", yellow amber . . . . $300–$400
Iron Bitters, square, 8¹/₂", amber. . . . . $30–$40
Isham's Stomach Bitters, I-35, 9³/₈", yellow amber. . . . . $175–$250
J Dingle's Tonic Bitters, (on base), D-77, 11¹/₂", olive green, IP . . . . $120–$140
J Rose's Orizaba Bitters, clear lady's leg, 11¹/₂". $200–$300
Jackson's Aromatic Life Bitters, J-4, 8³/₄", deep yellow olive . . . . $1300–$1900
Jackson's Stonewall Bitters, J-8, yellow amber cabin, 9⁵/₈" . . . . $1500–$2000
Jacob's Tonic Bitters, J-13, clear cabin, 7⁵/₈", OP . . . . $14,000–$17,500
James W Price's Aromatic Stomach Bitters, P-137, 9³/₄", yellow amber . . . .
. . . . $200–$250
Jenkin's Stomach Bitters, J-28, 9³/₈", red amber . . . . $700–$900
Jim's Bitters Place & Co, J-40, 10¹/₂", amber . . . . $150–$200
John Moffat Phoenix Bitters Price $1.00, M-114, full labels, 6³/₈", aqua . . . .
. . . . $400–$600
John Moffat Phoenix Bitters, M-110, base chip, 5³/₈", yellow olive, OP . . $175–$250
John Moffat Phoenix Bitters Price $1.00, M-110, 5¹/₂", olive green, OP. . . . .
. . . . $300–$400
John Moffat Phoenix Bitters Price $1.00, M-112, 5¹/₂", aqua, OP . . . . $70–$85
John Moffat Phoenix Bitters Price $1.00, M-114, 6³/₈", aqua, OP . . . . $70–$85
John Moffat Phoenix Bitters Price 2 Dollars, M-108, 7¹/₈", olive amber, OP . . . .
. . . . $1750–$2250
John Moffat Phoenix Bitters Price 2 Dollars, M-108, aqua, OP . . . . $750–$1250
John Moffat Phoenix Bitters Price 2 Dollars, M-109, 7⁷/₈", olive amber, OP . . . .
. . . . $1500–$2000
John Moffat Phoenix Bitters, Price $1.00, M-112, 6¹/₄", aqua, OP . . . . $80–$120
John Root's Bitters 1834 Buffalo NY, J-90.4, 10¹/₄", amethystine . . . . . . $500–$750
John Root's Bitters 1834 Buffalo NY, J-90.4, 10", deep olive yellow . . $1400–$1900
John Root's Bitters 1834 Buffalo NY, J-90.4, full label, 10¹/₄", clear. . . . $900–$1250
John Root's Bitters 1834 Buffalo NY, J-90.4, 10¹/₄", medium blue green . . . .
. . . . $900–$1250
John Root's Bitters, R-90, 9¹/₂", aqua. . . . . $3500–$4200
John W Steele's Niagara Star Bitters, S-182, 10¹/₄", bright yellow olive . . . .
. . . . $1600–$2200

John W Steele's Niagara Star Bitters, S-183, 10", amber . . . . $275–$400
John W Steele's Niagara Star Bitters, S-183, 10", golden amber . . . . $450–$750
Johnson's Calisaya Bitters, J-45, 9³/₄", red puce, amber tone . . . . $550–$700
Johnson's Calisaya Bitters, J-45, 9³/₈", amber. . . . . $40–$60
Johnson's Indian Dysteptic Bitters, J-46, 6¹/₂", aqua, OP. . . . . $300–$400
Jones Universal Stomach Bitters, J-53, potstone crack, 9", amber . . . . $150–$250
JM Laroque's Anti Bilious Bitters, L-29, 9⁷/₈", medium amber . . . . $800–$1200
JP Brady's Family Bitters, 9³/₄", yellowish olive amber . . . . $100–$140
JT Higby Tonic Bitters Milford Ct, T-40, 9¹/₂", amber . . . . $80–$120
JT Wiggin's Herb Bitters, unlisted, 9⁵/₈", amber. . . . . $150–$225
JV Mattison Washington NJ Excelsior Herb Bitters, E-65, 10", gold amber . . . .
. . . . $450–$700
JW Colton's Nervine Strengthening Bitters, C-197, label, 8", yellowish amber. . . . .
. . . . $175–$250
JW Hutchinson's Tonic Bitters, H-220, 9", yellow amber, olive tone . . . . $125–$175
Kagy's Superior Stomach Bitters, K-3, 9¹/₂", deep amber . . . . $125–$175
Kaiser Wilhelm Bitters Co, K-5, 10¹/₈", amber . . . . $30–$40
Kaufmann's World Premium Bitters, K-17, 9⁵/₈", amber . . . . $200–$250
Kelly's Old Cabin Bitters, golden amber cabin, 9" . . . . $1300–$1750
Kennedy's East India Bitters, K-28, sample, 4¹/₈", clear . . . . $250–$340
Kennedy's East India Bitters Iler & Co, K-26, 8⁷/₈", clear . . . . $50–$75
Keystone Bitters, K-36, barrel, 9³/₄", amber . . . . $350–$500
Khoosh Bitters, K-38, full labels, 12¹/₂", amber . . . . $225–$300
Kimball's Jaundice Bitters, K-42, 6⁷/₈", yellow olive, IP . . . . $375–$500
King Solomon's Bitters, K-49, full label, 8¹/₄", amber. . . . . $400–$600
King's 25 Cent Bitters, K-56, 6¹/₂", aqua . . . . $40–$50
Knapp's Health Restorative Bitters, K-62, 8¹/₈", aqua, OP . . . . $400–$600
Ko Hi Bitters, K-68, round, 9", amber . . . . $200–$300
Ko Hi Bitters, similar to K-68, rectangular, 9", gold amber . . . . $250–$350
Lackey's Iron Bitters, L-1, 6³/₈", aqua . . . . $75–$110
Lacour's Bitters Sarsapariphere, L-3, 9", yellow amber . . . . $500–$750
Landberg's Century Bitters, L-13, 11¹/₄", golden amber . . . . $3000–$4000
Lash's Bitters, L-32, full labels, 9¹/₄", amber . . . . $20–$30
Lash's Kidney & Liver Bitters, L-36, 9", amber . . . . $25–$35
Lash's Kidney & Liver Bitters, L-38, 9", amber . . . . $25–$35
Laughlin's & Bushfield Old Home Bitters, 0-35, 9⁵/₈", amber . . . . $800–$1100
Lediard's Celebrated Stomach Bitters, L-60, 10", blue green . . . . $500–$750
Lediard's OK Plantation Bitters 1840, L-62, 10¹/₈", medium yellow amber . . . .
. . . . $2000–$3000
Mrs Leonard's Dock & Dandelion Bitters, L-74, full label, 8¹/₈", clear . . $175–$250
Leopold Sahl's Aromatic Stomach Bitters, S-7, 10¹/₈", yellow amber. . . . .
. . . . $3000–$3750
Life Everlasting Bitters Atlanta Ga, L-91, 9¹/₂", golden amber . . . . $400–$550
Life of Man Bitters, CG Gates & Co, G-7, labelled, 8¹/₄", sapphire blue . . . .
. . . . $150–$225
Lippman's Great German Bitters, L-98, 9⁷/₈", yellow amber . . . . $500–$700
Lippman's Great German Bitters, L-99, 9⁷/₈", reddish amber . . . . $250–$375
Litthauer Stomach Bitters, L-102, milk glass, case gin form, 9³/₈" . . . . . . $100–$135
Litthauer Stomach Bitters, L-103, full label, 7", clear . . . . $75–$125
LN Kleinbrook's Bitters, K-78, 8¹/₈", amber . . . . $150–$200
Loftus Peach Bitters, unlisted, 11¹/₂", deep olive amber . . . . $100–$140

Log Cabin Figural, unembossed, similar to ST Drake's, sloping collar, 10", amber . . .
. . . . $125–$175
Lorimer's Juniper Tar Bitters, L-121, 9³/₈", rich yellow green . . . . $700–$1000
Lorimer's Juniper Tar Bitters, L-121, labeled, 9¹/₂", blue green . . . . . . $1000–$1500
Loveridge's Wahoo Bitters, L-127, yellow amber flask, 7" . . . . $700–$925
Lowell's Invigorating Bitters, L-128, 8", aqua . . . . $60–$85
Lutz's German Stomach Bitters (on label under glass), L-134, amber . . . .
. . . . $1800–$2400
Lyon's Bitters Co New Haven, L-141, 9", amber . . . . $70–$90
M Cziner Chemist Malabac Bitters, M-13, gold amber lady's leg, 11¹/₂" . . . .
. . . . $175–$245
Mack's Orange Tonic Bitters, M-3, 8⁷/₈", amber . . . . $200–$250
Magic Bitters, M-8, 7³/₄", amber . . . . $500–$650
Mahan Bitters, St Louis, Mo, M-10.5, 8¹/₂", aqua . . . . $50–$75
Malarion Bitters, M-18, 9¹/₄", amber . . . . $175–$235
Mansfield New Style Highland Stomach Bitters, M-33, 8³/₄", gold amber . . . .
. . . . $500–$700
Mark's Famous Stomach Bitters, M-38, 8⁷/₈", golden amber . . . . $200–$250
McConnon's Stomach Bitters, M-53, 8⁵/₈", red amber . . . . $150–$200
McKeever's Army Bitters, M-58, drum and cannonballs, 10¹/₈", golden amber . . . . . .
. . . . $1600–$2400
McKelvy's Stomach Bitters, M-59, aqua . . . . $250–$350
Milburn's Kola Bitters, M-81, 9¹/₂", medium amber . . . . $350–$450
Mill's Bitters, M-93, golden amber lady's leg, 11³/₈" . . . . $2400–$2900
Mishler's Herb Bitters, M-100, 8³/₄", amber . . . . $125–$160
Mishler's Herb Bitters, M-100, 8³/₄", gasoline peach . . . . $800–$1200
Mishler's Herb Bitters, M-100, 8³/₄", yellow with olive tones . . . . $250–$325
Mishler's Herb Bitters, M-100, 8³/₄", medium strawberry puce . . . . $300–$375
Mishler's Herb Bitters, M-101, 9", amber . . . . $100–$135
Mishler's Herb Bitters, M-99, 8⁷/₈", yellow amber . . . . $100–$125
Mohica Bitters, M-118, 9", amber . . . . $250–$300
Monongahela Rye Bitters, M-120.5, 9³/₄", olive amber . . . . $600–$800
Morning Star Bitters, M-135, 12¹/₂", medium amber, IP . . . . $200–$250
Morning Star Bitters, M-135, SB, 12¹/₂", light golden yellow . . . . $200–$275
Morning Star Bitters, M-135, yellow olive shades to yellow green in neck . . . .
. . . . $1200–$1800
Moulton's Oloroso Bitters, M-146, base edge chip, 11³/₈", deep blue aqua . . . .
. . . . $100–$135
Moulton's Oloroso Bitters, M-146, mint condition, 11³/₈", deep blue aqua . . . .
. . . . $175–$245
Mountain Herb & Root Bitters, M-150, 9¹/₄", yellow amber . . . . $700–$900
Moxie Bitters, M-156, 8⁷/₈", yellow amber . . . . $450–$650
Muller's Genuine Bismark Bitters, M-157, 7⁵/₈", amber . . . . $90–$125
Muller's Genuine Bismark Bitters, M-158, 6¹/₄", amber . . . . $45–$65
N Wood Portland Me, B-279L, full label, SB, 7¹/₂", aqua . . . . $140–$180
Napoleon Bitters 1866 Dingen Brothers Buffalo NY, N-2, 9⁷/₈", amber . . . .
. . . . $1800–$2500
National Bitters, N-7, ear of corn, sheared lip, 12", red amber . . . . $450–$650
National Bitters, N-8, ear of corn, amber tone 1/3 of bottle, 12¹/₂", yellow . . . .
. . . . $900–$1150
National Bitters, N-8, ear of corn, 12¹/₂", deep red amber . . . . $450–$550

National Bitters, N-8, ear of corn, 12¹/₂", puce....................... $750–$1000
National Bitters, N-8, ear of corn, deep burgundy .... $600–$850
National Bitters, N-8, ear of corn, grayish puce .... $1750–$2250
National Bitters, N-8, ear of corn, light golden yellow................ $800–$1100
National Bitters, N-8, ear of corn, yellow.......................... $800–$1000
National Bitters, N-8, ear of corn, 12¹/₂", medium yellow amber .... $350–$450
National Bitters, N-8, ear of corn, 95% label, 12⁵/₈", bluish aqua ...... $3500–$4500
National Tonic Bitters, N-13, 9³/₄", light blue green .... $1200–$1500
New York Hop Bitters Company, N-28, 9³/₈", greenish aqua........... $175–$240
Newman's Golden Fruit Bitters, 10³/₄", medium orange amber .... $600–$750
Night Cap Bitters, N-32, 8⁷/₈", clear............................... $200–$300
NK Brown Iron & Quinine Bitters, I-28, 7¹/₄", clear .... $30–$40
Normandy Herb & Root Stomach Bitters, N-38, 7³/₄", amber........... $40–$65
O'Hare Bitters Co, O-10, 9¹/₂", yellow amber .... $110–$150
O'Leary's 20th Century Bitters, O-55, 9³/₈", amber................... $60–$75
O'Marra's Fenian Bitters JB Wilder & Co, O-63, 9¹/₂", medium teal green........
.... $3500–$4000
OHP Rose Pat'd June 21 70, R-99, full label, 10⁵/₈", medium amber .... $750–$1000
OK 1840 Plantation, medium peach puce cabin, 9⁷/₈" .... $1500–$2000
Old Cabin Bitters, Patented 1863, 0-19, amber cabin, 9¹/₄" .... $1500–$2500
Old Carolina Bitters, 9⁷/₈", yellowish amber .... $500–$850
Old Continental Bitters, 0-25, 10", medium amber.................. $300–$375
Old Dr Aurent's IXL Stomach Bitters, unlisted, 8¹/₂", medium amber ... $450–$650
Old Dr Goodhue's Root & Herb Bitters, G-69, 8⁷/₈", aqua .... $125–$175
Old Dr Solomon's Great Indian Bitters, S-137, 8³/₈", aqua.............. $75–$95
Old Dr Solomon's Indian Wine Bitters, S-138, 8⁵/₈", aqua .... $75–$100
Old Dr Townsend's Celebrated Stomach Bitters, T-51, amber handled chestnut, OP, pontil crack, 8⁵/₈" .... $800–$1200
Old Dr Townsend's Magic Stomach Bitters, unlisted, 9³/₄", deep aqua...........
.... $800–$1000
Old Dr Warren's Quaker Bitters, W-48, 9¹/₂", aqua .... $40–$50
Old Hickory Celebrated Stomach Bitters, O-32, yellow amber sample, 4¹/₂".......
.... $150–$200
Old Hickory Celebrated Stomach Bitters, O-32, 9", amber............. $60–$80
Old Homestead Wild Cherry Bitters, O-37, 9⁵/₈", yellow, olive tone ... $800–$1200
Old Homestead Wild Cherry Bitters, O-37, deep golden yellow....... $750–$1250
Old Homestead Wild Cherry Bitters, O-37, amber cabin, base edge bruise, 9⁵/₈"....
.... $175–$225
Old Homestead Wild Cherry Bitters, O-37, amber cabin, full label, 9¹/₂".........
.... $2500–$3250
Old Homestead Wild Cherry Bitters, O-37, medium amber cabin, 9³/₄" .. $275–$375
Old Homestead Wild Cherry Bitters, O-37, medium strawberry puce cabin, 9³/₈" ...
.... $1000–$1500
Old Homestead Wild Cherry Bitters, O-37, yellow amber cabin, 9⁵/₈" ... $350–$450
Old Sachem Bitters and Wigwam Tonic, O-46, moss green barrel .... $2500–$3500
Old Sachem Bitters and Wigwam Tonic, medium yellow olive barrel, 9".........
.... $3500–$4500
Old Sachem Bitters and Wigwam Tonic, O-46, 9¹/₂", greenish aqua barrel........
.... $3000–$4000
Old Sachem Bitters and Wigwam Tonic, O-46, 9¹/₂", yellow with puce tint........
.... $375–$475

Old Sachem Bitters and Wigwam Tonic, O-46, 9³/₈", medium copper puce . . . .
. . . . $400–$500
Old Sachem Bitters and Wigwam Tonic, O-46, amber barrel, 9" . . . . . . $250–$350
Old Sachem Bitters and Wigwam Tonic, O-46, lip repair, 9¹/₄", golden amber. . . . . .
. . . . $125–$175
Old Sachem Bitters and Wigwam Tonic, O-46, medium yellow amber barrel, 9" . . .
. . . . $300–$350
Old Sachem Bitters and Wigwam Tonic, O-46, root beer amber barrel, OP . . . .
. . . . $750–$900
Old Sachem Bitters and Wigwam Tonic, O-47, root beer amber, OP . . . . $600–$800
Original Pocahontas Bitters, O-86, aqua barrel, 9¹/₄" . . . . $3000–$3500
Original Pocahontas Bitters, O-86, lip chip, potstone crack, 9", aqua . . . $900–$1200
Orolo Bitters Aug Knoefel, O-89, 8⁷/₈", amber . . . . $225–$300
Oxygenated Bitters For Dyspepsia. . ., 7¹/₄", aqua, OP. . . . . $100–$140
Palmer's Tonic Bitters, P-12, 10¹/₄", golden amber. . . . . $1300–$1750
Palmer's Tonic Bitters, P-12, 10¹/₄", medium emerald green . . . . $1400–$1800
Passquier's French Bitters, P-29, large crack, 10", deep amber . . . . $500–$700
Pendleton's Pine Apple Bitters, P-38, 9", amber. . . . . $1000–$1500
Penn's Pony Bitters, P-40, 9", root beer amber . . . . $250–$450
People's Favorite Bitters, P-41, golden amber barrel, 10³/₄" . . . . $10,000–$15,000
Pepsin Bitters RW Davis Drug Co., P-44, 8¹/₄", yellow green. . . . . $75–$95
Pepsin Bitters, RW Davis Drug Co., P-45, yellow green sample, 4³/₈" . . . . . $40–$50
Pepsin Calisaya Bitters, P-50, full labels, 8", yellow green. . . . . $80–$120
Pepsin Wild Cherry Bitters, P-54, 8", amber. . . . . $40–$65
Peruvian Bark Bitters, P-70, 8⁵/₈", aqua . . . . $600–$900
Peruvian Bitters Chas Noelle & Co, 9¹/₂", amber . . . . $125–$165
Peruvian Bitters Prepared by P Shaw (on label), P-66, yellow amber pumpkinseed
flask, 5¹/₈" . . . . $75–$110
Peruvian Tonic Bitters, P-72, 9¹/₂", medium amber. . . . . $200–$245
Peruvian Tonic Bitters, P-72, full labels, 9¹/₂", medium amber. . . . . $400–$525
Peychaud's American Aromatic Bitter Cordial, cylinder, 10", amber . . . . . $30–$45
Peychaud's American Bitters New Orleans, P-83, 10¹/₄", dark yellow olive, OP . . . .
. . . . $1500–$2250
Philadelphia Hop Bitters, P-89, 9¹/₂", aqua . . . . $375–$475
Phoenix Bitters (SEE John Moffat). . . . .
Prickly Ash Bitters, P-140, ABM, 9⁵/₈", medium yellowish amber. . . . . $20–$30
Prickly Ash Bitters, P-140, full label, 9⁵/₈", amber. . . . . $60–$90
Prickly Ash Bitters, P-141, 9¹/₄", medium yellowish amber . . . . $35–$50
Prof Leonard's Celebrated Nectar Bitters, L-75, 9¹/₄", amber . . . . $250–$300
Professor BE Manns Oriental Stomach Bitters, M-29, 10", medium amber. . . . . . .
. . . . $800–$950
Prussian Bitters, P-152, 9", yellow amber . . . . $175–$250
Quinine Tonic Bitters, Q-6, 8", clear . . . . $30–$40
Ramsay's Virginia Tonic Bitters, R-5, 8³/₈", aqua, OP . . . . $750–$1000
Ranche Bitters JK ISH Omaha, R-10, 9", yellow root beer amber. . . . . . . $600–$800
RC Ridgeway & Co (on base), olive amber lady's leg, IP, 10⁷/₈" . . . . $125–$160
Red Jacket Bitters, R-19, 9⁵/₈", yellow amber . . . . $140–$190
Red Jacket Bitters, R-20, 9¹/₈", medium amber . . . . $35–$45
Red Star Stomach Bitters, R-25, 11¹/₄", amber . . . . $150–$200
Reed's 1878 Tonic Bitters, amber square, 9" . . . . $25–$40
Reed's Bitters, medium orange amber lady's leg, 12³/₄" . . . . $300–$425

RH Becker's Russian Bitters, B-45, 10⅝", clear .... $250–$300
Rising Sun Bitters, R-66, 7", greenish aqua, OP...................... $90–$120
Rising Sun Bitters, R-66, SB, medium yellow amber................... $70–$95
Ritz's Juniper & Wild Lemon Bitters, 10", deep amber.............. $700–$950
Rivaud's Cocktail Bitters, R-68, amber 8-sided lady's leg, 12⅝" ...... $800–$1200
RL Edgerton's Stomach Bitters, E-25, 10", yellow amber............. $500–$650
Romaine's Crimean Bitters, R-87, 9¾", golden amber .... $300–$450
Rose Hill Stomach Bitters, R-92, 9¾", amber..................... $125–$175
Rosenheim's Bitters The Great Western Remedy, R-96, 10", copper, puce tone....
.... $275–$375
Rosswinkle's Crown Bitters, R-102, 9", golden yellow amber .... $300–$375
Roth & Co San Francisco Mohica Bitters, M-118, 9", yellow amber .... $300–$400
Royal Bitters, The, Geo A Clement, Niagara, Ont, unlisted, 8⅝", aqua.. $300–$360
Royal Italian Bitters, R-111, 13½", medium pinkish amethyst.......... $500–$650
Royal Pepsin Stomach Bitters, R-113, 8¾", amber .... $70–$95
Royal Pepsin Stomach Bitters, R-114, 7⅜", amber .... $65–$85
Royal Pepsin Stomach Bitters, R-115, 6⅜", amber .... $65–$90
Royal Pepsin Stomach Bitters, R-116, amber sample, 3⅞" .... $200–$250
Royal Pepsin Stomach Bitters, R-116, sample bottle, golden amber ..... $125–$175
RS Gardner & Co, T-4, Chinaman figural, small crack, 11¼", yellow amber ....
.... $3250–$4250
Rush's Bitters AH Flanders MD New York, R-124, 8¾", aqua .... $175–$250
Rush's Bitters AH Flanders MD New York, R-124, labeled, 9", amber .... $35–$50
Russ St Domingo Bitters, R-125, 9⅞", light topaz .... $750–$1100
Russian Imperial Tonic Bitters, R-133, 9½", bluish aqua .... $800–$1200
S & S Bitters Der Doktor 1/3 Gal, S-4, 9½", clear................... $275–$400
Saint Jacob's Bitters, S-13, 8¾", amber .... $100–$125
Salmon's Perfect Stomach Bitters, S-19, 9½", amber .... $75–$90
San Diego Wine Bitters, S-25, 10¾", yellow, olive tints.............. $500–$625
San Joaquin Wine Bitters, S-26, 9¾", yellow amber .... $275–$375
Sanborn's Kidney and Liver Vegetable Laxative Bitters, S-28, 9", amber ....
.... $160–$190
Sandheger's Famous Stomach Bitters (acid etched on glass), 10", clear ....
.... $100–$150
Sarasina Stomach Bitters, S-32, 8¾", amber .... $40–$50
Sarracenia Life Bitters, S-34, 9", yellow green .... $250–$400
Sarracenia Life Bitters, S-35, 8¾", yellow, olive tone .... $100–$150
Sarracenia Life Bitters, S-34, 9", amber .... $140–$200
Sazerac Aromatic Bitters, S-47, amber lady's leg, 12" .... $1000–$1500
Sazerac Aromatic Bitters, S-47, milk glass lady's leg, 12" .... $200–$250
Sazerac Aromatic Bitters, S-48, amber lady's leg, heavy wear, 10⅛" .... $200–$250
Sazerac Aromatic Bitters, S-48, olive green lady's leg, 10⅛" .... $850–$1050
Schroeder's Bitters Henry H Shufeldt & Co, S-71, amber lady's leg, 11½" ....
.... $500–$650
Schroeder's Bitters Louisville and Cincinatti, S-70, amber lady's leg, 5⅛".......
.... $350–$450
Schroeder's Bitters Louisville Ky, S-62, amber lady's leg, 9" .... $400–$550
Schroeder's Bitters Louisville Ky, S-64, 11¾", amber................ $350–$450
Schroeder's Bitters Louisville Ky, S-64, 11⅞", light yellow amber...... $400–$600
Schroeder's Bitters, S-68.5, amber lady's leg, 9".................... $250–$350

Seaworth Bitters Co Cape May NJ, S-82, medium amber lighthouse, 11" . . . .
. . . . $3000–$3750
Seaworth Bitters Co Cape May NJ, S-82, sample amber lighthouse, 6³/₈" . . . .
. . . . $2750–$3250
Seaworth Bitters Co Cape May NJ, S-81, lighthouse, 11", aqua . . . . . . $3250–$4250
Seaworth Bitters Co Cape May NJ, S-82, lip chip, 6¹/₄", golden amber . . . .
. . . . $1000–$1300
GC Segur's Golden Seal Bitters, S-84, 8", aqua, OP. . . . . $75–$125
Senour's Calisaya Bitters, unlisted, 9⁵/₈", yellow amber . . . . $350–$450
Shedd's Spring Bitters, S-97, full labels, 9³/₄", medium amber. . . . . $475–$650
Shurtleff's Bitters, S-104, yellow amber lady's leg, large crack, 12³/₈". . . . $175–$240
Simon's Centennial Bitters, S-110, 10", aqua . . . . $500–$625
Simon's Centennial Bitters, S-110, 10", golden amber . . . . $1400–$1800
Simon's Centennial Bitters, S-110, potstone crack, 10", golden amber . . $850–$1250
Simon's Centennial Bitters, S-110, 10", reddish amber. . . . . $1200–$1500
Sir Robert Edgar's English Life, E-18, 8³/₄", amber. . . . . $350–$475
Smith's Druid Bitters, S-124, cherry puce barrel, 9¹/₂" . . . . $1100–$1500
Smith's Druid Bitters, S-124, olive tone barrel, yellow. . . . . $1800–$2500
Smith's Druid Bitters, S-124, puce tint barrel, 9³/₈", copper . . . . $1000–$1350
Snyder's Celebrated Bitter Cordial, 9⁵/₈", amber. . . . . $125–$175
SO Richardson's Bitters, R-57, 6⁷/₈", aqua, OP. . . . . $50–$65
Sol Frank's Panacea Bitters, F-79, medium amber lighthouse, 9⁷/₈" . . . . . $400–$600
Solomon's Strengthening & Invigorating Bitters, S-139, small body cracks, exterior
heavily cleaned, 9⁵/₈", cobalt . . . . $400–$500
Solomon's Strengthening & Invigorating Bitters, S-140, 9³/₄", cobalt . . . .
. . . . $1200–$1700
Southern Aromatic Cock Tail Bitters, S-149, medium amber lady's leg, 13" . . . .
. . . . $400–$550
ST Drake's 1860 Plantation Bitters, common variant, beer bottle amber. . . . $50–$75
ST Drake's 1860 Plantation Bitters, D-102, 10", deep chocolate amber . . $300–$375
ST Drake's 1860 Plantation Bitters, D-102, 9⁵/₈", deep amthyst . . . . $500–$700
ST Drake's 1860 Plantation Bitters, D-103, 10", black amethyst. . . . . $350–$450
ST Drake's 1860 Plantation Bitters, D-103, 10", medium amber. . . . . $75–$95
ST Drake's 1860 Plantation Bitters, D-104, 10¹/₈", medium amber. . . . . . $175–$250
ST Drake's 1860 Plantation Bitters, D-105, 10", deep cherry puce . . . . . . $175–$250
ST Drake's 1860 Plantation Bitters, D-105, 10", deep root beer amber. . . $110–$150
ST Drake's 1860 Plantation Bitters, D-105, 10", yellow amber, olive tone. . . . .
. . . . $225–$300
ST Drake's 1860 Plantation Bitters, D-105, 10", yellow with puce tone . . $400–$525
ST Drake's 1860 Plantation Bitters, D-105, 9⁵/₈", yellowish lime green . . . .
. . . . $5000–$7000
ST Drake's 1860 Plantation Bitters, D-105, medium gasoline puce (topaz), 10". . . . .
. . . . $225–$325
ST Drake's 1860 Plantation Bitters, D-105, root beer amber, olive tone, 10" . . . .
. . . . $180–$260
ST Drake's 1860 Plantation Bitters, D-105, wide mouth, 9¹/₈", amber . . . .
. . . . $2000–$2500
ST Drake's 1860 Plantation Bitters, D-106, 10", bright yellow olive . . . $750–$1000
ST Drake's 1860 Plantation Bitters, D-106, 10", deep puce. . . . . $200–$275
ST Drake's 1860 Plantation Bitters, D-106, 10", root beer amber . . . . $110–$150
ST Drake's 1860 Plantation Bitters, D-108, 10", cherry puce . . . . $250–$325

ST Drake's 1860 Plantation Bitters, D-108, 10", medium amber......... $70–$90
ST Drake's 1860 Plantation Bitters, D-108, 10", medium apricot puce... $350–$475
ST Drake's 1860 Plantation Bitters, D-108, 10", medium reddish puce .. $160–$220
ST Drake's 1860 Plantation Bitters, D-108, 10", medium yellow apricot . $300–$340
ST Drake's 1860 Plantation Bitters, D-108, 10", yellow with amber tint. . $200–$290
ST Drake's 1860 Plantation Bitters, D-108, 10", light to medium yellow apricot ....
.... $250–$300
ST Drake's 1860 Plantation Bitters, D-108, 10", medium yellow amber, olive tone. .
.... $110–$150
ST Drake's 1860 Plantation Bitters, D-110, 10", light to medium apricot..........
.... $450–$600
ST Drake's 1860 Plantation Bitters, D-110, 10", yellow amber, olive tone.........
.... $700–$900
ST Drake's 1860 Plantation Bitters, D-110, 10", burst lip bubbles, yellow amber ...
.... $75–$100
ST Drake's 1860 Plantation Bitters, D-110, full labels, yellow amber.... $600–$800
St Gotthard Bitters, S-12, 9", amber .... $70–$85
St Nicholas Stomach Bitters, S-16, 9¼", amber, IP .... $4000–$6000
Steinfeld's French Cognac Bitters, S-186, 9¾", medium yellowish amber.........
.... $4500–$5500
Steketee's Blood Purifying Bitters, S-188, 6⅝", amber .... $225–$325
Stomach Bitters Sanford Chamberlain and Albers, P-157, 9½", amber ....
.... $1250–$1750
Suffolk Bitters, Philbrook & Tucker, S-217, yellow amber pig, lip chips, 9¾" .....
.... $450–$650
Suffolk Bitters, Philbrook & Tucker, S-217, 10⅛", yellow amber ...... $650–$825
Suffolk Bitters, Philbrook & Tucker, S-217, 9⅞", yellow, light olive tone........
.... $1500–$2100
Suffolk Bitters, Philbrook & Tucker, S-217, 9⅝" ½" jaw bruise, yellow amber pig .
.... $250–$300
Sumter Bitters Dowie Moise and Davis, S-221, 9¾", medium amber.... $500–$650
Sumter Bitters Dowie Moise and Davis, S-221, 9¾", yellow amber ..... $525–$700
Sun Kidney & Liver Bitters, S-222, 9¼", full label, contents, amber....... $30–$45
Sunny Castle Stomach Bitters, S-223, 9", amber .... $70–$90
Texas Blood Purifier and Tonic Bitters, T-14, 9¾", amber.......... $1000–$1400
Thad Waterman Warsaw Stomach Bitters, W-54.5, 9¾", yellow amber..........
.... $275–$375
Tilton's Dandelion Bitters (on label under glass), T-30L, 11⅜", amber..........
.... $800–$1100
Tinkham's Golden Sherry Wine Bitters, painted label, 10½", clear..... $300–$400
Tip Top HR & Co Bitters, T-31, 9", yellow, olive tone............... $200–$350
Tippecanoe HH Warner & Co, 9", yellow amber log.................. $70–$85
Tippecanoe HH Warner & Co, 9", full labels, yellow amber log........ $300–$500
Tonic Bitters Graves & Son, T-96, 10", amber .... $150–$200
Tonola Bitters, T-47, 8¼", aqua.................................... $85–$115
Traveler's Bitters, T-54, man walking, 10½", yellow amber .... $2500–$3500
Tyler's Standard American Bitters, T-72, 9⅜", root beer amber .... $150–$200
Ulmer's Mountain Ash Bitters New German Remedy, U-2, 7", aqua, OP.........
.... $800–$1100
Uncle Marb's OB Bitters, U-3, 6⅞", amber coffin flask............... $650–$900
Uncle Tom's Bitters, U-5, 10", yellowish amber .... $275–$350

Universe Bitters, U-12, olive green lady's leg, 12" . . . . $8000–$12,000
Upper Ten Bitters, U-15, 9$1/2$", yellow amber . . . . $175–$250
VerMuth Stomach Bitters, V-19, 9", clear . . . . $40–$55
Verno Stomach Bitters, V-15, 9$1/4$", full labels, clear . . . . $30–$40
Von Humboldt's German Bitters, V-30, 7", labeled, aqua, IP . . . . $400–$525
W & Co, P-100, 8$3/8$", medium yellow olive, IP . . . . $900–$1200
W & Co, P-100, 8$5/8$", golden amber pineapple, OP . . . . $350–$450
W & Co, P-100, 8$3/8$", deep olive green pineapple, OP . . . . $1200–$1500
Wahoo & Calisaya Bitters, W-3, 10$1/4$", golden amber . . . . $600–$825
Wakefield's Strengthening Bitters, W-7, 8$1/4$", aqua. . . . . $50–$65
Walker's Tonic Bitters, W-13, 12$1/8$", red amber lady's leg . . . . $250–$375
Walton's Bitters, W-22, 9$3/8$", medium amber . . . . $175–$245
Wampoo Bitters, W-24, 9$3/4$", medium amber . . . . $150–$200
Wampoo Bitters, W-25, 9$5/8$", amber . . . . $125–$165
Warner's Safe Tonic Bitters, W-34, 9$1/2$", reddish amber . . . . $600–$750
Warner's Safe Tonic Bitters, W-34, 9$1/2$", full rear label, amber . . . . . . $1000–$1750
Warner's Safe Tonic Bitters, W-34, 9$1/2$", potstone cracks, amber . . . . $275–$350
Warner's Safe Tonic, W-36, 7$3/8$", full label, amber . . . . $850–$1100
Warner's Safe Tonic, W-36, 9$1/2$", label badly stained, amber. . . . . $300–$400
Warsaw Stomach Bitters, W-54.5, 10$3/4$", amber . . . . $1250–$1750
WC Bitters Brobst & Rentschler, W-57, 10$5/8$", amber . . . . $450–$650
Weis Bros Knickerbocker Stomach Bitters, W-68, 12", amber lady's leg . . . .
. . . . $800–$1150
Weis Bros Knickerbocker Stomach Bitters, W-68, 12", orange amber lady's leg. . . .
. . . . $1500–$2000
West India Stomach Bitters, W-79, 8$3/4$", amber. $60–$80
WF Severa Stomach Bitters, S-88, 9", amber . . . . $70–$90
Wheeler's Berlin Bitters, 6-sided, 9$3/8$", aqua, OP . . . . $1000–$1400
Wheeler's Berlin Bitters, W-83, 9$3/8$", clear, OP . . . . $2000–$2500
Wheeler's Berlin Bitters, W-83, 9$1/2$", IP yellow olive green . . . . $5000–$6500
Wheeler's Genuine Bitters, W-85, 8$3/4$", aqua. . . . . $30–$45
Wheeler's Genuine Bitters, W-85, 8$3/4$", light green . . . . $350–$500
White's Angostura Bitters (on base), W-96, 4$1/8$", sample, olive green . . . . . $40–$45
White's Stomach Bitters, W-101, 9$1/2$", golden amber . . . . $125–$175

Lady's Leg-shaped Bitters. PHOTO COURTESY OF GLASS WORKS
AUCTIONS.

Whitwell's Temperance Bitters Boston, W-105, 7", aqua, OP . . . . $85–$105
Whitwell's Temperance Bitters Boston, W-105, 9½", medium amber . . . . . $70–$85
Edw Wilder's Stomach Bitters, W-116, 10½", clear . . . . $275–$400
William Allen's Congress Bitters, A-29, 10", blue aqua . . . . $250–$350
William Allen's Congress Bitters, A-29, 10¼", deep emerald green . . . $1250–$1500
Winter's Stomach Bitters, W-141, 9⅝", amber. . . . . $60–$80
WL Richardson Bitters, S-58, 6½", aqua, OP . . . . $50–$75
Wm Ritmeier's California Wine Bitters, R-67, 9", golden amber . . . . $150–$200
Wm Ward's Eureka Tonic Bitters, W-28, 8¾", clear . . . . $60–$85
Wood's Tonic Wine Bitters, W-153, 9¼", aqua . . . . $50–$75
Woodcock Pepsin Bitters Schroeder's Med Co, W-159, 8", amber. . . . . $45–$65
Woodcock Pepsin Bitters, W-158, 8", amber. . . . . $45–$60
WR Tyree's Chamomile Bitters, T-75, 9½", amber . . . . $400–$500
Wryghte's Bitters, London, W-165, 5¾", olive green, OP . . . . $375–$475
Yazoo Valley Bitters, Fulton M McRae, Y-2, 8⅝", yellow amber. . . . . $140–$180
Yerba Buena Bitters SF Cal, pint, yellow amber flask . . . . $80–$125
Yochim Bros Celebrated Stomach Bitters, Y-5, 8¾", labeled, amber. . . . . . $40–$55
Zingari Bitters, Z-4, 11⅞", amber lady's leg, faded label . . . . $200–$275
Zoeller's Stomach Bitters, Z-7, 9⅝", full labels, amber . . . . $225–$275
Zwack Jes Tarsan Unicum Budapest, U-9, 3¼", sample, full labels, olive green . . . .
. . . . $35–$45

BLOWN BOTTLES, INCLUDING BLACK GLASS AND CHESTNUT BOTTLES

Blown bottles, or free-blown bottles, are those which are made without the use of any molds and are totally shaped by the glassblower during formation. Blown bottles are the earliest types of bottles made, and it is often difficult to know the origin or date of a given blown bottle since the forms were made overseas as well as in the United States for a long period of time. The novice and experienced collector alike should be wary when purchasing free-blown types of bottles, since it is fairly easy to reproduce such bottles. Become familiar with how the bottles were made and what forms and colors were originally used, and then watch for indicators such as wear and methods of manufacture. The reader is referred to *American Bottles and Flasks and their Ancestry* by McKearin and Wilson.

Please keep in mind the following when buying and collecting blown bottles:

- Valuation of blown bottles depends on many factors, including age (is it 17th, 18th or 19th century); color, although most early blown bottles are shades of green; lip treatment (is it a standard lip treatment for this type of bottle, or unusual); and form. Many collectors, including yours truly, like their blown bottles to be as crude as possible, with crooked sides, uneven lips, bubbly glass, and showing huge open pontils, sometimes so large of a pontil that the item will not even stand straight. The novice collector needs to see and handle as many free blown bottles as possible in order to know what constitutes a rare form, or a common form.
- Even though the sequence of manufacturing innovations made the need to blow bottles free-hand unnecessary by the mid to late 19th century, bottles continued to be blown into the 20th century in the United States and overseas, and continue to be made today. Be very careful when buying blown bottles, and remember that genuinely old bottles were made to be functional; always question a bottle that "does not work," such as one with too narrow a mouth opening, or of very heavy weight; and always watch for legitimate wear on the base, sides, and lips of bottles to ascertain age.

Blacking bottle, square, 4³/₄", sheared lip, OP, olive amber . . . . $40–$60
Bulbous bodied, 5", 2" neck, applied lip, thinly made, OP, olive green . . . . $200–$300
Case gin, square, slightly tapering sides, 9¹/₂", applied lip, OP, 9¹/₂", olive amber. . . . .
. . . . $40–$55
Case gin, square, slightly tapering sides, 14¹/₂", applied lip, OP, olive amber . . . .
. . . . $200–$300
Case gin, square, slightly tapering sides, 16¹/₂", applied lip, OP, olive green . . . .
. . . . $375–$550
Chestnut bottle, flattened sides, 3¹/₄", miniature, OP, olive amber. . . . . $450–$450
Chestnut bottle, flattened sides, 5", applied lip, OP, olive green . . . . $100–$150
Chestnut bottle, flattened sides, 6¹/₄", applied lip, OP, olive green . . . . $100–$150

Blown, Chestnut, with flattened sides. PHOTO COURTESY OF NEIL GROSSMAN.

Demijohn or "carboy." These large bottles were often used to transport chemicals or spirits, and were often encased within wicker to protect the bottle from breakage and to keep sunlight away from the contents, since light might diffuse the potency of the contents. These bottles are available both pontiled and unpontiled, with pontiled worth more. This particular example measures 16" in height and 17" in width and has semiflattened sides. PHOTO COURTESY OF LYNDA MAGDITS.

Chestnut Bottle, flattened sides, 9¹/₈", applied lip, OP, olive green . . . . . . $125–$195

Cylinder, free blown, 4¹/₂", squared off shoulder, straight neck, flaring lip, OP, olive green . . . . $38–$50

Cylinder, free blown, 5⁷/₈", uneven sides (indicates an early piece), OP, applied string ring below lip, olive amber . . . . $400–$400

Cylinder, free blown, tooled pouring spout, 8", olive amber, OP . . . . $80–$125

Cylinder, free blown, 6⁵/₈", wide mouth, folded over lip, OP, olive amber . $150–$200

Cylinder, hock-wine form, 10¹/₂", high kick up in base, OP, laid on ring below lip, olive green. . . . . $30–$50

Cylinder, straight sided, 12", sloping collar, OP, olive amber . . . . $40–$60

Cylinder, straight sided, 7", blown from a two-piece bottle mold, wide flaring mouth, OP, olive green . . . . $450–$700

Cylinder, free blown, 4¹/₂", squared off shoulder, straight neck, sheared lip, OP, olive amber. . . . . $35–$45

Cylinder, free blown, 4¹/₂", squared off shoulder, straight neck, sheared lip, OP, olive green . . . . $35–$45

Decanter, flaring lip, undecorated, period stopper, OP, quart, clear . . . . $40–$70

Decanter, quart, two bands of chainlike decoration around body, with stopper, OP, clear. . . . . $250–$350

Decanter, heavy ring lip, "Wine" engraved on side, two neck rings, quart, clear. . . . . $150–$250

Left: *blown, Dutch squat.* Right: *blown, globular form.* PHOTOS COURTESY OF NEIL GROSSMAN.

Decanter, heavy ring lip, neck rings, OP, quart, olive amber . . . . $400–$600

Decanter, two bands of triple neck rings, OP, period stopper, quart, clear . . . . $60–$90

Demijohn, bulbous form, OP, 16", olive amber . . . . $125–$175

Demijohn, pear shaped, 17$1/2$", olive green . . . . $125–$175

Demijohn, pear shaped, 17$1/2$", olive green . . . . $75–$125

Dutch, ca. 1740, squat, laid on ring below lip, 6$1/2$", OP, olive green . . . . $50–$90

Dutch, ca. 1740, squat, laid on ring below lip, 6$1/2$", OP, inner stain, heavy wear, small lip chips, olive green . . . . $20–$40

Flask, coffin shape, sloping collar, SB, pint, clear . . . . $5–$10

Flask, diamond shaped, flattened sides, sheared lip, OP, 6$1/4$", olive green. . . . . $125–$175

Flask, strap sided, double collar, SB, pint, clear . . . . $3–$6

Flask, tear drop shape, applied lip, OP, 5$1/4$", clear . . . . $40–$60

Fly Trap, three ball feet, clear stopper, 7", clear . . . . $100–$145

Globular Form, long neck, applied lip, OP, 9", olive green . . . . $80–$150

Globular Form, miniature, applied lip, OP, 3$3/4$", olive amber. . . . . $400–$600

Handled Bulbous bodied Bottle, bulbous bodied, sloping collar, OP, 5$1/2$", strawberry puce. . . . . $140–$220

Handled Bulbous bodied Bottle, sloping collar, OP, 5$1/2$", deep amber . . . . $75–$125

Handled Chestnut, flattened sides, 8$1/4$", laid on ring below lip, OP, amber . . $30–$40

Handled Chestnut, flattened sides, 7$3/4$", laid on ring below lip, OP, olive green . . . . $50–$75

Hexagonal, 4$1/4$", slightly flared lip, OP, olive green. . . . . $350–$500

Hexagonal, 5$1/4$", slightly flared lip, OP, olive amber . . . . $400–$550

Hexagonal, flaring lip, OP, 4", aqua . . . . $15–$20

Lady's Leg Whiskey Bottle, cylinder, 10$1/2$", olive green . . . . $20–$30

Mallet Form, ca. 1720, laid on ring below lip, OP, 6$1/4$", olive amber . . . . . $140–$180

Mallet Form, laid on ring below lip, OP, chips on string ring, heavy wear on sides, olive amber. . . . . $75–$125

Miniatures (see Shape category), Miniatures are often very rare and quite valuable; under 4" and you might have a miniature, but remember that certain medicine and pill bottles were normally issued in small sizes, so these are not truly miniatures; under 3" bottles in color and pontile . . . .

Onion Form, OP, 5$3/4$", olive green. . . . . $175–$225

Rectangular, beveled edges, 1" wide mouth, OP, 4", olive amber . . . . $40–$50

Rectangular, beveled edges, 1" wide mouth, rolled lip, 6$1/2$", aqua . . . . $75–$150

Blown, mallet-shaped wine, ca. 1720. PHOTO COURTESY OF NEIL GROSSMAN.

Rectangular, beveled edges, double collared lip, medicine shaped, OP, 7^1/$_4$", olive green . . . . $100–$135

Rectangular, early, beveled edges, 1" wide mouth, crude applied lip, postone crack, 6^1/$_2$", olive green . . . . $80–$125

Rectangular, early, beveled edges, OP, 1" wide mouth, curde applied lip, 6^1/$_2$", olive green . . . . $175–$200

Rectangular, rolled lip, OP, 4^1/$_2$", aqua. . . . . $12–$16

Round, blown in three-piece mold, glass, OP, beer bottle form, lady's leg neck, 7", black . . . . $10–$20

Round, blown in three-piece mold, whittled sides, straight sided, straight neck, tooled collar, OP, 7^1/$_2$", aqua . . . . $12–$18

Round, rolled lip, 4^3/$_4$", OP, aqua . . . . $10–$14

Shaft & Globe, rounded bottom, 7^1/$_4$", OP, wear, small lip chips, 7^1/$_4$", olive green . . . . $1500–$2200

Shaft & Globe, rounded bottom, 7", string ring chips, OP, 7", olive amber . . . . $1500–$2200

Shaft & Globe, tapering "V" shaped base, 6^7/$_8$", OP, wear, olive amber . . . . $1750–$2500

Square, blacking bottle, sheared lip, OP, 4^3/$_4$", olive amber . . . . $40–$60

Square, snuff, 1" wide mouth, OP, 4", olive green . . . . $125–$165

Square, snuff, 1" wide open mouth, bubbly, OP, 5^1/$_2$", olive amber . . . . $250–$325

BLOWN GLASS

Blown glass refers to blown tableware such as pitchers, bowls, creamers, sugar bowls, etc. that were made at 18th- and 19th-century American glasshouses. It was not uncommon for glassblowers to be given free time at the end of a shift to use the furnaces to make things for themselves and their families. This type of work is often called "offhand." Many of these items were not commercial (not made for resale) but rather made for the glassblowers family or for gifts or presentation pieces; some were made to be sold in the company's stores, or for distribution to retail outlets around the state or country, or for possible export. Most of the pieces were unpatterned ("free blown"), while some were blown into ribbed, diamond, ogival or other molds ("pattern molded"). Items also included within this classification are gadrooned, lily pad, and threaded. Legitimately old offhand pieces would almost always have an open pontil mark, although some of the items blown for commercial sale might have a polished or ground-down pontil. Free blown and patterned molded bottles are not covered under this section; see Blown, and Pattern Molded Bottles sections. This section deals strictly with blown tableware, such as sugar bowls, bowls, mugs, wines, etc.

Yes, this is a book on bottles, but blown glass is one of those crossover areas a bottle collector might run into, so this will serve as general information for both glass and bottle collectors. Blown glass is an *extremely* difficult area, since the same techniques and equipment used to blow a piece of glass in 1750, 1850, 1900 or 1950 are still used today. As you read this, there are numerous glasshouses across the country, and around the world, that continue to free blow and mold blow pieces in the same forms and colors as originally made 100 or 200 years ago. Sometimes the items are marked, making it easier to identify as a reproduction; usually, however, the pieces are unmarked, making it difficult to determine the authenticity of a piece.

Finding early blown glass can prove to be quite a challenge. In fact, if someone had a million dollars to spend and wished to start collecting quality and rare blown glass examples today, they would probably not get very far; the stuff is simply not available for sale. A great deal of the rare and desirable pieces are in museum collections, or in private collections that are rarely sold. Sure, you can get lucky and find something at an estate sale or auction, but don't count on it. About five years ago, while I was working for Skinner's Auctioneers, I took in for consignment an olive amber lily pad bowl with a blown funnel foot that was purchased at an upstate New York estate sale for the grand sum of $100; we sold the piece, which the consignor found on the top shelf of the pantry, for about $10,000. You are more likely to encounter the more common pieces, such as clear pillar mold decanters, which are worth about $40 to $60, or clear free blown bowls, valued at maybe $80 to $150, or tons of finger bowls in every color imaginable, most worth in the $20 to $50 range. But good luck trying to find something rare! There are several auction houses that cater to the bottle and glass collector (they are listed in the auction section in this book) but even they rarely have any truly great blown glass for sale. You can try the antique show route, and you will see plenty of clear wines with button knop stems or with paneled bowls, and loads of wine rinsers, and bunches of clear cut or pressed decanters, and quantities of English blue and emerald green wines or decanters, but quality American blown glass is almost impossible to find even there.

So how does one tell an old piece from a 20th-century reproduction? Learning blown glass is truly a hands-on experience, and is something which is difficult to impart well through these few paragraphs. You have to learn about form, and what types of pieces were made when; get a copy of *American Glass* by McKearin, the finest book ever on American blown glass, and visit the museums to look at the pieces. Be aware that the great majority of blown glass that you see in antique shops and at antique shows is 20th-century; old glass is simply hard to find. Go to the major glass shows such as those held in Old Greenwich, CT, each April, and in Hyannis, MA, each August and *handle* the items, and don't be afraid to ask questions of the dealers. Old blown glass sometimes surfaces at bottle shows, but there are reproductions mixed in there along with it. Be *very* careful before you spend any money. Some of the reproductions you will encounter were done in the 1920s–1940s and are often very difficult for the uninitiated to distinguish from the pre-Civil War era blown glass, since these reproductions might have 75 years of wear on them. After all these "warnings," if you still get excited about blown glass, if you catch the "fever," reconcile yourself to the fact that even after you collect for ten or more years, you will still be fooled by a piece, still see those pieces that defy dating or attribution. So enjoy, but beware!

BLOWN THREE-MOLD

Blown three-mold is a term given to bottles and glass which was produced between 1820 and 1840 in the New England and Midwestern areas and blown into three-piece molds (although molds with two or four or more pieces were also used); however, blown three-mold was also produced in France, Portugal, and England and is often difficult to differentiate from American pieces.

It is very important for the collector to differentiate between blown three-mold glass and pressed three-mold glass. On blown three-mold glass, since the impression was obtained by the glass blower blowing a bubble into a mold, the mold impression can always be felt on the inside, as well as the outside, of the piece. On pressed three-mold pieces, the impression can only be felt on the outside of the piece.

Blown three-mold glass was made in a wide variety of patterns and colors. The colors vary from amethyst, sapphire blues, and a wide assortment of greens. All blown three-mold pieces should have rough pontil scars. Collectors should become familiar with the patterns listed in *American Glass* by McKearin, as there are many foreign lacy patterns to be contended with, as well as numerous reproductions and outright fakes. The Metropolitian Museam of Art has been selling well-made and realistic blown three-mold reproductions which should have the initials "MMA" roughly engraved on or next to the pontil mark. Collectors should also become familiar with the products of the Clevenger Brothers Glassworks, which began operations in New Jersey in the 1920s, and which made faithful reproductions, but often in unusual colors not characteristic of the originals.

Anyone who is seriously considering pursuing blown three-mold glass collecting is well advised to obtain a copy of the article "Unmasking an American Glass Fraud" by Dwight Lanmon (*Antiques Magazine,* Jan. 1983), which goes into great detail on some extremely well-made blown three-mold fakes. The reader is also referred to *American Glass* by McKearin, which the letter "G" refers to below.

Bird Fountain, GI-12, flattened knop finial, 5¼", clear . . . . $100–$150
Bird Fountain, GI-12, hen finial . . . . $200–$300
Bowl, GII-18, 4½", rare color, olive amber . . . . $7500+
Bowl, GI-5, 4½", clear . . . . $60–$90
Bowl, GI-5, 6", clear . . . . $90–$125
Bowl, GI-30, aqua . . . . $1500–$2000
Bowl, GII-18, 4¼", clear . . . . $50–$80
Bowl, GII-18, 5½", clear . . . . $50–$70
Bowl, GII-18, 5¾", clear . . . . $60–$90
Bowl, GII-18, rare color, 4½", olive amber . . . . $7500+
Bowl, GII-19, 5⅜" . . . . $60–$80
Bowl, GII-21, 4⅞" . . . . $80–$100
Bowl, GII-21, 5½", clear . . . . $60–$80
Bowl, GII-28, 4", clear . . . . $125–$150
Bowl, GIII-8, 5¾", clear . . . . $60–$85
Bowl, GIII-20, 6⅝", clear . . . . $100–$150
Bowl, GIII-20, 8¾", clear . . . . $250–$300
Bowl, GIII-21, 5¾", clear . . . . $70–$95
Bowl, GIII-22, 4¾" . . . . $80–$100
Bowl, GIII-23, 5¼", clear . . . . $60–$90
Bowl, GIII-24, 4⅞" . . . . $60–$80
Carafe, GI-29, quart, blue green . . . . $1500–$2500
Castor Bottle, GI-11, 4½", clear . . . . $40–$70
Castor Bottle, with original peaked and sided stopper, GI-10, clear . . . . $40–$70
Castor Set, GI-20, four pieces, silver plated holder . . . . $200–$300
Celery Vase, GII-22, 7½", clear . . . . $650–$900
Celery Vase, GIII-34, clear . . . . $900–$1250
Celery Vase, GV-21, 8¼", clear . . . . $700–$900
Creamer, GI-07-03, 3", opaque robin's egg blue . . . . $300–$400
Creamer, GI-07-03, 3", opaque white . . . . $250–$325
Creamer, GI-29, 4¼", cobalt . . . . $1500–$2200
Creamer, GI-29, amethyst . . . . $2500–$4000
Creamer, GI-29, applied foot, 4⅜", cobalt . . . . $2750–$3750
Creamer, GI-29, blue . . . . $2000–$3000
Creamer, GII-3, 2½", clear . . . . $350–$400

Creamer, GII-3, clear. . . . . $300–$400
Creamer, GII-18, 2³/₄", clear. . . . . $250–$300
Creamer, GII-21, 2⁷/₈", clear. . . . . $300–$400
Creamer, GII-21, 3", clear. . . . . $250–$350
Creamer, GII-22, 2³/₄", clear. . . . . $300–$400
Creamer, GIII-6, 4¹/₄", clear . . . . $350–$450
Creamer, GIII-6, 4³/₈", clear . . . . $300–$375
Creamer, GIII-6, small chip inside spout, 4". . . . . $350–$450
Creamer, GIII-14, 4¹/₂", clear . . . . $300–$400
Creamer, GIII-14, clear. . . . . $300–$350
Creamer, GIII-21, clear . . . . $300–$350
Creamer, GIII-21, miniature, 2³/₄", clear. . . . . $300–$375
Creamer, GIII-26, 4³/₄", cobalt . . . . $2000–$2500
Creamer, GIII-26, 4³/₄", cobalt with clear handle . . . . $2000–$3000
Creamer, GV-8, 4¹/₂", clear. . . . . $350–$450
Creamer, GV-14, 4⁷/₈", clear. . . . . $500–$750
Creamer, GV-14, clear . . . . $600–$900
Decanter, GII-6, globular form, 8³/₄", aqua. . . . . $2000–$3000
Decanter, GI-15, original stopper, quart, clear . . . . $150–$200
Decanter, GI-27, quart, clear. . . . . $125–$175
Decanter, GI-29, correct stopper, 6¹/₂", cobalt . . . . $300–$425
Decanter, GI-29, half pint, cobalt . . . . $1000–$1500
Decanter, GI-29, period stopper, quart, clear . . . . $100–$140
Decanter, GI-29, quart, blue green . . . . $1000–$1500
Decanter, GI-29, quart, clear. . . . . $100–$150
Decanter, GI-8, "Brandy," quart, clear . . . . $250–$300
Decanter, GII-2-1, half pint, clear . . . . $125–$175
Decanter, GII-3, half pint, dark olive green. . . . . $3000–$5000
Decanter, GII-06, globular form, 8³/₄", aqua. . . . . $2000–$3000

Kent decanter, globular body, GII-6. PHOTO
COURTESY OF GLASS WORKS AUCTIONS.

Decanter, GII-7, barrel shaped, 8¹/₂", olive green . . . . $1500–$2000
Decanter, GII-7, barrel shaped, 9¹/₈", aqua . . . . $2000–$2500

Decanter, GII-7, barrel shaped, 9", aqua . . . . $1600–$2300
Decanter, GII-7, barrel shaped, glass, 8½", black. . . . . $1750–$2500
Decanter, GII-7, barrel shaped, pint, clear. . . . . $125–$175
Decanter, GII-7, barrel shaped, quart, clear. . . . . $100–$150
Decanter, GII-7, pouring spout, handled, 11½", clear . . . . $250–$350
Decanter, GII-10, quart, clear . . . . $125–$175
Decanter, GII-10, stopper is diamond patterned shot glass, quart, clear . . . . $200–$300
Decanter, GII-12, miniature, original stopper, 3½", clear . . . . $400–$600
Decanter, GII-18, quart, clear . . . . $90–$120
Decanter, GII-18, sunburst stopper, 5" (including stopper), quarter pint . . . $200–$300
Decanter, GII-18, three quilled neck rings, blown stopper, quart . . . . $70–$95
Decanter, GII-22, pint . . . . $100–$125
Decanter, GII-22, quart, clear . . . . $90–$120
Decanter, GII-22, quart, clear . . . . $80–$110
Decanter, GII-24, quart, clear . . . . $200–$250
Decanter, GII-26, pint, clear . . . . $150–$200
Decanter, GII-27, quart, clear . . . . $90–$120
Decanter, GII-28, flaring lip, mushroom stopper, quart, deep emerald green. . . . .
. . . . $2500–$4000
Decanter, GII-28, no stopper, square quart, clear . . . . $100–$125
Decanter, GII-28, square pint, clear. . . . . $150–$200
Decanter, GII-28, square quart, olive green. . . . . $2000–$3000
Decanter, GII-28, square, 10", medium olive yellow . . . . $1600–$2200
Decanter, GII-28, square, 8", light lime green, stopper. . . . . $1100–$1400
Decanter, GII-28, square, pint, clear . . . . $100–$150
Decanter, GII-29, 7", deep emerald green. . . . . $9000+
Decanter, GII-29, 7", medium violet purple . . . . $9000+
Decanter, GII-30, pint, emerald green. . . . . $3000–$4000
Decanter, GII-30, square, sea green. . . . . $2500–$3500
Decanter, GII-33, miniature, 5¼" matching stopper, ¼" pint, clear . . . . . . $500–$600
Decanter, GII-43, pineapple shaped, aqua. . . . . $2500–$3500
Decanter, GII-43, pineapple shaped, quart, yellow green . . . . $2500–$3750
Decanter, GII-43, quart, clear . . . . $800–$1200
Decanter, GII-46, half pint, clear. . . . . $250–$350

Left: *"Pineapple" decanter.*
Right: *Keene decanter,*
PHOTOS COURTESY OF GLASS
WORKS AUCTIONS.

Decanter, GIII-2-1, pint, deep yellow olive.......................... $2000+
Decanter, GIII-2-1, pint, olive green............................ $1750–$2500
Decanter, GIII-2-1, quart, olive green........................... $1500–$2250
Decanter, GIII-2-2, mismatched stopper, pint, clear................... $100–$140
Decanter, GIII-5, stained, quart, clear............................... $70–$90
Decanter, GIII-5, threaded neck, acorn stopper, quart, clear............ $600–$900
Decanter, GIII-6, 7¼", olive amber .... $375–$475
Decanter, GIII-6, half pint, clear................................. $200–$300
Decanter, GIII-6, quart, olive green.............................. $350–$400
Decanter, GIII-9, half pint, clear................................. $300–$375
Decanter, GIII-9, pint, clear...................................... $90–$125
Decanter, GIII-9, wheel stopper, pint, clear .... $100–$150
Decanter, GIII-12, miniature, original stopper, 3⅞", clear.............. $450–$750
Decanter, GIII-16, flared lip (rare), pint, amber .... $1500–$2000
Decanter, GIII-16, flaring lip (rare), 7", forest green................. $1500–$2000
Decanter, GIII-16, pint, olive green.............................. $325–$400
Decanter, GIII-16, pint, olive green.............................. $350–$450
Decanter, GIII-19, base crack, quart, yellow olive .... $225–$300
Decanter, GIII-19, quart, olive amber............................. $600–$750
Decanter, GIII-19, quart, olive green............................. $400–$600
Decanter, GIII-2, "Wine," quart, clear............................ $400–$600
Decanter, GIII-23, quart, clear................................... $125–$175
Decanter, GIII-24, body bruise, quart, clear .... $50–$70
Decanter, GIII-26, original stopper, quart, clear .... $100–$150
Decanter, GIII-26, period stopper, quart, clear .... $150–$200
Decanter, GIII-26, quart, clear.................................... $90–$140
Decanter, GIII-5, Mutzer repro, 1920s, quart, clear .... $125–$175
Decanter, GIV-5, quart, clear..................................... $150–$200
Decanter, GIV-7, quart, clear..................................... $100–$140
Decanter, GIV-7, rayed stopper, pint, clear.......................... $70–$95
Decanter, GV-8, matching stopper, pint, sapphire blue.............. $2000–$3000
Decanter, GV-8, quart, clear .... $150–$250
Decanter, GV-8, unpatterned blue stopper, OP, quart, sapphire blue .... $2000–$2750
Decanter, GV-9, quart, clear .... $175–$225
Decanter, GV-10, quart, clear .... $125–$175
Decanter, GV-12, matching stopper, quart, clear .... $200–$325
Decanter, GV-13, quart, clear .... $225–$300
Decanter, GV-14, quart, clear .... $275–$350
Decanter, GV-14, quart, clear .... $400–$500
Decanter, GV-17, matching stopper, quart, clear .... $400–$475
Flask, GI-22, pint, yellow green................................. $4000–$6000
Flask, GII-7, 9¾", clear....................................... $1200–$1600
Flask, GIII-24, pale blue .... $3000–$4000
Flip Glass, GII-18, 5¾", clear.................................. $150–$200
Flip Glass, GII-22, 6¼", clear.................................. $100–$145
Flip Glass, GIII-22, 6", clear .... $200–$300
Hat, GII-13, clear... $100–$150
Hat, GII-18, 2", clear .... $100–$160
Hat, GIII-3, 2⅜", clear....................................... $90–$125
Hat, GIII-3, clear .... $75–$125
Hat, GIII-3, 2⅜", cobalt...................................... $375–$500

Hat, GIII-4, 2¹/₄", cobalt. . . . . $400–$475
Hat, GIII-5, 2¹/₂". . . . . $60–$90
Hat, GIII-7, 2¹/₄", clear. . . . . $75–$100
Hat, GIII-7, 2¹/₈". . . . . $80–$100
Hat, GIII-8, with vertical ribbing (rare), clear . . . . $250–$350
Hat, GIII-23, 2¹/₄", cobalt. . . . . $400–$475
Hat, GIII-23, 2³/₈", clear. . . . . $90–$125
Hat, GIII-23, 2", cobalt . . . . $350–$500
Hat, GIII-23, clear . . . . $90–$120
Hat, GIII-23, sapphire blue . . . . $375–$500
Hat, GIII-25, 2³/₈", cobalt. . . . . $450–$650
Hat, GIII-29, folded rim, 4¹/₂" long, olive amber . . . . $9000+
Hat, GIII-29, olive amber. . . . . $7000+
Ink, GII-2, 1⁷/₈", olive green . . . . $120–$150
Ink, GII-15, 1³/₄", medium olive green . . . . $600–$850
Ink, GII-15, olive amber. . . . . $300–$375
Ink, GII-16, 1⁵/₈", amber . . . . $100–$145
Ink, GII-18, 1³/₄", olive amber . . . . $150–$190
Ink, GII-18, 2", olive amber. . . . . $125–$165
Ink, GII-18, deep olive amber . . . . $150–$190
Ink, GII-18, olive green . . . . $100–$135
Ink, GII-26, olive amber. . . . . $2500–$4000
Ink, GIII-29, 1¹/₂", amber. . . . . $100–$145
Ink, GIII-29, olive amber . . . . $200–$275
Lamp, GI-7, lacy square stepped base, 5¹/₂", clear . . . . $300–$350
Lamp, GI-15, triangular base, clear . . . . $400–$550
Miniature Cordial, GII-16, small lip chip, 2³/₄" . . . . $70–$90
Miniature Decanter, GIII-12, unpatterned stopper, 3¹/₄" . . . . $140–$180
Miniature Pitcher, GIII-12, handle curl missing, 2¹/₈". . . . . $75–$100
Miniatures, See by type of item, pitcher, decanter, etc.
Mug, GII-18, barrel shaped, 2⁷/₈", clear. . . . . $175–$275
Mug, GII-18, clear . . . . $300–$450
Mug, GIII-13, 2³/₄", clear. . . . . $275–$400
Mug, GIII-18, 3¹/₂", clear. . . . . $275–$375

Pitcher (note nice handle tail curl). PHOTO COURTESY OF GLASS WORKS AUCTIONS.

Mug, GIII-29, 2^1/$_2$", aqua .... $6000–$9000
Mustard Bottle, GI-7-3, matching lid, clear .... $125–$175
Mustard Bottle, GI-24, no lid, clear .... $50–$70
Mustard Jar, GIII-28, rare mold, original ribbed blown stopper, 4^1/$_2$" .... $275–$350
Pitcher, GI-25, probably not of period, milk glass .... $300–$450
Pitcher, GII-18, 4^1/$_2$", clear .... $400–$475
Pitcher, GII-22, 6^1/$_4$", clear .... $600–$850
Pitcher, GII-22, 7", clear .... $500–$800
Pitcher, GII-26, made from decanter mold, 5^3/$_4$", deep olive green .... $9000+
Pitcher, GII-27, 6", clear .... $400–$600
Pitcher, GII-33, 6^3/$_8$", clear .... $500–$700
Pitcher, GIII-1, made from decanter mold, 7^5/$_8$", aqua .... $9000+
Punch Bowl, GII-21, footed, 5"(h)x8^1/$_2$"(w), clear .... $2500–$3750
Salt, GI-6, drawn foot, 2", blue .... $400–$550
Salt, GII-16, clear .... $125–$175
Salt, GII-18, drawn foot, 2^3/$_8$", clear .... $210–$270
Salt, GII-18, applied foot, 2^1/$_2$", amethyst .... $2000–$3000
Salt, GII-18, drawn stem and foot, 2^3/$_4$", olive amber .... $8000+
Salt, GII-19, drawn foot and tapering in bowl, 2^1/$_2$", clear .... $150–$200
Salt, GII-19, drawn foot, double ogee form, 2^1/$_2$", clear .... $150–$200
Salt, GII-21, clear .... $200–$300
Salt, GII-21, drawn foot and flaring lip, 2^1/$_4$", blue .... $500–$800
Salt, GII-21, drawn foot, flaring mouth, 1^7/$_8$ (h) x 2^5/$_8$ (w), amethyst .... $1600–$2300
Salt, GIII-3, drawn foot, 2^3/$_4$", blue .... $450–$750
Salt, GIII-3, drawn foot, flaring lip, 2^1/$_4$", clear .... $250–$325
Salt, GIII-7, drawn foot, 2^1/$_8$" .... $150–$200
Salt, GIII-13, drawn foot, 3", blue .... $500–$700
Salt, GIII-13, drawn foot, double ogee form, 3^3/$_4$", sapphire blue .... $600–$800
Salt, GIII-15, drawn foot and tooled in and flaring lip, 2^1/$_4$", blue......... $500–$700
Salt, GIII-21, drawn foot, clear .... $200–$300
Salt, GIII-21, drawn foot, wide mouth, 2^1/$_4$", sapphire blue .... $350–$450
Salt, GIII-23, drawn foot, double ogee form, sapphire blue............. $550–$750
Salt, GIII-23, ogee form, cobalt .... $550–$750
Salt, GIII-25, drawn foot, cobalt .... $700–$950
Salt, GIII-25, drawn foot, flaring lip, 2^1/$_8$", cobalt .... $400–$550
Salt, GIII-25, drawn foot, tapering in lip, 2", cobalt .... $500–$650
Salt, GIII-25, drawn foot, wide mouth, 1^3/$_4$", clear .... $175–$245
Shaker Bottle, GI-24, original cap, 4^1/$_2$" .... $45–$65
Shaker Bottle, GII-13, brass cap, clear .... $75–$125
Shaker Bottle, GII-44, metal cap, clear............................ $60–$90
Shaker Bottle, GII-5, clear with brass cap, 4^1/$_4$", clear .... $40–$65
Shaker Bottle, GIII-27, 4^3/$_4$", metal cap .... $75–$125
Shaker Bottle, GIV-4, 4^1/$_4$", clear................................. $60–$90
Sugar Bowl, GI-29, cobalt .... $4000–$6000
Sugar Bowl, GII-18, applied funnel foot, patterned lid, 5^1/$_2$", clear .... $5000+
Sugar Bowl, GII-18, applied pad foot, matching lid, 4^7/$_8$" (h), clear.......... $5000+
Sugar Bowl, GII-22, clear .... $4000–$6000
Syrup Jug, GV-11, pewter spout and lid........................... $300–$425
Toilet Water, GI-3-1, with stopper, lip lightly ground, sapphire .... $90–$125
Toilet Water, GI-3-2, lip flake, sapphire blue...................... $100–$150
Toilet Water, GI-3-2, with stopper, cobalt .... $150–$200

Toilet water bottle with tam o'shanter stopper. PHOTO COURTESY OF GLASS WORKS AUCTIONS.

Toilet Water, GI-3-2, with stopper, cobalt . . . . $200–$300
Toilet Water, GI-3-2, with stopper, sapphire blue . . . . $250–$325
Toilet Water, GI-7, lip flakes, no stopper, amethyst . . . . $200–$250
Toilet Water, GI-7-4, ground lip, no stopper, violet . . . . $80–$120
Toilet Water, GI-7-4, lip flake, no stopper, sapphire blue . . . . $100–$140
Toilet Water, GI-7-4, no stopper, medium amethyst . . . . $200–$300
Toilet Water, GI-7-4, no stopper, sapphire blue . . . . $125–$200
Toilet Water, GI-7-4, with stopper, clear . . . . $90–$125
Toilet Water, GI-7-4, with stopper, deep lavendar . . . . $250–$350
Toilet Water, GI-7-4, with stopper, deep lavendar . . . . $250–$350
Toilet Water, GI-7-4, with stopper, sapphire blue . . . . $250–$300
Toilet Water, GI-7-4, with stopper, violet . . . . $250–$300
Toilet Water, GI-7-4, without stopper, clear . . . . $40–$75
Toilet Water, GI-13, smooth base, 6", amethyst . . . . $275–$375
Toilet Water, GI-29, no stopper, clear . . . . $40–$70
Toilet Water, GI-3-2, 6¾", clear with tam o'shanter stopper . . . . $50–$70
Toilet Water, with stopper, midnight blue . . . . $250–$300
Tumbler, GI-20, 2⅞", clear . . . . $150–$200
Tumbler, GI-24, with blue rim (rare), clear . . . . $400–$500
Tumbler, GI-30, aqua . . . . $3000–$5000
Tumbler, GII-16, 1¾", clear . . . . $150–$225
Tumbler, GII-18, barrel shaped, 3¼", clear . . . . $100–$160
Tumbler, GII-18, olive green . . . . $5000+
Tumbler, GII-18, straight sided, lightly polished rim, 3" . . . . $50–$65
Tumbler, GIII-13, 2¾", clear . . . . $150–$250
Tumbler, GIII-18, 2¾", clear . . . . $80–$120
Tumbler, GIII-20, 3½", clear . . . . $80–$120
Tumbler, GIII-21, barrel shaped, 2½" . . . . $125–$175
Tumbler, GIII-21, barrel shaped, 3½", clear . . . . $70–$120
Tumbler, GIII-23, 4½", clear . . . . $200–$300
Tumbler, GV-4, 3½", clear . . . . $150–$200
Whiskey Taster, GII-19, 2¼" . . . . $70–$90
Wine, GII-16, 2⅝", clear . . . . $250–$350
Witch Ball, (rare), clear (very rare), aqua, green & ambers (even rarer) . . . . . . $3000+

CANDY CONTAINERS

Figural glass candy containers are an area of bottle collecting that is becoming more and more popular. The first candy container is believed to be the Liberty Bell which was sold at the 1876 Centennial Exhibition in Philadelphia. From the 1890s up until around 1960, when glass candy containers were all but discontinued, thousands of different figural candy containers in all shapes, sizes, and colors were made. Though some candy containers were sold to merchants already filled with candy, it is uncertain which ones came filled and which ones were filled by the merchants at their stores.

When collecting and buying candy containers, be watchful for original paint and original closures. Try to be certain that all the parts and accessories are present and, if possible, that they are original to the piece. The reader is referred to *The Compleat American Glass Candy Containers Handbook* by George Eikelberner and Serge Agadjanian, which the numbers below refer to. Be mindful of the reproductions made over the past few years.

Airplane, 306, complete with cap and wing .... $50–$75
Airplane, 4A, with contents .... $40–$70
Airplane, Spirit of Goodwill, 8A, complete and painted .... $125–$200
Airplane, Spirit of Goodwill, 8C, complete and painted, contents .... $125–$200

Candy container, Liberty Motor. PHOTO COURTESY OF NEIL GROSSMAN.

Auto, 43, with tin roof and wheels .... $70–$100
Automobile, 35, colored glass, complete .... $30–$50
Automobile, 37, colorless glass, complete .... $35–$50
Automobile, 38, colorless glass, complete, painted .... $50–$60
Automobile, 45, tin wheels .... $50–$80
Baby Sweeper, 132, complete with contents and handle .... $450–$700
Barney Google, 72A, with closure and some paint .... $175–$250

Billiken, 90, with original paint, closure .... $60–$90
Boat Candy Containers, various shapes and sizes .... $30–$70
Boat, The Colorado, complete with rigging and tin cover .... $150–$250
Boot, 111, with closure... $20–$30
Building, 324B, closure .... $60–$90
Building, 807, with glass insert and pin........................... $110–$150
Bureau, 112, with original paint, closure.......................... $100–$150
Cannon, Rapid Fire, 129, tin, with glass walls, in working order .... $200–$300
Cars, Various Types, colorless glass .... $20–$90
Charlie Chaplin, 137, closure and contents .... $80–$120
Chick, 145A, with all paint, contents............................... $75–$125
Chicken, 147A, with original paint, no closure .... $40–$60
Chicken, 147C, with original paint, closure......................... $45–$65
Chicken, 148A, with closure .... $30–$50
Chicken, 149B, with closure .... $40–$60
Clock, 162, with some paint, white .... $80–$130
Clock, 163, colorless glass, octagonal, no closure..................... $40–$60
Clock, 164A, paper dial, closure, colorless .... $40–$60
Dirigible, 176A, with closure...................................... $150–$200
Dog Shaped, various shapes and sizes, colorless or blue................. $5–$50
Dog, Seated Bulldog, 189A, with black paint, closure .... $40–$65
Dog, Seated Bulldog, 189A, with gold paint, closure .... $40–$65
Drum Mug, 543, with some paint .... $25–$40
Duck with Large Bill, 199, with most of its paint..................... $100–$150
Duck, 197, complete and with some paint .... $30–$40
Duck, 198, complete and with contents .... $30–$45
Fat Boy on Drum, 208, original paint.............................. $175–$250
Fire Engine, 213C, with contents .... $30–$50
Fire Engine, 217, with contents and paint........................... $50–$70
Fire Engine, 219, complete with contents and closure .... $125–$175
Fire Engine, 221B, complete, colorless.............................. $30–$45
Fire Engine, 223B, complete, colorless.............................. $30–$45
Gay Head Lighthouse, colorless.................................... $60–$90
Gun, Colt, 285, with black paint .... $40–$60

Candy Container, Colt pistol.
PHOTO COURTESY OF NEIL
GROSSMAN.

Gun, Indian Head Handle, 285, with cap .... $40–$55
Guns, various shapes and sizes, colorless glass .... $10–$50
Hat, Uncle Sam's, milk glass with original paint .... $30–$40
Horn, 313, complete and full .... $25–$40
House, 324A, original paint, closure .... $90–$120
Iron, 343, with closure .... $20–$30
Jack O'Lantern, original paint, no cap .... $200–$300
Liberty Bell, 87A, closure, yellow amber .... $25–$40
Liberty Bell, 87A, with closure, blue.............................. $25–$40
Locomotive, various types, glass, colorless.......................... $10–$50
Mail Box, 521, complete and painted............................... $60–$90
Mail Box, 521-1, complete, no closure .... $50–$75
Mail Box, 521-2, milk glass, no closure............................ $40–$60
Moon Mullins, 534, complete with some paint .... $40–$60
New York Central Rail Car Set, 495, all three cars, minor damage .... $400+
Opera Glasses, with closures, milk glass .... $70–$95
Owl, 566B, complete with closure .... $30–$42
Piano, 577, with tin closure .... $80–$120
Rabbit, 606A, complete with contents, some paint..................... $30–$45
Rabbit, 609, glass, with no closure, colorless .... $20–$25
Rabbit, 617A, with closure, contents, glass, colorless.................. $25–$35
Rabbit in Egg Shell, 608B, with closure, contents .... $70–$95
Rabbit Pushing Chick in Shell Cart, 602A, original paint, closure .... $400+
Rabbit Running on a Log, 603A, with closure .... $80–$120
Rabbit with Wheelbarrow, 601B, with some paint..................... $45–$75
Radio, 643, missing closure .... $50–$80
Radio, 643B, with closure and some paint........................... $90–$110
Rocking Horse with Clown, glass, blue tint.......................... $90–$135
Rocking Horse with Clown, glass, colorless .... $75–$100
Santa, 670, with original candy and cotton, closure .... $150–$200
Santa, 671, with some paint, closure .... $100–$150
Santa, Leaving Chimney, 673B, with paint, closure .... $75–$125
Spark Plug, Horse Figural, colorless................................ $75–$100
Spark Plug, Horse Shaped, with some original paint, no closure......... $100–$140
Spirit of Goodwill, 8A, complete and painted........................ $100–$150
Spirit of Goodwill, 8C, complete and painted, contents .... $100–$150
Spirit of St. Louis, with original paint .... $500+
Suitcase, 707, milk glass, original paint .... $100+
Suitcase, 707A, with handle and closure .... $30–$50
Suitcase, 707F, with handle and closure, contents..................... $35–$55
Tank, assorted shapes and sizes, colorless glass .... $20–$45
Top with Winder, 776, complete .... $100+
Village Building, 812, missing glass insert and pin.................... $20–$25
Village Building, 813, missing glass insert and pin.................... $20–$25
Village Building, 815, missing glass insert and pin.................... $20–$25
Wagon, 323, colorless glass....................................... $30–$50
Wagon, 539A, complete and full .... $35–$55
Wagon, 539D, complete and full .... $35–$55
Wagon, 822, complete and full .... $30–$50
Windmill, 843B, with contents .... $70–$90

COLOGNE BOTTLES

Cologne bottles were used by both ladies and gentlemen, and the shapes and colors of the bottles were as varied as the colognes that filled them. Though colognes were popular in 17th- and 18th-century America, most of the fancy bottles encountered by collectors are from 1830 to 1880 period. The reader is referred to *American Bottles and Flasks and Their Ancestry* by McKearin and Wilson, pgs. 378–407.

Bunker Hill Monument Form, 6³/₈", cobalt. . . . . $150–$250
Bunker Hill Monument Form, 9³/₄", full label, amethyst . . . . $1000–$1500
Bunker Hill Monument Form, 6¹/₂", milk glass . . . . $75–$125
Bunker Hill Monument Form, octagonal, round corset waist hourglass, SB, 5³/₄", cobalt. . . . . $400–$600
Bunker Hill Monument Form, round corset waist hourglass, OP, SB, 6", cobalt / amethyst . . . . $550–$700
Bunker Hill Monument Form, stopper (rare to find with bottle), 12", teal green . . . . $1500–$1800
Bunker Hill Monumental Form, flattened, modified corset waist, SB, 4", amethyst . . . . $125–$175
Bunker Hill Monumental Form, round corset waist, hourglass, SB, 3" base crack, 6⁷/₈", cobalt . . . . $100–$150
Cylinder, unpatterned, unembossed, 10⁷/₈", milk glass, OP, powder blue . . . . $55–$75
Dolphins Supporting Urn, OP, 4³/₄", opalescent lavender. . . . . $300–$500
Petal Form, six petals, long drawn neck, OP, 3⁷/₈", cobalt . . . . $100–$135
Poodle Sitting on Hassock, OP, 7", fiery opal . . . . $600–$800
Round, vertical beaded flutes, 10¹/₄", SB, emerald green . . . . $750–$1250
Round, vertical beaded flutes, 5¹/₂", SB, shoulder chip, electric blue . . . . . . $100–$200

Left: *Twelve-sided cologne.* Center: *Six-sided, flattened, waisted.* Right: *Monument cologne.* PHOTOS COURTESY OF GLASS WORKS AUCTIONS.

Round, vertical beaded flutes, 5⅝", SB, cobalt . . . . $350–$450
Round, vertical beaded flutes, 7¼", milk glass . . . . $60–$85
Square, arrow shaped pointed edges, SB, 7½", amethyst . . . . $300–$400
Square, beveled corners, wide central vertical rib on three sides, SB, double collared lip, 12", puce . . . . $400–$650
Square, decorative leaf motif on three sides, SB, 7⅝", lavender . . . . $200–$300
Square, herringbone edges, thumbprint pattern on four sides, SB, medium cobalt . . . . .
. . . . $150–$200
Square, rope edges, floral embossing, milk glass, 8¾" . . . . $100–$150
Square, rope edges, three stars in panels, milk glass, 5½" . . . . $60–$80
Twelve Sided, 4¾", teal green . . . . $80–$120
Twelve Sided, OP, angular shoulder, 7⅛", medium lavender . . . . $400–$600
Twelve Sided, OP, angular shoulder, 7⅜", pale blue green . . . . $300–$450
Twelve Sided, SB, 11", teal green . . . . $500–$750
Twelve Sided, SB, 4¾", amethyst . . . . $75–$125
Twelve Sided, SB, 5½", opalescent turquoise blue . . . . $300–$400
Twelve Sided, SB, 5", medium blue green . . . . $70–$100
Twelve Sided, SB, 6½", cobalt blue . . . . $80–$120
Twelve Sided, SB, 7½", opalescent light blue . . . . $300–$500
Twelve Sided, SB, 7¼", amethyst . . . . $150–$250
Twelve Sided, SB, 8¾", cobalt . . . . $250–$350
Twelve Sided, SB, 8⅝", sapphire blue . . . . $250–$325
Twelve Sided, SB, 9", sapphire blue . . . . $275–$375
Twelve Sided, SB, angular shoulder, 4¾", cobalt blue . . . . $80–$120
Twelve Sided, SB, wider body, angular shoulder, 6", amethyst . . . . $250–$350

COSMETIC BOTTLES

See the section on Hair Bottles for information on most cosmetic bottles.

ENAMELED BOTTLES

Enamel has been used as a glass decoration for many hundreds of years. Enamel is painted onto the glass and then the item is reheated which fires or bakes the decoration on. Most of the enameled pieces you will see are 18th and early 19th century, and generally of European origin. The bottles are almost always done in the half post method and are usually found with a pewter screw lip. The most common form of bottle is rectangular with beveled edges in shape, and clear glass is the most common; next is fiery opal, then cobalt, then amber. It is unusual to find the pewter cap with the bottle, and it is not uncommon to find damaged or missing threaded portions. Sometimes the entire pewter portion is missing. The most common enameled decor is floral, next are birds, and then people. Among the rarest of decor is that of a person performing some function, such as hunting. Several years ago, an enameled bottle was auctioned off overseas that depicted a glass blower; that piece sold in excess of $10,000. Be mindful of reproductions of enameled bottles, which continue to be made. The quality of the glass is very clear and shiny, with little or no wear; reproductions are often heavier in weight than 18th century pieces.

Bottle, dated 1767, half post, pewter threaded top, rectangular form, enameled man on side, 6" . . . . $290–$390
Bottle, half post, pewter threaded top, no cap, rectangular form, multicolored floral, 5¹/₂", clear . . . . $250–$350
Bottle, half post, pewter threaded top, rectangular form, enameled floral, 5¹/₂", cobalt blue . . . . $500–$700
Bottle, half post, pewter threaded top, rectangular form, enameled floral, 5³/₄", fiery opal . . . . $350–$500
Bottle, half post, pewter threaded top, rectangular form, enameled floral, amber (rare) . . . . $700–$850
Bottle, half post, pewter threaded top, rectangular form, enameled floral, no pewter on neck but rather flaring lip, 5¹/₂", clear. . . . . $250–$325
Bottle, half post, pewter threaded top, rectangular form, enameled heart on one side, floral, 5⁵/₈" . . . . $300–$425
Bottle, half post, pewter threaded top, rectangular form, enameled woman on one side, 5³/₄" . . . . $275–$375
Bottle, half post, pewter threaded top, rectangular form, no cap, 6¹/₂" . . . . . $250–$375

Two examples of late 18th-century bottles. PHOTO COURTESY OF GLASS WORKS AUCTIONS.

Bottle, half post, pewter threaded top, rectangular form, with original pewter cap.....
.... $275–$375
Mug, applied handle, enameled floral, 5", clear...................... $400–$575
Mug, applied handle, floral and rooster, 5¹/₂", clear................... $450–$600
Mug, applied handle, floral decor, 6¹/₄", fiery opal .... $400–$600
Mug, applied handle, floral decor, crack at handle attachment, 5¹/₂", clear. . $125–$175
Mug, ca. 1840, applied handle, florals and "Remember Me," ribbed lower body, star patterned base, probably Spanish, cobalt blue .... $55–$80
Mug, ca. 1840, applied handle, florals and "Remember Me," ribbed lower body, star patterned base, probably Spanish, clear .... $35–$55
Tumbler, floral and bird decor, 4", clear .... $275–$375
Tumbler, floral and woman holding bouquet, 4", clear................. $300–$425
Tumbler, floral decor, 3¹/₄", clear .... $175–$275

FIGURAL BOTTLES

Figural bottles include figures of people, famous personalities, animals, guns, and other objects, all in a wide range of colors. Most of the collectible figural bottles were produced in the late 19th and early 20th centuries, and were manufactured both in the United States and abroad. Please keep the following in mind:

- There are other bottle categories under which your figural may be listed if it doesn't appear below; look for embossing such as "Bitters" or "Whiskey" on your bottle and then check those categories.

- As with other bottles, color and condition are important variables for determining the value and rarity of figural bottles.

- Just because a figural has a pontil mark does not mean it is an early bottle; figural bottles continue to be made today in the old manner of blowpipe and pontil rod.

- Many of the newer figural bottles have a yellowish tint to the glass.

- Many figural bottles came with stoppers or metal screw caps, the lack of which can greatly impact the value.

- Early screw-top figurals often have ground lips, with the top of the lip frosted and rough from being ground down on a metal wheel, which was part of the bottle finishing process around the turn of the century; newer screw-top figurals usually have smooth polished lips, due to later advancements in bottle making technology. While modern and common figurals may have little value from a bottle collecting perspective, they are popular from a decorative perspective and may have more value at a tag sale or flea market than at a bottle show.

"Aspasia-Aonaoia,", woman's face on sides, 9³/₄", mint green . . . . $500–$700
Acorn, 2³/₄", clear. . . . . $15–$20
Adolph Thier Bust, OP, 11", clear . . . . $125–$150
Alligator, standing, "Deponirt," frosted, 10", clear . . . . $400–$500
Baby Head, milk glass, 2⁵/₈" . . . . $250–$300
Barrel, 9¹/₂", sapphire blue. . . . . $800–$1200
Barrel, 9³/₄", amber . . . . $125–$165
Barrel, Lancaster Glassworks, Lancaster NY (on base), olive yellow . . . . . $250–$300
Barrel, Lancaster Glassworks, Lancaster NY (on base), orange amber . . . . $175–$225
Barrel, lying on side, footed, ABM, 6", root beer amber . . . . $30–$45
Basket Decanter, 6¹/₄", clear . . . . $100–$125
Bather on Rocks, "Depose," no stopper, 11⁵/₈", clear. . . . . $50–$75
Bear Bottle, applied face (rare), OP, 10¹/₄", deep purple blue. . . . . $1000–$2000
Bear Bottle, Kummel bear, applied lip, 10", black . . . . $25–$35
Bear Bottle, Kummel bear, applied lip, milk glass, 10" . . . . $90–$120
Bear Bottle, on haunches, metal screw cap, 11", clear with black paint . . . . . $25–$35
Bear Hanging onto Lamp Post, "Depose," milk glass, 11". . . . . $250–$350
Bear Pomade Jar, 3³/₄", glass head lid, clambroth . . . . $350–$450
Bear Pomade Jar, 3³/₄", glass head lid, FB Strouse (on base), black . . . . . . $200–$300
Bear Pomade Jar, 3³/₄", glass head lid, milk glass . . . . $375–$450
Bear Pomade Jar, 3³/₄", glass head lid, nose/foot chips, black. . . . . $70–$100
Bear Pomade Jar, 3³/₄", glass head lid, rim chips, black . . . . $90–$145
Bear Pomade Jar, 3³/₄", glass head lid, light opaque blue . . . . $500–$700
Bear Pomade Jar, 3³/₄", glass head lid, no base embossing, black. . . . . $200–$275
Bear Pomade Jar, 4¹/₂", glass head lid, paws folded between legs, black . . . .
. . . . $800–$1000
Bear, 5¹/₂", jar, wide mouth, clear with screw cap . . . . $10–$15
Beecher Bust, 5", clear. . . . . $30–$40
Bell, "Gayner Glass Works Salem NJ," metal handle, screw lid, 6¹/₄", clear . . . .
. . . . $90–$125
Bell, "Proclaim Liberty Throughout all the Land. . . ," 8³/₄", aqua . . . . $150–$200
Billy Club, metal screw cap, amber . . . . $45–$60
Bob Fitzsimmons, fighter, flesh colored upper body, frosted lower, 14¹/₂" . . . .
. . . . $900–$1250
Book, pottery, "Bennington Battle," 10¹/₂", brown / cream / green . . . . . $1000–$1450
Book, pottery, "Departed Spirits," glaze, 5³/₄", brown / orange. . . . . $275–$375
Book, pottery, "Departed Spirits," lip chips, glaze, 5³/₄", brown / orange. . . $145–$195
Book, pottery, "History of Holland," blue glaze, 5¹/₂" . . . . $200–$300
Book, pottery, unembossed, glazes, 10¹/₂", brown / cream / green . . . . $400–$600
Book, pottery, unembossed, glazes, 5³/₄", brown / cream / green . . . . $200–$300
Boot, "Saratoga Dressing," 4¹/₄", aqua. . . . . $30–$50
Boot, lady's, 3³/₄", clear . . . . $8–$12
Boot, lady's, nailsea type, clear with white looping, OP, 6¹/₄" . . . . $150–$250
Bullet Shaped Smelling Salts Bottle, 3⁷/₈", cobalt . . . . $80–$120
Bunker Hill Monument, 12", clear. . . . . $25–$35
Cannon, Phalon & Son, 7¹/₈", clear. . . . . $45–$55
Carrie Nation, clear. . . . . $8–$12

Castle, "Depose," OP, with stopper, 12", clear .... $80–$110
Cat, 8", clear... $8–$12
Cat, head is stopper, modern, 9¹/₂", yellow amber........................ $5–$7
Cavalier Pomade Jar, wide brimmed hat, clambroth................. $700–$1000
Cavalier Pomade Jar, wide brimmed hat, light opaque blue .... $900–$1400
Charlie Chaplin, 11", clear... $55–$75
Cherub Holding Medallion, 14¹/₄", clear............................. $15–$20
Cherub Holding Medallion, 14¹/₄", deep cobalt....................... $200–$300
Cherubs, three, holding a sphere, 10", clear .... $20–$25
Children Climbing Tree, 12", clear .... $25–$35
Chinaman, "Indestructible Trade Mark Japanese Gloss...," 4³/₈", amber...........
.... $150–$190
Cigar, 5³/₈", light amber... $20–$35
Cigars, bunch of, screw cap, 5", light amber.......................... $35–$45
Clam Flask, metal cap, 5¹/₄", amber .... $65–$85
Clam Flask, metal cap, 5¹/₄", clear .... $20–$35
Clam Flask, metal cap, 5¹/₄", cobalt .... $300–$400
Clam Flask, metal cap, with original white paint, 5¹/₄", clear.............. $30–$40
Clock Flask, applied lip, 5¹/₂", clear .... $15–$25
Clock, grandfather, "Depose," milk glass, original stopper, 12¹/₄" .... $150–$200
Clock, grandfather, 7³/₄", clear....................................... $12–$18
Coachman, pottery, Bennington mark on base, boot tip chipped, 10¹/₂" ... $100–$135
Coachman, pottery, Bennington mark on base, glaze, 10¹/₂", brown / tan ....
.... $250–$350
Coachman, Van Dunck's, glass, 8¹/₂", black.......................... $65–$85
Columbus Column, metal figural closure, milk glass, 18" .... $350–$450
Coming Through the Rye, female figure, clear frosted, 13¹/₂" .... $700–$900
Crying Baby, 5³/₄", opaque white .... $500–$750
Crying Baby, 6", clear.. $35–$55
Czar, milk glass, 10¹/₂" .... $400–$600
Czarina Alexandra, milk glass, 10¹/₂" .... $400–$600
Dagger, clear with metal screw cap, 8¹/₂" .... $25–$35
Dice Bottle, milk glass, glass stopper, 5¹/₈".......................... $100–$125
Dice Bottle, one die atop another, 8⁷/₈" .... $75–$95
Dice Bottle, one die atop another, milk glass, 5¹/₄" .... $40–$45
Dice Bottle, square, 1¹/₁₆", clear.................................... $30–$35
Dog, 3" metal screw cap, ink bottle, cobalt .... $5–$7
Dog, modern, 9¹/₂", green.. $4–$5
Dolphins, three, holding sphere, frosted, 12", clear.................... $40–$55
Dolphins, three, holding sphere, OP, 12", clear....................... $40–$50
Duck, Atterbury, "Patd April 11th 1871" (base), milk glass, 11⁵/₈" .... $250–$350
Duck, standing, shot glass stopper, 9³/₄", clear .... $50–$75
Ear of Corn, 5¹/₂", clear.. $12–$16
Ear of Corn, 9⁵/₈", amber.. $80–$120
EG Booz Cabin Bottle, (See Figured Flasks GVII items; beware of reproductions!!)..
....
Eiffel Tower, OP, 7³/₈", clear.. $200–$250
Eiffel Tower, 11⁷/₈", electric blue .... $450–$600
Elephant and Tree, 3⁷/₈", clear...................................... $35–$55
Elephant Seated on a Drum, frosted, "Depotnirt", 9³/₄", clear .... $200–$300
Elephant With Uplifted Trunk, frosted, 18", clear .... $125–$150

Ear of Corn figural. PHOTO COURTESY OF GLASS WORKS
AUCTIONS.

Elephant, 10¹/₂", amber . . . . $9–$12
Elk's Bust With Clock, frosted, 11³/₄" . . . . $70–$90
Elk's Tooth Flask, 4", opaque white . . . . $75–$110
Eye Opener, eyeball figure, flask, 5¹/₄", opaque white . . . . $150–$175
Face, before and after, frosted, 12", clear. . . . . $30–$50
Fat Dutchman, milk glass, 10" . . . . $500–$700
Fiddle, (See Violin, this listing)
Fish, 11", aqua . . . . $12–$18
Fish, 7¹/₂", clear . . . . $10–$12
Fish, ABM, 4", clear. . . . . $2–$4
Fish, ABM, 6¹/₄", amber. . . . . $12–$16
Fish, ABM, 8¹/₄", amber. . . . . $15–$20
Fish, ABM, 9⁷/₈", amber. . . . . $20–$30
Fish, ca. 1900, ground lip, clear metal screw cap, full paint, 8¹/₂". . . . . $40–$50
Fish, ground lip, clear metal screw cap, no paint, 8¹/₂" . . . . $20–$30
Galliano, Alleroe, bust, 11³/₄", clear . . . . $15–$19
Garibaldi, bust, ABM, 11³/₄", clear. . . . . $12–$18
Girl, with hands at waist, early, 7", clear. . . . . $50–$75
Globe, jar form, metal screw cap, clear . . . . $4–$6
Goat, 11¹/₂", clear. . . . . $6–$8
Gold Nugget, milk glass, lacking paint, metal screw cap, 6" . . . . $45–$65
Gold Nugget, milk glass, metal screw cap, original paint, 6" . . . . $55–$75
Gold Nugget, with original paint, screw cap, clear . . . . $25–$35
Golf Bag, with original paint, 3³/₄", clear. . . . . $25–$35
Good Night, smiling face milk glass flask, metal screw cap, 4" . . . . $120–$150
Grant's Tomb, milk glass, lacking metal top, 8" . . . . $85–$95
Grant's Tomb, milk glass, with original metal top, 8" . . . . $350–$500
Grapes, bunch of, ground lip, 6", clear . . . . $10–$20
Grapes, bunch of, original metal cap and chain, 7", yellow amber. . . . . $35–$50
Grim Reaper Decanter Set, "Poison," glazed ceramic, decanter, four skull cups. . . . .
. . . . $80–$120
Grover Cleveland, figural bust, frosted, OP, 9¹/₂", clear. . . . . $95–$125
Ham, metal screw cap, original paint, amber. . . . . $40–$55

Hand Holding Bottle, 13⁷/₈", clear .... $20–$30
Hand Holding Bottle, OP, 7¹/₈", yellowish amber .... $125–$175
Hand Holding Bottle, with frosted hand, OP, 11¹/₈", clear .... $40–$55
Hand, 5¹/₄", clear .... $30–$40
Hand, ink bottle, milk glass, 5³/₈" .... $125–$150
Harrison, President, clear frosted bust on black fluted column, 16" ...... $250–$350
Henry Clay, OP, 11", clear .... $150–$250
Hessian Soldier, 7", clear... $30–$50
Hobo, 7¹/₂", clear .... $25–$35
Jester, standing, 6", clear.. $20–$30
Joan of Arc, milk glass, "Bonbons John Tavernier" (shield), 16¹/₂"....... $300–$400
John Bull, fat man, 11³/₈", golden amber.......................... $195–$245
Kate Klaxton, bust, clear... $55–$65
King Victor Emmanuel III, bust, 11³/₄", clear....................... $15–$20
Kummel Bear, 11¹/₄", black .... $30–$45
Kummel Bear, milk glass, 11¹/₄".................................. $90–$120

Figural, kummel bear. PHOTO COURTESY OF NEIL GROSSMAN.

Liberty Bell, "Proclaim Liberty," 8³/₄", yellow olive .... $80–$120
Life Preserver, milk glass, 5¹/₂" .... $150–$250
Lighthouse, "Cay Head Light," 6", clear........................... $100–$150
Lincoln Bank Bottle, metal screw cap, clear........................ $10–$15
Little Girl Reading Book, milk glass, 4¹/₄" .... $125–$175
Lorraine DD, "Depose SS" (around base), milk glass woman figural, 13" ....
.... $350–$500
Madonna Bottle, handled, with stopper, OP, 12", cobalt .... $20–$25
Man Leaning on Stump, clear .... $25–$35
Man Sitting on Barrel, painted, 11¹/₂", clear .... $15–$20
Man With Shoes Under Arm, 13¹/₄", clear .... $25–$45
Marie Antoinette, 11³/₄", clear .... $125–$175
Mermaid, glazed ceramic, 7³/₄", brown............................ $75–$110
Milk Bottles in Basket, milk glass, 3⁷/₈".......................... $75–$150
Monkey, (on front), woman's buttocks on rear, "Chest-Nuts," clear flask, 5¹/₂" ......
.... $50–$75
Monkey, jar, screw lid, ABM, clear................................ $10–$13
Monkey, sitting, milk glass, 4¹/₂"................................ $100–$145

Monkey, sitting, milk glass, 4¹/₂", clear...............................$15–$20
Moses in Bulrushes, baby sitting, 4³/₄", clear.........................$40–$60
Moses, ABM, 11", green...$20–$40
Moses, Poland Spring Water, applied lip, 11", amber..................$350–$450
Moses, Poland Spring Water, applied lip, 11", aqua...................$80–$120
Moses, Poland Spring Water, applied lip, 11", honey amber............$375–$450
Moses, Poland Spring Water, flaring lip, 11", green..................$150–$225
Moses, Poland Spring Water, OP, 11", clear.........................$75–$95

Figural, Moses spring water. PHOTO COURTESY OF NEIL GROSSMAN.

Mr. Pickwick, clear..$8–$12
Mrs. Butterworth, screw cap, amber................................$1–$2
Mu Mu, dirigible, frosted, screw cap, 9³/₈", clear....................$80–$120
Napoleon, (standing soldier), 7¹/₄", clear...........................$40–$60
Negro Gentleman, frosted, painted, 12³/₄", clear....................$500–$700
Negro Waiter, with black head, 14¹/₂", clear........................$150–$225
Night Cap, man with stocking cap, milk glass flask, metal cap, 4"......$150–$225
Night Stick, screw cap, 10¹/₂", amber..............................$45–$60
Oriental, oriental figure atomizer, metal head, milk glass body, 5¹/₂".....$120–$170
Owl, jar, milk glass, original glass lid with eagle, 6"...................$75–$100
Owl, jar, screw cap, 5", clear....................................$8–$12
Oyster, with metal screw cap, clear................................$20–$30
Pickle, 4¹/₂", medium green......................................$75–$100
Pig, ceramic, unembossed, glaze, blue eyes, 6¹/₂", tan................$200–$275
Pig, dated 1882, pottery, Anna railroad pig, railroad map, 7"..............$2000+
Pig, glass, "Drink while it lasts from the hogs...," 6³/₄"..............$100–$145
Pineapple, 4³/₄", clear..$10–$15
Pineapple, 7¹/₂", clear..$12–$18
Pineapple, W & Co, OP, 8¹/₂", amber..............................$200–$300
Pipe, 10¹/₂", turquoise blue......................................$75–$95
Pistol, ground lip, original metal cap, 7³/₄", purple amethyst...........$200–$250
Pistol, metal screw cap, 5¹/₂", clear..............................$15–$20
Pistol, metal screw cap, 7¹/₂", medium sapphire blue.................$300–$400
Pistol, screw cap, amber...$40–$65
Policeman, hand in air is stopper, painted, 13", cobalt.................$125–$225
Policeman, no stopper, painted, 13", cobalt.........................$30–$40

Potato, 4¹/₄", aqua. . . . . $25–$35
Potato, with brown paint, screw cap, clear . . . . $20–$30
Powder Horn, with metal cap, 5", clear . . . . $15–$20
Pretzel, cork top, ceramic. . . . . $40–$60
Queen Margherita, ABM, 11³/₄", clear . . . . $10–$15
Rabbit, jar, screw cap, 5", clear . . . . $8–$12
Sad Hound Dog, some original paint, 10³/₄", citron . . . . $30–$35
Santa With Tree, original paint, 7³/₈", clear . . . . $400–$600
Santa, tooled lip, 12", clear . . . . $40–$55

Figural, Santa. PHOTO COURTESY OF NEIL GROSSMAN.

Scallop Shell, screw cap, 5", aqua . . . . $20–$30
Scallop Shell, with metal screw cap, clear. . . . . $20–$30
Seated Bear, glass, 11", black . . . . $20–$30
Seated Bear, milk glass, 11" . . . . $30–$45
Seated Wolf With Book, ceramic, Germany (on base), glaze, 5", brown. . . . . $40–$60
Senorita, 13¹/₂", clear. . . . . $20–$30
Shells, (scallops), stacked atop one another, ABM, 12⁷/₈", aqua . . . . $30–$45
Shirt Flask, milk glass, metal screw cap, 4³/₄" . . . . $75–$125
Shoe, fancy, applied lip, 5¹/₂", clear . . . . $30–$40
Shoe, glass, 3¹/₂", black . . . . $40–$65
Shoe, with floral buckle, 3¹/₂", clear. . . . . $15–$20
Shoe, with toe showing, metal screw cap, black amethyst. . . . . $150–$225
Smiling Jack, large smiling face, original paint . . . . $30–$35
Snake, coiled, ABM, 5", clear . . . . $45–$65
Soldier's Bust, 10¹/₂", clear . . . . $15–$20
Soldier, standing, 11¹/₂", clear . . . . $20–$25
Spanish Senorita, 12", clear . . . . $8–$12
Statue of Liberty, milk glass, complete with metal top, 9¹/₄". . . . . $325–$425
Statue of Liberty, milk glass, lacking metal top, 9¹/₄" . . . . $45–$60
Sweet Potato, ceramic, 7" . . . . $50–$75
Tear Drops, milk glass eye flask, metal cap, 3⁷/₈". . . . . $100–$145
Three Busts, 13¹/₄", medium yellow amber. . . . . $40–$60
Three Busts, milk glass encased in, 13³/₄", clear. . . . . $70–$90
Turkey Claw Clutching Egg, 14", clear. . . . . $20–$30
Turkey, metal screw cap, 4⁵/₈", amber. . . . . $70–$90

Turtle, "Merry Xmas" (on base), metal screw cap, 5¹/₄", clear . . . . $25–$35
Uncle Sam, "Pat Apld For" (on base), 9¹/₂", clear . . . . $65–$95
Van Dunck's Coachman, 8¹/₂", deep amber . . . . $75–$85
Violin, ABM, 8", cobalt . . . . $10–$15
Violin, glass with wooden shaft, strings, 8", amber . . . . $95–$125
WC Fields, 11¹/₄", clear . . . . $35–$50
Whisk Broom, "Dust Remover," pottery, 6¹/₄" . . . . $40–$60
Wickered Demijohn, OP, 3", aqua . . . . $20–$30
Windmill, ceramic, decorated, 9¹/₂", blue . . . . $12–$15
Woman's Torso, screw cap, 6¹/₂", clear . . . . $20–$30
Woman, fancy dress, OP, 13¹/₂", deep sapphire blue . . . . $800–$1200
Woman, figural, full body, milk glass, 10¹/₂" . . . . $300–$400
Woman, holding a water pitcher, milk glass, 11¹/₈" . . . . $150–$200
Woman, in Victorian dress, hands at sides, stopper, OP, 13³/₈", yellowish olive green .
. . . . $1500–$2250
Woman, seated on wicker basket, OP, 8¹/₂", clear. $75–$125
Woman, standing on head on top of ball, "Depose," 16", clear . . . . $30–$35
Woman, with crossed arms, 14³/₄", clear. . . . . $10–$15

FIGURED, AND OTHER, FLASKS

FIGURED FLASKS (Also referred to as "Historical Flasks")

Among the most highly prized and sought after of all bottles are the figured
flasks, which make up the group of decorative, Masonic, historical, and picto-
rial flasks. No other area of bottles comes close to equaling the wide variety of
design and colors used, as is evidenced by the record prices set for these types
of bottles.

Figured flasks first appeared in the United States about 1815 in Connecticut,
and then spread to glasshouses across the country, which produced these items
into the 20th century. Generally speaking, the earlier the flasks, the more skill-
fully and elaborately made was the design. Around the mid 19th century, the
flasks began to become thinner in shape with less attention given to design
detail and eye appeal. Among the earliest flasks made were those which pictured American heroes such as George Washington, Jackson, and Taylor, as
well as eagles, Masonics, cornucopias and urns, and sunburst flasks. These

types of flasks continued to be made into the mid to late 19th century, when other types such as scroll flasks, Pike's Peak varieties, and those with the glasshouse name embossed became more common.

Nowhere in the field of bottle collecting does color have such an effect on the rarity and value of a given bottle than it does in the area of figured flasks. For example, a Columbia-Eagle flask in aqua can be purchased for approximately $300 to $400, whereas the same flask in cobalt blue will be well in excess of $30,000. In the area of flasks, many collectors attempt to specialize in a given area, such as sunbursts or eagle flasks, whereas others attempt to obtain every color known for a given type of flask.

Because of the immense interest in figured flasks, the collector should also be aware of the wide range of both legitimate reproductions and outright fakes available on the market. While most of the reproductions and fakes are easily distinguished from the originals, there are several which are very difficult to identify as 20th century. It is strongly recommended that interested parties become familiar with the reproductions and fakes by reading the previous chapter on "Fakes, Reproductions, and Repairs," and by studying the well-written chapters in *American Bottles and Flasks and Their Ancestry* by McKearin and Wilson, from which all references in this chapter are drawn.

Note: An asterisk (*) following an entry title means that the item has been reproduced. OP means open pontil, SB means smooth based, and IP means iron pontil mark.

Adams / Eagle, GI-62, OP, sheared lip, pint, greenish aqua .... $8000–$10,000
American System; see Steamboat / Sheaf of Rye ....
Anchor / Reverse Plain, GXIII-64, SB, double collar, quart, golden amber .. $25–$35
Anchor / Reverse Plain, GXIII-65, SB, double collar, pint, golden amber ... $25–$35
Anchor / Reverse Plain, GXIII-66, SB, double collar, half pint, aqua .... $20–$30
Anchor / Reverse Plain, GXIII-68, SB, double collar, half pint, amber ...... $25–$35
Anchor Isabella / Glass Factory, GXIII-57, OP, sheared lip, half pint, aqua ....
.... $350–$450
Army Officer / Daisy, GXIII-15, IP, sloping collar, quart, aqua .... $65–$90
Army Officer / Daisy, GXIII-15, IP, sloping collar, quart, deep aqua ..... $120–$150
Army Officer / Daisy, GXIII-15, IP, sloping collar, quart, light blue green . $100–$130
Balt. Anchor / Resurgam, GXIII-53, 1/2" lip chip, pint, yellowish olive ... $250–$300
Balt. Anchor / Resurgam, GXIII-53, pint, aqua .... $70–$85
Balt. Anchor / Resurgam, GXIII-53, pint, golden amber .... $275–$375
Balt. Anchor / Resurgam, GXIII-53, SB, applied lip, pint, olive green .... $700–$800
Balt. Anchor / Resurgam, GXIII-54, double collar, pint, yellow amber ... $275–$400
Balt. Monument / Capt Bragg, GV-1, OP, sheared lip, half pint, aqua .... $275–$350
Balt. Monument / Capt Bragg, GV-1, OP, sheared lip, half pint, olive green ....
.... $1600–$2200
Balt. Monument / Capt Bragg, GVI-1, OP, sheared lip, half pint, medium copper apricot .... $4000–$5000
Balt. Monument / Capt Bragg, GVI-1, OP, sheared lip, half pint, strawberry puce ...
.... $6000–$7500

Calabash form. PHOTO COURTESY OF GLASS WORKS AUCTIONS.

Balt. Monument / Corn, GVI-4, IP, applied ring, quart, copper puce . . . . . $700–$925
Balt. Monument / Corn, GVI-4, IP, double collar, quart, olive yellow . . . . $450–$600
Balt. Monument / Corn, GVI-4, SB, applied lip ring, quart, blue green . $1500–$2500
Balt. Monument / Corn, GVI-4, SB, applied lip ring, quart, ice blue . . . . . $150–$200
Balt. Monument / Corn, GVI-4, SB, applied lip, quart, golden amber . . . . $325–$375
Balt. Monument / Corn, GVI-4, SB, applied lip, quart, light yellow amber . . . . $275–$400
Balt. Monument / Corn, GVI-4, SB, applied ring, quart, aqua . . . . $90–$135
Balt. Monument / Corn, GVI-4, SB, double collar, quart, ice blue . . . . $250–$350
Balt. Monument / Corn, GVI-4, SB, double collar, quart, yellow amber . . $325–$375
Balt. Monument / Corn, GVI-4, SB, double collar, quart, yellow apricot . . . . $750–$950
Balt. Monument / Corn, GVI-4, SB, quart, cornflower blue . . . . $400–$600
Balt. Monument / Corn, GVI-4, SB, quart, medium green . . . . $600–$900
Balt. Monument / Corn, GVI-5, OP, quart, aqua . . . . $90–$145
Balt. Monument / Corn, GVI-5, SB, quart, aqua . . . . $70–$90
Balt. Monument / Corn, GVI-6, OP, sheared lip, pint, aqua . . . . $175–$225
Balt. Monument / Corn, GVI-7, SB, tooled lip, half pint, aqua . . . . $60–$90
Balt. Monument / Corn, GVI-7, SB, tooled lip, half pint, bright green . . . . $450–$500
Balt. Monument / Fells Point Sloop, GVI-2, OP, sheared lip, half pint, amethyst . . . . $2500+
Balt. Monument / Fells Point Sloop, GVI-2, OP, sheared lip, half pint, aqua . . . . $200–$300
Balt. Monument / Fells Point Sloop, GVI-2, OP, sheared lip, half pint, citron . . . . $2200–$2500
Balt. Monument / Fells Point Sloop, GVI-2, OP, sheared lip, half pint, deep aqua . . . . $250–$350
Balt. Monument / Fells Point Sloop, GVI-2, OP, sheared lip, half pint, olive green . . . . $3000+
Balt. Monument / Fells Point Sloop, GVI-2, OP, sheared lip, half pint, strawberry puce . . . . $3500–$4200
Balt. Monument / Liberty & Union, GVI-3, OP, pint, greenish aqua . . . . . $130–$180
Binningers Clock, GXIII-87, OP, double collar, amber . . . . $450–$550

Binningers Clock, GXIII-87, OP, double collar, aqua . . . . $250–$325
Bryan Sewall / Eagle, GI-126, coin shaped, SB, double collar, yellow amber. . . . . . .
. . . . $1000–$1400
Bryan Sewall / Eagle, GI-126, SB, double collar, clear . . . . $800–$1200
Cannon / Capt Bragg, GX-4, OP, sheared lip, pint, copper . . . . $5500–$6500
Cannon / Capt Bragg, GX-4, OP, sheared lip, pint, olive green . . . . $4500–$5500
Cannon / Capt Bragg, GX-5, OP, sheared lip, pint, aqua. . . . . $175–$250
Cannon / Capt Bragg, GX-5, OP, sheared lip, pint, bright blue green. . . . . $400–$600
Cannon / Capt Bragg, GX-5, OP, sheared lip, pint, olive . . . . $2500–$3000
Cannon / Capt Bragg, GX-6, OP, sheared lip, half pint, aqua . . . . $140–$190
Cannon / Capt Bragg, GX-6, OP, sheared lip, half pint, bright green . . . . . $200–$290
Cannon / Capt Bragg, GX-6, OP, sheared lip, half pint, deep olive yellow . . . .
. . . . $650–$900
Cannon / Capt Bragg, GX-6, OP, sheared lip, half pint, pale clear green . . $225–$325
Cannon / Capt Bragg, GX-6, OP, sheared lip, half pint, strawberry puce . . . .
. . . . $2750–$3250
Cherub With Floral Decor, bell form, milk glass, 7³/₄", OP . . . . $100–$150
Clasped Hands / Cannon, GXII-38, SB, quart, yellow amber . . . . $650–$950
Clasped Hands / Cannon, GXII-39, SB, laid on ring, pint, amber. . . . . . . $575–$675
Clasped Hands / Cannon, GXII-39, SB, pint, aqua . . . . $70–$85
Clasped Hands / Cannon, GXII-39, SB, sheared lip, pint, amber . . . . $400–$500
Clasped Hands / Cannon, GXII-39, sheared lip, pint, gold amber . . . . $350–$425
Clasped Hands / Cannon, GXII-40, pint, amber . . . . $150–$225
Clasped Hands / Cannon, GXII-40, pint, aqua . . . . $70–$95
Clasped Hands / Cannon, GXII-40, pint, deep aqua . . . . $100–$140
Clasped Hands / Cannon, GXII-40, pint, golden amber . . . . $175–$225
Clasped Hands / Cannon, GXII-40, pint, olive yellow . . . . $350–$450
Clasped Hands / Cannon, GXII-40, pint, olive yellow . . . . $350–$450
Clasped Hands / Cannon, GXII-41, inner haze, pint, amber . . . . $100–$145
Clasped Hands / Cannon, GXII-41, pint, aqua . . . . $60–$80
Clasped Hands / Cannon, GXII-41, pint, golden amber . . . . $200–$250
Clasped Hands / Cannon, GXII-41, pint, medium citron. . . . . $900–$1300
Clasped Hands / Cannon, GXII-43, IP, double collar, quart, deep amber. . . . .
. . . . $350–$450
Cleve & Steve / Rooster, GI-124, half pint, golden amber . . . . $400–$600
Cleve & Steve / Rooster, GI-124, half pint, yellow amber . . . . $450–$650
Cleveland / Hendricks, GI-128, pint, clear. . . . . $600–$850
Clyde Glassworks NY / Plain, GXV-1, SB, applied lip, quart, amber. . . . . $80–$120
Clyde Glassworks NY / Plain, GXV-2, SB, applied lip, pint, amber. . . . . . $80–$120
Clyde Glassworks NY / Plain, GXV-3, AB, applied lip, half pint, amber. . $100–$140
Clyde Glassworks, NY, SB, applied lip, quart, aqua . . . . $50–$60
Columbia / Eagle, GI-117, OP, lip chip, sheared lip, pint, aqua. . . . . $225–$295*
Columbia / Eagle, GI-117, OP, sheared lip, pint, aqua. . . . . $350–$440*
Columbia / Eagle, GI-117, OP, sheared lip, pint, gray blue . . . . $17,500–$22,000*
Columbia / Eagle, GI-117, OP, sheared lip, pint, pale aqua . . . . $350–$500*
Columbia / Eagle, GI-118, OP, lip flake, half pint, aqua . . . . $400–$550
Columbia / Eagle, GI-118, OP, sheared lip, half pint, citron . . . . $3500+
Columbia / Eagle, GI-118, OP, sheared lip, half pint, cobalt . . . . $3500+
Columbia / Eagle, GI-118, OP, sheared lip, half pint, pale vaseline. . . . . $4000–$5000
Columbia / Eagle, GI-118, OP, sheared lip, half pint, sapphire blue . . . . $3500+
Columbia / Eagle, GI-118, OP, sheared lip, half pint, aqua . . . . $700–$1000

Columbia / Eagle, GI-119, OP, sheared lip, pint, cobalt . . . . $27,500–$35,000
Columbia / Eagle, GI-121, OP, sheared lip, pint, aqua . . . . $275–$375
Columbia / Eagle, GI-121, OP, sheared lip, pint, greenish aqua . . . . $275–$400

Figured flask, Columbia-Eagle, GI-121. PHOTO COURTESY
OF NEIL GROSSMAN.

Columbia / Eagle, GI-121, OP, sheared lip, pint, light blue green . . . . $3500+
Columbia / Eagle, GI-122, OP, sheared lip, pint, clear . . . . $4500–$7000
Columbia / Eagle, GI-122, OP, sheared lip, pint, clear . . . . $4500–$7000
Columbus / Reverse unembossed, GI-127, screw cap, half pint, clear . . . . $250–$325
Concentric Ring Eagle, GII-76, OP, sheared lip, quart, light green . . . . $3750–$5000*
Concentric Ring Eagle, GII-76, reproduction, OP, registration # on base, quart, green
. . . . $60–$80*

Figured flask, Eagle-Willington, GII-64. PHOTO COURTESY
OF NEIL GROSSMAN.

Concentric Ring Eagle, GII-76a, OP, tooled lip, pint, yellow green . . . $8500–$10,500
Concentric Ring Eagle, GII-77, OP, tooled lip, quart, deep yellow green $12,500–$17,500
Connell McGill Liquors, strap flask, quart, aqua . . . . $20–$30
Cornucopia / Beaded Medallion, GIII-1, OP, sheared lip, half pint, aqua. . $2300–$2800
Cornucopia / Beaded Medallion, GIII-1, OP, sheared lip, half pint, pale blue green . . . .
. . . . $2500–$3500
Cornucopia / Cornucopia, GIII-2, OP, half pint, aqua . . . . $90–$145
Cornucopia / Cornucopia, GIII-3, OP, sheared lip, 1¹/₂ pints, pale yellow green . . . . .
. . . . $4000–$5500
Cornucopia / Urn, GIII-4, OP, sheared lip, large lip chip, pint, olive green . $30–$35*
Cornucopia / Urn, GIII-4, OP, sheared lip, pint, bright green . . . . $200–$300*
Cornucopia / Urn, GIII-4, OP, sheared lip, pint, deep olive amber . . . . $50–$70*
Cornucopia / Urn, GIII-4, OP, sheared lip, pint, greenish aqua . . . . $125–$170*
Cornucopia / Urn, GIII-4, OP, sheared lip, pint, light yellow, olive tone . $250–$325*
Cornucopia / Urn, GIII-4, OP, sheared lip, pint, olive amber . . . . $55–$75*
Cornucopia / Urn, GIII-4, OP, sheared lip, pint, olive green . . . . $55–$75*
Cornucopia / Urn, GIII-4, OP, sheared lip, pint, teal green . . . . $200–$275*
Cornucopia / Urn, GIII-4, OP, sheared lip, pint, yellow amber . . . . $55–$75*

Figured flask, Cornucopia-Urn, GIII-4. PHOTO COURTESY OF SKINNER'S, INC.

Cornucopia / Urn, GIII-4, OP, sheared lip, pint, yellow olive . . . . $65–$90*
Cornucopia / Urn, GIII-4, OP, sheared lip, potstone crack, pint, olive amber . . . .
. . . . $30–$45*
Cornucopia / Urn, GIII-5, OP, sheared lip, pint, olive amber . . . . $125–$150
Cornucopia / Urn, GIII-6, OP, pint, olive amber . . . . $45–$60
Cornucopia / Urn, GIII-7, OP, sheared lip, half pint, amber . . . . $60–$80
Cornucopia / Urn, GIII-7, OP, sheared lip, half pint, bright green. . . . . $90–$135
Cornucopia / Urn, GIII-7, OP, sheared lip, half pint, forest green . . . . $75–$125
Cornucopia / Urn, GIII-7, OP, sheared lip, half pint, medium emerald green . . . .
. . . . $125–$195
Cornucopia / Urn, GIII-7, OP, sheared lip, half pint, olive amber . . . . $50–$65
Cornucopia / Urn, GIII-7, OP, sheared lip, half pint, olive green . . . . $50–$60
Cornucopia / Urn, GIII-7, OP, sheared lip, half pint, yellow olive . . . . $55–$70
Cornucopia / Urn, GIII-7, OP, sheared lip, lip chip, half pint, olive amber . . . $30–$45
Cornucopia / Urn, GIII-7, OP, sheared lip, olive yellow shading to black in shoulder area, half pint . . . . $90–$110
Cornucopia / Urn, GIII-7, OP, sheared lip, pontil chip, half pint, olive green . . . .
. . . . $30–$45
Cornucopia / Urn, GIII-8, OP, sheared lip, half pint, olive amber . . . . $55–$65
Cornucopia / Urn, GIII-8, OP, sheared lip, half pint, olive green . . . . $55–$65
Cornucopia / Urn, GIII-9, OP, sheared lip, half pint, olive amber . . . . $55–$65
Cornucopia / Urn, GIII-10, OP, sheared lip, half pint, olive amber . . . . $50–$60
Cornucopia / Urn, GIII-10, OP, sheared lip, half pint, olive green . . . . $50–$60
Cornucopia / Urn, GIII-10, OP, sheared lip, half pint, yellow olive amber . . . $55–$65
Cornucopia / Urn, GIII-11, OP, sheared lip, half pint, olive green . . . . $55–$65
Cornucopia / Urn, GIII-11, OP, sheared lip, half pint, yellow amber . . . . . . $60–$75
Cornucopia / Urn, GIII-11, OP, sheared lip, lip chip, half pint, olive green . . . .
. . . . $30–$35
Cornucopia / Urn, GIII-12, OP, sheared lip, half pint, golden amber . . . . . . $90–$135
Cornucopia / Urn, GIII-12, OP, sheared lip, half pint, olive amber . . . . $75–$95
Cornucopia / Urn, GIII-12, OP, sheared lip, half pint, olive green . . . . $65–$80
Cornucopia / Urn, GIII-13, OP, sheared lip, half pint, medium yellow green . . . .
. . . . $475–$575
Cornucopia / Urn, GIII-14, OP, sheared lip, half pint, blue green . . . . $325–$375
Cornucopia / Urn, GIII-14, OP, sheared lip, half pint, emerald green . . . . . $325–$375
Cornucopia / Urn, GIII-14a, OP, sheared lip, half pint, aqua. . . . . $145–$200
Cornucopia / Urn, GIII-15, OP, sheared lip, half pint, aqua. . . . . $100–$150

Cornucopia / Urn, GIII-15, OP, sheared lip, half pint, clear . . . . $400–$625
Cornucopia / Urn, GIII-16, IP, sheared lip, pint, ice blue . . . . $800–$1200
Cornucopia / Urn, GIII-16, OP, sheared lip, pint, aqua . . . . $125–$185
Cornucopia / Urn, GIII-16, OP, sheared lip, pint, blue green. . . . . $450–$575
Cornucopia / Urn, GIII-16, OP, sheared lip, pint, bluish aqua. . . . . $175–$210
Cornucopia / Urn, GIII-16, OP, sheared lip, pint, golden amber . . . . $2500–$3500
Cornucopia / Urn, GIII-17, OP, double collared lip, pint, deep aqua. . . . . $140–$200
Cornucopia / Urn, GIII-17, OP, double collared lip, pint, deep blue green . . . .
. . . . $300–$450
Cornucopia / Urn, GIII-17, OP, double collared lip, pint, light blue green . . . .
. . . . $150–$200
Cornucopia / Urn, GIII-17, OP, double collared lip, pint, teal blue . . . . $225–$325
Cornucopia / Urn, GIII-17, OP, sheared lip, lip flakes, pint, aqua . . . . $80–$120
Cornucopia / Urn, GIII-17, OP, sheared lip, pint, aqua . . . . $140–$190
Cornucopia / Urn, GIII-17, OP, sheared lip, pint, blue green. . . . . $250–$325
Cornucopia / Urn, GIII-17, OP, sheared lip, pint, deep olive yellow . . . . . . $300–$450
Cornucopia / Urn, GIII-17, OP, sheared lip, pint, grass green . . . . $350–$500
Cornucopia / Urn, GIII-18, OP, sheared lip, pint, light blue green . . . . $500–$700
Cornucopia / Urn, GIII-18, OP, sheared lip, potstone cracks, pint, light blue green . . .
. . . . $300–$375
Dancing Sailor / Banjo Player, GXIII-8, OP, sheared lip, half pint, aqua. . . . $60–$80
Dancing Sailor / Banjo Player, GXIII-8, OP, sheared lip, half pint, yellow olive. . . . .
. . . . $525–$675
Dandy, The, SB, 5¹/₄", clear pumpkinseed . . . . $30–$45
Drake, John B, Tremont House, Chicago, inner screw thread, half pint, amber . . . . .
. . . . $200–$250
Draped Bust / Draped Bust, GI-114, OP, sheared lip, half pint, golden amber. . . . . . .
. . . . $125–$175
Draped Bust / Draped Bust, GI-114, OP, sheared lip, half pint, olive green. . . . .
. . . . $125–$165
Draped Bust / Draped Bust, GI-114, OP, sheared lip, half pint, olive yellow. . . . .
. . . . $125–$150
Draped Bust / Draped Bust, GI-114, sheared lip, lip flake, half pint, olive amber . . . .
. . . . $90–$110
Draped Bust, E-35, 8", clear . . . . $100–$140
Duck / Reverse Plain, GXIII-27, SB, laid on ring, quart, pale blue green . . . .
. . . . $475–$600
Duck / Reverse Plain, GXIII-27, SB, string lip, aqua. . . . . $210–$245
Duck / Reverse Plain, GXIII-29, pint, deep greenish aqua. . . . . $200–$240
Duck / Reverse Plain, GXIII-29a, SB, tooled lip, half pint, aqua. . . . . $600–$750
Duck / Reverse Plain, GXIII-29a, SB, tooled lip, half pint, pale blue green . . . .
. . . . $650–$800
Duck / Reverse Plain, GXIII-30, half pint, aqua. $100–$160
Eagle / Anchor, New London, GII-67, OP, applied lip, half pint, orange amber. . . . . .
. . . . $900–$1100
Eagle / Anchor, New London, GII-67, SB, applied lip, half pint, yellow amber. . . . . .
. . . . $750–$950
Eagle / Bunch of Grapes, GII-55, OP, sheared lip, quart, aqua . . . . $120–$170*
Eagle / Bunch of Grapes, GII-55, OP, sheared lip, quart, deep gold amber. . . . .
. . . . $1100–$1325*
Eagle / Bunch of Grapes, GII-55, OP, sheared lip, quart, olive yellow . $2000–$2400*

Eagle / Bunch of Grapes, GII-56, OP, sheared lip, half pint, aqua . . . . . . $175–$250*
Eagle / Bunch of Grapes, GII-56, OP, sheared lip, half pint, yellow olive . . . .
. . . . $3500–$4100*
Eagle / Coffin & Hay, GII-48, flag, OP, sheared lip, large lip chip, quart, aqua . . . . . .
. . . . $65–$95
Eagle / Coffin & Hay, GII-48, flag, OP, sheared lip, quart, deep blue green . . . .
. . . . $2000–$2500
Eagle / Coffin & Hay, GII-48, flag, OP, sheared lip, quart, emerald green . . . .
. . . . $1200–$1600
Eagle / Coffin & Hay, GII-48, flag, OP, sheared lip, quart, medium green . . . .
. . . . $700–$800
Eagle / Coffin & Hay, GII-48, flag, OP, sheared lip, small crack, quart, light citron . . .
. . . . $200–$230
Eagle / Coffin & Hay, GII-48, OP, flag, sheared lip, quart, aqua . . . . $125–$175
Eagle / Cornucopia, GII-6, OP, sheared lip, pint, aqua . . . . $210–$245
Eagle / Cornucopia, GII-6, OP, sheared lip, pint, greenish aqua . . . . $275–$325
Eagle / Cornucopia, GII-6, OP, sheared lip, pint, pale green . . . . $300–$350
Eagle / Cornucopia, GII-11, OP, sheared lip, half pint, aqua . . . . $220–$240
Eagle / Cornucopia, GII-11, OP, sheared lip, half pint, clear . . . . $500–$800
Eagle / Cornucopia, GII-11, OP, sheared lip, half pint, deep aqua . . . . $220–$270
Eagle / Cornucopia, GII-11, OP, sheared lip, half pint, greenish aqua . . . . . $200–$275
Eagle / Cornucopia, GII-11, OP, sheared lip, heavy inner stain, half pint, aqua . . . . . .
. . . . $120–$165
Eagle / Cornucopia, GII-11, OP, sheared lip, lip flakes, half pint, aqua . . . . $125–$175
Eagle / Cornucopia, GII-11a, OP, sheared lip, half pint, aqua . . . . $200–$275
Eagle / Cornucopia, GII-11a, OP, sheared lip, half pint, light yellow green . . . .
. . . . $750–$950
Eagle / Cornucopia, GII-11a, OP, sheared lip, shoulder crack, half pint, aqua . . . .
. . . . $100–$135
Eagle / Cornucopia, GII-13, OP, sheared lip, aqua . . . . $550–$750
Eagle / Cornucopia, GII-14, OP, sheared lip, deep bluish aqua . . . . $350–$475
Eagle / Cornucopia, GII-15a, OP, sheared lip, half pint, aqua . . . . $350–$450
Eagle / Cornucopia, GII-15a, OP, sheared lip, half pint, greenish aqua . . . . $400–$525
Eagle / Cornucopia, GII-16, OP, sheared lip, half pint, aqua . . . . $225–$325*
Eagle / Cornucopia, GII-16, OP, sheared lip, half pint, deep aqua . . . . $250–$375*
Eagle / Cornucopia, GII-16, OP, sheared lip, half pint, sapphire . . . $15,000–$20,000*
Eagle / Cornucopia, GII-17, OP, half pint, aqua . . . . $200–$275*
Eagle / Cornucopia, GII-44, OP, half pint, aqua . . . . $150–$225
Eagle / Cornucopia, GII-45, OP, half pint, aqua . . . . $150–$200
Eagle / Cornucopia, GII-45, OP, half pint, greenish aqua . . . . $140–$190
Eagle / Cornucopia, GII-46, OP, half pint, aqua . . . . $125–$175*
Eagle / Cornucopia, GII-58, OP, sheared lip, half pint, olive yellow . . . . $5000–$7000
Eagle / Cornucopia, GII-69, OP, sheared lip, half pint, blue green . . . . $450–$575
Eagle / Cornucopia, GII-69, OP, sheared lip, half pint, clear . . . . $700–$900
Eagle / Cornucopia, GII-69, OP, sheared lip, half pint, pale green . . . . $400–$575
Eagle / Cornucopia, GII-73, OP, sheared lip, base crack, pint, olive green . . . $45–$60
Eagle / Cornucopia, GII-73, OP, sheared lip, pint, amber . . . . $80–$95
Eagle / Cornucopia, GII-73, OP, sheared lip, pint, deep green . . . . $120–$140
Eagle / Cornucopia, GII-73, OP, sheared lip, pint, greenish aqua . . . . $75–$110
Eagle / Cornucopia, GII-73, OP, sheared lip, pint, olive green . . . . $75–$90
Eagle / Cornucopia, GII-73, OP, sheared lip, pint, yellow amber . . . . $80–$95

Eagle / Cornucopia, GII-73a, OP, pint, forest green. . . . . $150–$250
Eagle / Cornucopia, GII-74, OP, sheared lip, pint, olive amber. . . . . $100–$125
Eagle / Cornucopia, GII-75, OP, sheared lip, pint, olive amber. . . . . $1800–$2200
Eagle / Cornucopia, GII-75, OP, sheared lip, pint, olive green . . . . $1850–$2250
Eagle / Dyottsville Glassworks, GII-38, OP, pint, aqua. . . . . $100–$145
Eagle / Eagle in Flight, GII-9, OP, sheared lip, pint, pale vaseline . . . . . $6500–$7500
Eagle / Eagle, GII-24, OP, sheared lip, pint, deep aqua. . . . . $125–$175
Eagle / Eagle, GII-1, OP, sheared lip, pint, aqua. $200–$265
Eagle / Eagle, GII-1, OP, sheared lip, pint, deep aqua. . . . . $225–$300
Eagle / Eagle, GII-1, OP, sheared lip, pint, greenish aqua. . . . . $225–$285
Eagle / Eagle, GII-1, OP, sheared lip, pint, pale green . . . . $250–$290
Eagle / Eagle, GII-1, OP, sheared lip, shoulder crack, pint, aqua . . . . $90–$145
Eagle / Eagle, GII-2, OP, sheared lip, pint, aqua. $190–$240
Eagle / Eagle, GII-2, OP, sheared lip, pint, bluish aqua . . . . $225–$275
Eagle / Eagle, GII-2, OP, sheared lip, pint, greenish aqua. . . . . $190–$240
Eagle / Eagle, GII-3, OP, sheared lip, pint, aqua. $175–$235
Eagle / Eagle, GII-4a, OP, sheared lip, pint, pale green . . . . $275–$325
Eagle / Eagle, GII-4a, OP, sheared lip, lip chips, pint, greenish aqua. . . . . . $75–$110
Eagle / Eagle, GII-4a, OP, sheared lip, pint, aqua. . . . . $250–$300
Eagle / Eagle, GII-5, OP, sheared lip, pint, light yellow green . . . . $3000–$4000
Eagle / Eagle, GII-128, SB, light olive tone, half pint, yellow . . . . $500–$650
Eagle / Eagle, GII-130, SB, laid on ring, pint, aqua . . . . $55–$65
Eagle / Eagle, GII-20, OP, sheared lip, pint, bluish aqua . . . . $2000–$2400
Eagle / Eagle, GII-24, OP, sheared lip, inner stain, pint, aqua . . . . $75–$95
Eagle / Eagle, GII-24, OP, sheared lip, lip edge bruise, pint, medium yellow green . . .
. . . . $260–$290
Eagle / Eagle, GII-24, OP, sheared lip, small lip chips, pint, aqua . . . . $60–$85
Eagle / Eagle, GII-24, OP, sheared lip, pint, aqua. . . . . $110–$130
Eagle / Eagle, GII-24, OP, sheared lip, pint, blue green . . . . $2000–$3500
Eagle / Eagle, GII-24, OP, sheared lip, pint, cornflower blue . . . . $275–$350
Eagle / Eagle, GII-24, OP, sheared lip, pint, golden amber. . . . . $600–$850
Eagle / Eagle, GII-24, OP, sheared lip, pint, greenish aqua. . . . . $100–$145
Eagle / Eagle, GII-24, OP, sheared lip, pint, ice blue . . . . $225–$325
Eagle / Eagle, GII-24, OP, sheared lip, pint, medium yellow amber. . . . . $1900–$2300
Eagle / Eagle, GII-24, OP, sheared lip, pint, medium yellow green . . . . $350–$450
Eagle / Eagle, GII-24, OP, sheared lip, pint, pale blue . . . . $300–$400
Eagle / Eagle, GII-24, OP, sheared lip, pint, sapphire blue. . . . . $200–$2400
Eagle / Eagle, GII-24, OP, sheared lip, points wear, pint, aqua. . . . . $75–$95
Eagle / Eagle, GII-24, OP, sheared lip, side edge bruise, pint, sapphire . . . $900–$1350
Eagle / Eagle, GII-25, OP, sheared lip, pint, pale blue green . . . . $250–$300
Eagle / Eagle, GII-26, OP, sheared lip, quart, blue green . . . . $650–$850
Eagle / Eagle, GII-26, OP, sheared lip, heavy inner stain, quart, aqua . . . . . . $85–$120
Eagle / Eagle, GII-26, OP, sheared lip, quart, aqua. . . . . $125–$175
Eagle / Eagle, GII-26, OP, sheared lip, quart, clambroth, gray tint. . . . . . . $600–$900
Eagle / Eagle, GII-26, OP, sheared lip, quart, deep amber . . . . $1250–$1500
Eagle / Eagle, GII-26, OP, sheared lip, quart, deep aqua. . . . . $135–$200
Eagle / Eagle, GII-26, OP, sheared lip, quart, deep golden amber . . . . . . $1000–$1600
Eagle / Eagle, GII-26, OP, sheared lip, quart, deep green. . . . . $700–$1100
Eagle / Eagle, GII-26, OP, sheared lip, quart, emerald green . . . . $1500–$2750
Eagle / Eagle, GII-26, OOP, sheared lip, quart, ice blue. . . . . $275–$350
Eagle / Eagle, GII-26, OP, sheared lip, quart, medium green . . . . $375–$500

Eagle / Eagle, GII-26, OP, sheared lip, quart, moonstone . . . . $500–$725
Eagle / Eagle, GII-26, OP, sheared lip, quart, olive yellow . . . . $2000–$2600
Eagle / Eagle, GII-26, OP, sheared lip, quart, pale yellow green . . . . $200–$325
Eagle / Eagle, GII-40, OP, sheared lip, blue green . . . . $675–$875
Eagle / Eagle, GII-40, OP, sheared lip, deep yellow green . . . . $600–$800
Eagle / Eagle, GII-40, OP, sheared lip, emerald green . . . . $650–$850
Eagle / Eagle, GII-40, OP, sheared lip, light yellow green . . . . $200–$235
Eagle / Eagle, GII-70, OP, sheared lip, pint, olive amber . . . . $100–$135
Eagle / Eagle, GII-70, OP, sheared lip, pint, olive green . . . . $100–$140
Eagle / Eagle, GII-70, OP, sheared lip, pint, yellow olive . . . . $110–$155
Eagle / Eagle, GII-70, OP, sheared lip, side rib chip, pint, olive amber . . . . . . $75–$95
Eagle / Eagle, GII-71, OP, sheared lip, half pint, olive amber . . . . $100–$140
Eagle / Eagle, GII-71, OP, sheared lip, half pint, olive green . . . . $100–$140
Eagle / Eagle, GII-71, OP, sheared lip, half pint, yellow olive . . . . $110–$150
Eagle / Eagle, GII-71, OP, sheared lip, lip chip, half pint, olive green . . . . $65–$90
Eagle / Eagle, GII-72, OP, sheared lip, pint, olive amber . . . . $90–$110
Eagle / Eagle, GII-72, OP, sheared lip, pint, olive green . . . . $90–$110
Eagle / Eagle, GII-72, OP, sheared lip, pint, yellow amber . . . . $90–$110
Eagle / Eagle, GII-72, OP, sheared lip, pontil chip, pint, olive amber . . . . $65–$90
Eagle / Eagle, GII-78, OP, sheared lip, quart, yellow olive . . . . $150–$190
Eagle / Eagle, GII-79, OP, sheared lip, quart, amber . . . . $90–$135
Eagle / Eagle, GII-82, OP, pint, olive amber . . . . $65–$90
Eagle / Eagle, GII-83, OP, sheared lip, pint, amber . . . . $65–$90
Eagle / Eagle, GII-83, OP, sheared lip, pint, olive amber . . . . $65–$90
Eagle / Eagle, GII-83, OP, sheared lip, pint, olive green . . . . $65–$90
Eagle / Eagle, GII-84, OP, sheared lip, pint, amber . . . . $65–$90
Eagle / Eagle, GII-84, OP, sheared lip, pint, olive amber . . . . $65–$90
Eagle / Eagle, GII-85, OP, sheared lip, pint, green . . . . $75–$95
Eagle / Eagle, GII-85, OP, sheared lip, pint, yellow amber . . . . $80–$110
Eagle / Eagle, GII-86, OP, sheared lip, half pint, olive amber . . . . $60–$85
Eagle / Eagle, GII-86, OP, sheared lip, half pint, olive green . . . . $60–$85
Eagle / Eagle, GII-86a, OP, sheared lip, half pint, olive green . . . . $65–$90
Eagle / Eagle, GII-87, OP, sheared lip, half pint, olive amber . . . . $65–$90
Eagle / Eagle, GII-88, OP, sheared lip, half pint, amber . . . . $65–$90
Eagle / Eagle, GII-88, OP, sheared lip, half pint, olive green . . . . $65–$90
Eagle / Eagle, GII-88, OP, sheared lip, lip flake, half pint, olive amber . . . . . . $45–$55
Eagle / Eagle, GII-89, OP, sheared lip, half pint, amber . . . . $65–$90
Eagle / Eagle, GII-91, IP, laid on ring, quart, aqua . . . . $45–$65
Eagle / Eagle, GII-91, SB, laid on ring, quart, brown amber . . . . $150–$190
Eagle / Eagle, GII-92, IP, laid on ring, pint, golden yellow amber . . . . $110–$135
Eagle / Eagle, GII-92, SB, laid on ring, pint, aqua . . . . $30–$35
Eagle / Eagle, GII-93, IP, laid on ring, pint, medium sapphire blue . . . . . . $800–$1200
Eagle / Eagle, GII-93, SB, laid on ring, pint, aqua . . . . $30–$40
Eagle / Eagle, GII-93, SB, laid on ring, pint, light green . . . . $150–$190
Eagle / Eagle, GII-94, SB, laid on ring, pint, aqua . . . . $35–$45
Eagle / Eagle, GII-95, SB, tooled lip, half pint, light apple green . . . . $80–$115
Eagle / Eagle, GII-97, SB, laid on ring, half pint, aqua . . . . $30–$35
Eagle / Eagle, GII-98, SB, laid on ring, quart, aqua . . . . $45–$65
Eagle / Eagle, GII-99, SB, laid on ring, quart, amber . . . . $80–$110
Eagle / Eagle, GII-100, laid on ring, SB, quart, aqua . . . . $35–$45
Eagle / Eagle, GII-102, SB, laid on ring, quart, aqua . . . . $55–$65

Eagle / Eagle, GII-103, SB, laid on ring, quart, aqua . . . . $30–$40
Eagle / Eagle, GII-103, SB, laid on ring, quart, deep olive amber . . . . $120–$140
Eagle / Eagle, GII-103, SB, laid on ring, quart, forest green. . . . . $2500–$350
Eagle / Eagle, GII-105, SB, laid on ring, pint, medium emerald green. . . . . $110–$135
Eagle / Eagle, GII-105, SB, ring lip, pint, aqua. . . . . $35–$45
Eagle / Eagle, GII-105, SB, ring lip, pint, olive green. . . . . $150–$200
Eagle / Eagle, GII-106, SB, laid on ring, pint, aqua . . . . $45–$55
Eagle / Eagle, GII-106, SB, laid on ring, pint, deep olive green . . . . $90–$110
Eagle / Eagle, GII-106, SB, laid on ring, pint, medium yellow olive green . . . .
. . . . $110–$130
Eagle / Eagle, GII-107, SB, laid on ring, pint, dark olive green . . . . $150–$190
Eagle / Eagle, GII-108, laid on ring, pint, deep olive green . . . . $140–$195
Eagle / Eagle, GII-108, SB, laid on ring, pint, deep aqua . . . . $50–$60
Eagle / Eagle, GII-108, SB, laid on ring, pint, emerald green. . . . . $125–$150
Eagle / Eagle, GII-108, SB, laid on ring, pint, forest green. . . . . $130–$200
Eagle / Eagle, GII-109, half pint, emerald green. . . . . $200–$325
Eagle / Eagle, GII-116, quart, aqua . . . . $55–$70
Eagle / Eagle, GII-117, SB, laid on ring, aqua. . . . . $40–$55
Eagle / Eagle, GII-118, pint, golden amber . . . . $125–$175
Eagle / Eagle, GII-118, SB, laid on ring, pint, aqua . . . . $35–$50
Eagle / Eagle, GII-118, SB, laid on ring, pint, yellow. . . . . $350–$550
Eagle / Eagle, GII-120, SB, laid on ring, pint, aqua . . . . $35–$50
Eagle / Eagle, GII-122, SB, laid on ring, half pint, aqua. . . . . $30–$40
Eagle / Eagle, GII-124, SB, laid on ring, half pint, aqua. . . . . $30–$40
Eagle / Eagle, GII-125, half pint, aqua . . . . $30–$45
Eagle / Eagle, GII-126, SB, laid on ring, half pint, aqua. . . . . $30–$40
Eagle / Eagle, GII-126, SB, laid on ring, half pint, golden amber. . . . . $130–$180
Eagle / Eagle, GII-126, SB, laid on ring, half pint, yellow amber. . . . . $225–$300
Eagle / Eagle, GII-126, SB, laid on ring, lip chip, half pint, aqua. . . . . $10–$20
Eagle / Eagle, GII-127, IP, laid on ring, half pint . . . . $35–$45
Eagle / Eagle, GII-128, SB, laid on ring, half pint, aqua. . . . . $65–$80
Eagle / Farley & Taylor, GII-27, OP, 2$^1/_2$ quart, deep golden amber. . . . . . . $20,000+
Eagle / Farley & Taylor, GII-27, OP, sheared lip, 2$^1/_2$ quart, aqua . . . . . $3500–$4500
Eagle / Flag, GII-52, OP, sheared lip, inner stain, pint, aqua . . . . $90–$120
Eagle / Flag, GII-52, OP, sheared lip, pint, aqua. . . . . $120–$160
Eagle / Flag, GII-52, OP, sheared lip, pint, golden amber. . . . . $4000–$4500
Eagle / Flag, GII-53, OP, sheared lip, pint, aqua. . . . . $140–$175
Eagle / Flag, GII-54, OP, sheared lip, pint, aqua. . . . . $100–$125
Eagle / Flag, GII-54, OP, sheared lip, very bubbly glass, pint, aqua. . . . . . . $125–$165*
Eagle / Floral Medallion, GII-23, OP, sheared lip, pint, aqua . . . . $450–$700
Eagle / Floral Medallion, GII-23, OP, sheared lip, pint, aqua . . . . $250–$325
Eagle / Floral Medallion, GII-23, OP, sheared lip, pint, greenish aqua . . . $750–$1000
Eagle / Frigate, GII-42, OP, pint, aqua . . . . $145–$195
Eagle / Indian, GII-141, quart, aqua . . . . $140–$240
Eagle / Indian, GII-142, lip chip, quart, aqua . . . . $60–$85
Eagle / Indian, GII-142, quart, aqua . . . . $100–$150
Eagle / Louisville Eagle, GII-114, quart, medium yellow green. . . . . $400–$650
Eagle / Louisville Eagle, GII-115, SB, laid on ring, pint, aqua. . . . . $45–$60
Eagle / Lyre, GII-22, OP, sheared lip, pint, light green. . . . . $600–$850
Eagle / Lyre, GII-22, OP, sheared lip, pint, pale blue green . . . . $400–$600
Eagle / Medallion, GII-8, OP, sheared lip, pint, clear. . . . . $3500–$6500

Eagle / Morning Glory & Vine, GII-19, OP, double collar lip, pint, aqua . . . .
. . . . $475–$600
Eagle / Morning Glory & Vine, GII-19, OP, pottery, pint . . . . $190–$240
Eagle / Morning Glory & Vine, GII-19, OP, sheared lip, pint, aqua . . . . . . $300–$400
Eagle / New London Glassworks, GII-66, SB, quart, yellow amber . . . . . . $700–$950
Eagle / New London Glassworks, GII-68, OP, pint, golden amber . . . . $600–$775
Eagle / New London Glassworks, GII-68, OP, pint, light blue green . . . . . $350–$500
Eagle / Pikes Peak Prospector, GII-21, pint, aqua . . . . $65–$95
Eagle / Pikes Peak Prospector, GII-21, pint, deep aqua . . . . $100–$175
Eagle / Ravenna, GII-37, IP, laid in ring, anchor, pint, olive yellow . . . . . $900–$1250
Eagle / Ravenna, GII-37, IP, pint, deep olive green . . . . $600–$900
Eagle / Ravenna, GII-37, OP, pint, deep aqua . . . . $140–$200
Eagle / Ravenna, GII-37, OP, small lip chip, pint, aqua . . . . $80–$95
Eagle / Ravenna, GII-37, SB, laid on ring, anchor, pint, aqua . . . . $125–$165
Eagle / Reverse Plain, GII-135, quart, aqua . . . . $25–$35
Eagle / Reverse Plain, GII-138, half pint, red amber . . . . $45–$70
Eagle / Reverse Plain, GII-138, half pint, yellow amber . . . . $40–$60
Eagle / Reverse Plain, GII-139, half pint, yellow amber . . . . $40–$55
Eagle / Reverse Plain, GII-28, OP, 2¹/₂ quarts, aqua . . . . $1200–$1750
Eagle / Stag, GII-49, Coffin & Hay, OP, sheared lip, pint, aqua . . . . $125–$170
Eagle / Stag, GII-49, Coffin & Hay, OP, sheared lip, pint, clambroth . . . $1500–$1750
Eagle / Stag, GII-50, Coffin & Hay, OP, sheared lip, half pint, aqua . . . . . $225–$275
Eagle / Sunburst, GII-7, OP, sheared lip, pint, yellow green . . . . $3000–$3750
Eagle / Sunburst, GII-7, OP, sheared lip, pint, clear . . . . $2400–$3000
Eagle / Sunburst, GII-7, OP, sheared lip, pint, light blue green . . . . $800–$1200
Eagle / Tree, GII-41, OP, sheared lip, edge bruise, pint, aqua . . . . $60–$85
Eagle / Tree, GII-41, OP, sheared lip, lip flakes, pint, aqua . . . . $75–$90
Eagle / Tree, GII-41, OP, sheared lip, pint, aqua . . . . $110–$130
Eagle / Tree, Liberty, GII-60, OP, sheared lip, half pint, amber . . . . $800–$1100
Eagle / Tree, Liberty, GII-60, OP, sheared lip, half pint, aqua . . . . $350–$500
Eagle / Tree, Liberty, GII-60, OP, sheared lip, half pint, deep greenish aqua . . . .
. . . . $300–$475
Eagle / Tree, Liberty, GII-60, OP, sheared lip, half pint, golden amber . . $900–$1150
Eagle / Tree, Liberty, GII-60, OP, sheared lip, half pint, pale yellow green . . . .
. . . . $600–$850
Eagle / Tree, Liberty, GII-60, OP, sheared lip, lip chip, half pint, amber . . $600–$800
Eagle / Tree, Liberty, GII-60, OP, sheared lip, medial rib crack, half pint, aqua . . . . . .
. . . . $175–$225
Eagle / Unembossed, GII-136, SB, quart, clear . . . . $35–$40
Eagle / Unembossed, GII-143, IP, laid on ring, quart, grass green . . . . $225–$315
Eagle / Unembossed, GII-143, IP, laid on ring, quart, yellow green . . . . . . $200–$300
Eagle / Westford, GII-65, OP, sheared lip, half pint, olive amber . . . . $240–$280
Eagle / Westford, GII-65, SB, sheared lip, half pint, green . . . . $90–$125
Eagle / Willington, GII-61, SB, sloping collar, quart, bluish emerald green . . . .
. . . . $360–$460
Eagle / Willington, GII-61, SB, sloping collar, quart, deep green . . . . $160–$185
Eagle / Willington, GII-61, SB, sloping collar, quart, olive amber . . . . $125–$175
Eagle / Willington, GII-61, SB, sloping collar, quart, red amber . . . . $170–$260
Eagle / Willington, GII-61, SB, sloping collar, quart, yellow olive . . . . $140–$190
Eagle / Willington, GII-62, OP, sheared lip, pint . . . . $300–$360
Eagle / Willington, GII-62, SB, double collar, pint . . . . $125–$140

Eagle / Willington, GII-63, OP, sheared lip, half pint, olive amber . . . . $325–$375
Eagle / Willington, GII-63, OP, sheared lip, half pint, olive green . . . . $300–$365
Eagle / Willington, GII-63, SB, double collar, half pint, olive amber . . . . . $120–$150
Eagle / Willington, GII-63, SB, double collar, half pint, olive green . . . . . . $120–$145
Eagle / Willington, GII-63, SB, double collar, half pint, yellow olive . . . . $125–$170
Eagle / Willington, GII-63, SB, half pint, emerald green . . . . $110–$145
Eagle / Willington, GII-63a, SB, double collar, half pint, yellow amber . . . $120–$155
Eagle / Willington, GII-64, SB, sheared lip, pint, red amber . . . . $125–$175

Figured flask, Eagle-Willington, GII-64. PHOTO
COURTESY OF NEIL GROSSMAN.

Eagle / Willington, GII-64, SB, sloping collar, pint, green . . . . $110–$150
Eagle / Willington, GII-64, SB, sloping collar, pint, olive amber . . . . $100–$150
Eagle FL / Cornucopia, GII-15, OP, sheared lip, half pint, deep bluish aqua . . . .
. . . . $475–$650
Eagle Ihmsens / Agriculture, GII-10, OP, sheared lip, pint, greenish aqua . . . .
. . . . $750–$1000
Eagle in Circle, strap flask, clear . . . . $40–$60
Eagle JPF / Cornucopia, GII-57, OP, sheared lip, pint, yellow green . . . .
. . . . $42,000–$52,000
Eagle Kirkpatrick / Reverse Plain, GII-134, quart, aqua . . . . $450–$700
Eagle TWD / Cornucopia, GII-43, OP, sheared lip, clear . . . . $700–$900
Eagle WC / Cornucopia, GII-12, OP, sheared lip, half pint, aqua . . . . $600–$825
Eagle WC / Cornucopia, GII-12, OP, sheared lip, half pint, greenish aqua . . . .
. . . . $500–$800
Eagle WC / Cornucopia, GII-12, OP, sheared lip, heavy exterior wear, half pint, aqua
. . . . $375–$500
Eagle With Shield / Plain, GII-39, SB, applied lip, pint, yellow green . . $1600–$2200
Eagle With Stars / Tree, GII-47, OP, sheared lip, quart, aqua . . . . $350–$450
Eagle Zanesville / Cornucopia, GII-18, OP, sheared lip, half pint, aqua . . . .
. . . . $450–$650
Eagle Zanesville / Cornucopia, GII-18, OP, sheared lip, half pint, deep red amber . . .
. . . . $1900–$2300
Eagle Zanesville / Cornucopia, GII-18, OP, sheared lip, half pint, golden amber . . . . .
. . . . $2200–$3500
Eagle, Cunningham / Eagle, GII-110, SB, laid on ring, quart, aqua . . . . $55–$75
Eagle, Cunningham / Eagle, GII-111, SB, laid on ring, pint, aqua . . . . $55–$70

Eagle, Cunningham / Eagle, GII-112, SB, laid on ring, lip flake, pint, aqua . . . .
. . . . $30–$40
Eagle, Granite Glass Co / Eagle, GII-80, Stoddard NH, OP, sheared lip, quart, amber
. . . . $375–$450
Eagle, Granite Glass Co / Eagle, GII-80, Stoddard NH, OP, sheared lip, quart, olive
amber. . . . . $375–$475
Eagle, Granite Glass Co / Eagle, GII-80, Stoddard NH, OP, sheared lip, quart, yellow
olive. . . . . $425–$525
Eagle, Granite Glass Co / Eagle, GII-81, Stoddard NH, OP, sheared lip, pint, yellow
amber. . . . . $140–$175
Eagle, McC & Co / Eagle, GII-113, SB, laid on ring, pint, aqua . . . . $45–$60

Figured flask, EG Booz cabin, GVII-3. PHOTO COURTESY
OF SKINNER'S, INC.

EG Booz's Old Cabin Whiskey, GVII-3, SB, sloping collar, amber . . . $1200–$1800*
EG Booz's Old Cabin Whiskey, GVII-3, SB, sloping collar, golden amber . . . .
. . . . $1300–$1800*
EG Booz's Old Cabin Whiskey, GVII-4, SB, sloping collar, golden amber . . . .
. . . . $1400–$1800
EG Booz's Old Cabin Whiskey, GVII-5, SB, round collar, greenish aqua . . . .
. . . . $2500–$3500
Erie Distilling Co., clear . . . . $20–$25
Eye Opener, eyeball figure on flask, 5¹/₄", opaque white . . . . $150–$250
Flag / Stoddard, GX-27, OP, sheared lip, pint, olive amber . . . . $6500–$7500
Flag / Stoddard, GX-28, OP, sheared lip, half pint, olive amber . . . . $6250–$8250
Flag / Stoddard, GX-29, OP, sheared lip, half pint, light amber . . . . $6250–$8250
Flora Temple, handled, GXIII-19, SB, laid on ring, quart, dark red amber. . . . .
. . . . $200–$260
Flora Temple, handled, GXIII-19, SB, laid on ring, quart, strawberry puce . . . .
. . . . $240–$280
Flora Temple, handled, GXIII-21, SB, laid on ring, pint, red amber. . . . . . $200–$240
Flora Temple, handled, GXIII-21, SB, laid on ring, pint, yellow copper . . $375–$455
Flora Temple, handled, GXIII-24, SB, laid on ring, pint, cherry puce . . . . $425–$500
Flora Temple, handled, GXIII-24, SB, laid on ring, pint, smoky olive. . . . $450–$525
Flora Temple, no handle, GXIII-20, SB, laid on ring, quart, blue green. . . $450–$550
Flora Temple, no handle, GXIII-20, SB, laid on ring, quart, copper puce . . . .
. . . . $325–$400

Flora Temple, no handle, GXIII-23, SB, laid on ring, pint, blue green . . . . $350–$400
Flora Temple, no handle, GXIII-23, SB, laid on ring, pint, yellow olive . . $225–$250
For Pikes Peak / Eagle & Co., GXI-39, SB, laid on ring, half pint, clear . . $350–$400
For Pikes Peak / Eagle, Ceredo, GXI-35, SB, laid on ring, pint, light cornflower blue
. . . . $850–$1100
For Pikes Peak / Eagle, Ceredo, GXI-34, SB, laid on ring, quart, aqua . . . . . $40–$50
For Pikes Peak / Eagle, Ceredo, GXI-34, SB, laid on ring, quart, citron . . $400–$600
For Pikes Peak / Eagle, Ceredo, GXI-34, SB, laid on ring, quart, greenish yellow . . .
. . . . $1000–$1500
For Pikes Peak / Eagle, Ceredo, GXI-34, SB, laid on ring, quart, yellow olive . . . . . .
. . . . $650–$900
For Pikes Peak / Eagle, Ceredo, GXI-35, SB, laid on ring, pint, yellow green . . . .
. . . . $500–$750
For Pikes Peak / Eagle, Ceredo, GXI-36, SB, laid on ring, half pint, aqua . . . $35–$45
For Pikes Peak / Eagle, GXI-21, SB, laid on ring, pint, aqua. . . . . $45–$55
For Pikes Peak / Eagle, GXI-22, SB, laid on ring, pint, aqua. . . . . $45–$60
For Pikes Peak / Eagle, GXI-22, SB, laid on ring, pint, medium golden amber . . . . . .
. . . . $600–$800
For Pikes Peak / Eagle, GXI-24, SB, quart, golden amber. . . . . $550–$750
For Pikes Peak / Eagle, GXI-25, SB, laid on ring, pint, aqua. . . . . $40–$55
For Pikes Peak / Eagle, GXI-26, OP, half pint, aqua . . . . $200–$300
For Pikes Peak / Eagle, GXI-27, SB, laid in ring, pint, light apple green . . $175–$225
For Pikes Peak / Eagle, GXI-27, SB, laid on ring, pint, aqua. . . . . $50–$60
For Pikes Peak / Eagle, GXI-28, SB, laid on ring, pint, aqua. . . . . $45–$55
For Pikes Peak / Eagle, GXI-30, quart, olive yellow . . . . $600–$900
For Pikes Peak / Eagle, GXI-31, SB, laid on ring, pint, aqua. . . . . $40–$55
For Pikes Peak / Eagle, GXI-33, SB, laid on ring, half pint, aqua . . . . $40–$50
For Pikes Peak / Eagle, GXI-37, SB, laid on ring, pint, aqua. . . . . $35–$45
For Pikes Peak / Eagle, GXI-43, SB, laid on ring, pint, aqua. . . . . $40–$55
For Pikes Peak / Eagle, Ihmsen, GXI-29, SB, laid on ring, pint, aqua . . . . . . $55–$60
For Pikes Peak / Hunter, GXI-46, SB, laid on ring, lip flake, quart, aqua. . . $80–$100
For Pikes Peak / Hunter, GXI-46, SB, laid on ring, quart, deep blue aqua . . . .
. . . . $160–$200
For Pikes Peak / Hunter, GXI-46, SB, laid on ring, quart, root beer amber . . . .
. . . . $1750–$2250
For Pikes Peak / Hunter, GXI-46, SB, laid on ring, quart, yellow amber . . $450–$575
For Pikes Peak / Hunter, GXI-46, SB, laid on ring, quart, yellow olive green . . . .
. . . . $500–$700
For Pikes Peak / Hunter, GXI-47, SB, laid on ring, quart, golden amber . . $400–$550
For Pikes Peak / Hunter, GXI-48, SB, laid on ring, quart, aqua . . . . $90–$115
For Pikes Peak / Hunter, GXI-50, IP, laid on ring, pint, aqua. . . . . $225–$295
For Pikes Peak / Hunter, GXI-50, pint, deep golden amber . . . . $600–$775
For Pikes Peak / Hunter, GXI-50, pint, light blue green . . . . $200–$300
For Pikes Peak / Hunter, GXI-50, pint, yellow green . . . . $500–$800
For Pikes Peak / Hunter, GXI-50, SB, laid on ring, pint, deep yellow olive. . . . .
. . . . $650–$825
For Pikes Peak / Hunter, GXI-51, SB, laid on ring, pint, olive green . . . . $800–$1200
For Pikes Peak / Hunter, GXI-51, SB. laid on ring, pint, aqua . . . . $40–$50
For Pikes Peak / Hunter, GXI-52, OP, sheared lip, half pint, aqua . . . . $150–$225
For Pikes Peak / Hunter, GXI-52, OP, sheared lip, half pint, deep blue aqua. . . . .
. . . . $200–$260

For Pikes Peak / Hunter, GXI-52, OP, sheared lip, half pint, light yellow green . . . . .
. . . . $800–$1100
For Pikes Peak / Hunter, GXI-52, OP, sheared lip, inner stain, half pint, aqua . . . . . .
. . . . $90–$130
For Pikes Peak / Hunter, GXI-54, quart, aqua . . . . $1000–$1500
For Pikes Peak, GXI-1, SB, laid on ring, quart, aqua . . . . $35–$55

Pike's Peak with laid on ring below lip. PHOTO COURTESY
OF GLASS WORKS AUCTIONS.

For Pikes Peak, GXI-2, SB, laid on ring, pint, aqua . . . . $35–$45
For Pikes Peak, GXI-3, SB, laid on ring, pint, aqua . . . . $35–$45
For Pikes Peak, GXI-5, SB, laid on ring, half pint . . . . $40–$60
For Pikes Peak, GXI-7, SB, laid on ring, quart, deep olive amber . . . . $700–$900
For Pikes Peak, Old Rye, GXI-8, SB, laid on ring, quart, teal green . . . . . $800–$1200
For Pikes Peak, Old Rye, GXI-8, SB, laid on ring, lip chip, stain, quart, aqua . . . .
. . . . $40–$45
For Pikes Peak, Old Rye, GXI-8, SB, laid on ring, quart, aqua . . . . $75–$100
For Pikes Peak, Old Rye, GXI-9, SB, laid on ring, pint, aqua . . . . $35–$40
For Pikes Peak, Old Rye, GXI-9, SB, laid on ring, pint, pale yellow green . . . .
. . . . $150–$225
For Pikes Peak, Old Rye, GXI-10, SB, laid on ring, half pint . . . . $35–$40
Franklin / Franklin, GI-97, OP, sheared lip, quart, aqua . . . . $125–$175
Franklin / Franklin, GI-97, OP, sheared lip, quart, bright green . . . . $1800–$2300
Franklin / Franklin, GI-97, OP, sheared lip, quart, emerald green . . . . . $2300–$2800
Franklin / Franklin, GI-97, OP, sheared lip, small lip chip, quart, aqua . . . . $80–$120
Franklin / TW Dyott, GI-94, OP, sheared lip, pint, aqua . . . . $140–$180
Franklin / TW Dyott, GI-94, OP, sheared lip, pint, black . . . . $2000–$3000
Franklin / TW Dyott, GI-94, OP, sheared lip, pint, clear with blue tint . . . . $125–$175
Franklin / TW Dyott, GI-94, OP, sheared lip, small lip chip, pint, aqua . . . . $80–$110
Franklin / TW Dyott, GI-94, sheared lip, pint, deep golden amber . . . . . $3250–$3850
Franklin / TW Dyott, GI-95, OP, sheared lip, pint, aqua . . . . $140–$180
Franklin / TW Dyott, GI-96, OP, sheared lip, pint, aqua . . . . $150–$200
Franklin / TW Dyott, GI-96, OP, sheared lip, pint, greenish aqua . . . . $125–$175
Franklin / TW Dyott, GI-96, OP, sheared lip, small lip chip, pint, aqua . . . . $90–$125

Franklin / Dyott, GI-98, Wheeling, sheared lip, pint, light green....... $2500–$3000
Full Measure, SB, double collar, pint, amber .... $20–$25
General Taylor Flasks, see Washington / Taylor or Taylor section
Girl Riding Bicycle / Eagle, GXIII-3, SB, pint, aqua.................. $150–$250
Girl Riding Bicycle / Plain, GXIII-1, SB, laid on ring, pint, gold amber... $350–$450
Girl Riding Bicycle / Plain, GXIII-2, SB, laid on ring, pint, aqua........ $110–$140
Good Game Stag / Tree, GX-1, OP, sheared lip, high point wear, pint, aqua . $70–$90
Good Game Stag / Tree, GX-1, OP, sheared lip, pint, aqua............. $125–$175
Good Game Stag / Tree, GX-2, OP, sheared lip, half pint, aqua .... $200–$265
Good Night, smiling face on milk glass flask, metal screw cap, 4"........ $120–$150
Granite Glass Co / Stoddard NH, GXV-6, OP, sheared lip, quart, olive amber......
.... $500–$700
Granite Glass Co / Stoddard NH, GXV-7, SB, applied lip, pint, amber... $150–$200
Grant / Eagle, GI-79, lip chip, pint, aqua .... $100–$125
Grant / Eagle, GI-79, pint, aqua .... $150–$250
Grover Cleveland / Rooster, GI-123a, SB, sloping collar, pint, aqua ..... $180–$220
Hagerty Glassworks (on base), SB, applied lip, quart, gold amber......... $30–$40
Handmade Sour Mash, clear, half pint, pumpkinseed .... $30–$45
Harrison / Log Cabin, GI-63, OP, sheared lip, pint, aqua .... $22,000–$30,000*
Horse / Gentry Shote & Co., GXIII-25, IP, applied lip, pint, olive amber ....
.... $1300–$1700
Horse and Rider / Hound, GXIII-16, IP, applied lip, olive tone, quart, yellow.......
.... $350–$450
Horse and Rider / Hound, GXIII-16, OP, applied lip, olive tone, quart, yellow......
.... $300–$375
Horse and Rider / Hound, GXIII-17, OP, sheared lip, pint, root beer amber ....
.... $450–$600
Horse and Rider / Hound, GXIII-17, SB, double collar, pint, yellow amber ....
.... $300–$360
Horse and Rider / Hound, GXIII-17, SB, laid on ring, pint, pale yellow green ......
.... $175–$225
Hotel Statler, clear, 3$^1/_2$", pumpkinseed .... $25–$35
Hunter / Fisherman, GXIII-4, IP, sloping collar, quart, deep puce apricot . $250–$350
Hunter / Fisherman, GXIII-4, IP, sloping collar, quart, golden amber .... $175–$225
Hunter / Fisherman, GXIII-4, IP, sloping collar, quart, strawberry puce .. $275–$325
Hunter / Fisherman, GXIII-4, IP, sloping collar, quart, yellow amber .... $200–$225
Hunter / Fisherman, GXIII-4, OP, sloping collar, quart, red amber ...... $300–$335
Hunter / Fisherman, GXIII-4, SB, sloping collar, quart, light blue green .. $200–$275
Hunter / Fisherman, GXIII-4, SB, sloping collar, quart, medium blue green ....
.... $300–$350
Hunter / Fisherman, GXIII-5, OP, sloping collar, quart, aqua............ $85–$110
Hunter / Fisherman, GXIII-6, OP, sloping collar, quart, aqua............ $80–$110
Hunter / Hounds, GXIII-7, OP, pint, olive yellow .... $250–$295
I Got My Fill at Jake's..., man and dog at lamppost, clear, pint, pumpkinseed......
.... $300–$450
Jackson / Eagle, GI-64, OP, sheared lip, pint, aqua .... $850–$1050
Jackson / Eagle, GI-65, JT & Co., OP, sheared lip, pint, greenish aqua... $800–$1200
Jackson / Eagle, GI-65, OP, sheared lip, pint, blue green............. $900–$1250
Jackson / Eagle, GI-66, OP, pint, clear......................... $1250–$1950
Jackson / Eagle, GI-67, B&M, OP, sheared lip, pint, clear .... $9000–$12,000
Jackson / Eagle, GI-69, OP, pint, aqua .... $20,000+

Jackson / Flowers, GI-68, lip chip, OP, pint, aqua . . . . $400–$550
Jackson / Flowers, GI-68, OP, sheared lip, pint, deep greenish aqua . . . . $1100–$1350
Jackson / Masonis, GI-70, OP, pint, aqua . . . . $20,000+
Jacobs Cabin Tonic Bitters, GVII-6, OP, tooled lip, clear . . . . . . $12,000–$15,000*
Jared Spencer / Manchester, GX-24, OP, sheared lip, pint, yellow olive . . . .
. . . . $50,000+

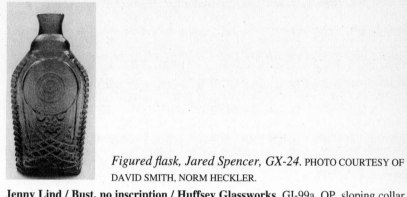

Figured flask, Jared Spencer, GX-24. PHOTO COURTESY OF
DAVID SMITH, NORM HECKLER.

Jenny Lind / Bust, no inscription / Huffsey Glassworks, GI-99a, OP, sloping collar,
quart, aqua. . . . . $5000–$6000
Jenny Lind / Fislerville, GI-107, IP, sloping collar, quart, aqua . . . . $80–$110
Jenny Lind / Fislerville, GI-107, OP, sloping collar, quart, aqua. . . . . $80–$110
Jenny Lind / Glass Factory Building, GI-103, OP, sloping collar, inner stain, quart,
aqua. . . . . $35–$50
Jenny Lind / Glass Factory Building, GI-103, OP, sloping collar, lip chip, quart, aqua
. . . . $35–$55
Jenny Lind / Glass Factory Building, GI-103, OP, sloping collar, quart, aqua. . $60–$85
Jenny Lind / Glass Factory Building, GI-104, IP, sloping collar, lip chip, quart, aqua
. . . . $40–$65
Jenny Lind / Glass Factory Building, GI-104, IP, sloping collar, quart, aqua . . . .
. . . . $75–$100
Jenny Lind / Glass Factory Building, GI-104, IP, sloping collar, quart, blue green. . .
. . . . $275–$375
Jenny Lind / Glass Factory Building, GI-104, IP, sloping collar, quart, deep blue . . .
. . . . $1400–$1800
Jenny Lind / Glass Factory Building, GI-104, OP, quart, root beer amber . . . .
. . . . $10,000–$13,500
Jenny Lind / Glass Factory Building, GI-104, OP, sloping collar, quart, aqua . . . . . .
. . . . $75–$100
Jenny Lind / Glass Factory Building, GI-104, OP, sloping collar, quart, cornflower
blue. . . . . $200–$325
Jenny Lind / Glass Factory Building, GI-104, OP, sloping collar, quart, deep aqua . .
. . . . $75–$125
Jenny Lind / Glass Factory Building, GI-104, OP, sloping collar, quart, light sapphire
blue . . . . $800–$1100
Jenny Lind / Glass Factory Building, GI-105, IP, sloping collar, quart, deep teal . . . .
. . . . $400–$550

Jenny Lind / Glass Factory Building, GI-105, IP, sloping collar, quart, pale blue green . . . . $225–$265

Jenny Lind / Glass Factory Building, GI-105, OP, sloping collar, quart, aqua . . . . $80–$110

Jenny Lind / Glass Factory, GI-102, IP, sloping collar, quart, aqua . . . . . . $110–$150

Jenny Lind / Glass Factory, GI-102, OP, sloping collar, quart, aqua . . . . . $110–$150

Jenny Lind / Glass Factory, GI-107a, reproduction calabash, OP, amber. . . . $25–$35

Jenny Lind / Glass Factory, GI-107a, reproduction calabash, OP, aqua. . . . . $10–$25

Jenny Lind / Glass Factory, GI-107a, reproduction calabash, OP, cobalt blue. . . . . $25–$35

Jenny Lind / Glass Factory, GI-107a, reproduction calabash, OP, emerald green . . . . $25–$35

Jenny Lind / Huffsey Glassworks, GI-99, sloping collar, quart, blue green. . . . . $200–$275

Jenny Lind / Huffsey Glassworks, GI-99, IP, sloping collar, quart, aqua. . . . . $100–$140

Jenny Lind / Huffsey Glassworks, GI-99, OP, sloping collar, quart, aqua . . . . $110–$140

Jenny Lind / Huffsey Glassworks, GI-99, OP, sloping collar, quart, emerald green . . . . $800–$1200

Jenny Lind / Huffsey Glassworks, GI-99, OP, sloping collar, quart, lime / citron . . . . $1300–$1800

Jenny Lind / Huffsey Glassworks, GI-99, OP, sloping collar, quart, yellow olive tint. . . . . $750–$1000

Jenny Lind / Huffsey Glassworks, GI-99, sloping collar, lip chip, quart, emerald green . . . . $450–$650

Jenny Lind / Huffsey Glassworks, GI-99, sloping collar, quart, bright yellow. . . . . $1500–$2500

Jenny Lind / Jenny Lind, GI-108, OP, sheared lip, pint, aqua. . . . . $575–$725

Jenny Lind / Jenny Lind, GI-108, OP, sheared lip, pint, deep aqua . . . . . . $600–$800

Jenny Lind / Jenny Lind, GI-109, OP, sheared lip, quart, deep aqua . . . $1000–$1350

Jenny Lind / Jenny Lind, GI-110, OP, sheared lip, quart, aqua. . . . . $900–$1300

Jenny Lind / Jenny Lind, GI-110, OP, sheared lip, quart, pale blue green . . . . $750–$1250

Jenny Lind / Kossuth, GI-100, OP, sloping collar, quart, aqua . . . . $110–$150

Jenny Lind / Millfora, GI-101, OP, sloping collar, lip chip, quart, aqua . . . . . $60–$80

Jenny Lind / Millfora, GI-101, OP, sloping collar, quart, aqua . . . . $85–$120

Jenny Lind / Tree, GI-106, OP, aqua calabash. . . . . $6000+

JR & Son Waisted Corset, GIX-43, OP, pint, aqua. . . . . $375–$475

JR & Son Waisted Corset, GIX-43, OP, pint, greenish aqua. . . . . $390–$440

JR & Son Waisted Corset, GIX-43, OP, pint, medium amethyst . . . . $5000+

Kline, JN & Co, Aromatic Digestive Cordial, 5", cobalt . . . . $275–$325

Kossuth / Frigate, GI-112a, OP, sloping collar, quart, aqua. . . . . $90–$115

Kossuth / Steam Frigate Huffsey, GI-112, IP, sloping collar, lip chip, quart, aqua . . . . $90–$140

Kossuth / Steam Frigate Huffsey, GI-112, IP, sloping collar, quart, aqua . $180–$225

Kossuth / Steam Frigate Huffsey, GI-112, IP, sloping collar, quart, deep olive yellow . . . . $1300–$1750

Kossuth / Steam Frigate Huffsey, GI-112, OP, quart, emerald green . . . $1750–$2500

Kossuth / Steam Frigate Huffsey, GI-112, OP, sloping collar, lip crack, quart, aqua. . . . . $75–$110

Kossuth / Tree, GI-113, IP, base edge chip, quart, yellow olive . . . . $175–$200
Kossuth / Tree, GI-113, IP, sloping collar, quart, pale green . . . . $60–$90
Kossuth / Tree, GI-113, OP, sloping collar, quart, aqua . . . . $90–$135
Kossuth / Tree, GI-113, OP, sloping collar, quart, aqua . . . . $65–$85
Kossuth / Tree, GI-113, OP, sloping collar, quart, blue green . . . . $190–$225
Kossuth / Tree, GI-113, OP, sloping collar, quart, olive yellow . . . . $275–$350
Kossuth Bridgton / Sloop, GI-111, OP, sheared lip, pint, aqua . . . . $150–$225
Kossuth Bridgton / Sloop, GI-111, OP, sheared lip, pint, light green . . . . . $550–$675
Lafayette / Dewitt Clinton, GI-82, OP, sheared lip, half pint, olive yellow . . . .
. . . . $2500–$3500
Lafayette / Eagle, GI-92, Wheeling Know McKee, OP, sheared lip, pint, pale green . .
. . . . $2500–$3500
Lafayette / Eagle, GI-93, OP, sheared lip, pint, clear green . . . . $2300–$2800
Lafayette / Eagle, GI-90, OP, sheared lip, inner stain, pint, aqua . . . . $160–$200
Lafayette / Eagle, GI-90, OP, sheared lip, large lip chip, pint, aqua . . . . . . $100–$145
Lafayette / Eagle, GI-90, OP, sheared lip, medial rib crack, pint, aqua . . . . . $90–$135
Lafayette / Eagle, GI-90, OP, sheared lip, pint, aqua . . . . $210–$250
Lafayette / Eagle, GI-91, OP, "TWD," sheared lip, pint, aqua . . . . $290–$390
Lafayette / Eagle, GI-93, OP, sheared lip, pint, greenish aqua . . . . $1200–$1500
Lafayette / Eagle, GI-93, OP, sheared lip, pint, light blue green . . . . $1500–$2000
Lafayette / Liberty Cap, GI-85, OP, sheared lip, lip chip, pint, olive amber . . . .
. . . . $225–$295
Lafayette / Liberty Cap, GI-85, OP, sheared lip, pint, olive amber . . . . $350–$475
Lafayette / Liberty Cap, GI-85, OP, sheared lip, pint, olive green . . . . $375–$525
Lafayette / Liberty Cap, GI-85, OP, sheared lip, pint, yellow amber . . . . . . $375–$500
Lafayette / Liberty Cap, GI-85, OP, sheared lip, pint, yellow olive . . . . . . $675–$875
Lafayette / Liberty Cap, GI-86, OP, sheared lip, half pint, forest green . . . $475–$575
Lafayette / Liberty Cap, GI-86, OP, sheared lip, half pint, olive amber . . . $400–$475
Lafayette / Liberty Cap, GI-86, OP, sheared lip, half pint, olive green . . . . $425–$525
Lafayette / Liberty Cap, GI-86, OP, sheared lip, half pint, yellow olive . . . $440–$540
Lafayette / Liberty Cap, GI-86, OP, sheared lip, lip chip, half pint, olive amber . . . . .
. . . . $275–$345
Lafayette / Liberty Cap, GI-86, OP, sheared lip, stain, half pint, olive amber . . . .
. . . . $295–$375
Lafayette / Liberty Cap, GI-87, no stars, OP, sheared lip, half pint, yellow green . . . .
. . . . $3750–$4750
Lafayette / Masonic, GI-88, OP, sheared lip, cracked, pint, olive green . . . $450–$550
Lafayette / Masonic, GI-88, OP, sheared lip, pint, olive green . . . . $1400–$1700
Lafayette / Masonic, GI-88, OP, vertical ribs, sheared lip, pint, olive green . . . .
. . . . $12,000–$18,000
Lafayette / Masonic, GI-89, OP, sheared lip, half pint, yellow olive . . . . $1250–$1650
Lafayette / Masonic, GI-89, OP, sheared lip, weak impression, half pint, olive amber
. . . . $600–$900
Lafayette S&C / Dewitt Clinton, GI-81, OP, sheared lip, half pint, olive yellow . . . . .
. . . . $800–$1150
Lafayette S&C / Dewitt Clinton, GI-81, OP, sheared lip, half pint, yellow olive . . . . .
. . . . $750–$1100
Lafayette S&C / Dewitt Clinton, GI-81a, OP, sheared lip, half pint, yellow olive . . . .
. . . . $2500+
Lafayette S&C, Dewitt Clinton, GI-81, OP, sheared lip, chip, half pint, olive amber .
. . . . $600–$850

Lafayette TS / De Witt Clinton, GI-80, OP, sheared lip, chip, pint, olive green . . . . . .
. . . . $275–$350
Lafayette TS / De Witt Clinton, GI-80, OP, sheared lip, pint, light olive amber . . . . .
. . . . $375–$475
Lafayette TS / De Witt Clinton, GI-80, OP, sheared lip, pint, medium olive green . . .
. . . . $400–$500
Lafayette TS / De Witt Clinton, GI-80, OP, sheared lip, pint, olive amber . . . .
. . . . $400–$525
Lafayette TS / De Witt Clinton, GI-80, OP, sheared lip, pint, olive green . . . .
. . . . $400–$500
Lafayette TS / De Witt Clinton, GI-80, OP, sheared lip, pint, yellow olive . . . .
. . . . $450–$550
Lafayette TS / De Witt Clinton, GI-80, OP, sheared lip, rib chip, pint, yellow olive . .
. . . . $300–$375
Lafayette TS / Masonic, GI-83, OP, sheared lip, pint, yellow olive . . . . . $3250–$4250
Lafayette TS / Masonic, GI-83, OP, sheared lip, pint, yellow olive . . . . . $1800–$2400
Lafayette TS / Masonic, GI-84, OP, sheared lip, half pint, forest green . . . .
. . . . $3400–$3800
Large Key / Reverse Plain, GXIII-75, SB, round collar, pint, aqua . . . . $20–$30
LG CO (on base), SB, applied lip, pint, olive yellow . . . . $25–$35
Life Preserver, clear, pumpkinseed . . . . $30–$45
Life Preserver, milk glass flask, 5½" . . . . $150–$250
Lion / Cluster of Grapes, OP, sheared lip, pint, cobalt . . . . $150–$200
Lion With Shield, Ornberg & Anderson / Gothebarc, OP, sheared lip, cobalt . . . .
. . . . $150–$180
LK & Co, Syracuse, strap flask, half pint, amber . . . . $30–$40
Locomotive / Winged Figure, GV-12, OP, sheared lip, pint, clear . . $25,000–$35,000
Log Cabin / Anchor, Spring Garden, GXIII-58, pint, aqua . . . . $70–$90
Log Cabin / Anchor, Spring Garden, GXIII-58, pint, deep red amber . . . . $300–$500
Log Cabin / Anchor, Spring Garden, GXIII-58, SB, double collar, pint, light amber .
. . . . $325–$375
Log Cabin / Anchor, Spring Garden, GXIII-58, SB, pint, medium strawberry puce . .
. . . . $2000–$3000
Log Cabin / Anchor, Spring Garden, GXIII-60, SB, applied lip, half pint, aqua . . . . .
. . . . $115–$145
Log Cabin / Anchor, Spring Garden, GXIII-61, half pint, yellow amber . $375–$475
Log Cabin / Hard Cider, Flag, GX-22, OP, sheared lip, pint, deep aqua . . . .
. . . . $5000–$6000
Louisville Ky Glassworks / Plain, GXV-13, SB, applied lip, pint, aqua . . . . . $55–$75
Lowell Railroad / Eagle, GV-10, OP, sheared lip, half pint, olive amber . . $160–$195
Lowell Railroad / Eagle, GV-10, OP, sheared lip, half pint, olive green . . . $140–$185
Lowell Railroad / Eagle, GV-10, OP, sheared lip, half pint, yellow amber . . . .
. . . . $175–$200
Masonic / Eagle, GIV-1, OP, sheared lip, pint, blue green . . . . : $200–$325*
Masonic / Eagle, GIV-1, OP, sheared lip, pint, clear . . . . $650–$825*
Masonic / Eagle, GIV-1, OP, sheared lip, pint, light blue green . . . . $225–$265*
Masonic / Eagle, GIV-1, OP, sheared lip, pint, olive green . . . . $950–$1250*
Masonic / Eagle, GIV-1a, OP, sheared lip, moonstone cast, pint, clear . . . . $400–$600
Masonic / Eagle, GIV-1a, OP, sheared lip, pint, blue green . . . . $350–$475
Masonic / Eagle, GIV-1a, OP, sheared lip, pint, medium blue green . . . . . . $350–$450
Masonic / Eagle, GIV-2, OP, sloping collar, pint, light green . . . . $450–$550

Masonic / Eagle, GIV-2, OP, sloping collar, pint, medium green......... $300–$400
Masonic / Eagle, GIV-2, OP, sloping collar, pint, pale greenish aqua ..... $400–$600
Masonic / Eagle, GIV-2, OP, sloping collar, pint, yellow olive .... $3200–$3800
Masonic / Eagle, GIV-3, OP, tooled lip, pint, greenish aqua .... $300–$375
Masonic / Eagle, GIV-3, OP, rolled collar, deep yellow olive mouth and base, pint, greenish aqua body... $3900–$4300
Masonic / Eagle, GIV-3, OP, tooled lip, pint, medium emerald green ..... $750–$950
Masonic / Eagle, GIV-3, OP, tooled lip, pint, yellow green .... $800–$1150
Masonic / Eagle, GIV-4, OP, tooled lip, gray neck shades to clear body, pint, clear body... $800–$1200
Masonic / Eagle, GIV-4, OP, tooled lip, pint, light green.............. $375–$475
Masonic / Eagle, GIV-5, OP, tooled lip, pint, yellowish green.......... $400–$450
Masonic / Eagle, GIV-6, OP, tooled lip, pint, light green.............. $375–$475
Masonic / Eagle, GIV-7, OP, tooled lip, amethyst streaks, pint, clear ..... $500–$600
Masonic / Eagle, GIV-7, OP, tooled lip, lip chip, pint, blue green .... $160–$225
Masonic / Eagle, GIV-7, OP, tooled lip, pint, blue aqua............... $175–$225
Masonic / Eagle, GIV-7, OP, tooled lip, pint, clear................... $375–$475
Masonic / Eagle, GIV-7, OP, tooled lip, pint, emerald green.............. $3000+
Masonic / Eagle, GIV-7, OP, tooled lip, pint, medium greenish aqua ..... $400–$550
Masonic / Eagle, GIV-7, OP, tooled lip, pint, medium yellow green ...... $500–$700
Masonic / Eagle, GIV-7a, pint, light blue green .... $400–$600
Masonic / Eagle, GIV-8, OP, pint, yellow green..................... $400–$600
Masonic / Eagle, GIV-8a, OP, tooled lip, light yellow green .... $400–$500
Masonic / Eagle, GIV-8a, OP, tooled lip, medium yellow green .... $400–$600
Masonic / Eagle, GIV-9, OP, tooled lip, light yellow green .... $400–$525
Masonic / Eagle, GIV-1, OP, sheared lip, pint, aqua.................. $175–$250
Masonic / Eagle, GIV-10, OP, tooled lip, light blue green .... $275–$375
Masonic / Eagle, GIV-11, OP, pint, clear .... $400–$600
Masonic / Eagle, GIV-12, OP, tooled lip, pint, blue green .... $3500–$4250
Masonic / Eagle, GIV-13, OP, half pint, clear...................... $1000–$1500
Masonic / Eagle, GIV-14, aqua................................... $400–$600
Masonic / Eagle, GIV-14, greenish aqua........................... $300–$400
Masonic / Eagle, GIV-14, light green .... $400–$525
Masonic / Eagle, GIV-14, OP, yellow green........................ $400–$500
Masonic / Eagle, GIV-15, OP, tooled lip, pint, greenish aqua .... $3500–$4250
Masonic / Eagle, GIV-16, OP, sloping collar, pint, deep yellow olive ... $2400–$2800
Masonic / Eagle, GIV-17, OP, sheared lip, pint, pure olive .... $300–$360
Masonic / Eagle, GIV-17, OP, sheared lip, pint, olive amber............ $130–$180
Masonic / Eagle, GIV-18, OP, sheared lip, lip chip, pint, yellow amber ..... $60–$80
Masonic / Eagle, GIV-18, OP, sheared lip, pint, olive amber............ $125–$175
Masonic / Eagle, GIV-18, OP, sheared lip, pint, pure olive .... $130–$180
Masonic / Eagle, GIV-19, OP, sheared lip, lip flakes, pint, olive green ..... $80–$100
Masonic / Eagle, GIV-19, OP, sheared lip, pint, olive amber............ $125–$175
Masonic / Eagle, GIV-19, OP, sheared lip, pint, yellow amber .... $125–$160
Masonic / Eagle, GIV-19, OP, sheared lip, pint, yellow amber .... $130–$180
Masonic / Eagle, GIV-20, OP, sheared lip, pint, olive amber .... $130–$175
Masonic / Eagle, GIV-20a, OP, sheared lip, pint, olive amber .... $125–$175
Masonic / Eagle, GIV-21, OP, sheared lip, pint, yellow olive .... $125–$160
Masonic / Eagle, GIV-22, OP, sheared lip, pint, clear .... $5000–$6000
Masonic / Eagle, GIV-23, OP, tooled lip, pint, medium yellow green .... $800–$1000
Masonic / Eagle, GIV-24, OP, sheared lip, lip chip, pint, olive amber..... $110–$145

Masonic / Eagle, GIV-24, OP, sheared lip, pint, deep yellow olive . . . . $225–$250
Masonic / Eagle, GIV-24, OP, sheared lip, pint, greenish aqua . . . . $400–$600
Masonic / Eagle, GIV-24, OP, sheared lip, pint, olive green . . . . $175–$205
Masonic / Eagle, GIV-24, OP, sheared lip, pint, redware pottery . . . . $400–$700
Masonic / Eagle, GIV-25, OP, half pint, olive amber . . . . $600–$900
Masonic / Eagle, GIV-26, half pint, olive green . . . . $400–$575
Masonic / Eagle, GIV-26, OP, half pint, deep yellow olive . . . . $400–$550
Masonic / Eagle, GIV-27, half pint, blue green. . . . . $275–$375
Masonic / Eagle, GIV-27, half pint, greenish aqua . . . . $150–$200
Masonic / Eagle, GIV-27, half pint, ice blue. . . . . $450–$700
Masonic / Eagle, GIV-27, half pint, pale blue. . . . . $450–$650
Masonic / Eagle, GIV-31, OP, sheared lip, pint, greenish aqua . . . . $3000–$4000
Masonic / Eagle, GIV-32, OP, sheared lip, burst side bubble, pint, yellow amber. . . . .
. . . . $350–$400

Figured flask, Masonic-Eagle, GIV-32. PHOTO
COURTESY OF NEIL GROSSMAN.

Masonic / Eagle, GIV-32, OP, sheared lip, inner stain, pint, red amber . . . . $300–$385
Masonic / Eagle, GIV-32, OP, sheared lip, pint, amber . . . . $375–$475
Masonic / Eagle, GIV-32, OP, sheared lip, pint, dark red amber . . . . $350–$425
Masonic / Eagle, GIV-32, OP, sheared lip, pint, deep aqua . . . . $190–$280
Masonic / Eagle, GIV-32, OP, sheared lip, pint, deep golden amber . . . . . . $350–$450
Masonic / Eagle, GIV-32, OP, sheared lip, pint, golden amber . . . . $900–$1200
Masonic / Eagle, GIV-32, OP, sheared lip, pint, light blue green. . . . . $275–$375
Masonic / Eagle, GIV-32, OP, sheared lip, pint, orange amber . . . . $375–$500
Masonic / Eagle, GIV-32, OP, sheared lip, pint, pale blue green . . . . $200–$245
Masonic / Eagle, GIV-32, OP, sheared lip, pint, red amber . . . . $400–$550
Masonic / Eagle, GIV-32, OP, sheared lip, pint, yellow . . . . $700–$1000
Masonic / Eagle, GIV-32, OP, sheared lip, pint, yellow amber . . . . $450–$550
Masonic / Eagle, GIV-32, OP, sheared lip, pint, yellow green . . . . $600–$900
Masonic / Eagle, GIV-33, OP, sheared lip, pint, deep blue green. . . . . . . $2500–$3500
Masonic / Eagle, GIV-33, OP, sheared lip, pint, greenish aqua . . . . $1500–$2500
Masonic / Eagle, GIV-37, OP, sheared lip, neck crack, pint, aqua . . . . $90–$135
Masonic / Eagle, GIV-37, TWD, OP, sheared lip, pint, aqua . . . . $175–$225
Masonic / Eagle, GIV-37, TWD, OP, sheared lip, pint, deep aqua. . . . . $175–$250
Masonic / Eagle, GIV-40, OP, pint, golden amber . . . . $250–$300
Masonic / Eagle, GIV-41, clasped hands, OP, half pint, aqua. . . . . $100–$145
Masonic / Masonic, GIV-28, OP, sheared lip, half pint, blue green . . . . $300–$400
Masonic / Masonic, GIV-28, OP, sheared lip, half pint, deep aqua . . . . $200–$265

Masonic / Masonic, GIV-28, OP, sheared lip, half pint, light green . . . . . . $225–$325
Masonic / Masonic, GIV-28, OP, sheared lip, half pint, medium blue green . . . .
. . . . $250–$350
Masonic / Masonic, GIV-28, OP, sheared lip, half pint, medium grass green . . . .
. . . . $800–$1200
Masonic / Masonic, GIV-28, OP, sheared lip, half pint, olive green . . . . $1000–$1400
Masonic / Masonic, GIV-28a, OP, sheared lip, half pint, emerald green . . . $500–$625
Masonic / Masonic, GIV-28a, OP, sheared lip, half pint, greenish aqua . . . $275–$335
Masonic / Masonic, GIV-28a, OP, sheared lip, pontil chip, half pint, light blue green .
. . . . $225–$250
Masonic / Ship, Franklin, GIV-34, OP, sheared lip, high point wear, pint, aqua . . . . .
. . . . $125–$150
Masonic / Ship, Franklin, GIV-34, OP, sheared lip, pint, aqua . . . . $180–$220
Masonic / Ship, Franklin, GIV-34, OP, sheared lip, pint, emerald green . . . .
. . . . $4500+
Masonic / Ship, Franklin, GIV-34, OP, sheared lip, pint, pale yellow green . . . .
. . . . $500–$700
Masonic Crossed Keys / Compass, GIV-30, OP, sheared lip, half pint, olive yellow. .
. . . . $15,000+
Masonic Hourglass / Compasses, GIV-29, OP, sheared lip, half pint, olive green . . . .
. . . . $6000–$7500
Masonic Union / Eagle, GIV-38, SB, laid on ring, quart, gold amber . . . . . $150–$235
Masonic Union / Eagle, GIV-39, OP, flat collar, quart, yellow olive . . . . . $800–$1150
Masonic Union / Eagle, GIV-42, OP, sloping collar, inner stain, quart, aqua . . . .
. . . . $30–$45
Masonic Union / Eagle, GIV-42, OP, sloping collar, quart, aqua. . . . . $50–$60
Masonic Union / Eagle, GIV-42, SB, sloping collar, quart, citron . . . . $200–$225
McKinley / Honey Bee, GI-125, clear coin, SB, half pint, clear. . . . . $675–$900
Medallion / Medallion, GX-25, OP, sheared lip, pint, yellow olive . . . . $40,000+
Medallion, Pearls / Medallion, Pearls, GX-26, OP, sheared lip, large body cracks,
pint, yellow amber . . . . $4500–$5500
Medallion, Pearls / Medallion, Pearls, GX-26, OP, sheared lip, pint, light olive . . . . .
. . . . $25,000+
Men Arguing / Grotesque Head, GX-12, half pint, aqua . . . . $175–$245
Men Arguing / Grotesque Head, GX-12, OP, half pint, cobalt . . . . $500–$650
Merry Christmas, A, woman sitting, Happy New Year, rooster, half pint, amber . . . .
. . . . $250–$350
Murdock & Cassel / Zanesville, GX-14, OP, sheared lip, pint, light blue green . . . . . .
. . . . $1500–$1800
Murdock & Cassel / Zanesville, GX-14, OP, sheared lip, pint, light green. . . . .
. . . . $1200–$1500
Newburgh Glass Co, Pat'd Feb 27, 1866, GXV-15, double collar, half pint, black . . . .
. . . . $1200–$1700
Newburgh Glass Co, Patd Feb 27, 1866, GXV-15, laid on ring, half pint, yellow olive
. . . . $1350–$1800
Night Cap, man with stocking cap on, milk glass flask, metal cap, 4" . . . . . $150–$225
Ornberg & Anderson / Gothebarc, OP, sheared lip, cobalt . . . . $150–$180
Patent (on face), SB, double collar, pint, amber . . . . $40–$55
Picnic, 5¹/₄", amber pumpkinseed . . . . $75–$95
Pikes Peak Flasks, see For Pikes Peak, and Prospector / Eagle
Portchester Wine & Liquor, clear . . . . $20–$25

Prospector / Eagle, Arsenal, GXI-13, SB, laid on ring, quart, aqua .... $60–$85
Prospector / Eagle, Arsenal, GXI-15, SB, laid on ring, pint, medium yellow green...
.... $1200–$1500
Prospector / Eagle, GXI-11, OP, string lip, pint, yellow olive........ $2600–$3400
Prospector / Eagle, GXI-11, SB, laid on ring, pint, aqua................. $60–$90
Prospector / Eagle, GXI-17, SB, laid on ring, pint, aqua .... $50–$60
Prospector / Eagle, GXI-17, SB, laid on ring, pint, deep yellow olive..... $700–$850
Prospector / Eagle, GXI-19, SB, laid on ring, half pint, aqua .... $45–$60
Prospector / Eagle, GXI-20, half pint, deep yellow green .... $1200–$1700
Prospector / Eagle, GXI-40, SB, laid on ring, quart, aqua .... $70–$90
Prospector / Eagle, GXI-41, pint, aqua................................ $50–$65
Prospector / Eagle, GXI-41, pint, bluish aqua .... $50–$80
Prospector / Eagle, GXI-44, IP, applied lip, pint, aqua .... $1250–$1750
Railroad Horse and Cart, GV-7, OP, sheared lip, lip chips, pint, olive amber.......
.... $80–$110
Railroad Horse and Cart, GV-7, OP, sheared lip, pint, olive amber...... $160–$195
Railroad Horse and Cart, GV-7, OP, sheared lip, pint, olive green ..... $175–$225
Railroad Horse and Cart, GV-7a, OP, sheared lip, pint, olive amber..... $185–$240
Railroad Horse and Cart / Eagle, GV-9, OP, sheared lip, pint, olive amber.. $160–$190
Railroad Horse and Cart / Eagle, GV-9, OP, sheared lip, pint, olive green.........
.... $150–$190
Ravenna Glass Works, GXIII-83, SB, applied lip, pint, yellow olive ... $1100–$1550
Ravenna Glassworks / Plain, GXV-17, SB, double collar, pint, amber.... $150–$250
Rib Pattern, no embossing, half pint, amber........................... $15–$20
Ribbed Eagle / Ribbed Eagle, GII-29, OP, sheared lip, pint, aqua .... $375–$475
Ribbed Eagle / Ribbed Eagle, GII-30, OP, sheared lip, half pint, aqua.... $250–$350
Ribbed Eagle / Ribbed Eagle, GII-30, OP, sheared lip, half pint, greenish aqua .....
.... $250–$360
Ribbed Eagle / Ribbed Eagle, GII-30, OP, sheared lip, lip chip, half pint, aqua......
.... $140–$185
Ribbed Eagle / Ribbed Eagle, GII-31, OP, double collar, quart, aqua..... $275–$400
Ribbed Eagle / Ribbed Eagle, GII-31, OP, double collar, quart, yellow green.......
.... $3000–$3600
Ribbed Eagle / Ribbed Eagle, GII-32, OP, lip flakes, pint, aqua......... $120–$145
Ribbed Eagle / Ribbed Eagle, GII-32, OP, pint, aqua .... $190–$270
Ribbed Eagle / Ribbed Eagle, GII-31, OP, double collar, quart, emerald green ......
.... $3100–$3750
Ribbed Eagle / Ribbed Louisville, GII-33, SB, double collar, half pint, aqua........
.... $80–$100
Ribbed Eagle / Ribbed Louisville, GII-33, SB, double collar, half pint, deep amber ..
.... $800–$1200
Ribbed Eagle / Ribbed Louisville, GII-33, SB, double collar, half pint, deep yellow
green .... $1200–$1500
Ribbed Eagle / Ribbed Louisville, GII-33, SB, double collar, half pint, pale blue green
.... $125–$150
Ribbed Eagle / Ribbed Louisville, GII-34, IP, double collar, pint, aqua... $290–$360
Ribbed Eagle Louisville / Plain, GII-35, SB, laid on ring, quart, aqua ..... $80–$110
Ribbed Eagle Louisville / Plain, GII-36, SB, laid on ring, pint, aqua .... $75–$90
CA Richards Co, 99 Washington St Boston, pint, aqua................. $35–$45
Geo W Robinson Main St W Va / Plain, GXV-18, SB, applied lip, quart, aqua .....
.... $125–$175

Roosevelt / TVA, GI-129, sloping collar, quart, aqua . . . . $125–$145
Safe / Reverse Plain, GXIII-80, half pint, aqua. . . . . $30–$40
SC Dispensary, clear, half pint . . . . $100–$120
SC Dispensary, clear, pint . . . . $80–$100

Figured flask, scroll, GIX-1. PHOTO COURTESY OF
NEIL GROSSMAN.

Scroll, GIX-1, IP, sheared lip, quart, aqua . . . . $40–$60
Scroll, GIX-1, IP, sheared lip, quart, golden amber . . . . $500–$700
Scroll, GIX-1, IP, sheared lip, quart, olive yellow . . . . $500–$750
Scroll, GIX-1, IP, sheared lip, quart, spruce green. . . . . $1500–$2000
Scroll, GIX-1, OP, sheared lip, quart, blue aqua . . . . $40–$65
Scroll, GIX-1, OP, sheared lip, quart, medium sapphire blue . . . . $1000–$1400
Scroll, GIX-1, OP, sheared lip, quart, moonstone . . . . $500–$600
Scroll, GIX-2, IP, quart, deep yellow green . . . . $650–$775
Scroll, GIX-2, IP, sheared lip, pink tint, quart, moonstone . . . . $450–$550
Scroll, GIX-2, IP, sheared lip, quart, cobalt blue . . . . $1500–$2500
Scroll, GIX-2, IP, sheared lip, quart, deep golden amber . . . . $500–$600
Scroll, GIX-2, IP, sheared lip, quart, olive amber . . . . $400–$600
Scroll, GIX-2, IP, sheared lip, rib crack, large rib chip, quart, sapphire . . . . $300–$450
Scroll, GIX-2, OP, sheared lip, large lip chip, quart, aqua. . . . . $30–$35
Scroll, GIX-2, OP, sheared lip, lavender tint, quart, moonstone . . . . $475–$550
Scroll, GIX-2, OP, sheared lip, quart, bright green . . . . $250–$350
Scroll, GIX-2, OP, sheared lip, quart, medium green . . . . $500–$700
Scroll, GIX-2, OP, sheared lip, quart, olive yellow . . . . $500–$750
Scroll, GIX-2, sheared lip, OP, quart, spruce green. . . . . $750–$1000
Scroll, GIX-3, OP, sheared lip, lip chips, quart, amber . . . . $200–$275
Scroll, GIX-3, OP, sheared lip, lip crack, quart, aqua . . . . $15–$20
Scroll, GIX-3, OP, sheared lip, lip flakes, quart, sapphire blue . . . . $600–$800
Scroll, GIX-3, OP, sheared lip, quart, aqua . . . . $35–$55
Scroll, GIX-3, OP, sheared lip, quart, black. . . . . $750–$1000
Scroll, GIX-3, OP, sheared lip, quart, grass green . . . . $275–$400
Scroll, GIX-3, OP, sheared lip, quart, light green . . . . $200–$300
Scroll, GIX-3, OP, sheared lip, quart, olive . . . . $500–$750
Scroll, GIX-3, OP, sheared lip, quart, sea green . . . . $325–$475
Scroll, GIX-3, sheared lip, quart, sapphire blue. $1100–$1450
Scroll, GIX-4, OP, applied lip ring, quart, aqua. . . . . $40–$60
Scroll, GIX-4, OP, applied lip ring, quart, blue green . . . . $300–$450
Scroll, GIX-4, OP, applied lip ring, quart, root beer amber . . . . $500–$600

Scroll, GIX-5, OP, sheared lip, quart, aqua . . . . $40–$55
Scroll, GIX-5, OP, sheared lip, quart, light green . . . . $175–$275
Scroll, GIX-6, IP, sheared lip, quart. . . . . $100–$145
Scroll, GIX-7, IP, quart, citron . . . . $600–$800
Scroll, GIX-8, IP, lip roughness, pint, aqua . . . . $45–$60
Scroll, GIX-8, IP, pint, aqua. . . . . $75–$90
Scroll, GIX-8, IP, pint, greenish aqua . . . . $80–$120
Scroll, GIX-8, IP, pint, yellow green . . . . $700–$950
Scroll, GIX-9, IP, sheared lip, pint, amber. . . . . $600–$900
Scroll, GIX-9, IP, sheared lip, pint, aqua . . . . $80–$95
Scroll, GIX-10, OP, sheared lip, pint, light yellow green . . . . $175–$300*
Scroll, GIX-10, IP, sheared lip, lip bruise, pint, deep sapphire . . . . $1100–$1450*
Scroll, GIX-10, IP, sheared lip, lip flakes, pint, deep golden amber . . . . . $175–$275*
Scroll, GIX-10, IP, sheared lip, pint, aqua . . . . $40–$50*
Scroll, GIX-10, IP, sheared lip, pint, bluish aqua. . . . . $40–$60*
Scroll, GIX-10, IP, sheared lip, pint, cobalt blue . . . . $1300–$1800*
Scroll, GIX-10, IP, sheared lip, pint, deep golden amber . . . . $300–$400*
Scroll, GIX-10, IP, sheared lip, pint, moonstone . . . . $300–$400*
Scroll, GIX-10, IP, sheared lip, pint, yellow green . . . . $350–$475*
Scroll, GIX-10, OP, sheared lip, dark olive amber . . . . $400–$600*
Scroll, GIX-10, OP, sheared lip, pint, amber . . . . $300–$400*
Scroll, GIX-10, OP, sheared lip, pint, blue green. . . . . $250–$350*
Scroll, GIX-10, OP, sheared lip, pint, clear . . . . $200–$300*
Scroll, GIX-10, OP, sheared lip, pint, clear vaseline tint . . . . $160–$200*
Scroll, GIX-10, OP, sheared lip, pint, cobalt blue . . . . $1300–$1800*
Scroll, GIX-10, OP, sheared lip, pint, golden amber . . . . $375–$475*
Scroll, GIX-10, OP, sheared lip, pint, medium blue . . . . $400–$600*
Scroll, GIX-10, OP, sheared lip, pint, sapphire . . . . $1800–$2300*
Scroll, GIX-10, sheared lip, lip flake, pint, olive yellow . . . . $400–$550*
Scroll, GIX-10, sheared lip, pint, deep olive green . . . . $375–$500*
Scroll, GIX-10a, OP, pint, deep aqua. . . . . $60–$85
Scroll, GIX-10a, OP, pint, sage green . . . . $600–$800
Scroll, GIX-10a, OP, pint, sapphire blue . . . . $1150–$1600
Scroll, GIX-10b, OP, pint, deep olive yellow . . . . $40–$600
Scroll, GIX-10b, OP, pint, medium yellow green . . . . $250–$400
Scroll, GIX-10b, OP, pint, olive amber . . . . $550–$700
Scroll, GIX-10b, OP, pint, olive yellow. . . . . $500–$750
Scroll, GIX-10b, OP, pint, yellow green . . . . $400–$600
Scroll, GIX-10c, OP, pint, aqua . . . . $75–$95
Scroll, GIX-10c, OP, pint, blue green . . . . $600–$900
Scroll, GIX-10c, OP, pint, medium citron . . . . $400–$550
Scroll, GIX-10d, OP, pint, aqua . . . . $55–$70
Scroll, GIX-10e, OP, pint, aqua . . . . $55–$70
Scroll, GIX-11, OP, large lip chip, pint, aqua . . . . $30–$35*
Scroll, GIX-11, OP, pint, amber. . . . . $200–$300*
Scroll, GIX-11, OP, pint, aqua. . . . . $70–$85*
Scroll, GIX-11, OP, pint, bright olive green . . . . $350–$550*
Scroll, GIX-11, OP, pint, golden amber. . . . . $250–$350*
Scroll, GIX-11, OP, pint, light yellow olive. . . . . $750–$900*
Scroll, GIX-11, OP, pint, yellow amber. . . . . $325–$500*
Scroll, GIX-11, OP, pint, yellow green . . . . $425–$600*

Scroll, GIX-11, pint, ice blue . . . . $150–$250*
Scroll, GIX-11a, IP, pint, aqua . . . . $40–$55
Scroll, GIX-11a, IP, pint, medium golden amber . . . . $250–$350
Scroll, GIX-11a, IP, pint, olive green . . . . $300–$450
Scroll, GIX-11a, IP, pint, olive green . . . . $300–$450
Scroll, GIX-12, OP, pint, yellowish olive green . . . . $350–$500
Scroll, GIX-13, IP, pint, aqua . . . . $40–$55
Scroll, GIX-13, IP, pint, yellow olive . . . . $500–$775
Scroll, GIX-13, pint, olive green . . . . $375–$450
Scroll, GIX-14, OP, grayish tint, pint, clear . . . . $300–$550
Scroll, GIX-14, OP, pint, aqua . . . . $40–$50
Scroll, GIX-14, OP, pint, deep golden amber . . . . $300–$350
Scroll, GIX-14, OP, pint, deep yellow green . . . . $750–$950
Scroll, GIX-14, OP, pint, yellow olive . . . . $500–$750
Scroll, GIX-14, pint, light green . . . . $90–$135
Scroll, GIX-15, OP, pint, aqua . . . . $60–$85
Scroll, GIX-15, OP, pint, greenish yellow . . . . $450–$500
Scroll, GIX-15, OP, pint, medium citron . . . . $600–$750
Scroll, GIX-16, IP, pint, aqua . . . . $50–$75
Scroll, GIX-16, IP, pint, olive amber . . . . $300–$400
Scroll, GIX-16, OP, pint, clear . . . . $200–$275
Scroll, GIX-16a, OP, pint, aqua . . . . $40–$60
Scroll, GIX-17, OP, pint, aqua . . . . $40–$55
Scroll, GIX-18, OP, pint, aqua . . . . $40–$60
Scroll, GIX-18, OP, pint, sapphire blue . . . . $900–$1300
Scroll, GIX-18, OP, pint, yellow . . . . $500–$800
Scroll, GIX-19, OP, pint, aqua . . . . $50–$70
Scroll, GIX-19, OP, pint, deep tobacco amber . . . . $450–$600
Scroll, GIX-19, OP, pint, pale yellow green . . . . $250–$375
Scroll, GIX-19, OP, pint, sapphire . . . . $1600–$1900
Scroll, GIX-2, OP, double collar, quart, aqua . . . . $60–$80
Scroll, GIX-20, OP, pint, amber . . . . $350–$475
Scroll, GIX-20, OP, pint, aqua . . . . $50–$70
Scroll, GIX-20, OP, pint, yellow olive . . . . $800–$1150
Scroll, GIX-21, OP, pint, aqua . . . . $40–$55
Scroll, GIX-22, OP, pint, aqua . . . . $75–$95
Scroll, GIX-23, OP, medium yellow green . . . . $900–$1250
Scroll, GIX-23, OP, pint, aqua . . . . $60–$90
Scroll, GIX-24, OP, pint, aqua . . . . $60–$90
Scroll, GIX-24, OP, pint, yellow green . . . . $2500+
Scroll, GIX-25, OP, pint, aqua . . . . $80–$100
Scroll, GIX-25, OP, pint, deep aqua . . . . $80–$110
Scroll, GIX-25, OP, small lip chips, pint, aqua . . . . $45–$70
Scroll, GIX-26, OP, pint, greenish aqua . . . . $650–$775
Scroll, GIX-28, OP, pint, aqua . . . . $2750–$3750
Scroll, GIX-29, OP, sheared lip, two quarts, aqua . . . . $475–$600
Scroll, GIX-30, IP, sheared lip, gallon, aqua . . . . $500–$750
Scroll, GIX-31, OP, sheared lip, half pint, amber . . . . $450–$650
Scroll, GIX-31, OP, sheared lip, half pint, aqua . . . . $70–$90
Scroll, GIX-31, OP, sheared lip, half pint, bluish aqua . . . . $75–$95
Scroll, GIX-31, OP, sheared lip, half pint, deep amber . . . . $550–$700

Scroll, GIX-31, OP, sheared lip, half pint, medium green . . . . $275–$400
Scroll, GIX-31, OP, sheared lip, half pint, yellow green . . . . $400–$550
Scroll, GIX-32, IP, applied disc lip, yellow olive green . . . . $1000–$1500
Scroll, GIX-32, IP, half pint, deep aqua . . . . $80–$110
Scroll, GIX-33, IP, half pint, light yellow green . . . . $300–$400
Scroll, GIX-33, IP, round collar, half pint, medium sapphire . . . . $3200–$4000
Scroll, GIX-33, OP, double collared lip, half pint, aqua . . . . $50–$70
Scroll, GIX-33, OP, half pint, blue green . . . . $400–$550
Scroll, GIX-33, OP, sheared lip, half pint, aqua . . . . $40–$50
Scroll, GIX-34, OP, sheared lip, half pint, golden amber . . . . $400–$550
Scroll, GIX-34, OP, sheared lip, half pint, medium amber . . . . $350–$400
Scroll, GIX-34, OP, sheared lip, half pint, root beer amber . . . . $425–$475
Scroll, GIX-34, OP, sheared lip, half pint, yellow amber . . . . $500–$600
Scroll, GIX-34, OP, sheared lip, lip repair, half pint, medium puce . . . . $450–$550
Scroll, GIX-34, OP, sheared lip, olive tone, half pint, yellow . . . . $1750–$2250
Scroll, GIX-34a, IP, sheared lip, half pint, olive green . . . . $2000–$2500
Scroll, GIX-36, half pint, light sapphire blue . . . . $650–$950
Scroll, GIX-36, OP, half pint, aqua . . . . $75–$95
Scroll, GIX-36, OP, half pint, golden amber . . . . $375–$475
Scroll, GIX-36, OP, half pint, light yellow green . . . . $450–$700
Scroll, GIX-36, OP, half pint, medium emerald green . . . . $600–$900
Scroll, GIX-36, OP, half pint, pink moonstone . . . . $350–$550
Scroll, GIX-36, OP, half pint, sapphire blue . . . . $2000–$3000
Scroll, GIX-37, OP, sheared lip, half pint, aqua . . . . $60–$85
Scroll, GIX-37, OP, sheared lip, half pint, black . . . . $800–$1200
Scroll, GIX-37, OP, sheared lip, half pint, deep yellow green . . . . $2000–$3000
Scroll, GIX-37, OP, sheared lip, half pint, golden yellow . . . . $500–$650
Scroll, GIX-37, OP, sheared lip, half pint, sapphire blue . . . . $2000–$3000
Scroll, GIX-38, OP, half pint, aqua . . . . $200–$250
Scroll, GIX-39, OP, sheared lip, half pint, aqua . . . . $75–$95
Scroll, GIX-39, OP, sheared lip, half pint, light green . . . . $1200–$1600
Scroll, GIX-39, OP, sheared lip, half pint, light moonstone . . . . $400–$450
Scroll, GIX-39, OP, sheared lip, lip chip, half pint, aqua . . . . $40–$45
Scroll, GIX-40, miniature, 2$^1/_2$ inches, clear . . . . $600–$900
Scroll, GIX-41, OP, sheared lip, half pint, deep aqua . . . . $200–$275
Scroll, GIX-41, OP, sheared lip, half pint, light golden yellow . . . . $4000–$6000
Scroll, GIX-42, OP, sheared lip, amethyst tint, half pint, clear . . . . $1400–$2000
Scroll, GIX-42, OP, sheared lip, half pint, greenish aqua . . . . $440–$490
Scroll, GIX-44, OP, corset waisted, sheared lip, pint, aqua . . . . $400–$500
Scroll, GIX-45, OP, corset waisted, lip crack, pint, aqua . . . . $200–$245
Scroll, GIX-45, OP, corset waisted, pint, aqua . . . . $325–$425
Scroll, GIX-45, OP, corset waisted, pint, deep aqua . . . . $400–$550
Scroll, GIX-45, OP, corset waisted, pint, greenish aqua . . . . $350–$450
Scroll, GIX-45, OP, corset waisted, pint, light blue green . . . . $700–$950
Scroll, GIX-46, OP, sheared lip, quart, aqua . . . . $675–$825
Scroll, GIX-46, OP, sheared lip, quart, emerald green . . . . $3000+
Scroll, GIX-47, OP, sheared lip, quart, pale yellow green . . . . $550–$750
Scroll, GIX-48, OP, sheared lip, quart, deep aqua . . . . $650–$850
Scroll, GIX-49, OP, sheared lip, quart, deep aqua . . . . $900–$1100
Scroll, GIX-50, OP, sheared lip, quart, aqua . . . . $550–$700
Scroll, GIX-50, OP, sheared lip, quart, pale blue green . . . . $675–$900

Scroll, Hearts & Flowers, GIX-51, OP, sheared lip, aqua . . . . $1750–$2250
Scroll, Hearts & Flowers GIX-51, OP, sheared lip, greenish aqua . . . . . $2000–$2750
Scroll, IP, sheared lip, quart, sapphire blue . . . . $2000–$2500
Seeing Eye AD / GRJA, GIV-43, OP, sheared lip, pint, yellow amber . . . . $175–$250
Seeing Eye AD / GRJA, GIV-43, OP, sloping collar, pint, yellow amber . . . .
. . . . $200–$245
Sheaf of Grain / Balt, Anchor, GXIII-48, SB, double collar, quart, blue green . . . . . .
. . . . $450–$550
Sheaf of Grain / Balt, Anchor, GXIII-48, SB, double collar, quart, deep amber. . . . . .
. . . . $500–$650
Sheaf of Grain / Balt, Anchor, GXIII-49, SB, double collar, quart, deep olive yellow.
. . . . $350–$475
Sheaf of Grain / Balt, Anchor, GXIII-49, SB, double collar, quart, olive amber . . . . .
. . . . $275–$350
Sheaf of Grain / Isabella Glasshouse, GXIII-56, OP, sheared lip, pint, aqua . . . .
. . . . $175–$225
Sheaf of Grain / Mechanicsville, GXIII-34, OP, sheared lip, quart, aqua . . . .
. . . . $275–$325
Sheaf of Grain / Mechanicsville, GXIII-34, OP, sheared lip, quart, deep green . . . . . .
. . . . $500–$700
Sheaf of Grain / Sheets & Duffy, GXIII-43, OP, sloping collar, quart, aqua . . . .
. . . . $75–$95
Sheaf of Grain / Sheets & Duffy, GXIII-43, OP, sloping collar, quart, light yellow
green. . . . . $150–$200
Sheaf of Grain / Star, GXIII-38, OP, sheared lip, quart, medium blue green . . . .
. . . . $225–$290
Sheaf of Grain / Star, GXIII-39, OP, double collar, pint, yellow green. . . . $750–$900
Sheaf of Grain / Star, GXIII-40, OP, sheared lip, half pint, deep aqua . . . . $350–$450
Sheaf of Grain / Star, GXIII-40, OP, sheared lip, half pint, deep aqua . . . . $350–$450
Sheaf of Grain / Star, GXIII-40, OP, sheared lip, half pint, yellowish grass green. . . .
. . . . $1300–$2000
Sheaf of Grain / Star, GXIII-41, OP, quart, aqua. $75–$100
Sheaf of Grain / Star, GXIII-45, calabash, IP, handled, golden amber . . . . $350–$450
Sheaf of Grain / Star, GXIII-45, calabash, IP, handled, seedy glass, amber . . . .
. . . . $350–$475
Sheaf of Grain / Tree, GXIII-46, OP, double collar, quart, black . . . . $650–$850
Sheaf of Grain / Tree, GXIII-46, OP, sloping collar, quart, aqua . . . . $60–$75
Sheaf of Grain / Tree, GXIII-46, OP, sloping collar, quart, burgundy. . . . . $550–$675
Sheaf of Grain / Tree, GXIII-47, OP, double collar, quart, light green . . . . $160–$210
Sheaf of Grain / Tree, GXIII-47, OP, double collar, quart, medium emerald green . . .
. . . . $400–$475
Sheaf of Grain / Westford, GXIII-35, SB, double collar, pint, amber. . . . . . . $70–$85
Sheaf of Grain / Westford, GXIII-35, SB, double collar, pint, olive amber . . $75–$95
Sheaf of Grain / Westford, GXIII-35, SB, double collar, pint, red amber. . . . $70–$95
Sheaf of Grain / Westford, GXIII-36, SB, double collar, pint, olive green. . . . .
. . . . $80–$110
Sheaf of Grain / Westford, GXIII-37, SB, double collar, half pint, olive amber. . . . . .
. . . . $80–$110
Sheaf of Grain / Westford, GXIII-37, SB, double collar, half pint, red amber . . . .
. . . . $80–$120

Sheaf of Grain / Westford, GXIII-37, SB, double collar, lip bruise, half pint, amber. .
.... $40–$50
Sheaf of Rye / Grapes, GX-3, OP, sheared lip, half pint, aqua........... $145–$185
Sheaf of Rye / Grapes, GX-3, OP, sheared lip, half pint, light apple green ....
.... $325–$375
Sheaf of Rye, Liberty / Star, GX-10, OP, sheared lip, pint, aqua .... $350–$425
Sheaf of Rye, Liberty / Star, GX-11, sheared lip, half pint, aqua .... $350–$425
Sheaf of Wheat / Reverse Plain, GXIII-31, pint, aqua.................. $60–$90
Sheaf of Wheat / Tibby Brothers, GXIII-33, pint, clear .... $150–$250
Sheaf of Wheat / Sheaf of Wheat, GXIII-32, pint, aqua .... $60–$90
Shield, Clasped Hands / Eagle, GXII-1, SB, laid on ring, quart, aqua ...... $35–$45
Shield, Clasped Hands / Eagle, GXII-2, OP, laid on ring, quart, aqua ...... $55–$65
Shield, Clasped Hands / Eagle, GXII-3, SB, laid on ring, quart, aqua ...... $35–$45
Shield, Clasped Hands / Eagle, GXII-4, SB, laid on ring, quart, aqua ...... $35–$45
Shield, Clasped Hands / Eagle, GXII-5, SB, laid on ring, quart, aqua ...... $35–$45
Shield, Clasped Hands / Eagle, GXII-7, SB, laid on ring, quart, aqua ...... $35–$45
Shield, Clasped Hands / Eagle, GXII-7, SB, laid on ring, quart, yellow olive ....
.... $150–$225
Shield, Clasped Hands / Eagle, GXII-8, SB, laid on ring, quart, olive yellow ....
.... $125–$175
Shield, Clasped Hands / Eagle, GXII-9, SB, laid on ring, quart, aqua ...... $35–$45
Shield, Clasped Hands / Eagle, GXII-10, SB, laid on ring, quart, aqua ..... $35–$45
Shield, Clasped Hands / Eagle, GXII-12, SB, laid on ring, quart, aqua ..... $35–$45
Shield, Clasped Hands / Eagle, GXII-13, SB, laid on ring, quart, aqua ..... $45–$55
Shield, Clasped Hands / Eagle, GXII-13, SB, laid on ring, quart, golden amber .....
.... $300–$450
Shield, Clasped Hands / Eagle, GXII-13, SB, laid on ring, quart, yellow...........
.... $250–$375
Shield, Clasped Hands / Eagle, GXII-15, SB, laid on ring, quart, light blue green....
.... $450–$650
Shield, Clasped Hands / Eagle, GXII-15, SB, laid on ring, quart, yellow green......
.... $350–$400
Shield, Clasped Hands / Eagle, GXII-17, SB, laid on ring, pint, aqua ...... $35–$45
Shield, Clasped Hands / Eagle, GXII-18, SB, laid on ring, pint, aqua ...... $35–$45
Shield, Clasped Hands / Eagle, GXII-21, SB, laid on ring, pint, medium amber .....
.... $110–$140
Shield, Clasped Hands / Eagle, GXII-23, SB, laid on ring, pint, medium yellow green
.... $350–$450
Shield, Clasped Hands / Eagle, GXII-24, SB, laid on ring, pint, amber ... $125–$150
Shield, Clasped Hands / Eagle, GXII-25, SB, laid on ring, pint, aqua ...... $45–$55
Shield, Clasped Hands / Eagle, GXII-27, SB, laid on ring, pint, golden amber ......
.... $250–$350
Shield, Clasped Hands / Eagle, GXII-28, SB, laid on ring, pint, amber ... $100–$125
Shield, Clasped Hands / Eagle, GXII-29, SB, laid on ring, half pint, amber........
.... $90–$125
Shield, Clasped Hands / Eagle, GXII-29, SB, laid on ring, half pint, golden yellow ..
.... $100–$135
Shield, Clasped Hands / Eagle, GXII-30, SB, laid on ring, half pint, amber........
.... $250–$350
Shield, Clasped Hands / Eagle, GXII-31, laid on ring, half pint, aqua ...... $40–$50

Shield, Clasped Hands / Eagle, GXII-33, SB, laid on ring, half pint, amber . . . .
. . . . $70–$90
Shield, Clasped Hands / Eagle, GXII-35, SB, laid on ring, half pint, aqua . . . .
. . . . $45–$55
Shield, Clasped Hands / Eagle, GXII-37, SB, laid on ring, olive tone, quart, yellow . .
. . . . $500–$575
Shield, Clasped Hands / Eagle, GXII-37, SB, laid on ring, quart, aqua . . . $150–$200
Shield, Clasped Hands / Shield, GXII-31, SB, laid on ring, half pint, amber . . . .
. . . . $190–$235
Shirt Shaped Flask, milk glass, metal screw cap, 4³/₄" . . . . $200–$300
Sloop / Bridgeton, GX-7, OP, half pint, aqua . . . . $150–$250
Sloop / Star, GX-8, OP, sheared lip, half pint, aqua . . . . $90–$120
Sloop / Star, GX-9, OP, sheared lip, half pint, aqua . . . . $90–$120
Sloop / Star, GX-9, OP, sheared lip, half pint, medium greenish aqua . . . . . $250–$325
Soldier / Ballet Dancer, GXIII-11, SB, sheared lip, pint, aqua. . . . . $50–$70
Soldier / Ballet Dancer, GXIII-12, OP, sheared lip, pint, aqua . . . . $80–$115
Soldier / Ballet Dancer, GXIII-13, SB, sheared lip, pint, olive green . . . . . $475–$675
Soldier / Ballet Dancer, GXIII-14, SB, laid on ring below lip, pint, yellow olive . . . .
. . . . $700–$950
St Wolfgang (on staff) of Bishop / Mountain, House, pewter screw on stopper, OP,
cobalt. . . . . $375–$475
Star in Circle, strap flask, half pint, yellow green. $15–$20
Steamboat / Sheaf of Rye, GX-21, OP, sheared lip, aqua . . . . $13,000–$15,000
Stoddard-Flag; see Flag / Stoddard Success to the Railroad flasks, also see Railroad Horse and Cart
Success to the Railroad, GV-1, OP, sheared lip, pint, light amber. . . . . . $1200–$1800
Success to the Railroad, GV-1, OP sheared lip, pint, golden yellow amber . . . .
. . . . $3500+
Success to the Railroad, GV-1, OP, sheared lip, lip chips, pint, medium sapphire . . . .
. . . . $2100–$2450
Success to the Railroad, GV-1, OP, sheared lip, pint, apricot . . . . $3500+
Success to the Railroad, GV-1, OP, sheared lip, pint, aqua . . . . $150–$200
Success to the Railroad, GV-1, OP, sheared lip, pint, blue green . . . . . . $1500–$2000
Success to the Railroad, GV-1, OP, sheared lip, pint, bluish aqua. . . . . . . $175–$225
Success to the Railroad, GV-1, OP, sheared lip, pint, deep blue green . . . .
. . . . $1800–$2200
Success to the Railroad, GV-1, OP, sheared lip, pint, light citron . . . . . . $1800–$2200
Success to the Railroad, GV-1, OP, sheared lip, pint, medium blue sapphire . . . .
. . . . $2200–$3300
Success to the Railroad, GV-1, OP, sheared lip, pint, olive green . . . . . $1500–$2500
Success to the Railroad, GV-1, OP, sheared lip, pint, red amber. . . . . . . $1500–$2500
Success to the Railroad, GV-1, OP, sheared lip, pint, yellow olive . . . . . $1500–$2750
Success to the Railroad, GV-2, OP, sheared lip, pint, aqua . . . . $350–$450
Success to the Railroad, GV-3, OP, sheared lip, heavy stain, pint, olive amber . . . . . .
. . . . $80–$110
Success to the Railroad, GV-3, OP, sheared lip, lip chip, pint, olive amber . . . .
. . . . $90–$120
Success to the Railroad, GV-3, OP, sheared lip, pint, aqua . . . . $450–$650
Success to the Railroad, GV-3, OP, sheared lip, pint, forest green . . . . $175–$275
Success to the Railroad, GV-3, OP, sheared lip, pint, olive amber . . . . $125–$185
Success to the Railroad, GV-3, OP, sheared lip, pint, olive green. . . . . $125–$175

Figured flask, Success to the Railroad, GV-5. PHOTO
COURTESY OF NEIL GROSSMAN.

Success to the Railroad, GV-3, OP, sheared lip, pint, yellow amber . . . . . . $180–$220
Success to the Railroad, GV-3, OP, sheared lip, pint, yellow olive . . . . $160–$225
Success to the Railroad, GV-3, OP, sheared lip, very bubbly glass, pint, green . . . . . .
. . . . $200–$350
Success to the Railroad, GV-4, OP, sheared lip, olive tone, pint, gold yellow . . . .
. . . . $550–$650*
Success to the Railroad, GV-4, OP, sheared lip, pint, olive amber . . . . . . $140–$180*
Success to the Railroad, GV-4, OP, sheared lip, pint, olive green . . . . $140–$190*
Success to the Railroad, GV-5, OP, sheared lip, pint, aqua . . . . $750–$1250*
Success to the Railroad, GV-5, OP, sheared lip, pint, deep forest green . . $300–$400*
Success to the Railroad, GV-5, OP, sheared lip, pint, deep yellow olive. . $150–$180*
Success to the Railroad, GV-5, OP, sheared lip, pint, light yellow olive. . $250–$350*
Success to the Railroad, GV-5, OP, sheared lip, pint, deep olive amber . . $150–$180*
Success to the Railroad, GV-5, OP, sheared lip, pint, olive green . . . . . . $190–$225*
Success to the Railroad, GV-6, OP, sheared lip, lip chips, pint, olive amber . . . .
. . . . $75–$100
Success to the Railroad, GV-6, OP, sheared lip, pint, medium yellow olive . . . .
. . . . $160–$185
Success to the Railroad, GV-6, OP, sheared lip, pint, olive amber . . . . . . $135–$185
Success to the Railroad, OP, sheared lip, pint, sapphire blue . . . . $2500–$3500
Success to the Railroad / Eagle, GV-8, OP, sheared lip, base crack, pint, olive amber.
. . . . $90–$115
Success to the Railroad / Eagle, GV-8, OP, sheared lip, pint, olive amber . . . .
. . . . $140–$190
Success to the Railroad / Eagle, GV-8, OP, sheared lip, pint, olive green . . . .
. . . . $140–$190
Success to the Railroad / Eagle, GV-8, OP, sheared lip, pint, yellow amber . . . .
. . . . $160–$190
Summer Tree / Winter Tree, GX-15, OP, double collar, pint, greenish citron . . . .
. . . . $500–$700
Summer Tree / Winter Tree, GX-15, OP, double collar, pint, pale green . . . .
. . . . $150–$200
Summer Tree / Winter Tree, GX-15, OP, double collar, shading to yellow amber,
pint, medium amber . . . . $1400–$1800
Summer Tree / Winter Tree, GX-15, OP, sheared lip, pint, aqua . . . . $60–$70

Summer tree flask with round collar with bevel lip. PHOTO COURTESY OF GLASS WORKS AUCTIONS.

Sunburst with sloping collar with bevel-type lip.
PHOTO COURTESY OF GLASS WORKS AUCTIONS.

Summer Tree / Winter Tree, GX-15, OP, sheared lip, pint, medium olive yellow. . . .
. . . . $300–$450
Sunburst, GVIII-1, OP, sheared lip, green tint, pint, clear . . . . $350–$450
Sunburst, GVIII-1, OP, sheared lip, large lip chip, pint, light green. . . . . . . $175–$200
Sunburst, GVIII-1, OP, sheared lip, pint, clear . . . . $500–$600
Sunburst, GVIII-1, OP, sheared lip, pint, deep emerald green . . . . $2500+
Sunburst, GVIII-1, OP, sheared lip, pint, medium lavender. . . . . $900–$1150
Sunburst, GVIII-1, OP, sheared lip, pint, pale blue green . . . . $350–$390
Sunburst, GVIII-1, OP, sheared lip, pint, yellow green . . . . $750–$1000
Sunburst, GVIII-2, OP, sheared lip, pint, clear . . . . $400–$550*
Sunburst, GVIII-2, OP, sheared lip, pint, grass green. . . . . $450–$500*
Sunburst, GVIII-2, OP, sheared lip, pint, light green . . . . $375–$445*
Sunburst, GVIII-2, OP, sheared lip, pint, medium green . . . . $400–$550*
Sunburst, GVIII-2, OP, sheared lip, pint, medium yellow green . . . . $400–$575*

Sunburst, GVIII-3, OP, sheared lip, lip chip, pint, olive green . . . . $175–$200
Sunburst, GVIII-3, OP, sheared lip, pint, amber . . . . $300–$425
Sunburst, GVIII-3, OP, sheared lip, pint, medium olive amber . . . . $250–$350
Sunburst, GVIII-3, OP, sheared lip, pint, medium yellow olive . . . . $400–$575
Sunburst, GVIII-3, OP, sheared lip, pint, yellow olive . . . . $450–$575
Sunburst, GVIII-3, OP, sheared lip, pint, olive green . . . . $275–$350
Sunburst, GVIII-3a, OP, sheared lip, pint, olive amber . . . . $275–$375
Sunburst, GVIII-4, OP, pint, blue green . . . . $7500+
Sunburst, GVIII-5, OP, pint, olive green . . . . $425–$550
Sunburst, GVIII-5a, OP, pint, light yellow olive . . . . $1300–$1600
Sunburst, GVIII-5a, OP, pint, olive green . . . . $700–$800
Sunburst, GVIII-5a, OP, pint, yellow amber . . . . $800–$1000
Sunburst, GVIII-6, OP, pint, yellow olive . . . . $2500+
Sunburst, GVIII-7, pint, olive amber . . . . $1000–$1450
Sunburst, GVIII-8, heavy wear, pint, medium yellow olive . . . . $200–$240
Sunburst, GVIII-8, lip chip, pint, olive amber . . . . $200–$235
Sunburst, GVIII-8, OP, pint, olive amber . . . . $300–$450
Sunburst, GVIII-8, OP, pint, olive green . . . . $350–$450
Sunburst, GVIII-8, pint, dark olive green . . . . $300–$450
Sunburst, GVIII-8, pint, medium yellow olive amber . . . . $400–$500
Sunburst, GVIII-9, half pint, amber . . . . $225–$300
Sunburst, GVIII-9, base crack, half pint, olive amber . . . . $125–$175
Sunburst, GVIII-9, half pint, olive amber . . . . $200–$325
Sunburst, GVIII-9, half pint, olive green . . . . $200–$325
Sunburst, GVIII-9, half pint, yellow amber . . . . $275–$325
Sunburst, GVIII-9, lip chip, half pint, olive amber . . . . $150–$200
Sunburst, GVIII-9, lip flake, half pint, olive amber . . . . $180–$210
Sunburst, GVIII-10, lip chips, half pint, olive green . . . . $100–$175
Sunburst, GVIII-10, OP, half pint, olive amber . . . . $250–$325
Sunburst, GVIII-10, OP, half pint, olive green . . . . $250–$325
Sunburst, GVIII-11, sheared lip, half pint, emerald green . . . . $600–$850
Sunburst, GVIII-11, sheared lip, half pint, olive amber . . . . $1400–$2200
Sunburst, GVIII-11, sloping collar, half pint, sea green . . . . $3000–$3600
Sunburst, GVIII-12, sheared lip, pint, deep olive green . . . . $5500–$6500
Sunburst, GVIII-12, sheared lip, OP, pint, greenish aqua . . . . $750–$1000
Sunburst, GVIII-13, OP, half pint, clear . . . . $3000+
Sunburst, GVIII-14, OP, sheared lip, half pint, medium blue green . . . . $650–$725
Sunburst, GVIII-14, OP, sheared lip, half pint, medium emerald green . . . . $700–$850
Sunburst, GVIII-14a, OP, sheared lip, half pint, bright green . . . . $1100–$1350
Sunburst, GVIII-15, OP, sheared lip, half pint, emerald green . . . . $1300–$1800
Sunburst, GVIII-15a, OP, sheared lip, half pint, pale green . . . . $800–$1150
Sunburst, GVIII-16, OP, sheared lip, half pint, deep emerald green . . . . . . $500–$850
Sunburst, GVIII-16, OP, sheared lip, half pint, deep green . . . . $250–$350
Sunburst, GVIII-16, OP, sheared lip, half pint, forest green . . . . $300–$360
Sunburst, GVIII-16, OP, sheared lip, half pint, light olive yellow . . . . $250–$300
Sunburst, GVIII-16, OP, sheared lip, half pint, medium olive green . . . . . . $275–$325
Sunburst, GVIII-16, OP, sheared lip, half pint, medium yellow olive . . . . . $250–$290
Sunburst, GVIII-16, OP, sheared lip, half pint, moss green . . . . $325–$425
Sunburst, GVIII-16, OP, sheared lip, half pint, olive amber . . . . $250–$300
Sunburst, GVIII-16, OP, sheared lip, lip flakes, half pint, olive amber . . . . $150–$200
Sunburst, GVIII-17, OP, half pint, clear . . . . $2500+

Sunburst, GVIII-18, OP, half pint, light yellow olive.................. $290–$330
Sunburst, GVIII-18, OP, half pint, olive amber .... $245–$295
Sunburst, GVIII-18, OP, half pint, yellow amber.................... $275–$325
Sunburst Snuff, GVIII-19, OP, sheared lip, wide mouth, pint, green .. $8500–$10,500
Sunburst, GVIII-20, OP, sheared lip, lip chips, pint, aqua .... $80–$110
Sunburst, GVIII-20, OP, sheared lip, pint, aqua...................... $130–$160
Sunburst, GVIII-21, OP, sheared lip, pint, aqua...................... $225–$325
Sunburst, GVIII-22, OP, sheared lip, pint, pale green .... $150–$200
Sunburst, GVIII-23, amethyst tint, pint, clear......................... $4500+
Sunburst, GVIII-24, sheared lip, pint, aqua .... $150–$200
Sunburst, GVIII-25, OP, sheared lip, half pint, medium pink puce ..... $2750–$3250
Sunburst, GVIII-25, OP, sheared lip, half pint, aqua .... $150–$200
Sunburst, GVIII-25, OP, sheared lip, half pint, deep wine .... $2800–$3300
Sunburst, GVIII-25, OP, sheared lip, half pint, medium green .... $3000+
Sunburst, GVIII-25, OP, sheared lip, lip chips, half pint, aqua .... $80–$120
Sunburst, GVIII-26, OP, sheared lip, pint, clear..................... $225–$275
Sunburst, GVIII-26, OP, sheared lip, pint, deep yellow olive .... $3000–$3600
Sunburst, GVIII-26, OP, sheared lip, pint, greenish aqua............... $225–$300
Sunburst, GVIII-26, OP, sheared lip, pint, ice blue .... $800–$925
Sunburst, GVIII-26, OP, sheared lip, pint, light blue green .... $340–$385
Sunburst, GVIII-26, OP, sheared lip, pint, medium yellow green ...... $1200–$1500
Sunburst, GVIII-27, OP, sheared lip, half pint, pale yellow green........ $600–$800
Sunburst, GVIII-27, OP, sheared lip, half pint, aqua .... $125–$185
Sunburst, GVIII-27, OP, sheared lip, half pint, clear .... $250–$350
Sunburst, GVIII-27, OP, sheared lip, half pint, emerald green.......... $900–$1250
Sunburst, GVIII-27, OP, sheared lip, half pint, medium green .... $2400+
Sunburst, GVIII-27, OP, sheared lip, lip chipping, half pint, clear........ $125–$185
Sunburst, GVIII-28, OP, half pint, aqua .... $130–$190
Sunburst, GVIII-28, OP, half pint, clear .... $130–$190
Sunburst, GVIII-28, OP, half pint, deep aqua........................ $150–$225
Sunburst, GVIII-28, OP, half pint, light lavender..................... $400–$500
Sunburst, GVIII-28, OP, half pint, light yellow olive.................. $275–$375
Sunburst, GVIII-29, OP, tooled lip, 3/4 pint, aqua.................. $125–$185
Sunburst, GVIII-29, OP, tooled lip, 3/4 pint, blue green .... $250–$300
Sunburst, GVIII-29, OP, tooled lip, 3/4 pint, blue green .... $150–$225
Sunburst, GVIII-29, OP, tooled lip, 3/4 pint, bluish emerald green....... $150–$225
Sunburst, GVIII-29, OP, tooled lip, 3/4 pint, clear.................... $575–$725
Sunburst, GVIII-29, OP, tooled lip, 3/4 pint, deep aqua .... $130–$195
Sunburst, GVIII-29, OP, tooled lip, 3/4 pint, deep greenish aqua .... $175–$200
Sunburst, GVIII-29, OP, tooled lip, 3/4 pint, medium green .... $250–$400
Sunburst, GVIII-29, OP, tooled lip, 3/4 pint, medium yellow olive ..... $1500–$2500
Sunburst, GVIII-29, OP, tooled lip, lip bruised, 3/4 pint, blue green........ $80–$110
Sunburst, GVIII-29, OP, tooled lip, lip flakes, 3/4 pint, blue green........ $100–$135
Sunburst, GVIII-30, OP, 3/4 pint, light blue green .... $750–$1250
Taylor / Corn for the World, GI-74, OP, sheared lip, lip chip, pint, aqua .. $80–$110
Taylor / Corn for the World, GI-74, OP, sheared lip, pint, apricot.......... $4000+
Taylor / Corn for the World, GI-74, OP, sheared lip, pint, aqua......... $150–$200
Taylor / Corn for the World, GI-74, OP, sheared lip, pint, greenish aqua ....
.... $150–$200
Taylor / Corn for the World, GI-74, OP, sheared lip, pint, olive yellow ....
.... $4500+

Taylor / Corn for the World, GI-75, OP, sheared lip, pint, aqua . . . . $250–$350
Taylor / Eagle, GI-76, OP, sheared lip, pint, deep blue aqua . . . . $3950–$4750
Taylor / Eagle, GI-77, Masterson, OP, sheared lip, lip chip, quart, deep aqua . . . .
. . . . $550–$850
Taylor / Eagle, GI-77, Masterson, OP, sheared lip, quart, deep aqua . . . . $1100–$1500
Taylor / Eagle, GI-77, Masterson, OP, sheared lip, quart, greenish aqua . . . .
. . . . $800–$1200
Taylor / Eagle, GI-77, Masterson, sheared lip, OP, quart, pale blue green . . . .
. . . . $900–$1250
Taylor / Fells Point Monument, GI-73, OP, lip chip, pint, aqua . . . . $70–$90
Taylor / Fells Point Monument, GI-73, OP, pint, aqua . . . . $90–$125
Taylor / Fells Point Monument, GI-73, OP, pint, deep grass green . . . . $2500+
Taylor / Fells Point Monument, GI-73, OP, sheared lip, pint, amethyst . . . .
. . . . $4000–$5500
Taylor / Ringgold, GI-71, OP, sheared lip, open side bubble, pint, aqua . . . . . $60–$70
Taylor / Ringgold, GI-71, OP, sheared lip, pint, aqua . . . . $80–$100
Taylor / Ringgold, GI-71, OP, sheared lip, pint, grayish clear . . . . $100–$125
Taylor / Ringgold, GI-72, OP, sheared lip, pint, aqua . . . . $80–$100
Taylor / Ringgold, pint, GI-71, OP, sheared lip, pint, pale lavender . . . . $1300–$1500
Taylor / Robt Ramsay, GI-78, OP, sheared lip, pint, aqua . . . . $1000–$1400
Tear Drops, milk glass flask with large eyeball, metal cap, 3⁷/₈" . . . . $100–$145
Tippecanoe / North Bend, sloping collar, cabin green . . . . $40,000–$50,000
Tippecanoe / North Bend, GVII-1, OP, sloping collar, cabin, green . . . .
. . . . $40,000–$50,000
Tippecanoe / Tippecanoe, GVII-2, cabin, OP, rounded collar, green . . . .
. . . . $40,000–$50,000
Trapper, Great Western / Buck, GX-30, SB, laid on ring, pint, aqua . . . . $250–$300
Travelers Companion / Plain, GXIV-8, IP, sheared lip, half pint, amber . . . .
. . . . : . . . . $450–$575
Travelers Companion / Railroad Guide, GXIV-9, OP, sheared lip, half pint, light
blue green . . . . $325–$385
Travelers Companion / Railroad Guide, GXIV-9, OP, sheared lip, half pint, olive
green . . . . $1800–$2300
Travelers Companion / Sheaf of Grain, GXIV-1, IP, tooled lip, quart, honey amber .
. . . . $400–$600
Travelers Companion / Sheaf of Grain, GXIV-1, SB, applied lip, quart, amber . . . . .
. . . . $325–$375
Travelers Companion / Sheaf of Grain, GXIV-1, SB, sloping collar, olive amber . . .
. . . . $240–$280
Travelers Companion / Sheaf of Grain, GXIV-1, sloping collar, deep red amber . . . .
. . . . $225–$300
Travelers Companion / Star, Lancaster, GXIV-4, pint, aqua . . . . $175–$225
Travelers Companion / Star, Lancaster, GXIV-5, SB, double collar, pint, aqua . . . . .
. . . . $275–$325
Travelers Companion / Star, Lancaster, GXIV-5, SB, double collar, pint, light blue
green . . . . $340–$400
Travelers Companion / Star, Lockport, GXIV-6, OP, double collar, pint, bright
yellow green . . . . $1300–$1750
Travelers Companion / Star, Lockport, GXIV-6, OP, double collar, pint, deep blue
green . . . . $1600–$2200

Travelers Companion / Star, Lockport, GXIV-6, OP, double collar, pint, light blue green . . . . $750–$1000
Travelers Companion / Star, Lockport, GXIV-7, IP, sheared lip, half pint, apricot yellow . . . . $1100–$1500
Travelers Companion / Star, Lockport, GXIV-7, IP, sheared lip, half pint, aqua . . . . $140–$190
Travelers Companion / Star, Lockport, GXIV-7, IP, sheared lip, half pint, golden amber. . . . . $400–$500
Travelers Companion / Star, Lockport, GXIV-7, IP, sheared lip, half pint, yellow . . . . $800–$1200
Travelers Companion / Star, Ravenna, GXIV-2, applied lip, quart, dark amber. . . . . $300–$360
Travelers Companion / Star, Ravenna, GXIV-2, IP, applied lip, quart, bright medium green . . . . $750+
Travelers Companion / Star, Ravenna, GXIV-2, IP, applied lip, quart, deep ice blue . . . . $275–$400
Travelers Companion / Star, Ravenna, GXIV-2, IP, applied lip, quart, gold amber . . . . $600–$725
Travelers Companion / Star, Ravenna, GXIV-2, IP, applied lip, quart, yellow green. . . . . $900–$1250
Travelers Companion / Star, Ravenna, GXIV-3, OP, pint, aqua . . . . $70–$90
Travelers Companion / Star, Ravenna, GXIV-3, OP, pint, deep aqua. . . . $140–$200
Travelers Companion / Star, Ravenna, GXIV-3, OP, rounded collar, pint, gold amber . . . . $400–$475
Travelers Companion / Star, Ravenna, GXIV-3, OP, sheared lip, pint, gold amber . . . . $375–$450
Travelers Companion / Star, Ravenna, GXIV-3, SB, sheared lip, pint, olive yellow . . . . $750–$975
Tree / Tree, GX-16, OP, double collar, half pint, aqua . . . . $125–$170
Tree / Tree, GX-17, OP, sheared lip, pint, deep aqua . . . . $70–$110
Tree / Tree, GX-17, OP, sheared lip, pint, medium green. . . . . $800–$1000
Tree / Tree, GX-17, OP, sheared lip, pint, olive yellow . . . . $750–$1000
Tree / Tree, GX-18, OP, double collar, quart, aqua . . . . $80–$110
Tree / Tree, GX-18, OP, double collar, quart, bright green. . . . . $500–$700
Tree / Tree, GX-18, OP, double collar, quart, cobalt . . . . $6500+
Tree / Tree, GX-18, OP, sloping collar, quart, yellow green (citron) . . . . . $750–$1000
Tree / Tree, GX-19, OP, double collar, quart, medium green. . . . . $900–$1100
Tree / Tree, GX-19, OP, sheared lip, large lip chip, quart, sapphire. . . . . . . $375–$450
Tree / Tree, GX-19, SB, double collar, quart, aqua. . . . . $100–$150
Tree / Tree, GX-19, SB, sheared lip, quart, burnt orange amber . . . . $800–$975
Try It, SB, 4$^{1}/_{2}$", amber pumpkinseed . . . . $50–$75
Unembossed, unpatterned, amber, green, yellow green . . . . $10–$30
Union Glassworks New London / Plain, GXV-23, SB, applied lip, pint, olive green . . . . $600–$750
Warranted Flask, SB, double collar, clear, pint, quart, half gallon . . . . $6–$12
Washington, GI-18, Baltimore Glassworks, monument, OP, sheared lip, chip, pint, aqua. . . . . $60–$90
Washington, GI-18, Baltimore Glassworks, monument, OP, sheared lip, pint, aqua . . . . $125–$175
Washington, GI-18, Baltimore Glassworks, monument, OP, sheared lip, pint, yellow green . . . . $2500+

Washington, GI-19, Baltimore Glassworks, monument, OP, pint, aqua.... $200–$300
Washington, GI-19, Baltimore Glassworks, monument, OP, pint, puce.............
.... $2500–$4000
Washington, GI-20, Baltimore monument, OP, clear, pint, blue tint ...... $100–$175
Washington, GI-20, Baltimore monument, OP, pint, aqua............... $90–$125
Washington, GI-20, Baltimore monument, OP, pint, greenish aqua....... $100–$165
Washington, GI-20, Baltimore, monument, OP, pint, medium cobalt ....
.... $25,000–$30,000
Washington, GI-20, Baltimore monument, OP, lip chip, pint, aqua......... $60–$90
Washington, GI-21, Baltimore monument, OP, inner stain, quart, aqua...... $60–$90
Washington, GI-21, Baltimore monument, OP, lip chip, quart, aqua........ $40–$65
Washington, GI-21, Baltimore monument, OP, quart, aqua.............. $90–$110
Washington, GI-21, Baltimore monument, OP, quart, light amethyst ... $2200–$2700
Washington, GI-30, Albany Glassworks, OP, half pint, bright green...... $300–$450
Washington, GI-30, Albany Glassworks, OP, half pint, aqua............ $200–$250
Washington, GI-30, Albany Glassworks, OP, half pint, greenish aqua .... $200–$250
Washington, GI-60, Lockport/Washington, IP, double collar, quart, ice blue........
.... $750–$975
Washington, Taylor, GI-41, OP, sheared lip, large crack, half pint, medium emerald
green.. $75–$125
Washington / Tree, GI-35, calabash, OP, sloping collar, quart, sapphire blue........
.... $4000–$5000
Washington / Classical Bust, GI-22, OP, lip chip, quart, aqua .... $75–$95
Washington / Classical Bust, GI-22, OP, quart, aqua .... $125–$175
Washington / Classical Bust, GI-22, OP, quart, greenish aqua .... $125–$185
Washington / Classical Bust, GI-23, OP, quart, strawberry puce ...... $3000–$4500
Washington / Classical Bust, GI-25, Bridgeton, OP, inner stain, quart, aqua........
.... $75–$110
Washington / Classical Bust, GI-25, Bridgeton, OP, quart, aqua .... $140–$190
Washington / Classical Bust, GI-25, Bridgeton, OP, quart, blue green.... $775–$975
Washington / Double Headed Sheaf of Rye, GI-59, OP, half pint, aqua .... $50–$75
Washington / Eagle, GI-1, OP, sheared lip, lip chip, pint, aqua.......... $100–$150
Washington / Eagle, GI-1, OP, sheared lip, pint, aqua................. $240–$280
Washington / Eagle, GI-1, OP, sheared lip, pint, deep aqua............. $250–$300
Washington / Eagle, GI-1, OP, sheared lip, pint, greenish aqua.......... $240–$280
Washington / Eagle, GI-1, OP, sheared lip, pint, pale blue green .... $750–$950
Washington / Eagle, GI-2, OP, pint, deep greenish aqua .... $275–$375
Washington / Eagle, GI-2, OP, pint, pale green .... $250–$350
Washington / Eagle, GI-2, OP, sheared lip, pint, greenish aqua.......... $295–$345
Washington / Eagle, GI-2, OP, small lip chip, pint, aqua............... $150–$195
Washington / Eagle, GI-2, sheared lip, OP, pint, aqua............... $180–$240
Washington / Eagle, GI-3, OP, sheared lip, pint, aqua................. $450–$650
Washington / Eagle, GI-3, OP, sheared lip, pint, greenish aqua.......... $475–$675
Washington / Eagle, GI-3, small lip chip, OP, pint, aqua............... $250–$350
Washington / Eagle, GI-4, OP, sheared lip, pint, aqua................ $500–$700
Washington / Eagle, GI-5, sheared lip, OP, pint, greenish aqua........ $3500–$4500
Washington / Eagle, GI-6, "JR," OP, sheared lip, clear, pint, amethyst tint.........
.... $800–$975
Washington / Eagle, GI-6, "JR," OP, sheared lip, pint, clear............ $300–$400
Washington / Eagle, GI-6a, "JR," OP, sheared lip, clear, pint, purple tint.. $1600–$1900

Washington / Eagle, GI-7, "FL," OP, sheared lip, lip ding, pint, green aqua.........
.... $300–$360
Washington / Eagle, GI-8, faces left, "FL," sheared lip, pint, aqua .. $16,000–$22,000
Washington / Eagle, GI-9, OP, sheared lip, pint, greenish aqua.......... $700–$900
Washington / Eagle, GI-9, OP, sheared lip, pint, pale yellow green ...... $650–$950
Washington / Eagle, GI-10, OP, pint, greenish aqua .... $200–$300
Washington / Eagle, GI-10, OP, pint, pale blue green .... $250–$350
Washington / Eagle, GI-10, OP, sheared lip, pint, aqua .... $225–$325
Washington / Eagle, GI-10, OP, sheared lip, pint, deep aqua............ $550–$750
Washington / Eagle, GI-10, OP, small lip bruise, pint, aqua .... $150–$250
Washington / Eagle, GI-11, OP, sheared lip, lip chip, pint, aqua......... $200–$245
Washington / Eagle, GI-11, OP, sheared lip, pint, aqua .... $310–$420
Washington / Eagle, GI-11, OP, sheared lip, pint, deep aqua............ $575–$725
Washington / Eagle, GI-11, OP, sheared lip, pint, greenish aqua......... $300–$450
Washington / Eagle, GI-11, OP, sheared lip, shoulder crack, pint, aqua ... $125–$175
Washington / Eagle, GI-12, OP, sheared lip, pint, deep aqua........... $900–$1200
Washington / Eagle, GI-13, "BK," OP, sheared lip, pint, pale green .... $1500–$2000
Washington / Eagle, GI-14, "TWD," shear lip, OP, polished lip chip, pint, aqua .....
.... $100–$125
Washington / Eagle, GI-14, "TWD," sheared lip, OP, pint, gray amethyst tone ......
.... $1200–$1500
Washington / Eagle, GI-14, "TWD," sheared lip, OP, major chip side of bottle # on
eagle figure, pint, emerald green.................................... $700–$900
Washington / Eagle, GI-14, "TWD," sheared lip, OP, pint, aqua......... $130–$180
Washington / Eagle, GI-14, "TWD," sheared lip, OP, pint, clear amethyst tint.......
.... $800–$1200
Washington / Eagle, GI-14, "TWD," sheared lip, OP, pint, emerald green..........
.... $4200–$5200
Washington / Eagle, GI-14, "TWD," sheared lip, OP, pint, greenish aqua ....
.... $200–$260
Washington / Eagle, GI-14, "TWD," sheared lip, OP, pint, medium green..........
.... $1500–$2500
Washington / Eagle, GI-14, "TWD," sheared lip, outer stain, OP, pint, aqua ....
.... $100–$145
Washington / Eagle, GI-15, OP, pint, aqua.......................... $125–$175
Washington / Eagle, GI-16, "TWD," OP, sheared lip, inner stain, pint, aqua ....
.... $75–$125
Washington / Eagle, GI-16, "TWD," OP, sheared lip, lip chip, pint, aqua.... $60–$90
Washington / Eagle, GI-16, "TWD," OP, sheared lip, pint, aqua......... $130–$190
Washington / Taylor, GI-24, Bridgeton, N Jersey, OP, pint, deep gold amber ....
.... $325–$385
Washington / Eagle, GI-26, OP, inner stain, quart, aqua .... $75–$125*
Washington / Eagle, GI-26, OP, lip chip, quart, aqua.................. $75–$95*
Washington / Eagle, GI-26, OP, quart, aqua........................ $120–$150*
Washington / Eagle, GI-26, OP, quart, citron....................... $600–$900*
Washington / Eagle, GI-26, OP, quart, medium emerald green .... $1200–$1500*
Washington / Eagle, GI-26a, OP, quart, deep blue green............. $1400–$1750
Washington / Eagle, GI-27, OP, quart, aqua........................ $120–$155
Washington / Eagle, GI-27, OP, quart, deep olive yellow .... $2500–$3500
Washington / Eagle, GI-27, OP, quart, medium blue green .... $800–$1200
Washington / Eagle, GI-27, OP, rib bruise, quart, aqua .... $75–$95

Washington / Jackson, GI-31, OP, pint, olive amber . . . . $110–$130
Washington / Jackson, GI-31, OP, forest green . . . . $250–$300
Washington / Jackson, GI-31, OP, pint, olive green . . . . $110–$130
Washington / Jackson, GI-31, OP, pint, yellow amber . . . . $130–$160
Washington / Jackson, GI-31, OP, pint, yellow olive . . . . $150–$200
Washington / Jackson, GI-32, OP, lip chip, pint, olive amber . . . . $80–$100
Washington / Jackson, GI-32, OP, pint, olive amber . . . . $120–$150
Washington / Jackson, GI-32, OP, pint, olive green . . . . $120–$150
Washington / Jackson, GI-32, OP, pint, yellow olive . . . . $135–$195
Washington / Jackson, GI-33, OP, pint, olive amber . . . . $100–$130
Washington (facing right) / Jackson, GI-34, OP, lip chip, pint, yellow green . . . .
. . . . $85–$100
Washington (facing right) / Jackson, GI-34, OP, pint, olive amber . . . . . . $135–$185
Washington (facing right) / Jackson, GI-34, OP, pint, olive green. . . . . . . $145–$195
Washington / Reverse Side Unembossed, GI-47 OP, sheared lip, quart, medium teal
blue . . . . $250–$300
Washington / Reverse Side Unembossed, GI-48, lip chip, OP, pint, aqua . . . $30–$35
Washington / Reverse Side Unembossed, GI-48, OP, pint, blue green. . . . $150–$200
Washington / Reverse Side Unembossed, GI-48, OP, sheared lip, pint, medium blue
green . . . . $50–$300
Washington / Reverse Side Unembossed, GI-48, OP, sheared lip, pint, medium blue
teal. . . . . $225–$250
Washington / Reverse Side Unembossed, GI-47, OP, sheared lip, quart, aqua . . . $50–$65
Washington / Reversed Side Unembossed, GI-48, OP, pint, aqua . . . . $45–$55
Washington / Sheaf of Rye, GI-57, OP, sheared lip, quart, aqua . . . . $45–$65
Washington / Sheaf of Rye, GI-57, SB, sloping collar, quart, deep olive green . . . . . .
. . . . $425–$575
Washington / Sheaf of Rye, GI-58, OP, sheared lip, pint, aqua . . . . $45–$65
Washington / Taylor, GI-17, Balimore Glassworks, sheared lip, OP, lip chip, pint, aqua
. . . . $30–$40
Washington / Taylor, GI-17, Baltimore Glassworks, OP, sheared lip, pint, aqua . . . . .
. . . . $55–$75
Washington / Taylor, GI-17, Baltimore Glassworks, OP, sheared lip, pint, pale yellow
green . . . . $300–$500
Washington / Taylor, GI-24, Bridgeton, N Jersey, OP, pint, aqua. . . . . . . $125–$175
Washington / Taylor, GI-24, Bridgeton, N Jersey, OP, pint, blue green . . . .
. . . . $500–$650
Washington / Eagle, GI-26, OP, quart, deep aqua . . . . $175–$245
Washington / Taylor, GI-37, OP, quart, burgundy . . . . $2100–$2750*
Washington / Taylor, GI-37, OP, quart, golden yellow . . . . $500–$625*
Washington / Taylor, GI-37, OP, quart, medium pink amethyst . . . . . . $2500–$3000*
Washington / Taylor, GI-37, OP, quart, medium puce. . . . . $2200–$2800*
Washington / Taylor, GI-37, OP, sheared lip, quart, medium sapphire blue . . . .
. . . . $2600–$3400*
Washington / Taylor, GI-37, OP, sloping collar, quart, aqua. . . . . $60–$85*
Washington / Taylor, GI-37, OP, sloping collar, quart, plum amethyst. . . . .
. . . . $2600–$3200*
Washington / Taylor, GI-37, SB, round collar, quart, light yellow green . . . .
. . . . $225–$325*
Washington / Taylor, GI-37, SB, round collar, quart, medium yellow green . . . .
. . . . $300–$425*

Washington / Taylor, GI-37, SB, sloping collar, quart, aqua . . . . $45–$60*
Washington / Taylor, GI-37, SB, sloping collar, quart, copper topaz . . . $900–$1150*
Washington / Taylor, GI-37, OP, double ring lip, quart, aqua . . . . $60–$85
Washington / Taylor, GI-37, OP, sheared lip, quart, aqua . . . . $60–$75
Washington / Taylor, GI-38, OP, pint, blue green . . . . $200–$300

Figured flask, Washington-Taylor, GI-38. PHOTO
COURTESY OF NEIL GROSSMAN.

Washington / Taylor, GI-38, OP, pint, emerald green . . . . $250–$400
Washington / Taylor, GI-38, OP, pint, strawberry puce . . . . $800–$1200
Washington / Taylor, GI-38, OP, quart, amethyst . . . . $2200–$2700
Washington / Taylor, GI-38, OP, quart, deep yellow olive . . . . $675–$850
Washington / Taylor, GI-38, OP, sheared lip, pint, medium sage green . . . $300–$375
Washington / Taylor, GI-38, OP, sheared lip, quart, aqua . . . . $45–$60
Washington / Taylor, GI-38, OP, sloping collar, quart, aqua . . . . $60–$75
Washington / Taylor, GI-38, SB, sheared lip, pint, aqua . . . . $40–$50
Washington / Taylor, GI-38, SB, sloping collar, pint, aqua . . . . $45–$65
Washington / Taylor, GI-38, SB, sloping collar, pint, light sapphire (not aqua) . . . . . .
. . . . $275–$375
Washington / Taylor, GI-39, OP, quart, blue green . . . . $200–$300
Washington / Taylor, GI-39, OP, quart, clear . . . . $40–$65
Washington / Taylor, GI-39, OP, quart, deep blue green . . . . $250–$375
Washington / Taylor, GI-39, OP, quart, emerald green . . . . $200–$300
Washington / Taylor, GI-39, OP, sheared lip, quart, aqua . . . . $50–$70
Washington / Taylor, GI-39, OP, sloping collar, pint, aqua . . . . $55–$75
Washington / Taylor, GI-39, SB, sheared lip, quart, aqua . . . . $40–$50
Washington / Taylor, GI-40, OP, polished lip chip, lightly cleaned, sheared lip, pint,
medium sapphire . . . . $300–$450
Washington / Taylor, GI-40, OP, sheared lip, pint, aqua . . . . $40–$50
Washington / Taylor, GI-40, OP, sloping collar, pint, aqua . . . . $75–$85
Washington / Taylor, GI-40, SB, sheared lip, pint, aqua . . . . $35–$40
Washington / Taylor, GI-40a, OP, sheared lip, pint, aqua . . . . $40–$55
Washington / Taylor, GI-40a, OP, sheared lip, pint, cobalt . . . . $1800–$2300
Washington / Taylor, GI-40b, base edge chip, heavy wear, pint, medium cobalt . . . . .
. . . . $1000–$1200
Washington / Taylor, GI-40b, OP, sheared lip, pint, cobalt . . . . $1900–$2250
Washington / Taylor, GI-41, OP, sheared lip, half pint, aqua . . . . $40–$55
Washington / Taylor, GI-41, OP, sheared lip, half pint, olive green . . . . $1800–$2200
Washington / Taylor, GI-41, SB, sheared lip, half pint, aqua . . . . $35–$40

Washington / Taylor, GI-42, Little More Grape Capt Bragg, OP, medium blue green .
. . . . $750–$950
Washington / Taylor, GI-42, Little More Grape Capt Bragg, OP, sheared lip, medium
blue . . . . $3000+
Washington / Taylor, GI-43, blue striations, OP, sheared lip, quart, med. smoky gray
amethyst . . . . $4000–$4750
Washington / Taylor, GI-43, OP, quart, emerald green . . . . $250–$350
Washington / Taylor, GI-43, OP, sheared lip, quart, aqua . . . . $45–$60
Washington / Taylor, GI-43, OP, sheared lip, quart, blue green . . . . $200–$300
Washington / Taylor, GI-43, SB, sheared lip, quart, aqua . . . . $35–$45
Washington / Taylor, GI-43, SB, sloping collar, quart, aqua . . . . $45–$55
Washington / Taylor, GI-44, OP, lip chip, pint, aqua. $25–$35
Washington / Taylor, GI-44, OP, pint, cobalt blue. . . . . $1200–$1500
Washington / Taylor, GI-44, OP, pint, golden yellow . . . . $500–$700
Washington / Taylor, GI-44, OP, sheared lip, pint, aqua . . . . $45–$55
Washington / Taylor, GI-44, OP, sheared lip, pint, citron . . . . $750–$950
Washington / Taylor, GI-44, SB, pint, golden amber. . . . . $350–$500
Washington / Taylor, GI-45, OP, sheared lip, quart, aqua . . . . $45–$65
Washington / Taylor, GI-45, SB, double collar, quart, light yellow green . $200–$240
Washington / Taylor, GI-46, OP, sheared lip, quart, aqua . . . . $45–$60
Washington / Taylor, GI-46, SB, sheared lip, quart, aqua . . . . $35–$45
Washington / Taylor, GI-46, SB, sloping collar, quart, black . . . . $1500–$1850
Washington / Taylor, GI-49, OP, sloping collar, pint, aqua. . . . . $45–$60
Washington / Taylor, GI-49, SB, sheared lip, pint, aqua . . . . $35–$40
Washington / Taylor, GI-50, OP, sheared lip, deep green . . . . $400–$600*
Washington / Taylor, GI-50, OP, sheared lip, lip chip, aqua . . . . $25–$35*
Washington / Taylor, GI-50, OP, sheared lip, pint, aqua . . . . $40–$50*
Washington / Taylor, GI-50, OP, sheared lip, pint, emerald green . . . . . . $300–$500*
Washington / Taylor, GI-51, base edge chip, side bruise, OP, sheared lip, deep pink
puce. . . . . $750+
Washington / Taylor, GI-51, OP, round collar, quart, sapphire . . . . $2500–$2900
Washington / Taylor, GI-51, OP, sheared lip, quart, aqua . . . . $45–$55
Washington / Taylor, GI-51, SB, sloping collar, quart, aqua . . . . $40–$60
Washington / Taylor, GI-52, IP, double collar, deep amber. . . . . $500–$725
Washington / Taylor, GI-52, OP, sheared lip, pint, aqua . . . . $45–$50
Washington / Taylor, GI-52, OP, sheared lip, yellow amber . . . . $375–$465
Washington / Taylor, GI-53, OP, sheared lip, half pint, aqua . . . . $50–$70
Washington / Taylor, GI-53, OP, sloping collar, half pint, aqua . . . . $80–$100
Washington / Taylor, GI-54, OP, quart, blue green . . . . $200–$265
Washington / Taylor, GI-54, OP, quart, copper . . . . $450–$650
Washington / Taylor, GI-54, OP, quart, sapphire blue. . . . . $1500–$2500
Washington / Taylor, GI-54, OP, sheared lip, quart, aqua . . . . $45–$55
Washington / Taylor, GI-54, OP, sheared lip, quart, deep wine. . . . . $1900–$2400
Washington / Taylor, GI-54, OP, sheared lip, quart, emerald green . . . . . . $250–$350
Washington / Taylor, GI-54, SB, double collared lip, quart, aqua . . . . $40–$50
Washington / Taylor, GI-54, SB, sloping collar, lip bruise, quart, cobalt . . . .
. . . . $900–$1100
Washington / Taylor, GI-54, SB, sloping collar, quart, olive yellow. . . . . . $425–$525
Washington / Taylor, GI-54, sheared lip, OP, lip chip, quart, aqua . . . . $25–$35

Washington / Taylor, GI-54, sheared lip, OP, quart, pinkish amethyst . . $2200–$3000
Washington / Taylor, GI-54, sloping collar, SB, quart, golden amber. . . . $800–$1200
Washington / Taylor, GI-55, OP, pint, deep amber . . . . $350–$450
Washington / Taylor, GI-55, OP, pint, emerald green . . . . $250–$325
Washington / Taylor, GI-55, OP, pint, olive yellow . . . . $350–$550
Washington / Taylor, GI-55, OP, sheared lip, lip chip, pint, aqua . . . . $25–$35
Washington / Taylor, GI-55, OP, sheared lip, pint, aqua . . . . $40–$50
Washington / Taylor, GI-56, OP, sheared lip, half pint, aqua . . . . $50–$65
Washington / Taylor, GI-56, OP, sheared lip, olive tone, half pint, yellow. . . . .
. . . . $8000–$10,000
Washington / Taylor, GI-56, SB, sheared lip, half pint, aqua . . . . $40–$50
Washington / Tree, GI-35, calabash, inner stain, OP, sloping collar, quart, aqua . . . . .
. . . . $75–$95
Washington / Tree, GI-35, calabash, OP, sloping collar, quart, aqua. . . . . . $110–$150
Washington / Tree, GI-36, calabash, OP, sloping collar, quart, aqua. . . . . . $110–$150
Washington / Washington, GI-61, OP, quart, aqua . . . . $75–$125
Washington / Washington, GI-61, OP, quart, blue green . . . . , . . $125–$195
Washington, Albany / Ship, GI-28, IP, double collar lip, pint, gold amber. . . . .
. . . . $900–$1200*
Washington, Albany / Ship, GI-28, IP, double collar lip, pint, light green . . . .
. . . . $2000–$2400*
Washington, Albany / Ship, GI-28, IP, pint, aqua . . . . $175–$225*
Washington, Albany / Ship, GI-28, OP, lip chip, stain, pint, aqua . . . . $60–$75*
Washington, Albany / Ship, GI-28, OP, medial rib chip, pint, aqua . . . . . . $70–$90*
Washington, Albany / Ship, GI-28, OP, pint, blue green. . . . . $600–$750*
Washington, Albany / Ship, GI-28, OP, pint, greenish aqua . . . . $150–$225*
Washington, Albany / Ship, GI-28, OP, pint, light sapphire blue . . . . . $3000–$4000*
Wheat Price / Fairview Works, GI-115, OP, sheared lip, pint, blue green . . . .
. . . . $1750–$2500
Wheat Price / Fairview Works, GI-115, OP, sheared lip, pint, pale blue green . . . . . .
. . . . $1600–$1900
Wheat Price / Fairview Works, GI-116, OP, sheared lip, pint, blue green . . . .
. . . . $5000+
Wheat Price / Fairview Works, GI-116, OP, sheared lip, pint, deep aqua . . . .
. . . . $3000–$4250
Wheeling Va / Old Rye, GXV-25, SB, applied lip, pint, deep yellow olive. . . . .
. . . . $700–$900
Whitney Glassworks (on base), SB, double collar or inner screw thread, half pint,
amber. . . . . $20–$25
Whitney Glassworks (on base), SB, double collar or inner screw thread, pint, amber .
. . . . $20–$25
Winchell & Davis Importing, Albany, NY, clear . . . . $20–$25
Winchell & Davis, Full Measure, W&D, strap flask, aqua . . . . $20–$30
Worthman Bros., NY, clear . . . . $20–$25
Zanesville City Glassworks / Plain, GXV-28, SB, applied lip, pint, aqua . . . .
. . . . $100–$145

OTHER FLASKS

CA Richards Co, 99 Washington St Boston, pint, aqua . . . . $35–$45
Clyde Glassworks, NY, quart, SB, applied lip, aqua . . . . $50–$60

Connell McGill Liquors, strap flask, aqua, quart .... $20–$30

Dandy, The, clear pumpkinseed, 5¼", SB .... $30–$45

Drake, John B, Tremont House, Chicago, ½ pint, amber, inner screw thread, ...
.... $200–$250

Eagle in Circle, clear strap flask .... $40–$60

Erie Distilling Co, clear... $20–$25

Eye Opener, eyeball figure on flask, 5¼", opaque white .... $150–$250

Full Measure, pint, amber, SB, double collar .... $20–$25

Good Night, smiling face on milk glass flask, 4", metal screw cap......... $120–$150

Hagerty Glassworks (on base), gold amber, SB, quart, applied lip........ $30–$40

Handmade Sour Mash, clear, half pint, pumpkinseed.................... $30–$45

Hotel Statler, clear pumpkinseed, 3½"............................. $25–$35

I Got My Fill at Jake's . . . , man and dog at lamppost, pint, clear pumpkinseed .....
.... $300–$450

Kline, JN & Co, Aromatic Digestive Cordial, 5", cobalt .... $275–$325

LG CO (on base), SB, applied lip, olive yellow, pint................... $25–$35

Life Preserver, clear pumpkinseed .... $30–$45

Life Preserver, 5½", milk glass flask .... $150–$250

Lion/Cluster of Grapes, pint, OP, sheared lip, cobalt .... $150–$200

Lion With Shield, Ornberg & Anderson/Gothebarc, cobalt, OP, sheared lip, ...
.... $150–$180

LK & Co, Syracuse, amber strap flask, half pint .... $30–$40

Merry Christmas, A, woman sitting, **Happy New Year**, rooster, half pint, amber....
.... $250–$350

Night Cap, man with stocking cap on 4" milk glass flask, metal cap ...... $150–$225

Ornberg & Anderson/Gothebarc, cobalt, OP, sheared lip .... $150–$180

Patent (on face), pint, amber, SB, double collar .... $40–$55

Picnic, amber pumpkinseed, 5¼" .... $75–$95

Portchester Wine & Liquor, clear .... $20–$25

Rib Pattern, no embossing, amber, half pint .... $15–$20

SC Dispensary, half pint, clear .... $100–$120

SC Dispensary, pint, clear....................................... $80–$100

Shirt Shaped Flask, 4¾", milk glass, metal screw cap .... $200–$300

Star in Circle, light yellow green strap flask, half pint.................. $15–$20

St Wolfgang (on staff) of Bishop/Mountain, House, pewter screw on stopper, cobalt,
OP.. $375–$475

Tear Drops, milk glass flask with large eyeball, 3⅞", metal cap......... $100–$145

Try It, amber pumpkinseed, 4½", SB .... $50–$75

Unembossed, unpatterned, amber, green, yellow green .... $10–$30

Warranted Flask, pint, quart, half gallon, clear, SB, double collar .... $6–$12

Whitney Glassworks (on base), pint, amber, SB, double collar or inner screw thread .
.... $20–$25

Whitney Glassworks (on base), half pint, amber, SB, double collar or inner screw
thread.. $20–$25

Winchell & Davis Importing, Albany, NY, clear .... $20–$25

Winchell & Davis, Full Measure,W&D, aqua strap flask .... $20–$30

Worthman Bros, NY, clear....................................... $20–$25

FIRE GRENADES

Fire extinguisher bottles are bottles that held a special fluid which, when the fire grenade and contents were smashed into a fire, would put the fire out. Most of the fire grenades were made after 1870 and come in a wide variety of shapes, sizes, and colors. Since the extinguisher bottles were made to be destroyed, they are fairly rare. Many can be found with the original closures, contents, and labels, which enhance their value.

Acme Fire Extr, Pat'd June 29 1869, $5^7/_8$", yellow amber . . . . $2500+

Ajax Fire Engine Works, $11^1/_4$", deep aqua . . . . $100–$145

American Fire Extinguisher Co Hand Grenade, clear, $6^1/_4$" . . . . $175–$225

Babcock Hand Grenade Non Freezing, quart, cobalt . . . . $1200–$1500

Barnum's Hand Fire Ext Diamond, Pat'd June 26 1869, 6", yellow amber . . . .
. . . . $300–$350

Barnum's Hand Fire Ext Diamond, Pat'd June 26 1869, aqua . . . . $375–$500

Boer's & CP Delft Flesschenfabriek, diamond pattern, $2^3/_4$", light green . . . .
. . . . $1200–$1600

C & NWRY, clear, $17^1/_2$" . . . . $60–$85

Descours & Co Fire Watcher Grenade (on label), clear, wire carrier, $5^1/_4$" . . . .
. . . . $300–$425

Extingteur Grenade Protector, nine pointed stars on four sides, $5^3/_4$", cobalt . . . .
. . . . $800–$1200

Fire Dept Throw Into Fire, figural fire plug, clear, $4^3/_8$" . . . . $200–$300

Firex Grenade, original box, $3^3/_4$", cobalt blue . . . . $60–$80

Flaggs Fire Extinguisher, Pat'd 1868, $6^1/_4$", orange amber . . . . $450–$600

Grenade Francais, pint, $6^5/_8$", yellow green . . . . $900–$1300

Grenade L'Urbaine, amber tones, $6^1/_2$", yellow . . . . $600–$900

Grenade L'Urbaine, labels, $6^1/_2$", medium yellow amber . . . . $500–$750

Grenade L'Urbaine, with hint of olive, labels, $6^1/_2$", yellow . . . . $500–$750

Grenades Du Progres Extincives, OP, $5^1/_8$", golden amber . . . . $800–$1100

Grenades Du Progres Extincives, yellow amber . . . . $650–$900

Harden Hand Grenade Fire Extinguisher, Star, $6^3/_8$", sapphire blue . . . . $100–$125

Harden Hand Grenade Fire Extinguisher, Star, $7^7/_8$", medium turquoise . . . .
. . . . $75–$110

Harden Hand Grenade Fire Extinguisher, Star, May 27 84 (on base), 8", yellow
green . . . . $200–$275

Harden Hand Grenade Fire Extinguisher, Star, May 27 84 (on base), clear, 8" . . . .
. . . . $500–$600

Harden Hand Grenade Fire Extinguisher, Star, neck label, $6^1/_2$", medium cobalt . . .
. . . . $175–$245

Harden Star Hand Grenade Fire Extinguisher, $6^5/_8$", aqua . . . . $175–$250

Harden Star Hand Grenade Fire Extinguisher, label, $6^1/_2$", medium cobalt . . . .
. . . . $160–$220

Harden Star Hand Grenade Fire Extinguisher, label, 6⁵/₈", cobalt. . . . . . $175–$225
Harden Star Tubular Grenade, clear tube, 16⁷/₈". . . . . $200–$300
Harden's Hand Fire Extinguisher Grenade, 4⁷/₈", electric cobalt blue . . . $175–$245
Harden's Hand Fire Extinguisher Grenade, Aug 8 1871, Patented No 2, 5", turquoise
. . . . $80–$120
Harden's Hand Fire Extinguisher Grenade, Pat'd Aug 14, 83, Star, 6", turquoise . . .
. . . . $300–$400
Harden's Hand Fire Extinguisher Grenade, Patented, 4³/₄", cobalt . . . . . $150–$210
Harden's Hand Fire Extinguisher Grenade, Patented, 4³/₄", purple . . . . . $150–$200
Harden's Improved Grenade Fire Extinguisher, Pat'd Oct 7, 1884, two pieces, clear,
5". . . . . $150–$250
Harden's Improved Grenade Fire Extinguisher, Pat'd Oct 7, 1884, top half of
grenade only, 2³/₈", cobalt. . . . . $250–$350
Harden's Improved Hand Grenade Fire Extinguisher, 6⁵/₈", medium amber . . . . . .
. . . . $800–$1200
Harkness Fire Destroyer, 6¹/₄", deep cobalt. . . . . $400–$500
Harkness Fire Destroyer, 6", sapphire blue . . . . $450–$600
Hayward Grenade Fire Extinguisher, No 407, Broadway, NY, clear, 6" . . $90–$125

Hayward's fire grenade. PHOTO COURTESY OF
GLASS WORKS AUCTIONS.

Hayward Hand Grenade Fire Extinguisher New York, clear, 6¹/₂" . . . . . $100–$125
Hayward Hand Grenade Fire Extinguisher, 5⁷/₈", aqua . . . . $125–$175
Hayward's Hand Fire Grenade SF Hayward, 407 Broadway NY, 6", cobalt. . . . . . .
. . . . $200–$250
Hayward's Hand Fire Grenade SF Hayward, 407 Broadway NY, 6", light yellow . .
. . . . $160–$210
Hayward's Hand Fire Grenade SF Hayward, 407 Broadway NY, label, 6", light sap-
phire . . . . $180–$255
Hayward's Hand Fire Grenade, 6", cobalt . . . . $250–$300
Hayward's Hand Fire Grenade, Pat'd Aug 8 1871, 1" neck crack, 6", turquoise. . . . .
. . . . $125–$175
Hayward's Hand Fire Grenade, Pat'd Aug 8 1871, 6¹/₄", turquoise blue . . $150–$225
Hayward's Hand Fire Grenade, Pat'd Aug 8 1871, 6¹/₈", medium apple green . . . . . .
. . . . $110–$150

Hayward's Hand Fire Grenade, Pat'd Aug 8 1871, 6$^1/_8$", medium yellowish green . .
. . . . $150–$300
Hayward's Hand Fire Grenade, Pat'd Aug 8 1871, 6", amber . . . . $100–$150
Hayward's Hand Fire Grenade, Pat'd Aug 8 1871, 6", deep yellow olive . . . .
. . . . $100–$145
Hayward's Hand Fire Grenade, Pat'd Aug 8 1871, 6", light apple green. . . . .
. . . . $150–$200
Hayward's Hand Fire Grenade, Pat'd Aug 8 1871, 6", medium yellow olive . . . .
. . . . $125–$165
Hayward's Hand Fire Grenade, Pat'd Aug 8 1871, 6", yellow amber . . . . $125–$150
Hayward's Hand Fire Grenade, Pat'd Aug 8 1871, applied lip (rare), 6$^1/_4$", aqua . . . .
. . . . $250–$325
Hayward's Hand Fire Grenade, Pat'd Aug 8 1871, clear, 6" . . . . $200–$300
Hayward's Hand Fire Grenade, Pat'd Aug 8 1871, clear, full label, 6" . . . $275–$375
Hayward's Hand Fire Grenade, Pat'd Aug 8 1871, olive tint, 6", straw yellow. . . . . .
. . . . $150–$200
Hayward's Hand Fire Grenade, Pat'd Aug 8 1871, olive tone, 6", light yellow. . . . . .
. . . . $125–$175
Hazelton's High Pressure Chemical Fire Keg, neck band, 11", yellow amber barrel .
. . . . $200–$275
Healy's Hand Fire Extinguisher, 11$^1/_2$", yellow amber. . . . . $650–$900
Heathman's (fire hat) Swift Fire Grenade, 6$^1/_4$", medium pink gasoline puce . . . . . .
. . . . $700–$850
HNS, 7$^1/_8$", diamond pattern, clear, 7$^1/_8$" . . . . $200–$260
HNS, 7$^1/_8$, yellow amber. . . . . $240–$320
HNS, 7$^1/_8$", diamond pattern, 7$^1/_8$", medium amber . . . . $250–$350
Imperial Fire Extinguisher Co Ltd, 6$^5/_8$", medium green. . . . . $150–$185
Kalamazoo Automatic & Hand Fire Extinguisher, Patent Applied For, 11", cobalt
. . . . $250–$325
LB, vertical ribs, 5$^3/_8$", cobalt blue. . . . . $400–$600
London Fire Appliance Co, Glascow London & Manchester, 8$^3/_4$", yellow olive . . . .
. . . . $375–$500
London Fire Appliance Co, Glascow London & Manchester, amber . . . . . $450–$575
Magic Fire Extinguisher Co, amber tone, 6$^1/_8$", yellow. . . . . $400–$525
Magic Fire Grenade, 6$^1/_4$", yellow amber. . . . . $400–$525
Merryweather London, MS, neck label, 6$^1/_2$", root beer amber. . . . . $800–$1200
NHS (monogram), quart, yellow amber. . . . . $110–$150
Pat'd Nov 28 1884, pint, yellowish amber. . . . . $400–$500
Pat'd Sept 25 1877 (on shoulder), grainy surface, 2$^5/_8$", light olive green. . . . .
. . . . $1800–$2300
Prevoyante Extinguisher Grenade, vertical ribs, 5$^5/_8$", orange amber . . . . $300–$400
PSN (monogram), diamond pattern, quart, 6$^3/_4$", aqua . . . . $250–$350
Rockford Kalamazoo Automatic & Hand Fire Extinguisher, 11", cobalt . . . .
. . . . $325–$425
Sinclair Fire Grenade, Toot (on base), 7$^1/_4$", cobalt . . . . $300–$400
Star Harden's Grenade Sprinkler, 17$^3/_4$", cobalt . . . . $800–$1200
Systeme Labbe Grenade Extingteur L'Incombustibilite, 5$^1/_2$", light topaz yellow . .
. . . . $250–$300
Systeme Labbe Grenade Extingteur L'Incombustibilite, 5$^5/_8$", orange amber. . . . . .
. . . . $300–$350
Unembossed, 11horizontal rings, label panel, 6", cobalt. . . . . $175–$250

Unembossed, clear neck label, 5¹/₂"................................... $600–$800
Unembossed, many vertical ribs, central band, similar in form to Harden's but without any embossing, clear, 6⁷/₈"....................................... $700–$1000
Unembossed, quilted pattern, round label panel, 6¹/₂", amber............ $300–$400
Unembossed, quilted pattern, round label panel, 6³/₈", aqua.............. $250–$350
Unembossed, round, unpatterned but with circular label panel, 6", cobalt...........
.... $800–$1200
Unembossed, vertical rib pattern, 5¹/₂", light straw yellow.............. $400–$525
Unembossed, vertical rib pattern, 5¹/₂", turquoise blue.................. $400–$600
Unembossed, vertical rib pattern, frosted clear, neck label, 5¹/₄"......... $500–$750
Unic Grenade Extintrice, ribbed body, 5⁷/₈", orange amber............. $400–$600
Universal Fire Extinguisher, OP, 7¹/₄", light sapphire blue............ $800–$1150
WD Allen Manufacturing Company Chicago Illinois, clear, 8"........ $375–$475

FOOD BOTTLES

Food bottles come in a wide variety of shapes and sizes. Peppersauce bottles come in a wide range of colors and are very collectible. References preceded with a "Z" are for *Ketchup, Pickles and Sauces* by Betty Zumwalt, and those prefaced by an "H" are from *American Bottles and Flasks and Their Ancestry* by McKearin and Wilson.

A Doufour & C Bordeaux, jar, pewter screw cap, OP, label, 4³/₄", light yellow green.
.... $60–$85
A1 Sauce, applied lip, clear, 10"....................................... $6–$9
Alfred Jones Sons, Bangor, Maine (on label only), cylinder, 11", yellow green......
.... $90–$120
Arrow Brand Pickles (on label only), square pickle, 8¹/₂", amber........ $90–$135
Arrow Brand Pickles JJ Wilson Chicago (on label only), 7³/₄", amber pickle......
.... $90–$135
Atmore's (on two panels), cathedral pickle, SB, 11¹/₄", apple green...... $250–$350
Atmore's, Z-32, cathedral pickle, square, 11³/₈", aqua.................. $125–$150
B & L, barrel shaped jar, SB, 5", aqua.................................. $30–$40
Baker Flavoring Extract, clear, OP, 5"................................ $9–$14
Barrel Shaped, 3¹/₂", amber.. $25–$35
Barrel Shaped, milk glass, 3¹/₂"..................................... $25–$35
Bastine & Co Pure Flavoring Extracts, New York, cylinder, 9³/₄", deep blue green.
.... $40–$60
Berry Bottle, tall cylinder with fluted shoulder panels, SB, 11¹/₄", amber...........
.... $375–$475
Berry Bottle, tall cylinder with fluted shoulder panels, SB, 11¹/₄", aqua... $150–$190
Bertin Pure Olive Oil, 7¹/₂", dark green............................. $14–$19

Berry bottle, fluted shoulder. PHOTO COURTESY OF GLASS WORKS AUCTIONS.

Boiled Maple Sap & Apple Cider Vinegar, E Rindge, NH, quart, cobalt . . . . $1200–$1450
Burnett's Standard Flavoring Extract, 6³/₄", aqua . . . . $4–$5
Burnett's Standard Flavoring Extract, 6³/₄", light green . . . . $5–$7
Carlton's HP Sauce, applied top, 8¹/₄", aqua . . . . $9–$12
CD Brooks Boston, wide mouth, 9¹/₂", amber . . . . $50–$70
CGO (on base), horizontally ribbed sauce bottle, 6", aqua . . . . $15–$20
Choice Family Pickles Trade Mark Hawkeye Vinegar & Pickle Works (on label), square, 11", aqua . . . . $20–$30
Chow Chow from Grosse & Blackwell (on label), cylinder, 8¹/₂", golden amber . . . . $30–$40
Coleman Bros Gherkins, Packed in Pure Malt Vinegar (on label), square, clear, 11" . . . . $15–$20
Cowdrey, tall cylinder, clear, 11¹/₈" . . . . $35–$45
Cruikshank Bros Co Preserves, Jellies Fruit Butters, stoneware jar, lid, wire handle, 7" . . . . $75–$125
Cruikshank Bros Highest Grade (on label), stoneware pickle jar, lid, wire handle, 5¹/₂" . . . . $75–$110
Curtice, square pickle, SB, 7", aqua . . . . $40–$45
CWS Grill Sauce, applied lip, 7", green . . . . $6–$8
CWS Sauce, 8", aqua . . . . $6–$8
Daddie's Favourite Sauce, 8", dark aqua . . . . $10–$12
Daddies Sauce, applied lip, 7³/₄", aqua . . . . $10–$12
Dill's Family Extracts, clear, 6¹/₄" . . . . $1–$2
Dodson Hills St Louis, cathedral peppersauce, SB, 8⁵/₈", aqua . . . . $80–$120
Dr Fenner's Concentrated Flavors, 6", aqua . . . . $2–$4
Dr Price Delicious Flavoring Extract, clear, 5" . . . . $3–$4
Dr Price Delicious Flavoring Extract, clear, 6³/₄" . . . . $4–$6
East India Pickles (on neck), quart, aqua . . . . $15–$22
EHVB, cathedral pickle, six sided, IP, 9¹/₄", deep aqua . . . . $400–$600
Eiffel Tower Fruit Juices, 4", aqua . . . . $1–$3
Eskays Albuminized Foot Patd (on base), vacuum cap, pint, amber . . . . $4–$6
Espy (arched) Philad, cylinder, sloping collar, SB, 10", aqua . . . . $25–$30

Espy (arched) Philad, wide mouthed cylinder, SB, 9³/₄", aqua . . . . $25–$30
Espy Philad, Z434 lower right, cylinder, SB, 9", aqua . . . . $35–$45
ET Cowdrey & Co Boston, SB, 7⁵/₈", amber . . . . $50–$70
Evergreen Pickle Works, pickle stoneware crock, no lid, 9¹/₂" . . . . $40–$60
Extra Pickles Wm Underwood & Co (on label only), square pickle, 11", aqua . . . . .
. . . . $90–$125
FE McAllister's Mocking Bird Food, New York, labeled, screw top, 7", aqua . . . . . .
. . . . $8–$12
Fletcher's Indian Sauce, 8", dark aqua . . . . $10–$13
Fletcher's Shipley Sauce, 5", aqua . . . . $8–$11
Fletcher's Shipley Sauce, 6", aqua . . . . $8–$11
Fletcher's Tiger Sauce, 5¹/₂", aqua . . . . $10–$13
Fletcher's Tiger Sauce, 8¹/₄", aqua . . . . $8–$12
Fletcher's Tomato Sauce, oval, applied lip, 8", aqua . . . . $10–$13
Forbes Delicious Flavoring Extract, clear, 5" . . . . $4–$6
Frank Miller's Crown Dressing New York USA, full label, cork top, 5¹/₂", aqua . . . .
. . . . $20–$30
Garton's, round, applied lip, 8¹/₂", aqua . . . . $6–$8
Gelfand's Mayonnaise Baltimore Md, glaze stoneware jar, no lid, 9", brown and tan
. . . . $45–$70
Gerkin's from Lewis & Bros, 93 Broad Street (on label only), square pickle, 13³/₄",
aqua . . . . $75–$95
Giessens Union Mustard NY (eagle), barrel shaped, OP, 5", aqua . . . . $50–$70
Golden Tree Maple Syrup, clear, screw cap, 20 oz . . . . $1–$2
Golden Tree Pure Honey, clear, screw cap, 4 oz . . . . $1–$2
GP Sanborn & Son Union Brand Boston Pickles, 5", yellow amber . . . . . $125–$165
GP Sanborn & Son Union Brand Boston Pickles, 5", aqua . . . . $60–$70
GP Sanborn & Son Union Brand Boston Pickles, 8", yellow amber . . . . . $130–$175
GP Sanborn & Son Union Brand Boston Pickles, SB labeled, 8", yellow amber . . . .
. . . . $125–$150
Grand Union Tea Co, clear, 5" . . . . $1–$3
Granny's Delicious Relish, 8", dark aqua, aqua . . . . $10–$12
Great Atlantic & Pacific Tea Co, clear, 5¹/₂" . . . . $1–$2
Great Seal, Styron Beggs Co, clear, 9" . . . . $1–$2
Chas Gulden, NY, mustard jar, clear, 4³/₄" . . . . $1–$2
Chas Gulden, NY, sauce bottle, clear, 11¹/₂" . . . . $50–$80
Hallocks Pure Extracts, clear, 6" . . . . $1–$2
Harris Pure Flavors, clear, 5¹/₂" . . . . $1–$2
Heinz & Noble Pittsburgh Pa, square pickle, 7³/₈", aqua . . . . $70–$90
Heinz Bros & Co (with cross), on front, four sided oval, clear . . . . $10–$15
Heinz No 26 (on base), cylinder, clear . . . . $5–$7
Heinz, frosted glass barrel, ground lip, 10" . . . . $150–$200
Hires Improved Root Beer, four panels, clear . . . . $1–$2
HJ Heinz (keystone, key), on front, Patd June 17 1890 (base), clear ketchup, paneled
base . . . . $8–$12
HJ Heinz Co Patd (base), flattened ovoid form, olive jar, clear . . . . $2–$3
HJ Heinz Co Patd (base), paneled ketchup bottle, clear . . . . $2–$4
HJ Heinz Patented 69 (on base), sided jar, clear . . . . $4–$6
HJ Heinz Patented 69 (on base), sided jar, clear, with original label . . . . $5–$7
HJ Heinz, Pittsburgh (on ground lid), six sided jar, clear, 9¹/₂" . . . . $100–$145
HJ Neuhauser, mustard jar, barrel shaped, clear, OP, 5" . . . . $70–$90

Hoe's Sauce, eight sided, $7^1/2$", aqua . . . . $6–$9

Horlick's Malted Milk, clear jar, tin screw cap, various sizes . . . . $1–$9

Hormel Good Food (in frame), oval, glass lid, clear . . . . $5–$7

Horse Raddish Warranted Pure by Remington & Co (on label), square, cross hatching, OP, 6", aqua . . . . $70–$95

J Fau Bordeaux, clear, OP, Z-143, $6^1/2$" . . . . $25–$150

J Fau Prunes Dente Bordeaux, Z-143 upper, OP, $8^1/2$", smoky aqua . . . . . $100–$130

J McCollick & Co New York, circular, IP, $11^1/2$", aqua . . . . $750+

J McCollick & Co New York, square, IP, $8^1/2$", deep greenish aqua . . . . . . $175–$225

Jesse H Lippincott Pittsburgh, Pa, peppersauce, four sided pyramid form, OP, $8^1/2$", aqua . . . . $35–$45

JM Clark & Co, Louisville, Ky, $5^1/4$", yellow amber. . . . . $60–$75

JM Clark & Co, Louisville, Ky, $6^7/8$", yellow amber. . . . . $60–$75

JM Clark & Co, Louisville, Ky, $8^1/2$", yellow amber. . . . . $75–$100

John Thomas Yonkers, NY, square wide mouthed jar, $6^1/2$", aqua . . . . $20–$30

John W Stout X New York, globular body, 6", aqua. . . . . $30–$40

Joseph Campbell, slug plate, crown top, clear, $8^3/8$" . . . . $15–$20

JP Smith & Co Pittsburgh, smooth base, quart, aqua . . . . $40–$60

JR, bell shaped bottle, OP, $6^1/2$", aqua . . . . $65–$90

Jumbo $10^1/2$" oz Peanut Butter, clear, pint . . . . $4–$6

Jumbo Brand 7 oz Net Peanut Butter, dated on base, clear . . . . $4–$7

JV Sharp Williamstown New Jersey, full label, $9^1/4$", aqua . . . . $150–$250

JVS (monogram), labeled, $9^1/4$", aqua. . . . . $80–$120

King's Flavoring Extract, clear, $6^3/4$". . . . . $3–$4

Labeled Pickle, square, no embossing, $10^1/2$", aqua . . . . $60–$85

Lansches Superior C Mustard, cylinder, OP, 5", aqua . . . . $30–$45

Lansdale & Bros (on panel), cathedral pickle, OP, $8^7/8$", aqua . . . . $450–$650

Lea & Perrins (vertically) Worcestershire Sauce, (around shoulder), aqua . . . $2–$3

Libby's Trademark Camp Sauce (on shoulder), clear paneled base ketchup, crown top . . . . $6–$9

Libby's Trademark Tomato Sauce (on shoulder), clear paneled base ketchup. . . . . $6–$9

Liberty Brand Celebrated Pickles Put up By E Edesheimer (on label), square, 9", aqua. . . . . $20–$25

M & GM (on base), round, ribbed, OP, 10", aqua . . . . $40–$65

Maple Sap & Boiled Cider Vinegar, cylinder, $11^3/8$", cobalt . . . . $650–$900

Marceau Spanish Olives (on label), clear barrel, $7^1/2$" . . . . $13–$17

Marcelin David (on seal), straight sided cylinder, OP, thinly made, $9^1/2$", aqua . . . . $175–$250

MB Espy Philada, square, $11^1/4$", medium teal blue. . . . . $200–$300

MB Espy, square, no "Phila" at base edge, IP, $8^7/8$", aqua . . . . $110–$145

Mellin's Food Co Boston USA Small Size Mellins Food, labeled, 5", aqua . . . . $25–$30

Mellin's Infant's Food Doliber Goodale Co Boston, round jar, aqua . . . . $3–$4

Milwaukee Pickle Co, Wauwatosa Wis, cylinder, $12^5/8$", orange amber . . $175–$245

Milwaukee Pickle Co, Wauwatosa Wis, cylinder, lip chip, $9^5/8$", orange amber . . . . $100–$140

Monadnock Brand Fancy Pickles, The Holbrook Grocery Co (on label), square, 11", aqua. . . . . $20–$30

Monticello Reckhow Preserving Co (on label), square, clear, tapered, $7^3/8$" . . . . $125–$175

Mrs Chapin's Mayonnaise, clear, pint . . . . $3–$4
New England Pickles Manufactured by Skilton Foote & Co (on label), clear, 11"
. . . . $25–$33
Newman's Pure Cold Extracts, clear, 5½" . . . . $1–$2
Old Reliable Tea Bags (on label), glass, tumbler, 8oz, 4½", red . . . . $15–$25
Old Style Mustard, clear, labeled, pint . . . . $5–$7
Peppersauce, cathedral, four sided, four fancy panels, OP, 7½", aqua . . . . . . $45–$70

Peppersauce, cathedral. PHOTO COURTESY OF GLASS WORKS
AUCTIONS.

Peppersauce, cathedral, four sided, four fancy panels, OP, 7½", medium green . . . . . .
. . . . $120–$165
Peppersauce, cathedral, four sided, four fancy panels, SB, 7½", aqua . . . . . . $12–$18
Peppersauce, cathedral, four sided, four fancy panels, SB, 7½", medium green . . . . . .
. . . . $90–$135
Peppersauce, cathedral, OP, 8¾", medium blue green . . . . $100–$135
Peppersauce, cathedral, OP, six sided, 8¾", light blue green . . . . $150–$200
Peppersauce, cathedral, six sided, six fancy panels, SB, 7½", aqua . . . . $25–$35
Peppersauce, cathedral, wide squared body like a pickle, SB, 10¼", aqua . . . $60–$85
Peppersauce, cathedral, wide squared body like a pickle, SB, 10¼", medium blue
green . . . . $160–$220
Peppersauce, thick horizontal rings from shoulder on down, SB, 7", deep aqua . . . . . .
. . . . $10–$17
Peppersauce, thick horizontal rings from shoulder on down, SB, 7", emerald green . . .
. . . . $25–$35
Pickle, cathedral, fleur de lis-like pattern in panels, 11¾", light green . . . . . $325–$425
Pickle, cathedral, four fancy panels, SB, 8½", aqua . . . . $65–$85
Pickle, cathedral, SB, leaf pattern outlines panels, four sided, 7½", aqua . . . . . $30–$45
Pickle, cathedral, six sided, five fancy panels, one plain, clear, SB, 8½" . . . . . $45–$75
Pickle, cathedral, six sided, five fancy panels, one plain, OP, 12½", aqua . . $125–$185
Pickle, cathedral, six sided, five fancy panels, one plain, SB, 12½", aqua . . . $80–$130
Pickle, cathedral, six sided, SB, full label, 13", light green . . . . $150–$225
Pickle, cathedral, six sided, WT & CO (on base), 13¼", golden amber . . . $800–$1200
Pickle, cathedral, square with chain decor on panel edges, IP, 11", light green . . . .
. . . . $250–$350

Pickle, cathedral, square with chain decor on panel edges, IP, 9", aqua . . . . $160–$220
Pickle, cathedral, square with chain decor on panel edges, SB, 11", aqua . . $125–$165
Pickle, cathedral, square with chain decor on panel edges, SB, 11", light green. . . . . . .
. . . . $135–$185
Pickle, cathedral, square, cross hatching in one panel, IP, 7$^1/_2$", emerald green . . . .
. . . . $600–$800
Pickle, cathedral, square, four fancy panels with cross hatching, IP, 12$^1/_2$", aqua. . . . . .
. . . . $140–$200
Pickle, cathedral, square, four fancy panels with cross hatching, OP, 12$^1/_2$", aqua. . . . .
. . . . $140–$200
Pickle, cathedral, square, four fancy panels with cross hatching, OP, 12$^1/_2$", emerald
green . . . . $800–$1200
Pickle, cathedral, square, four fancy panels with cross hatching, OP, 6$^1/_2$", aqua . . . . . .
. . . . $65–$95
Pickle, cathedral, square, four fancy panels with cross hatching, OP, 9$^1/_2$", aqua . . . . . .
. . . . $90–$145
Pickle, cathedral, square, four fancy panels with cross hatching, OP, 9$^1/_2$", emerald
green . . . . $700–$900
Pickle, cathedral, square, four fancy panels with cross hatching, SB, 12$^1/_2$", aqua. . . . .
. . . . $80–$130
Pickle, cathedral, square, four fancy panels with cross hatching, SB, 6$^1/_2$", aqua . . . . . .
. . . . $40–$45
Pickle, cathedral, square, four fancy panels with cross hatching, SB, 9$^1/_2$", emerald
green . . . . $550–$700
Pickle, cathedral, square, four fancy panels, IP, 12$^1/_2$", aqua. . . . . $125–$185
Pickle, cathedral, square, four fancy panels, IP, 9$^1/_2$", aqua. . . . . $115–$155
Pickle, cathedral, square, four fancy panels, OP, 11$^1/_2$", amber (rare color) . . . .
. . . . $10,000+
Pickle, cathedral, square, four fancy panels, OP, 8$^1/_2$", amber (rare color) . . . .
. . . . $3000–$4500
Pickle, cathedral, square, four fancy panels, OP, 9$^1/_2$", aqua. . . . . $115–$155
Pickle, cathedral, square, four fancy panels, SB, 12$^1/_2$", aqua . . . . $80–$110
Pickle, cathedral, square, four fancy panels, SB, 5$^1/_2$", aqua . . . . $35–$55
Pickle, cathedral, square, three fancy panels, one panel plain, OP, 11$^1/_2$", emerald green
. . . . $800–$1000
Pickle, cathedral, square, three fancy panels, one panel plain, OP, 6$^1/_2$", aqua . . . .
. . . . $80–$100
Pickle, cathedral, square, three fancy panels, one panel plain, OP, 8$^1/_2$", emerald green
. . . . $650–$900
Pickle, cathedral, square, three fancy panels, one panel plain, OP, 9$^1/_2$", aqua . . . .
. . . . $110–$150
Pickle, cathedral, square, three fancy panels, one unpatterned panel, OP, 9$^1/_2$", aqua. . .
. . . . $115–$155
Pickle, square, four unpatterned panels, SB, 8$^1/_2$", aqua . . . . $30–$40
Pickle, cathedral, square, four fancy panels, SB, 8$^1/_2$", aqua . . . . $65–$85
Pure Horse Radish HD Geer, Z-1661, square, 7", aqua . . . . $14–$17
Purity Oats, with flower, clear, screw cap jar, quart. $12–$15
Remember The Maine, milk glass jar, milk glass and tin screw cap, pint. . . . .
. . . . $140–$190
Richilieu Brand Mince Meat (on label), glaze stoneware jar, lid and wire, 8", brown
and tan. . . . . $25–$30

Rivera Brand Fruit Butter Distributed by Sears Roebuck (on label), stoneware jar, with lid, 7". $50
RJC (on one panel of six sided jar), OP, 6¹/₄", aqua . . . . $35–$45
RJC, six sided mustard jar, Z-66, OP, 6¹/₄", aqua . . . . $40–$55
Roanoke Pure Apple Cider Vinegar Co, cruet, clear, half pint . . . . $8–$12
Round Pickle, fluted shoulder, IP, 11¹/₄", aqua. . . . . $125–$175
Rowat's Superior Pickles in Pure Vinegar (on label), square, 9", yellow amber . . . .
. . . . $30–$35
Royal Mint Sauce HC Mfg Co Detroit, labeled, 6⁷/₈", bright green . . . . . . $100–$125
S & P Pat App For (on base), spiral ribbed pepper sauce, emerald green. . . . $30–$40
Sauers Extracts, clear, 6" . . . . $3–$5
Schmidt Patent, tapered cylinder, OP, 6", cobalt . . . . $90–$135
Shaker Brand Pickles ED Pettengill & Co (on label), square, 7¹/₄", amber. . . . .
. . . . $300–$400
Shaw's Huddersfield Relish, 8", deep aqua . . . . $8–$12
SJG, cathedral pickle, SB, 7¹/₄", aqua . . . . $65–$95
Skilton Foote & Co Bunker Hill Pickles, clear, 5¹/₄" . . . . $4–$7
Skilton Foote & Co Bunker Hill Pickles, lighthouse, Z376-3, 11¹/₄", light yellow
green . . . . $400–$500
Skilton Foote & Co Bunker Hill Pickles, lighthouse, Z376-3, 11¹/₄", medium amber .
. . . . $400–$500
Skilton Foote & Co Bunker Hill Pickles, square, 50% label, Z377, 6³/₄", amber. . . . .
. . . . $65–$85
Skilton Foote & Co Bunker Hill Pickles, square, SB, 6³/₄", yellow olive. . . . .
. . . . $100–$150
Skilton Foote & Co Bunker Hill Pickles, square, SB, labeled, 6³/₄", yellow olive. . . .
. . . . $200–$250
Skilton Foote & Co Bunker Hill Pickles, Z377, round, 5¹/₂", aqua. . . . . $25–$35
Skilton Foote & Co Bunker Hill Pickles, Z377, round, clear, 6¹/₂" . . . . $20–$30
Skilton Foote & Co Bunker Hill Pickles, Z377, square, 6³/₄", yellow amber. . . . .
. . . . $50–$75
Skilton Foote & Co Bunker Hill Pickles, Z378, cylinder, 7⁷/₈", olive yellow . . . .
. . . . $140–$190
Sol Wangenheim & Co, San Fran, square, beveled edges, 11¹/₄", aqua . . . . . $40–$55
CL Stickney, peppersauce, OP, 9", aqua . . . . $90–$125
Sunnyside Ketchup (on label only), clear, 9⁷/₈". . . . . $30–$40
Superior Pickles (on label only), six sided cathedral pickle, SB, 13", aqua . . . .
. . . . $70–$90
Superior Pickles Jekkies Katsups Etc. (on label), square, 8", aqua. . . . . $15–$20
Superior Pickles JP & D Plummer Boston Mass (on label), square pickle, 11", aqua
. . . . $20–$30
TA Bryan & Cos Perfection Tomato Sauce, 8¹/₄", yellow amber . . . . $175–$250
TB Smith & Co Philada, cathedral pickle, square, OP, 9¹/₄", aqua . . . . $300–$400
TB Smith & Co, Philada, cylinder, OP, 10⁵/₈", aqua . . . . $50–$75
TB Smith & Co, Philada, square, beveled edges, fluted shoulder, OP, 9¹/₄", aqua . . . .
. . . . $260–$360
TB Smith & Co., Philada, OP, half gallon, emerald green. . . . . $1000–$1500
Teitchell Champlin Cos Flavoring Extract, clear, 4¹/₂" . . . . $4–$6
Thompson & Taylor Root Beer Flavoring, clear, 4" . . . . $2–$4
Tourist Brand The Fee & Brown Co, clear, labeled, 11" . . . . $15–$25
Twin Hills Pickles (on label), on Kerr fruit jar, clear, quart. . . . . $5–$7

US Navy Mustard, sided, SB, 5$^1/_2$", aqua . . . . $50–$75

US Navy Pepper, sided, SB, 5$^1/_2$", aqua . . . . $50–$75

Valentine's Meat Juice, egg shape, 3", amber . . . . $4–$6

W & E, Z-433, square peppersauce, OP, 8$^7/_8$", aqua . . . . $150–$200

Waterford House Yorkshire Relish, 4$^1/_2$", aqua . . . . $7–$9

WDS NY, square pickle, OP, 7$^1/_2$", light apple green . . . . $250–$350

Welch's Grape Juice, clear, crown top . . . . $2–$3

Wellman Groceries Distributors (in circle), 7$^3/_4$", aqua . . . . $15–$25

Wellman Groceries Wellman Peck & Co Distributors, clear, round, 6". . . . $15–$20

Wells & Miller, Z428-1, square, unpatterned, OP, 6$^3/_8$", medium emerald green. . . . . .
. . . . $300–$400

Wells Miller & Provost (on flutes), peppersauce, OP, 9", aqua. . . . . $40–$55

Wells Miller & Provost (on shoulder), heavy ribbed peppersauce, OP, 8", medium
emerald green . . . . $300–$425

Wells Miller & Provost, Z428-2, square, fluted shoulders, IP, 11$^1/_2$", aqua. . . . .
. . . . $250–$375

Wendell & Espy Mince Meat, 152 So Front Philada, square, OP, 8", aqua . . . .
. . . . $300–$425

Wendell & Espy, on shoulder, Z434-top left, cylinder, OP, 9$^1/_2$", aqua . . . . . . $70–$95

White House Apple Vinegar, with pour spout, clear, gallon . . . . $40–$52

White House Apple Vinegar, with pour spout, quart, clear . . . . $25–$30

White House Brand Vinegar, with pour spout, clear. . . . . $40–$50

White House Brand Vinegar, with pour spout, clear, half gallon . . . . $12–$16

White House Brand Vinegar, with pour spout, clear, half pint . . . . $50–$60

White House Brand Vinegar, with pour spout, clear, pint. . . . . $12–$16

White House Brand Vinegar, with pour spout, clear, quart. . . . . $12–$16

White House Brand Vinegar, with pour spout, quart, light green . . . . $40–$45

White House Jug, without pour spout, clear, gallon . . . . $35–$45

White House Jug, without pour spout, clear, half gallon . . . . $15–$25

White House Jug, without pour spout, clear, pint . . . . $10–$14

White House Jug, without pour spout, clear, quart. $12–$18

White House Tusk Vinegar, clear, quart . . . . $15–$20

Wine Cured Pickles, Manhattan Pickle Co, clear, quart . . . . $4–$6

WK Lewis & Co (on shoulder), fluted body peppersauce, OP, 8", aqua . . . . . $40–$55

WKL & Co, Z-277-2, cathedral peppersauce, 10", aqua. . . . . $300–$425

WM & P NY (on shoulder), cylinder, OP, 6", aqua. $40–$50

WM & P NY (on shoulder), cylinder, OP, 8", aqua. $30–$42

WM & P NY, square pickle, wide ribbed corners, OP, 7$^3/_4$", aqua . . . . $60–$80

WM Underwood & Co (around base edge), peppersauce, 7$^1/_4$", emerald green . . . . .
. . . . $30–$35

Wm Underwood & Co, (embossed at bottom edge), fluted shoulder, OP, round, 11$^1/_2$"
x 4", aqua . . . . $300–$425

Wm Underwood & Co, (embossed at bottom edge), square, SB, 32 oz, 7$^1/_2$", aqua . . . .
. . . . $35–$50

Wm White Newport Garden, cylinder, OP, 11", aqua . . . . $40–$55

Worcestershire Sauce, (around shoulder), aqua . . . . $5–$7

World's Fair, 1939, (on banner across globular body), milk glass vinegar bottle . . . . .
. . . . $15–$25

FRUIT JARS

Due to the lack of refrigeration and the spoilage of foods, ways had to be found to store and preserve foods. The earliest food jars were not airtight and were made principally to keep the food moist and to prevent dirt and dust from mixing with the food. In the early 1800s, a Frenchman discovered a way to preserve food by enclosing it in an airtight container. The earliest fruit jars were free-blown vessels which were covered with a wax cloth or with a tightly fitting cork. In the mid 19th century, "wax sealer" jars led to jars with clamps and then screw threads.

The jars come in a wide variety of sizes, from as small as half pints to as large as five-gallon jars. Aqua and clear jars are fairly common, whereas jars made of milk glass, greens, blacks, blues or ambers are very rare. Jars with their original lids, covers, and metal bails can significantly add to the price and rarity. It is not uncommon to see replaced wire bails and other metal parts on jars. The reader is referred to *Red Book #7 on Fruit Jars* by Alice Creswick.

A & DH Chambers Union Fruit Jar, #580, quart, aqua . . . . $50–$75
A Kline, Pat'd Oct 27 1863, Use a Pin (on stopper), #1424, pint, aqua . . . . $20–$30
A Kline, Pat'd Oct 27 1863, Use a Pin (on stopper), #1428, side lugs, quart, aqua . . . . .
. . . . $20+
A Stone & Co Philada (in arch), #2750.1, two inner lugs, quart, aqua . . . . $475–$550
A Stone & Co Philada Manufactures by Cunninghams, IP, #2753, quart, aqua . . . .
. . . . $400+
A Stone & Co Philada, #2743, IP, wax sealer, quart, aqua . . . . $150–$250
A Stone & Co Philada, #2743, iron pontil, quart, aqua . . . . $100–$150
A Stone & Co Philada, #2744, wax sealer, pint, aqua . . . . $400–$500
A Stone & Co Philada, #2748.1, threaded glass stopper, pint, aqua . . . . $1200–$1600
A Stone & Co Philada, pint, aqua. . . . . $400–$500
ABC, #4.1, potstone crack, half gallon, aqua. . . . . $150–$200
ABC, #4.1, quart, aqua . . . . $200–$300
ABC, large letters, no periods between letters, #4, pint, aqua . . . . $225–$300
Absolutely Pure Milk, Milk Protector, clear, wire clamp, glass lid, pint . . . .
. . . . $500–$650
Ackers HG Registered Finley Acker & Co, stoneware. . . . . $75–$100
Acme (on shield), stars and stripes, #12, clear, half gallon . . . . $10–$12
Acme (on shield), stars and stripes, #12, clear, pint . . . . $2–$4
Acme (on shield), stars and stripes, #12, clear, quart . . . . $2–$4
Adlam Patent Boston Mass (on base), clear, metal cap, bail, half gallon . . . . $30–$45
Adler Progress (on base), #26, clear, quart . . . . $3–$5
AG Smalley & Co Boston (on base), #2644, quart, amber . . . . $35–$40
Agee Special, #37, no base mark, quart, amber. . . . . $25–$35
Agee, #29, quart, amber . . . . $20–$35

Air Tight Fruit Jar, #51, iron pontil, quart, aqua . . . . $400–$600

Air Tight Fruit Jar, #51, iron pontil, quart, deep aqua . . . . $400–$600

Airtight, #50, clear, quart . . . . $35–$45

All Right, #59, Pat'd Jan 26, 1868 (base), quart, light blue . . . . $125–$150

All Right, Patd Nov 26 1867, #59, repro lid, quart, light cornflower blue . . $150–$200

Allens, #57, original top, Pat'd June 1871 (on base), quart, aqua . . . . $150–$250

Allens, #57, repro top, Pat'd June 1871 (on base), quart, aqua . . . . $100–$150

Amazon Swift Seal, #69, clear, quart . . . . $8–$10

Amazon Swift Seal, #70, Pat'd July 14, 1908, clear, pint . . . . $8–$10

American (NAGCo), Porcelain Lined, #79, midget, aqua . . . . $125–$175

American Fruit Jar, Eagle and Flag, #73, quart, aqua . . . . $100–$150

American Malt Cream Co, 6", aqua. . . . . $8–$10

American NAG Co, #75, midget, aqua . . . . $125–$175

American NAG Co, #75, midget, greenish aqua . . . . $125–$175

Anchor Hocking (H in anchor) Mason, #81, clear, pint. . . . . $1–$1.5

Anchor Mason's Patent, #86, clear, quart . . . . $15–$20

ARS (fancy script), #94, quart, aqua . . . . $60–$75

ARS, #94, glass closure, quart, aqua . . . . $50–$65

Atherholt Fisher & Co Philada, #103, original Kline's stopper, quart, aqua . . . .
. . . . $400–$600

Atlas (clover) Good Luck, #130, clear, quart . . . . $2–$3

Atlas (clover), Good Luck, #130, clear, pint . . . . $2–$3

Atlas (HA in circle) Mason, #134, clear, half gallon . . . . $2–$4

Atlas EZ Seal, #109, amber swirled, half gallon, olive green . . . . $30–$40

Atlas EZ Seal, #109, clear, half gallon . . . . $2–$3

Atlas EZ Seal, #109, half gallon, aqua . . . . $2–$3

Atlas EZ Seal, #109, half gallon, cornflower blue. . . . . $30–$40

Atlas EZ Seal, #109, quart, apple green . . . . $6–$8

Atlas EZ Seal, #109, quart, aqua . . . . $2–$3

Atlas EZ Seal, #109, quart, cornflower blue . . . . $20–$25

Atlas EZ Seal, #111, quart, amber. . . . . $20–$24

Atlas EZ Seal, #116, squatty, pint, green. . . . . $10–$12

Atlas EZ Seal, #117, pint, light green . . . . $10–$12

Atlas EZ Seal, #124, quart, aqua . . . . $8–$12

Atlas EZ Seal, Atlas Trademark Red (on base), #118, half pint, aqua . . . . $8–$10

Atlas EZ Seal, bell shaped, lip flakes, pint, aqua. . . . . $3–$4

Atlas HA EZ Seal, #132, quart, clear . . . . $4–$6

Atlas HA Mason, #133, mini bank, clear . . . . $8–$12

Atlas Mason (non-serrified lettering), #141, quart, aqua . . . . $4–$5

Atlas Mason (serrified lettering), #140, quart, aqua . . . . $4–$5

Atlas Mason, #161, pint, apple green . . . . $5–$6

Atlas Mason, #161, quart, cornflower blue . . . . $11–$18

Atlas Masons, Patent Nov 30 1858, #154, half gallon, medium green . . . . $6–$7

Atlas Masons, Patent Nov 30 1858, #154, half gallon, aqua. . . . . $6–$7

Atlas Masons, Patent, #150, pint, aqua . . . . $3–$5

Atlas Masons, Patent, #150, pint, aqua . . . . $2–$4

Atlas Masons, Patent, #150, quart, aqua . . . . $1–$2

Atlas Special Mason, #158, half gallon, aqua. . . . . $7–$9

Atlas Special Mason, #158, quart, greenish aqua . . . . $6–$8

Atlas Strong Shoulder Mason, #162, clear, pint . . . . $1–$2

Atlas Strong Shoulder Mason, #162.1, mini bank, clear. . . . . $15–$25

Atlas Strong Shoulder Mason, #163, pint, aqua .... $1–$2
Atlas Strong Shoulder Mason, #164, half gallon, cornflower blue .... $12–$15
Atlas Strong Shoulder Mason, #164, pint, cornflower blue............... $15–$25
Atlas Strong Shoulder Mason, #164, quart, aqua .... $1–$2
Atlas Strong Shoulder Mason, #164, quart, light cobalt blue .... $125–$175
Atlas Whole Fruit, #170, clear, half gallon........................... $7–$9
Atlas Whole Fruit, #170, clear, pint .... $1–$3
Atlas Whole Fruit, #170, clear, quart .... $1–$3
Automatic Sealer, Clayton Bottle (on base), #177, half gallon, aqua..... $120–$150
Baker Bros & Co Baltimore Md (on base), #196, half gallon, aqua........ $30–$40
Ball (script) Masons, Patent Nov 30th 1858, quart, aqua .... $4–$6
Ball (Stippled Lettering), ribbed, clear, modern jar, quart............... $2–$3
Ball (Three L Loop), #191, half gallon, aqua .... $2–$4
Ball (Three L Loop), #191, quart, aqua .... $1–$2
Ball (Three L Loop), #191, quart, olive green .... $50–$75
Ball (Three L Loop), #191, quart, olive green .... $50–$75
Ball Deluxe Jar, #199, clear, quart .... $5–$7
Ball Eclipse Wide Mouth, #202, clear, quart .... $1–$3
Ball Eclipse, #200, clear, pint .... $2–$4
Ball Eclipse, #200, clear, quart .... $2–$4
Ball Freezer Jar, #207.1, clear, pint .... $1–$3
Ball Home Canning, William H Hannah, modern, quart, teal green ...... $75–$100
Ball Ideal, #208, clear, half gallon.................................. $1–$3
Ball Ideal, #209, square, half gallon, light blue....................... $3–$6
Ball Ideal, Edmund A Ball (in medallion), #242, modern, quart, aqua...... $35–$50
Ball Ideal, Pat'd July 14, 1908, #218, clear, pint .... $1.5–$2.5
Ball Ideal, Pat'd July 14, 1908 (all on front), #220, pint .... $1.5–$2.5
Ball Ideal, Pat'd July 14, 1908, #218, clear, half gallon .... $1.5–$2.5
Ball Ideal, The Fischer Years, (man's bust), clear, modern, quart .... $35–$50
Ball Improved, #246, pint, aqua .... $3–$4
Ball Jar Masons, Patent 1858, #269, half gallon, aqua.................... $8–$12
Ball Mason (3 L Loop), #280, half gallon, aqua......................... $2–$4
Ball Mason (Three L Loop), #279.4, quart, aqua........................ $2–$4
Ball Mason (Three L Loop), #280, clear, quart .... $7–$12
Ball Mason (Three L Loop), #280, half gallon, aqua..................... $2–$4
Ball Mason (Three L Loop), #280, pint, aqua .... $2–$4
Ball Mason, #290, no crossbar on A, pint, greenish aqua .... $6–$9
Ball Mason, #290, no crossbar on A, quart, aqua .... $6–$9
Ball Mason, beaded neck, #279, quart, aqua........................... $1–$2
Ball Mason, sipper, unthreaded, clear, metal handle .... $6–$9
Ball Masons, Patent 1858, #305, quart, aqua........................... $5–$6
Ball Masons, Patent, #303, beaded neck, clear, quart .... $4–$5
Ball Perfect Mason, #339, beaded neck seal, quart, aqua................. $1–$3
Ball Perfect Mason, #339, beaded neck seal, quart, olive green............ $45–$55
Ball Perfect Mason, #340, round, eight ribs, quart, aqua .... $6–$8
Ball Perfect Mason, #356, no crossbar on A, pint, aqua................. $6–$9
Ball Perfect Mason, #356, no crossbar on A, quart, aqua................ $6–$9
Ball Perfect Mason, square, quart, aqua .... $5–$6
Ball Sanitary Sure Seal, #369, no base date, quart, aqua................. $10–$15
Ball Special, #372, half gallon, aqua .... $12–$15
Ball Special, Made in USA, #375, clear, gripper ribs, quart .... $2–$3

Ball Standard, #385, clear, quart. . . . . $15–$25
Ball Standard, RG Simpson, 1952–1982, clear, new, quart . . . . $40–$50
Ball Sure Seal, Packed in St Johnsbury, #395, aqua . . . . $30–$40
Ball Sure Seal, Pat'd July 14, 08 (on base), #394, pint, aqua . . . . $20–$30
Ball, #191, quart, clambroth aquamarine . . . . $100–$125
Banner (encircled by), Patd Feb 9th 1864, quart, aqua . . . . $125–$175
Battleship Maine Mustard Jar, #3086, clear, original, tin and glass lid. . . . $90–$135
Battleship Maine Mustard Jar, #3086, milk glass, tin and glass lid. . . . . . $250–$300
BBGM Co (monogram), #195-1, quart, aqua. . . . . $50–$90
BBGM Co, #195, midget, aqua . . . . $375–$475
BBGM Co, #195-1, quart, golden amber. . . . . $3000–$5000
BBGM Co, #196, half pint, aqua . . . . $300–$500
Beaver, #424, midget, pint, aqua . . . . $50–$75
Beaver, #424, quart, golden amber . . . . $400–$550
Bee Hive, #433, midget, clear, pint . . . . $400–$500
Bell Shaped, wax sealer, #3061, quart, ice blue . . . . $250–$350
Belle, Pat'd Dec 14 1869, #438, quart, aqua. . . . . $750–$1000
Bennett's No 2, #446, backward two, original clear lid, quart, aqua. . . . . $1000–$1500
Benton Myers & Co Cleveland Ohio (on base), #450, clear, half gallon. . . . . $9–$12
Best Fruit Keeper, #460, quart, aqua . . . . $30–$40
Best Fruit Keeper, Pat May 5 1896 (on lid), quart, aqua . . . . $30–$40
Best, #453, original amber insert, quart, root beer amber . . . . $250–$350
Bloesser Jar, #468, correct lid and wire, quart, aqua. . . . . $350–$500
Bloesser Jar, #468, quart, aqua . . . . $200–$250
Bloesser, #467.1, quart, aqua . . . . $350–$450
Blown in Two Piece Mold, folded lip, OP, 5³/₄", medium blue . . . . $250–$350
Bostwick Perfect Seal (in script), #487, clear, quart . . . . $40–$50
Boyd Mason (Mason in banner over faint Genuine), #491, clear, half gallon . . . . . .
. . . . $8–$10
Boyd Perfect (error jar), #502, half gallon, aqua. . . . . $5–$10
Boyd Perfect Mason, #500, quart, aqua . . . . $5–$6
Boyd Perfect Mason, Non-slanted lettering, quart, greenish aqua . . . . $6–$7
Braun Safety Mason, #508, clear, pint . . . . $6–$8
Brighton, Clamp, Pat March 30 (on lid), #512, clear, repro lid, pint . . . . $60–$70
Brighton, Clamp, Pat March 30 (on lid), #512, clear, original lid, pint . . . . $125–$160
Brockway Clear Vu Mason, #514, clear, quart. . . . . $0.5–$1
Brockway Sur Grip Mason, #514, clear, quart . . . . $0.75–$1.25
Brockway Sur Grip Mason, #515, clear, half gallon. . . . . $5–$8
Brockway Sur Grip Mason, #515, clear, pint . . . . $2–$3
Brockway Sur Grip Mason, #515, clear, quart . . . . $0.75–$1.25
Buck Glass Co (on lid), clear, quart . . . . $4–$5
Buckeye 1, #528, clamp missing, quart, aqua . . . . $50–$60
Buckeye 3, #528, correct Adams glass lid, repro metal yoke, quart, aqua. . . . .
. . . . $150–$200
Buckeye, #527, repro clamp, quart, aqua. . . . . $175–$225
Burns Mfg Co Limt North East Pa Pat'd . . ., quart, aqua. . . . . $300–$500
C Burnham & Co Manufacturers, #544, quart. . . . . $750–$1000
Calcutts Patent Apr 11th (on cap), #549, clear, quart. . . . . $30–$35
Canadian Jewel Made in Canada, #1331, clear, pint . . . . $2–$3
Canadian Jewel Made in Canada, #1331, clear, quart . . . . $2–$3
Canadian Mason Jar Made in Canada, #556, clear, pint . . . . $0.75–$1

Canton Domestic Fruit Jar, #565, clear, original clamp, quart . . . . $100–$125
Canton Domestic Fruit Jar, #565, clear, original lid, quart. . . . . $70–$80
Canton Electric Fruit Jar, #568, half gallon, medium cobalt . . . . $4000+
CF Spencers Improved Jar, #2685, quart, aqua . . . . $250–$350
CF Spencers Pat 1868 Improved, #2685, repro metal lid . . . . $150–$200
CF Spencers Patent Rochester NY, #2682, repro lid, quart, aqua . . . . $70–$95
CF Spencers Patent Rochester NY, #2682, repro lid, two quarts, aqua . . . . . $70–$95
Champion Pat Aug 31, 1869, #583, no lid, repro clamp . . . . $100–$150
Champion Pat Aug 31, 1869, #583, original lid and clamp . . . . $150–$225
Chas M Higgins & Co, Brooklyn, NY, clear, screw cap, 3oz . . . . $3–$4
Chef (in frame), Berdan & Co, #589, pint, aqua . . . . $5–$7
Chef (in frame), Berdan & Co, #589, quart, aqua . . . . $5–$7
Chicago Fruit Jar, #592, quart, aqua . . . . $250–$350
Chief, The, #594, original tin lid, half gallon, deep aqua . . . . $250–$325
Clarks Peerless, #605, half gallon, aqua . . . . $12–$15
Clarks Peerless, #605, pint, aqua . . . . $5–$7
Clarks Peerless, #605, quart, aqua . . . . $5–$7
Clyde Mason's Improved, #622, clear, quart . . . . $12–$15
Cohansey Glass Mfg Co Mould #2 (on base), #625, pint, amber . . . . $22–$26
Cohansey Glass Mfg Co Pat Feb 12 1867 (on base), #630, lid, 1.5 quart, aqua . . . . . .
. . . . $60–$90
Cohansey Glass Mfg Co Pat Feb 12 1867 (on base), #630, metal lid, pint, aqua . . . . .
. . . . $50–$65
Cohansey Glass Mfg Co Pat Mch 20 77 (on base), #633.1, barrel, quart, aqua . . . . . .
. . . . $100–$150
Cohansey Glass Mfg, #631, pint, aqua . . . . $100–$125
Cohansey, #628, original glass lid, wire clamp, pint, aqua . . . . $60–$90
Cohansey, #628, quart, aqua . . . . $20–$25
Cohansey, slug plate on reverse, half pint . . . . $80–$110
Cohansey, slug plate on reverse, pint. . . . . $20–$35
Columbia, #641, clear, pint . . . . $18–$24
Columbia, #641, quart, aqua . . . . $18–$24
Commodore, #646, original lid, quart, aqua . . . . $1500+
Common Sense Jar, #648, with original yoke clamp, quart, aqua . . . . $800+
Conserve Jar, #652, clear, half gallon. . . . . $12–$16
Conserve Jar, #652, clear, pint . . . . $4–$5
Conserve Jar, #652, clear, quart . . . . $4–$5
CPU (on milk glass lid), #660, clear, quart. . . . . $12–$16
Crown Cordial and Extract Co New York, #671, half gallon, aqua . . . . $9–$11
Crown Crown, (ring crown), #680, half gallon, aqua. $13–$17
Crown Crown, (ring crown), #680, quart, aqua . . . . $10–$13
Crown Emblem, (tall and slim version), #682, midget, aqua . . . . $30–$35
Crown Mason, #703, clear, pint . . . . $3–$5
Crown Mason, #711, clear, pint . . . . $12–$15
Crown, #675, midget, pint, greenish aqua . . . . $20–$30
Crown, (crown, no dot crown variety), quart, aqua. . . . . $12–$15
Crown, (no dot crown variety), #672, quart, aqua . . . . $12–$15
Crown, (no dot crown variety), midget, aqua . . . . $325–$375
Crown, (with E in diamond, over Toronto), #698, clear, pint . . . . $7–$9
Crystal, #705, Pat Nov 26 67/ Pat Feb 4 1873 (base), quart, aqua . . . . $60–$90
Cunningham & Co Pittsburgh Pa (on base), IP, quart, medium sapphire . . . . $2000+

Cunningham & Co Pittsburgh Pa (on base), pint, aqua.............. $140–$180
Cunningham & Ihmsen Pittsburgh Pa (on base), #729, quart, yellow amber.......
.... $150–$200
Curtice & Moore Trade Mark Boston, #733, clear jar, two quart........ $20–$25
Daisy Fe Ward & Co, #762, pint, aqua.............................. $8–$10
Daisy Fe Ward & Co, #762, quart, aqua............................ $8–$10
Daisy Fe Ward (in circle), #744, quart, aqua........................ $8–$12
Daisy Jar, #745, clear, original clamp, quart....................... $140–$180
Daisy Jar, #745, clear, repro clamp, quart........................ $100–$130
Dexter (fruit), #775, quart, aqua................................. $50–$80
Dexter, #772, quart, aqua...................................... $25–$30
Diamond Form Embossed on Side, #781, half gallon, aqua.............. $18–$23
Diamond Fruit Jar Improved Trademark, #778, clear, pint............ $1.5–$2.5
Diamond Fruit Jar Improved Trademark, #778, clear, quart........... $1.5–$2.5
Diamond Symbol (on front), #781, mideget, aqua..................... $25–$30
Dictator, 1869, Patented DI Holcomb, #783, quart, aqua.................. $55–$75
DOC (on base), #795, olive tone, half gallon, medium yellow........... $150–$175
Dodge Sweeney & Co California Butter, #796, quart, aqua.............. $40–$60
Dodge Sweeney & Co California Butter, #796, quart, blue aqua.......... $40–$60
Doolittle (block letters), #809, quart, aqua........................... $35–$45
Doolittle (script), #811, clear, pint................................. $30–$40
Doolittle Self Sealer, GJ Co (on base), #813, original lid, pint, aqua..... $300–$375
Double Safety, SKO (on base), #815, clear, pint...................... $3–$5
Double Safety, SKO (on base), #815, clear, quart..................... $3–$5
Drey (in script) Mason, #839, clear, quart.......................... $1–$2
Drey Improved Ever Seal Patd (on neck), clear, pint.................. $6–$7
Drey Improved Ever Seal, #835, clear, quart........................ $5–$6
Drey Improved Ever Seal, #838, clear, half gallon..................... $4–$7
Drey Improved Ever Seal, #838, clear, quart........................ $1.5–$2.5
Drey Improved Ever Seal, Pat Sept 7 1920 (reverse), #836, clear, pint...... $5–$10
Drey Improved Ever Seal, Pat Sept 7 1920 (reverse), #836, clear, quart..... $5–$10
Drey Mason (long underline), #839, clear, quart...................... $3–$5
Drey Pat'd 1920 Improved Ever Seal, #834, clear, glass "ears," pint........ $8–$12
Drey Pat'd 1920 Improved Ever Seal, #834, clear, quart................. $4–$5
Drey Square Mason, in carpenter's square, #847, clear, quart.............. $2–$4
Dunkley (on base), #855, clear, pint............................... $6–$9
Eagle Mason (on both sides), clear, modern, quart..................... $2–$4
Eagle Patd Dec 28th 1858, #873, quart, aqua........................ $150–$200
Eagle, #874, with patent date, original lid and yoke, quart, aqua......... $150–$200
Eagle, #874, with patent date, original lid and yoke, two quart, aqua..... $150–$225
EC Hazard & Co Shrewsbury NJ (on base), #1220, clear, quart.......... $10–$12
Eclipse, The, #884, quart, aqua................................... $90–$125
Economy (underlined) TM Portland Ore (base), #885, clear, quart........ $2–$3
EGC Imperial, with circle, quart, aqua............................ $18–$21
EGC Imperial, without circle, quart, aqua.......................... $18–$21
EHE 7 (on heel), SK & Co (on base), quart, aqua...................... $3–$4
Electric (script, in circle), #916, pint, aqua........................ $10–$14
Electric Fruit Jar (around globe), #921, original clamp, pint, aqua..... $150–$200
Electric Fruit Jar (around globe), #921, repro clamp, quart, aqua....... $110–$150
Electric Fruit Jar (around globe), #921, repro clamp, two quart, aqua... $110–$150
Empire (with stippled cross, in frame), #925, clear, pint................ $4–$6

Empire (with stippled cross, in frame), #925, clear, quart . . . . $7–$8
Empire (with stippled cross, in frame), #925, clear, two quart. . . . . $10–$15
Empire, The, #927, glass closure and yoke, quart, aqua . . . . $100–$150
Empire, The, clear, pint . . . . $25–$35
Empire, The, patent date on base, repro clamp, quart, greenish aqua . . . . $75–$90
Eureka (in script on jar side), #947, clear, half pint . . . . $25–$35
Eureka (script), #947, clear, half pint . . . . $25–$35
Eureka 6 Patd Dec 27th 1864, #948, original tin lid, quart, aqua . . . . $100–$150
Eureka Pat'd Dec 27 1864, #948, original tin closure, quart, aqua . . . . $135–$160
Eureka Pat'd Dec 27 1864, #948, original tin lid, quart, aqua . . . . $135–$160
Eureka Pat'd Dec 27 1864, #948, repro closure, 1.5 quart, aqua . . . . $60–$80
Eureka Pat'd Dec 27 1864, #948, repro closure, 1.5 quart, aqua . . . . $60–$80
Eureka Pat'd Dec 27 1864, #948, repro closure, quart, aqua . . . . $60–$80
Eureka Pat'd Dec 27 1864, #948, repro closure, quart, aqua . . . . $65–$80
Eureka Pat'd Dec 27 1864, #948, repro closure, two quart, aqua. . . . . $65–$80
Eureka Pat'd Dec 27 1864, #948, repro closure, two quart, aqua. . . . . $60–$80
Eureka, #945, clear, pint . . . . $8–$10
Excelsior Improved (in two straight lines), #959, two quart, aqua. . . . . $35–$45
Excelsior Improved (in two straight lines), #959, two quart, greenish aqua . . . .
. . . . $35–$45
Excelsior, milk bottle shaped, #956, quart, aqua . . . . $250–$300
Excelsior, Pat'd Aug 3 1858 (on lid), #958, two quart, greenish aqua. . . . . . $40–$50
Exwaco (on base), #965, pint, amber. . . . . $25–$30
Exwaco (on base), #965, pint, emerald green . . . . $20–$30
EZ Seal (no Atlas), EZ Seal Reg (on base), quart, aqua . . . . $12–$15
F & J Bodine Manufacturers, Phila, #473, original lid, quart, aqua. . . . . . $125–$175
F & J Bodine Manufacturers, Phila, #473, repro lid, quart, aqua. . . . . $100–$150
F & S (in circle), #1043, pint, aqua . . . . $18–$23
F & S (in circle), #1043, quart, aqua . . . . $18–$20
Family Fruit Jar, #975, clear, original lid, quart . . . . $250–$350
Farley Chicago, #978, clear, quart . . . . $4–$5
Farley, squat, clear, metal screw cap, pint . . . . $4–$5
Farm Family (on lid), clear, round, pint . . . . $8–$10
FB Co / 2 (on base), #987, wax sealer, quart, yellow amber. . . . . $100–$150
FCG Co 1 (on base), #988, half gallon, citron . . . . $200–$250
Flaccus Bros (steer head) Wheeling W Va, #1006, clear, quart . . . . $75–$100
Flaccus Bros Mustard Fruit Jar, #1011, clear, no cover, pint . . . . $75–$110
Flaccus Bros Steers Head Fruit Jar, #1012, clear, pint . . . . $100–$125
Flaccus Bros Steers Head Fruit Jar, #1013, milk glass, pint . . . . $200–$250
Flaccus Bros Steers Head Fruit Jar, #1014, clear, pint . . . . $40–$50
Flaccus Bros Steers Head Fruit Jar, #1014, milk glass, pint . . . . $200–$350
Flaccus Bros Steers Head Fruit Jar, #1014, pint, yellow amber . . . . $250–$350
Flaccus Bros Steers Head Fruit Jar, #1014, screw on lid, pint, yellow . . . $300–$450
Flaccus Bros Steers Head Fruit Jar, clear, pint . . . . $75–$125
Flaccus type, vines and fancy decoration, milk glass, half pint. . . . . $13–$16
Flaccus type, vines and fancy decoration, milk glass, half pint, blue . . . . $30–$35
Foster Sealfast, Foster (on base), #2580, clear, half pint. . . . . $6–$8
Franklin Fruit Jar, #1033, clear, quart. . . . . $50–$70
Freeblown, cylinder, rolled lip, OP, 6½", light sapphire blue . . . . $2000–$3000
Freeblown, cylinder, wax sealer mouth, OP, 10", medium blue . . . . $2000–$3500
Fresherator (in rectangle), #1037.5, clear, squat, pint. . . . . $6–$8

Fridley & Cormans Ladies Choice, #1038, original iron rim, pint, aqua . . . .
. . . . $800–$1200
From Your Friends at Ball, John W Erichson, clear, pint . . . . $15–$20
Fruit Commonwealth Jar, #650, clear, 1.5 quart. . . . . $100–$140
Fruit Commonwealth Jar, #650, clear, quart. . . . . $100–$140
Fruitkeeper GCCo, #1042, quart, greenish aqua . . . . $35–$40
Fruitkeeper GCCo, #1042, two quart, greenish aqua. . . . . $40–$45
G & D (on base), #1044, quart, aqua. . . . . $25–$35
Gayner Glass Top, #1049, clear, pint . . . . $7–$9
Gem (cross), #1059, midget, aqua . . . . $40–$45
Gem (in arch), #1058.1, midget, aqua. . . . . $20–$35
Gem (on 1 line), #1053, one base date, quart, aqua. . . . . $6–$8
Gem (on 1 line), #1054, more than one base date, quart, aqua . . . . $4–$6
Gem CFJ Co, quart, aqua . . . . $6–$8
Gem, #1053, midget, aqua . . . . $25–$30
Gem, hourglass on reverse, #1057, half gallon, aqua. . . . . $16–$22
Gem, hourglass on reverse, #1057, quart, aqua . . . . $16–$22
Genuine Mason (Mason in flag), #1103, quart, apple green . . . . $4–$6
Geo D Brown, #525, clear, repro clamp, half gallon. . . . . $35–$45
Geo D Brown, #525, clear, repro clamp, pint . . . . $35–$45
Geo D Brown, #525, clear, repro clamp, quart . . . . $35–$45
Gilberd's (star) Improved Jar, #1108, original glass lid, quart, aqua. . . . . $200–$300
Gilberd's (star) Improved Jar, #1108, wire clamp, quart, aqua . . . . $100–$145
Gilberd's (star), #1107, original lid (rare), quart, aqua. . . . . $250–$350
GJ Co, #1109, large engraved lid, pint, aqua. . . . . $30–$35
Glassboro Trade Mark Improved, #1114, pint, aqua. . . . . $12–$16
Glenshaw G Mason, #1122, clear, pint. . . . . $3–$6
Globe, #1123, quart, aqua. . . . . $11–$15
Globe, Patented May 25, 1886 (on lid), #1123, pint, amber . . . . $48–$55
Globe, Patented May 25, 1886 (on lid), #1123, pint, aqua . . . . $19–$24
Globe, Patented May 25, 1886 (on lid), #1123, quart, amber . . . . $55–$60
Globe, Patented May 25, 1886 (on lid), #1123, quart, aqua . . . . $11–$15
Globe-shaped Jar, clear, screw cap, pint . . . . $4–$5
Gold Brand Pure Leaf Lard, #1129, quart, aqua. $55–$65
Good House Keepers Mason, #1142, clear, quart . . . . $6–$8
Great Eastern Philada Whitehead, #1150, glass stopper, quart, aqua . . . .
. . . . $1300–$1800
Green Mountain CA Co (in frame), #1151, clear, pint. . . . . $10–$15
Green Mountain CA Co (in frame), #1151, clear, quart. . . . . $10–$15
Green Mountain CA Co (in frame), #1152, clear, half gallon . . . . $16–$24
Green Mountain CA Co (in frame), #1152, clear, pint. . . . . $16–$20
Green Mountain, #1152, pint, light aqua . . . . $10–$13
Griffens Patent Oct 7 1862, #1154, half gallon, aqua . . . . $100–$150
Griswold's Patent 1862, #1156, amethyst tint, light clambroth. . . . . $1500+
Hamilton, #1188, clear, quart . . . . $50–$70
Hamilton, #1188, Patd Feb 1886 (on lid), clear, pint . . . . $40–$60
Hansees PH Palce Home Jar, #1206, clear, pint . . . . $90–$110
Hartell & Letchworth (on metal cap), #1213, half gallon, aqua. . . . . $100–$150
Hartell-Letchworth Patent 1866, #1213, repro lid, quart, aqua . . . . $65–$80
Hartell-Letchworth Patent 1866, #1213, repro lid, two quart, aqua . . . . $65–$80
Hartells Glass Air Tight Cove (on lid), #1211, pint, aqua. . . . . $50–$75

Hartells, #1211, quart, greenish aqua .... $40–$50
Harvest Mason, #1215, clear, quart ..../............................ $7–$8
Haserot Company Cleveland Mason, #1216, quart, aqua................. $7–$9
Hazel (on metal lid), #1226, quart, amber......................... $45–$60
Hazel Atlas EZ Seal, #1227, quart, aqua........................... $10–$14
Hazel Atlas Lightning Seal, #1228, pint, aqua...................... $10–$15
Hazel Atlas Lightning Seal, #1228, quart, aqua.................... $10–$15
Hazel HA Preserve Jar, #1231, clear, pint......................... $4–$6
Heinz, with star design inside (on base), clear, oval, half pint .... $12–$15
Helmes Railroad Mills, #1235, pint, amber .... $18–$21
Hereo Improved, #1246, quart, aqua .... $20–$25
Hereo Improved, #1246, two quart, aqua........................... $20–$25
Hero (above cross), #1240, quart, deep aqua .... $35–$50
Hero (cross), #1240, quart, aqua .... $30–$35
Hero (cross), #1241, pint, aqua .... $17–$20
Hero (cross), #1241, quart, aqua .... $25–$30
Hero, multiple patent dates on base, #1244, quart, aqua .... $45–$55
Hero, multiple patent dates on base, #1244, two quart, aqua......... $45–$55
Hero, The, #1244, quart, aqua .... $30–$35
Heroine, #1248, tin insert, quart, aqua........................... $45–$55
Heroine, The, #1248, quart, aqua .... $30–$35
Hiltons Pat Mar 10th 1868, #1256, repro clamp, quart, aqua .... $750+
HJ Heinz Co Pickling & Preserve Works, #1234, stoneware, 5" x 6" .... $120–$150
HJH Co Patd (on base), four sides, clear, ABM, half pint................. $3–$4
HK Mulford Chemists Philadelphia, #2215, pint, amber .... $25–$35
Holmegaard (on base), clear, Dansig, quart .... $9–$12
Holt-Lyon Jar Cream Whip Mayonnaise Mixer, #1258.1, metal beater, pint, aqua..
.... $200+
Honest Mason Jar Patent 1858, #1264, clear, pint .... $15–$18
Howe Jar, Scranton, Pa, #1274, pint, aqua .... $40–$60
Howe Jar, The, Scranton, Pa, #1274, original glass lid, bail, quart, aqua.... $30–$40
HW Petit Salem NJ (on base), #2363, two quart, aqua .... $10–$13
HW Petit Westville NJ (on base), #2362, pint, aqua................ $9–$12
HW Petit Westville NJ (on base), #2362, quart, aqua............... $12–$15
HW Petit Westville NJ (on base), #2362, two quart, aqua............ $12–$15
HW Petit, #2362, Westville NJ (base), pint, cornflower blue .... $35–$50
Ideal, C & E Co Monogram, no lid, quart, light green .... $7–$9
Imperial Pat April 20th 1886, #1293, clear, pint................. $150–$200
Improved (Keystone), #1299, half gallon, aqua..................... $25–$35
Improved (Keystone), #1299, pint, aqua .... $20–$23
Improved (Keystone), #1299, quart, aqua .... $15–$23
Improved Gem Made in Canada, #1094, clear, pint................... $1.5–$2.5
Improved Gem Made in Canada, #1094, clear, quart.................. $1.5–$2.5
Improved Mason Jar, #1305, clear, pint .... $4–$6
Independent Jar, #1308, clear midget .... $40–$50
J & B (within octagon) Fruit Jar, #1321, original lid, quart, aqua ...... $75–$95
J & B (within octagon) Fruit Jar, #1321, repro lid, quart, aqua .... $35–$40
J & B (within octagon), Fruit Jar, #1321, repro lid, pint, aqua............ $35–$40
J & B Fruit Jar Pat'd June 14th 1898, #1321, pint, aqua .... $60–$75
J & B Fruit Jar Pat'd June 14th 1898, #1321, quart, aqua.......... $50–$65
J & B Fruit Jar, #1321, repro lid, pint, aqua .... $40–$50

JC Baker's Patent Aug 14 1860, #188, repro clamp, quart, pale blue green . . $150–$250

JC Baker's Patent Aug 14 1860, #188, stained, no clamp, quart, deep aqua. . . $75–$100

JC Leffert's Patented Feby 15th 1859, #1470.1, iron, no lid, quart . . . . . . $200–$300

JD Willoughby Patd Jan 4, 1859 (on repro stopper), quart, aqua . . . . $40–$50

JD Willoughby Patd Jan 4, 1859, #3016, proper stopper, quart, aqua . . . . $140–$175

JE Taylor & Co Pure Food (in circle), #2787, quart, aqua . . . . $17–$21

Jeannette J (in square) Mason Home Packer, #1324, clear, quart. . . . . $2–$3

Jewell Jar Made in Canada, #1328, clear, half gallon. . . . . $8–$10

Jewell Jar Made in Canada, #1328, clear, quart. $2.5–$4

JFG Products, #1333, clear, figural globe, pint . . . . $10–$12

John M Moore & Co Patd 1861 (on front), #2206, small mouth, quart, deep aqua . . .

. . . . $300+

Johnson & Johnson New Brunswick NJ USA, half pint, amber . . . . $9–$12

Johnson & Johnson New York, square, 5½", cobalt. . . . . $30–$35

Johnson & Johnson New York, square, quart, amber . . . . $9–$11

Johnson & Johnson, #1340, quart, amber. . . . . $12–$15

Jos Middleby Jr Inc, #2175, clear, two quart . . . . $6–$8

Joshua Wright, Philada, #3035, IP, two quart, aqua . . . . $300–$400

KC Finest Quality Mason, #1354, clear, quart. . . . . $5–$6

KERR Self Sealing Mason, 65th anniversary, #1387, clear, quart, blue streak . $30–$35

KERR Self Sealing Wide Mouth, clear, modern jar, half pint. . . . . $2–$3

KERR Self Sealing Wide Mouth, modern jar, quart, light green. . . . . $5–$6

KERR Self Sealing, #1370, clear, quart . . . . $2–$3

Kilner Jar Improved Regd, #1409, clear, quart. . . . . $8–$12

Kilner Jar, No Regd, #1407, clear, quart . . . . $8–$12

King (on banner below crown), #1414, clear, pint . . . . $8–$10

King (on banner below crown), #1414, clear, quart . . . . $8–$10

Kinsella 1874 True Mason, #1421, clear, quart . . . . $5–$7

Kline, #1423, quart. . . . . $18–$25

Knowlton Vacuum (star) Fruit Jar, #1432, quart, aqua . . . . $15–$25

Knowlton Vacuum (star) Fruit Jar, #1432, quart, aqua . . . . $75–$90

Knowlton Vacuum (star) Fruit Jar, #1432, two quart, aqua . . . . $30–$35

L & W Manufacturer for Rice & Burnett, #1529, glass stopper, quart, aqua . . . .

. . . . $300–$450

L & W's XL, #1523, quart, aqua . . . . $65–$95

Lafayette (in script), #1452, clear, pint. . . . . $125–$150

Fruit jar, Lafayette. PHOTO COURTESY OF SKINNER'S, INC.

Lafayette (in script), #1452, clear, quart. . . . . $125–$150
Lafayette (in script), #1452, original glass lid, closure, quart, aqua. . . . . . $100–$145
Lafayette (in script), #1452, quart, aqua. . . . . $90–$125
Lafayette (profile), #1450, quart, aqua . . . . $600+
Lafayette Fruit Jar, quart, aqua . . . . $500–$600
Lafayette, #1452, Patented Sept 2 1884/Aug 4 1885 (on lid), quart, aqua . . . . $60–$90
Lamb Mason, #1455, large letters, clear, zinc cap, quart . . . . $1.75–$2.5
Lamb Mason, #1455.1, small letters, clear, zinc cap, quart . . . . $2–$4
Lamb Mason, clear, pint . . . . $2–$4
Leader (in two lines), #1466, clear, repro wire, pint. . . . . $40–$45
Leader, The, #1466, correct lid & wire closure, quart, yellowish amber . . . $175–$250
Legrand Ideal Trade, LIJ monogram, #1472, repro lid, quart, aqua . . . . . . $80–$100
Leifheit Confiture, Ring of Fruit, modern German jar, painted screw cap . . . .
. . . . $10–$15
Leotric (in circle), #1476, clear, half gallon . . . . $14–$18
Leotric (in circle), #1476, clear, quart. . . . . $8–$12
Leotric (in circle), #1476, pint, aqua. . . . . $3–$4
Leotric (in circle), #1476, quart, aqua. . . . . $3–$5
Leotric (in circle), #1477, two quart, aqua . . . . $6–$8
Leotric (with erased trademark Electric), #1478, pint, aqua. . . . . $7–$9
Leotric, #1473, base embossed, smooth lip, pint, aqua . . . . $6–$8
Leotric, #1473, embossed, ground lip, pint, aqua . . . . $7–$9
Leotric, #1473, no base embossing, clear, pint . . . . $7–$9
LG Co (on base), #1482, half gallon, deep golden amber. . . . . $250–$300
Lightning, with H over anchor, #81, clear, pint . . . . $2–$3
Lightning, with H over anchor, #81, clear, quart . . . . $2–$3
Lindell Glass Co (on base), #1509, wax sealer, quart, amber . . . . $125–$150
Lockport Mason Improved, #1514, pint, aqua . . . . $4–$5
Lockport Mason, #1512, clear, quart . . . . $6–$8
Lockport Mason, #1512, half gallon, aqua. . . . . $8–$12
Lockport Mason, #1512, pint, aqua . . . . $6–$8
Lockport Mason, #1512, quart, aqua . . . . $6–$8
Longlife Mason, #1515, quart, amber . . . . $10–$15
Longlife, Obear Nester (on base), #1516, clear, pint. . . . . $2–$3
Ludlows Patent June 28 1858 (on lid), #1546, half gallon, aqua . . . . $70–$100
Ludlows Patent June 28 1858 (on lid), #1546, quart, aqua . . . . $125–$165
Lustre, RE Tongue & Bros, #1555, pint, aqua. . . . . $6–$8
Lustre, RE Tongue & Bros, #1556, fancy frame, quart, aqua . . . . $6–$8
Lynchburg Standard Mason, #1594, quart, aqua . . . . $15–$20
Lyon & Bossard's Jar, East Stroudsburg, #1595, correct lid, yoke, quart, aqua. . . . .
. . . . $400–$450
Lyon & Bossard's Jar, Stroudsburg, Pa, #1595, original clamp, quart, aqua . . . .
. . . . $400–$475
Lyon & Bossard's Jar, Stroudsburg, Pa, #1595, repro clamp, quart, aqua . . . .
. . . . $175–$275
Magic Fruit Jar, #1606, half gallon, aqua . . . . $125–$150
Mansfield Improved Mason, #1621, clear, quart. . . . . $10–$12
Marian Jar Masons Patent 1858, #1624, pint, aqua . . . . $10–$14
Marstons Restaurant, Boston (in circle), #1627, clear, quart. . . . . $20–$30
Mascot Trademark Patd Improved, #1630, clear, quart, tudor rose . . . . . $175–$225
Mason (Keystone in circle), #1682, quart, aqua. . . . . $10–$15

Mason (shield) Union, #2133, period lid, quart, aqua. . . . . $100–$150
Mason (shield) Union, #2133, quart, aqua . . . . $150–$200
Mason Fruit Jar (in three lines), #1667, clear, half gallon . . . . $7–$10
Mason Fruit Jar (in three lines), #1667, clear, pint. $6–$9
Mason Fruit Jar (in three lines), #1667, clear, quart. . . . . $4–$6
Mason Fruit Jar (in three lines), #1667, pint, aqua. . . . . $8–$12
Mason Fruit Jar, #1665, pint, medium amber . . . . $150–$175
Mason Fruit Jar, #1667, pint, medium amber . . . . $200–$225
Mason HG Co, midget, pint, aqua. . . . . $250–$325
Mason Improved, #1690, half gallon, aqua . . . . $4–$5
Mason Improved, #1690, quart, aqua. . . . . $2–$3
Mason Jar (arched design), #1742, clear, quart. . . . . $9–$12
Mason Jar of 1872, #1749, pint, aqua. . . . . $60–$80
Mason Jar of 1872, #1749, quart, aqua. . . . . $25–$35
Mason Jar of 1872, #1749, two quart, aqua . . . . $25–$35
Mason Jar of 1872, The, #1749, quart, aqua . . . . $30–$40
Mason Jar of 1872, The, #1750, half gallon, aqua . . . . $30–$45
Mason Patent Nov 30th 1858, (keystone in circle), quart, aqua. . . . . $7–$9
Mason Patent Nov 30th 1858, (no s), #1789, clear, quart . . . . $6–$8
Mason Vacuum Knowlton Patent, #2134, original clamp, pint, aqua. . . . . . . $70–$95
Mason Vacuum Knowlton Patent, #2134, repro clamp, two quart, aqua . . . . $40–$50
Mason's CFJ Co Improved Butter Jar, #1688, aqua . . . . $75–$100
Mason's CFJ Co Improved Butter Jar, #1688, clear . . . . $75–$100
Mason's Improved, #1695/1, half gallon, medium amber . . . . $125–$175
Mason's Patent Nov 30th 1858, #1758.1, quart, aqua . . . . $3–$5
Mason's Patent Nov 30th 1858, #1787, clear midget, original zinc lid . . . . $125–$175
Mason's Patent Nov 30th 1858, #1787, half gallon, deep amber. . . . . $175–$250
Mason's Patent Nov 30th 1858, #1787, half gallon, yellow amber . . . . $100–$145
Mason's Patent Nov 30th 1858, #1787, quart, yellow olive . . . . $400–$600
Mason's Patent / Mason's Improved, salesman's closure display jar, clear. . . . .
. . . . $2000+
Mason, with shepherd's crook, #1637, half gallon, aqua . . . . $12–$18
Mason, with shepherd's crook, #1637, pint, aqua. . . . . $12–$18
Mason, with shepherd's crook, #1637, quart, aqua. . . . . $4–$6
Masons (arched) Patent (straight), half gallon, greenish aqua . . . . $7–$9
Masons (cross) Improved, #1725, midget, aqua. . . . . $15–$18
Masons (cross) Patent Nov 30th 1858, #1939, quart, medium golden amber . . . . . .
. . . . $75–$100
Masons (cross) Patent Nov 30th 1858, #1940, half gallon, yellow green . . . . $70–$90
Masons (cross), 1858, quart, amber. . . . . $100–$125
Masons (keystone) Improved, #1736, midget, aqua . . . . $30–$35
Masons (keystone) Keystone, #1737, correct lide, quart, aqua . . . . $90–$125
Masons (keystone) Patent Nov 30th 1858, #1964, midget, aqua. . . . . $25–$35
Masons (keystone) Patent Nov 30th 1858, #1965, midget, aqua. . . . . $25–$35
Masons (star) Patent Nov 30th 1858, reproduction, four gallon, aqua . . . . . . $20–$25
Masons 1 Patent Nov 30th 1858, #2027, quart, aqua. . . . . $10–$14
Masons 111 Patent Nov 30th 1858, #2117, midget, aqua . . . . $125–$175
Masons 2 Patent Nov 30th 1858, #2030, quart, aqua. . . . . $10–$14
Masons 2 Patent Nov 30th 1858, HCT (on base), #2030.1, half gallon, aqua. . . . . . .
. . . . $20–$30
Masons 2 Patents Nov 30th 1858, #2030, half gallon, aqua. . . . . $14–$18

Masons 25 Patent Nov 30th 1858, quart, aqua . . . . $11–$14
Masons 404 Patent Nov 30th 1858, midget, aqua . . . . $125–$175
Masons A Patent Nov 30th 1858, midget, aqua . . . . $200–$250
Masons BGCo Improved, pint, light green . . . . $75–$90
Masons C Patent Nov 30th 1858, quart, aqua . . . . $8–$12
Masons CFJ Co Improved Clyde NY, #1712, midget, aqua. . . . . $25–$35
Masons CFJ Co Improved Clyde NY, #1712, pint, aqua . . . . $6–$8
Masons CFJ Co Improved, #1711, clear, quart . . . . $6–$7
Masons CFJ Co Improved, #1711, original lid, half gallon, amber . . . . . . $100–$145
Masons CFJ Co Patent Nov 30th 1858, #1920, half gallon, aqua. . . . . $3–$5
Masons CFJ Co Patent Nov 30th 1858, #1920, midget, aqua. . . . . $12–$15
Masons CFJ Co Patent Nov 30th 1858, #1920, olive tone, quart, yellow. . . . .
. . . . $300–$450
Masons CFJ Co Patent Nov 30th 1858, #1920, quart, aqua . . . . $2–$3
Masons CFJ Co Patent Nov 30th 1858, #1920, quart, golden amber . . . . . $150–$200
Masons CFJ Co Patent Nov 30th 1858, #1920, quart, medium yellow amber . . . .
. . . . $175–$200
Masons Cross Patent Nov 30th 1858, #1938, pint, aqua. . . . . $3–$5
Masons Cross Patent Nov 30th 1858, #1938, quart, aqua . . . . $2–$2.5
Masons Cross, #1938, half gallon, amber . . . . $125–$150
Masons Cross, #1938, quart, amber . . . . $80–$110
Masons GC Co Patent Nov 30th 1858, #1934, pint, aqua. . . . . $8–$12
Masons GC Co Patent Nov 30th 1858, #1934, pint, light green . . . . $7–$9
Masons III Patent Nov 30th 1858, #2042, midget, aqua . . . . $110–$140
Masons III Patent Nov 30th 1858, #2042, quart, aqua . . . . $20–$25
Masons Improved (shield emblem), midget, aqua. $50–$60
Masons Improved (with cross), #1723, half gallon, aqua . . . . $3–$5
Masons Improved Patd, quart, aqua. . . . . $4–$6
Masons Improved, (ghosted Mascot), #1695, half gallon, medium amber. . . . .
. . . . $125–$175
Masons Improved, CFJ (on reverse), #1709, clear midget. . . . . $12–$15
Masons Improved, CFJ (on reverse), #1709, half gallon, aqua . . . . $3–$5
Masons Improved, The, #1694, clear, disk immenser, pint . . . . $70–$90
Masons Improved, The, #1694, clear, two quart . . . . $30–$40
Masons Improved, The, #1694, half gallon, yellow amber . . . . $100–$125
Masons Improved, The, #1695, two quart, amber . . . . $100–$125
Masons KBG Co Patent Nov 30th 1858, clear, pint . . . . $15–$20
Masons KBG Co Patent Nov 30th 1858, pint, aqua . . . . $15–$20
Masons Keystone Improved, #1736, half gallon, aqua . . . . $23–$27
Masons Keystone Patent Nov 30th 1858, #1964, half gallon, medium amber . . . .
. . . . $450–$550
Masons Keystone Patent Nov 30th 1858, #1965, pint, aqua . . . . $6–$7
Masons LGW Improved, clear, quart. . . . . $18–$23
Masons Patent 1858, #1766, clear, quart . . . . $2–$4
Masons Patent 1858, half gallon, honey amber . . . . $110–$135
Masons Patent 1858, quart, yellow amber . . . . $75–$100
Masons Patent Nov 30th 1858—Hero Glassworks, three gallon, aqua . . . $500–$700
Masons Patent Nov 30th 1858—Tudor Rose, midget, aqua. . . . . $30–$40
Masons Patent Nov 30th 1858 Clyde NY (on base), midget, aqua. . . . . $80–$100
Masons Patent Nov 30th 1858 Dupont, #1848, half gallon, aqua. . . . . $200–$250
Masons Patent Nov 30th 1858 Moore Bros Glass (on base), quart, aqua . . . . . $5–$7

Masons Patent Nov 30th 1858, #1787, half gallon, yellow amber . . . . $200–$300
Masons Patent Nov 30th 1858, #1798, midget, aqua . . . . $30–$50
Masons Patent Nov 30th 1858, #1833, midget, aqua . . . . $30–$50
Masons Patent Nov 30th 1858, #1836, pint, medium yellow olive . . . . $400–$500
Masons Patent Nov 30th 1858, #1872, midget, aqua . . . . $30–$50
Masons Patent Nov 30th 1858, (with cross), clear, quart . . . . $7–$8
Masons Patent Nov 30th 1858, (with cross), quart, aqua . . . . $5–$6
Masons Patent Nov 30th 1858, ball on reverse, quart, aqua. . . . . $6–$7
Masons Patent Nov 30th 1858, clear midget, disk immenser, tudor rose . . . $125–$150
Masons Patent Nov 30th 1858, clear, two reversed "N's," quart . . . . $13–$18
Masons Patent Nov 30th 1858, half gallon, aqua . . . . $4–$5
Masons Patent Nov 30th 1858, half gallon, greenish aqua. . . . . $3–$4
Masons Patent Nov 30th 1858, heart on base, quart, aqua . . . . $50–$70
Masons Patent Nov 30th 1858, midget, large star on base, aqua . . . . $50–$60
Masons Patent Nov 30th 1858, midget, medium blue . . . . $1000–$1500
Masons Patent Nov 30th 1858, midget, small star on base, aqua. . . . . $50–$60
Masons Patent Nov 30th 1858, milk glass lid Ball embossed, midget, aqua . . . .
. . . . $110–$130
Masons Patent Nov 30th 1858, Pat Nov 26, 67 (on base), quart, aqua . . . . $5–$7
Masons Patent Nov 30th 1858, Port (on base), two quarts, aqua . . . . $5–$7
Masons Patent Nov 30th 1858, quart, aqua . . . . $7–$9
Masons Patent Nov 30th 1858, quart, yellow amber . . . . $100–$150
Masons Patent Nov 30th 1858, with amber striations, half gallon, green . . . .
. . . . $350–$400
Masons Patent Nov 30th 1858, with reversed 9, quart, aqua . . . . $15–$20
Masons Patent Nov 30th 1858, with reversed N's, midget, aqua. . . . . $45–$55
Masons Patent Nov 30th 1858, with underlined 5, midget, aqua. . . . . $25–$45
Masons Patent, #1756, quart, ball blue . . . . $3–$5
Masons SG Co Patent Nov 30th 1858, #1974, half gallon, aqua. . . . . $10–$12
Masons SG Co Patent Nov 30th 1858, #1974, pint, aqua . . . . $10–$12
Masons Union, with shield, #2133, quart, aqua . . . . $90–$125
McMechens Always the Best Old Virginia, clear, milk glass lid . . . . $90–$110
McMechens Always the Best Old Virginia, quart, aqua . . . . $50–$75
Medford Preserved Fruit Buffalo NY, #2163, two quarts, pale cornflower blue . . . . .
. . . . $225–$250
Michigan Mason, #2172, no side embossing, clear, pint . . . . $18–$22
Michigan Mason, with side embossing, #2172, pint, aqua . . . . $30–$40
Millville Atmospheric Fruit Jar, #2181, 1 and $\frac{1}{2}$ quart, aqua . . . . $25–$35
Millville Atmospheric Fruit Jar, #2181, 1 and $\frac{1}{2}$ quart, aqua . . . . $35–$50
Millville Atmospheric Fruit Jar, #2181, half gallon, aqua . . . . $35–$50
Millville Atmospheric Fruit Jar, #2181, half gallon, aqua . . . . $25–$35
Millville Atmospheric Fruit Jar, #2181, high shoulder, lid clamp, quart, aqua . . . . . .
. . . . $150–$175
Millville Atmospheric Fruit Jar, #2181, pint, aqua. $25–$35
Millville Atmospheric Fruit Jar, #2181, quart, aqua. . . . . $25–$35
Millville Atmospheric Fruit Jar, #2181, quart, aqua. . . . . $25–$35
Millville Atmospheric Fruit Jar, #2183, lid, clamp, pint, aqua. . . . . $60–$95
Millville Atmospheric Fruit Jar, #2183, square shoulder, pint, aqua . . . . . $110–$140
Millville Atmospheric Fruit Jar, #2183, square shoulder, quart, aqua . . . . $110–$125
Millville Atmospheric Fruit Jar, #2183, square shoulder, two quart, aqua. . . . .
. . . . $130–$160

Millville jar, square shoulder variety. PHOTO COURTESY OF GLASS WORKS AUCTIONS.

Millville Whitall's Patent, #2185, correct lid, yoke, half pint, aqua . . . . . . $150–$220
Millville WT Co Improved, correct lid, quart, aqua. . . . . $40–$50
Millville, #2185, with iron yoke clamp, half pint, aqua . . . . $150–$225
Mission Mason, with bell, #2191, clear, quart. . . . . $6–$8
Model Jar Patd Aug 27 1867, #2194, half gallon, aqua. . . . . $125–$160
Model Jar Patd Aug 27 1867, #2194, quart, aqua . . . . $200–$300
Monarch (in shield), #2199, clear, quart. . . . . $8–$10
Moores Patent Dec 3d 1861, #2204, 1.5 quart, aqua . . . . $70–$85
Moores Patent Dec 3d 1861, #2204, 1861 lid, correct yoke, quart, aqua. . . . $80–$120
Moores Patent Dec 3d 1861, #2204, correct lid, yoke, quart, aqua . . . . $75–$100
Moores Patent Dec 3d 1861, #2204, pint, aqua . . . . $110–$135
Moores Patent Dec 3d 1861, #2204, quart, aqua . . . . $70–$85
Moores Patent Dec 3d 1861, #2204, two quart, aqua. . . . . $70–$85
Mothers Jar Trade Mark RE Tongue (on front), #2211, pint, aqua . . . . $40–$45
Mothers Jar Trade Mark RE Tongue (on front), #2211, quart, aqua . . . . . . $25–$30
Mountain Mason, #2212, no base mark, clear, quart . . . . $25–$30
Mrs Chapins Mayonnaise, clear, pint. . . . . $3–$5
Mrs GE Haller Patd Feb 25, 73 (on stopper), #1178, quart, aqua . . . . $125–$150
Myer's Test Jar, #2218, rusting on lid, quart, deep aqua . . . . $300–$500
NE Plus Ultra Air Tight Fruit Jar, Bodine, #478, IP, pint, aqua . . . . $600–$850
New Paragon, #2289, quart, aqua . . . . $120–$165
New Perfection, IG Co, #2246, clear, two quarts . . . . $40–$55
Newmans Pure Gold Baking Powder, #2239, pint, aqua . . . . $30–$35
Norton Bros Chicago (on lid), #2252, tin handle, pint. . . . . $45–$55
Norton Bros Chicago (on lid), #2252, tin handle, quart. . . . . $40–$50
OC, #2255, fruit on bottle, quart, aqua. . . . . $38–$50
Old Style Mustard, #2272, clear, full label, pint . . . . $5–$6
P Lorillard (on base), #1543, quart, amber. . . . . $9–$12
Pacific San Francisco Glass Work Patd Feby 9th 1864, #2895, half gallon, aqua . . .
. . . . $150–$175

Pat Jan 12 1886, #482, quart, aqua . . . . $120–$140
Pat'd Feb 9th 1864 WW Lyman 27, #1575.8, correct tin lid, quart, aqua. . . . $50–$65
Pat'd Oct 1864 JJ Squire March Sept 1865, #2696, original lid, quart, aqua . . . .
. . . . $125–$175
Patd Aug 5th 1862 & Feb 9th 1864 WW Lyman, #1579, no lid, pint, aqua . . . .
. . . . $30–$40
Patd Aug 5th 1862 & Feb 9th 1864 WW Lyman, #1579, original lid, pint, aqua . . . .
. . . . $70–$80
Patd Feb 9th 1864 WW Lyman, #157, with lid, pint, aqua . . . . $60–$90
Patd March 26th 1867 1 BB Wilcox, #3001, two quart, aqua . . . . $50–$60
Patent Applied For by Lutz & Schramm Co (on heel), pottery, quart . . . . . $20–$25
Patent Sept 18, 1860, #2295, wax sealer, quart, aqua . . . . $75–$90
Patented Aug 8th 1882 (on lid), narrow mouth, 1¹/₂ pint, aqua . . . . $50–$60
Patented Aug 8th 1882 (on lid), repro wire, pint, aqua . . . . $40–$60
Patented Aug 8th 1882 (on lid), repro wire, quart, aqua . . . . $50–$60
Patented Aug 8th 1882 (on lid), wide mouth, two quarts, aqua . . . . $40–$50
Patented July 19, 1919 by Jos H Schramm, ten panels, pottery, quart . . . . . . $20–$25
Patented July 27th 1886 (on base), Greek Key, #2308, half gallon, emerald green. . .
. . . . $275–$325
Patented Jun 9, 03, June 23, 03 (on base), clear, 2¹/₂" . . . . $2–$3
Patented Oct 19 1858 (on screw lid), #1212, quart, deep amethyst. . . . . $1200–$1500
Patented Oct 19th 1858 (on lid), quart, black . . . . $900–$1200
Patented Oct 19th 1858 (on lid), quart, deep amethyst . . . . $500–$700
Pearl, #2318, quart, aqua . . . . $30–$40
Pearl, The, #2319, quart, aqua. . . . . $50–$75
Peerless, #2322, quart, aqua. . . . . $40–$60
Peerless, #2322, quart, aqua. . . . . $125–$150
Penn, Phillips & Co Pitts Pa, wax sealer, quart, aqua . . . . $150–$200
Peoria Pottery (on base), eight sided, wax sealer, #2329, glaze, quart, brown . . . .
. . . . $40–$60
Perfect Seal (in script), clear, #2336, pint . . . . $4–$6
Perfect Seal, #2334, Pat Pend (on base), quart, amber . . . . $100–$140
Pet, #2359, patent date on lid, repro wire, quart, aqua. . . . . $60–$80
Pet, #2359, patent date on lid, repro wire, two quart, aqua . . . . $60–$80
Petal Jar, #3067, IP, half gallon, deep olive green . . . . $2000–$2500
Petal Jar, #3067, IP, quart, aqua . . . . $250–$300
Petal Jar, #3067, quart, deep olive green . . . . $1000–$1250
Petal Jar, IP, #3067, half gallon, aqua. . . . . $250–$300
Petal Jar, IP, quart, medium cobalt . . . . $1000–$1500
Phoenix Surgical Dressing Co., #2364, quart, amber. . . . . $250–$350
Pine P Mason, #2367, clear, pint. . . . . $6–$8
Pine P Mason, #2367, clear, quart. . . . . $6–$8
Porcelain Lined, #2373, midget, aqua. . . . . $150–$200
Porcelain Lined, #2374, arched lettering, half gallon, aqua . . . . $18–$23
Porcelain Lined, #2374, arched lettering, midget, aqua . . . . $90–$120
Porcelain Lined, #2374, arched lettering, quart, aqua. . . . . $12–$15
Porcelain Lined, #2374, arched lettering, two quart, aqua . . . . $15–$18
Porcelain Lined, #2374, midget, aqua. . . . . $100–$150
Potter & Bodine, Philadelphia, #2381, new closure, quart, aqua . . . . $45–$65
Potter & Bodine, Philadelphia, #2381, tin closure, quart, aqua . . . . $120–$160
Potter & Bodines Air Tight, #2382, pint, aqua . . . . $600–$750

Fruit jar, Potter and Bodine wax sealer. PHOTO COURTESY OF SKINNER'S, INC.

Potter & Bodines Air Tight, #2382, quart, aqua .... $500–$700
Potter & Bodines Air Tight, #2382, quart, aqua .... $500–$700
Princess (on shield in frame), #2418, clear, pint .... $18–$22
Princess (on shield in frame), #2418, clear, quart .... $15–$20
Protector (one panel recessed), #2421.1, repro clamp, quart, aqua .... $24–$28
Protector (panels recessed), #2421, original lid, pint, aqua .... $70–$90
Protector (panels recessed), #2421, repro lid, quart, aqua .... $24–$26
Puritan Trademark Fruit Jar, #2426, original closure, quart, aqua ...... $300–$375
Puritan Trademark Fruit Jar, #2426, repro metal closure, pint, aqua .... $200–$300
Purity Oats, with flowers, clear, quart .... $12–$15
Putnam (on base), #1492, 4³/₄", 2¹/₂", half pint, aqua .... $65–$80
Putnam (on base), #2427, pint, amber .... $25–$30
Putnam Glassworks, Zanesville (on base), #2428, quart, aqua.............. $5–$6
Queen, #2433, quart, aqua .... $15–$18
Queen, encircled by Patd 1858, 1868, #2432, quart .... $30–$35
Quick Seal Patd July 14, 1908, #2454, quart, aqua .... $4–$5
Quick Seal Patd July 14, 1908, #2454, quart, light aqua .... $3–$4
Quick Seal, no circle, #2453, pint, aqua .... $3–$4
Quick Seal, within circle, #2451, pint, aqua.......................... $3–$4
RAC, #2461.1, clear, pint.. $15–$20
RE Tongue & Bros Co Inc Lustre, #1553, clear, pint.................... $10–$12
RE Tongue & Bros Co Inc Lustre, #1553, clear, quart.................... $8–$10
Red Crown Dried Beef (on label), 2¹/₂ oz, pink......................... $4–$5
Reg US Patent Office (on heel), half pint, aqua .... $7–$10
Reservoirs To Open Admit Air, #2496, original glass stopper, quart, aqua ....
.... $400–$525
Rex, No 3, (on base), Siemens Glass (on lid), clear, quart .... $8–$10
Robert Arthurs Patent, #98, pottery, lip chip, pint .... $90–$120
Robert Arthurs Patent, #98, pottery, pint .... $200–$250
Royal Trademark Full Measure (on front), quart, amber .... $45–$60
Safe Seal (in circle above date), #2530, pint, aqua..................... $4–$5
Safe Seal (in circle above date), #2531, quart, aqua.................... $4–$6
Safety Valve Patd 1895 HC (over triangle), 7¹/₂" x 2³/₈", pint, aqua .... $75–$95
Safety Valve Patd 1895 HC (over triangle), clear, ¹/₄ pint .... $30–$35
Safety Valve Patd 1895 HC (over triangle), clear, half pint.............. $8–$10

Safety Valve Patd 1895 HC (over triangle), clear, squat, half pint......... $40–$45
Safety Valve Patd 1895 HC (over triangle), half pint, aqua.............. $20–$25
Safety Valve Patd 1895 HC (over triangle), pint, cornflower blue......... $30–$35
Safety Valve, #2538, clear, half pint.................................. $8–$10
Safety Valve, #2538, clear, half quart................................. $6–$7
Safety Valve, Greek Key Design, #2539, aqua........................ $25–$30
Safety Valve, Greek Key Design, #2539, clear....................... $30–$35
Safety Valve, Greek Key Design, #2539, green...................... $120–$160
Safety Valve, with Greek Key Design, emerald green................. $300–$350
Safety Wide Mouth Mason Salem, #2549, quart, aqua.................. $12–$15
Safety, #2534, quart, amber....................................... $125–$175
Salem Jar, The, Holz Clark & Taylor, #2544, glass screw stopper..... $800–$1200
Samco Super Mason (Mason in plate), #2548, clear, quart............... $5–$7
Sanety Wide Mouth Mason Salem, #2549, quart, aqua................. $12–$15
SB Dewey Jr 65 Buffalo St, #771, quart, aqua......................... $800+
Schaffer Jar Rochester NY, #2561, dated lid, original wire, pint, aqua ... $375–$460
Schram Auto B Sealer, #2569, clear, pint........................... $8–$10
Schutz Marke (on base), Kieffer (on lid), clear, quart.................... $9–$12
Scranton Jar, #2576, original glass lid, quart, aqua................... $400–$600
Scranton Jar, The, #2576, original metal & wood lid, quart, aqua....... $500–$700
Sealfast, Foster, #2580, clear, quart................................. $4–$5
Security Seal, #2608, clear, pint.................................... $5–$6
Security Seal, #2608, clear, quart.................................. $4–$5
Selco Surety Seal (in circle), #2611, patented 1908, pint, bluish........... $12–$15
Selco Surety Seal (in circle), #2611, patented 1908, quart, bluish........... $8–$10
Silicon (in circle), #2629, quart, aqua................................ $12–$15
Silicon Glass Co (in circle), #2630, quart, aqua....................... $10–$12
Simplex Mason, #2635, clear, pint.............................. $100–$135
Simplex, #2634, in diamond, clear, pint.............................. $7–$10
SKQ Queen Trademark Wide Mouth, clear, half pint.................. $14–$18
SKQ Queen, half pint, sun colored amethyst.......................... $8–$9
Smalley AGS, #2648, quart, amber................................ $50–$65
Smalley Full Measure AGS, #2648, clear, pint...................... $12–$15
Smalley Full Measure AGS, #2648, clear, quart...................... $9–$12
Smalley Full Measure AGS, #2648, engraved zinc lid, quart, amber....... $60–$75
Smalley Full Measure AGS, #2648, pint, aqua...................... $15–$18
Smalley Full Measure AGS, #2648, plain zinc lid, quart, amber.......... $50–$60
Smalley Jar, repro metal, quart, aqua............................. $280–$350
Standard, #2699, quart, amber................................... $300–$450
Tight Seal (in circle above date), quart, aqua.......................... $4–$5
Tight Seal (in circle), dated on reverse, pint, aqua...................... $5–$6
TM Banner Warranted (in circle), quart, aqua........................ $7–$8
TM Keystone Reg, clear, pint..................................... $5–$6
Trade Mark Advance, half gallon, aqua.......................... $200–$260
Trade Mark Lightning (on base), pint, aqua.......................... $4–$6
Trade Mark Lightning Putnam (on base), pint, aqua................... $3–$5
Trade Mark Lightning, #1496, half pint, aqua...................... $80–$110
Trade Mark Lightning, #1499, half gallon, golden yellow amber........ $90–$135
Trade Mark Lightning, #1499, original lid, closure, quart, yellow amber ... $75–$95
Trade Mark Lightning, #1499, original lid, quart, medium amber........ $50–$75
Trade Mark Lightning, #1499, original lid, quart, yellowish amber........ $50–$75

Trade Mark Lightning, #1499, quart, yellow olive . . . . $80–$110
Trade Mark Lightning, half gallon, amber . . . . $40–$60
Trade Mark The Dandy, #751, amber tone, matching lid, quart, yellow . . . .
. . . . $275–$375
Trade Mark The Dandy, patented 1885, glass lid, quart, yellow amber . . . . $80–$120
Trade Mark VR Lightning, #1506, quart, sun colored amethyst . . . . $150–$200
Trademark Banner Registered, clear, half pint. . . . . $30–$40
Trademark Banner Warranted (in circle), quart, bluish . . . . $4–$6
Trademark Electric, pint, aqua. . . . . $12–$15
Trademark Electric, quart, aqua. . . . . $8–$10
Trademark Keystone Registered, clear, pint. . . . . $6–$8
Trademark Keystone Registered, clear, quart. . . . . $6–$8
Trademark Lightning, pint, aqua. . . . . $4–$6
Trademark Lightning, Putnam (on base), 1½ pint, aqua . . . . $30–$35
Trademark Lightning, Putnam (on base), quart, amber. . . . . $30–$35
Trademark Lightning, Putnam (on base), two quart, aqua . . . . $9–$12
Triumph No 1, #2814, three piece mold, quart, aqua . . . . $500–$700
Triumph No 2, #2815, three piece mold, quart, aqua . . . . $500–$700
Unembossed Wax Sealer, clear, quart . . . . $7–$10
Unembossed Wax Sealer, quart, aqua. . . . . $8–$12
Unembossed, #3063, three piece mold, rough sheared lip, medium blue . . . $400–$550
Unembossed, barrel shaped wax sealer, pottery, half gallon, yellow . . . . $20–$25
Unembossed, bell shaped wax sealer, quart, aqua. $60–$80
Unembossed, round, cork seat, quart, aqua . . . . $13–$17
Union No 1, quart, aqua. . . . . $200–$275
Valve Jar Co Philadelphia Patent March 10th 1868, #2874, lid, quart, aqua . . . .
. . . . $175–$250
Valve Jar Philadelphia, original lid and clamp, quart, aqua . . . . $300–$350
Van Vliet Jar of 1881, #2879, original lid with wire, quart, aqua . . . . $350–$450

Van Vliet jar with unusual clamp. PHOTO COURTESY OF
GLASS WORKS AUCTIONS.

Van Vliet Jar of 1881, The, #2880, correct lid, metal yoke, quart, aqua . . . $400–$650
Victor Patented 1899, pint, aqua. . . . . $50–$65
Victor Patented 1899, quart, aqua. . . . . $40–$45

Victory (encircled by dates), quart, aqua . . . . $10–$12
Victory (encircled by Patd 1864 & 1867 on front), Pacific SF Glassworks . . . .
. . . . $200–$250
Victory (in shield), Victory Jar (on lid), clear, ¼ pint . . . . $25–$35
Victory (in shield), Victory Jar (on lid), clear, half pint . . . . $12–$16
Wan Eta Cocoa Boston, pint, amber. . . . . $10–$13
Wan Eta Cocoa Boston, quart, aqua . . . . $7–$9
Wears (in circle), pint, bluish . . . . $12–$16
Wears Jar (in circle), clear, pint . . . . $9–$13
Wears Jar (in circle), clear, quart . . . . $9–$13
Wears Jar (in stippled frame), clear, quart . . . . $9–$13
Wears Jar (in stippled oval), clear, quart. . . . . $9–$13
Weir Patd Mar 1st 1892 (on lid), pottery, pint. . . . . $20–$30
Weir Patd Mar 1st 1892 (on lid), pottery, quart. . . . . $20–$25
Weir Patd March 1st 92, April 16 1901 (on lid), pottery, pint . . . . $25–$30
Wells & Provost, Spratts Patent, two raised knobs, quart. . . . . $300–$500
Western Pride, pint, aqua . . . . $150–$200
WH Glenny Son & Co Importers . . ., #1120, damaged stopper, quart, aqua . . . .
. . . . $120–$150
Whitall Tatum & Co (on glass lid), clear, OP, half gallon . . . . $20–$30
Whitmore's Patent, #2966, with glass lid, wire bail, quart, aqua. . . . . $150–$225
Whitney Glass Works / Whitney, quart, deep aqua. . . . . $400–$600
Widemouth Famous Jar (in circle), pint, aqua . . . . $15–$25
Wilcox, quart . . . . $50–$80
Winslow Improved Valve Jar, repro clamp, quart, deep aqua. . . . . $300–$400
Winslow Jar, #3023, correct lid, wire clamp, 1½ pint, aqua . . . . $55–$75
Winslow Jar, #3023, correct lid, wire clamp, quart, aqua. . . . . $55–$75
Winslow Jar, pint, aqua. . . . . $120–$160
Winslow Jar, quart, aqua. . . . . $60–$90
Winslow Patented 1870 Pat 1873, pint, aqua. . . . . $80–$120
Wm L Haller Carlisle Pa, #1179, original glass lid, screw, quart, aqua . . . $400–$550
Woodbury, quart, aqua . . . . $25–$30
Woodbury, two quart, aqua . . . . $25–$30
Woodbury, WGW monogram, clear, pint . . . . $35–$45
Woodbury, WGW monogram, two quarts, aqua . . . . $35–$45
WW Lyman, Patd Feb 9th 1864, repro lid, quart, aqua . . . . $25–$35

GIN BOTTLES

Gin was invented by a Dutch doctor whose original concoction was first used
as a medicine to promote kidney function. Shortly thereafter, the distinctive
flavoring of gin became popular and distilling became more widespread.

Case gin bottles are tall square shaped bottles, so called because they were often shipped in specially made wooden cases. They were made both in America and Continental Europe, and it is very difficult to determine where a given bottle was made. Also, because of the standard shape of these bottles, it is often difficult to determine exactly how old a given case gin bottle is, as they continued to be made for hundreds of years.

ACA Nolet Schiedam, 10", olive green. . . . . $30–$40
AM Bininger & Co NY, Superior London Dock Gin (on label), see Bininger Bottles, 9¼", emerald green . . . .
Asparagus Gin, The Rothenberg Co, colorless. . . . . $10–$12
Avan Hoboken & Co, Rotterdam, dark green. . . . . $25–$35
Blankenheym & Nolet, 6½", olive. . . . . $13–$16
Booths High & Dry Gin, 10¼", light blue . . . . $4–$5
Case Gin Bottle with Label, OP, 9¾", olive green . . . . $45–$70

Gin bottle, case gin. PHOTO COURTESY OF NEIL GROSSMAN.

Case Gin, OP, 9⅝", olive amber . . . . $40–$60
Case Gin, OP, 9⅞", green with yellow tint. . . . . $35–$50
Case Gin, 9⅞", olive amber. . . . . $40–$60
Case Gin, 13", olive amber . . . . $200–$300
Case Gin, OP, 13⅞", olive amber . . . . $250–$400
Case Gin, OP, 15½", olive amber . . . . $300–$550
Case Gin, OP, 19⅝", olive amber . . . . $450–$700
Charles London Cordial Gin, 8", medium blue green. . . . . $70–$100
Coachman, Van Duncks, glass, 8½", black. . . . . $50–$80
Daniel Visser & Zonen, Schiedam, 9", olive green . . . . $35–$45
EN Cook & Co Distillers Buffalo NY, 10", amber . . . . $125–$150
Gin, Back Bar Bottle, with cap, ten ribs, with silver letters, 11", golden yellow . . . . $90–$110
Gordon Dry Gin, London, England, 9", light green . . . . $2–$3
Gordons London Dry Gin, 9", colorless . . . . $2–$3
Herman Jansen Schiedam, 9½", olive green. . . . . $30–$40
J Ferd: Nagel, with Medallion and Bust, 1873, pale yellow green. . . . . $40–$60
Old Holland Gin, Greene & Glading, emerald green . . . . $55–$70
Royal Imperial Gin London, 9¾", medium cobalt . . . . $200–$240

Royal Imperial Gin London, square, 9³/₄", medium cobalt blue . . . . $100–$135
The Olive Tree, Case Gin Form, 9¹/₂", olive green . . . . $150–$200
Udolpho Wolfes Schiedam Aromatic Schnappes, IP, 9³/₄", olive amber. . . . $50–$70
Udolpho Wolfes Schiedam Schnapps, 8", yellow olive . . . . $40–$60
Udolpho Wolfes, Aromatic Schnapes, 9", green . . . . $15–$20
W Haskamp & Co, 9", olive green . . . . $30–$40
WA Gilbey Silver Stream Schnapes, 8", colorless . . . . $5–$7

HAIR BOTTLES

Hair bottles are a popular collecting category mainly because of the beautiful colors the bottles are found in, such as dark blues, amethysts, and ambers. Many of the bottles are pontiled.

A Grandjeans Composition for the Hair, clear, OP, 3" . . . . $150–$200
AH Brown Hair Specialist Southhampton, 6¹/₈", cobalt . . . . $35–$50
Altenheim Medical Dispensary for Hair & Scalp, clear, 8". . . . . $8–$12
Arnold's Vegetable Hair Balsam, clear, 6³/₈" . . . . $15–$25
AV Possnicker Hair Specialist, Balsam SW, 7¹/₂", cobalt . . . . $70–$100
Ayer's Ague, 7", aqua . . . . $8–$12
Ayer's Hair Vigor, no stopper. . . . . $30–$45
Ayer's Hair Vigor, no stopper, cobalt. . . . . $75–$95
Ayer's Hair Vigor, stopper, 7¹/₄", peacock blue . . . . $40–$55
Ayer's Hair Vigor, stopper, cobalt . . . . $90–$125
Bancroft's Hair Restorer, 6¹/₂", cobalt. . . . . $75–$110
Barne's Phenomenal Hair Restorer, 7¹/₄", cobalt. . . . . $125–$175
Barrow Evans Hair Restorer, 6", aqua . . . . $10–$20
Barry's Pearl Cream, milk glass, 4³/₄". . . . . $8–$12
Barry's Safe Hair Dye New York, 4¹/₈", cobalt. $75–$110
Barry's Tricopherous for the Skin, OP, 6", aqua . . . . $20–$30
Barry's Tricopherous for the Skin, SB, 6", aqua . . . . $10–$15
Batchelor's Liquid Hair Dye No 2, OP, aqua . . . . $20–$25
Bears Oil, OP, aqua . . . . $60–$90
Bishop's Hair Restorer, 6¹/₂", cobalt . . . . $75–$125
Bogle's Hyperion Fluid for the Hair, aqua . . . . $10–$14
Boswell & Warners Colorific, 5¹/₂", cobalt . . . . $150–$200
Boswell & Warners Colorific, amethyst. . . . . $100–$150
Buckingham Whisker Dye, 3³/₄", amber . . . . $4–$6
Burger's Hair Restorative New York, 6⁷/₈", fiery opal. . . . . $600–$850
Bush's Argentine Hair Dye #2, OP, aqua. . . . . $30–$50
Cameron's Kephalia For The Hair, OP, 7³/₈", aqua . . . . $175–$245
CAP Mason Alpine Hair Balm Providence RI, OP, 6⁷/₈", olive green . . . .
. . . . $5000–$6000

Carpenter Morton Co Colorite, clear, 4¼"...........................$7–$10
Catalan Hair Renewer, six sided, 6", cobalt ....$90–$135
Church's Circassian Hair Restorer, 7½", puce ....$400–$700
Church's Circassian Hair Restorer, 7⅜", yellow amber..............$80–$110
Circassian Hair Restorer Cincinnati, 7½", golden amber............$150–$200
Clirehughs Tricopherous for the Hair & Skin, 7", aqua ....$50–$75
Clock's Excelsior Hair Restorer, aqua ....$20–$30
D Mitchell's Tonic for the Hair, OP, 6¼", deep aqua.................$80–$110
Damschinsky Liquid Hair Dye, 3½", aqua..........................$4–$6
Damschinsky Liquid Hair Dye, NY, 4¼", aqua.......................$5–$7
Dodge Brothers Melanine Hair Tonic, 7½", medium amethyst.........$450–$600
Dodge Brothers Melanine Hair Tonic, 7¼", deep amethyst ....$375–$475
Dr Campbell's Hair Invigorator, OP, aqua..........................$60–$90
Dr Chaussier's Empress, SB, 5¼", cobalt...........................$75–$100
Dr D Jayne's Hair Tonic Philada, OP, aqua.......................$15–$22
Dr Gorhams Gray Hair Restorer, 5½", light amber ....$25–$35
Dr Hays Hair Health, 6½", light amber............................$25–$35
Dr Leon's Electric Hair Renewer, 7½", amethyst ....$300–$450
Dr Tebbetts Physiological Hair Regenerator, 7½", deep amethyst......$200–$250
Dr Tebbetts Physiological Hair Regenerator, 7¼", light amber ....$70–$90
Dr Tebbetts Physiological Hair Regenerator, 7¼", medium puce ......$300–$450
Dr Wm Korong Hair Coloring Mfg Chemist, clear, 4½" ....$9–$14
EE Russell's Castanine for the Hair, 6¾", red amber ....$300–$400
Eureka Hair Restorative San Francisco, SB, 7½", aqua.............$500–$750
Excelsior Hair Tonic, OP, 6½", olive amber....................$2000–$2500
Farr's Gray Hair Restorer, 5½", amber ....$25–$35
Fish's Hair Restorative, clear, 7¼" ....$600–$800
Florida Water Druggists, NY, clear, 9¼" ....$10–$14
Frixie Hair Oil, Howard Drugs & Medicine, clear, 2¼" ....$3–$5

Left: *Dr. Tebbett's bottle.* Center: *Jerome's bottle.* Right: *Mrs. Allen's bottle.*
PHOTOS COURTESY OF GLASS WORKS AUCTIONS.

Gallagher's Magical Hair Oil, aqua............................... $15–$20
Geller's Hair Producer, Boston, Mass., 7", golden amber .... $150–$250
Hagans Magnolia Balm, milk glass .... $8–$12
Hair Restorer, The, 7¼", cobalt.................................... $140–$190
Halls Vegetable Hair Renewer, 6½", teal blue .... $150–$200
Harry D Harber's Magic Hair Coloring, 6", cobalt.................... $55–$75
Hays Hair Health, labeled with box, amber .... $10–$15
Hiawatha Hair Restorative, 6¾", aqua .... $75–$125
Hills Hair Dye, aqua .... $8–$12
Hood's Tooth Powder, clear, 3½" .... $5–$7
Humphrey's Marvel Witch Hazel, ABM, clear, 5½".................... $4–$6
Hurd's Hair Restorer, OP, 8⅛", aqua................................ $75–$100
Ideal Dandruff Remover, clear, 6"................................. $5–$7
Imperial Hair Regenerator, New York, 4½", light green .... $7–$11
J Myers Bavarian Hair Tonic, 7", aqua.............................. $30–$40
Jefferson's Hair Renewer Agent Blunts Northampton, 7½", cobalt ..... $75–$110
Jerome's Hair Color Restorer, 6½", cherry amethyst .... $750–$950
Jerome's Hair Color Restorer, cobalt.............................. $300–$350
Sackett's Magic Coloris, 6⅜", cobalt............................. $100–$150
JL Giofray & Co Hair Renovator Rockland Me, 8", red amber ...... $1600–$2200
John Fitch Co, Youngstown, Ohio, clear, 5¾"...................... $7–$11
John Hart & Co, heart form, 7¼", medium amber .... $200–$250
Kelley's Petroline Hair Cream, 4⅞", cobalt........................ $60–$85
Kickapoo Sage Hair Tonic, 4½", cobalt .... $125–$175
Klinker's Hair Tonic, Cleveland, clear, 6" .... $8–$12
Larkin Co. Buffalo, NY, waisted, stopper, 3½", emerald green .... $15–$20
Larkin Co., Buffalo, clear, cylinder, 3¾"........................... $3–$4
Larkin Co., Buffalo, clear, cylinder, 6" .... $4–$6
Larkin Co., Buffalo, clear, oblong, 5" .... $4–$6
Le Renovateur De La Femme Lucien Pratt Waterbury Conn, 9½", cobalt ....
.... $75–$125
London Hair Restorer, 7", aqua.................................... $25–$35
Lorrimer's Excelsior Hair Enforcer, 6⅜", light amber .... $20–$30
Lucky Tiger for Scalp & Hair, clear, screw cap, 7½".................. $7–$11
Lyons Kathairon for the Hair, OP, aqua............................ $12–$18
Lyons Powder, OP, 4⅜", deep amethyst............................. $100–$140
Mennen's Liquid Soap, stopper, label, 6⅜", cobalt................... $55–$75
Mexican Hair Renewer, The, SB, 5½", cobalt .... $75–$100
Morley's Hair Restorer, flask shaped, amber....................... $60–$80
Mrs SA Allen's Worlds Hair Restorer, 7", amber .... $75–$95
Mrs SA Allen's Worlds Hair Restorer, 7", deep amethyst............. $80–$120
Mrs SA Allen's Worlds Hair Restorer, 7", olive green .... $350–$500
Mrs SA Allen's Worlds Hair Restorer, OP, 7", amber................. $20–$25
Mrs SA Allen's Worlds Hair Restorer, yellow, amber and olive tone, 7" ....
.... $125–$175
Nattans Crystal Discovery for the Hair, 7½", cobalt................ $175–$275
Nature's Hair Oil, White Rock Oil Co., 5½", amber.................. $35–$45
Natures Hair Restorative, 7", aqua .... $25–$35
Newbros Herpicide for the Scalp, clear, 6¼" .... $6–$8
Newbros Herpicide for the Scalp, clear, 7"......................... $8–$12
Newbros Herpicide Kills the Dandruff Germ, clear, 7"................ $15–$25

Newhall's Magic Hair Restorer, 7^1/$_2$", cobalt . . . . $150–$250
Noonan's Hair Petrole, 7", aqua. . . . . $25–$35
Noonan's Hair Petroleum, Boston, 6^1/$_2$", aqua . . . . $25–$35
Noxzema (on base), screw cap, cobalt . . . . $0.50–$1
Obliterine, The Ideal Hair Remover, six sided, stopper, 3^1/$_2$", emerald green . . . .
. . . . $125–$150
Oldridge's Balm of Columbia for Restoring Hair, OP, 5^1/$_8$", apple green . . . .
. . . . $450–$700
Oldridge's Balm of Columbia for Restoring Hair, OP, 5^1/$_8$", aqua . . . . . . $175–$250
Palmolive Shampoo, BJ Johnson, ABM, clear, 7^1/$_4$" . . . . $4–$6
Palmolive Shampoo, BJ Johnson, ten paneled, ABM, 4", aqua . . . . $3–$5
Parisian Sage & Hair Tonic, 7^1/$_4$", aqua . . . . $8–$12
Parkers Hair Balsam, 6^5/$_8$", yellow green . . . . $30–$50
Parkers Hair Balsam, New York, 6^1/$_2$", emerald green. . . . . $8–$14
Parkers Hair Balsam, New York, rect., 6^1/$_2$", amber. . . . . $8–$12
Paul Westphal Auxiliator for the Hair, clear, 6^3/$_4$" . . . . $10–$16
Paul Westphal Auxiliator for the Hair, clear, 8" . . . . $15–$20
Perry's Hungarian Balm for the Hair, OP, 5^3/$_4$", aqua. . . . . $40–$60
Phalon's Magic Hair Dye, No 1, OP, aqua. . . . . $15–$20
Pond's Extract, clear, 5^1/$_2$" . . . . $8–$12
Prof JR Tilton the Great Hair Producer, 7", cobalt. . . . . $200–$275
Professor Benbow Specialist for the Hair, 6^1/$_4$", deep cobalt . . . . $50–$80
Professor Wood's Hair Restorative, OP, aqua . . . . $25–$30
R Douglas's Hair Wash, 8^1/$_4$", cobalt. . . . . $100–$125
Renovo for the Hair, 7^3/$_4$", amethyst . . . . $1200–$1800
Riker's American Hair Restorer, 6^3/$_4$", medium amber . . . . $50–$75
Rose Hair Tonic & Dandruff Cure, label under glass, clear, 7^1/$_2$" . . . . $50–$75
Royal Foot Wash, Eaton Drug Co. . . . . $8–$12
Royal Hair Restorer, 7^7/$_8$", cobalt. . . . . $75–$110
RP Hall's Improved Preparation for the Hair, 7^1/$_2$", cobalt . . . . $250–$350
Rubifoam for the Teeth, clear, 4". . . . . $7–$10
Russian Hair Dye, OP, 2^5/$_8$", aqua . . . . $50–$75
S Barrow Evans Hair Restorer, 6", light blue. . . . . $40–$55
Sandell's Hair Restorer, 6", light amethyst . . . . $100–$150
Sanford's Extract of Hammelis or Witch Hazel, 7^1/$_2$", cobalt . . . . $85–$125
Sanitol for the Teeth, clear, 4^1/$_2$" . . . . $7–$10
Saratoga Aperient, 5^7/$_8$", medium cobalt blue . . . . $80–$130
Scheffler Hair Cologne, clear, 4" . . . . $5–$7
Shaker Hair Restorer, 7^1/$_2$", golden amber . . . . $200–$300
St Clair's Hair Lotion, 7^1/$_2$", cobalt . . . . $100–$150
Sterling's Ambrosia for the Hair, 6", aqua . . . . $60–$90
Sutherland 7 Sisters Hair Grower, 6", aqua . . . . $10–$20
Sutherland 7 Sisters Hair Grower, clear, 6" . . . . $10–$16
Sutherland 7 Sisters Hair Grower, clear, ABM, 6" . . . . $7–$9
Swire's Hair Restorer, 7^1/$_4$", cobalt . . . . $125–$200
Teaberry for the Teeth & Breath, clear, 3^1/$_2$" . . . . $6–$9
W Fitch Co, This Bottle Loaned By, clear, lady's leg, 7^3/$_4$" . . . . $15–$20
Wagner's for the Hair Sapajo, 6", deep cobalt . . . . $100–$135
Walnut Leaf Hair Restorer, 7^1/$_2$", yellow amber. $75–$100
WC Montgomery's Hair Restorer, 7^1/$_2$", black amethyst. . . . . $200–$300
WC Montgomery's Hair Restorer, 7^3/$_4$", puce . . . . $350–$450

WC Montgomery's Hair Restorer, 7⁵/₈", medium amber . . . . $75–$90
WH Harris Hair Restorative, 7¹/₄", aqua. . . . . $70–$100
Wildroot Company, Buffalo, NY, 6", amber . . . . $6–$9
Zemo Antiseptic Lotion for Skin & Scalp, clear, 6" . . . . $8–$11

HOUSEHOLD BOTTLES

This category covers the various utility bottles with contents such as ammonia, blacking (which is actually a shoe polish), and various other oils and liniments for lubrication. Blacking bottles are very popular and are commanding higher and higher prices.

AA Cooley, Hartford, Conn, Blacking Bottle, OP, 4⁵/₈", olive green . . . . . . $60–$80
American Bluing Co, Buffalo, NY, colorless, 5¹/₄" . . . . $3–$4
Ammonia . . . SF Gaslight Co, 7⁷/₈", deep aqua . . . . $40–$50
Ammonia . . . SF Gaslight Co, 9¹/₈", amber . . . . $100–$120
Ammonia . . . SF Gaslight Co, 9¹/₈", yellow amber . . . . $50–$70
Ammonia . . . SF Gaslight Co, 9", aqua . . . . $75–$90
Ammonia . . . SF Gaslight Co, 9", citron . . . . $100–$150
Anthony Flint Varnish For Negatives, colorless, cylinder, 5¹/₂" . . . . $4–$6
Bengal Bluing, 5³/₄", aqua . . . . $2–$3
BF Stinson & Co, Buffalo, NY, colorless, 4¹/₂" . . . . $0.5–$1
Black Cat Stove Enamel, colorless, 6" . . . . $2–$3
Blacking Bottle, square, OP, 4⁵/₈", deep yellow amber . . . . $45–$60
Blacking Bottle, square, OP, 4⁷/₈", olive amber . . . . $70–$100
Blown Cylinder, OP, heavy collared lip, 6¹/₄", olive amber . . . . $70–$90
Boot, Saratoga Dressing, 4¹/₄", aqua . . . . $30–$45
Carbona, 5", aqua . . . . $2–$3
Cocoa Nut Oil, C Toppan, violin shape, OP, 5⁷/₈", aqua . . . . $100–$120
Cosmoline Registered, Globe, colorless, 3" . . . . $1–$2
Curtis & Brown Co Mfg, NY, colorless, 3" . . . . $1–$2
Dutchers Dead Shot For Bed Bugs, with label, OP, 4⁷/₈", aqua . . . . $60–$80
Eastman Kodak Chemicals, 5¹/₄", amber. . . . . $5–$8
Eastman Kodak, Rochester, NY, 3", amber . . . . $3–$4
Eclipse French Stain Gloss, 4¹/₂", apple green . . . . $3–$5
Electrical Bicycle Lubricating Oil, colorless, oval, 4¹/₄" . . . . $175–$200
French Gloss, colorless, 4" . . . . $1–$2
FS Pease Sewing Machine Oil, OP, 5³/₈", light cornflower blue . . . . $300–$500
Furst-McNess Co, Freeport, Ill, colorless, 8³/₈" . . . . $1–$2
Greever-Lolspeich Mfg Co, colorless, 4¹/₂" . . . . $0.25–$0.5
Hercules Disinfectant, 6", amber . . . . $3–$4
Home Relief Co, Jameston, NY, 4¹/₂", aqua. . . . . $2–$3

Hutchins & Mason Keene NH Waterproof Blacking, OP, square, 5⁵/₈", olive amber
.... $1500+
Keasbey & Mattison Co, 5¹/₄", light blue .... $4–$5
Lake Shore Seed Co, 5¹/₂", aqua .... $0.5–$1
Liquid Stove Polish, colorless, 6¹/₄" .... $1–$2
Liquozone-Mfg, 6", amber .... $3–$4
Melvin & Badger Co, Boston, colorless, 2³/₄" .... $0.5–$1
National Casket Co, colorless, embossed eagle and capitol .... $18–$23
Nontoxo Chemical Co, 2³/₄", amber .... $1–$2
Osborns Liquid Polish, OP, 3³/₄", olive yellow .... $350–$450
Patent Gutta Percha Oil Blacking, OP, 5¹/₂", yellow amber .... $1500+
Patent Oil Blacking Gutta Percha Forbes & Co, OP, rectangular, 5¹/₄", olive amber.
.... $2000+
Prices Patent Candle Company Limited, 7¹/₈", cobalt .... $75–$100
Prices Patent Candle Company Limited, OP, 7¹/₈", cobalt .... $125–$175
Prof Callans World Renowned, 4", aqua .... $2–$3
Race & Sheldon Boot Polish, eight sided, OP, green .... $250–$350
Saratoga Dressing, shoe figural, 4¹/₂", aqua .... $30–$50
Shulife-For Shoes, 3³/₄", olive green .... $4–$5
Simons-Binghamton, NY, 7", light green .... $4–$5
Spauldings Glue, OP, aqua .... $16–$22
Special Battery Oil, Thomas Edison, colorless, 4¹/₂" .... $3–$4
Sperm Sewing Machine Oil, colorless, 4³/₄" .... $2–$3
Standardised Disinfectant Co, 4¹/₄", light amber .... $1–$2
Triump Superior Clock Oil, colorless, 3¹/₂" .... $2–$3
Uptons Refined Liquid Glue, C-1753, OP, twelve sided, 2⁷/₈", aqua .... $45–$65
USA Hosp. Dept., 9¹/₄", yellow olive .... $250–$300
Utility Bottle, square, OP, lip opening, 1³/₄", 11¹¹/₁₆" (h), green .... $225–$280
Utility Bottle, square, straight sided, OP, 9⁵/₈", greenish aqua .... $350–$450

INK BOTTLES

Ink bottles and inkwells were among the earliest-produced bottles in America, certainly going back to at least the 18th century. The early ink bottles were generally small in size, as the cost of the ink used to fill them was quite expensive. Usually the black ink was the least costly, whereas blues, greens, and reds were indeed extravagant.

Up until the mid 19th century, ink was made and sold mainly by chemists and apothecary shops. Most of these early bottles were unembossed and would carry only a label mentioning the type of ink and the manufacturer. Molded ink bottles appeared in the United States probably around 1815, with blown three-mold ink bottles becoming very popular through the 1840s. Around this time, also, appeared one of the most commonly found shapes in ink bottles—the umbrella type. This is a multisided conical form of bottle, which is readily found both pontiled and with smooth bases.

Beginning around the mid 19th century, ink bottle manufacturers began to use more unusual colors and employ various unusual shapes, such as figurals of all sorts. One of the more highly collected type of ink bottle is the so-called tea kettle type, in which the neck extends upward at an angle from the base. These were made in an incredible assortment of shapes and colors, and it is very difficult to determine the origin of a given ink bottle since they were made in England, France, and the United States.

Collectors should also become familiar with some of the deceptive reproductions on the market, such as some of the free-blown funnel-type inkwells. The reader is referred to *Ink Bottles and Inkwells* by William E. Covill, Jr., which the letter "C" refers to below.

A & F, C-610, offset dome, 1$^1/_2$", aqua .... $40–$45
AB Laird's Ink, eight sided, OP, 2$^1/_4$", aqua. .... $200–$300
AB Laird's Ink, eight sided, OP, 2$^1/_8$", blue green .... $1800–$2500
Adrian Maurin, boot shaped, 2$^3/_4$", aqua .... $175–$250
Allings Patd Apl 25 1871, C-704, offset dome, 1$^3/_4$", aqua .... $30–$35
AM & Co NY, clear cottage form, 3$^5/_8$" .... $150–$200
Am Bertinguiot, round, squat, labeled, OP, 2$^1/_2$", dark amber .... $200–$275
American Standard Ink Frederick Md, SB, 10", grass green .... $300–$375
Bank of England Ink, cottage shaped, 3$^5/_8$", aqua .... $1500–$1900
Barrel, Pat March 17 1870, C-672, clear, 2$^1/_2$" .... $25–$35
Barrel, Pat Oct 17 1865, C-669, clear, 2$^1/_4$" .... $25–$35
Barrel, unembossed, clear, 2$^1/_2$". .... $20–$30
BB & Co, umbrella, OP, 1$^3/_4$", cornflower blue .... $375–$475
BD, on teakettle panel, clear, 1$^1/_2$" .... $300–$360
Ben Franklin Bust, teakettle, C-1291, 2$^3/_4$", aqua. .... $125–$175
Ben Franklin Bust, teakettle, C-1291, 2$^3/_4$", cobalt .... $1200–$1500
Bertinguiot, C-575, OP, 2$^1/_2$", aqua. .... $150–$250
Bertinguiot, C-575, OP, 2$^1/_8$", olive amber .... $210–$260
Bertinguiot, C-575, OP, 2$^1/_2$", sapphire blue .... $600–$900
Billing's Mauve Ink, dome shaped, 2$^1/_2$" .... $30–$50
Black Writing Fluid Prepared by Maynard & Noyes (on label), OP, 5$^5/_8$", olive amber. .... $200–$275
Blackwood & Co London, paneled shoulder dome, 2", cobalt. .... $200–$265
Blackwood's Patent London, 2", aqua. .... $20–$30
Blake & Herring NY, eight sided umbrella, OP, 3", aqua .... $110–$160
Blake & Herring NY, eight sided umbrella, OP, 3", light emerald green ....
.... $600–$800
Blake NY, umbrella, OP, 3", aqua .... $200–$250
Blown Ink, C-1064, with lid and finial, OP, 2", blue. .... $100–$125
Blown Ink, dome shaped, inverted spout, similar to C-1030, OP, 2$^1/_4$", olive amber...
.... $400–$550
Blown Ink, dome shaped, similar to C-1128, OP, 2", olive amber .... $300–$400

Blown Three Mold (see Geometric, this listing)

Boss Patent, six sided, OP, 2³/₈", aqua. . . . . $250–$300

Bowman's American Ink Co's Ink (on label), umbrella, OP, 2¹/₄", medium root beer amber. . . . . $275–$350

Butler Cinci, teakettle, eight sided, 1⁷/₈", aqua . . . . $400–$650

Butler's Ink Cincinnati, C-519, twelve sided, OP, 2¹/₂", yellow olive . . $4000–$6000

Butler's Ink Cincinnati, C-519, twelve sided, OP, rolled lip, 2³/₈", aqua . . $100–$150

Butler's Ink Cincinnati, C-519, twelve sided, rolled lip, ¹/₄", pale apple green. . . . . $250–$350

Butler's Ink Cincinnati, cylinder, OP, 5¹/₈", aqua . . . . $150–$225

Butler's Ink Cincinnati, OP, cylinder, 5¹/₄", yellow green . . . . $450–$700

Cabin, SB, clear, 3¹/₄" (h) . . . . $400–$600

Cabin ink. PHOTO COURTESY OF GLASS WORKS AUCTIONS.

Cabin, unembossed, C-680, clear, 2¹/₂" . . . . $350–$500

Cabin, unembossed, C-688, 2¹/₂", aqua . . . . $300–$350

Cal Ink Co SF, schoolhouse, 2¹/₂", amber. . . . . $2500–$3000

Carter's (on base), C-555, ABM, 2³/₄", cobalt . . . . $90–$120

Carter's (on base), Carter Ink Products, full labels, with stopper, 8¹/₂", cobalt . . . . $70–$100

Carter's cathedral. PHOTO COURTESY OF GLASS WORKS AUCTIONS.

Carter's (on base), David's Black Writing Ink (on label), ABM, 7", cobalt. . . . . $25–$30

Carter's Inks, stoneware, embossed at base edge, 9¼" . . . . $35–$45
Carter's, C-819, six sided, cathedral arches, 7⁷/₈", cobalt . . . . $125–$150
Carter's, embossed metal screw lid, clear, 3⁵/₈" . . . . $30–$50
Carter, C-820, ABM, cathedral panels, 9³/₄", cobalt . . . . $100–$140
Carter, C-820, ABM, cathedral panels, pour spout, 7⁷/₈", cobalt . . . . $125–$190
Carter, C-820, ABM, cathedral panels, wider mouth, 6¼", cobalt . . . . $200–$260
Carter, C-820, tooled mouth, 6¼", cobalt . . . . $150–$200
Centennial Ink, (see Patented. . . . this listing) . . . .
CF, eight flaring panels, OP, 2¹/₂", black . . . . $400–$550
Clark's Superior Record Ink, C-749, OP, 5⁷/₈", olive green . . . . $1400–$1900
Cone Ink, 2¹/₂", amber . . . . $10–$15
Cone Ink, ABM, unembossed, 2¹/₂", cobalt, green, amber . . . . $5–$20
Cone Ink, C-18, X on base, amber tone, OP, 2³/₈", olive green . . . . $100–$145
Cone Ink, C-18, X on base, olive tone, OP, 2¹/₈", yellow . . . . $250–$350
Cone Ink, C-23, OP, lightly cleaned, 2¹/₄", light emerald green . . . . $120–$150
Cone Ink, C-25, ribbed, SB, 2¹/₈", aqua . . . . $30–$40
Cone Ink, C-25, with vertical rib pattern, OP, lightly cleaned, 2¹/₈", aqua . . $100–$135
Cone Ink, clear, 2¹/₂" . . . . $8–$10
Cone Ink, OP, 2¹/₄", amber . . . . $300–$360
Cone Ink, OP, 2¹/₄", deep forest green . . . . $750–$950
Cone Ink, OP, 2¹/₄", light apricot yellow amber . . . . $400–$475
Cone Ink, OP, 2¹/₄", light blue green . . . . $325–$400
Cone Ink, OP, 2¹/₄", medium apricot amber . . . . $300–$400
Cone Ink, OP, 2¹/₄", medium emerald green . . . . $450–$550
Cone Ink, OP, 2³/₈", medium olive green . . . . $125–$155
Cone Ink, OP, 2³/₈", medium root beer amber . . . . $125–$165
Cone Ink, OP, 2³/₈", medium yellow amber . . . . $225–$285
Cone Ink, OP, 2³/₈", olive amber . . . . $250–$290
Cone Ink, unembossed, rolled lip, open pontil, 2", aqua . . . . $40–$55
Cone Ink, vertical shoulder ribs, three piece mold, SB, 2¹/₂", aqua . . . . $40–$60

Left: *Cone ink.* Right: *Cottage ink.* PHOTOS COURTESY OF GLASS WORKS AUCTIONS.

Cottage, C-684, 2⁵/₈", aqua . . . . $350–$450
Cottage, C-688, lip bruise, 2¹/₂", aqua . . . . $150–$190
Cottage, C-693, domed roof, SB, 2¹/₂", medium blue green . . . . $1500–$2000
Cottage, similar to C-689, no roof embossing, 2⁵/₈", aqua . . . . $400–$500
Cottage, unembossed, two story house, milk glass, 4³/₄" . . . . $400–$500
Cowle's Inc, three piece mold, SB, 9¹/₂", deep amber . . . . $125–$185
David's & Black New York, cylinder, OP, sloping collar, 5⁷/₈", emerald green . . . . . .
. . . . $250–$350

David's & Black New York, cylinder, pour spout, OP, 8³/₄", blue green. . . . .
. . . . $180–$250
David's & Black New York, cylinder, sloping collar, OP, 4", light green. . . . $60–$90
David's & Black New York, OP, sloping collar, 4⁵/₈", light green . . . . $125–$175
David's, C-617, offset dome, 1⁵/₈", medium blue green . . . . $350–$475
Davis & Miller, eight sided umbrella, OP, 2¹/₂", aqua . . . . $400–$600
De Halsey Patente, OP, 3", olive amber . . . . $450–$650
Diamond Patterned, ten diamond, midwestern, C-1332, 2", aqua . . . . . . $5000–$7500
Dog Pottery Inkwell, C-1593, reclining dog, 3³/₄" . . . . $175–$250
Dr Blossom's Chemical Warehouse Zanesville, twelve sided, OP, 4¹/₄", aqua . . . . . .
. . . . $200–$250
Dr Sheet's Ink, cylinder, pour spout, SB, 9³/₄", sapphire blue . . . . $500–$600
Drape Pattern Cone Ink, C-27, OP, 2¹/₄", aqua. . . . . $250–$325
E Eichele, twelve sided, OP, umbrella, 2³/₄", aqua . . . . $200–$300
E Waters A, OP, vertical ribbed, OP, 3¹/₈", aqua . . . . $400–$475
E Waters B, square, ribbed, OP, 3", aqua . . . . $100–$150
E Waters Inde. Le Ink Troy, clear, rect., ribbed, OP, 2¹/₂" . . . . $150–$200
E Waters Troy NY, C-207, cylinder, OP, 2¹/₄", aqua. . . . . $150–$210
E Waters Troy NY, C-208, cylinder, OP, 3⁷/₈", light green . . . . $250–$350
E Waters Troy NY, C-208, cylinder, OP, 4", aqua. . . . . $250–$350
E Waters Troy NY, C-773, OP, 4¹/₄", aqua . . . . $400–$550
E Waters Troy NY, C-773, OP, 5¹/₈", aqua . . . . $600–$800
E Waters Troy NY, C-774, OP, 6³/₄", aqua . . . . $500–$600
E Waters Troy NY, OP, fluted shoulders, 6¹/₂", aqua. . . . . $500–$650
E Waters Troy NY, sixteen shoulder flutes, OP, 5¹/₄", green . . . . $1000–$1500
EB Estes Metropolitan Ink No 88 John St NY, stoneware jug, handled, 8" . . . .
. . . . $275–$375
Enamel Decorated, square, clear, flaring lip, OP, 2³/₈". . . . . $125–$175
Enamel Decorated, square, milk glass, flaring lip, OP, 2¹/₂" . . . . $200–$300
Encre De La Grande Vertu Bordeau, round, OP, 2", deep amethyst . . . . . $250–$325
Encre Francaise Lefils Par, snail shaped, 1⁷/₈", aqua. . . . . $400–$500
Estes NY Ink, C-117, OP, eight sided, 4", aqua . . . . $1000–$1300
Estes NY Ink, C-756, OP, eight sided, 6³/₄", aqua . . . . $350–$500
Estes NY Ink, conical umbrella, 4", aqua . . . . $200–$300
Estes NY Ink, eight sided, OP, 6¹/₄", medium blue green . . . . $600–$800
Estes, umbrella, OP, 3", aqua. . . . . $900–$1200
F Kidder Improvd Indelible Ink, C-481, square, OP, 2³/₈", aqua. . . . . $100–$135
F Xlett & Co Superior Ink, cylinder, OP, 4¹/₄", aqua . . . . $175–$250
Fahnestock's Neutral Ink, six concave panels, OP, 4¹/₈", aqua. . . . . $250–$350
Farley's Ink, C-528, eight sided, 3⁵/₈", yellowish amber . . . . $1100–$1400
Farley's Ink, eight sided, 80% label, tooled lip, OP, 3", olive amber . . . . . . $550–$800
Farley's Ink, eight sided, OP, 1⁷/₈", olive amber. . . . . $600–$900
FH Metzger, cylinder, OP, 2", aqua . . . . $90–$135
Fine Black Ink Made & Sold By JL Thompson Troy NY, cylinder, flared lip, OP,
5⁷/₈", straw yellow. . . . . $1800–$2500
Funnel Ink, similar to C-1341, OP, 2¹/₈", golden amber. . . . . $300–$400
G & R American Writing Fluid, cone, OP, 2⁵/₈", aqua. . . . . $300–$400
GA Miller Quicy III, eight sided, 2¹/₂", aqua . . . . $175–$275
GA Miller Quincy III, octagon, applied lip, SB, 2¹/₂", aqua . . . . $200–$300
Gaylord's Superior Record Ink Boston, cylinder, flared lip, OP, 5¹/₈", olive green . .
. . . . $750–$1000

Farley's, paneled or sided. PHOTO COURTESY OF GLASS WORKS AUCTIONS.

Geometric, C-1173, milky opalescent, SB, 1⁵/₈"................... $225–$275
Geometric, C-1175, OP, 1³/₄", deep yellowish olive amber............ $150–$180
Geometric, C-1182, OP, 1⁵/₈", deep olive amber.................... $150–$190
Geometric, C-1194, OP, base edge flake, 1³/₄", deep olive amber....... $100–$115
Geometric, C-1196, 2¹/₈", deep olive green........................ $100–$135
Geometric, C-1196, OP, 1⁷/₈", deep olive amber.................... $110–$145
Geometric, C-1200, OP, 2", deep yellowish amber................... $110–$145
Geometric, C-1221, lip edge chip, 1¹/₂", olive green................. $80–$95
Geometric, C-1221, OP, 1¹/₂", deep yellowish olive amber............ $110–$140
Geometric, GI-7, C-1172, cobalt blue.............................. $2500+
Geometric, GII-15, OP, 1³/₄", medium olive green.................. $600–$750
Geometric, GII-15, OP, 1⁷/₈", medium green...................... $2000–$3000
Geometric, GII-15, OP, olive amber.............................. $250–$350
Geometric, GII-16, OP, 1¹/₂", dark olive amber..................... $100–$140
Geometric, GII-16, OP, 1¹/₂", yellow olive........................ $125–$165
Geometric, GII-18, 1⁵/₈", yellow olive .... $130–$175
Geometric, GII-18, OP, 1¹/₂", deep olive amber.................... $140–$180
Geometric, GII-18, OP, base edge flake, olive green .... $90–$110
Geometric, GII-18, OP, cobalt blue............................... $15,000+
Geometric, GIII-23, corset shaped, OP, sapphire blue .... $5000+
Geometric, GIII-29, base edge chip, OP, 1¹/₂", yellow olive .... $90–$110
Geometric, GIII-29, OP, 1¹/₂", deep olive........................ $130–$190
Geometric, GIII-29, OP, upper body chip, 1³/₈", yellowish olive......... $80–$100
Globe Shaped Ink, SB, 3", aqua................................ $100–$140
Golden Treasure, barrel, 4⁷/₈", aqua............................. $75–$100
Gross & Robinsons American Writing Fluid, cylinder, OP, 7¹/₄", aqua ....
.... $750–$1000
Gross & Robinsons American Writing Fluid, IP, cylinder, 6", aqua..... $500–$750
H & T Red Ink, OP, cone, 2", aqua.............................. $100–$140
Harrison / Tippecanoe, C-676, clear cabin, OP, 3⁷/₈" .... $10,000–$15,000
Harrison's Columbian Ink Patent, twelve sided, OP, 7", cobalt..... $5000–$10,000
Harrison's Columbian Ink, C-194, cylinder, 2", cobalt .... $500–$750
Harrison's Columbian Ink, C-194, cylinder, OP, 2", cobalt........... $450–$650

Harrison's Columbian Ink, C-194, cylinder, OP, exterior stain, 2$^1/_8$", cobalt. . . . . $300–$375
Harrison's Columbian Ink, C-195, cylinder, full label, OP, 4", cobalt. . . $750–$1000
Harrison's Columbian Ink, C-195, cylinder, OP, 4", cobalt . . . . $400–$525
Harrison's Columbian Ink, C-529, eight sided, 1$^7/_8$", medium blue green . . . . $400–$600
Harrison's Columbian Ink, C-529, eight sided, OP, 1$^3/_8$", aqua . . . . $160–$210
Harrison's Columbian Ink, C-529, eight sided, OP, 1$^7/_8$", light bluish green . . . . $100–$135
Harrison's Columbian Ink, C-530, eight sided, OP, 1$^3/_4$", blue aqua . . . . . $150–$190
Harrison's Columbian Ink, C-530, eight sided, OP, 1$^5/_8$", aqua . . . . $80–$120
Harrison's Columbian Ink, C-530, eight sided, OP, surface stain, 1$^3/_4$", aqua . . . . $75–$95
Harrison's Columbian Ink, C-530, OP, 1$^7/_8$", medium yellow green . . . . . $600–$900
Harrison's Columbian Ink, C-531, eight sided, OP, 2", aqua . . . . $150–$200
Harrison's Columbian Ink, C-536, eight sided, OP, 3$^3/_4$", aqua . . . . $75–$125
Harrison's Columbian Ink, C-537, reversed "N" in Ink, OP, 2$^1/_2$", aqua . . . . $100–$175
Harrison's Columbian Ink, C-538, 95% label, OP, twelve sided, 5", aqua . . . . $300–$400
Harrison's Columbian Ink, C-623, igloo, 1$^5/_8$", aqua . . . . $300–$400
Harrison's Columbian Ink, C-624, eight sided offset dome, 1$^7/_8$", aqua. . . $300–$400
Harrison's Columbian Ink, C-624, eight sided offset dome, $^1/_2$" lip chip, 2", aqua . . . . $200–$240
Harrison's Columbian Ink, C-760, twelve sided, OP, 4$^1/_2$", aqua. . . . . $80–$120
Harrison's Columbian Ink, C-761, eight sided, OP, lip chips, 7$^1/_8$", aqua . . . . $100–$125
Harrison's Columbian Ink, C-761, twelve sided, OP, 7$^1/_8$", aqua. . . . . $375–$500
Harrison's Columbian Ink, C-761, twelve sided, OP, 9", aqua. . . . . $550–$750
Harrison's Columbian Ink, C-762, twelve sided, OP, 11$^1/_2$", aqua. . . . . . $750–$1150
Harrison's Columbian Ink, C-763, twelve sided, IP, 11$^1/_2$", medium blue. . . . . $15,000–$25,000
Harrison's Columbian Ink, C-764, cylinder, OP, 5$^3/_4$", cobalt . . . . $575–$800
Harrison's Columbian Ink, C-765, cylinder, $^1/_2$" lip chip, cleaned, 7", cobalt . . . . $450–$575
Harrison's Columbian Ink, C-765, cylinder, OP, 7", cobalt . . . . $1200–$1500
Harrison's Columbian Ink, C-765, OP, 5$^3/_4$", cobalt. . . . . $800–$1200
Harter's Black Letter Ink (on label), OP, flared lip, 5$^1/_4$", black . . . . $140–$190
Herron's Ink Newville Pa, cylinder, conical, shoulders, OP, 2$^1/_2$", aqua. . . $400–$600
Higg's Ink, twelve sided, umbrella, OP, 2$^7/_8$", aqua . . . . $150–$200
Hodgson Philada (on base), clear cone, OP, 2" . . . . $100–$150
Hohenthal Brothers & Co Indelible Writing Ink NY, cylinder, pour spout, OP, 9", olive amber. . . . . $800–$1100
Horse & Rider Figure embossed on sides, round, squat, flattened lip, OP, 1$^3/_8$"(h), aqua. . . . . $8000+
Hover Phila, cylinder, flared lip, OP, 5$^1/_4$", sapphire. . . . . $500–$800
Hover Phila, cylinder, pour spout, SB, 9", aqua . . . . $125–$175
Hover Phila, cylinder, tooled lip, OP, 5$^1/_2$", medium green . . . . $150–$240
Hover Phila, eight sided umbrella, OP, 2$^1/_4$", light blue green . . . . $300–$375
Hover Phila, eight sided umbrella, OP, 2$^3/_8$", emerald green . . . . $650–$900
Hover Phila, OP, 9", medium emerald green . . . . $400–$600

Hover Phila, twelve sided umbrella, OP, 1³/₄", blue green . . . . $250–$325
Hyde London, cone, 2³/₄", cobalt . . . . $80–$120
Ink for Boot & Shoemaker's (on label), cylinder, 7⁵/₈", olive amber . . . . . $100–$150
J & IEM, C-627, offset blue, bright blue . . . . $900–$1250
J & IEM, C-627, offset dome, 1⁵/₈", yellow amber . . . . $325–$450
J & IEM, C-627, offset dome, olive tone, 2", yellow . . . . $1250–$1600
J & IEM, C-628, offset dome, 1⁵/₈", amber . . . . $125–$165
J & IEM, C-628, offset dome, 1⁵/₈", light yellow apple green . . . . $325–$425
J & IEM, C-629, offset dome, 1¹/₂", aqua . . . . $20–$25
J & IEM, C-632, offset dome, 2", aqua . . . . $30–$45
J & IEM, C-647, offset dome, 1⁵/₈", aqua . . . . $20–$25
J Butler Cin, C-478, OP, 2⁷/₈", aqua . . . . $100–$145
J Guidry Cincinnati, umbrella, twelve sided, OP, 3¹/₂", aqua . . . . $250–$350
J Raynald, globe figural, 2¹/₂", aqua . . . . $150–$225
JA Williamson Chemist, cylinder, 6¹/₂", blue green . . . . $150–$200
James P Scott's Ink, square, OP, 2¹/₂", aqua . . . . $90–$135
James S Mason & Co, eight sided umbrella, OP, 2³/₈", aqua . . . . $350–$450
JB Fondersmith's Ink, eight panels, embossed domed shoulders, OP, 3¹/₈", aqua . . . .
. . . . $90–$135
JJ Butler Cin O, cylinder, embossed on shoulder, OP, 2⁵/₈", aqua . . . . $80–$125
JJ Butler Cin, C-478, rectangular, OP, 2³/₄", aqua . . . . $60–$80
JJ Butler Cinct Ohio, unlisted, cone form, OP, 2¹/₂", aqua . . . . $350–$475
JK Palmer Chemist Boston, C-770, pour spout OP, 9", olive amber . . . . . $350–$450
JM & S, greenish aqua, offset dome, C-644, 1³/₄" . . . . $75–$90
JM & S, offset dome, C-633, 1⁵/₈", aqua . . . . $70–$80
Jones Empire Ink NY, 12 sided, C-769, IP, emerald green . . . . $2500–$3500
Jones Empire Ink NY, 12 sided, C-769, IP, lip chip, emerald green . . . . . $800–$1200
Jones No 1, vertically ribbed, rect., SB, 3¹/₂", aqua . . . . $110–$145
Josiah Johnson Japan Writing Fluid, C-1242, pottery teakettle, 2¹/₄" . . . . $100–$150
Joy's Ink, C-289, SB, 2¹/₄", cobalt . . . . $150–$225
JS Dunham & Co, umbrella, OP, 2³/₈", bluish aqua . . . . $400–$550
JS Dunham, C-116, umbrella, OP, 2¹/₂", bluish aqua . . . . $200–$250
JS Mason Philada, cylinder, sloping collar, OP, 6", aqua . . . . $100–$150
JS Mason Philada, OP, flared lip, cylinder, 4³/₈", medium emerald green . . $350–$475
JW Ely Cincinnati, OP, rolled lip, 2⁵/₈", aqua . . . . $275–$375
JW Seaton Louisville Ky, twelve sided, OP, 2¹/₄", light emerald green . . . . $550–$750
Kirtland's Ink W&H (on base), C-622, offset dome, aqua . . . . $150–$200
Kirtland's Writing Fluid Poland Ohio, domed cylinder, OP, 2⁷/₈", aqua . . . .
. . . . $300–$375
L Poingelet, OP, 1⁷/₈", deep amber . . . . $450–$650
Laughlin and Bushfield Wheeling Va, eight sided, OP, 2⁷/₈", aqua . . . . . . $150–$200
Levinson's Inks St Louis, cabin, 1⁷/₈", amber . . . . $300–$400
LH Thomas Ink, C-76, cone shaped, SB, 2¹/₂", aqua . . . . $30–$45
Liberty Bell Shaped, frosted clear, 2³/₈" . . . . $75–$125
Locomotive Figural Ink Bottle, 3", aqua . . . . $1000–$1250
Locomotive Ink (embossed), C-714, locomotive form, 2⁷/₈", aqua . . . . . $1500–$2000
LW (on base), umbrella, C-162, SB, 2¹/₂", aqua . . . . $50–$75
M & C Ltd, square, 2⁷/₈", medium emerald green . . . . $75–$125
M & P New York, eight sided umbrella, OP, 2¹/₂", light greenish aqua . . . . $120–$175
MA & Pa Carter, C-1619, painted porcelain figural's, pair . . . . $250–$350
Matthew & Bro's Albany Ia N, eight sided, OP, 2¹/₂", aqua . . . . $375–$450

Maxwell's Record & Copying Ink (on label), OP, 9$\frac{1}{2}$", olive amber .... $125–$165
Melon Shaped, 26 vertical ribs, C-1129, OP, 1$\frac{3}{4}$", olive green .... $2000–$2500
NA Paris Depose, square semi-building form, SB, 2$\frac{3}{4}$", cobalt .... $100–$140
NE Plus Ultra Fluid, C-689, cabin, 2$\frac{1}{2}$", aqua. .... $300–$400
NJ Simond's Lawrence Mass, twelve sided, OP, pour spout, 8", aqua ... $750–$1000
North & Warren's Fine Ink, cylinder, OP, 4$\frac{1}{2}$", slag green .... $500–$700
Offset Dome (Turtle Ink), C-638, bird on branch, 1$\frac{5}{8}$", aqua .... $35–$45
Offset Dome (Turtle Ink), C-645, 1$\frac{5}{8}$", amber .... $150–$210
Offset Dome (Turtle Ink), C-647, 1$\frac{3}{4}$", cobalt .... $1200–$1500
Offset Dome (Turtle Ink), C-647, 2", deep amber .... $210–$270

Offset dome or "turtle." PHOTO COURTESY OF GLASS WORKS AUCTIONS.

Offset Dome, unembossed, aqua .... $10–$25
Opdyke Bros Ink, C-664, barrel, 2$\frac{1}{2}$", aqua. .... $150–$225
Paneled (see Sided Ink, this listing)
Paris Depose Na, 2$\frac{3}{4}$", cobalt .... $125–$175
Pat March 17 1870, medium barrel ink, clear, 2" .... $40–$60
Patd Apl (on side), cabin, 2$\frac{3}{4}$", deep amber .... $1200–$1500
Patd Mar 14 1871, schoolhouse, 2$\frac{3}{4}$", aqua .... $300–$375
Patented April 11 1876, building shaped, C-695, clear, 3$\frac{3}{8}$". .... $375–$450
Patterson's Excelsior Ink, OP, eight sided, 2$\frac{5}{8}$", aqua .... $325–$450
Perine Guyot & Cie, round, squat, OP, 2$\frac{1}{4}$", deep amethyst .... $250–$325
Pitkin Type, 36 ribs swirled, all sides equal size, square .... $4000+
Pitkin Type, 36 ribs swirled, round, 1$\frac{1}{2}$", olive amber................ $350–$500
Pitkin Type, 36 ribs swirled, round, $\frac{1}{4}$" mouth chip, 1$\frac{1}{2}$", olive green .... $125–$175
Pitkin Type, 36 ribs swirled, round, OP, 1$\frac{7}{8}$", yellow olive............. $400–$500
Pitkin Type, 36 ribs swirled, square sided, 1$\frac{1}{2}$", olive green .... $900–$1300

Left: *Pitkin ink.* Right: *Ringed or "annular."* PHOTOS COURTESY OF GLASS WORKS AUCTIONS.

Potter Champlin Westerly RI, eight sided umbrella, OP, 2$\frac{7}{8}$", aqua .... $800–$1100
RB Snow St Louis, twelve sided umbrella, OP, 2", aqua .... $200–$300
Redg April 3 1869 (on base), cottage, crizzled, 2$\frac{3}{8}$", aqua .... $60–$90

Revolving Ink Stand, brass base, pottery barrel shaped bottle, blue .... $75–$100
Revolving Ink Stand, C-1451, cast iron rope / anchor motif, clear snail bottle, $4^3/8$" ..
.... $80–$110
Revolving Ink Stand, fancy iron stand with two clear snail inkwells...... $125–$175
RF, C-203, OP, $2^1/8$", black amethyst............................... $125–$165
Ribbed Ink, 24 vertical ribs, OP, funnel shaped, medium blue green.... $1500–$2000
Ringed Inkwell, C-1167, five rings, OP, $1^3/8$", olive green............. $700–$900
Ross's Excelsior Ink, 12 sided, OP, $7^1/4$", emerald green............. $2750–$3750
Round, unembossed, sharp shoulder, ABM, $3^1/4$", cobalt.................. $2–$3
Round, unembossed, sharp shoulder, ring at top and bottom edges, 3", cobalt... $4–$6
Round, unembossed, sharp shoulder, SB............................. $5–$7
S Fine Blk Ink, C-193, OP, 3", medium olive green................... $350–$400
S Fine Blk Ink, OP, 3", deep orange amber........................ $750–$1000
S Fine Blk Ink, OP, 3", medium emerald green .... $400–$475
S Fine Blk Ink, OP, cylinder, $3^1/4$", light green...................... $150–$250
Sanford's Inks One Quart & Library Paste, C-890, full label, ABM, $9^3/8$", amber ..
.... $70–$90
Sheet's Writing Fluid, six sided, corset shaped, OP, $2^5/8$", aqua .... $550–$750
Shoe Figural, lady's slipper, $3^1/2$", fiery opal .... $400–$500
SI Comp, barrel, milk glass, $2^1/2$" .... $325–$425
SI Comp, C-683, milk glass, cottage shaped, $2^3/4$" .... $300–$400
SI Comp, clear cottage shaped ink, $2^5/8$".......................... $250–$350
SI Comp, cottage shaped ink, $2^5/8$", aqua.......................... $100–$150
Sided Ink, 10 sided, OP, $2^1/4$", blue green....................... $275–$375
Sided Ink, 12 sided, OP, $1^3/4$", emerald green....................... $85–$110
Sided Ink, 12 sided, OP, 2", light emerald green..................... $75–$100
Sided Ink, 12 sided, pour spout, OP, $5^3/4$", olive green............... $700–$950
Sided Ink, 12 sided, pour spout, OP, 8", olive green.................. $800–$1200
Snow & Quirk St Louis, 12 paneled, OP, $2^1/4$", aqua.................. $175–$250
SO Dunbar Taunton Mass, C-754, OP, cylinder, sloping collar, $8^3/8$", aqua ....
.... $100–$150
SO Dunbar Taunton Mass, C-755, OP, $8^1/2$", aqua................... $100–$175
SO Dunbar Taunton, C-115, eight sided umbrella, OP, $2^3/8$", aqua....... $150–$200
SO Dunbar Taunton, C-115, eight sided umbrella, OP, lightly cleaned but retains
ground wear, $2^3/8$", aqua...................................... $60–$75
Soc G Rizzo, round, long neck, rough sheared, SB, $2^3/8$", honey yellow .... $90–$135
Square, 2 oz on neck, ABM, cobalt................................. $3–$4
Square, unembossed, rough sheared lip, English, 2", aqua, greens, blues .... $10–$40
Square, unembossed, rough sheared lip, English, ribbed, 2", various colors .. $20–$50
SS Stafford's Inks Made in USA, pour spout, $4^5/8$", cobalt............... $30–$35
SS Stafford's Inks Made in USA, pour spout, $5^1/2$", cobalt............... $30–$40
SS Stafford's Inks Made in USA, pour spout, $7^1/2$", cobalt............... $40–$50
SS Stafford's Inks Made in USA, pour spout, $9^3/8$", cobalt............... $50–$65
Stoneware, unembossed, cylinder, ring lip, $2^1/4$", tan colored................ $4–$6
T & M, square, rolled lip, $2^1/2$", bright green....................... $140–$190
TDA (on base), C-611, offset dome, $1^5/8$", aqua..................... $35–$50
Teakettle, C-1229, clear, $1^5/8$" .... $50–$75
Teakettle, C-1231, flat top, $2^1/4$", cobalt .... $375–$500
Teakettle, C-1232, clear, $1^3/4$"................................. $250–$325
Teakettle, C-1233, floral pattern, 2", cobalt........................ $600–$750
Teakettle, C-1233, milk glass, 2", fiery opal....................... $275–$375

Teakettle, C-1235, silver overlay, flat top, 2", black amethyst .... $300–$375
Teakettle, C-1237, $2^3/8$", light opaque blue .... $450–$650
Teakettle, C-1237, $2^5/8$", deep opaque powder blue .... $500–$750
Teakettle, C-1237, electric yellow green........................... $300–$375
Teakettle, C-1237, milk glass, fancy domed top, $2^5/8$" .... $375–$450
Teakettle, C-1239, milk glass, raised floral decoration, six sided, $2^1/4$" .... $300–$400
Teakettle, C-1242, Josiah Johnson Writing Fluid, pottery, $2^1/4$".......... $100–$150
Teakettle, C-1248, marble base, $1^1/4$", emerald green.................. $500–$750
Teakettle, C-1248, rounded top, $1^5/8$", aqua .... $70–$90
Teakettle, C-1250, flat top, $2^1/8$" .... $125–$175
Teakettle, C-1250, lip chip, $2^1/8$", deep cobalt........................ $225–$275
Teakettle, C-1251, flat top, $1^5/8$", amethyst tint........................ $40–$60
Teakettle, C-1252, flat top, $1^7/8$", bright yellow green.................. $400–$600
Teakettle, C-1253, flat top, $2^1/2$", medium honey amber................ $500–$650
Teakettle, C-1254, flat top, 2", cobalt .... $125–$175
Teakettle, C-1255, 2", smoky lavender .... $400–$500
Teakettle, C-1257, 2", emerald green .... $300–$450
Teakettle, C-1257, 2", medium cobalt blue........................... $350–$450
Teakettle, C-1257, flat top, 2", deep purple amethyst .... $350–$450
Teakettle, C-1257, flat top, 2", medium sapphire .... $325–$425
Teakettle, C-1257, overall dullness & ground wear, 2", cobalt........... $160–$220
Teakettle, C-1257, several body bruises, 2", medium teal blue .... $70–$95
Teakettle, C-1259, flat top, 2", bright yellowish green .... $400–$550
Teakettle, C-1259, with gilt decoration, 2", deep green .... $400–$525
Teakettle, C-1261, flat top, 2", light–medium blue green................ $200–$250
Teakettle, C-1261, two top corner chips, 2", amethyst .... $90–$120
Teakettle, C-1262, clear with three blue enamel base bands, 2" .... $250–$350
Teakettle, C-1262, milk glass, dome top, $2^1/8$" .... $225–$300
Teakettle, C-1262, milk glass, enamel floral decoration, $2^1/8$" .... $325–$400
Teakettle, C-1263, clear, flat top, 2" .... $125–$150
Teakettle, C-1263, flat top, 2", deep yellowish green .... $275–$375
Teakettle, C-1265, flat top, $2^3/8$", powder blue opalescent .... $325–$425
Teakettle, C-1266, $2^1/4$", opalescent powder blue..................... $250–$350
Teakettle, C-1267, $2^1/4$", sapphire blue .... $800–$1200
Teakettle, C-1267, beehive form, $2^1/4$", medium greenish aqua .... $600–$850
Teakettle, C-1268, $2^3/4$", amethyst............................... $250–$325
Teakettle, C-1278, raised floral design, panel edge chip, $2^1/2$", fiery opal ....
.... $375–$475
Teakettle, C-1285, barrel, $2^1/8$", deep sapphire .... $800–$1000
Teakettle, C-1286, barrel, $2^1/8$", amethyst...................... $800–$1100
Teakettle, C-1286, barrel, $2^1/8$", cobalt .... $800–$1100
Teakettle, C-1288, turtle shell form, $1^7/8$", aqua .... $400–$550
Teakettle, C-1291, Ben Franklin bust, $2^1/2$", aqua.................... $300–$400
Teakettle, C-1294, clear, $1^3/8$" .... $70–$90
Teakettle, domed top, $2^1/4$", grayish clambroth .... $350–$450
Teakettle, flat top, $2^1/8$", bright canary yellow...................... $275–$375
Teakettle, pottery, brown mottled glaze, $2^1/8$", tan with white .... $100–$145
Teakettle, stoneware, hotel advertisement on side, $2^1/2$"................ $200–$300
Teakettle, stoneware, whiskey advertising on side, $2^1/2$" .... $500–$600
Teakettle, unlisted, clear, unpaneled, 2" .... $45–$60
Teakettle, unlisted, cut and polished, diamonds, 2", amethyst to clear..... $500–$650

Teakettle, unlisted, flat top, 2", aqua . . . . $50–$75
Teakettle, unlisted, free blown, acorn finial, 2¹/₄", medium lime green . . . . $350–$425
Thaddeus Davids Co Premium Writing Fluid, stoneware, 26" . . . . $1300–$1900
Tippecanoe / Harrison, clear cabin, OP, 4" . . . . $10,000–$15,000
Tippecanoe Extract Hard Cider, clear barrel, 1⁷/₈". . . . . $600–$900
Titcomb's Ink Cin, 12 sided, paneled shoulder, OP, 2⁷/₈", aqua . . . . $250–$350
Titcomb, eight sided umbrella, OP, 2¹/₂", aqua . . . . $650–$850
Titcomb, eight sided umbrella, OP, 2⁵/₈", aqua . . . . $400–$550
Turtle Inks (see Offset Dome, or J & IEM, this listing)
Umbrella, C-149, 12 sided, OP, 2¹/₈", light green . . . . $45–$55
Umbrella, 16 sided, OP, 2", amber . . . . $300–$400
Umbrella, 8 or 12 sided, open pontil, 2" thru 2¹/₂", aqua . . . . $25–$40
Umbrella, 8 or 12 sided, open pontil, 2" thru 2¹/₂", greenish aqua . . . . $25–$50
Umbrella, 8 or 12 sided, smooth base, 2" thru 2¹/₂", aqua. . . . . $15–$20
Umbrella, 8 or 12 sided, smooth base, 2" thru 2¹/₂", greenish aqua . . . . $20–$30
Umbrella, ABM, 2", aqua . . . . $8–$12
Umbrella, C-123, eight sided, OP, 2¹/₂", medium emerald green . . . . $225–$325
Umbrella, C-123, eight sided, OP, 80% label, 2¹/₂", medium blue green . . . $200–$250
Umbrella, C-129, eight sided, IP, 2³/₈", medium yellowish green . . . . $350–$450
Umbrella, C-134, SB, 2¹/₄", black amethyst . . . . $400–$550
Umbrella, C-135, eight sided, OP, 2¹/₈", deep root beer amber. . . . . $110–$145
Umbrella, C-135, eight sided, OP, medium yellow, 2¹/₈", root beer amber . . . .
. . . . $150–$200
Umbrella, C-137, eight sided, OP, 2¹/₂", medium cobalt. . . . . $500–$675
Umbrella, C-137, SB, 2¹/₂", cobalt blue . . . . $500–$600
Umbrella, C-139, OP, 2¹/₄", light sapphire blue . . . . $800–$1200
Umbrella, C-143, eight sided, OP, 2¹/₈", forest green . . . . $450–$550
Umbrella, C-143, eight sided, OP, 2¹/₈", light yellowish green. . . . . $100–$135
Umbrella, C-143, eight sided, OP, 2¹/₈", medium blue green . . . . $100–$140
Umbrella, C-144, eight sided, OP, 2¹/₂", deep yellowish olive green . . . . . $225–$285
Umbrella, C-145, eight sided, OP, 2¹/₂", orange amber. . . . . $175–$200
Umbrella, C-145, eight sided, OP, 2³/₈", root beer amber. . . . . $175–$225
Umbrella, C-145, eight sided, OP, 2³/₈", root beer amber. . . . . $175–$225
Umbrella, C-145, OP, 2⁵/₈", reddish amber. . . . . $175–$225
Umbrella, C-150, 12 sided, OP, 2¹/₈", light yellowish green. . . . . $200–$300
Umbrella, C-150, OP, 2¹/₈", medium emerald green. . . . . $225–$285
Umbrella, C-153, OP, 16 sided, 2", deep olive amber. . . . . $400–$500
Umbrella, C-167, eight sided, SB, 2⁵/₈", light apple green . . . . $175–$245
Umbrella, C-179, eight sided, SB, 1/₈" lip flake, 2⁵/₈", medium sapphire . . . $175–$225
Umbrella, C-179, olive tone, eight sided, SB, 2¹/₂", bright yellow . . . . $600–$900
Umbrella, C-180, eight sided, OP, 2¹/₄", yellow amber. . . . . $600–$800
Umbrella, C-180, eight sided, OP, 2³/₈", medium blue green . . . . $85–$110
Umbrella, C-180, eight sided, SB, 2¹/₂", medium yellow amber. . . . . $90–$125
Umbrella, C-180, eight sided, SB, 2¹/₂", purple amethyst. . . . . $700–$900
Umbrella, C-182, 12 sided, OP, 2¹/₄", medium emerald green . . . . $350–$475
Umbrella, C-182, 12 sided, OP, 2", aqua. . . . . $20–$30
Umbrella, concave panel, eight panels, OP, 2¹/₂", deep puce . . . . $2000+
Umbrella, concave panel, eight panels, OP, 2⁵/₈", medium blue. . . . . $750–$1150
Umbrella, concave panel, eight panels, OP, 2⁵/₈", sapphire blue . . . . $1400–$1900
Umbrella, eight sided, OP, 2¹/₂", deep ruby red . . . . $750–$1000
Umbrella, eight sided, OP, 2⁵/₈", deep amethyst . . . . $750–$1000

Umbrella, eight sided, OP, deep yellow olive . . . . $210–$260

Umbrella, eight sided, OP, lightly cleaned, $2^3/8$", medium cobalt blue . . . . . $400–$550

Umbrella, eight sided, SB, $2^1/2$", deep cobalt blue . . . . $400–$525

Umbrella, giant size, eight sided, OP, 3", sapphire . . . . $3500+

Umbrella, long tooled neck, possibly unique, OP, $2^5/8$", emerald green . . . $800–$1200

Umbrella, OP, eight sided, medium apricot amber . . . . $250–$350

Underwood Inks, C-914, cylinder, pour spout, $9^1/4$", cobalt. . . . . $150–$240

Underwood Inks, C-916, full label, pour spout, $9^1/2$", cobalt . . . . $50–$60

Unembossed Master Ink, three piece mold, pouring spout, smooth base, straight sided cylinder, 7", olive green . . . . $50–$75

Unembossed Master, three piece mold, SB, pour spout, blue green . . . . $35–$45

Unembossed, clear cylinder, screw cap, ABM, 3" . . . . $1–$3

Unembossed, square, pour spout, SB, $8^1/4$", golden amber . . . . $160–$220

USV Kukison, pottery, three quill holes, $1^3/4$". . . . . $50–$75

Ward's Ink Boston, cylinder, pour spout, SB, $7^3/4$", green. . . . . $100–$135

Warren's Congress Ink, eight sided, OP, $2^7/8$", olive yellow. . . . . , . . $1500–$2000

Warren's Congress Ink, eight sided, OP, 5", aqua. $150–$225

Warren's Congress Ink, octagonal, IP, pour spout, $7^1/4$", yellow olive . . . .
. . . . $1500–$2250

Water's Ink, Troy NY, C-132, six sided, OP, $2^5/8$", aqua . . . . $800–$1200

Water's Ink, Troy NY, C-132, six sided, OP, lip repair, $2^3/4$", aqua . . . . . . $200–$275

Water's Ink, Troy NY, C-171, SB, $2^1/2$", aqua. . . . . $600–$800

WE Bonney, barrel, SB, 6", aqua. . . . . $200–$225

WE Bonney, barrel, SB, $7^1/2$, aqua . . . . $225–$300

WE Bonney, C-653, barrel, SB, $2^5/8$", aqua. . . . . $75–$95

Western Ink Co, The, Bloomington Ills, square, $3^1/8$", aqua. . . . . $75–$100

Williston's Superior Indelible Ink, C-488, OP, square, $2^1/2$", aqua . . . . . . $300–$375

Wood's Black Ink Portland, C-12, cone ink, OP, $2^1/2$", aqua . . . . $200–$275

Wood's Black Ink Portland, cone, OP, $2^1/2$", dark root beer amber . . . . $1000–$1350

Writing Fluid JJ Butler Cincinnati, round, OP, $2^7/8$", aqua . . . . $150–$250

Zieber & Co's Excelsior Ink, 12 sided, IP, $5^7/8$", emerald green . . . . $3000–$4000

Zieber & Co's Excelsior Ink, 12 sided, IP, $7^1/2$", yellow olive . . . . $3250–$4500

LABEL-UNDER-GLASS BOTTLES

Label-under-glass bottles are those which have a thin piece of glass covering the labeled area. This type of bottle was popular in the late 19th and early 20th centuries and is a very collectible area with rapidly increasing prices. Look for the colorful and unusual labels, and check to see if the glass strip covering the label is in good condition.

A Merry Christmas Corking Good Stuff, 1891 Rye, man corking a bottle, clear flask, metal screw cap, 6".. $500–$700

A Merry Christmas, Happy New Year, birds on branch, clear flask, metal screw cap, 5"... $375–$500

Admiral Dewey Picture With Eagle, flags, clear flask, metal screw cap, hairline crack in label, 5¹/₄".. $300–$400

Bay Rum / HM Pownall, milk glass barber bottle, some label panel cracks, 9¹/₂".....
.... $175–$235

Boy Leaning Against Pillar, clear flask, metal screw cap, 5³/₄"......... $250–$300

Brandy, bust of pretty woman, rect., clear, minor glass cover cracks, 10³/₄" .. $800–$1100

Brandy, bust of pretty woman, round, clear, label, panel edge broken off, small crack also, 11³/₄".. $300–$400

C Sandheger Peach & Honey, pretty woman, amber in wicker, label cover hairline crack, 11³/₄".. $225–$300

Catawba, bust of pretty woman, round, clear, 11¹/₂"................ $900–$1200

Com WS Schley USN, on clear pocket flask, photo & flag, screw cap..... $350–$450

Dewey Photo, flags, swords, clear flask, metal screw cap, 5¹/₈".......... $300–$400

Doughterty's Old Rye Whiskey, bust of young girl, clear, some label cover damage, 8³/₄".. $175–$250

Drink Gin Gera Trade Mark 5c, clear cylinder, 11¹/₂"................ $160–$220

Eau De Cologne, bust of pretty woman, clear cylinder, stopper missing, small label panel crack, 6".. $100–$150

For Vallie, with photo, clear decanter, stopper, 6¹/₄".................. $200–$250

Gentleman, well dressed, clear flask, metal screw cap, 5¹/₂" .... $400–$550

Green River, clear decanter, slight label discoloration, 11³/₄" .... $100–$140

Hick's Capudine Trade Mark Liquid for Headaches, stopper, 7⁵/₈", amber ....
.... $275–$375

Holland Gin, bust of young girl, amber in wicker, label cover cracks, 11¹/₄".........
.... $140–$175

Horlick's Malted Milk, clear jar, ground stopper, 6³/₄" .... $250–$325

Horlick's Malted Milk, That's Meat and Drink to Me, clear jar, stopper, 8".......
.... $350–$450

Four label-under-glass back bar bottles. PHOTO COURTESY OF GLASS WORKS AUCTIONS.

Kummel, bust of pretty woman, clear, rect., large glass cover cracks, 11¼" . . . .
. . . . $550–$700
Kummel, bust of pretty woman, minor edge cover crack, 11¼" . . . . $950–$1250
Kummel, bust of pretty woman, mint, no cracks, stopper, 11¼" . . . . . . $1100–$1400
Life Preserver, clear flask, "A Merry Christmas" under glass label, no cap, 4¼" . . . . .
. . . . $80–$120
Lightner's White Rose Perfumes, milk glass cylinder, stopper, section of label panel
broken off, 6¼" . . . . $125–$150
London Shrub, cylinder, pewter stopper with figural finial, 11⅛", amber. . . . .
. . . . $150–$200
Major General Fitzhugh Lee, with photo, clear flask, metal screw cap, 5¼" . $325–$400
Merry Christmas, bird on branch, clear flask, metal screw cap, 4⅞" . . . . . $150–$250
Okolona Rye Whiskey, clear cylinder, 9⅛" . . . . $475–$675
Our Candidates, picture of Bryan and Stevenson, "Whiskey," clear, 10⅝" . . . .
. . . . $1400–$1700
Our Candidates, picture of McKinley and Roosevelt, "Whiskey," clear, 10¾" . . . . . .
. . . . $1400–$1700
Peppermt, two hairline cover cracks, 8⅜", amber . . . . $100–$145
Pointer Maryland Rye, with setter dog, clear, 11" . . . . $1250–$1750
Pretty Woman, bust, clear flask encased in bark, metal screw cap, 6" . . . . $175–$250
Pretty Woman, bust, clear round flask, metal screw cap, 5⅛" . . . . $600–$800
Pretty Woman, in costume dress, clear flask, label discoloration, 5¾" . . . $100–$140
Pretty Woman, standing, clear flask, 5¾" . . . . $300–$400
Sachette Jockey Club, clear apothecary bottle, ground stopper, 7" . . . . . . $175–$250
Sallie Cologne, with bust of woman, clear cylinder, ground stopper, 7½" . . . . $150–$200
Shac for Headache, man with headache Band Aid, clear jar, ground lid, 5⅞" . . . .
. . . . $800–$1200
Smoke Wilcox Bros & Co's Handmade Cigar . . . , clear flask, pewter screw cap, 5"
. . . . $125–$175
TDA (on base), C-611, offset dome, 1⅝", aqua . . . . $1600–$1900
Time to Take a Drink, clear flask, clock in face, metal screw cap, 5⅛" . . . $250–$300
Victorian Jockey Club Perfumes, clear cylinder, stopper, small label panel cracks,
8⅛" . . . . $125–$165
Victorian White Rose Perfumes, clear cylinder, stopper, minor label panel damage, 8"
. . . . $125–$165
Woman Photo (See Pretty Woman, this listing)
Yriarte Sherry, bust of pretty woman, amber in wicker, mint, 11⅝" . . . . . $300–$400

MARBLES

Marbles is another one of those crossover areas that bottle collectors will
almost certainly run into at a bottle show, flea market, or the bottom of a privy.
This is in no way intended to be a concise treatment of such a complicated and

diverse area but is meant to merely provide a few points to consider when handling marbles. Those interested in obtaining a much greater understanding of marbles, along with their values, are advised to obtain a copy of *Marbles: Identification and Price Guide* by Robert Block. Following are the categories of marbles that we will briefly touch upon here:

- Bennington's—This group includes the highly glazed brown and blue clay marbles, along with the white glazed and unglazed varieties (china's) which often have red or blue circles or flowers drawn/painted upon them. This type of marble is very common and usually quite inexpensive, with clays sold by the handful for a few dollars. Some china's with ornate flowers can be worth several hundred dollars, however, and the large "carpet balls," which measure about 3"+ in diameter, often bring in the $50–$75 range.
- Handmade's—These are the swirls, end-of-days- (onion skins), lutz swirls, sulfides, etc., which were handmade in Germany during the 1860–1910 era. These types of marbles would always show a pontil mark, which, unlike the rough and jagged pontil found on a bottle or piece of blown glass, is often ground down to a soft frosted area on the tip of a marble, or shows itself as a group of little bevels cut into the glass. Handmade's are down in value from a few years ago.
- Transitionals—These are slag-type marbles made with a combination of hand and machinemade techniques, and are usually from around the 1900–1920 era.
- Machine-mades—These marbles were made from the 1910s until today in the United States and other countries. The marbles made in the 1920–1930 era by such firms as Christensen, Peltier, and Akro are the hottest things on the market today.

Following is some information on what to look for, what is hot, and what is not:

- Size is important, with larger marbles commanding higher prices. What is a larger marble? Sulfides and end-of-days in excess of 2 inches would be considered very large, and Lutz marbles $3/4$ inch and larger are hard to find. Most machine-made marbles are in the $1/2$ inch to $5/8$ inch range and anything larger is more unusual.
- Condition is very important, with heavy wear, chips, dings, moons or shiners detracting from the value of any marble, with the decrease in value dependent on the severity of the damage.
- Scratches, wear, dings, and chips in marbles can be polished off. On an old marble, the pontil is often polished off, detracting from the value. A polished sulfide usually falls about 40% in value, whereas an end-of-day or swirl might depreciate over half. Most old marbles you encounter will show at least minor surface wear and scratching, and if a marble looks too clean, suspect polishing and check to see whether the pontil has been polished off. Sometimes a marble can be polished with the pontil left alone; if polishing is

suspected, roll the marble slowly across the floor, and if it rolls cockeyed, it's probably been polished.

- Cracked sulfides decrease the value by at least a third, whereas painted sulfides can be worth a thousand dollars or more. Sulfides made of colored glass are very rare and extremely valuable. Reproduction sulfides are out there, and the glass is extremely clear and without bubbles, impurities, and wear you normally always see on the old pieces.
- Reproduction swirls are also made; check for glass clarity, unusually bright colors, and wear.
- End-of-day marbles, also known as onion skins, which contain mica chips, are worth up to double, triple or more times the value of a similar marble without mica. The more mica the better, and the higher the value. "Lobed" onion skins, which show even ridges or ribs within the marble, are also worth considerably more.
- Cardboard boxed sets of marbles from the 1920's to 1940's are quite rare and valuable. The plastic bags used in the 1950's to modern day are much more common and thus much lower priced.

Some average prices for mint condition marbles are:

- $1/2$" Bennington brown pottery marble, glazed, $0.20
- $3/4$" sulfide, standing dog, $150–$200
- $1 1/2$" sulfide, standing dog, $100–$150
- $1 1/2$" sulfide, standing dog, painted, $800–$1500
- 1" latticino swirl, average colors, $25–$35
- $3/4$" Lutz, gold and red bands on clambroth body, $175–$250
- $1/2$" Guinea, $300–$400

Three Bennington clay marbles at left, three painted and decorated china marbles on the right. These are among the earliest types of marbles, possibly dating back to the 18th century and earlier, although they continued to be made into the 20th century. PHOTO COURTESY OF GLASS WORKS AUCTIONS.

- ⁵/₈" corkscrew, average colors, $3–$5
- Akro Agate boxed set, cardboard box, 100 marbles, $400–$500

Marble enthusiasts should consider joining the Marble Collectors Society of America, PO Box 222, Trumbull, CT, 06611.

Akro Agate Boxed Set, cardboard box, 100 marbles . . . . $400–$500
Bennington, pottery marble, glazed, ¹/₂", brown . . . . $0.20+
Christensen and Peltier Cardboard Boxed Sets, are rare and worth at least $1000. . .
Corkscrew, average colors, ⁵/₈" . . . . $3–$5
Guinea, ¹/₂". . . . . $300–$400
Latticino Swirl, average colors, 1" . . . . $25–$35

Left: *Latticino core swirl.* Right: *Three early swirled marbles.* PHOTOS COURTESY OF GLASS WORKS AUCTIONS.

Lutz, gold and red bands on clambroth body, ³/₄" . . . . $175–$250

Left: *A Lutz marble, which characteristically shows a wide central band of gold on either side of the marble, in this case on a base color of black with yellow bands. This is a more unusual color combination for a Lutz, with the average Lutz being on a clear body.* Center: *An onion skin, otherwise known as an end-of-day.* Right: *Another onion skin, this one showing a slight swirl to the pattern.* PHOTOS COURTESY OF GLASS WORKS AUCTIONS.

Sulphide, standing dog, 1¹/₂" . . . . $100–$150
Sulphide, standing dog, ³/₄" . . . . $150–$200

Left: *Sulphide rooster marble.* Right: *Sulphide seated dog figure. Note that the sulphide has been painted black and white, with a patch of green grass underneath. Painted sulphides are* extremely *rare and valuable.* PHOTOS COURTESY OF GLASS WORKS AUCTIONS.

Sulphide, standing dog, painted, $1^1/2$" . . . . $800–$1500

MEDICINE AND CURES BOTTLES

Medicine bottles comprise one of the largest areas of bottle collecting, and this area encompasses bottles such as ointments, cures, liniments, panaceas, balsams, remedies, and all sorts of drug bottles. Though medicine bottles were certainly among the products of the earliest American glasshouses, it was not until the late 18th century that the embossed medicine bottle appeared. Turlingtons Balsam, originally imported from England, was probably one of the first embossed medicines produced in America. Even with the production of this bottle around the year 1800, the vast majority of medicine bottles were unembossed and carried only a paper label until about 1840/1850. Many of these early unembossed pontiled medicines, usually in shades of dark greens and amber, can still be found at reasonable prices. The embossed medicines of the 1830s and 1840s are fairly common in clear and aqua, whereas the embossed greens, ambers, and blues often fetch sums in the thousands of dollars. Starting around the middle of the 19th century and up until the Pure Food and Drug Act of 1906, an amazing assortment of so-called patent medicine bottles were produced which purported to heal any number of maladies, ranging from the common cold to cancer.

When buying and collecting medicine bottles, look for original labels and boxes, and watch for those early unusually embossed bottles. Those which are embossed "Shaker" or "Indian" are usually quite collectible and oftentimes quite valuable. The reader is referred to *Great American Pontiled Medicines* by Frederick Nielsen, which the letter "N" refers to below.

A McEckrons Ring Bone Liniment NY, N-425, OP, $6^5/8$", aqua .... $65–$95
A Mosher, ovoid form, sloping collar, IP, $8^5/8$", blue green .... $600–$900
A Trask's Magnetic Ointment, OP, $2^1/2$", aqua....................... $25–$35
A Trask's Magnetic Ointment, SB, $2^1/2$", aqua........................ $3–$5
A Trask's Magnetic Ointment, SB, $3^1/4$", aqua........................ $3–$5
A Warner & Co's Sepia, rectangle, SB, $6^5/8$", golden amber........... $100–$140
AB Holmes, Pharmacist, clear, 4" .... $1–$2
Abbott Aikal Co, Chicago, clear, $2^1/2$"............................ $4–$6
Abigail M Littlefield Pharmacist Troy NY, $5^5/8$", cobalt .... $110–$140
ABL Myer's Rock Rose, New Haven, IP, $9^1/2$", emerald green........ $800–$1200
ABL Myer's Rock Rose, New Haven, OP, $9^1/2$", aqua .... $200–$250
Abner Royce Co, clear, $5^1/2$"..................................... $3–$5
Absorbine, Springfield, Mass, $7^1/2$", amber .... $5–$8
Acid Iron Earth Nature's Own Remedy, Mobile, Alabama, $6^5/8$", amber ....
.... $30–$50
Agua Perubinat Cordial, clear, labeled, $10^1/2$"........................ $6–$9
AJ Thompson Carminative, OP, aqua .... $20–$24
Alden's Extract of Coffee, cylinder, IP, 6", blue green .... $750–$900
Alexander's Silameau, OP, $6^1/4$", cobalt........................... $400–$600
Alexander's Silameau, OP, light blue............................... $300–$450
Allen's Essence of Jamaica Ginger, $5^1/2$", aqua...................... $7–$11
Allen's Nerve & Bone Liniment, 4", aqua .... $7–$10
Allenbury's Castor Oil, 7", amber .... $6–$9
Alvatunder, the Hisey Dental Mfg., clear, $3^3/4$"..................... $2–$3
American Compound Coventry, Auburn, NY, N-7, OP, 7", aqua........ $60–$90
American Cough Drops, OP, clear, $5^1/4$" .... $125–$175
American Eagle Liniment, N-8, six sided, OP, $5^1/4$", aqua .... $125–$175
American Expectorant, N-9, eight sided, OP, 6", aqua .... $80–$120
American Rob Dr's J & M New York, OP, $7^5/8$", aqua .... $200–$275
Anderson's Dermador, N-18, OP, $4^7/8$", medium cornflower blue .... $90–$120
Anderson's Dermador, OP, $4^7/8$", aqua .... $40–$65
Anderson's Dermador, SB, $4^1/4$", aqua .... $3–$5
Anderson's Dermador, SB, $5^3/4$", aqua .... $4–$6
Andrew's Herpetic Lotion (on seal), SB, $5^1/2$", olive amber......... $2000–$3000
Anthlophoros, Toilet Extract, square, clear, $8^1/4$" .... $15–$25
Armour's Vigorals, Chicago, squat body, amber....................... $4–$6
Arnica & Oil Liniment, $6^1/2$", aqua .... $4–$6
AS Hind's, Portland, Me, clear, $5^1/2$"............................. $4–$6
Astyptodyae Chemical Co, clear, $4^1/2$"............................ $4–$5
AT & SF Chemical Dept, clear, $10^3/4$"............................ $175–$225
Athieus Cough Syrup .... $4–$6
Atlanta Chemical Co., $8^1/2$", amber .... $6–$9
Atlas Medicine Co, Henderson, NC, $9^1/4$", amber.................... $10–$15
Ayer's Ague Cure, Lowell, OP, 7", aqua .... $125–$175

Ayer's Ague Cure, Lowell, SB, 5³/₄", aqua .... $10–$14
Ayer's Cherry Pectoral, OP, aqua .... $20–$30
Ayer's Cherry Pectoral, SB, aqua .... $7–$10
Ayer's Lowell, Mass, USA, 8¹/₂" .... $2–$4
Ayer's Pills, Lowell, Ma, rectangular, 2", aqua .... $7–$10
Ayer's Pills, square, clear, 2¹/₂" .... $1–$3
B Denton Aurburn, NY, OP, 6¹/₂", aqua .... $60–$80
B Denton Healing Balsam, eight sided, OP, 4¹/₄", aqua .... $40–$50
B Denton Healing Syrup, eight sided, OP, 3³/₄", aqua .... $80–$120
B Fosgate's Anodyne Cordial, cylinder, OP, 4³/₄", aqua .... $15–$24
B Fosgate's Anodyne, 4¹/₂", aqua .... $6–$9
Bach's American Compound Auburn NY, N-32, OP, 7³/₈", aqua .... $80–$100
Baker's Celery Kola, 10", amber .... $40–$60
Baker's Vegetable Blood & Liver Cure, 9³/₄", amber................. $175–$275
Ballard Snow Liniment Co, clear, 4¹/₂" .... $4–$6
Balsam of Wild Cherry and Tar ..., N-38, OP, 7⁵/₈", aqua............ $75–$100
Balsam Vegetable Pulmonary, 5", aqua.............................. $8–$11
Barclay's American Balsam, OP, 5³/₄", aqua........................ $30–$50
Barker, Moore & Mein, Druggist, 5¹/₄", aqua......................... $4–$6
Barker, Moore & Mein, Druggist, 6¹/₂", aqua......................... $3–$4
Barker, Moore & Mein, Druggist, 6", aqua .... $2–$3
Barker, Moore & Mein, Druggist, 8", clear .... $2–$4
Barrill's Cold Cure, 7", aqua .... $90–$125
Barry's Tricopherous for the Skin, OP, 5¹/₄", aqua .... $20–$25
Barry's Tricopherous for the Skin, SB, 5¹/₄", aqua .... $7–$10
Bartow Drug Co, clear, 3¹/₂".. $3–$5
Batchelor's, clear, 3" .... $3–$5
Bayer, twice in cross design front of bottle, clear, screw cap .... $2–$4
BBB Atlanta, Ga, 3³/₄", amber .... $10–$13
BBB Phila & St Louis, aqua .... $25–$35
Bear's Oil, OP, 2³/₄", light to medium citron........................ $300–$375
Bear's Oil, OP, 2⁵/₈", aqua.. $75–$125
Bee Dee Liniment, Chattanooga, Tn, clear, 5¹/₂" .... $5–$8
Beekman's Pulmonic Syrup, New York, N-45, eight sided, OP, 7³/₈", olive green ...
.... $3000+
Begg's Cherry Cough Syrup, rect., 5³/₄", aqua .... $5–$8
Begg's Diarrhea Balsam, 5¹/₂", aqua .... $8–$12
Bell Ans, ABM, 3³/₄", amber .... $1–$2
Benjamin Green Apothecarty Portsmouth NH, 7¹/₄", cobalt........... $100–$150
Bennett's Magic Cure, 5¹/₄", deep cobalt............................ $450+
Bennett's Pharmacy, St Petersburg, Fla, clear........................ $2–$4
Berlin Series, OP, 9¹/₈", aqua...................................... $25–$35
Berry Bros., 11¹/₄", aqua .... $6–$9
Bigelow's Alternative, CW Bleecker, OP, 5³/₄", aqua .... $70–$95
Billing's Rheumatic Liniment, OP, 6", aqua .... $125–$175
Bisatuarted Magnesia, clear cylinder, 4³/₄" .... $2–$3
Black Gin for the Kidneys, 8⁷/₈", amber............................. $40–$55
Blodgett's Persian Balm, OP, 4⁷/₈", aqua............................ $100–$145
Blud Life, clear, ABM .... $1–$2
BM & EA Whitlock & 7 Co Owners NY, IP, 9", aqua................. $150–$250
Boericke & Runyon Company, clear, 7".............................. $2–$3

Bon Opto for the Eyes, clear, 3¹/₄" .... $3–$4
Bonpland's Fever & Ague Remedy, OP, 5¹/₄", aqua .... $35–$45
Bower's Infant Cordial, OP, aqua .... $40–$45
Bragg's Arctic Liniment, OP, 4", aqua .... $120–$150
Brandriff's Vegetable Antidote for Ague, aqua .... $30–$40
Brant's Indian Balsam, OP, 7¹/₂", aqua .... $75–$95
Brant's Indian Pulmonary Balsam, eight sided, OP, 6⁷/₈", aqua .... $40–$60
Brant's Indian Pulmonary Druggist, NY, OP, aqua .... $50–$75
Brant's Purifying Extract, OP, 10", aqua .... $80–$120
Bridge's Lung Tonic, aqua .... $15–$20
Bristol Myers Co, 7³/₄", amber .... $2–$4
Bromo Caffeine, ABM, 3¹/₂", cobalt.................................. $1–$3
Bromo Seltzer, 3¹/₂", cobalt....................................... $3–$6
Bromo Seltzer, 5", cobalt... $4–$8
Bromo Seltzer, corker top, 2", cobalt .... $3–$5
Brook's Drug Co, clear, 8" .... $2–$3
Brown Forman & Co, clear, 4¹/₂"................................... $2–$3
Brown Household Panacea & Family Liniment, SB, 5¹/₈", aqua........... $5–$8
Brown's Instant Relief for Pain, 5¹/₄", aqua .... $5–$7
Bryant's Purifying Extract MT Wallace & Co, N-70, OP, 10¹/₈", aqua ....
.... $200–$250
Buchan's Hungarian Balsam of Life, OP, 5³/₄", aqua.................. $60–$75
Buchan's Tonic Mixture, OP, 6³/₈", aqua............................ $50–$65
Budd's Wound, Nerve and Bone Liniment, OP, 5³/₈", aqua .... $250–$375
Bumstead's Worm Syrup, Philada, 4¹/₂", aqua....................... $10–$14
Burke & James, clear, 6¹/₄"....................................... $2–$3
Burlington Drug Co, Burlington, Vt, clear, labeled, 5¹/₄"................ $6–$9
Burnett's Cocaine, OP, aqua...................................... $25–$40
Burnett's Cocaine, SB, aqua...................................... $10–$12
Burnett, clear, 6³/₄" .... $3–$4
Burnham's Beef, Wine & Iron, 9¹/₂", aqua .... $8–$11
BW Hair & Son Asthma Cure, London, 5", aqua...................... $25–$35
By AA Cooley Hartford, Conn, OP, ovoid, 4³/₈", olive green........... $200–$250
By The King's Royal Patent, Turlington, OP, 2¹/₂", aqua .... $60–$90
C Brinckerhoff's Health Restorative Price $1.00 New York, OP, 7", olive green ...
.... $450–$550
C Brinckerhoff's Health Restorative Price $1.00 New York, OP, 7", olive yellow ..
.... $450–$650
C Heimstreet & Co, eight sided, 7", cobalt blue...................... $30–$40
C Heimstreet & Co, Troy, NY, eight sided, OP, 7", cobalt .... $125–$175
C Mathewson's Remedy, OP, 6⁷/₈", aqua........................... $80–$110
C Sines Tar Wild Cherry Hoar Hound, N-581, OP, 5¹/₈", aqua.......... $25–$45
CA Newman Druggist, OP, aqua .... $12–$17
Caldwell's Syrup Pepsin, rect., 3", aqua............................ $3–$5
California Fig Syrup, clear, ABM .... $3–$5
Calvert's Derby Cure for Influen, 5¹/₂", aqua....................... $30–$45
Campbell VV, clear, 5¹/₈ .... $3–$4
Capudine Chemical Co, Raleigh, NC, ABM, 7¹/₂", amber .... $2–$4
Carbona & Carbona Products Co, 12 panels, 5¹/₈", aqua................ $7–$11
Carbona (on base), 5¹/₂", aqua .... $2–$4
Carlsbad AH (on bottom), clear, 4"................................ $2–$3

Medicine, C. Heimstreet & Co. PHOTO COURTESY OF NEIL GROSSMAN.

Carson's Blood Purifier, Jamestown, NY, SB, 6¹/₂", aqua .... $25–$35
Carter's Extract of Smartweed, OP, 5³/₈", aqua .... $60–$90
Carter's Little Pills, clear, ABM. .... $2–$4
Carter's Spanish Mixture, N-108, full label, IP, 8¹/₄", medium olive green ....
.... $450–$600
Carter's Spanish Mixture, N-108, IP, 8¹/₄", medium olive green .... $300–$375
Cauvin's Syrup for Babies .... $20–$30
CC Pendleton's Tonic, 9¹/₂", amber .... $80–$110
Celery Compound (Celery Stalk), 10", yellow amber................... $60–$80
Celery Compound (Celery Stalk), base edge chip, 10", amber........... $20–$30
CG Clark Co New Haven Ct, 12 panels, 5¹/₂", aqua .... $3–$5
CG Clark Restorative, 7³/₄", aqua .... $5–$8
CH Phillip's, NY, 9¹/₄", amber .... $3–$5
CH Weigle's, sides embossed, clear .... $7–$9
Chamberlain's Colic, Cholera & Diarrhea Remedy, 4¹/₂", aqua.......... $9–$13
Chamberlain's Cough Remedy, clear, ABM, 7"......................... $2–$3
Chamberlain's Cough Remedy, rect., 5³/₄", aqua .... $2–$3
Chamberlain's Immediate Relief, N-111, OP, 4³/₄", aqua .... $75–$110
Chamberlain's Medicine Co., Des Moines, Iowa, clear, 5³/₄" .... $4–$5
Chapman's Genuine Boston, OP, 8", olive green .... $1500–$2200
Chapman's Genuine Essence, OP, 8¹/₄", light olive amber .... $1500–$2500
Chapman's Genuine No Salem St, Boston, OP, 8¹/₄", olive amber .... $1000–$1500
Chas D Cooper Pharmacist, Walden, NY, clear, 4¹/₂" .... $3–$5
Chas E Lathrop Pharmacist, Omaha, clear, 5³/₄"...................... $3–$5
Chas H Phillip's Chem Co., screw cap, 11", cobalt.................... $15–$25
Chattanooga Medicine Co., screw top, 8³/₈", light green............... $2–$3
Chattanooga Medicine Co., Woman's Tonic, 8¹/₂", aqua................. $6–$9
Chemist's Rushton Clark & Co., OP, 10", aqua .... $25–$32
Chloride Calcium St Catharines Canada, OP, 5³/₄", deep aqua......... $125–$175
Christie's Ague Balsam New York, N-119, OP, 7", deep aqua.......... $90–$120
Christie's Magnetic Fluid, N-120, OP, 4³/₄", aqua.................... $30–$45
Circassian Lymph, violin form, OP, 6⁵/₈", aqua..................... $150–$200
Citrate of Magnesia, clear cylinder, lightning stopper .... $7–$11
Citrate of Magnesia, OP, clear, 6³/₄" .... $75–$125
City Drug Company, Anaconda, Mt, clear, 4" .... $2–$4
City Drug Company, Meridian, Texas, 3¹/₄" .... $2–$3

CK Donnell MD, Lewiston, Me, clear, 6¹/₄" .... $4–$5
Clark's Infallible Worm Syrup, Phila, OP, aqua .... $40–$55
Clarke's Lincoln World Famed Blood Mix, 7¹/₄", grayish blue .... $25–$35
Clemen's Indian Tonic, embossed and full label, OP, 5¹/₄", aqua .... $400–$550
Clewley's Miraculous Cure for Rheumatism, 6", aqua .... $35–$50
Cloud's Cordial, 10³/₄", yellow..................................... $125–$150
CO Michaelis Apothecary, Charleston, SC, aqua....................... $3–$4
Cod Liver Oil (fish in center), square, ABM, 6", amber .... $3–$4
Cod Liver Oil (fish in center), square, ABM, 9", amber .... $3–$5
Cod Liver Oil, 9³/₄", aqua .... $4–$6
Colt's Foot Expectorant, clear, 6" .... $3–$5
Compound Elixer of Phosphate & Calisaya, square, aqua............... $9–$12
Compound Elixir, 8³/₄", aqua .... $5–$8
Compound Extract of Hops & Boneset, OP, 4¹/₂", aqua................. $40–$55
Compound Extract Pine Splinters, Atlanta, Ga, clear, 7¹/₂" .... $6–$9
Comstock Morse's Root Pills, amber............................... $10–$14
Constitutional Beverage, 10¹/₄", amber............................. $50–$70
Constock & Co Indian Vegetable Elixer, OP, 4¹/₄", aqua.............. $125–$175
Converse Co, Columbus, Ohio, eight sided, clear, 6" .... $2–$3
Cordial Balm of Gilead Prepared Only by Dr Solomon, OP, 6⁷/₈", olive amber ....
.... $3500–$4500
Cowan's Lithontriptic, OP, 7³/₄", cherry puce.................... $7000–$8000
Craig Kidney Cure Company, 9¹/₂", amber......................... $125–$175
Crosby's Balsamic Cough Elixer, 4¹/₂", aqua .... $6–$9
Crumpton's Strawberry Balsam, OP, 5", aqua...................... $175–$250
Cullen's Remedies Rowland & Walton, OP, 6", aqua .... $35–$45
Cummings Vegetine, 10", aqua.................................... $9–$13
Cuticure Cure for Constitutional Humors, 80% label, 9", aqua .... $18–$23
CW Atwell, Portland, Me, 8", aqua .... $5–$8
CW Snow & Co Druggists, 6¹/₂", cobalt blue......................... $75–$100
D Miller & Co Shaker Syrup, OP, 7¹/₄", aqua....................... $200–$300
D Zeublin's Safe & Quick Cure, OP, 3¹/₂", aqua.................... $125–$175
D Zeublin's Safe & Quick Cure ..., OP, 3⁵/₈", aqua .... $200–$300
Dalby's Carminative, conical form, OP, 3¹/₂", emerald green .... $1500–$1600
Dalby's Carminative, N-156, OP, 4", aqua .... $35–$45
Dam's Sanatorium, Cure for the Tobacco Habit, 5¹/₄", cobalt .... $600–$800
Davis & Millers American Worm Syrup, OP, six sided, 4", aqua .... $125–$175
Davis 3 Cornered Bottle Pile Remedy, triangular, 3¹/₂", amber .... $90–$120
Davis Botanic Cholagogue Buffalo, OP, 6", aqua .... $200–$275
Davis Pain Killer, N-164, OP, aqua .... $15–$24
Davis Vegetable Pain Killer, SB, 5³/₄", aqua....................... $2–$4
Diaphoratic Compound, HA Tucker, MD, 5¹/₂", aqua.................. $6–$9
Dickie's Iceland Balm for Coughs, OP, 5⁷/₈, aqua................... $50–$60
Dill's Balm of Life, 6", aqua .... $5–$8
Ditchett's Remedy for the Piles, OP, double collar, 8", olive green .... $3800–$4400
Doct Curtis Sherry Syrup, OP, clear, 7³/₈" .... $40–$60
Doct Fowler's Anti Ericholic, OP, 6", aqua......................... $60–$90
Doct Harrisons Chalybeate Tonic, 9¹/₈", blue green.................. $75–$110
Doct Marshall's Aromatic Catarrh, OP, 3³/₈", aqua.................. $50–$70
Doct Robt B Folgers Olosaonian, N-223, OP, 7", aqua............... $80–$95
Doctor Frank's Turkey Febrifuge, OP, 5", aqua..................... $175–$250

Donald Kennedy & Co, Roxbury, Mass, labeled, $6^1/2$", aqua . . . . $4–$6
Donnaud's Gout Remedy, IP, 6", aqua . . . . $40–$60
Donnell's Rheumatic Liniment, $7^1/4$", aqua . . . . / . . $7–$10
DPS Co, $3^1/2$", amber . . . . $2–$3
Dr A Bochie's German Syrup, square, $6^3/4$", aqua . . . . $5–$7
Dr A Fowler Syracuse, OP, $4^3/8$", aqua . . . . $30–$50
Dr A Roe's Cough Syrup, OP, 5", aqua . . . . $50–$70
Dr Adolf Hommels Haematogen, aqua . . . . $10–$15
Dr Alexander Lung Healer, rect., $6^1/2$", aqua . . . . $8–$12
Dr Atherton's Wild Cherry Syrup, OP, $5^1/4$", aqua . . . . $100–$145
Dr AW Coleman's Anti Dyspeptic, IP, $9^1/4$", deep green . . . . $1500–$2000
Dr Baker's Compound New York, OP, $7^3/4$", aqua . . . . $250–$350
Dr Baker's Pain Panacea, N-34, OP, 5", aqua . . . . $30–$45
Dr Baker's Pain Panacea, N-34, OP, 5", light blue green . . . . $45–$65
Dr Bell's Pine Tar Honey, $5^1/2$", aqua . . . . $9–$12
Dr Birmingham's Antibilious Blood Purifyer, SB, $8^1/2$", yellow green . . . .
. . . . $600–$750
Dr Bosanko's Pile Remedy, Phila, Pa, $2^1/2$", aqua . . . . $6–$9
Dr Bosher's German Syrup, SB, 7", aqua . . . . $3–$5
Dr Brown's Ruterba, 8", amber . . . . $10–$15
Dr Bull's Herbs & Iron, patent date on base, $9^1/2$", aqua . . . . $18–$25
Dr C Grattan's Diptheria Remedy, 7", aqua . . . . $25–$35
Dr Caldwell's Laxative Senna, clear, rect., 7" . . . . $3–$5
Dr Caldwell's Pepsin Syrup, with label and contents, aqua . . . . $12–$16
Dr Carter's Compound Pulmonary Balsam, N-107, OP, $5^1/8$", aqua . . . . . . $35–$45
Dr CF Brown Young American Liniment, 4", aqua . . . . $9–$13
Dr Clark N York, beveled edges, IP, square, $9^1/4$", deep green . . . . $800–$1000
Dr Conver's Invigorating Cordial, N-138, OP, 6", aqua . . . . $75–$125
Dr Culver's Malarial Germ Destroyer, pour spout, 8", medium amber . . . $175–$225
Dr Cummings Vegetine, aqua . . . . $12–$16
Dr CW Roback's Scandinavian Blood Purifier, 7", aqua . . . . $25–$35
Dr D Jayne's Carmenative, Phila, 5", aqua . . . . $5–$7
Dr D Jayne's Carminitive Balsam, Phila, OP, aqua . . . . $25–$35
Dr D Jayne's Carminitive Balsam, SB, 5", aqua . . . . $7–$9
Dr D Jayne's Expectorant Philada, N-337, OP, $6^7/8$", aqua . . . . $35–$45
Dr D Jayne's Expectorant, clear, $6^1/2$" . . . . $3–$4
Dr D Jayne's Life Preservative, OP, $5^1/2$", aqua . . . . $400+
Dr D Jayne's Tonic Vermifuge, oval, $4^3/8$", aqua . . . . $8–$11
Dr Dadirrian's Zoolak, cylinder, aqua . . . . $4–$6
Dr Daniel's Cough, Cold & Fever Drops, clear, $4^1/2$" . . . . $7–$9
Dr Davis's Depurative, SB, $9^5/8$", medium emerald green . . . . $850–$1150
Dr Davis's Depurative, Phila, N-165, IP, $9^3/4$", bluish emerald green . . . .
. . . . $1500–$2500
Dr Davis's Depurative, Phila, N-165, IP, $9^3/4$", medium teal blue . . . . . . $1800–$2500
Dr DB Vincent's Angel of Life for the Blood, 8", aqua . . . . $750–$1000
Dr DC Kellinger NY, rect., OP, $7^1/4$", medium sapphire . . . . $1000–$1500
Dr DC Kellinger's Remedies New York, OP, $8^3/4$", aqua . . . . $150–$225
Dr Drake's Group Remedy, clear, $6^1/4$" . . . . $5–$6
Dr EE Dixon, clear, $6^1/2$" . . . . $3–$4
Dr Evan's Camomile Pills, OP, $3^3/4$", aqua . . . . $18–$26
Dr Fahrney's Uterine, clear, $8^1/2$" . . . . $12–$15

Dr Faust's German Aromatic Wine, 11", orange amber . . . . $150–$250
Dr Fenner's Concentrated Extract . . . . $3–$6
Dr Fenner's Peoples Remedy's, oval, 8¹/₂", amber . . . . $14–$19
Dr Foord's Pectoral Syrup, OP, 5¹/₂", aqua. . . . . $75–$90
Dr Foord's Tonic & Anodyne Cordial, OP, 5³/₄", aqua . . . . $45–$65
Dr Foord's Tonic Cordial Cazenovia, NY, OP, 4¹/₄", aqua . . . . $60–$80
Dr Fraga's Cuban Vermifuge, eight panels, 3³/₄", aqua . . . . $6–$8
Dr Friend's Cough Balsam, OP, 6", aqua . . . . $50–$80
Dr G Gould's Pin Worm Syrup, OP, 5", aqua. . . . . $45–$65
Dr Gesteria Regulator, eight sided, 5", amber . . . . $10–$14
Dr Gordak's Iceland Jelly, OP, 6³/₄", aqua . . . . $100–$145
Dr Grove's Anodyne for Infants, clear, 5³/₄". . . . . $5–$7
Dr Guysott's Compound Extract of Yellow Dock & Sarsaparilla, square, IP, 9¹/₂",
    emerald green . . . . $2000–$2500
Dr H Swayne's Compound Syrup of Wild Cherry, OP, 6", aqua . . . . $80–$120
Dr HA Ingram's Vegetable Pain Extractor, 4¹/₂", aqua. . . . . $8–$12
Dr Harter's Fever & Ague Specific, SB, 6", aqua. . . . .
Dr Harter's Iron Tonic, amber. . . . . $15–$25
Dr Harter's Iron Tonic, aqua. . . . . $15–$20
Dr HB Myer's Dandelion Wild Cherry, OP, 9¹/₂", aqua . . . . $300–$500
Dr HB Skinner Boston, rect., OP, 5³/₄", medium green . . . . $600–$750
Dr J Hedge's Fever & Ague Annihilator, OP, 7¹/₄", aqua . . . . $125–$225
Dr HF Perry's Dead Shot Vermifuge, 4", amber . . . . $5–$7
Dr Hill's Pain Killer, 5¹/₄", aqua. . . . . $20–$25
Dr Hooker's Cough & Croup Syrup, OP, 5¹/₂", aqua. . . . . $80–$110
Dr HW Jackson Druggist Vegetable Home Syrup, OP, 5³/₄", olive green . . . .
    . . . . $800–$1200
Dr Ira Warren's Inhaling Balm, OP, 7¹/₂", aqua. . . . . $140–$190
Dr J Blackman's Genuine Healing Balsam, N-53, clear, OP, 5⁵/₈" . . . . $60–$80
Dr J Pettit's Canker Balm, clear flask shaped, 3¹/₄" . . . . $8–$12
Dr J Webster's Cerevesia, OP, 7¹/₄", emerald green . . . . $90–$1250
Dr JA Sherman's Rupture Curative Compound, 8¹/₄", cobalt blue . . . . $900–$1200
Dr James Cherry Tar Syrup, 5³/₄", aqua. . . . . $6–$8
Dr James McClintock Family Medicines, OP, clear, 8¹/₂" . . . . $45–$65
Dr James Rainey Vitality Tablets, 3¹/₄", amber . . . . $4–$6
Dr James Worm Syrup, 5¹/₂", aqua . . . . $6–$8
Dr JAS McClintock's Family Medicines, clear, OP, 8¹/₂" . . . . $25–$35
Dr JB Lynar & Son, Logansport, Ind. (on seal), clear, 6" . . . . $8–$10
Dr JB Lynar & Son, Logansport, Ind., clear, 6". . . . . $3–$5
Dr JF Churchhill's Specific Remedy, OP, 6⁷/₈", aqua. . . . . $90–$135
Dr JH McLean's Volcanic Oil Liniment, 6¹/₂", aqua . . . . $7–$9
Dr JN Keeler's Vegetable Panacea Philada, OP, 7¹/₈", aqua . . . . $600–$900
Dr Johnson's Horse Remedies, 6³/₄", aqua . . . . $8–$12
Dr Johnston's Indian Compound Herbaline, ovoid, 10", aqua . . . . $100–$125
Dr Jones Australian Oil, 5", amber . . . . $8–$12
Dr Jones Red Clover Tonic, 8³/₄", amber. . . . . $65–$90
Dr JR Miller's Balm, clear, 4³/₄" . . . . $4–$5
Dr JS Wood's Elixer Albany NY, N-700, chips, hole, 8³/₄", emerald green . . . .
    . . . . $400–$575
Dr JS Wood's Elixer Albany NY, N-700, IP, 8³/₄", emerald green. . . . . $2800–$3800
Dr Jugs Medicine for Lungs, Liver & Blood, jug, 6¹/₄", brown . . . . $35–$50

Dr JW Bull's Vegetable Baby Syrup, round, aqua . . . . $5–$6
Dr Kay's Lung Balm, rect., 7³/₄", aqua. . . . . $7–$10
Dr Keeley's Double Chloride of Gold Cure for Opium Habit, clear, 6" . . . .
. . . . $400+
Dr Kellinger's Magic Fluid New York, OP, 4⁷/₈", aqua . . . . $100–$145
Dr Kennedy's Favorite Remedy, clear, 7". . . . . $3–$5
Dr Kennedy's Medical Discovery, Roxbury, Mass, square, 9" . . . . $5–$7
Dr Kennedy's Rheumatic Liniment, 6¹/₂", aqua . . . . $8–$12
Dr Kiesow's Essence of Life, clear, 5" . . . . $5–$7
Dr Kilmer's Cough Cure Consumption Oil, SB, 8³/₄", aqua . . . . $400–$600
Dr Kilmer's Female Remedy Binghamton NY, 8⁵/₈", aqua . . . . $70–$90
Dr Kilmer's Indian Cough Cure Consumption Oil, 7¹/₂", aqua . . . . $70–$90
Dr Kilmer's Indian Cough Remedy Consumption Oil, 5¹/₂", aqua. . . . . $10–$15
Dr Kilmer's Ocean Weed Heart Remedy, SB, 8¹/₂", aqua . . . . $85–$125
Dr Kilmer's Swamp Root Diuretic to the Kidneys, ABM, aqua . . . . $10–$15
Dr Kilmer's Swamp Root Kidney Cure . . . . $5–$10
Dr Kilmer's Swamp Root Kidney Cure, Sample . . . . $8–$14
Dr Kilmer's Swamp Root Kidney Liver & Bladder Cure, 7", aqua . . . . $7–$9
Dr Kilmer's Swamp Root Kidney Liver & Bladder Cure, 8", aqua . . . . $8–$12
Dr Kilmer's Swamp Root Kidney Remedy, Sample, 4¹/₄", aqua. . . . . $9–$13
Dr Kilmer's U & O Oinitment, 1³/₄", aqua . . . . $4–$6
Dr King's Groups Cough Syrup, OP, aqua . . . . $50–$75
Dr King's New Discovery for Coughs & Colds, clear, 6³/₄" . . . . $4–$6
Dr King's New Discovery, 4", aqua . . . . $3–$5
Dr King's New Discovery, clear, 4" . . . . $2–$4
Dr King's New Life Pills, clear, 2¹/₂" . . . . $2–$4
Dr King's Pills, labeled . . . . $7–$12
Dr Koch Vegetable Tea Co., clear, 9" . . . . $5–$7
Dr L William's Universal Pain Extractor, OP, aqua . . . . $30–$45
Dr Larookah's Indian Vegetable Pulmonic Syrup, OP, 8⁵/₈", aqua . . . . . $110–$150
Dr LE Keeley's Gold Cure for Drunkenness (on label), clear, 5¹/₂" . . . . . $125–$225
Dr Linack's Malt Extract, clear, 6" . . . . $5–$7
Dr Lindsay's Blood Searcher, clear, 8¹/₂" . . . . $15–$25
Dr LR Park's Egyptian Anodyne, OP, 5", aqua . . . . $80–$120
Dr LR Stafford Olive Tar, clear, 6" . . . . $5–$7
Dr M Bowman's Healing Balsam, clear, 6¹/₂" . . . . $5–$6
Dr MA Simmon's Liver Medicine, aqua . . . . $5–$8
Dr Mann's Celebrated Ague Balsam, OP, 6³/₄", aqua . . . . $90–$135
Dr Maskeker's Balm of Gilead, N York, rect., OP, 9¹/₂", honey amber . . . .
. . . . $9000–$10,000
Dr McMunn's Elixer of Opium, N-437, OP, 4¹/₄", aqua. . . . . $20–$25
Dr Mile's Heart Treatment, 8¹/₄", aqua. . . . . $20–$25
Dr Mile's Heart Treatment, full labels, aqua. . . . . $150–$200
Dr Mile's Remedy for the Heart, 8¹/₄", aqua. . . . . $7–$10
Dr Mile's Restorative Nervine, 8", aqua . . . . $2–$4
Dr Mile's Restorative Nervine, clear, 8" . . . . $1–$3
Dr Mile's Restorative Tonic, aqua . . . . $14–$19
Dr MM Fenner's People's Remedies, clear, 6" . . . . $5–$8
Dr Nywall's Family Medicine, 7¹/₂", amber . . . . $14–$18
Dr O Phelps Brown, 2³/₄", aqua . . . . $3–$5
Dr Park's Indian Liniment, clear, 5³/₈" . . . . $7–$10

Dr Perkin's Syrup, Albany, rect., IP, 9¹/₄", teal green . . . . $500–$800
Dr Peter Fahrney's & Sons Chicago, clear, 9" . . . . $2–$3
Dr Peter's Kuriko, 8³/₄", aqua . . . . $5–$7
Dr Peter's Kuriko, clear, square, 9" . . . . $4–$5
Dr Pierce's Anuric, cylinder, 3", aqua . . . . $10–$14
Dr Pierce's Favorite Prescription, 8¹/₄", aqua . . . . $8–$10
Dr Pierce's Golden Medical Discovery, square, 8¹/₄", aqua . . . . $5–$8
Dr Pierce's Golden Medical Discovery, square, sun colored amethyst . . . . . . $14–$20
Dr Pinkham's Emmanogogue, Op, 6⁷/₈", aqua . . . . $45–$65
Dr Porter New York, OP, 5", aqua . . . . $15–$20
Dr R Sappington Flaxseed Syrup, 7¹/₂", aqua . . . . $8–$12
Dr Rabell Emulsion, 9¹/₂", aqua . . . . $4–$6
Dr RC Flower's Scientific Remedies, 9¹/₈", amber . . . . $60–$80
Dr Roback Swedish Remedy, eight sided, OP, 4¹/₂", aqua . . . . $80–$120
Dr Roback Swedish Remedy, OP, 6¹/₄", aqua . . . . $150–$225
Dr Robb's Hippodrome Liniment, OP, 5¹/₄", aqua . . . . $100–$140
Dr Rose's Antidyspeptic Vermifuge Phila, OP, aqua . . . . $90–$140
Dr Rose's for the Lung & Throat Disease, OP, 5³/₈", aqua . . . . $75–$95
Dr Rose's Philada for All Lung & Throat . . . , N-533, OP, 5³/₈", aqua. . . $125–$165
Dr S Feller's Eclectic Treatment, OP, 4¹/₄", aqua . . . . $125–$175
Dr S Feller's Lung Balsam, IP, 6¹/₂", deep aqua . . . . $150–$250
Dr S Fitch, 707 Bway, NY, rect., OP, 4³/₄", aqua . . . . $15–$25
Dr S Hardy's Woman's Friend, aqua . . . . $20–$30
Dr S Pitcher's Castoria, 6", aqua . . . . $5–$8
Dr SA Tuttle's, Boston, Mass, 12 panels, 6³/₄", aqua . . . . $5–$8
Dr SA Weaver's Canker & Salt Syrup, 7³/₄", aqua . . . . $20–$30
Dr Sage's Catarrh Remedy . . . . $15–$20
Dr Sanford's Liver Invigorator, OP, 7¹/₂", aqua . . . . $60–$80
Dr Sanford's Liver Invigorator, SB, 7¹/₂", aqua . . . . $30–$40
Dr SBH & Co, PR (on base), clear cylinder, 9" . . . . $8–$10
Dr Schenck's Pine Tar for Throat and Lungs, 6", aqua . . . . $10–$15
Dr Schultz, 6¹/₂", aqua . . . . $3–$4
Dr Schwartze's Compound Extract of Sarsaparilla, OP, 7³/₄", aqua . . . . $300–$450
Dr Seth Arnold's Balsam . . . . $5–$6
Dr Seth Arnold's Balsam, 3³/₄", amethyst . . . . $7–$9
Dr Seth Arnold's Balsam, 7", aqua . . . . $10–$15
Dr Seth Arnold's Balsam, IP, 3³/₄", amethyst . . . . $7–$9
Dr SF Stowe's Ambrosial Nectar, 8", light yellow green . . . . $70–$85
Dr Shoop's Family Medicines, 5¹/₂", aqua . . . . $2–$4
Dr Shoop's Family Medicines, 6¹/₂", aqua . . . . $3–$5
Dr Shoop's Family Medicines, 7", aqua . . . . $6–$9
Dr Simmon's Squaw Vine & Wine Compound, 8¹/₂", aqua . . . . $9–$13
Dr Smith's Colombo Tonic, 9³/₈", amber . . . . $35–$50
Dr SS Fitch & Co, 714 Broadway NY, OP, aqua . . . . $15–$22
Dr SS Fitch, 707 Bway, NY, OP, aqua . . . . $20–$25
Dr SS Fitch, NY, OP, 5", aqua . . . . $20–$25
Dr Swett's Panacea Exeter NH, OP, 8", deep yellow amber. . . . . $1750–$2750
Dr Syke's Specific Blood Medicine, clear, 6¹/₂" . . . . $4–$6
Dr Taft's Asthmalene, NY, 3¹/₂", aqua . . . . $4–$6
Dr Thacher's Liver & Blood Syrup, rect., 7¹/₄", amber . . . . $5–$7
Dr Thacher's Liver & Blood Syrup, sample, 3¹/₂", amber . . . . $7–$10

Dr Thacher's Vegetable Syrup, clear, 7"..............................$6–$9
Dr Thacher's Worm Syrup, square, $4^1/4$", aqua........................$5–$7
Dr Tichenor's Antiseptic, $3^1/2$", aqua..............................$5–$7
Dr Tobias Venetian Liniment, OP, 5", aqua..........................$12–$18
Dr Tobias Venetian Liniment, SB, 5", aqua...........................$5–$7
Dr Tobias, New York, SB, $4^1/4$", aqua.............................$4–$6
Dr Townsend's Aromatic Hollands Tonic, square, 9", amber..........$100–$145
Dr True's Elixer Established 1851, clear, ABM, $5^1/2$"...................$2–$3
Dr True's Elixer Established 1851, clear, ABM, $7^3/4$"...................$3–$4
Dr True's Elixer Worm Expeller, aqua..............................$10–$16
Dr True's Elixer, clear, $5^1/2$"..................................$4–$6
Dr Tutt's Asparagine, New York, $10^1/4$", aqua.....................$12–$16
Dr TW Graydon, Diseases of the Lungs, 6", light amber.................$8–$12
Dr Von Wert's Balsam, Watertown, NY, rect., 6", aqua..................$6–$8
Dr Walsh's Invigorator, 7", amber.................................$30–$50
Dr WB Caldwell's Syrup Pepsin, clear, 7"............................$6–$8
Dr WB Farrell's Arabian Liniment, Chicago, Ill's, cylinder, OP, $7^5/8$", yellow green
....$1300–$1500
Dr WB Farrell's Arabian Liniment, OP, $7^1/2$", aqua ....$150–$190
Dr WG Little's Ring Worm & Tetter Ointment, OP, 3", aqua.........$350–$475
Dr WH Alexander's Wonderful Healing Oil, aqua......................$4–$7
Dr White's Dandelion Alternative, $9^1/4$", deep aqua....................$50–$75
Dr William's Anti Dyspeptic Elixer, OP, $6^3/8$", aqua..................$75–$125
Dr Wilson's Horse Ointment, OP, $4^1/4$", emerald green..................$2000+
Dr Wistar's Balsam of Wild Cherry, IP, $6^1/4$", deep aqua...........$35–$50
Dr Wm A Sabine New York, OP, aqua...............................$15–$20
Dr WN Handy Easton NY, 12 sided, SB, $8^1/2$", olive green..........$2000–$2600
Dr WS Love's Vegetable Elixer, Baltimore, cylinder, OP, 7", olive green.........
....$3500–$4500
Drs D Fahrney & Son Preparation for Cleansing the Blood, SB, 9", medium apricot
amber...$325–$425
Drs EE & JA Greene, New York, & Boston, $7^1/2$", aqua.................$8–$11
Druggist's Lindsay Ruffin & Co., clear, $6^1/4$"........................$5–$7
Dudley's Emulsion Pure Cod Liver Oil, $10^1/4$", cobalt...............$150–$190
Duff Gordon Sherry Medical Department, $9^3/4$", olive amber..........$300–$375
Dunbar & Co Wormwood Cordial, SB, $9^1/2$", greenish aqua...........$150–$200
Durfee Mfg Co, Grand Rapids, Mich., clear, 7"........................$1–$3
Dutcher's Dead Shot for Bed Bugs St Albans Vt, N-184, OP, 5", aqua...........
....$250–$325
Dutton's Vegetable Discovery, 6", aqua.............................$7–$10
Dyer's Healing Embrocation, N-185, OP, $6^1/8$", aqua................$80–$100
Dyer's Healing Embrocation, OP, 6", aqua...........................$70–$90
Dyspeptic Cordial, N-187, OP, $6^3/8$", deep aqua...................$100–$140
E Bloch & Co WB (on base), clear, $3^1/2$"...........................$3–$5
EA Buckout's Dutch Liniment, Mechanicville, NY, OP, $4^5/8$", aqua.....$400–$500
Ebenezer A Pearls Tincture of Life, $7^3/4$", aqua.....................$8–$12
Eddy & Eddy, clear, 5"...$2–$3
Edw S Burnham Apothecary, Charleston, SC, $4^1/4$", aqua.............$5–$8
EE Dyer & Co Extract of Dandelion Boston Mass, double collar, pour spout, IP,
$5^7/8$", light blue..$600–$850
EE Sutherland Medical Co., Paducah, Ky, $6^3/4$", aqua.................$6–$9

A variety of cologne bottles, including sided varieties, a corset-waisted example (third from left), two monument forms (center), and some rare figural pomade jars (left). PHOTO COURTESY OF CHARLES MOORE AMERICANA.

Assortment of Midwestern globular bottles, with the rarest being the green example (left) and the vertically ribbed example (second from right). PHOTO COURTESY OF CHARLES MOORE AMERICANA.

Fantastic colorful assortment of scroll flasks. PHOTO COURTESY OF CHARLES MOORE AMERICANA.

Grouping of pickle and food bottles. Note the deep amber square pickle, fourth from the right. This type is attributed to Willington, Conn., and is valued in excess of $10,000. PHOTO COURTESY OF GLASS WORKS AUCTIONS.

Colorful assortment of beer and soda water bottles. PHOTO COURTESY OF CHARLES MOORE AMERICANA.

Colorful grouping of historical and pattern molded flasks. Note the amethyst Stiegel-type at left. PHOTO COURTESY OF GLASS WORKS AUCTIONS.

A nice assortment of rare target balls showing the diverse colors in which they are found. PHOTO COURTESY OF GLASS WORKS AUCTIONS.

Rare colored bottles, including a green cone (top left) next to a group of umbrellas, with the second shelf of teakettles, and (bottom left) a "submarine" poison and a shield bottle (second from the left). PHOTO COURTESY OF GLASS WORKS AUCTIONS.

Shown here, a wide variety in forms and colors of barber bottles. PHOTO COURTESY OF GLASS WORKS AUCTIONS.

A nice grouping of pint-sized early mineral water bottles. PHOTO COURTESY OF CHARLES MOORE AMERICANA.

An assortment of beautifully colored hair bottles. PHOTO COURTESY OF CHARLES MOORE AMERICANA.

Label under glass bottles. PHOTO COURTESY OF GLASS WORKS AUCTIONS.

A selection of rare soda bottles, including sided, round bottomed, and ten pin form. PHOTO COURTESY OF GLASS WORKS AUCTIONS.

Three rare, blown, three-mold decanters with two extremely rare historical flasks in between. While aqua is usually the most common and least valuable of colors found in bottles in general, aqua blown three-mold is extremely rare, and the aqua flask at left is possibly unique. PHOTO COURTESY OF CHARLES MOORE AMERICANA.

Colorful assortment of squats, torpedos, and sided, mineral waters, beers, and sodas. PHOTO COURTESY OF CHARLES MOORE AMERICANA.

Rare black glass, including some rare and dated seal bottles. PHOTO COURTESY OF CHARLES MOORE AMERICANA.

A nice grouping of rare and colored bottles, including rare colored pontiled medicines. PHOTO COURTESY OF CHARLES MOORE AMERICANA.

Rare and colored inks dominate the scene, with a rare colored and threadless insulator at left. PHOTO COURTESY OF CHARLES MOORE AMERICANA.

Beautiful grouping of rare and colored blown three-mold decanters, flasks, medicines, and a miniature shaft and globe (foreground). PHOTO COURTESY OF CHARLES MOORE AMERICANA.

Bitters bottles in extremely rare colors, with a green Drakes Plantation cabin (third from right) and a light green barrel (center). PHOTO COURTESY OF CHARLES MOORE AMERICANA.

Egyptian Chemical Co., Boston, Mass, ABM, screw cap, clear, 7¹/₂" .... $1–$2
Ehrlicher Bros Pharmacists, clear, 4¹/₄" .... $5–$8
Elixir Alimentare Ducro A Paris, 8", light green .... $5–$7
Elixir Babek for Malaria Chills, aqua .... $10–$15
Elliman's Embrocation, 5¹/₂", aqua .... $3–$5
Elliman's Royal Embrocation for Horses, 7", light aqua .... $4–$6
Ely's Nasal Cream Balm, amber .... $3–$5
Empire State Drug Co., clear, 6¹/₂" .... $2–$4
Eno's Fruit Salt Derivative Compound, eight sided, 7", blue aqua .... $8–$12
Evan's Chemical Co., clear, 6¹/₄" .... $3–$4
Ever Ready Drug Co, Hollywood, 5³/₄", amber...................... $50–$65
Extract Valerian Shaker Fluid, OP, 3⁷/₈", aqua .... $100–$150
F Brown's Essence of Jamaica Ginger, 5¹/₂", aqua.................. $5–$7
Farquar's Medicated California Wine & Brandy, SB, 9", puce .... $750–$950
Farrell's Arabian Liniment, OP, aqua............................. $40–$60
Father John's Medicine, Lowell, 7¹/₄", dark amber..................... $3–$5
Father John's Medicine, wide mouth, 9", amber........................ $4–$7
FC Allen Concentrated Electric Past or Arabian Pain Extractor, Lancaster, Pa., square, OP, 3", yellow green.. $600–$750
Fellow's & Co Chemists, St John, NB, 8", aqua .... $8–$12
Fellow's & Co Chemists, St John, NB, ABM, 8", aqua .... $4–$5
Fellow's Syrup of Hypophosphates, oval .... $1–$3
Ferrol The Iron Oil Food Cod Liver Oil, 9¹/₄", amber.................. $8–$13
Flagg's Good Samaritan, five sided, OP, pale cornflower blue .... $100–$145
Flagg's Good Samaritan, OP, five sided, 3³/₄", aqua................... $60–$85
Fletcher's Castoria, 6", aqua....................................... $4–$6
Fletcher's Castoria, clear, 6" .... $3–$4
Fluid Extract of Sarsaparilla New York (on label), OP, aqua............ $50–$75
Foley & Co, clear sample, 2¹/₂" .... $1–$2
Foley & Co, clear, 5 1//4" .... $1–$2
Foley's Cream, Foley & Co, Chicago, USA, clear, 5¹/₄"................ $1–$2
Foley's Honey & Tar, 5¹/₄", aqua .... $4–$5
Foley's Kidney Pills, Foley & Co, Chicago, clear, 2¹/₂" .... $3–$5
Folger's Olosaonean, OP, aqua..................................... $35–$50
Foster's Mountain Compound, OP, 6¹/₄", aqua.................... $80–$120
Fougera's Compound Ionized Cod Liver Oil, three sided, clear .... $3–$5
Frank HE Eggleston Pharmacy, Laramie, Wy, clear .... $5–$8
Frank Whitmore Prescription Druggist, Conneaut, Ohio, clear .... $6–$8
Franklin Howes Medical Discovery, aqua.......................... $15–$20
Fred KW Hale Natures Herbal Remedies, aqua...................... $10–$14
Frederick Stearns & Co, Detroit, 4", amber .... $3–$4
Frey's Vermifuge, Baltimore, square, OP, 4¹/₂", aqua................. $25–$40
Friedenwald's Buchu Gin for Kidney & Liver Troubles, full label, 9⁷/₈", deep yellow green .... $200–$275
Friend's Rheumatic Dispeller Buffalo NY, OP, 6¹/₄", aqua .... $125–$185
Frog Pond Chill & Fever Cure, ABM, 7", cobalt .... $60–$90
Frog Pond Chill & Fever Cure, rect., 7", apricot amber .... $300–$450
From the Laboratory of GW Merchant, 5⁵/₈", yellowish green......... $350–$425
From the Laboratory of GW Merchant, IP, 5¹/₂", medium blue green ... $175–$250
From the Laboratory of GW Merchant, OP, 5¹/₂", emerald green ...... $125–$225
From the Laboratory of GW Merchant, OP, 5³/₈", aqua .... $160–$210

Fulton's Radical Remedy, 8³/₄", amber .... $300–$500
Furst McNess Co, Freeport, Ill, 8¹/₄", aqua .... $2–$4
G Facella (on base), 6", aqua. .... $2–$3
Gardner's Liniment, OP, 3⁷/₈", aqua .... $40–$65
Gargling Oil Lockport NY, 7¹/₈", emerald green...................... $200–$300
Gay's Compound Extract of Canchalagua New York, rect., OP, 6¹/₂", aqua ....
.... $140–$180
General Infirmary at Leeds, The, oval, 7¹/₄", aqua...................... $6–$9
Genesee Liniment, OP, 5¹/₄", aqua .... $40–$65
Genuine Essence, OP, 4¹/₂", aqua .... $15–$22
Genuine Essence, OP, medium yellow olive .... $550+
Genuine Fluid Extracts, HT Hembold, 7¹/₄", aqua...................... $6–$8
Genuine Swaim's Panacea, N-610, OP, 7⁵/₈", aqua................. $400–$600
Geo E Fairbanks No 10 Druggists Front St Worcester, amber......... $125–$150
German Fir Cough Cure, labeled and in box, 6³/₈", aqua .... $50–$75
German Magnetic Liniment, OP, 5", aqua .... $50–$75
GF Hedrich Apothecary, Charleston, SC, clear, 4¹/₂" .... $3–$5
GH Holtzman, Pharmacist, clear, 5¹/₂" .... $3–$5
Gibb's Bone Liniment, 6¹/₂", olive amber .... $650–$825
Gibb's Bone Liniment, 6¹/₂", medium olive amber .... $675–$850
Gibb's Bone Liniment, OP, 6¹/₂", olive green .... $700–$900
Ginseng Panacea, OP, 4³/₈", aqua................................. $80–$100
Glaser, Kohn & Co Mfg Chemists, clear, 4¹/₄" .... $1–$2
Glover's Imperial Mange, rect., 6¹/₂", amber.......................... $3–$5
Glover's Imperial Medicine, screw top, amber .... $2–$3
Glyco Thymoline, clear, 2¹/₂" .... $1–$2
Goff's Indian Vegetable Cough Syrup, aqua .... $35–$50
Golden Eye Lotion Leonardis, Tampa, Fla, ABM, 4¹/₂", aqua .... $3–$5
Golden Eye Lotion, Leonardis, Tampa, Fla, 4¹/₂", aqua .... $7–$12
Golden Eye Lotion, New York, 4¹/₂", aqua .... $7–$12
Gombault's JE Caustic Balsam, 6¹/₂", aqua .... $4–$6
GPR, clear, 6¹/₄" .... $3–$4
Graffenberg Children's Panacea, OP, 4¹/₄", aqua.................... $90–$135
Granular Citrate of Magnesia, 6", cobalt .... $30–$40
Gray's Celebrated Sparkling Spray, clear .... $7–$12
Gray's Syrup of Red Spruce Gum, ABM, 5¹/₂", aqua .... $2–$3
Great English Sweeny Specific, 4", aqua .... $6–$9
Great Western Liniment, OP, 4¹/₄", aqua .... $125–$175
Grecian Fancheronian Drops JS Fancher New York, N-204, IP, 7⁵/₈", aqua.......
.... $100–$125
Grober's Botanic Dyspepsia Fluid .... $20–$28
Gross Cereal Extract of Oats and Barley, 10¹/₂", amber .... $50–$75
Guide to Health Avery & Co, book figural, 9¹/₄", medium amber........ $300–$400
GW Merchant Carbonic Mineral Water Lockport NY, OP, 5¹/₂", emerald green...
.... $3000+
GW Merchant Chemist Lockport NY, IP, 7³/₈", medium emerald green..........
.... $150–$250
GW Merchant Chemist Lockport NY, OP, 5¹/₂", emerald green.......... $50–$70
GW Merchant Chemist Lockport NY, SB, 7¹/₄", deep blue green........ $90–$120
GW Merchant Lockport NY, OP, 5", aqua......................... $75–$125
GW Merchant Lockport NY, OP, 5", deep emerald green .... $85–$135

Medicine, GW Merchant. PHOTO COURTESY OF NEIL GROSSMAN.

GW Merchant Lockport NY, OP, blue green . . . . $100–$135
GW Merchant Lockport NY, OP, lip bruise, 5", deep blue green. . . . . $50–$60
GW Stone's Cough Elixir Boston Mass, N-607, OP, 6", aqua . . . . $75–$90
GW Stone's Liquid Cathartic & Family Physic, Lowell Mass, rect., 8³/₄", olive amber. . . . . $6000–$8000
GW Stones Cough Elixir, OP, 6³/₈", aqua . . . . $70–$95
H & G Co, Phila, cylinder, clear, 4" . . . . $8–$12
H Lakes Indian Specific, OP, 8", aqua . . . . $550–$750
HA Cassebeer Apothecary New York, 6¹/₂", cobalt . . . . $90–$125
Hagan's Magnolia Balm, rect., milk glass . . . . $8–$15
Hall's Balsam for the Lungs, 7¹/₄", aqua . . . . $5–$7
Hall's Catarrh Cure, cylinder, 4¹/₂", aqua . . . . $3–$6
Hall's Great Discovery, A Texas Wonder, clear, 3¹/₂" . . . . $5–$7
Haller Propietary Co, Blair, Neb., clear, 7¹/₂". . . . . $4–$6
Hampton's Vegetable Tincture, Baltimore, labeled, olive amber . . . . . $1800–$2200
Hampton's Vegetable Tincture, Baltimore, medium yellow amber. . . . . $800–$1200
Hampton's Vegetable Tincture, Baltimore, olive amber . . . . $800–$1100
Hampton's Vegetable Tincture, Baltimore, yellow green . . . . $1500–$1800
Hance Brothers & White, Phila, 7", amber. . . . . $8–$10
Hand Med Co, Phila, 5¹/₄", aqua . . . . $4–$6
Handyside's Consumption Cure, 7¹/₄", aqua. . . . . $30–$45
Hardy's Elixir Prepared by McKinstry, Hudson, NY, aqua . . . . $15–$20
Haskin's Nervine, Binghamton, NY, 8¹/₄", aqua . . . . $5–$7
Hawe's Healing Extract, N-287, OP, original wrapper, 3³/₈", aqua. . . . . . $200–$250
Haynes & Co Blue Bottle Extracts Montour Falls NY, 6³/₄", cobalt. . . . . . $30–$40
HC Farrell's Arabian Liniment, N-208, OP, aqua . . . . $40–$50
Healy & Bigelow Kickapoo Indian Sagwa, full label, 8⁵/₈", aqua. . . . . $70–$95
Healy & Bigelow Kickapoo Oil . . . . $12–$16
Heceman & Co Chemists New York, 10¹/₂", aqua . . . . $5–$7
Henry K Wampole & Co, clear, 4³/₄". . . . . $2–$4
Henry Wampole & Co Phila, clear, 8¹/₄". . . . . $2–$4
Henry's Three Chlorides, 7¹/₄", amber. . . . . $3–$5
Herb Med Co, Weston, W Va, 9¹/₂", aqua. . . . . $6–$9
Herbine, St, St Louis, clear, rect., 6³/₄". . . . . $3–$4
HF Clark Pharmacist, Carbondale, clear, 5" . . . . $3–$5
HH Warner & Co Tippecanoe, canoe shaped, 9", amber . . . . $70–$90

HHH Medicine, Celebrated DDT, 1869, aqua. . . . . $6–$9
Hick's Capudine for Headaches, 3³/₈", amber. . . . . $1–$3
Higby & Stearns Detroit Mich, SB, 7¹/₄", medium sapphire blue. . . . . $400–$575
Hillside Chem Co (on base), 7¹/₂", amber. . . . . $3–$4
Himalaya, The Kola Compound, Natures, 7¹/₄", yellow amber. . . . . $40–$45
Hit, Elmira, NY, clear, rect. . . . . $2–$3
HK Mulford Co Chemist, Phila, 5¹/₂", amber . . . . $3–$5
Hobo Med Co Beaumont, Texas, clear, screw cap, 8¹/₂" . . . . $2–$3
Hoff's German Liniment, 12 panels, 5³/₄", aqua . . . . $6–$9
Hoffman's Anodyne, clear, 5". . . . . $3–$4
Holland Drug Co, Prescriptions a Specialty, clear, 4³/₄" . . . . $3–$4
Holland Harlem Oil, clear, 3¹/₂" . . . . $3–$5
Hollis Balm of America, 5", aqua . . . . $5–$8
Holman's Natures Grand Restorative, OP, 6³/₄", olive green . . . . $2500–$3750
Holton's Electric Oil, clear, 3¹/₄" . . . . $3–$5
Hood's Tooth Powder, CI Hood & Co, clear, 3¹/₂". . . . . $4–$6
Hoof Liniment Prepared by Baker & Co New Rochelle, rect., OP, 5", aqua . . . .
. . . . $200–$300
Hoof's Liniment, Goodrich Drug Co., 12 panels, ABM, 7", aqua . . . . $3–$4
Hop Tonic, 9³/₄", amber. . . . . $70–$90
Hope's Magnetic Oil, OP, 2⁷/₈", aqua. . . . . $40–$65
Houses Indian Tonic (Indian), N-309, OP, 5³/₈", aqua . . . . $1400–$1800
Howard's Vegetable Cancer and Canker Syrup, rect., with beveled edges, OP, 7¹/₄",
olive amber . . . . $1500–$2500
Howland's Cough Remedy, OP, 4⁷/₈", aqua. . . . . $90–$135
Howland's Ready Remedy, OP, aqua. . . . . $110–$150
Humphrey's Homeopathic, clear, 3¹/₂" . . . . $4–$6
Humphrey's Marvel of Healing, clear, 5¹/₂" . . . . $4–$6
Humphrey's Marvel Witch Hazel, clear, ABM, 5¹/₂". . . . . $3–$4
Hurd's Cough Balsam, N-321, OP, full label, 4¹/₂", aqua . . . . $100–$160
Husband's Calcined Magnesia, 4¹/₄", aqua . . . . $5–$8
Husband's Calcined Magnesia, clear, 4¹/₄" . . . . $3–$4
Hyatt's Infallible Life Balsam, N-322, IP, 9¹/₂", medium yellow green . . . .
. . . . $900–$1200
Hyatt's Infallible Life Balsam, N-322, OP, 9¹/₂", aqua . . . . $100–$150
Hyatt's Infallible Life Balsam, N-322, SB, 9¹/₂", aqua . . . . $20–$30
I Covet Balm of Life, N-142, 5⁵/₈", olive green . . . . $500–$700
I Newton's Panacea Purifier of the Blood, N-469, OP, olive amber . . . $1000–$1250
ID Bulls Ext of Sarsaparilla Hartford Con, rect., OP, 6³/₄", aqua . . . . $100–$150
Indian's Panacea, OP, 9", olive amber . . . . $3000–$3750
Iodine, 2¹/₄", amber . . . . $1–$2
J & C Maguire Chemists & Druggists, 9³/₈", medium cobalt. . . . . $100–$140
J Jungmann Apothecary 1047 Third Ave, 6⁷/₈", cobalt . . . . $100–$150
JA Richardson Apothecary, Phila, clear, 7" . . . . $6–$9
Jackson's Antizyme or Fever Cure, 4¹/₄", aqua . . . . $15–$20
Jacob's Cholera & Dysentery Cordial, OP, aqua . . . . $80–$120
Jamaica Ginger, clear, labeled, 5³/₄". . . . . $3–$4
James Anodyne Expectorant or Cough Pills, OP, 2³/₈", aqua . . . . $225–$325
James S Robinson, Memphis, Tn, clear, 7". . . . . $3–$4
Jaynes & Co, Boston, screw cap, 9¹/₂", amber . . . . $2–$3
JC Maguire Chemists & Druggists, 7³/₄", cobalt . . . . $40–$50

Left: *Medicine, Indian Sagwa.* Right: *Medicine, Jacob's cordial.* PHOTOS COURTESY OF NEIL GROSSMAN.

Jelly of Pomegranate, by Dr Gordak, OP, 6³/₄", aqua . . . . $60–$90
Jenk's Vegetable Extract, OP, 4", aqua . . . . $60–$85
Jewett's Liniment for Fever, OP, 4", deep bluish aqua . . . . $300–$350
Jewett's Liniment for Headache, OP, 2¹/₄", aqua . . . . $45–$60
Jewett's Nerve Liniment, OP, 3", aqua . . . . $40–$55
Jewett's Stimulating Liniment, OP, 3", aqua . . . . $40–$55
JF Hart & Co Limited Toronto, 8", cobalt . . . . $150–$250
JJ Hunt's Modern Remedy, OP, 6¹/₂", aqua . . . . $100–$145
JJ Mapes No 61 Front St N York, OP, rect., 4¹/₂", yellow olive amber . . . .
 . . . . $650–$1000
JK Palmer Chemist Boston, OP, 9¹/₄", olive amber. . . . . $425–$575
JK Palmer Chemist Boston, OP, full label, 9¹/₄", olive amber . . . . $1000–$1350
JL Curtis Syrup of Sassafras, OP, 4⁵/₈", aqua . . . . $75–$110
Jno T Barbee & Co, clear, 6" . . . . $3–$4
Jno Wyeth & Bro Hypophosphites, 8³/₄", medium cobalt . . . . $40–$50
Joe Evan Apothecary, Westchester, Pa, clear, 5" . . . . $3–$5
John Bull's King of Pain New York . . . , OP, 5", aqua. . . . . $70–$100
John Gilbert & Co Druggists, OP, 6", aqua. . . . . $25–$30
John H Pope Druggist N Orleans, ovoid, OP, 5¹/₂", sapphire blue . . . . $550–$750
John J Smith Louisville Ky, cylinder, OP, 5⁵/₈", deep green . . . . $400–$525
John J Tufts Apothecary, Plymouth, NH, clear, 6¹/₄" . . . . $3–$5
John M Winslow Rochester, NY, OP, 6", aqua . . . . $75–$100
John P Lee, clear, 4¹/₂" . . . . $2–$3
John Wyeth & Bro Take Next Dose at, dose cap, 5³/₄", cobalt. . . . . $12–$18
John Wyeth & Bro, Pat May 16th 1899, 3¹/₂". . . . . $8–$12
John Wyeth & Bro, Pat May 16th 1899, 6¹/₂", cobalt. . . . . $14–$19
John Wyeth & Brother Liquid Malt Extract, 9", amber . . . . $8–$12
Johnson & Johnson Oil (label), 5", aqua . . . . $4–$6
Johnson's American Anodyne Liniment, OP, 4¹/₂", aqua . . . . $15–$19
Johnson's American Anodyne Liniment, SB, 4¹/₂", aqua. . . . . $4–$7
Johnson's Chill & Fever Tonic, aqua. . . . . $12–$16
Jone's Drops for Humors or Anti Impetigines, N-352, OP, 4³/₄", aqua. . . . .
 . . . . $125–$175
Jozeau Pharmacien, OP, ovoid, 4¹/₄", olive green . . . . $250–$450
JR Burdsall's Arnica Liniment, New York, N-92, OP, 5¹/₂", aqua . . . . $45–$60
JR Nichols & Co Chemists Boston, 9¹/₄", cobalt. . . . . $110–$160

JR Spalding's Rosemary & Castor Oil, OP, 4⁷/₈", aqua . . . . \$40–\$55
JW Bull's Compound Pectoral Baltimore, N-89, OP, 5¹/₂", aqua . . . . \$80–\$110
JW Kelly & Co, clear, 6" . . . . \$2–\$3
KA Konka the Great Indian Remedy . . . . \$13–\$19
Kay's Compound Essence of Linseed, 5", aqua . . . . \$8–\$12
Keasbey & Mattison Co Chemists, Ambler, Pa, 5", light blue . . . . \$6–\$8
Keasbey & Mattison Philadelphia, 6", cobalt blue . . . . \$7–\$10
Keeley Remedy Neurotene, clear, 5¹/₂" . . . . \$6–\$8
Kemp's Balsam for Throat and Lungs, Leroy, NY, 5³/₄", aqua . . . . \$6–\$9
Kemp's Balsam for Throat and Lungs, 8", blue green . . . . \$15–\$24
Kemp's Balsam for Throat and Lungs, aqua . . . . \$3–\$4
Kemp's Balsam for Throat and Lungs, clear . . . . \$4–\$6
Kemp's Balsam, flask shaped, 2³/₄", aqua . . . . \$10–\$15
Kendall's Spavin Cure, 12 sided, 5¹/₂", amber . . . . \$5–\$8
Kendall's Spavin Treatment, 5¹/₄", aqua . . . . \$4–\$5
Kennedy's Favorite Remedy . . . . \$6–\$8
Kennedy's Medical Discovery, clear, 6" . . . . \$3–\$4
Keystone Drug Co, So Boston, Va, clear, 9" . . . . \$6–\$9
Kickapoo Sage Hair Tonic, 4¹/₂", cobalt blue . . . . \$90–\$130
Klinker's Hair Tonic, Cleveland, clear, 6" . . . . \$7–\$9
Knapp's Extract of Roots, NY, 5¹/₂", aqua . . . . \$7–\$9
Kola Cardinette, aqua . . . . \$7–\$11
Kutnow's Powder, 4³/₄", aqua . . . . \$4–\$6
Lactopeptine, clear, 4" . . . . \$3–\$4
Lactopeptine, small lip chip, 7¹/₂", cobalt . . . . \$20–\$25
Laine Chem Co., 6¹/₂", amber . . . . \$3–\$4
Langenbach's Dysentery Cure, labeled, aqua . . . . \$20–\$30
Langley & Michaels, San Francisco, 6¹/₄", aqua . . . . \$4–\$6
Langley's Red Bottle Elixir of Life, N-370, OP, 4⁷/₈", aqua . . . . \$60–\$90
Lanman & Kemp Cod Liver Oil, 10¹/₂", aqua . . . . \$6–\$9
Larkin & Co, ground stopper, rect., waisted, Seven-up green . . . . \$20–\$25
Laxacure, Something New Under the Sun, label and box . . . . \$12–\$15
Laxol, AJ White, 7", cobalt . . . . \$9–\$13
Le Jung, 11", amber . . . . \$2–\$3
Lediard's Morning Call, 9³/₄", olive green . . . . \$60–\$90
Legrande's Arabian Catarrh Remedy, New York, oval, 9", aqua . . . . \$30–\$40
Lennon, 3", aqua . . . . \$4–\$5
Leonardis Blood Elixer, Tampa, Fla, 8¹/₄", amber . . . . \$18–\$25
Leonardis Worm Syrup, 5", aqua . . . . \$6–\$9
Lewis Cough Syrup, Rochester, NY, eight sided, OP, 6¹/₂", yellow green . . . .
. . . . \$7000–\$8000
LF Ganter's Magic Chicken Cholera Cure, 6", amber . . . . \$50–\$65
Li, canoe shaped, 9", amber . . . . \$70–\$90
Lie Big Cos Coca Beef Tonic, aqua . . . . \$10–\$14
Lightning Hot Drops No Relief No Pay, 5", aqua . . . . \$7–\$10
Lightning Kidney & Liver Cure, 9¹/₂", aqua . . . . \$40–\$55
Lindsay's Blood Searcher, OP, 8³/₈", aqua . . . . \$60–\$95
Liniment Oil for Life, clear, 16 oz, 10¹/₂" . . . . \$8–\$12
Liquid Franconia of Woodward, clear, 4¹/₄" . . . . \$4–\$5
Liquid Opodeldoc, N-388, OP, 4¹/₂", aqua . . . . \$15–\$20
Liquid Opodeldoc, N-388, SB, 4¹/₂", aqua . . . . \$4–\$5

Liquid zone, 5¹/₂", amber... $3–$5
Liquid zone, 8", amber... $4–$5
Listerine, clear, varying sizes .... $3–$4
Listerine, clear, varying sizes, ABM .... $1–$2
Listerine, Lambert Pharmacal Co, cylinder, 5¹/₂" .... $2–$3
Listerine, Lambert Pharmacal Co, cylinder, clear, 3" .... $2–$3
Listerine, Lambert Pharmacal Co, cylinder, clear, 6³/₄" .... $2–$4
Litchfield's Diptheria Vanquisher, aqua............................. $12–$15
Little Giant Sure Death to All Bugs, 8¹/₂", aqua..................... $9–$12
Live & Let Live Cut Rate Drug Co, clear, 3¹/₂" .... $4–$5
LM Green Prop., Woodbury, NJ, clear................................. $3–$4
LM Green Woodbury NJ, clear, 4¹/₄" .... $2–$3
Log Cabin Cough & Consumption Remedy, amber.................... $100–$145
Log Cabin Extract, amber.. $140–$190
Log Cabin Scalpine, Rochester, NY, full label, 8⁵/₈", amber .... $350–$425
Log Cabin Scalpine, Rochester, NY, lip flake, 9", amber .... $200–$240
Long's Vegetable Pain Cure .... $10–$15
Longley's Panacea, beveled edges, double collar, IP, 6¹/₄", olive green ....
.... $800–$1200
Loomis's Cream Liniment, corset shap, OP, 4⁷/₈", emerald green ..... $1250–$1500
Lord's Opeldoc, (embossed man and crutches), 5", aqua.................. $6–$10
Louden & Co Vermifuge Philada, N-400, OP, 4³/₄", aqua .... $35–$45
Louden & Co's Indian Expectorant, N-399, OP, 7¹/₂"................ $100–$135
Louden & Cos Cherokee Liniment, OP, 5³/₈", aqua .... $175–$225
Louden & Cos Cure for Piles, OP, 6³/₄", aqua...................... $200–$275
Louis Daudelin Co, clear, 8³/₄" .... $3–$4
LP Dodge Rheumatic Liniment Newburg, OP, 6", olive green ...... $2000–$2500
LP Dodge Rheumatic Liniment Newburg, rect., OP, 5⁷/₈", medium amber.........
.... $1400–$1750
LQC Wishart's Pine Tree Tar Cordial Patent, 7³/₄", emerald green..... $150–$200
LQC Wishart's Pine Tree Tar Cordial Patent, 7³/₄", medium blue green.........
.... $225–$350
LQC Wishart's Pine Tree Tar Cordial Patent, 9¹/₂", yellow olive ...... $300–$350
LQC Wishart's Pine Tree Tar Cordial Patent, 9³/₈", emerald green..... $200–$275
LQC Wishart's Pine Tree Tar Cordial Patent, olive tone, 7³/₄", yellow green......
.... $150–$200
LQC Wishart's Trade Mark Pine Tree Cordial, 10¹/₄", blue green ..... $110–$150
LQC Wishart's Trade Mark Pine Tree Cordial, 9³/₄", amber........... $70–$90
Lucien Scott Cholera Curate, 3⁷/₈", aqua .... $35–$50
Lufkin Eczema Remedy, clear, 7" .... $5–$7
Luytie's, 6¹/₂", amber... $2–$3
Lydia Pinkham's Medicine, clear, 8"................................ $2–$3
Lydia Pinkham's Medicine, oval, 8", aqua .... $4–$6
Lydia Pinkham's Vegetable Compound, oval, 9", aqua............... $6–$9
Lyon's Laxative Syrup, clear, 6¹/₄" .... $4–$6
Lyon's Powder, KX-1, OP, 4¹/₄", deep puce....................... $90–$125
Lyon's Powder, KX-1, OP, 4¹/₄", olive green...................... $100–$140
Macassar Oil, rect., OP, 3¹/₂", aqua............................... $12–$15
Main Line Drug Store, clear, 5¹/₄" .... $3–$4
Marine Hospital Service 1798 USA 1871, 6", amber .... $150–$195
MB Roberts Vegetable Embrocation, N-524, 4¹/₈", blue green .... $100–$145

MB Roberts Vegetable Embrocation, N-524, OP, 4^1/$_8$", emerald green. . . $150–$200
MB Roberts Vegetable Embrocation, N-524, OP, 4^1/$_8$", light emerald green . . . .
. . . . $120–$140
McBurney's Kidney & Bladder Cure, 4^7/$_8$", aqua . . . . $30–$50
McCormick B Brand Extract, 5", sun colored amethyst. . . . . $12–$16
McCormick B Brand Extract, clear, flask shaped, 8" . . . . $18–$24
McKesson & Robbins, NY (on base), cylinder, 6^1/$_4$", amber. . . . . $3–$4
McNeal & Libby, Chicago, square, milk glass. . . . . $35–$45
Mead & Carrington's Fever & Ague Cure, OP, 6^1/$_2$", aqua. . . . . $150–$200
Medico Salt, Syracuse, NY, 7^3/$_4$", amber . . . . $5–$6
Mendenhall's Cough Remedy, OP, 4^3/$_8$", aqua . . . . $60–$90
Mexican Mustang Liniment Lyon Mfg Co, SB, 7^3/$_4$", aqua . . . . $6–$8
Mexican Mustang Liniment, N-444, OP, aqua . . . . $20–$30
Meyer Dillon Drug Co, Omaha, clear, 3^3/$_4$" . . . . $3–$4
Millard Hotel, Merritt's Pharmacy, clear, 6^3/$_4$" . . . . $4–$6
Miniard's Liniment, clear, 5^1/$_8$" . . . . $6–$9
Mitchell's Eye Salve, cobalt . . . . $7–$10
Mitchell's Eye Salve, square, OP, 1^7/$_8$", aqua . . . . $60–$80
Mixer's Cancer & Scrofula Syrup, aqua. . . . . $15–$20
MM Fenner MD, established 1872, 5^3/$_4$", aqua . . . . $4–$5
Monell's Teething Cordial, NY, eight sided, 6", aqua. . . . . $5–$8
Moore's Revealed Remedy, 8^3/$_4$", amber . . . . $15–$20
Moore's Revealed Remedy, 9", amber . . . . $30–$40
Moore's Tree of Life, full labels and wraps, 8^3/$_4$", aqua. . . . . $450–$650
Morse's Celebrated Syrup, OP, 9^1/$_2$", aqua . . . . $75–$125
Mortimer's Rheumatic Compound & Blood Purifier, OP, 6^3/$_4$", med yellowish apple
green . . . . $2200–$2700
Mortimore's Bitter Cordial . . . , N-461, OP, 7^7/$_8$", aqua . . . . $200–$285
Morton & Co, clear, 5^1/$_2$" . . . . $4–$5
Moses Hotchkiss Specific for Inflammation, 2^1/$_2$", aqua. . . . . $3–$5
Moses Indian Root Pills, 2^1/$_2$", amber. . . . . $15–$20
Mother's Friend, Pradfield Recl Co, rect., 7", aqua . . . . $5–$8
Mother's Relief, SB, 8", aqua . . . . $5–$7
Mounsey's Preston Salts, cylinder, SB, 1^3/$_4$", white opalescent. . . . . $75–$125
Moxie Nerve Food, 10^1/$_2$", aqua . . . . $4–$6
Moxie Nerve Food, 10", green . . . . $7–$9
Moyer's Bros Wholesale Druggists, clear, 8^1/$_2$" . . . . $3–$5
Moyer's Oil of Gladness, 5^1/$_2$", aqua . . . . $6–$9
Mrs Dinsmore's Cough & Croup Balsam, 6", aqua. . . . . $8–$11
Mrs E Kidder Dysentery Cordial, N-361, OP, 7^3/$_8$", aqua . . . . $90–$125
Mrs E Kidder Dysentery Cordial, N-361, OP, 8", olive green . . . . $1750–$2000
Mrs Porter's Hygienic Supply, 2", amber . . . . $3–$5
Mrs Winslow's Soothing Syrup, OP, 5^1/$_4$", aqua. $13–$19
Mrs Winslow's Soothing Syrup, SB, 5^1/$_4$", aqua . . . . $3–$4
Mulford's Digestive Malt Extract, 8^3/$_4$", amber . . . . $4–$6
Munyon's Germicide Solution, 3^1/$_4$", green. . . . . $4–$5
Munyon's Homeopathic, clear, 3^1/$_4$" . . . . $1–$2
Murine Eye Remedy, Chicago Usa, clear, 3^1/$_2$". . . . . $1–$2
Murine for Your Eyes, cylinder, clear, ground lip, screw cap, 4^1/$_8$" . . . . $1–$3
Murphy Bros, SB, 4^7/$_8$", aqua . . . . $3–$4
Myer's Rock Rose New Haven, N-466, OP, 9", aqua . . . . $225–$300

Myer's Rock Rose New Haven, N-466, OP, 9", deep emerald green ... $1200–$1500
N Wood, Portland, Me, rect., beveled edges, OP, 7", medium olive yellow ....
.... $750–$1000
Nankin's Specific, Bordentown, NY, 6¹/₂", aqua .... $9–$12
National Remedy Co, 2, aqua, 5¹/₂" .... $2–$3
Nelson's Chill Cure, Natchez, Miss, clear, 6" .... $20–$30
Nerve & Bone Liniment, cylinder, OP, 4", yellow green .... $450–$650
Nerve & Bone Liniment, cylinder, SB, 4", aqua .... $3–$5
NK Brown's Aromatic Essence, 4¹/₂", aqua .... $5–$7
Nyal's Emulsion of Cod Liver Oil, 9", amber ....
Nyal's Liniment, amber .... $4–$6
Oakland Chemical Co, 4", amber .... $3–$4
Oakland Chemical Co, 5¹/₄", amber .... $3–$5
OD Chemical Co, NY, 6¹/₄", amber .... $3–$5
Oldridge's Balm of Columbia for Restoring Hair, OP, 6¹/₄", aqua .... $45–$65
Oldridge's Balm of Columbia, OP, 5¹/₄", aqua .... $40–$60
Olds Ersipias Syrup, IP, square, 10¹/₂", olive green .... $3000–$4000
Omega Chemical Co, (embossed tree), clear, 5³/₄" .... $3–$5
Omega Oil It's Green, 4¹/₂", light green .... $12–$18
Omega Oil It's Green, clear, 4¹/₂" .... $2–$3
Omega Oil It's Green, screw cap, ABM, clear, 6" .... $2–$3
OO Woodman New Orleans, OP, 3³/₄", aqua .... $60–$90
Opodeldoc Liquid, cylinder, OP, 4¹/₂", aqua .... $12–$18

Medicine, liquid Opodeldoc, flaring lip. PHOTO COURTESY OF NEIL GROSSMAN.

Original Dr Craig's Kidney Cure, 9³/₄", medium amber .... $200–$325
Original Kidney & Liver Cure, 9³/₄", medium amber .... $300–$500
Osgood Indian Cholagoue New York, OP, aqua .... $40–$60
Otis Clapp & Sons Malt & Cod Liver Compound, 7¹/₄", amber .... $6–$9
Owbridge's Lung Tonic, 5", aqua .... $5–$7
Owl Drug Co (owl) San Francisco Cal, 9³/₄", Seven-up green .... $125–$175
Owl Drug Co (owl), 6¹/₄", cobalt blue .... $75–$95
Owl Drug Co (owl), milk glass, 4¹/₈" .... $40–$50
Owl Drug Co (owl), milk glass, 5" .... $45–$55
Owl Drug Co (owl), San Francisco, 9¹/₂", bright green .... $60–$80
Owl Drug Co (owl), square, 8¹/₂", amber .... $50–$60
Ozomulsion, 8³/₄", amber .... $6–$7

Pain Expeller, FA Richter & Co New York, rect., 5", aqua . . . . $4–$5
Paine's Celery Compound, amber . . . . $7–$10
Paine's Celery Compound, aqua . . . . $8–$12
Paine's Celery Compound, labeled, amber . . . . $9–$14
Palace Drug Store, clear, 4¹/₂" . . . . $3–$4
Palace Drug Store, clear, 6" . . . . $3–$5
Palmetto Pharmacy, Charleston, SC, aqua . . . . $4–$5
Palmolive Shampoo, BJ Johnson, clear, ABM, rect., 7¹/₄" . . . . $4–$5
Palmolive Shampoo, BJ Johnson, tenpaneled, ABM, 4", aqua . . . . $5–$7
Panopepton, 7³/₄", amber. . . . . $3–$4
Pardee's Rheumatic Remedy, 8¹/₂", aqua . . . . $6–$7
Park's Kidney & Liver Cure, 9³/₈", aqua. . . . . $100–$150
Parke Davis & Co, 3¹/₂", black . . . . $4–$5
Parke Davis & Co, 5", amber . . . . $4–$5
Parker's Ginger Tonic, aqua . . . . $8–$12
Parker's Hair Balsam, New York, rect., 6¹/₂", amber . . . . $8–$12
Pawnee Indian Ta Ha, Price 25c, 8¹/₂", aqua. . . . . $25–$35
PD & Co (on base), 3¹/₄", amber . . . . $2–$3
Pease's Eye Water, Newman, Ga, 4¹/₄", aqua . . . . $4–$6
People's Cure, Not a Patent Medicine, 8", deep aqua. . . . . $125–$175
Peptenzyme, 2¹/₂", cobalt. . . . . $12–$15
Pepto Mangan Guide, six panels, aqua. . . . . $5–$8
Pepto Mangan, six panels, 7", aqua . . . . $3–$4
Peptonoids the Arlington Chemist, Yonkers, NY, 6", amber. . . . . $4–$5
Perrine's Apple Ginger Phila, cabin, 10", amber . . . . $175–$275
Perrine's Ginger Depot No 37, medium amber, 10" . . . . $150–$250
Perry's Hungarian Balm for the Hair, OP, 5¹/₄", aqua. . . . . $40–$60
Peruvian Syrup, IP, 9⁵/₈", medium blue green . . . . $700–$950
Peruvian Syrup, OP, aqua. . . . . $60–$85
Peter Moller's Pure Cod Liver Oil, clear, 5³/₄" . . . . $2–$3
Petet's American Cough Cure, 7", aqua . . . . $8–$12
Phelp's Arcanum Genuine, six sided, OP, olive amber . . . . $12,000–$18,000
Phelp's Arcanum Worcester Mass, cylinder, indented panels, OP, 8¹/₂", olive amber
. . . . $900–$1250
Phillip's Milk of Magnesia, screw cap, 6", cobalt . . . . $1–$3
Pike & Osgood Alterative Syrup, Boston Mass, rect., OP, 8¹/₂", olive amber . . . .
. . . . $2500–$3000
Piso Company, 5", emerald green . . . . $5–$7
Piso Company, clear . . . . $3–$4
Piso's Cure for Consumption, aqua. . . . . $4–$8
Piso's Hazelton & Co, Warren, Pa, 6", amber . . . . $3–$5
PL Abbey Co, clear, 8³/₄" . . . . $6–$9
Pohls Drug Store, Tremont, Neb, clear, 6¹/₄" . . . . $6–$8
Polar Star Cough Cure, 5¹/₂", aqua . . . . $5–$8
Pond's Extract, N-499, OP, 4⁵/₈", aqua. . . . . $40–$50
Pond's Extract, SB, aqua . . . . $2–$4
Pond's Pain Destroyer, OP, 3³/₈", aqua . . . . $125–$150
Porter's Pain King, clear, 6¹/₂" . . . . $5–$7
Powell's American Liniment, OP, 4", aqua . . . . $60–$80
Pratt's Abolition Oil for Abolishing Pain, 6", deep aqua . . . . $200–$300
Prepared by HH Reynolds Batavia, OP, 5¹/₄", olive green . . . . $900–$1250

Prescribed by RV Pierce MD, 7", aqua . . . . $4–$6
Preston's Veg Purifying Catholicon Portsm NH, N-504, OP, 9¹/₂", aqua . . . .
. . . . $200–$225
Primley's Iron & Wahoo Tonic, 9¹/₂", dark amber . . . . $50–$75
Prof WH Peeks Remedy, amber . . . . $15–$20
Professor Callan's World Renowned Brazilian Gum, 4", aqua . . . . $4–$6
PT Wright & Co Pectoral Syrup Philada, OP, 6¹/₄", aqua . . . . $80–$120
Pure & Genuine Four Fold Liniment, clear, 5¹/₄" . . . . $4–$6
Pynchon, Boston, OP, aqua . . . . $14–$19
Races Indian Blood Renovator, aqua . . . . $35–$50
Ramson's Nerve & Bone Oil, Brown Mfg, rect., 5³/₄", aqua . . . . $8–$11
Ransom's Hive Syrup & Tolu, Buffalo, NY, square, 4¹/₂", aqua . . . . $9–$12
Rawleigh, ABM, 6", amber . . . . $1–$2
Rawleigh, clear, ABM, 6¹/₄" . . . . $1–$2
RE Stieraux Pills, clear, 1³/₄" . . . . $4–$5
RE Woodward's Vegetable Tincture, OP, 5⁷/₈", aqua . . . . $125–$175
Red Balsam, Taunton, Mass, 12 sided, clear, screw cap, 4¹/₄" . . . . $2–$4
Red Cross Family Liniment, clear, 5¹/₂" . . . . $2–$4
Red Heart Mfg & Med Co, Camden, NJ, clear, 8" . . . . $3–$5
Reed & Carnrick Peptenzyme, 4¹/₂", cobalt . . . . $10–$15
Reed & Carnrick Pharmacists, New York, 7¹/₂", amber . . . . $5–$8
Reed & Carnrick, NY, 4³/₄", amber . . . . $5–$6
Reed & Cutler Druggists Boston, OP, 7¹/₂", aqua . . . . $30–$35
Reinhardt's German Vegetable Bitter Elixer, OP, 3⁷/₈", aqua . . . . $80–$120
Renee's Magic Oil . . . . $5–$7
Resinal Balto Md Chemical Co, milk glass, 3¹/₄" . . . . $3–$5
Restoroff & Bettman, six panels, 4¹/₄", aqua . . . . $3–$5
Rev Gates Magamoose, Philada, aqua . . . . $10–$15
Rheumatic Syrup 1882 RS Co, 9³/₄", amber . . . . $75–$100
Rhodes Antidote to Malaria Fever and Ague Cure, N-515, OP, 8⁵/₈", aqua . . . .
. . . . $125–$165
Rhodes Antidote to Malaria Fever and Ague Cure, N-516, OP, 8", aqua . . . .
. . . . $400–$525
Rhodes Fever & Ague Cure, OP, 8³/₈", aqua . . . . $80–$120
Riccardi Ideal Tonic Blood Purifier, amber . . . . $9–$14
Ridakoff Cures Coughs, 5", aqua . . . . $40–$45
Ridgeway's Acme Liniment, 7¹/₂", amber . . . . $12–$16
Risley's Extract Buchu New York, OP, 7", aqua . . . . $50–$80
RN Searles Athlophoros, rect., 6³/₄", aqua . . . . $7–$10
Robert Gibson & Son Lozenge Makers, clear, 13" . . . . $30–$40
Robinson's American Horse Liniment, OP, 6", aqua . . . . $100–$150
Robt E Sellers Vermifuge, OP, 4³/₈", aqua . . . . $16–$22
Roche's Embrocation for Whooping Cough, clear, 4³/₄" . . . . $10–$15
Roderick's Wild Cherry Cough Balsam, ABM, 5¹/₂", amber . . . . $3–$5
Roderick's Wild Cherry Cough Balsam, ABM, clear, 5¹/₂" . . . . $3–$4
Rodericks Wild Cherry Balsam, clear, 3¹/₄" . . . . $8–$12
Roessmer Pharmacy, Phila, clear, 5¹/₂" . . . . $5–$7
Rohrer's Expectoral Wild Cherry Tonic, 10³/₈", golden amber . . . . $250–$350
Rohrer's Expectoral Wild Cherry Tonic, IP, 10³/₈", medium amber . . . . . $225–$325
Rohrer's Expectoral Wild Cherry Tonic, IP, olive tone, 10³/₈", bright yellow . . . .
. . . . $350–$500

Root Juice Med Co, 9", aqua... $3–$4
Root Juice Med Co, Fort Wayne, clear, 8¼" .... $3–$4
Rowand & Walton's Panacea Philada, OP, 6⅛", aqua .... $200–$250
Rowland's Macassar Oil, OP, aqua .... $35–$50
Royal Foot Wash, Eaton Drug Co, Atlanta, Ga........................ $9–$15
Royal Gall Remedy, ABM, 7½", dark amber.......................... $4–$6
Royce's Universal Relief, Wales Mass, OP, aqua .... $60–$90
RRR Radway & Co, OP, 4¾", aqua.................................. $15–$20
RRR Radway & Co, SB, full labels, 6½", aqua...................... $30–$40
Rubifoam for the Teeth, clear, 4"................................... $4–$6
Rumford Chem Works, eight sided, blue green....................... $15–$25
Rush's Buchu & Iron, aqua .... $14–$18
Rush's Remedy, AHF Monthly, 6", aqua .... $10–$14
Rushton's Cod Liver Oil New York, OP, 10", aqua .... $140–$190
S & D 100, clear, 2½" .... $2–$3
Sallade Magic Mosquito Bite Cure & Insect Exterminator .... $6–$9
Salvation Oil, AC Meyer & Co Baltimore, Md, 2¼", aqua........... $5–$7
Salvation Oil, AC Meyer & Co Trade Mark, 6¾", aqua.............. $4–$6
Sammy's Medicine Reaches Through the Entire System, 7", bluish aqua ....
.... $12–$20
San Cura Ointment, clear, 2½"..................................... $2–$3
Sanford's Extract of Hamamelis, 9⅜", cobalt .... $100–$150
Sanford's Radical Cure, 7½", cobalt................................ $40–$50
Sanford's Radical Cure, full label, 7½", cobalt.....................
Sanitol for the Teeth, clear, 4½" .... $5–$7
Sanitol for the Teeth, milk glass, 4"................................ $7–$9
Santalets, multipaneled, clear .... $10–$15
Sassafras Eye Lotion, Maugh Chunk, Pa, with eye cup, 6", cobalt .... $25–$35
Save the Baby, labeled.. $8–$12
Save the Horse Remedy, labeled .... $15–$20
SC Dispensary, with palm tree, aqua................................ $20–$35
SC Well's & Co, Leroy, NY, 5¼", aqua .... $1–$3
Schenck's Pulmonic Syrup, OP, 7", aqua .... $60–$90
Schenck's Seaweed Tonic, aqua .... $25–$35
Schmidt Pharmacist, Omaha, clear, 7¼" .... $5–$7
Scott's Emulsion Cod Liver Oil, Lime & Soda, 7½", aqua........... $2–$4
Scott's Emulsion, rect., aqua....................................... $2–$4
SD Baldwin's Liniment, 6", aqua................................... $40–$50
Seaver's Joint & Nerve Liniment, OP, 4", amber .... $1400–$2200
Selden's Magic Fluid NY, N-563, OP, 7⅜", aqua .... $125–$175
Shaker Cherry Pectoral Syrup No 1, N-569, OP, 5¼", aqua........... $150–$190
Shaker Fluid Extract Valerian, N-570, OP, 3¾", aqua .... $125–$175
Sherry & Iron, The Standard Tonic, 11", aqua .... $100–$125
Shiloh's Cure, Consumption Cure, 5½", aqua .... $8–$12
Short Stop for Coughs, HM O'Neil, NY, square, 4", aqua .... $5–$6
Silver Pine Healing Oil, 8⅛", aqua .... $18–$26
Silver Pine Healing Oil, Minn, clear, 6".......................... $6–$9
Simmon's Liver Regulator, 7", aqua .... $15–$20
Simmon's Liver Regulator, 9"...................................... $9–$13
Sirop Delacophosphate De Chaux, 7", aqua .... $5–$7
Skerret's Oil B Wheeler, OP, 6¼", emerald green .... $500–$650

SL Green Druggist Camden Ark, 3", amber.......................... $3–$4
Sloan's Liniment Kills Pain, 5", light blue............................ $4–$6
Sloan's Liniment, clear, screw cap .... $1–$2
Slocom's Colts Foot Expectorant, 2¹/₄", aqua .... $6–$8
Slocom's Colts Foot Expectorant, clear, 3"........................... $2–$4
Smith's Anodyne Cough Drops Montpelier, OP, 5⁵/₈", aqua............ $75–$110
Smith's Green Mountain Renovator, N-591, IP, 6³/₄", yellowish olive amber ......
.... $675–$900
Smith's Green Mountain Renovator, N-591, OP, 6³/₄", olive amber..... $625–$825
Smith's Green Mountain Renovator, SB, oval form, 7³/₄", aqua.......... $70–$95
SO Dunbar, Taunton, Mass, 6", aqua .... $4–$6
Solomon's Bros Branch Drug Stores, Bull St, 7", aqua .... $5–$6
Sozondont, clear, 2¹/₂" .... $2–$3
Spark's Perfect Health for Kidney & Liver Diseases, 4", aqua............ $8–$12
Spark's Perfect Health for Kidney & Liver Diseases, 9³/₈", amber...... $155–$255
Sparklene, 5", amber .... $3–$5
Spith San Francisco Pharmacy, 5¹/₄", aqua........................... $7–$11
Spohn's Distemper Cure, clear, 5"................................... $6–$9
Spooner's Hygeian Tonic, New York, Price $1.00, eight sided, OP, 6", olive amber .
.... $3500–$4500
St Andrew's Wine of Life Root, 9", dark red amber .... $55–$75
St Catherine's Chloride Calcium Canada, OP, 6", aqua .... $90–$125
St Jakob's Oil, Baltimore, Md, 6¹/₄", aqua .... $6–$8
Stabler & Co Druggists Baltimore, OP, 6⁵/₈", aqua .... $70–$90
Steelman & Archer, Phila, 6¹/₂", aqua................................ $1–$3
Steelman & Archer, Phila, clear, 6".................................. $1–$3
Stein & Co Apothecarier, Jersey City, clear, 5¹/₂" .... $3–$4
Stewart D Howe's Arabian Tonic, aqua .... $20–$25
Strong Cobb & Co Wholesale Druggists Cleveland O, 6¹/₄", cobalt...... $80–$120
Sultan Drug Co, St Louis & London, 7¹/₄", amber .... $5–$6
Swaim's Panacea Genuine, Phila, #610, OP, 7³/₄", aqua .... $300+
Swaim's Panacea Phila, N-612, OP, 7¹/₂", deep olive amber............ $250–$350
Swaim's Panacea, Philada, aqua .... $35–$45
Swaim's Panacea, SB, 8", olive green .... $90–$110
Swamp Chill & Fever Tonic, clear.................................... $6–$8
Sweet's Blk Oil Rochester NY, OP, 6¹/₈", medium emerald green .... $550–$850
Swift's Syphilitic Specific, oval, SB, 8⁷/₈", deep blue................. $250–$350
Syrup of Hypophosphites, 7¹/₄", aqua .... $5–$7
T & M, rect., OP, 2¹/₂", aqua .... $20–$25
T & M, rect., OP, 2¹/₂", deep emerald green .... $80–$130
T & M, rect., OP, 2¹/₂", medium emerald green .... $70–$95
T Elssier Provost A Paris (Bell), OP, 7³/₈", deep emerald green .... $150–$200
Tarrant & Co, clear, 5¹/₄" .... $2–$3
Taylor's Celebrated Oil, 6", aqua.................................... $6–$9
Taylor's Drug Store, clear, 5"....................................... $2–$3
Taylor's Indian Ointment, six sided, OP, 3", aqua .... $200–$260
Taylor's Opocura, OP, 3", aqua .... $45–$65
TB Smith Kidney Tonic, Cynthiana, KY, 10¹/₂", aqua.................. $12–$18
TE Jenkins & Co Chemists Louisville Ky, cylinder, double collar, OP, 6¹/₂", aqua ..
.... $90–$125
Teaberry for the Teeth & Breath, clear, 3¹/₂"........................ $6–$8

Tellssier Prevost A Paris, 7$^{1}/_{4}$", emerald green .... $45–$65
Tellssier Prevost A Paris, clear, OP, 7$^{1}/_{4}$" .... $12–$18
Thomas Electric Oil, clear, 4$^{1}/_{4}$".. $4–$6
Thompson & Crawford Druggists Phiada, OP, 5$^{1}/_{2}$", aqua .... $25–$35
Thompson's Dandelion & Celery Tonic, 9$^{3}/_{4}$", amber .... $20–$24
Thompson's Drug Store, The Market, clear, 5$^{1}/_{2}$" .... $4–$6
Thompson's Herbal Compound, 6$^{3}/_{4}$", aqua.......................... $4–$6
Thompson's Hygeia Wild Cherry Phosphate, 6$^{3}/_{4}$", aqua .... $25–$40
Thompsonian Appetizer (fat man), 9", yellowish amber .... $400–$575
Thorn's Hop & Burdock Tonic, 6$^{1}/_{4}$", yellow amber .... $35–$50
Tilden & Co, square, 7", amber.................................... $50–$70
Tilden, 7$^{1}/_{2}$", amber .... $3–$4
Tom's Russian Liniment, N-636, 4$^{1}/_{4}$", aqua..................... $50–$70
Tonsilene for Sore Throat, clear, 5$^{1}/_{2}$".............................. $4–$6
Townsend's Phosphated Cereal Tonic, 10", orange amber .... $75–$90
True Daffy's Elixer, OP, 3$^{3}/_{4}$", light yellow green .... $250–$300
Tucker Pharmacal, Brooklyn, NY, clear, 5"........................... $2–$3
Turkish Liniment, 4$^{3}/_{4}$", aqua.................................... $5–$7
Turlington's Balsam, OP, 2$^{1}/_{2}$", aqua................................. $70–$90
Turlington's Balsam, SB, 2$^{3}/_{4}$", aqua................................. $15–$20
Turner's Balsam, OP, eight sided, 4$^{7}/_{8}$", aqua.................... $60–$85
Tuttle's Elixir Co, Boston, Mass, 12 sided, clear, 6$^{1}/_{4}$" .... $6–$8
Umatilla Indian Relief, 5$^{1}/_{4}$", aqua................................. $80–$110
Unembossed, cylinder, flaring lip, OP, 5$^{1}/_{2}$", aqua .... $18–$24
Unembossed, cylinder, OP, flaring lip, 3$^{3}/_{4}$", aqua .... $10–$13
Unembossed, rect., beveled edges, applied tip, OP, 6$^{1}/_{2}$", olive green ..... $140–$210
Unembossed, rect., beveled edges, ring lip, OP, 5$^{1}/_{2}$", aqua .... $12–$16
Unembossed, rect., SB, 6", aqua .... $2–$3
US Marine Hospital Service, clear, 5$^{1}/_{2}$" .... $10–$15
USA Hosp Dept (in oval), 6", aqua.................................. $150–$200
USA Hosp Dept (in oval), 8$^{7}/_{8}$", bluish aqua......................... $275–$350

USA Hospital Dept. bottle. PHOTO COURTESY OF GLASS
WORKS AUCTIONS.

USA Hosp Dept, 2¹/₂", sapphire blue. . . . . $300–$400
USA Hosp Dept, 2" mouth, 7¹/₂", aqua . . . . $75–$95
USA Hosp Dept, 7¹/₂", aqua . . . . $125–$185
USA Hosp Dept, 7¹/₄", medium blue. . . . . $200–$275
USA Hosp Dept, 9¹/₂", clear yellow . . . . $450–$650
USA Hosp Dept, 9¹/₄", emerald green. . . . . $800–$1200
USA Hosp Dept, 9¹/₄", golden yellow amber . . . . $350–$425
USA Hosp Dept, 9¹/₄", yellow amber . . . . $300–$350
USA Hosp Dept, 9¹/₈", yellow olive . . . . $400–$500
USA Hosp Dept, 9³/₈", yellowish olive green . . . . $350–$400
USA Hosp Dept, 9⁷/₈", yellowish olive green . . . . $400–$600
USA Hosp Dept, 9", cobalt blue . . . . $900–$1300
USA Hosp Dept, 9", deep blue . . . . $900–$1400
USA Hosp Dept, 9", deep bluish aqua. . . . . $60–$80
USA Hosp Dept, amber tone, 9¹/₈", yellow. . . . . $250–$350
USA Hosp Dept, clear, 7¹/₂" . . . . $110–$150
USA Hosp Dept, cylinder, SB, 9¹/₄", yellow olive . . . . $375–$475
USA Hosp Dept, deep yellowish olive amber, 9³/₈" . . . . $250–$350
USA Hosp Dept, deep yellowish olive green, 9¹/₄" . . . . $350–$450
USA Hosp Dept, SDS (on base), 9¹/₂", apricot yellow. . . . . $400–$550
USA Hosp Dept, SDS (on base), 9¹/₄", deep red puce . . . . $600–$750
USA Hosp Dept, SDS (on base), 9", aqua . . . . $150–$190
USA Hosp Dept, very bubbly glass, olive tone, 8⁷/₈", yellow. . . . . $250–$350
USA Hosp Dept, wide mouth, 7¹/₂", aqua . . . . $125–$185
USA Med'l Dept, 9", aqua. . . . . $150–$200
V Roussin, Druggist, Muskegon, Mi, clear, 7¹/₄" . . . . $4–$6
Van Deusen's Improved Wahpene, OP, 8", aqua . . . . $125–$175
Van Deusen's Improved Wahpene, rect, OP, 8", aqua . . . . $150–$190
Vaughn's Vegetable Lithontriptic Mixture, 6¹/₈", medium emerald green. . . . .
. . . . $250–$340
Vaughn's Vegetable Lithontriptic Mixture, N-654, IP, 8", aqua. . . . . $175–$250
Vaughn's Vegetable Lithontriptic Mixture, N-654, OP, 8", aqua . . . . $175–$300
Vaughn's Vegetable Lithontriptic Mixture, OP, 6", deep aqua. . . . . $200–$275
Vaughn's Vegetable Lithontriptic Mixture, SB, 8¹/₈", aqua . . . . $80–$120
Vegetable & Hemlock Oil Medical Co, clear, 5". . . . . $3–$4
Vegetable Pulmonary Balsam, aqua . . . . $5–$9
Veno's Lightning Cough Cure, rect., 5¹/₄", aqua. . . . . $2–$4
Vernal Palemtona / Vernal Remedy Co, square, 9", aqua . . . . $15–$19
Voses's Celebrated Pile Dysentery, OP, aqua . . . . $125–$175
W & H Walker, Chemists, clear, 5³/₄" . . . . $2–$4
W Huff's Liniment, N-313, OP, 6", emerald green . . . . $2500–$3500
W Peets Salem Mass, cylinder, OP, 7", deep olive green. . . . . $1000–$1200
Warner's Bromo Soda, Phila, St Louis, 2³/₄", cobalt . . . . $10–$14
Warner's Safe Cure Frankfurt, 9", amber . . . . $400–$475
Warner's Safe Cure Frankfurt, 9", olive green . . . . $425–$600
Warner's Safe Cure Frankfurt, with contents, 9", green . . . . $425–$625
Warner's Safe Cure London, Eng, Toronto, Canada, Rochester, NY, 11", amber. .
. . . . $325–$450
Warner's Safe Cure Schutz Marke Pressburg, 9", red amber. . . . . $700–$875
Warner's Safe Cure Schutz Marke Pressburg, aqua. . . . . $1000–$1500
Warner's Safe Cure, London, 4⁵/₈", olive green . . . . $100–$135

Warner's Safe Cure, London, 4⁵/₈", yellow amber .... $325–$425
Warner's Safe Cure, London, 7¹/₄", yellow........................ $80–$95
Warner's Safe Cure, London, 9¹/₂", dark amber .... $55–$75
Warner's Safe Cure, London, 9¹/₂", olive green .... $80–$100
Warner's Safe Cure, London, medium amber........................ $35–$45
Warner's Safe Cure, Melbourne, 9¹/₂", amber .... $100–$135
Warner's Safe Cure, Melbourne, Aus, London, Eng, Toronto, Can, Rochester, NY, USA, 9" .... $110–$145
Warner's Safe Cure, Rochester, NY, London, England, Toronto, Canada, 9¹/₂", amber.. $40–$55
Warner's Safe Cure, Rochester, NY, with amber tint, 7¹/₄", yellow....... $90–$125
Warner's Safe Diabetes Cure, Frankfurt, 9³/₈", red amber .... $800–$1200
Warner's Safe Diabetes Cure, London, 9¹/₄", yellowish olive green ..... $200–$260
Warner's Safe Diabetes Cure, London, amber tone, 9³/₈", yellow....... $120–$165
Warner's Safe Diabetes Cure, Melbourne, 9¹/₂", golden amber .... $300–$390
Warner's Safe Diabetes Cure, Rochester, NY, 9¹/₂", amber .... $90–$120
Warner's Safe Diabetes Remedy, Rochester, NY, 16 oz, 9¹/₂", amber ..... $40–$50
Warner's Safe Kidney & Liver Cure, Rochester, NY, 9¹/₂", amber .... $15–$20
Warner's Safe Kidney & Liver Cure, Rochester, NY, 9¹/₂", orange....... $40–$50
Warner's Safe Kidney & Liver Cure, Rochester, NY, amber tone, 9¹/₂", yellow....
.... $60–$85
Warner's Safe Kidney & Liver Cure, Rochester, NY, labels, 9¹/₄", yellow amber...
.... $175–$275
Warner's Safe Kidney & Liver Remedy, Rochester, NY, 16 fl oz, 9", amber ......
.... $40–$50
Warner's Safe Log Cabin Liver Pills, with original wrapper .... $20–$30
Warner's Safe Nervine Rochester NY, 7¹/₂", medium amber............. $30–$40
Warner's Safe Remedies Co, Rochester NY, 6 Fl Oz, 7¹/₈", aqua......... $40–$60
Warner's Safe Remedies Co, Rochester, NY, 6 Fl oz, ABM, label, 7¹/₈", medium amber.. $45–$65
Warner's Safe Remedy Rochester NY, 8 fl oz, 7¹/₂", amber.............. $40–$50
Warner's Safe Remedy Rochester NY, 7¹/₂", medium amber .... $30–$45
Warner's Safe Rheumatic Cure Rochester, 9¹/₂", amber................ $45–$60
Warner's Safe Rheumatic Cure Rochester, 9⁵/₈", chocolate amber........ $75–$90
Warner's Safe Rheumatic Cure Rochester, full label, 9¹/₂", amber...... $125–$200
Warner's Safe Rheumatic Cure Rochester, USA, 9¹/₂", amber........... $35–$45
Warner's Safe Rheumatic Cure, Melbourne (slug plate), 9¹/₂", amber ....
.... $225–$325
Warner's Safe Tonic, Rochester NY, 9¹/₂", medium amber .... $200–$250
Warranted Cod Liver Oil Pure Medicinal, IP, 10¹/₂", deep aqua .... $150–$210
Wayne's Diuretic Elixir, 7", amber .... $60–$90
Wayne's Diuretic Elixir, square, SB, 7¹/₂", cobalt .... $200–$250
WB Sloan Instant Relief Chicago, aqua........................... $150–$190
WC Sweet HCR & L Rochester NY, OP, 6", aqua .... $15–$25
WE Brown, Druggist, Manchester, Ia, clear......................... $2–$3
WE Hagen & Co Troy NY, eight sided, 6³/₄", medium cobalt............. $60–$85
Web's Cathartic A No 1 Tonic, 9¹/₂", amber........................ $50–$70
Web's Liver & Kidney A No 1 Cathartic Tonic, 8⁵/₈", amber.......... $175–$225
Weiss Pharmacy, Phila, clear, embossed eagle, 6¹/₂"................... $9–$14
Westlake's Vegetable Ointment, 3", aqua.......................... $7–$9
Westlake's Vegetable Ointment, contents, wrapper, 3", aqua............ $30–$35

WH Bone Co CC Liniment, 6½", aqua .... $5–$6
WH Bull Medicine Co, 9½", amber .... $4–$7
WH Bull's Medicine Bottle, patent date on base, clear, 5" .... $3–$4
Wheaton's Sick Headache Remedy, IP, 6¼", deep aqua .... $400–$525
Wildfire Rheumatic Liniment, OP, 5⅞", aqua .... $200–$250
Wilford Hall Laboratories, Port Chester, NY, half pint, amber .... $15–$19
Winant's Indian Liniment, OP, 5", aqua .... $125–$175
Wishart's Pine Tree Cordial, clear, 9¾" .... $60–$80
Wm Jay Barker, Hirsutus, New York, pewter stopper, ABM, 5¼", aqua ..... $5–$8
Wm Jay Barker, Hirsutus, New York, pewter stopper, clear, ABM, 6⅝" ..... $5–$7
Wm R Warner & Co, Phila, 4", cobalt .... $8–$12
Wm R Warner & Co, Phila, 6" .... $12–$15
Wm Radam's Microbe Killer, 10⅜", amber .... $30–$50
Woodward Chemist-Nottingham, 6", light blue .... $5–$7
Worm Mixture Stabler, N-598, six sided, OP, 3⅝", aqua .... $125–$150

MILK BOTTLES

Milk bottles comprise an area of collecting that has grown dramatically in recent years. Milk bottles were originally made in the United States starting in the 1870s, but most of the collectible bottles found are from the 1920–1950 period. Up until about 1900 many of the milk bottles had tin cap-type closures. Around this time the common sense milk bottle was introduced. This bottle had a cap seat inside the neck near the lip, which held a paper cap. Up until the 1920s, most of the bottles used had embossed names on them. Around this time, pyroglazed bottles became popular. Pyroglazed bottles had paint or enamel-like decorations and writing on them, in various colors and scripts. The earliest milk bottles were generally cylindrical in form, with square milk bottles not coming into common usage until the late 1940s. Throughout the history of the milk bottle, the vast majority of the bottles were of colorless glass; however, at least 20 dairies used a green milk bottle, and amber milk bottles were even more common. Also, in 1950, Anchor Hocking Glass Company manufactured an experimental ruby red milk bottle for Borden's. These bottles were never used and are extremely rare.

Two of the more popular collectible types of milk bottles are baby-face and cop-the-cream bottles. The baby-face bottles had an embossed baby's face on the upper part of the neck, and are available in both cylindrical and square shapes. The cop-the-cream bottles, which enjoyed great popularity in the late

1930s and 1940s, have a policeman's head and cap embossed into the neck of the bottle. Both these types of bottles, along with early tin tops, are quite rare and command rising prices. A popular early grouping of bottles are A.G. Smalley bottles, with tin top and handle for pouring. Other popular pyroglazed types are war slogan bottles from World War II, Disney characters, nursery rhymes, colleges and institutions, display and souvenir giveaways from the glass companies, and two colored pictorials and Borden's bottles. Also in demand are those bottles from a collector's hometown or city, and the values reflected in this price guide might be low for collectors who have strong interest in a local creamery.

When collecting milk bottles, watch for unusual pyroglaze designs and colors, and remember that having two or more pyroglazed colors on a bottle makes it more unusual, and probably more valuable than single color pyroglazed bottles. On embossed milk bottles, be watchful for embossed standing animals or any unusual embossed figures. Since milk bottles were meant to be used over and over, often the bottles are found with wear, called case wear, which resulted from the bottles being transported about in wooden and metal cases. In general, bottles should be free of cracks and major chips. Some pyro bottles may even have the colors slightly dulled due to heavy usage. Prices can fluctuate widely depending on condition.

Adlam Glass Pail (On Tin Lid), pail shape, with tin bail, colorless, quart . . . . $250–$350
AG Smalley (On Base And Cap), no embossing on sides, colorless, with tin handle and cap, quart . . . . $75–$90
AG Smalley (On Base And Cap), with embossing on sides, colorless, tin handle and cap, quart. . . . . $125–$150
AG Smalley (On Base And Top), with side embossing, clear, tin handle and top, half pint . . . . $250–$300
Alex Bolin & Son, Bradford, PA, round, embossed, with original cap, pint. . . . $6–$7
Allvines Milk (In Script), Kansas City, Kan, round, pyro., with picture of full cow, quart, black . . . . $20–$25
Alta Crest Farms, colorless with blue pyro, quart . . . . $25–$50
Alta Crest Farms, quart, green . . . . $900–$1100
Andersons Creamery, embossed, 7oz. . . . . $3–$4
Aristocrat Dairy, Baltimore, MD, square, pyroglazed, quart . . . . $80–$85
Armour Creamers, Louisville, KY, cream jar, embossed . . . . $3–$5
Associate Dairies, Topeka, Kansas (On Base), round, embossed, state capitol and state, quart. . . . . $20–$25
Ausable Dairy Corporation, Ausable Forks, NY, round, embossed, pint . . . . . $5–$6
Bancroft, Madison, Wis, square, pyro, stubby, quart, red . . . . $4–$6
Beech Grove Dairy, Utica, NY, square, pyroglazed, quart. . . . . $75–$85
Beech Grove Dairy, Utican NY, pyroglazed, round, quart . . . . $150–$175
Belmont Dairy, Warren, Ohio, embossed, quart . . . . $125–$150
Bentleys Dairy, Fall River, Mass, pyroglazed, quart . . . . $125–$150
Big Elm Dairy Company, quart, green. . . . . $300–$500
Billings Dairy, creamer, round, pyro, green . . . . $15–$20

Milk bottles, colored. PHOTO COURTESY OF SKINNER'S, INC.

Blais For Mothers Who Care, with pyro, round, with baby drinking milk, quart, orange . . . . $125–$130
Blue Bell Dairy, Irvington, NJ, pint . . . . $150–$175
Bordens, 1939 World's Fair, pyro, half pint, blue/gray & red . . . . $300–$325
Bordens, Elsie Delivering Newspapers, pyro, extra cream added, quart, red . . . .
. . . . $75–$85
Bordens, experimental bottle, quart, ruby red . . . . $1000–$1200
Bowman Dairy Company, Chicago, Il, round, embossed, pint . . . . $5–$6
Brighton Place Dairy, embossed cow . . . . $1500–$2000
Brighton Place Dairy, quart, green . . . . $300–$350
Brogans Dairy, N Benton, Ohio, embossed, quart . . . . $125–$150
Brookfield Baby Top (Around Shoulder), square, double baby face, quart . . . .
. . . . $30–$45
Brookfield Dairy Hellertown, PA, embossed, round, half pint . . . . $25–$35
Brookfield Dairy, Hellertown, PA, square, pyroglazed, quart . . . . $45–$50
Brookfield, embossed only, no pyro, half pint . . . . $25–$35
Brookfield, embossed, quart . . . . $35–$48
Calhoun County Cremery, Birmingham, Ala, embossed, quart . . . . $12–$15
Carnation (Embossed on Shoulders), square, quart . . . . $12–$15
Carnation (Embossed on Shoulders), square, vertical embossing reads "Please Return," quart . . . . $12–$15
Cedar Grove Dairy, Hope, Ind, pyroglazed, quart . . . . $175–$200
Chipola Dairy, Marianna, Fla, round, pyro, stubby, quart, red . . . . $5–$7
Chris P Keller, Owatonna, Minn, square, pyroglazed, quart . . . . $85–$95
City Dairy Co, Statesboro, GA, embossed, round, quilted pattern, 7 ounce . . . . $4–$5
Clinton Milk Co, quart, light smokey beige . . . . $15–$20
Cloverdale Farms, Binghamton, NY, quart, amber . . . . $50–$70
Cloverleaf Dairy, Quincy, Mass, embossed, quart . . . . $90–$100
CMDA, Chillicothe, O, round, embossed, quart . . . . $9–$11
Coble (In Oblong Shield), Danda Process, General Mills Labs, square, quart, amber
. . . . $7–$9
Colonial Dairy Inc Milk, Albany, GA, round, embossed, quart . . . . $4–$6
Cooper Dairy, Elmer, NJ, embossed, pint . . . . $85–$90

Country Fresh Flavor of Winnisquam Farms, square, white pyro, gallon, amber . . .
. . . . $10–$13.5
Crescent Creamery, Tecumseh, NM, round, pyro, with nursery rhyme, quart, red . . .
. . . . $50–$75
Crescent Pasteurized Milk & Cream, creamer, round, pyro, ³/₄ ounce, yellow . . . . . .
. . . . $15–$20
Cummings Dairy, Arlington, Mass, square, pyroglazed, quart . . . . $90–$100
Cupps Dairy, Williamsport, PA, pyroglazed, quart. . . . . $175–$200
Dairylee Milk, You Can Whip The Cream, pyro, square, double baby face, quart, red
and yellow. . . . . $45–$50
Deluxe Cream Seperator, square, colorless with red pyroglaze, quart . . . . $300–$450
Deseret LDS Church Welfare Plan, Salt Lake City, with pictures of bee hives, pyro,
square, quart, red. . . . . $18–$22
Disney, Donald Hanging on Table, Purity Milk Co, Philipsburg, PA, pyro, half pint,
red . . . . $300–$350
Disney, Mickey Running, Bay View Dairy, Plattsburg, NY, pyro, quart, black . . . . .
. . . . $450–$500
Dixie Dairies, Macon, GA, round, embossed, quart . . . . $4–$5
Doc Stork Says Babies Do Better On Our Milk, round, pyro, Hazard, KY, quart,
orange . . . . $25–$30
Dresser Hill Farms, Charlton, Mass, pyroglazed, round, quart . . . . $150–$175
Drink Vallottons Milk, Its Better, Valdosta, GA, round, picture of doctor, case wear,
quart . . . . $6–$7
Drink Vallottons Milk, Its Better, Valdosta, GA, round, picture of doctor, pyro, quart
. . . . $8–$11
EF Mayer, quart, amber. . . . . $40–$60
Elmhurst Cream Co, half pint, light smoky beige . . . . $12–$15
Erdman & Sons, Lykens, Pa, pyroglazed, round, pint. . . . . $150–$175
Estes Park Creamery, Estes Park, Colo, round, pyro, with boy climbing stairs, quart,
red . . . . $35–$50
Fairfax Farms Dairy, Washington, DC, NW, round, 4620 First St, quart . . . $20–$25
Fairview Dairy Co, Lockhaven, Pa, embossed, half pint . . . . $150–$175
Fairview Dairy, Wallingford, square, pyroglazed, quart . . . . $85–$90
Ferg Co-34 (On Base), quart, amber. . . . . $30–$35
Fikes Dairy Farm, Meyersdale, Pa, round, slug plate embossed, straight-sided body,
quart . . . . $25–$35
Flanders Dairy, pyroglazed, quart. . . . . $135–$150
Florida Store Bottle, "3¢" around shoulder, round, embossed, large map of Florida,
quart . . . . $8–$10
Florida Universal Store Bottle, round, embossed, "5¢ deposit" on shoulder, pint . . . .
. . . . $4–$5
Fountain Head Dairy, Hagerstown, MD, pyroglazed, quart. . . . . $125–$150
Franklin Dairy, Tupperlake, NY, round, pyro, quart, red. . . . . $6–$7
Gabel-Ridson Famous Jersey Creamery Co, Milk And Ice Cream, embossed, pint.
. . . . $5–$6
Galena Dairy, Galena, Illinois, round, slug plate embossing, neck grips, pint . . . .
. . . . $7–$9
Gascoyne Dairy, Lockport, NY, square, pyro, crackle finish, screw top, quart, orange
. . . . $4–$6
George Signor, Keeseville, NY (On Bottom), round, embossed, pint. . . . . $4–$5
Glenside Dairy, Deepwater, NJ, embossed, pint . . . . $75–$90

Gold Crest Farms, Apollo, PA, embossed, quart...................... $75–$80

Golden Dawn Dairy, Westfield, NJ, square, pyroglazed, quart............ $85–$90

Good Rich Dairy Products, Mt Carmel, PA, embossed, half pint......... $85–$90

Good Rich Dairy Products, Mt Carmel, PA, embossed, pint............ $95–$100

Goodrich Pasteurized Dairy Products, square, pyro, picture of bottle, quart, chocolate.. $4–$6

Grand View Dairy, Canfield, Ohio, square, pyroglazed, quart.......... $100–$125

Grandma Wheatons Milkmaid, South Jerseys Best, modern bottle, 18oz .... $4–$5

Grayce Farms Dairy, Scranton, PA, square, pyroglazed, quart........... $85–$90

Green Acres Farms, Scottdale, PA, embossed, quart................. $125–$150

Greenleaf Dairy, Cop The Cream, square, pyro, Petersburg, VA, quart, green......
.... $20–$30

Greenleaf Dairy, Petersburg, PA, square, pyroglazed, quart............. $40–$60

Greenwood Dairy, Worcester, Mass, pyroglazed, quart............... $200–$250

Guimond Farms, Fall River, Mass, pyroglazed, quart................ $125–$150

Harshbarger Milk, PA, pyroglazed, pint........................... $100–$120

Hidden Acres Farms, Washington, NJ, pyro, square, with four-leaf clover, clear, quart, yellow.. $85–$90

Hillcrest Farm Dairy, Ticonderoga, NY, square, pyro, quart, orange........ $5–$6

Hillside Dairy, Middletown, Conn, half pint....................... $135–$150

Hillside Dairy, Middletown, Conn, square, embossed, quart............. $85–$90

Hillside Dairy, Middletown, Conn, square, pyroglazed, quart.......... $100–$125

Hillside Dairy, Middletown, Conn, square, pyroglazed, quart........... $95–$100

Hilton Harts Dairy, Ft Myers, Fla, round, embossed, quart.............. $12–$14

Hollywood Western Dairy Co . . ., round, embossed, quart.............. $15–$20

Holts Jar Cream Whips, fruit jar-shape with "Sanety Mason" on back, half gallon, aqua.. $200–$250

Hoover Milk Co, Perfectly Pasteurized Milk, round, New Bethlehem, PA, embossed, quart... $7–$9

Horlicks Malted Milk, Racine, Wisc, round jar, screw cap, stain, 10 ounce.... $3–$4

Hursts Dairy, EW Hurst, Manassas, VA, round, embossed, quart.......... $8–$10

Indian Head Farm, Framingham, Mass, colorless with embossed Indian head, pint .
.... $75–$90

JJ Brown Dairy, Troy, NY, pyroglazed, quart........................ $75–$80

Jolly Dairy Ice Cream Co, Tifton, GA, round, embossed stubby, quart....... $4–$5

Keating, Yankton, SD, with large shield and crown, pyro, baby holding milk bottle, quart, red... $25–$30

Kent Dairy, creamer, round, pyro, $3/4$ ounce, red...................... $15–$20

Lang Bros Dairy, square, pyroglazed, quart.......................... $75–$80

Lang's Creamery, Buffalo, New York, with Owen's mark, quart, green...........
.... $1000–$1200

Langs Creamery, Buffalo, New York, quart, green.................. $300–$350

Langs Creamery, quart, amber..................................... $50–$75

Lehigh Valley Cooperative Farmers, creamer, round, pyro, $3/4$ ounce, green .. $7–$9

Liberty Dairy Products Co, Chicago, Ill, round, Statue of Liberty embossed, quart ..
.... $10–$12

Liberty Dairy, Huron, Mich, pyroglazed, quart..................... $200–$250

Loux Dairy, Carthape, MO, round, pyro, with farm scene, quart, orange and blue ...
.... $9–$12

Margrove Inc Cream Craft Products, Newark, NY, square, pyro, quart, red.......
.... $4–$6

Martins Dairy, Lancaster, PA, square, pyroglazed, quart . . . . $95–$100
Mary Had A Litttle Lamb, Diamond Dairy, Port Jervis, NY, pyro, round, quart . . .
. . . . $75–$85
Mayer China, Est 1881, Curtis 18, creamer, ceramic, round, with saucer, $3/4$ ounce . .
. . . . $6–$8
Meadow Brook Products, Green River, Wyo, round, pyro, two cows, barn, silo,
cloud, quart, deep red . . . . $30–$35
Mechanicsburg Creamery, round, embossed, probably Ohio, pint . . . . $4–$5
Milts (In Script), creamer, round, pyro, $3/4$ oz, red . . . . $12–$15
Mirror Lake Farm, Herkimer, NY, pyroglazed, quart . . . . $150–$175
Mojonnier (In Script On Shield), with rubber stopper, 8 oz . . . . $3–$4
Murphys Dairy, Needham, Mass, embossed, half pint . . . . $95–$100
Nelsons Dairy, pyroglazed, square, quart . . . . $45–$60
Nicks Dairy Products, Old Forge, PA, pint . . . . $150–$175
NL Martin, square tin top, colorless, quart . . . . $350–$450
Nobhill Milk I X L, Colo. Springs, Colo, round, pyro, quart, green . . . . $12–$15
North Hampton Dairy, North Hampton, Mass, embossed, quart . . . . $85–$90
North Shore Dairy Co, Chicago, Ill, round, embossed, pint . . . . $4–$6
Norwalk Pure Milk, Norwalk, O, Uncle Sam, "War Bonds For Victory," pyro, quart
. . . . $65–$75
Old Home Milk Co, Reno, Nevada, round, pyro, with cow, half pint, orange . . . .
. . . . $8–$10
Old King Cole. . . , Proctor Dairy, Proctor, VT, pyro, square, quart . . . . $20–$25
Orchard Farm Dairy, AA Approved Ayrshire Milk, pyro, square, quart, red . . . . . .
. . . . $45–$65
Ori Smider Choice Dairy Product, Cresco, Michigan, pyro., with girl and boy,
orange . . . . $12–$14
Paramount, Wilkes Barre, PA, half pint . . . . $150–$175
Parkdale Dairy, Washington, NJ, pyroglazed, quart. . . . . $135–$150
Pecoras For Mothers Who Care, pyro, with baby on top of world, round, pint, orange
. . . . $150–$175
Pecoras For Mothers Who Care, pyro, with picture of cow and calf, square, quart, red /
black . . . . $70–$90
Penn Cross Mills, Cressen, PA, round, embossed, pint . . . . $8–$10
Penn Supreme Ice Cream, Penn Dairies, square, pyro, Quaker's head, quart, orange.
. . . . $4–$5
Phelp's Dairy, J Waycross, GA, round, pyro, quart, orange . . . . $6–$8
Plattsburg Dairy, Plattsburg, NY, round, pyro, quart, red . . . . $6–$8
Polly Meadows, with girl's head, creamer, round, pyro, blue . . . . $20–$22
Property Of Imdod Of Dayton Ohio, embossed, with black pyro, 3¢ store bottle, etc.,
quart . . . . $12–$15
Pure Milk, jar with tin screw-on cap, colorless, quart . . . . $750–$1000
Puritan Milk, Pasteurized, round, pyro, with housewife and food, quart, red . . . .
. . . . $20–$25
Purity Milk Co, Lewiston, Pa, pyroglazed, quart. $150–$175
Purity Milk Co, square, pyroglazed, quart . . . . $85–$90
Quality Dairy, None Better, creamer, round, pyro, red . . . . $10–$12
Randle Milk, Endicott, NY, pyroglazed, quart. . . . . $175–$200
Resorvoir Farm Dairy, Woonsocket, RI, square, pyroglazed, quart . . . . $75–$90
Rinehart Sunny Brae Farm, pyroglazed, quart . . . . $150–$175
Rosedale Dairy, Laramie, Wyo, round, pyro, quart, green . . . . $20–$25

Left: *Milk bottle, pyroglazed.* Right: *Milk bottles, with tin tops and one baby face.* PHOTOS COURTESY OF SKINNER'S, INC.

Rothermels (On Side), Minersville, PA (On Base), round, embossed cream separator, quart . . . . $60–$90
Royal Farm Dairy, embossed, quart . . . . $125–$150
Saco Dairy, Saco, Maine, embossed, pint . . . . $90–$95
Sanckens Dairies, Augusta, GA, round, embossed, pint . . . . $4–$5
Sanitary Dairy, creamer, square, pyro, ³/₄ ounce, orange . . . . $12–$15
Sawyers Farm, Gilford, NH, pyroglazed, quart . . . . $65–$70
Serve Cream Top Dairy Ice Cream, Cream Top, square, with pyro, quart, green and orange . . . . $15–$20
Shaws Dairy, Brattleboro, VT, square, pyroglazed, quart . . . . $60–$65
Solomons Dairy, Milk & Ice Cream, Qunicy, Fla, square, pyro, eye looking at bottle, quart, black . . . . $20–$25
Southern Maid Inc, Bristol, VA, round, embossed, pint . . . . $6–$8
Springdale Dairy Co, Jamestown, NY, round, dotted diamond design on bottle, pint .
. . . . $18–$24
State Road Dairy, Eldorado, Ill, pyroglazed, quart . . . . $175–$200
Studeys Dairy, Racine, Wisc, pyroglazed, quart . . . . $150–$175
Suncrest Farms, Providence, RI, pyroglazed, quart . . . . $150–$175
Sunny Dale Dairy, Union City, Ind, round, pyro, quart . . . . $8–$10
Sunshine Dairy, Framingham, Mass, square, pyroglazed, quart . . . . $85–$90
Sunshine Dairy, Orange Pyro, colorless, square, quart . . . . $40–$50
Superior Dairy, Millville, NJ, embossed, quart . . . . $85–$90
Superior Dairy, Pueblo, Colo, round, pyro, picture of man and cow's head, quart, orange . . . . $20–$25
Sweet Clover Dairy, Roosevelt, LI, pyroglazed, half pint . . . . $80–$90
Sweets Dairy, Fredonia, NY, pyroglazed, quart . . . . $175–$200
Thatcher's, With Man Milking Cow, with closure, quart, clear . . . . $400–$450
Thatchers, With Man Milking Cow, colorless, no closure, quart . . . . $200–$350
Tuscan Dairy, creamer, round, pyro, ³/₄ ounce, red . . . . $7–$9
Unembossed, Double Baby Face, no pyro, colorless, square, quart . . . . $20–$30
United Farms, Albany, NY, pyroglazed, quart . . . . $150–$175
United States Dairy System Inc, round, embossed, "United Store" on shoulder, pint .
. . . . $4.5–$5.5
Upton Farms, Bridgewater, Mass, pyro, pint, black . . . . $90–$95
Uptown Dairy, Charles City, IA, square base and round top, creamtop, pyro, orange .
. . . . $20–$25

VCS Visit Your Canteen For Quality, round, pyro, cottage cheese jar, white . . . .
. . . . $14–$18
Victory Bottle, Birmingham, Ala, round, embossed "a war bottle," case wear, quart .
. . . . $45–$50
Voegels Pasteurized, It Whips, pyro, square, quart, black. . . . . $65–$70
Waits Dairy, Belvidere, Ill, embossed, quart . . . . $85–$90
Wakefield Dairy, Washington, DC, square, embossed, quart . . . . $60–$70
Weber Dairy Co, Joliet, Illinois, round, slug plate embossed, $1/4$ pint. . . . . . . $14–$18
Weckerle, quart, green. . . . . $250–$300
Wells Dairy Cooperative, Columbus, GA, round, embossed stubby, quart . . . . $3–$4
West End Dairy, Jeannette, PA, pyroglazed, quart. . . . . $175–$200
Whitcombs Farm, Littleton, Mass, pyroglazed, quart. . . . . $150–$175
Whiteman (On Base), dome-type tip top, colorless, quart . . . . $250–$350
Whites Farm Dairy, Quality Products, square, pyro, quart, red and yellow . . . .
. . . . $40–$50
Willow Springs Farm, Thiensville, Wis, round, embossed, vertical grip bars, pint . . .
. . . . $7–$8
Winfield Dairy, Winfield, Kansas, Plane, "Buy Another War Bond," pyro, quart. . . .
. . . . $100–$125

MINERAL WATER
BOTTLES

For thousands of years, man has believed in the medicinal properties of natural
mineral waters. Mineral springs in America were discovered as early as the
17th century, and in the mid 18th century bottled spring water was being sold
in the Boston area. By the early 19th century, the spring waters of the Ballston
and Saratoga spas began a popularity which extended through the 19th and into
the 20th century.

It is unknown what types of bottles were used to sell mineral water in the
early days, but it was probably some type of free-blown globular bottles.
Starting around the 1830s, bottles with the embossed spring names began to
appear, and the demand was so great that several glasshouses were started in
the Saratoga area with the main purpose being to supply the mineral water
companies with enough bottles to sell their product. Many other glasshouses
from states such as Pennsylvania and Connecticut also supplied bottles for
these mineral water companies.

Many shapes and sizes of bottles were made, with an assortment of colors,
and a great deal of interest is directed towards those which have the name of

the glasshouse on the bottle, as well as those with embossed eagles and multi-sided bottles. The reader is referred to *Collectors Guide to Saratoga-Type Mineral Water Bottles* by Donald Tucker.

AD Schnackenberg & Co Mineral Water, Brooklyn, NY, pint, amber... $300–$400
Adirondack Spring, Westport, NY, N-1, quart, emerald green......... $225–$325
Adirondack Spring, Westport, NY, N-1, quart, forest green .... $200–$250
Adirondack Spring, Westport, NY, N-1, quart, yellow green........... $200–$275
Adirondack Spring, Whitehall, NY, N-2, pint, emerald green .... $125–$175
Adirondack Spring, Whitehall, NY, N-2-B, pint, emerald green .... $150–$225
Adirondack Spring, Whitehall, NY, N-2-B, potstone crack, pint, emerald green ....
.... $100–$150
Aetna Mineral Spouting Spring, AE, Saratoga, NY, pint, aqua ...... $1500–$2250
Akesion Spring, Owned by Sweet Springs Co, Saline Co, Mo, pint, yellow amber ..
.... $150–$250
Alburgh, A, Springs, VT, V-1, quart, orange amber .... $300–$400
Alburgh, A, Springs, VT, V-2, quart, yellow amber .... $300–$400
Aletic China Water, Discovered by Prof Lavender, half pint, yellow olive ....
.... $100–$125
Artesian Spring Co, Ballston NY, Ballston Spa, pint, green .... $100–$140
Artesian Spring Co, Ballston NY, Ballston Spa, S-5, pint, medium blue green......
.... $60–$80
Artesian Spring Co, Ballston NY, Ballston Spa, S-6, pint, greenish aqua ... $40–$50
Artesian Water, Louisville KY Dupont, IP, 12 sided base, olive amber .. $225–$325
Artesian Water, Louisville Ky Dupont, M-5, 12 sided base, IP, pint, root beer amber
.... $300–$400
Ballston Spa Lithia Mineral Water, S-6, pint, emerald green .... $100–$140
Bedford Springs, Co, M-7, quart, aqua............................. $125–$195
Blount Springs Natural Sulphur Water-Trade BS Mark, quart, cobalt...........
.... $150–$200
Blue Lick Water Co, KY, 12 paneled base, IP, pint, forest green ..... $2000–$3000
Bolen Waack & Co New York, Mineral Spring Water, M-8, half pint, emerald green
.... $150–$250
Boothay Medicinal Spring Water (on label), teal green................. $35–$40
Caledonia Spring, Wheelock, VT, quart, golden amber .... $500–$600
Caledonia Spring, Wheelock, VT, yellowish amber .... $475–$575
Campbell Mineral Spring Co, C, Burlington, VT, quart, aqua .... $800–$1200
Chalybeate Water of the American Spa Spring, NJ, blob top, M-10, aqua ....
.... $600–$900
Chalybeate Water of the American Spa Spring, NJ, M-10, pint, green aqua.......
.... $500–$700
Champion Spouting Spring, Saratoga Mineral Spring, S-11-B, pint, aqua........
.... $75–$125
Champion Spouting Spring, Saratoga, NY Champion Water, S-9, pint, aqua .....
.... $275–$350
Champlian Spring, Alkaline Chalybeate, Highgate, VT, quart, yellow green ......
.... $250–$350
Church Hill, Alum Water, VA, IP, pint, blue green .... $3000–$5000
Clark & White, C, New York, C-11-B-1, SB, quart, deep olive green ...... $40–$60

Mineral water, Clarke & White. PHOTO COURTESY OF NEIL GROSSMAN.

Clark & White, C, New York, C-11-B-5, SB, backwards N and &, quart, emerald green . . . . $150–$200
Clarke & Co, New York, C-6, quart, olive green. . . . . $150–$200
Clarke & Co, New York, C-7-2, quart, aqua . . . . $400–$600
Clarke & Co, New York, C-7-B, quart, green . . . . $250–$300
Clarke & Co, New York, C-8-E, quart, emerald green . . . . $100–$135
Clarke & Co, New York, C-9-3, IP, pint, blue green. . . . . $125–$175
Clarke & Co, New York, C-9-4, pint, deep olive amber . . . . $60–$80
Clarke & Co, New York, C-9-2, IP, pint, medium blue green. . . . . $200–$275
Clarke & Co, New York, C-9-2, OP, pint, yellowish olive amber. . . . . $100–$150
Clarke & Co, New York, C-9-3, IP, pint, deep blue green. . . . . $125–$175
Clarke & Co, New York, C-9-A, SB, pint, deep olive green. . . . . $50–$70
Clarke & Co, New York, C-9-A, SB, pint, olive green . . . . $50–$75
Clarke & Co, New York, IP, quart, clear green . . . . $300–$350
Clarke & White, C, New York, C-10-C, pint, olive amber . . . . $30–$45
Clarke & White, C, New York, C-10-C, pint, olive green. . . . . $30–$45
Clarke & White, C, New York, C-11, SB, quart, deep olive green. . . . . $50–$75
Clarke & White, C, New York, C-11-A, SB, quart, deep olive green. . . . . . . $50–$75
Clarke & White, C, New York, C-11-B-2, pint, olive green . . . . $30–$35
Clarke & White, New York, C-10-B-4, high shoulder, quart, deep olive green . . . . . .
. . . . $150–$200
Clarke & White, New York, C-10-B2, OP, quart, medium yellowish green. . . . .
. . . . $60–$90
Clarke & White, New York, NII, C-11-B, OP, pint, deep olive amber. . . . $150–$200
Cold Brook Medicinal, Spring Water, C, quart, lime citron. . . . . $1200–$1600
Congress & Empire Spring Co, Columbian Water, Saratoga, NY, pint, olive green
. . . . $450–$650
Congress & Empire Spring Co, E, Empire, Water, E-6-A, quart, olive green . . . . . .
. . . . $75–$100
Congress & Empire Spring Co, E, Empire, Water, E-6-A, quart, red amber. . . . . . .
. . . . $150–$220
Congress & Empire Spring Co, E, Empire, Water, E-6-B, pint, deep olive green. . .
. . . . $60–$90
Congress & Empire Spring Co, E, Empire, Water, E-6-B, pint, olive green . . . .
. . . . $90–$100

Congress & Empire Spring Co, E, Empire, Water, E-9-B, pint, emerald green. . . . .
. . . . $30–$40
Congress & Empire Spring Co, E, Empire, Water, pint, emerald green. . . . $30–$45
Congress & Empire Spring Co, E, Empire, Water, quart, emerald green. . . $30–$45
Congress & Empire Spring Co, Hotchkiss Sons, CW, S-14-C, half pint, emerald
green . . . . $300–$400
Congress & Empire Spring Co, Hotchkiss Sons, CW, S-14-C, half pint, olive green
. . . . $250–$350
Congress & Empire Spring Co, Hotchkiss Sons, E, New York, E-8-A, quart, forest
green . . . . $400–$550
Congress & Empire Spring Co, Hotchkiss Sons, E, New York, E-8-A, quart,
medium emerald green . . . . $150–$250
Congress & Empire Spring Co, Hotchkiss Sons, E, New York, E-8-A, quart, yel-
lowish green . . . . $150–$250
Congress & Empire Spring Co, Hotchkiss Sons, E, New York, E-8-B, pint, emerald
green . . . . $150–$200
Congress & Empire Spring Co, Hotchkiss Sons, E, New York, pint, brown amber. .
. . . . $400–$500
Congress & Empire Spring Co, Hotchkiss Sons, E, New York, pint, red amber . . . .
. . . . $400–$500
Congress & Empire Spring, Hotchkiss Sons, CW, New York, S-14-C, half pint,
yellow olive green. . . . . $250–$350
Congress & Empire Spring, Hotchkiss Sons, C, Congress Water, C-16-B, pint,
yellow olive. . . . . $100–$140
Congress & Empire Spring, Hotchkiss Sons, C, Congress Water, C-17-A, quart,
emerald green . . . . $100–$125
Congress & Empire Spring, Hotchkiss Sons, C, Congress Water, C-17-A, quart,
yellow green . . . . $125–$175
Congress & Empire Spring, Hotchkiss Sons, C, Congress Water, C-17-B, pint,
emerald green . . . . $100–$125
Congress & Empire Spring, Hotchkiss Sons, C, Congress Water, C-17-B, pint,
olive green. . . . . $140–$180
Congress & Empire Spring, Hotchkiss Sons, C, Congress Water, C-17-B-2, pint,
medium olive green. . . . . $110–$160
Congress & Empire Spring, Hotchkiss Sons, C, Congress Water, pint, medium
olive green. . . . . $120–$140
Congress & Empire Spring, Hotchkiss Sons, C, New York, C-15-B, pint, yellow
green . . . . $100–$150
Congress & Empire Spring, Hotchkiss Sons, C, New York, C-15-B, pint, yellow
olive. . . . . $150–$200
Congress & Empire Spring, Hotchkiss Sons, C, New York, C-16-B, pint, medium
olive green. . . . . $100–$140
Congress C & W Water, Corks of all Genuine Congress Water, pint, olive green . .
. . . . $1100–$1500
Congress Spring Co SS NY, 2 (on base), C-22, Congress label, quart, emerald green.
. . . . $60–$90
Congress Spring Co, C, Saratoga, NY, C-14-B, pint, blue green . . . . $30–$40
Congress Spring Co, C, Saratoga, NY, C-14-B, pint, emerald green . . . . $30–$45
Congress Spring Co, C, Saratoga, NY, C-14-B, pint, olive green . . . . $60–$90
Congress Spring Co, C, Saratoga, NY, C-15-B, pint, golden yellow olive . . . .
. . . . $75–$100

Mineral water, Congress Spring Co., sloping shoulder.
PHOTO COURTESY OF NEIL GROSSMAN.

Congress Spring Co, C, Saratoga, NY, C-15-B, pint, olive green .... $70–$100
Congress Spring Co, C, Saratoga, NY, C-15-B, pint, red amber .... $150–$200
Congress Spring Co, C, Saratoga, NY, C-19-A, quart, emerald green ...... $30–$45
Congress Spring Co, C, Saratoga, NY, C-19-B, pint, emerald green .... $30–$45
Congress Spring Co, C, Saratoga, NY, C-19-B, pint, olive green .... $40–$50
Congress Spring Co, C, Saratoga, NY, C-21-B, pint, emerald green .... $30–$35
Congress Water, C-13, three piece mold, SB, olive amber .... $175–$250
Cooper's Well Water, Miss, pint, red amber .... $150–$225
DA Knowlton, Saratoga, NY, E-5-B, quart, deep olive green .... $50–$75
DA Knowlton, Saratoga, NY, pint, deep olive green .... $40–$65
DA Knowlton, Saratoga, NY, pint, emerald green .... $65–$80
DA Knowlton, Saratoga, NY, quart, emerald green .... $65–$80
Darien Mineral Springs, Tifft & Perry, Darien Centre, NY, N-11, pint, aqua......
.... $225–$325
Darien Mineral Springs, Tifft & Perry, Darien Centre, NY, N-11, pint, blue green .
.... $250–$350
Deep Rock Spring, Oswego, NY, N-13, pint, amber .... $150–$250
Deep Rock Spring, Oswego, NY, N-13, pint, aqua .... $175–$275
Deep Rock Spring, Oswego, NY, N-13, very seedy glass, pint, teal blue ....
.... $300–$400
Deep Rock Spring, Oswego, NY, N-15-B, quart, aqua .... $250–$300
DJ Whelan, Troy, NY, M-58, quart, aqua .... $40–$60
Dr Struve's Mineral Water, half pint, olive green. .... $90–$125
Empire Spring Co, E, Saratoga, NY, Empire Water, E-11-A-2, quart, emerald green
.... $40–$65
Empire Spring Co, E, Saratoga, NY, Empire Water, E-11-B, pint, blue green .....
.... $30–$35
Empire Spring Co, E, Saratoga, NY, Empire Water, pint, emerald green ....
.... $30–$45
Empire Spring Co, E, Saratoga, NY, Empire Water, quart, amber ..... $400–$475
Empire Spring Co, E, Saratoga, NY, Empire Water, quart, red amber .. $200–$300
Eureka Spring Co, Saratoga, NY, S-20, ten pin form, pint, aqua........ $250–$350
Eureka Spring Co, Saratoga, NY, torpedo, 8⅞", deep aqua........... $400–$600
European Mineral Waters, After Dr Struve's Method, pint, pine green ....
.... $250–$350

Excelsior Rock Spring, Saratoga, NY, S-22-A-5, quart, ginger ale color. . . . .
. . . . $2000–$3000
Excelsior Rock Spring, Saratoga, NY, S-22-B, pint, topaz. . . . . $600–$800
Excelsior Spring, Saratoga, NY, S-21-B, pint, emerald green. . . . . $100–$160
Excelsior Spring, Saratoga, NY, S-21-B, pint, yellow olive . . . . $90–$150
Excelsior Spring, Saratoga, NY, S-26, quart, emerald green. . . . . $150–$200
Excelsior Spring, Saratoga, NY, S-26-A, pint, emerald green . . . . $150–$200
Excelsior Spring, Saratoga, NY, S-26A, lip bruise, quart, blue green. . . . . . . $60–$75
Excelsior Spring, Saratoga, NY-Saratoga Excelsior Spring Co, S-24, pint, red
amber. . . . . $500–$700
Franklin Spring Mineral Water, Ballston Spa, Saratoga, NY, S-28, pint, yellow
green . . . . '. . $300–$400
From the Magnetic and Medicinal Spring of CE Franklin, quart, red amber . . . . . .
. . . . $500–$800
Gettysburg Katalysine Water, M-18, quart, emerald green . . . . $90–$125
Gettysburg Katalysine Water, M-18, quart, yellowish olive . . . . $125–$175
Gettysburg Katalysine Water, M-18-A, quart, emerald green . . . . $80–$110
Gettysburg Katalysine Water, quart, yellow green. . . . . $80–$110
Geyser Spring, Saratoga Spring, The Saratoga Spouting Spring, S-29, quart, aqua.
. . . . $45–$65
Geyser Spring, Saratoga Spring, The Saratoga Spouting Spring, S-29-B, pint, aqua
. . . . $45–$65
Glacier Spouting Spring, Saratoga Springs, NY (drilling rig), S-32, pint, aqua . . . .
. . . . $1250–$2250
Guilford Mineral Spring Water, quart, blue green . . . . $60–$80
Guilford Mineral Spring Water, V-7, quart, yellowish green. . . . . $30–$40
GW Weston & Co, Saratoga, NY (around shoulder), OP, quart, olive green. . . . . . .
. . . . $175–$250
GW Weston & Co, Saratoga, NY, E-2-1, OP, quart, medium olive green . . . .
. . . . $100–$140
GW Weston & Co, Saratoga, NY, E-2-B-2, pint, deep olive green . . . . $80–$120
GW Weston & Co, Saratoga, NY, E-3-B, SB, pint, deep olive amber . . . . $100–$140
GW Weston & Co, Saratoga, NY, E-4-B, OP, with amber tone, pint, olive. . . . .
. . . . $100–$150
GW Weston & Co, Saratoga, NY, pint, yellow green. . . . . $150–$200
GW Weston & Co, Saratoga, NY, quart, olive green . . . . $200–$250
Hanbury Smith's Mineral Waters, M-22-A, pint, yellow green. . . . . $60–$85
Hanbury Smith's Mineral Waters, M-22-A, pint, yellow olive . . . . $35–$50
Hanbury Smith's Mineral Waters, pint, olive green. . . . . $50–$65
Haskins Spring Co, H, Shutesbury, Mass HS Co, MZ-4-B, pint, emerald green . . . .
. . . . $400–$600
Haskins Spring Co, H, Shutesbury, Mass HS Co, quart, emerald green . . $275–$425
Hathorn Spring, Saratoga, NY, pint, olive amber. $50–$60
Hathorn Spring, Saratoga, NY, S-33, quart, emerald green . . . . $40–$60
Hathorn Spring, Saratoga, NY, S-33-B, pint, emerald green . . . . $30–$50
Hathorn Spring, Saratoga, NY, S-33-B-1, pint, yellowish olive green. . . . . . $40–$65
Hathorn Spring, Saratoga, NY, S-33BII, pint, black amber. . . . . $35–$45
Hathorn Spring, Saratoga, NY, S-33BII, pint, dark amber. . . . . $30–$40
Hathorn Spring, Saratoga, NY, S-34, pint, yellow olive. . . . . $40–$60
Highrock Congress Spring (rock) C&W, Saratoga, NY, pint, emerald green . . . . . .
. . . . $120–$160

Highrock Congress Spring (rock) C&W, Saratoga, NY, pint, olive amber . . . .
. . . . $150–$225
Highrock Congress Spring (rock) C&W, Saratoga, NY, pint, reddish amber . . . . . .
. . . . / . . . . $100–$135
Highrock Congress Spring (rock) C&W, Saratoga, NY, pint, teal . . . . . . $200–$300
Highrock Congress Spring (rock) C&W, Saratoga, NY, pint, yellow olive green . . .
. . . . $125–$175
Highrock Congress Spring (rock) C&W, Saratoga, NY, quart, yellow green . . . . . .
. . . . $325–$400
Highrock Congress Spring (rock) C&W, Saratoga, NY, S-37, pint, emerald green. .
. . . . $120–$160
Highrock Congress Spring (rock) C&W, Saratoga, NY, S-37-A, pint, yellow green
. . . . $200–$300
Highrock Congress Spring (rock) C&W, Saratoga, NY, S-37-B, pint, amber . . . . . .
. . . . $125–$175
Highrock Congress Spring (rock) C&W, Saratoga, NY, S-37-B-3, pint, olive amber
. . . . $150–$250
Highrock Congress Spring 1767 (rock) C&W, Saratoga, NY, S-36, SB, pint, olive
amber. . . . . $150–$250
Highrock Congress Spring 1767 (rock) C&W, Saratoga, NY, S-36-A-1, pint, root
beer amber. . . . . $125–$175
Highrock Congress Spring 1767 (rock) C&W, Saratoga, NY, S-36-A-1, quart, red
amber. . . . . $150–$250
Highrock Congress Spring 1767 (rock) C&W, Saratoga, NY, S-36-C, pint, medium
amber. . . . . $100–$150
Highrock Congress Spring 1767 (rock) C&W, Saratoga, NY, S-36-C, pint, red
amber. . . . . $125–$175
Highrock Spring (rock), Saratoga, pint, dark olive amber . . . . $500–$700
ID Buttles, Rome, NY, quart, aqua . . . . $125–$195
Iodine Spring Water, L, South Hero Vt, quart, apricot amber . . . . $700–$1000
John Clarke New York, C-4-B-1, three piece mold, SB, quart, deep olive green . . . . .
. . . . $90–$125
John Clarke New York, C-4-B-2, OP, yellowish olive amber. . . . . $125–$165
John Clarke New York, C-4-B-2, three piece mold, SB, quart, olive green . . . .
. . . . $75–$125
John Clarke New York, C-5-B, OP, pint, yellowish olive amber . . . . $125–$200
John Clarke New York, C-9, OP, pint, olive green . . . . $75–$125
John Clarke New York, C-9A, pint, olive green . . . . $75–$90
John H Gardner & Son, Sharon Spring, NY, Sharon Sulphur Water, N-32, pint,
blue green . . . . $225–$325
John H Gardner & Son, Sharon Spring, NY, Sharon Sulphur Water, N-32, pint,
medium green . . . . $200–$250
John H Gardner & Son, Sharon Spring, NY, Sharon Sulphur Water, N-32, pint,
teal blue. . . . . $225–$300
Kissingen Water Hanbury Smith, M-21-2, pint, yellowish olive . . . . $75–$100
Kissingen Water Hanbury Smith, M-21-B, pint, yellow olive . . . . $80–$120
Kissingen Water Hanbury Smith, M-21-C, half pint, yellow olive green . . . $60–$90
Kissingen Water Hanbury Smith, pint, olive green . . . . $50–$65
Kissingen Water THD, The Spa Phila, pint, yellow. . . . . $200–$250
Korrylutz Lithia Water, Korrylutz Lithia Water Co, New York, 9", orange amber.
. . . . $75–$100

Three early mineral water bottles. PHOTO COURTESY OF GLASS WORKS AUCTIONS.

Lamoille Spring, Milton Vt, quart, amber . . . . $800–$1200
Lynch & Clark, New York, C-1-C, OP, quart, med yellowish olive amber . . $450–$600
Lynch & Clark, New York, C-2-A-1, SB, pint, yellowish olive amber. . . . . $75–$125
Lynch & Clarke, New York, C-2-A, OP, pint, dark olive green . . . . $300–$400
Lynch & Clarke, New York, C-2-A, potstone crack, OP, olive green. . . . . $125–$200
Lynch & Clarke, New York, C-2-B, OP, pint, olive green . . . . $140–$190
Lynch & Clarke, New York, C-2-B, OP, scratches, pint, olive green. . . . . $175–$250
Lynch & Clarke, New York, C-2-B-1, OP, pint, medium olive green . . . . $225–$275
Lynch & Clarke, New York, C-2-B-1, OP, pint, yellowish olive amber. . . $250–$300
Lynch & Clarke, New York, C-2-B-2, OP, pint, medium olive amber . . . . $225–$275
Lynch & Clarke, New York, OP, quart, olive amber. . . . . $300–$500
Magnetic Spring, Henniker, NH, V-10, quart, golden amber . . . . $550–$750
Massena Spring Water, N-22, quart, medium teal blue. . . . . $150–$225
Middletown Healing Springs, Grays & Clark, Middletown, Vt, quart, apricot amber
. . . . $550–$650
Middletown Healing Springs, Grays & Clark, Middletown, Vt, quart, golden amber
. . . . $100–$175
Middletown Healing Springs, Grays & Clark, Middletown, Vt, quart, olive amber .
. . . . $150–$250
Middletown Healing Springs, Grays & Clark, Middletown, Vt, quart, red amber . .
. . . . $140–$180
Middletown Healing Springs, Grays & Clark, Middletown, Vt, V-13, quart, golden
yellow amber. . . . . $500–$600
Middletown Mineral Spring Co, Natures Remedy, Middletown, Vt, full label, quart,
emerald green . . . . $350–$550
Middletown Mineral Spring Co, Natures Remedy, Middletown, Vt, quart, olive
green. . . . . $100–$125
Middletown Mineral Spring Co, Natures Remedy, Middletown, Vt, V-15a, quart,
emerald green . . . . $225–$325
Minnequa Water, Bradford Co, Pa, M-32-A, quart, aqua . . . . $200–$300
Missisquoi A Springs, (Indian woman, papoose), V-17-A, quart, lime green . . . .
. . . . $900–$1400

Missisquoi A Springs, quart, olive yellow .... $65–$85

Missisquoi A Springs, V-16-A, deep yellowish, quart, olive amber. .... $80–$120

Missisquoi A Springs, V-16-A, SB, quart, med yellowish olive amber ..... $80–$120

Missisquoi A Springs, V-16-B, quart, golden amber .... $60–$90

Missisquoi A Springs, V-16-B, quart, olive green .... $40–$60

Missisquoi A Springs, V-16-B, quart, yellowish green .... $80–$110

Oak Orchard, Acid Springs HW Bostwick, 574 Broadway, N-24, quart, blue green.
.... $75–$100

Oak Orchard, Acid Springs HW Bostwick, 574 Broadway, N-25, quart, golden
amber. .... $100–$175

Oak Orchard, Acid Springs HW Bostwick, 574 Broadway, N-25-A, quart, root beer
amber. .... $100–$150

Oak Orchard, Acid Springs HW Bostwick, 574 Broadway, N-25-B, quart, root beer
amber. .... $100–$150

Oak Orchard, Acid Springs HW Bostwick, 574 Broadway, quart, emerald green . . .
.... $90–$120

Pavilion & United States Spring, Aperient Pavilion Water, quart, emerald green . . .
.... $400–$600

Pavilion & United States Spring, P Pavilion Water, pint, yellow olive ....
.... $100–$150

Pavilion & United States Spring, P Pavilion Water, S-44-B, pint, deep blue green . .
.... $250–$350

Pavilion & United States Spring, P Pavilion Water, S-44-B, pint, medium blue green
.... $200–$275

Pavilion & United States Spring, P Pavilion Water, S-44B4, pint, yellow green ....
.... $125–$150

Pavilion & United States Spring, Pavilion Water, Aperient, pint, deep yellow green
.... $125–$175

Pavilion & United States Spring, Pavilion Water, Aperient, pint, emerald green . . .
.... $150–$250

Poland Water, H Ricker's & Sons, Moses figural, amber. .... $350–$450

Poland Water, H Ricker's & Sons, Moses figural, aqua .... $125–$165

Poland Water, M-38, quart, deep red amber. .... $1200–$1750

Saint Leon Spring Water, Earl W Johnson 27 Congress St Boston, pint, emerald
green .... $200–$350

Saratoga (star) Spring, quart, olive amber. .... $65–$85

Saratoga (star) Spring, S-52-A, quart, reddish amber .... $125–$175

Saratoga (star) Spring, S-52-B, pint, yellow green .... $400–$550

Saratoga (star) Spring, S-52-B, pint, yellowish amber .... $75–$95

Saratoga (star) Spring, S-53-A-II, SB, quart, amber .... $80–$110

Saratoga (star) Spring, S-53-A-II, SB, quart, emerald green. .... $150–$225

Saratoga Highrock Spring (rock), C&W, Saratoga NY, pint, emerald green. ......
.... $200–$275

Saratoga Highrock Spring (rock), C&W, Saratoga NY, S-40, pint, deep pine green.
.... $250–$325

Saratoga Highrock Spring 1767 (rock), Saratoga NY, S-39, quart, yellow green . . .
.... $1500–$2000

Saratoga Seltzer Water, S-51-B, pint, blue green .... $100–$125

Saratoga Seltzer Water, S-51-B, pint, blue green .... $75–$125

Saratoga Seltzer Water, S-51-B, pint, teal blue. .... $125–$175

Saratoga Seltzer Water, S-51-B, pint, teal blue. .... $125–$175

Saratoga Vichy Spouting Spring, V, Saratoga, NY, S-58-B, pint, aqua . . . . $75–$90
Saratoga Vichy Water, Saratoga, NY, V, S-60, quart, red amber . . . . $150–$250
Saratoga Vichy Water, Saratoga, NY, V, S-60-A, quart, aqua. . . . . $350–$500
Saratoga, A, Congress Carl H Schultz, NY, pint, emerald green. . . . . $1000–$1500
Saratoga, A, Spring Co, NY, S-1-A, pint, yellow olive. . . . . $150–$225
Saratoga, A, Spring Co, NY, S-1-B, yellow olive . . . . $100–$135
Saratoga, A, Spring Co, NY, S-1A, quart, yellow olive. . . . . $250–$350
Saratoga, A, Spring Co, NY, S-2-B, pint, emerald green. . . . . $100–$125
Saratoga, A, Spring Co, NY, S-2-B, pint, olive yellow . . . . $100–$165
Saratoga, Red, Spring, S-47, quart, medium green . . . . $65–$85
Saratoga, Red, Spring, S-47-A, quart, blue green . . . . $125–$200
Saratoga, Red, Spring, S-47-B, pint, emerald green . . . . $60–$80
Sheldon, A, Spring, Sheldon, Vt, V-19, quart, deep red amber . . . . $750–$1000
St Regis Water, Masasena Springs, N-21-A, overall haze, quart, blue green. . . . .
. . . . $100–$160
St Regis Water, Masasena Springs, N-21-A, pint, blue green . . . . $200–$250
St Regis Water, Masasena Springs, N-21-A, quart, medium bluish green . . . .
. . . . $200–$250
St Regis Water, Masasena Springs, N-21-B, clear, pint . . . . $400–$500
St Regis Water, Masasena Springs, quart, blue green. . . . . $160–$200
Star Spring Co (star), Saratoga, NY, S-54-B, black. . . . . $225–$350
Star Spring Co (star), Saratoga, NY, S-54-B, lip chip, pint, gold amber . . . . $70–$90
Star Spring Co (star), Saratoga, NY, S-54-B, lip chip, pint, yellowish amber. . . . . . .
. . . . $60–$90
Star Spring Co (star), Saratoga, NY, S-54-B, pint, honey amber. . . . . $70–$90
Star Spring Co (star), Saratoga, NY, S-54-B, pint, olive amber. . . . . $125–$175
Star Spring Co (star), Saratoga, NY, S-54-B, pint, red amber . . . . $60–$80
Star Spring Co (star), Saratoga, NY, S-54-B, pint, yellowish amber. . . . . . $90–$125
Star Spring Co (star), Saratoga, NY, S-54-B, quart, red amber . . . . $90–$135
Star Spring Co (star), Saratoga, NY, S-54-B, SB, root beer amber . . . . . . $100–$175
Stirling's Magnetic Mineral Spring, Eaton Rapids Mich, M-49, quart, red amber . .
. . . . $100–$175
Syracuse Springs Excelsior, N-33-B, pint, orange amber . . . . $150–$250
Syracuse Springs Excelsior, N-33-B, pint, yellowish amber . . . . $200–$300
Syracuse Springs Excelsior, quart, red amber . . . . $100–$160
Syracuse Springs, D, Excelsior AJ Delatour, New York, N-34-B, half pint, yellow
amber. . . . . $400–$600
Syracuse Springs, D, Excelsior AJ Delatour, New York, pint, red amber. . . . .
. . . . $200–$300
Triton Spouting Spring, T, Saratoga, NY-Triton Water, S-55, pint, aqua. . . . .
. . . . $750–$1200
Vermont Spring, Saxe & Co, Sheldon, Vt, C-21, quart, yellow green . . . . . . $40–$60
Vermont Spring, Saxe & Co, Sheldon, Vt, quart, citron. . . . . $250–$325
Vermont Spring, Saxe & Co, Sheldon, Vt, quart, olive green . . . . $60–$75
Vichy Water, Hanbury Smith, half pint, yellow olive. . . . . $50–$65
Vichy Water, Hanbury Smith, M-23-D, half pint, medium amber. . . . . $50–$75
Vichy Water, Patterson & Brazeau, NY, M-36, half pint, olive green. . . . . . $60–$90
Vichy Water, Patterson & Brazeau, NY, M-37, pint, olive green . . . . $40–$60
Washington Spring Co (Washington bust), Ballston Spa, C, S-61, pint, emerald
green . . . . $500–$750
Washington Spring, Saratoga, NY, S-64, lip bruise, pint, emerald green. . . $150–$200

Washington Spring, Saratoga, NY, S-64, pint, emerald green . . . . $250–$350
Washington Spring, Saratoga, NY, S-64-B, pint, medium olive amber . . . $300–$425
Washington Spring, Saratoga, NY, S-64-B-1, pint, yellow amber . . . . $450–$700
Washington, Lithia Well, Mineral Water, Ballston Spa, NY, S-62, pint, aqua . . . . .
. . . . $125–$175
Washington, Lithiawell, Mineral Water, Ballston Spa, NY, S-63, pint, aqua . . . . . .
. . . . $110–$160
Welden Spring, St Albans Vt, Alterative, Chalybeate, quart, forest green . . . .
. . . . $1500–$2500
White Sulphur Springs, Greenbrier, W Va, M-59, quart, medium emerald green . . .
. . . . $125–$185

NAILSEA-TYPE BOTTLES

Nailsea-type bottles are bottles which have white or colored looping. These were popular throughout the 19th century and are named for the Nailsea district in England where many of them were made. These bottles were also produced in the United States but it is difficult to tell which bottles are American and which are English or European. Look for unusual looping colors other than the more ordinary white and pink.

Bellows, applied stem & foot, red and white looping, OP, 11$\frac{1}{2}$", clear . . . . $250–$350
Bellows, cranberry body, white looping, clear rigaree, OP, 7" . . . . $110–$170
Bellows, red looping, clear rigaree & prunts, OP, 6$\frac{3}{4}$", clear . . . . $90–$150
Bellows, white looping, clear rigaree, OP, 7", clear. . . . . $80–$120
Boot shaped bottle, clear with white looping, OP, 8". . . . . $150–$225
Decanter, clear, white looping, round lip, thin neck rings, polished pontil, 11". . . . . . .
. . . . $150–$250

Nailsea type, looped flask. PHOTO COURTESY OF NEIL GROSSMAN.

Decanter, globular, heavy, donut lip, neck rings, applied pad foot, white looping, OP, aqua. . . . . $1000–$1400
Decanter, wide squat bottom, long neck, "Captain's bottle" form, flaring lip, white looping, stopper, cranberry . . . . $300–$450
Flask, clear pint with white looping, OP, 7½". . . . . $80–$135
Flask, milk glass with red and blue looping, OP, 6½" . . . . $150–$250
Flask, milk glass with red looping, tooled lip, OP, 7" . . . . $125–$175
Gemel, clear, white looping, clear rigaree, OP, 8" . . . . $100–$165
Pipe, clear with red & blue looping, 15" . . . . $160–$240
Pipe, milk glass with red looping, 17" . . . . $250–$400
Powder horn, clear with white looping, applied neck rings, 12" . . . . $100–$145
Powder horn, footed, clear, white looping, OP, 11¾" . . . . $200–$300
Powder horn, white looping, applied rings, 11", cobalt . . . . $150–$225
Powder horn, with white looping, applied rings, 10½", aqua . . . . $225–$350

PATTERN-MOLDED BOTTLES, INCLUDING MIDWESTERN AND STIEGEL-TYPE BOTTLES

Pattern molded-type bottles are those bottles that get their pattern by being blown into ribbed, diamond pattern, geometric or other patterned molds. Molds of this sort were used in the early Roman and Islamic glass factories thousands of years ago, by early European and English glass manufacturers for many hundreds of years, as well as in early America at least as far back as the 18th century. Among the rarest and most desirable of pattern-molded bottles are the Stiegel-type, many of which were blown at the Stiegel Glass Manufactory in Mannheim, Pennsylvania, in the late 18th century. Although Stiegel made various types of pattern-molded bottles, only the Diamond Daisy and Daisy and Hexagon variants can be positively attributed to Stiegel, since it has never been shown that these molds were used anywhere else. A physical examination of known Stiegel flasks would show you one of the distinctive features of Stiegel bottles, and that is the very wide and fat sides. Please note that virtually all of the known Stiegel flasks are amethyst in color and usually light in weight. However, other factories and countries also produced amethyst and lightweight glass. As such, remember that you should not make attributions based on color, but rather on form and design. Other patterns such as ribbed, diamond, and cells over flutes were also probably made at the Stiegel factories, but it is impossible to make a positive Stiegel attribution because other factories, including English and European, made similar products.

Included within this section are Midwestern-type bottles, which are often quite distinctive in form. Bottles and flasks under this group were generally made in either the Kent, Mantua or Zanesville factories of early Ohio in forms such as ribbed globular bottles, and diamond and ribbed patterned chestnut flasks. Midwestern bottles and flasks come in a range of colors but are usually found in shades of aqua or amber; other colors such as greens, blues, and amethysts are much more rare.

Glass made in the Pittsburgh area was often made pattern molded, such as the distinctive pillar molded items; pillar molded items are also known as "steamboat ware." Pittsburgh was one of the nation's earliest glass making centers and scores of factories operated in the late 18th into the mid 19th centuries making an incredible assortment of items. Pillar molded items are almost always found in clear; next most rare are those clear items that have a blue thread running down the center of each pillar; then comes the clambroth's, blues, amethysts, and the rare amber's and ruby colors. Just to show how the prices escalate based on color, here are estimates for a pillar molded decanter: Clear—$60; Clear with blue threads on each of the eight ribs—$800; Cobalt blue decanter—$2000–$2750; Amethyst decanter—$2500–$3250; Amber—$3500+.

Please consider the following points on pattern molded bottles and flasks:

- There are reproduction globular bottles. Reproductions are generally sloppy in appearance and often have flaring lips, which genuine globular bottles almost never have.
- Be suspicious of any Stiegel or Midwestern-type items that are heavy in weight and have flaring lips.
- There is a very good reproduction Diamond Daisy flask out there, excellent in form and color, but the fake has six daisies, whereas the original has five.
- Refer to the Reproduction section in this book for photos of pattern molded Clevenger reproductions from the 1930s and thereafter.
- Patterned molded flattened chestnuts and flasks were made in the early to mid 19th century in Europe in ribbed and diamond patterns, in very vibrant colors. Some of the items often exhibit forms uncharacteristic of Midwestern form, such as long tapering form, or very wide fronts with narrow sides.
- Globular bottles are usually found with swirled ribs; vertically ribbed items are rare and are generally much more valuable. As to color, the most common to rarest glob colors are aqua, amber, green, cobalt/sapphire, amethyst.
- The strength of a pattern is very important in determining the value of pat-

tern molded items. By strength of pattern, for example, we mean how pronounced the ribbing or diamond pattern is. A strong pattern can double, triple or more the value of an item. Consequently, weak patterned items are worth less.

• Pitkin flasks come in a variety of colors from shades of green and amber, to aquas and clears, and even cobalt; an amethsyt Pitkin flask is known. Color is not really the main determinant in Pitkin values, except for rare colors such as cobalt and amethyst. What drives the pricing is how strong the pattern is, overall appearance (is it an average or exceptional example), the shape, and size, with miniatures commanding thousands of dollars. I have seen an unusual Pitkin flask that is made from a two-piece mold, in other words, not really pattern molded, and is clear, but appears to have good age to it.

• Pattern molded flasks and chestnuts are still being made today. Reproductions are available at many museum and historical society gift shops. Upon handling these items and comparing them with known antique items, you will notice that the weight of the reproductions is generally noticeably heavier, the glass is of finer quality with fewer imperfections, bubbles, stones, etc., along with the obvious lack of wear and the "slippery" feel of new glass.

Beehive Bottle (See Club Bottles, this listing)
Cells Over Flutes, thick bodied flask, OP, $5^3/_8$", amethyst . . . . $2500–$3750
Chestnut "Grandfather's" Flask, 24 rib broken swirl, OP, $7^3/_4$", deep amber . . . .
. . . . $750–$1000
Chestnut "Grandfather's" Flask, 24 vertical ribs, OP, $8^1/_8$", medium amber . . . .
. . . . $800–$1000
Chestnut "Grandfather's" Flask, 24 vertical ribs, red tone, 8", medium amber . . . . .
. . . . $700–$950

Chestnut flask, swirled rib. PHOTO COURTESY OF
GLASS WORKS AUCTIONS.

Chestnut Flask, 10 diamonds, OP, 4$^7/_8$", golden amber . . . . $600–$900
Chestnut Flask, 10 diamonds, OP, very pronounced diamond pattern, 5$^1/_4$", deep red amber . . . . $2500+
Chestnut Flask, 10-diamond pattern, clear, OP, hairline crack, 4$^3/_4$" . . . . $80–$120
Chestnut Flask, 10-diamond pattern, clear, surface crack, 4$^3/_4$". . . . . $70–$90
Chestnut Flask, 16 vertical ribs, clear, OP, 6$^1/_2$" . . . . $300–$375
Chestnut Flask, 16 vertical ribs, coin shaped flask, OP, 6$^1/_8$", amethyst . . . $400–$550
Chestnut Flask, 16 vertical ribs, OP, 6$^1/_2$", medium amethyst . . . . $150–$225
Chestnut Flask, 16 vertical ribs, OP, light blue . . . . $175–$250
Chestnut Flask, 16 vertical ribs, OP, small lip chip, 5$^3/_4$", apple green . . . . $300–$400
Chestnut Flask, 18 diamonds, large lip chip, 5$^3/_4$", yellowish green . . . . $90–$120
Chestnut Flask, 18 swirled ribs, OP, weak impression, 5$^1/_8$", medium amber . . . .
. . . . $150–$200
Chestnut Flask, 18 swirled ribs, OP, weak impression, 5$^1/_8$", medium amber . . . .
. . . . $175–$250
Chestnut Flask, 18 swirled ribs, OP, weak impression, 6$^1/_2$", medium amber . . . .
. . . . $175–$240
Chestnut Flask, 20 rib broken swirl, OP, lip chip, bruise, 6$^7/_8$", yellow olive . . . .
. . . . $250–$350
Chestnut Flask, 20 swirled ribs, flaring lip, 3$^7/_8$", cobalt . . . . $250–$350
Chestnut Flask, 20 swirled ribs, flaring lip, OP, 4$^1/_2$", cobalt. . . . . $200–$275
Chestnut Flask, 20 vertical ribs, OP, 5$^3/_4$", deep amethyst. . . . . $1200–$1800
Chestnut Flask, 24 rib broken swirl, OP, 4$^3/_4$", aqua . . . . $140–$180
Chestnut Flask, 24 rib broken swirl, OP, weak impression, 5", deep reddish amber . . .
. . . . $300–$400
Chestnut Flask, 24 swirled ribs, 7", aqua . . . . $150–$200
Chestnut Flask, 24 swirled ribs, OP, 5$^1/_4$", golden amber. . . . . $150–$250
Chestnut Flask, 24 vertical ribs, 4$^7/_8$", golden amber . . . . $125–$175
Chestnut Flask, 24 vertical ribs, 5$^1/_8$", aqua . . . . $55–$80
Chestnut Flask, 24 vertical ribs, olive tint, OP, 5$^1/_4$", yellow. . . . . $300–$375
Chestnut Flask, 24 vertical ribs, OP, 4$^3/_4$", yellow olive . . . . $400–$550
Chestnut Flask, 24 vertical ribs, OP, 5", medium yellowish amber . . . . $250–$325
Chestnut Flask, 24 vertical ribs, OP, open $^3/_8$" neck bubble, 5$^1/_4$", medium amber . . . .
. . . . $75–$100
Chestnut Flask, 34 swirled ribs, handled, half post, applied lip, clear, OP, 5" . . . .
. . . . $140–$180
Chestnut Flask, handled, flattened, unpatterned, OP, laid on ring below lip, 7", amber
. . . . $40–$50
Chestnut Flask, handled, flattened, unpatterned, OP, laid on ring below lip, 7", puce. .
. . . . $75–$125
Chestnut Flask, handled, flattened, unpatterned, SB, molded lip, 6", amber . . . .
. . . . $20–$30
Chestnut Flask, unpatterned, 5$^1/_8$", yellowish amber . . . . $100–$140
Chestnut Flask, unpatterned, OP, 5$^1/_2$", orangish amber. . . . . $110–$150
Chestnut Flask, unpatterned, OP, 5$^1/_8$", yellow amber . . . . $100–$145
Chestnut Flask, unpatterned, SB, laid on ring below lip, 6$^5/_8$", deep cobalt. . . . .
. . . . $80–$125
Club Bottle, 16-rib broken swirl, OP, 8$^1/_2$", aqua . . . . $125–$175
Club Bottle, 24 swirled ribs, bluish aqua, 8", aqua . . . . $125–$175
Club Bottle, 24 swirled ribs, bold pattern, 7$^1/_2$", bluish aqua . . . . $200–$250
Club Bottle, 24 swirled ribs, olive tones, 8$^3/_4$", brilliant yellow . . . . $2000–$2750

Club Bottle, 24 swirled ribs, OP, 7³/₄", aqua . . . . $100–$150
Club Bottle, 24 swirled ribs, OP, 8¹/₈", aqua . . . . $125–$175
Club Bottle, 24 vertical ribs, IP, side bruise, 8¹/₄", deep bluish aqua . . . . $90–$125
Club Bottle, 24 vertical ribs, OP, 8¹/₄", aqua . . . . $80–$120
Club Bottle, 24 vertical ribs, OP, 8", deep aqua . . . . $150–$200
Club Bottle, 24-rib broken swirl, 8¹/₂", sapphire blue . . . . $4500–$7500
Club Bottle, 24-rib broken swirl, OP, 7⁷/₈", aqua . . . . $150–$200
Club Bottle, 24-rib broken swirl, OP, weak impression, 7³/₄", aqua . . . . $75–$95
Club Bottle, unpatterned, OP, 8¹/₄", aqua . . . . $30–$55
Club Bottle, unpatterned, OP, 9¹/₄", aqua . . . . $30–$50
Cruet, 16 swirled ribs, handled, clear with stopper, OP, 8¹/₄" . . . . $150–$200
Cruet, 16 swirled ribs, handled, original blue stopper, OP, 8¹/₄", sapphire blue . . . .
. . . . $1200–$1500
Cruet, 16 swirled ribs, handled, original stopper, OP, 8¹/₄", golden amber . . . .
. . . . $2000–$3000
Cruet, 16 vertical ribs, handled, original blue stopper, OP, 8¹/₄", sapphire blue . . . .
. . . . $1200–$1500
Daisy in Hexagon Flask, plump body, OP, 4³/₈", amethyst . . . . $5000–$7000

Left: *Pillar molded decanter*. Right: *Flask, diamond patterned*. PHOTOS COURTESY OF GLASS WORKS AUCTIONS.

Decanter, pillar mold, 8 heavy ribs, large donut lip, 11", ruby . . . . $1400–$1800
Decanter, pillar mold, 8 heavy ribs, large donut lip, 11", smoky blue . . . $2500–$3300
Decanter, pillar mold, 8 heavy ribs, large donut lip, clear, blue edge on ribs, 11" . . . . .
. . . . $550–$750
Decanter, pillar mold, 8 heavy ribs, large donut lip, clear, purple edge on ribs, 11" . . .
. . . . $600–$800
Decanter, pillar mold, 8 ribs, more slender form, narrower ribs, lighter weight, clear . .
. . . . $80–$125
Decanter, pillar molded, 8 heavy ribs, large donut lip, 11", sapphire blue . . $2000–$2600
Decanter, pillar molded, 8 heavy ribs, large donut lip, clear, 11¹/₄" . . . . $60–$90
Diamond Daisy Flask, plump body, OP, 4³/₄", amethyst . . . . $3000–$4000
Diamond Daisy Flask, plump body, OP, strong impression, 5³/₈", amethyst . . . .
. . . . $3500–$4750

Diamond Daisy Flask, plump body, OP, weak impression, 4³/₄", light amethyst . . . . .
. . . . $2000–$3000
Diamond Pattern Flask, 16 diamonds, teardrop form, clear, OP, 6¹/₄" . . . . . $80–$120
Diamond Pattern Flask, plump body, 12 diamond pattern, OP, 4¹/₄", amethyst . . . . . :
. . . . $2300–$3300
Diamond Pattern Flask, plump body, 12 diamond pattern, OP, 4³/₄", amethyst . . . . . .
. . . . $2000–$3000
Elongated Pocket Flask, 16 vertical ribs, OP, 6", medium green. . . . . $100–$145
Elongated Pocket Flask, 18 vertical ribs, OP, 6¹/₂", aqua . . . . $60–$80
Elongated Pocket Flask, 18 vertical ribs, OP, 6", light green . . . . $75–$95
Elongated Pocket Flask, 20 vertical ribs, 6¹/₄", aqua . . . . $50–$70
Elongated Pocket Flask, 20 vertical ribs, OP, 7", aqua . . . . $75–$95
Elongated Pocket Flask, 32 vertical ribs, OP, 6¹/₄", yellow green . . . . $125–$175
Elongated Pocket Flask, unpatterned, OP, 5¹/₂", yellow olive green . . . . . . $100–$145
Ewer, 15 vertical ribs, clear, no stopper, blown handle, 7³/₄" . . . . $80–$100

Left: *Pattern molded, globular bottle with rolled lip.* Right: *Pattern molded, globular bottle reproduction with flaring lip.* PHOTOS COURTESY OF NEIL GROSSMAN.

Globular Bottle, 24 swirled ribs, OP, 8³/₄", brilliant topaz . . . . $800–$1200
Globular Bottle, 24 swirled ribs, amber tone, OP, 7³/₄", yellow. . . . . $425–$575
Globular Bottle, 24 swirled ribs, amber tone, OP, bold impression, 7⁵/₈", yellow . . . . .
. . . . $500–$750
Globular Bottle, 24 swirled ribs, OP, ³/₄" crack, 7¹/₂", medium yellow green. $300–$375
Globular Bottle, 24 swirled ribs, OP, 7⁷/₈", aqua . . . . $200–$300
Globular Bottle, 24 swirled ribs, OP, 7⁷/₈", deep amber . . . . $350–$425
Globular Bottle, 24 swirled ribs, OP, 7", medium yellow amber . . . . $400–$575
Globular Bottle, 24 swirled ribs, OP, 8¹/₂", medium amber . . . . $350–$450
Globular Bottle, 24 swirled ribs, OP, 8¹/₂", medium amber . . . . $375–$450
Globular Bottle, 24 swirled ribs, OP, 8¹/₂", yellow green. . . . . $1000–$1450
Globular Bottle, 24 swirled ribs, OP, 8¹/₄", golden amber . . . . $300–$390
Globular Bottle, 24 swirled ribs, OP, 8¹/₄", medium amber . . . . $300–$400
Globular Bottle, 24 swirled ribs, OP, 8³/₄", citron . . . . $1200–$1500
Globular Bottle, 24 swirled ribs, OP, 9¹/₂", golden amber . . . . $450–$575
Globular Bottle, 24 swirled ribs, OP, 9¹/₄", medium amber . . . . $500–$675
Globular Bottle, 24 swirled ribs, OP, 9", golden amber . . . . $450–$575
Globular Bottle, 24 vertical ribs, 2" burst surface bubble, 7¹/₂", golden yellow amber .
. . . . $400–$500

Left: *Pattern molded, rare, vertically ribbed, globular bottle (left), club bottle (right), and ten-diamond patterned flask (right front).* PHOTO COURTESY OF GLASS WORKS AUCTIONS. Right: *Pattern molded, swirled, ribbed, toilet water bottle, ca. 1830.* PHOTO COURTESY OF NEIL GROSSMAN.

Globular Bottle, 24 vertical ribs, lip repaired, OP, $7^3/8$", greenish aqua. . . . $150–$200
Globular Bottle, 24 vertical ribs, OP, $7^1/2$", aqua . . . . $160–$220
Globular Bottle, 24 vertical ribs, OP, $7^7/8$", amber . . . . $2500–$3500
Globular Bottle, 24 vertical ribs, slightly melon shaped, OP, $6^7/8$", root beer amber. . .
. . . . $1200–$1500
Globular Bottle, 36 swirled ribs, OP, $7^1/2$", medium green. . . . . $1500–$2000
Globular Bottle, 36 swirled ribs, OP, $7^1/4$", light green . . . . $900–$1250
Globular Bottle, 36 swirled ribs, OP, $8^1/4$", puce . . . . $900–$1400
Globular Bottle, unpatterned, OP, $8^1/8$", medium amber . . . .$175–$240
Globular Bottle, unpatterned, OP, $9^1/8$", medium amber . . . . $225–$300
Globular Bottle, unpatterned, OP, 9", aqua. . . . . $60–$80
Globular Bottle, unpatterned, OP, 9", medium yellowish olive . . . . $100–$135
Globular Jug, handled, 24-rib broken swirl, OP, $6^1/8$", golden amber . . . .
. . . . $12,000–$16,000
Globular Jug, handled, unpatterned, IP, $5^1/8$", strawberry puce . . . . $125–$175
Globular Jug, handled, unpatterned, rolled lip, OP, 6", light amber. . . . . . $950–$1350
Globular Jug, handled, unpatterned, rolled lip, OP, handle tail broken off, 6", light
amber. . . . . $200–$300
Handled Swirled Rib Bottle, 16 ribs, OP, laid on ring below lip, $7^3/8$", puce . . . .
. . . . $350–$400
Handled Swirled Rib Bottle, 24 ribs, OP, laid on ring below lip, golden amber. . . . . .
. . . . $300–$425
Hobnail Pattern, half post, applied lip, OP, 18th-century form, $5^1/2$", light green. . . . .
. . . . $125–$250
Hobnail Pattern, half post, clear, applied lip, OP, 18th-century form, $6^1/2$". . . . .
. . . . $75–$125
Honeycomb Patterned Flask, half post, clear, OP, $4^3/4$" . . . . $125–$175
Melon Ribbed Flask, 20 vertical ribs, applied lip, OP, $7^1/2$", olive green. . . $700–$900
Melon Ribbed Flask, 20 vertical ribs, applied lip, OP, lip chip, $7^3/8$", olive green . . . .
. . . . $250–$325

Pinch bottle, half post neck, pewter stopper. PHOTO COURTESY OF GLASS WORKS AUCTIONS.

Nurser (See Elongated Pocket Flasks, this listing)
Pewter Screw Threaded Hobnailed Bottle, pear form, OP, 5^1/$_2$", cobalt . . . .
. . . . $3000–$4000
Pewter Screw Threaded Ribbed Bottle, tear drop shape, OP, 5^1/$_8$", amber . . . .
. . . . $1000–$1400
Pewter Screw Threaded Swirled Rib Bottle, 16 ribs, OP, 8^1/$_8$", sea green . . . .
. . . . $800–$1200
Pewter Screw Threaded Swirled Rib Bottle, OP, 6", cobalt . . . . $650–$900
Pewter Screw Threaded Swirled Rib Bottle, pinched center, 7^1/$_4$", light yellow green
. . . . $500–$675
Pewter Screw Threaded Vertically Ribbed Bottle, pinched center, OP, 8^1/$_4$", blue . .
. . . . $650–$900
Pewter Screw Threaded Vertically Ribbed Bottle, tear drop form, OP, 7^1/$_2$",
amethyst . . . . $1200–$1700
Pitkin Bottle, 36 swirled ribs, three sided, flaring lip, 4^7/$_8$", olive amber . . . . . $3000+
Pitkin Flask, 20 swirled ribs, clear, OP, probably Germany late 18th century, 5" . . . . .
. . . . $150–$250
Pitkin Flask, 24 swirled ribs, OP, 6^1/$_8$", light sea green . . . . $325–$400
Pitkin Flask, 24 vertical ribs, clear, OP, 4^5/$_8$" . . . . $300–$400
Pitkin Flask, 24 vertical ribs, OP, 5^1/$_2$", cobalt blue . . . . $1000–$1500
Pitkin Flask, 24 vertical ribs, OP, 5", cobalt . . . . $1000–$1500
Pitkin Flask, 28 swirled ribs, OP, 7^1/$_8$", bright yellowish green . . . . $350–$425
Pitkin Flask, 30-rib broken swirl, OP, 6^1/$_2$", bluish green. . . . . $150–$200
Pitkin Flask, 32-rib broken swirl, OP, 6^3/$_4$", bluish green. . . . . $150–$250
Pitkin Flask, 32-rib broken swirl, weak impression, 6^1/$_2$", root beer amber . $300–$375
Pitkin Flask, 32-rib broken swirl, OP, 6^1/$_4$", medium olive green . . . . $275–$350
Pitkin Flask, 32-rib broken swirl, OP, 6^5/$_8$", light green. . . . . $250–$300
Pitkin Flask, 32-rib broken swirl, OP, 6^7/$_8$", bluish green. . . . . $250–$325
Pitkin Flask, 32-rib broken swirl, OP, string impression, 6^5/$_8$", medium green . . . .
. . . . $275–$400
Pitkin Flask, 36-rib broken swirl, miniature, OP, 3^1/$_4$", olive green . . . . . $2000–$3000
Pitkin Flask, 36-rib broken swirl, OP, 5^3/$_4$", golden amber. . . . . $375–$450
Pitkin Flask, 36-rib broken swirl, OP, 5^5/$_8$", forest green . . . . $400–$475

Pitkin Flask, 36 swirled ribs, $^3/_8$" body bruise, OP, $4^3/_4$", light yellow olive . . . .
. . . . $200–$275

Pitkin Flask, 36 swirled ribs, OP, $5^3/_4$", forest green. . . . . $400–$650

Pitkin Flask, 36 vertical ribs (rare), OP, $5^1/_4$", olive green . . . . $600–$800

Pitkin Flask, 36-rib broken swirl, OP, $4^7/_8$", yellow olive. . . . . $240–$300

Pitkin Flask, 36-rib broken swirl, OP, $4^7/_8$", yellowish olive . . . . $275–$375

Pitkin Flask, 36-rib broken swirl, OP, $5^1/_4$", olive green. . . . . $250–$350

Pitkin Flask, 36-rib broken swirl, OP, $5^1/_4$", yellowish olive . . . . $240–$300

Pitkin Flask, 36-rib broken swirl, OP, $5^1/_4$", yellowish olive . . . . $250–$350

Pitkin Flask, 36-rib broken swirl, OP, $5^1/_8$", medium olive green . . . . $275–$375

Pitkin Flask, 36-rib broken swirl, OP, $5^3/_4$", sea green . . . . $350–$400

Pitkin Flask, 36-rib broken swirl, OP, $5^3/_8$", deep forest green. . . . . $400–$475

Pitkin Flask, 36-rib broken swirl, OP, $5^7/_8$", deep golden amber . . . . $375–$475

Pitkin Flask, 36-rib broken swirl, OP, $6^1/_2$", yellowish olive . . . . $250–$350

Pitkin Flask, 36-rib broken swirl, OP, inner milky stain, $5^1/_2$", greenish aqua . . . .
. . . . $150–$200

Pitkin Flask, 36-rib broken swirl, OP, olive tone, $6^3/_4$", yellow . . . . $325–$425

Pitkin Flask, 36-rib broken swirl, OP, shoulder bruise, $6^1/_2$", yellow olive . . . .
. . . . $225–$275

Pitkin Flask, miniature, approx. 3" . . . . $2000–$3000

Pitkin Ink, 36 swirled ribs, $2^1/_8$" (w), olive amber . . . . $375–$500

Pitkin Ink, 36 swirled ribs, OP, $1^1/_2$" (h) x $2^1/_4$", deep yellowish olive. . . . . $500–$725

Pitkin Ink, 36 swirled ribs, round, OP, $2^1/_4$", olive green . . . . $375–$500

Pitkin Ink, 36 swirled ribs, square (rare), OP, 2", olive green . . . . $800–$1100

Pitkin Jar, (ext. rare), wide mouth, OP, $5^3/_4$", olive green . . . . $5000+

Redware, Eagle E Pluribus Unum, glaze, $7^1/_4$", brown. . . . . $250–$300

Rib and Leaf Design, half post, flared lip, OP, $6^7/_8$", sapphire blue . . . . $250–$350

Ringed Inkwell, seven horizontal rings, $1^3/_8$" x $2^3/_8$", OP, forest green . . . . $700–$950

Scrolls and Petaled Flowers Flask, clear, OP, $5^3/_4$". . . . . $200–$300

Syrup Jug, pillar mold, eight ribs, pewter spout and lid, clear, footed, $8^3/_4$" . . . .
. . . . $350–$450

Pillar molded syrup. PHOTO COURTESY OF GLASS
WORKS AUCTIONS.

Vertically Ribbed Bottle, 16 vertical ribs, tall cylinder, stopper, 12", amethyst . . . . . .
. . . . $350–$425
Vertically Ribbed Bottle, 18 ribs, oval, clear, folded lip, OP, 2¹/₂" . . . . $125–$160
Vertically Ribbed Decanter, oval form, sloping collar, OP, 9³/₈", aqua . . . $125–$165
Vertically Ribbed Flask, 16 vertical ribs, no taper in body, OP, 5¹/₄", medium
amethyst . . . . $1500+
Vertically Ribbed Flask, 24 vertical ribs, straight sided, no taper, IP, pint, deep aqua .
. . . . $100–$135

PICKLE BOTTLES

Pickle bottles are among the most beautifully designed and largest in size of all
bottles. Pickle bottles, which ordinarily have wide mouths, are usually square,
but cylindrical and six and eight sided examples can also be found. One of the
most popular types of pickle bottles is the cathedral or gothic style, which often
has fancy gothiclike window panels on the sides. Pickle bottles ordinarily
come in aqua glass, and the collector should be on the lookout for the more
unusual-colored and pontiled examples. The reader is referred to *Ketchup,
Pickles and Sauces* by Betty Zumwalt.

Pickle, Cathedral, fleur de lis-like pattern in panels, 11³/₄", light green. . . . $325–$425
Pickle, Cathedral, four fancy panels with crosshatching, SB, 12¹/₂", aqua . . . .
. . . . $80–$130
Pickle, Cathedral, four sided, SB, leaf pattern outlines panels, 7¹/₂", aqua . . . $30–$45
Pickle, Cathedral, six sided, five fancy panels, one plain, clear, SB, 8¹/₂". . . . $45–$75
Pickle, Cathedral, six sided, five fancy panels, one plain, OP, 12¹/₂", aqua. . . . .
. . . . $125–$185
Pickle, Cathedral, six sided, five fancy panels, one plain, SB, 12¹/₂", aqua. . . . .
. . . . $80–$130
Pickle, Cathedral, six sided, SB, full label, 13", light green. . . . . $150–$225
Pickle, Cathedral, six sided, WT & CO (on base), 13¹/₄", golden amber. . . . .
. . . . $800–$1200
Pickle, Cathedral, square with chain decor on panel edges, IP, 11", light green . . . . . .
. . . . $250–$350
Pickle, Cathedral, square with chain decor on panel edges, IP, 9", aqua. . . $160–$220
Pickle, Cathedral, square with chain decor on panel edges, SB, 11", aqua . . . .
. . . . $125–$165
Pickle, Cathedral, square with chain decor on panel edges, SB, 11", light green . . . . .
. . . . $135–$185

Cathedral pickle, crosshatching in panel. PHOTO COURTESY OF GLASS WORKS AUCTIONS.

Pickle, Cathedral, square, crosshatching in one panel, IP, 7¹/₂", emerald green . . . . $600–$800

Pickle, Cathedral, square, three fancy panels, one panel plain, OP, 11¹/₂", emerald green . . . . $800–$1000

Pickle, Cathedral, square, three fancy panels, one panel plain, OP, 6¹/₂", aqua. . . . . $80–$100

Pickle, Cathedral, square, three fancy panels, one panel plain, OP, 8¹/₂", emerald green . . . . $650–$900

Pickle, Cathedral, square, three fancy panels, one panel plain, OP, 9¹/₂", aqua. . . . . $110–$150

Pickle, Cathedral, square, three fancy panels, one unpatterned panel, OP, 9¹/₂", aqua . . . . $115–$155

Pickle, Cathedral, square, four fancy panels with crosshatching, IP, 12¹/₂", aqua. . . . . $140–$200

Pickle, Cathedral, square, four fancy panels with crosshatching, OP, 12¹/₂", aqua . . . . $140–$200

Pickle, Cathedral, square, four fancy panels with crosshatching, OP, 12¹/₂", emerald green . . . . $800–$1200

Pickle, Cathedral, square, four fancy panels with crosshatching, OP, 9¹/₂", aqua . . . . $90–$145

Pickle, Cathedral, square, four fancy panels with crosshatching, OP, 9¹/₂", emerald green . . . . $700–$900

Pickle, Cathedral, square, four fancy panels with crosshatching, SB, 6¹/₂", aqua . . . . $40–$45

Pickle, Cathedral, square, four fancy panels with crosshatching, SB, 9¹/₂", emerald green . . . . $550–$700

Pickle, Cathedral, square, four fancy panels, IP, 12¹/₂", aqua . . . . $125–$185

Pickle, Cathedral, square, four fancy panels, IP, 9¹/₂", aqua . . . . $115–$155

Pickle, Cathedral, square, four fancy panels, OP, 11¹/₂", amber (rare color) . $10,000+

Pickle, Cathedral, square, four fancy panels, OP, 8¹/₂", amber (rare color). . . . . $3000–$4500

Pickle, Cathedral, square, four fancy panels, OP, 9½", aqua. . . . . : $115–$155
Pickle, Cathedral, square, four fancy panels, SB, 12½", aqua. . . . . $80–$110
Pickle, Cathedral, square, four fancy panels, SB, 5½", aqua. . . . . $35–$55
Pickle, Cathedral, square, four fancy panels, SB, 8½", aqua. . . . . $65–$85
Pickle, Cathedral, square, four panels with crosshatching, OP, 6½", aqua . . . $65–$95
Pickle, Square, four unpatterned panels, SB, 8½", aqua . . . . $30–$40

PITKIN-TYPE BOTTLES AND FLASKS

Pitkin-type bottles and flasks are so named because for years it was believed that they were made exclusively at the Pitkin Glassworks of Manchester, Connecticut. All Pitkin items were made by the half-post method, in which the second gather or dip of glass extended only to the lower neck of the bottle, leaving a noticeable edge around the lower neck or shoulder. Ironically, there is currently no proof that Pitkin-type flasks were ever made at the Pitkin Glassworks, though there is substantial evidence of this type of bottle being made in many other glasshouses. These include the Keene Marlborough Street Glassworks in Keene, New Hampshire; Coventry Glassworks in Coventry, Connecticut; numerous Midwestern glasshouses; at least one New Jersey glasshouse; and several other New England glassworks.

The Pitkin-type flasks and ink bottles are relatively common, whereas bottles, jugs, and jars are extremely rare. Also, it must be noted that the half-post method of blowing glass which was used for the Pitkin-type bottles originated in Germany, and Pitkin-type flasks from that area have shown up in the United States. As to attribution of Pitkin items, the New England Pitkins are more apt to have 32 or 36 ribs and are generally of a dark or olive green shading, along with having the elongated type of form; the Midwestern Pitkins are generally found in a wide range of colors and rib count, and are usually more oval shaped. The German Pitkin flasks are usually of a heavier straight ribbed variety, as opposed to the swirled or broken ribbed pattern which is generally found in the American items; they are often found in unusual colors such as dark blue.

The collector should be aware that there are a few reproduction Pitkins on the market, the most common one being a swirl ribbed variety which has mold seams on the side of the bottle; on genuine Pitkins, there would never be mold seams evident. Interested collectors should read *American Bottles and Flasks and Their Ancestry* by McKearin and Wilson for a much greater detailing of Pitkin-type products.

Pitkin Bottle, 36 swirled ribs, three sided, flaring lip, $4^7/8$", olive amber . . . . . . \$3000+

Pitkin Flask, 20 swirled ribs, clear, OP, probably Germany late 18th century, 5" . . . . \$150–\$250

Pitkin Flask, 24 swirled ribs, OP, $6^1/8$", light sea green . . . . \$325–\$400

Pitkin Flask, 24 vertical ribs, clear, OP, $4^5/8$" . . . . \$300–\$400

Pitkin Flask, 24 vertical ribs, OP, $5^1/2$", cobalt blue . . . . \$1000–\$1500

Pitkin Flask, 24 vertical ribs, OP, 5", cobalt . . . . \$1000–\$1500

Pitkin Flask, 28 swirled ribs, OP, $7^1/8$", bright yellowish green . . . . \$350–\$425

Pitkin Flask, 30-rib broken swirl, OP, $6^1/2$", bluish green. . . . . \$150–\$200

Pitkin Flask, 32-rib broken swirl, OP, $6^5/8$", light green . . . . \$250–\$300

Pitkin Flask, 32-rib broken swirl, OP, $6^1/4$", medium olive green . . . . \$275–\$350

Pitkin Flask, 32-rib broken swirl, OP, $6^3/4$", bluish green. . . . . \$150–\$250

Pitkin Flask, 32-rib broken swirl, OP, $6^7/8$", bluish green. . . . . \$250–\$325

Pitkin Flask, 32-rib broken swirl, OP, strong impression, $6^5/8$", medium green. . . . . \$275–\$400

Pitkin Flask, 32-rib broken swirl, weak impression, $6^1/2$", root beer amber . . . . \$300–\$375

Pitkin Flask, 36 rib broken swirl, OP, $6^1/2$", yellowish olive . . . . \$250–\$350

Pitkin Flask, 36 rib broken swirl, OP, olive tone, $6^3/4$", yellow . . . . \$325–\$425

Pitkin Flask, 36 swirled ribs, $3/8$" body bruise, OP, $4^3/4$", light yellow olive . . . . \$200–\$275

Pitkin Flask, 36 swirled ribs, OP, $5^3/4$", forest green. . . . . \$400–\$650

Pitkin Flask, 36 vertical ribs (rare), OP, $5^1/4$", olive green . . . . \$600–\$800

Pitkin Flask, 36-rib broken swirl, miniature, OP, $3^1/4$", olive green . . . . . \$2000–\$3000

Pitkin Flask, 36-rib broken swirl, OP, $4^7/8$", yellow olive. . . . . \$240–\$300

Pitkin Flask, 36-rib broken swirl, OP, $4^7/8$", yellowish olive . . . . \$275–\$375

Pitkin Flask, 36-rib broken swirl, OP, $5^1/4$", olive green. . . . . \$250–\$350

Pitkin Flask, 36-rib broken swirl, OP, $5^1/4$", yellowish olive . . . . \$240–\$300

Pitkin Flask, 36-rib broken swirl, OP, $5^1/4$", yellowish olive . . . . \$250–\$350

Pitkin Flask, 36-rib broken swirl, OP, $5^1/8$", medium olive green . . . . \$275–\$375

Midwestern Pitkin; note rounded body characteristic of Midwest Pitkins. PHOTO COURTESY OF GLASS WORKS AUCTIONS.

Pitkin Flask, 36-rib broken swirl, OP, 5³/₄", golden amber. . . . . $375–$450
Pitkin Flask, 36-rib broken swirl, OP, 5³/₄", sea green . . . . $350–$400
Pitkin Flask, 36-rib broken swirl, OP, 5³/₈", deep forest green. . . . . $400–$475
Pitkin Flask, 36-rib broken swirl, OP, 5⁵/₈", forest green . . . . $400–$475
Pitkin Flask, 36-rib broken swirl, OP, 5⁷/₈", deep golden amber . . . . $375–$475
Pitkin Flask, 36-rib broken swirl, OP, inner milky stain, 5¹/₂", greenish aqua . . . .
. . . . $150–$200
Pitkin Flask, 36-rib broken swirl, OP, shoulder bruise, 6¹/₂", yellow olive . . . .
. . . . $225–$275
Pitkin Flask, miniature, approx. 3", olive amber. . . . . $2000–$3000
Pitkin Ink, 36 swirled ribs, 2¹/₈" (w), olive amber . . . . $375–$500
Pitkin Ink, 36 swirled ribs, round, 1¹/₂" (h) x 2¹/₄", OP, deep yellowish olive . . . .
. . . . $500–$725
Pitkin Ink, 36 swirled ribs, round, OP, 2¹/₄", olive green . . . . $375–$500
Pitkin Ink, 36 swirled ribs, square (rare), OP, 2", olive green . . . . $800–$1100
Pitkin Jar, (ext. rare), wide mouth, OP, 5³/₄", olive green . . . . $5000+

Pitkin Note: For more ink prices please refer to Ink Bottles section.

POISON BOTTLES

Poisons of various sorts have been used for thousands of years. The first poison
bottles used in America may have been flasks blown in the half-post method
and pattern molded in a diamond or hobnail pattern.

Because there has always been a need to identify poison containers as such,
many of the poison containers from the 19th century clearly had "poison"
embossed on the bottle. It soon became evident, however, that it was necessary
to have a distinctive form of bottle, one with which someone who could not
read or who inadvertently grabbed the bottle at night would know that it was of
a toxic nature. Thus, a wide variety of bottle shapes were employed for poison,
such as skulls, coffins, bottles with a diamond- or lattice-type pattern, and
multisided bottles with very prominent vertical or horizontal ribbing. Also, it
was first felt that dark colors such as blues and browns were more identifiable,
but at some point in the 1930s it was determined that the strange shapes and
colors might actually be attracting the attention of children, and that more
attention should be given to finding safer closures on bottles.

When handling poison bottles extreme caution must be used, since it is quite
common to find poison bottles complete with original contents. When purchasing poison bottles, try to determine if the original poison bottle came with

a ground glass stopper, which can easily be determined by looking for a frosted area on the inside of the neck where the stopper was ground to form an airtight seal. If the glass stopper is missing, it can have a dramatic effect on the value of the bottle. Also, be on the lookout for unusual-size poison bottles and any of the unusual figurals such as the skull, leg bone, or coffin. The reader is referred to *Collectors Guide to Poison Bottles* by Roger Durflinger.

16 N Oz, KS-1, square, vertical ribs, stopper, 6³/₄", cobalt . . . . $60–$75
Caution—Not to be Taken, Patent, KT-3, three sided, vertical ribs, 6³/₄", medium emerald green . . . . $400–$600
Coffin Shape, KU-18, diamond pattern, vertical "Poison," 3¹/₂", medium amber . . . . .
. . . . $200–$250

Left: *Coffin shaped poison.* PHOTO COURTESY OF GLASS WORKS AUCTIONS.

Coffin Shape, KU-18, diamond pattern, vertical "Poison," 5", medium amber . . . .
. . . . $400–$600
Coffin Shape, KU-18, diamond pattern, vertical "Poison," 3¹/₂", amber . . . $175–$250
Coffin Shape, KU-18, diamond pattern, vertical "Poison," 3¹/₂", cornflower blue . . . . .
. . . . $100–$135
Coffin Shape, KU-18, diamond pattern, vertical "Poison," 3¹/₂", sapphire . . . $90–$110
Coffin Shape, KU-18, diamond pattern, vertical "Poison," ABM, 3¹/₂", cobalt . . . .
. . . . $50–$65
Coffin Shape, KU-18, diamond shape, vertical "Poison," full label, 3¹/₂", cobalt . . . . .
. . . . $75–$100
Coffin Shape, skull and crossbones on face, "Poison" on sides, 3", cobalt. . . . .
. . . . $800–$1200
Cylinder, KC-4, "Poison," with star above skull/crossbones, stars below, ABM, label, 2", cobalt. . . . . $175–$250
Cylinder, KC-49, wood closure, label, 2¹/₄", cobalt . . . . $60–$85
Doctor Oreste Sinanide's Medicinal Preparations Orestorine, coffin shaped, stopper, 4", cobalt. . . . . $200–$300

Dose Measuring Bottle, clear, 2 ounce, 4⁵/₈" . . . . $50–$75
Dual Sided Front, "Poison" both front panels, one sided back, KV-1, ABM, 2¹/₄",
amber. . . . . $10–$15
Dual Sided Front, "Poison" both front panels, one sided back, KV-1, ABM, full label,
3¹/₂", amber. . . . . $10–$15
Dual Sided Front, "Poison" both front panels, one sided back, KV-1, ABM, full label,
4⁷/₈", amber. . . . . $10–$20
Dual Sided Front, with "Poison" on one side, reverse one sided, oval, KD-1, 2⁵/₈",
amber. . . . . $20–$30
Dual Sided Front, with "Poison" on one side, reverse one sided, oval, KD-1, 3⁵/₈",
amber. . . . . $25–$35
Dykema's, KI-2, 6³/₈", yellowish green. . . . . $300–$400
Dykema's, KI-2, 7⁵/₈", yellowish green. . . . . $500–$750
FA Thompson & Co Detroit Poison, KU-4, coffin, 3", medium amber . . $800–$1200
Football Shaped, "Poison," KU-6, Reg No 336907 (base), 3" l., cobalt . . . $325–$425
Football Shaped, "Poison," KU-6, Reg No 336907 (base), lip repair, 4", cobalt. . . . . .
. . . . $150–$200
For External Use Only Prescription Reese Chem Co, KR-38, ABM, 5¹/₂", cobalt. . .
. . . . $35–$50
Friedgen, KI-2, 4", yellowish green. . . . . $675–$900
Hastings, 434 Slater Bldg, Worcester, Mass, rect., 5⁵/₈", yellowish green . . . .
. . . . $350–$450
Hexagonal, "Not to be Taken" on one panel, other panels ribbed, 4¹/₂", cobalt . . . .
. . . . $15–$25
Hexagonal, "Not to be Taken" on one panel, other panels ribbed, 5", green . . . .
. . . . $30–$35
Hexagonal, "PO/IS/ON" over three panels, upward arrow, KH-1, 4³/₈", cobalt . . . .
. . . . $15–$25
Hexagonal, "PO/IS/ON" over three panels, upward arrow, KH-1, 5¹/₂", cobalt . . . .
. . . . $15–$25
Hexagonal, "PO/IS/ON" over three panels, upward arrow, KH-1, 8", cobalt. . . . .
. . . . $30–$35
Hexagonal, "PO/IS/ON" over three panels, upward arrow, KH-1, 9⁷/₈", cobalt . . . .
. . . . $30–$40
Hexagonal, "PO/IS/ON" over three panels, upward arrow, KH-1, stopper, 5¹/₂", cobalt
. . . . $25–$40
HK Mulford Co Chemists Philadelphia, skull and crossed bones, 3¹/₄", cobalt
. . . . $75–$125
JF Hartz Co Limited Toronto, KS-15, heart, designs, 7³/₄", cobalt . . . . . . $250–$375
Kilner Bros Makers Poison, KC-16, vertical ribs, 6⁷/₈". . . . . $30–$40
Lattice, diamond pattern, KC-1, 13⁵/₈", cobalt . . . . $1250–$1550
Lattice, diamond pattern, KC-1, major crack, chip, 13⁵/₈", cobalt. . . . . $100–$150
Lattice, diamond pattern, KC-1, with stopper, 3³/₄", cobalt. . . . . $80–$100
Lattice, diamond pattern, KC-1, with stopper, 4⁵/₈", cobalt. . . . . $80–$100
Lattice, diamond pattern, KC-1, with stopper, 5¹/₂", cobalt. . . . . $125–$165
Lattice, diamond pattern, KT-1, HB & CO (on base), with stopper, 5⁵/₈", cobalt. . . . . .
. . . . $75–$100
Lattice, diamond pattern, KT-1, USPHS (on base), with stopper, 5¹/₈", cobalt. . . . . . .
. . . . $75–$100
Lattice, diamond pattern, KT-1, with stopper, 3³/₄", cobalt. . . . . $60–$80
Lattice, diamond pattern, KT-1, with stopper, 3³/₈", cobalt. . . . . $60–$80

Lattice, diamond patterned poison with stopper. PHOTO
COURTESY OF GLASS WORKS AUCTIONS.

Lattice, diamond pattern, KT-1, with stopper, 4³/₄", cobalt. . . . . $75–$100
Lattice, diamond pattern, KT-1, with stopper, 7¹/₈", cobalt. . . . . $75–$100
Lattice, diamond pattern, KT-1, with stopper, 7", cobalt . . . . $75–$100
Lattice, diamond pattern, KT-1, WT Co (on base), with stopper, 4¹/₂", cobalt. . . . .
. . . . $75–$100
Lattice, diamond pattern, KT-1, WT CO (on base), with stopper, 5¹/₂", cobalt . . . .
. . . . $75–$100
Lattice, diamond pattern, with stopper, KC-1, 7", cobalt . . . . $250–$300
McCormick & Co Balto (in circle around bee), KT-14, three sided, ABM, 2¹/₄",
cobalt. . . . . $15–$25
Melvin & Badger, on center panel of tri-paneled wide front with two outside panels
with horizontal ribbing, 5", cobalt . . . . $100–$165
Munyon's Germicide Solution, label, 3¹/₄", yellowish olive green . . . . $45–$65
Norwich (on base), coffin, diamond patterned body, 4⁷/₈", medium amber . . . .
. . . . $500–$650
Not to be Taken, KI-12, tri-sided front, flat back, 8 ounce, 7", cobalt . . . . . . $15–$20
Oval Shaped, "Poison" with band of stars running vertically, ABM, 2³/₄", cobalt. . . . .
. . . . $15–$25
Oval Shaped, "Poison," five pointed star above skull, crossed bones, 4⁵/₈", amber . . . .
. . . . $500–$600
Oval Shaped, Sharpe & Dome Baltimore Md (on base), 3", root beer amber . . . .
. . . . $40–$55
Oval Shaped, vertical ribs and squares pattern on one side, 8", cobalt . . . . . . $20–$30
Owl Drug Co, "Poison" (owl, mortar and pestle), three sided, KT-1, label, 9¹/₂", cobalt
. . . . $400–$550
Owl Drug Co, "Poison" (owl, mortar and pestle), three sided, label, KT-1, 5⁷/₈", cobalt
. . . . $120–$150
Owl Drug Co, "Poison" (owl, mortar and pestle), three-sided, KT-1, 2³/₄", cobalt . . . .
. . . . $40–$65
Owl Drug Co, "Poison" (owl, mortar and pestle), three-sided, KT-1, 3¹/₄", cobalt . . . .
. . . . $50–$75
Owl Drug Co, "Poison" (owl, mortar and pestle), three-sided, KT-1, 4¹/₂", cobalt . . . .
. . . . $50–$70

Owl Drug Co, "Poison" (owl, mortar and pestle), three-sided, KT-1, 4³/₄", cobalt . . . .
. . . . $60–$85
Owl Drug Co, "Poison" (owl, mortar and pestle), three-sided, KT-1, label, 3¹/₂", cobalt
. . . . $60–$80
Owl Drug Co, "Poison" (owl, mortar and pestle), three-sided, KT-1, label, 4¹/₈", cobalt
. . . . $70–$90
Owl Drug Co, "Poison" (owl, mortar and pestle), three-sided, KT-1, label, 5¹/₄", cobalt
. . . . $100–$145
Owl Drug Co, "Poison" (owl, mortar, and pestle), three-sided, KT-1, label, 7⁷/₈", cobalt
. . . . $100–$145
Poison Tinct Iodine, KR-3, rect., skull and crossed bones, 2³/₈", cobalt . . . . . $60–$90
Poison Tinct Iodine, KR-3, rect., skull and crossed bones, 3¹/₈", cobalt . . . . $90–$135
Poison Tinct Iodine, KR-3, rect., skull and crossed bones, ABM, 3", cobalt. . . . $5–$7
Poison Tinct Iodine, KR-3, rect., skull and crossed bones, ABM, 2¹/₂", amber. . . . . . .
. . . . $5–$7
Poison Tinct Iodine, KR-3, rect., skull and crossed bones, ABM, 3¹/₄", amber. . . . . . .
. . . . $5–$10
Rectangular, "Poison," two sided panels, label, KR-9, 5³/₄", yellow amber . . . .
. . . . $80–$120
Rectangular, KR-43, 2 ounce, vertical ribs one side, ABM, 2¹/₄", cobalt. . . . . . $5–$7
Rectangular, KR-43, 4 ounce, vertical ribs one side, ABM, 3", cobalt . . . . $5–$7
Rectangular, KR-50, vertical "Poison," amber tone, 4³/₄", yellow. . . . . . . $200–$300
Rectangular, KR-7, skull and crossbones on front, amber tone, 2⁵/₈", yellow . . . .
. . . . $90–$120
Rectangular, KR-9, "Poison," two sided panels, 7⁷/₈" . . . . $600–$900
Rectangular, KR-9, "Poison," two sided panels, 8", medium amber . . . . . . $100–$130
Rectangular, KR-9, "Poison," two sided panels, diamond edges, 7⁷/₈", yellow amber .
. . . . $250–$325
Rectangular, KR-9, "Poison," two sided panels, label, 5¹/₂", medium amber . . . .
. . . . $60–$75
Sharp & Dohme, Baltimore, Md (on side panels), round, unpatterned back, KV-6,
ABM, 2³/₈", cobalt . . . . $20–$30
Skeleton Figural in Cloak, ceramic, 5³/₄". . . . . $90–$125
Skull Figural, "Poison-Pat Appl'd For," ¹/₂" lip chip, 3¹/₂", cobalt. . . . . $500–$750
Skull Figural, "Poison-Pat Appl'd For," 2³/₄", cobalt . . . . $1400–$1900
Skull Figural, "Poison-Pat Appl'd For," ²/₃ of lip is gone, 4¹/₄", cobalt . . . . $300–$375

Poison, skull, cobalt blue. PHOTO COURTESY OF
SKINNER'S, INC.

Skull Figural, "Poison-Pat Appl'd For," 3¹/₂", cobalt . . . . $1400–$1900
Skull Figural, "Poison-Pat Appl'd For," 4¹/₈", cobalt . . . . $1200–$1500
Skull Figural, "Poison-Pat Appl'd For," lip chip, hole in nose, 2³/₄", cobalt . . . .
. . . . $350–$450
Skull Figural, "Poison-Pat Appl'd For," minor surface cracks, 4¹/₈", cobalt . . . .
. . . . $850–$1150
Skull Figural, ceramic, 1972 bottle show promotional, 3⁷/₈" . . . . $50–$65
Square, "Poison" and vertical lines on two sides, KS-2, 3³/₈", amber . . . . . . $75–$100
Square, ABM, "Poison" and vertical lines on two sides, KS-2, 3³/₈", cobalt . . $40–$55
Square, clear, "Poison" and vertical lines on two sides, KS-2, 3³/₈" . . . . $110–$135
Square, KS-2, "Poison" and vertical lines on two sides, 3³/₈", yellow amber . . . .
. . . . $110–$135
Square, KS-2, "poison" on sides with horizontal lines, 7³/₄", olive green . . . .
. . . . $1600–$2400
Square, KS-5, "Poison" on sides with diamond point edges, 6⁷/₈", amber . . . .
. . . . $1500–$2000
Square, KS-8, "Poison" and vertical lines on two sides, 2⁵/₈", cobalt . . . . $90–$115
Strychnia Poison, clear, 2³/₈" . . . . $125–$175
Submarine Shaped, "Poison" with horizontal lines, 2³/₈" (h), blue . . . . $600–$900
Sun Drug Co., KI-1, 2³/₄", yellowish green . . . . $125–$185
Three Sided, KT-10, Poison on one side, diamond edges, ABM, 3³/₄", cobalt . . . .
. . . . $20–$30
Three Sided, KT-3, "Poison" on one side, label, 5¹/₈", amber . . . . $450–$575
Three Sided, KT-5, "Poison" on one side, 5", reddish amber . . . . $500–$750
Three Sided, KT-5, "Poison" on one side, labeled, 3", amber . . . . $125–$150
Three Sided, rounded back, "Poison" on two front sides, KV-2, 10", orange amber . . .
. . . . $90–$120

Tri-paneled poison. PHOTO COURTESY OF GLASS WORKS AUCTIONS.

Tri-Paneled Front, two narrow panels with "Poison," wide center panel has star, skull and crossbones, star, reverse plain, ABM, 3¹/₈", cobalt . . . . $70–$90
Tri-Paneled Wide Front, horizontal ribbing, "Poison" on two panels, back plain, KI-1, 5¹/₂", yellow green . . . . $125–$175

Tri-Paneled Wide Front, horizontal ribbing, "Poison" on two panels, back plain, KI-1, 5", cobalt. . . . . $75–$125
Tri-Paneled Wide Front, horizontal ribbing, "Poison" on two panels, back plain, KI-1, 6$^1/_4$", cobalt. . . . . $90–$140
Tri-Paneled Wide Front, horizontal ribbing, "Poison" on two panels, back plain, KI-1, 7$^1/_2$", cobalt. . . . . $125–$175
Tri-Paneled Wide Front, horizontal ribs, "Poison," narrow sides, unpatterned back, KI-3, 2$^1/_2$", yellowish amber. . . . . $100–$175
Tri-Paneled Wide Front, horizontal ribs, "Poison," narrow sides, unpatterned back, KI-3, 3", yellowish amber. . . . . $125–$250
Tri-Paneled Wide Front, horizontal ribs, KI-2, narrow sides, unpatterned back, 5", cobalt. . . . . $150–$200
Tri-Paneled Wide Front, horizontal ribs, KI-2, narrow sides, unpatterned back, 5", turquoise blue . . . . $300–$400
Triloids / Poison, KT-9, three sided, ABM, 3$^1/_4$", cobalt . . . . $10–$20
Vapo Cresolene Co US Pat June 18th 1895, KS-14, 5$^1/_4$", medium cobalt . . . . $120–$150

POTTERY BOTTLES

Pottery bottles often are found in figural form and were popular in the 18th and 19th centuries. Collectors should be on the lookout for specific potters' marks such as those used in the Bennington Potteries in the 19th century, as well as the Anna Pottery of Anna, Illinois. The latter produced, among other items, the so-called Railroad Pig Bottles which have a railroad map incised in blue over the body of the pig. The reader is referred to *Decorated Stoneware Pottery of North America* by Donald Blake Webster.

Book, glaze, 4$^7/_8$", blue. . . . . $225–$275
Book, mottled glaze, corner edge chip, 8", brown and white. . . . . $100–$125
Coachman, mottled glaze, lip and boot tips repaired, Bennington mark on base, 10$^3/_4$", tan and brown . . . . $200–$250
Coachman, mottled glaze, lip repairs, unmarked, 10$^5/_8$", tan and brown . . . $100–$125
Coachman, mottled glaze, lip repairs, unmarked, 10$^5/_8$", tan and brown . . . $100–$125
Coachman, mottled glaze, unmarked, 9$^1/_4$", tan and brown . . . . $150–$200
Coachman, mottled glaze, unmarked, 9$^1/_4$", tan and brown . . . . $150–$200
Cylinder, blob lip, unembossed, 10" . . . . $8–$12
Cylinder, blob lip, unembossed, 10", blue. . . . . $30–$45
Cylinder, blob lip, various name on shoulder, 10", blue . . . . $50–$100
GA Potter, cylindrical, cobalt dots on shoulder, 9$^3/_8$", gray . . . . $140–$180
Queen With Crown, Fulton & Water 16 High St Lambeth, glazes, 9", tan and light brown . . . . $350–$450

Two early stoneware bottles. PHOTO COURTESY OF GLASS WORKS AUCTIONS.

Pottery, Bennington-type book. PHOTO COURTESY OF NEIL GROSSMAN.

Sided, 12 sides, unembossed . . . . $25–$35
Woman Holding Florals, BF & Co New York (near base), glaze, neck reglued, 10",
tan and green. . . . . $225–$275

PRESSED GLASS

Pressed glass is a complicated area of collecting, what with the hundreds of patterns and numerous reproductions and re-issuances over the years. This section

Left: *Early candlestick with arrow pointing to the "wafer," which is a blob of glass used to connect two pieces of pressed glass. Note that a mold seam will never run through a wafer. If a mold seam is evident within the wafer, then it is not an applied wafer but rather a molded wafer.* Right: *Another example of a wafer. Note that wafers were also used on early lamps, compotes, goblets, etc.* PHOTO COURTESY OF LYNDA MAGDITS.

is in no way intended to even remotely address this major collecting category, but hopes to give a few brief hints on things to look for with certain types of pressed glass, since pressed glass is something a bottle collector is certain to encounter at yard sales, flea markets, maybe even bottle shows. There are numerous excellent pressed glass references and price guides out there, and they are listed in the bibliography. Most of what will be covered on these few pages concerns the "wafer" and how it is often an easy way to identify a pre-Civil War piece of pressed glass. Other identification techniques will also be discussed.

Pressed glass was first made in America around 1820, and because of the complicated forms envisioned by early glass designers, pieces sometimes had to be made in several parts and then connected through the use of a hot blob of glass called a wafer. This technique had already been used on blown glass for thousands of years. Wafers were generally used on American pressed glass from the 1820s until about 1860, when full-sized one-piece molds became more prevalent. Thus, any pressed piece that has a wafer can usually be indicative of pre-Civil War manufacture.

One must be careful to make sure that a wafer is an applied wafer, which is an indication of an early piece, as opposed to a molded wafer, which was used through the 19th and into the 20th century. The easiest way to tell what type of wafer you are dealing with is to see whether a mold seam runs through the wafer. Since the pressed pieces which the wafer is holding together were made in molds, mold seams will be evident on the pressed portions, but on an applied wafer, the seams will not continue into the wafer.

Some points to remember about wafers and about pressed glass in general are:

- Applied wafers usually indicate pre-Civil War manufacture.
- Just because a piece has a molded wafer does not mean that it is new. The New England Glass Company, for example, did a quantity of pressed pieces in the 1840s and 1850s and employed molded wafers. Molded wafers are not being covered here because it is a complicated area with numerous reproductions.
- Just because a piece has an applied wafer does not mean it is valuable; use them merely as a tool to help date pieces.
- As in bottles and blown glass, color and condition are almost always the driving forces in determining the value of pressed glass; simply having a wafer means little.
- Wafers were also used by English and European pressed glass manufacturers.
- Wafers have been found on a few reproduction pieces. If you suspect a piece might be new, use the check points in this section to determine age and proceed with caution.
- Wafers were also used on candlesticks, compotes, vases, and to attach a blown font onto a pressed base on early lamps.
- Pre-Civil War American pressed glass is usually made of lead glass. Special types of black lights can be used to determine whether a piece is lead or non-lead. Some people "ring" the glass by gently tapping the edge with a finger, and if it rings, it is usually lead. Just because a piece is lead does not mean that it is early; lead pressed glass continues to be made today. You may want to become acquainted with the early (pre-1860) patterns, such as New England Pineapple, Horn of Plenty, Bulls Eye and Fleur de Lis, Ashburton, etc., all of which were ordinarily made of lead glass; later reproductions were non lead. Keep in mind that a large number of 1870s and later patterns were made of non-lead glass.
- Pre-Civil War American pieces often have polished pontils, although polished pontils are also found on 20th century pieces, including some 20th century reproductions of 19th century forms. A lot of early pressed glass did not have polished pontils, so don't "live or die" by the pontil. There are a lot of great early pieces that were not pontiled. Beware of a fake polished pontil that is out there. It's not really a polished pontil but rather a circular indentation about the size of a quarter on the base of some reproduction early patterned pieces. Just recently I found a set of four Horn of Plenty tumblers with this fake "pontil" at a local group shop.

- Pre-Civil War American pieces were often "fire polished," which means that after the piece was pressed it was reheated in the glory hole to smooth down the edges a bit. If you were to have an 1850s goblet next to a 20th century reproduction of the same pattern, it will often be obvious which is the old piece because of the smoothness of the pattern. Note that a lot of early pressed glass was not fire polished, however.
- Be suspicious if you find a set of four, six or eight pieces of an early pattern. It is hard enough to find a single old piece, but finding a set should make you suspicious that you have a 20th century grouping. Yes, old sets do show up, but be careful of all the new stuff that is out there.
- Some modern pressed pieces are marked. A few months ago I found a set of four Magnet and Grape water goblets that just didn't look right. They didn't have the wear they should have had, and they were too "clean" and absent of impurities. On the bottom of the bowl were the initials "MMA," indicating a Metropolitan Museum of Art reproduction. Watch out for 20th century reproduction pieces that have had the MMA or other signature ground off!
- Keep in mind that the original 19th-century pressed molds are sometimes used to re-make a pattern in the 20th century. The pieces might appear identical to the original, so look for lead content, wear on the bottom and top edges, polished pontil, ring, fire polishing, and the gray or blue cast that often is found on early glass, with reproductions often being much more "clear."

REPRODUCTION BOTTLES

Though many bottle collectors shudder when they hear the word reproduction, the collecting of reproduction bottles is attracting more and more people every year. Most interest in reproduction bottles centers around the products made by the Clevenger Glass Works of New Jersey, whose operations began in the 1930's, as well as the handcrafts of Emil Larsen, who operated around the same time period. Interested readers should review the chapter titled "Fakes, Reproductions, and Repairs" to become more comfortable with some of the signs of the reproduction pieces. The reader is referred to *American Bottles and Flasks and Their Ancestry* by McKearin and Wilson, pgs. 678–708.

Three whiskey bottles with glass seals. All three are in forms which one might actually see a genuinely old bottle in. The giveaway that these are late 20th century are unusual colors not found on 17th- and 18th-century bottles, the lack of open pontil marks, and the lack of wear, with extreme "shininess" and new look of the glass. PHOTO COURTESY OF LYNDA MAGDITS.

Three handled whiskey jugs, with the first and third very similar to original forms of early bottles. The center bottle is a fantasy item. When trying to detect good reproductions such as the first bottle on the left, remember to look for lack of wear, possibly a signature or registry number showing that the bottle was made in a limited series. Also check for weight, since reproduction bottles are usually heavier in weight than the genuine article (although lots of early bottles are heavy in weight!). PHOTO COURTESY OF LYNDA MAGDITS.

These two EG Booz cabins are 20th century. The one on the left has beveled edges which extend below the first row of shingles, whereas on the real ones, the bevel stays within the top row. The one on the right is much more difficult to tell and you are referred to American Bottles and Flasks and Their Ancestry *for detail.* PHOTO COURTESY OF LYNDA MAGDITS.

Here is a nice series of modern old-looking utility bottles. The four sided miniature at far left is one of the best reproductions I've ever seen. Remember that small and miniature bottles usually do not exhibit much wear; the heavier the bottle, the more wear. The glass is just too shiny and slippery feeling and with a total lack of wear. The next bottle is in a form which just does not seem right. It is unusual to see a flaring lip on a free-blown globular bottle, and again, the glass "feel" is not right, with no wear. The pickle is an oddball piece, with the wide mouth simply not found on the real McCoy. The seal bottle is a fantastic reproduction, but does not have a pontiled base. See how the lower side of the bottle bows out a bit? That is ordinarily the sign of a late 18-century piece, but this one again does not show the indicia of age. The case bottle is another great reproduction, and could be tough for a lot of people to spot as a fake. Check for signs of wear. PHOTO COURTESY OF LYNDA MAGDITS.

These three figurals should be fairly easy to spot as fakes. The Indian Queen has a headdress stopper; the real thing never came with a stopper. The bottle on the right has a passing resemblance to the Simon's Centennial Bitters, but the color (in this case blue), flattened lip, whittled nature of the glass, very weak embossing, and a pontil scar (real ones had smooth bases) show this to be new. PHOTO COURTESY OF LYNDA MAGDITS.

Fruit jar reproductions can be very hard to differentiate from the old ones, since they may have used original molds. There are often certain numbers on the bases of the reproductions which are a clue, and the weight is sometimes wrong, with fakes much heavier than the real thing. Again check for wear, and consider buying a copy of the Red Book of Fruit Jars *which goes into more detail on which jars were reproduced.* PHOTO COURTESY OF LYNDA MAGDITS.

Four flask forms. Left to right, the first is a fantasy bottle. The next calabash is a Jenny Lind, and these can be very difficult to differentiate from the real thing. You should read the information in the back of American Bottles and Flasks and Their Ancestry *by McKearin and Wilson for more information on this and many other reproduced flasks. The next flask is a Pike's Peak, but in amberina, which the genuine flask was not made in, and with a bottle club logo on the reverse side. The last flask is a Sunburst, and a very good copy, except the weight is light, with the originals generally heavier and showing more wear.* PHOTO COURTESY OF LYNDA MAGDITS.

Five flasks. Left to right, the first is a Cornucopia-Urn, which is a good copy but has a smooth base and no wear. The Scroll flask is a very good copy, and is pontiled. I recently saw one at a major bottle show on a dealers table listed as "extremely rare color" with a high price to boot. Next is another Cornucopia, and check for wear, pontil mark, and color, this color being a weird shade of blue green. Next is an Eagle/Flag, a very good copy. Watch for pitted surface of glass, almost a grainy texture, since some of these have been blown into plaster molds. The final flask is a fantasy piece, since no Abraham Lincoln flasks were made way back when. PHOTO COURTESY OF LYNDA MAGDITS.

*Five flasks, and some very good copies here. They are, left to right, a
Masonic/Eagle; Success to the Railroad, on the reproduction (the horse's
mane on the fake stands straight out, like he is being electrocuted); a
Columbia/Eagle (check for wear and possibly a registration number
scratched or molded into the bottom due to a limited edition); an
Eagle/Grapes (slightly different from the original, and note the stovepipe-
looking neck and lip, which is unusual to find on an old bottle); and
finally the Concentric Ring Eagle (a fantastic copy with a molded base
number, although some have it scratched in or polished out).* PHOTO
COURTESY OF LYNDA MAGDITS.

*Left to right: A Brookfield baby-face milk bottle in cobalt blue (also made in
pink, green, etc); a Borden's milk bottle in cobalt; a blown three-mold flip
glass in honey amber (we should be so lucky to find a real one in this color!!)
with MMA (Metropolitan Museum of Art) molded into the bottom, although
some museum copies have MMA or M scratched into the base, and some have
nothing on the bottom, so look for wear and signs of age!!; a marked MMA
three-mold decanter, and a very good copy.* PHOTO COURTESY OF LYNDA
MAGDITS.

Two Moses Poland Spring bottles—one is real, one isn't. The one on the right with the sloping collar is real, the weird looking tooled lip on left with mold seam running through it is new. PHOTO COURTESY OF LYNDA MAGDITS.

Four whiskey decanters from the 1960s/1970s. Note the glass and cork stoppers. These four can be called "fantasy" flasks, since they are not actually reproductions of an early bottle but rather stylized examples of such. PHOTO COURTESY OF LYNDA MAGDITS.

Five milk glass flasks, all of which are fantasy except for the middle, the Eagle/Flag. This flask was actually made in milk glass, but this example has a strange looking straight neck, no wear. PHOTO COURTESY OF LYNDA MAGDITS.

Four fantasy bottles which can be bought in many gift and florist shops today. Usually found in blue, although they might be found in other colors too. PHOTO COURTESY OF LYNDA MAGDITS.

Four clear reproductions. The three blown three-mold decanters can be determined to be fakes by the appearance of MMA or other base insignia; smooth bases as opposed to open pontil; no wear; being heavier in weight than the originals; having glass that is simply too "clear"; and without the gray or blue or green tints you would expect to find in 1830s glass. The enameled bottle is heavier in weight than the originals, shows no wear, shows very brilliant clear glass with no tints or imperfections you would expect to see on 18th-century glass, and has a weird looking glass stopper instead of the pewter caps you will usually see, although some new enameled pieces do have pewter screw threads and caps. PHOTO COURTESY OF LYNDA MAGDITS.

Six fantasy flasks, with none except the Scroll-type looking anything in form like old flasks. The Scroll is a commemorative and has a bust on the side, which is not found on the real thing. PHOTO COURTESY OF LYNDA MAGDITS.

SARSAPARILLA BOTTLES

Sarsaparilla originally gained its popularity in the 17th century as a blood purifier, and for many years it was believed to be a cure for syphilis. In the United
States, interest in sarsaparilla began in the 1820's when the drink was being
advertised as helping with the "perspiratory functions of the skin and imparting
tone and vigor to debilitated constitutions." As the century went on, the
boasted curative powers of sarsaparilla were elevated to the point of quackery.
Doctor Townsend's sarsaparilla, one of the more popular brands among bottle
collectors, was touted as being a "wonder and blessing of the new age / the
most extraordinary medicine in the world." Generally, sarsaparilla bottles are
of aqua or green coloration, but a few rare examples in blues and other colors
exist. The reader is referred to *American Sarsaparilla Bottles* by John
DeGrafft.

Adams & Carroll Sole Agents, D-1, $9^5/_8$", aqua. . . . . $55–$75
AH Bull Extract of Sarsaparilla, D-28 . . . . $75–$110
AH Bull Extract of Sarsaparilla, D-28, OP, lip chip, 7", aqua . . . . $20–$30
Allen Sarsaparilla Co., D-7, $9^1/_2$", aqua . . . . $35–$50
Allen's Sarsaparilla, D-8, $8^1/_4$", aqua . . . . $20–$25
Ayer's Sarsaparilla, ABM . . . . $2–$4
Ayer's Sarsaparilla, BIMAL . . . . $6–$9
Bell's Sarsaparilla, AM Robinson, D-18, labels, $9^1/_4$", aqua . . . . $60–$85
BF William's Syrup of Sarsaparilla, D-223, IP, $9^1/_2$", aqua . . . . $900+
Bristol's Extract of Sarsaparilla, D-22, OP, $5^3/_4$" . . . . $65–$90
Bristol's Extract of Sarsaparilla, OP, $5^1/_2$", aqua . . . . $45–$60
Bristol's Genuine Sarsaparilla, D-23, 11", aqua . . . . $15–$18
Bristol's Genuine Sarsaparilla, IP, $10^1/_2$", aqua . . . . $250–$300
Bristol's Genuine, D-23, aqua. . . . . $40–$60
Bristol's Sarsaparilla, D-22-2, OP, $5^1/_2$", aqua. . . . . $40–$48
Bristol's Sarsaparilla, D-24, $9^1/_4$", aqua. . . . . $10–$14
Cantrell's Compound Medicated Syrup, OP, 6", aqua. . . . . $400–$500
CD Cos Sarsaparilla Resolvent, D-40, $8^1/_2$", amber . . . . $40–$48
Charles Joly Philadelphia, D-114, crown top, 10", amber. . . . . $15–$22
Charles Joly Philadelphia, D-114, stain, yellow . . . . $12–$16
Corwitz Sarsaparilla, D-47, $9^1/_2$", aqua . . . . $40–$49
Crowell, Crane & Brigham Yellow Dock, D-51, OP, $9^1/_4$", aqua. . . . . $125–$185
Dalton's Sarsaparilla & Nerve Tonic, $9^1/_2$". . . . . $15–$20
Dalton's Sarsaparilla & Nerve Tonic, in box, $9^1/_2$", aqua. . . . . $40–$60
DeWitt's Sarsaparilla, Chicago, D-61, 9", aqua . . . . $25–$30
Dr AP Sawyer's Eclipse Sarsaparilla, D-63, 9", aqua . . . . $40–$55
Dr AS Hopkin's Compound Ext, D-103, 9", aqua . . . . $55–$75
Dr Bailey's Elliot Bros & Co Brisbane, aqua . . . . $80–$125

Dr Blackwell's Sarsaparilla, D-21-1, IP, 9³/₄", aqua .... $150–$200
Dr BW Hair's Sarsaparilla, OP, 9⁵/₈", bluish aqua .... $400–$600
Dr Cronk's Sarsaparilla Beer, 12 sided pottery, D-50, 10", gray .... $80–$125
Dr Cronk's Sarsaparilla Beer, eight sided pottery, D-50-4, gray .... $120–$170
Dr Cumming's Compound Ext of Sarsa, D-52, OP, 7", aqua .... $125–$175
Dr Cumming's Compound Ext of Sarsa, D-53, 7¹/₂", aqua .... $60–$80
Dr Guysott's Compound Extract of Yellow Dock & Sarsaparilla, OP, 9¹/₂", med yellowish olive amber .... $1500–$2250
Dr Guysott's Compound Extract, D-90, OP, mint, 9¹/₂", olive amber ....
.... $950–$1400
Dr Guysott's Compound Extract, D-90, OP, shoulder crack, 9¹/₂", olive amber .....
.... $200–$300
Dr Guysott's Compound Extract, D-90-9, OP, 9³/₈", aqua............. $125–$175
Dr Guysott's Yellow Dock, IP, deep aqua .... $80–$110
Dr Guysott's, B & P New York, DE-90-6, rect., 8³/₄", aqua .... $90–$145
Dr Guysott's, D-90-1, aqua....................................... $60–$80
Dr Ira Baker's, D-11, aqua....................................... $75–$110
Dr Ira Baker's, D-11, clear...................................... $75–$95
Dr J Rose's Sarsaparilla, JDG-182, IP, 9³/₈", aqua .... $150–$250
Dr Jarman's, D-113, aqua....................................... $25–$40
Dr Mile's Wine of Sarsaparilla, D-151, 9", aqua .... $35–$45
Dr Morley's Sarsaparilla & 100 Potash, D-155, 9¹/₂", aqua............. $55–$85
Dr Myer's Vegetable Extract, D-158, OP, 9⁷/₈", aqua................ $150–$225
Dr Pope's Sarsaparilla (on label), D-PL-71, OP, 6¹/₂", aqua .... $25–$38
Dr Russell's Balsam of Horehound, D-185, OP, 9³/₈", aqua............ $125–$165
Dr Stocker's Sarsaparilla, OP, 9¹/₂", pale greenish aqua............... $325–$425
Dr Thompson's Sarsaparilla, D-204, 9", aqua .... $40–$55
Dr Townsends Sarsaparilla Albany NY, 9³/₈", yellowish green........ $100–$125
Dr Townsends Sarsaparilla Albany NY, OP, 9¹/₂", yellowish olive green.........
.... $175–$225

Sarsaparilla, Old. Dr. Townsend's. PHOTO COURTESY OF NEIL GROSSMAN.

Dr Townsends Sarsaparilla Albany NY, OP, 9³/₄", emerald green ...... $175–$220
Dr Townsends Sarsaparilla Albany NY, OP, 9³/₈", medium blue green ....
.... $250–$300
Dr Townsends Sarsaparilla Albany NY, open surface bubbles, SB, 9", deep yellow
olive... $100–$125
Dr Townsends Sarsaparilla Albany NY, SB, 9¹/₂", teal blue .... $275–$350
Dr Townsends Sarsaparilla Albany NY, SB, 9³/₈", yellow green........ $100–$145
Dr Townsends Sarsaparilla Albany NY, with hint of olive, SB, 9", yellow amber ...
.... $275–$375
Dr Townsends Sarsaparilla Albany NY, OP, 9³/₄", olive amber .... $155–$215
Dr Townsends Sarsaparilla Albany NY, OP, 9³/₄", yellowish olive amber ....
.... $150–$200
Dr Townsends Sarsaparilla Albany NY, OP, 9³/₄", yellowish olive green..........
.... $175–$225
Dr Townsends Sarsaparilla Albany NY, SB, 4¹/₂", pale bluish aqua ..... $110–$160
Dr Townsends Sarsaparilla Albany NY, SB, 9³/₈", yellow olive .... $100–$140
Dr Townsends Sarsaparilla Albany NY, scratches, 9¹/₄", teal blue ...... $175–$215
Dr Tutt's, New York, D-209-2, 7¹/₂", amber .... $60–$85
Dr Webster's Sarsaparilla Ithica, OP, 6¹/₂", bluish aqua .... $250–$350
Dr Wilcox's Compound Extract of Sarsaparilla, IP, backwards S, D-221, 9³/₈", deep
blue green .... $500–$800
Dr Winslow's Sarsaparilla, D-225, 8⁷/₈", aqua .... $55–$65
Dr Woodworth's, Birmingham, Ct, D-229, OP, 9³/₄", aqua............ $125–$165
Dr Wynkoop's Katharismic Honduras Sarsaparilla, D-232, OP, 10", sapphire ....
.... $1200–$1750
Edwin N Joy Co San Francisco, D-115, 8³/₄", aqua .... $30–$50
Emerson's 50¢ Sarsaparilla, D-66, 9¹/₂", aqua .... $35–$45
Foley's Sarsaparilla, D-72, 9", amber............................. $25–$35
Gold Metal Sarsaparilla Albany NY, D-81, 9", amber................. $50–$70
Gooch's Extract of Sarsaparilla, D-82, clear, labeled, 9¹/₄" .... $30–$35
Graefenberg Co Sarsaparilla Compound, D-84, OP, 7", aqua .... $75–$125
Griffith's Sarsaparilla, aqua...................................... $80–$120
Hall's Sarsaparilla, D-92-2, aqua.................................. $60–$85
Hall's Sarsaparilla, JR Gates & Co, D-92, 9", aqua.................... $35–$45
Hambolt's (on label), D-PL-38, OP, aqua............................ $40–$60
ID Bull's Extract of Sarsaparilla Hartford Con, OP, 6⁷/₈", aqua .... $150–$250
Indian Sarsaparilla, JJ Mack & Co, D-110, double collar, 9", aqua ..... $150–$225
J Calegaris Compound Extract, D-36, 7", aqua .... $60–$90
JJ Mack & Co Indian Sarsaparilla, 9¹/₄", aqua .... $300–$425
John Bull's Extract of Sarsaparilla, 8³/₄", aqua .... $20–$30
John Bull's Extract of Sarsaparilla, D-30, 8³/₄", light green .... $75–$110
John Bull's Extract of Sarsaparilla, D-30-9, IP, 9", cornflower blue..... $400–$600
Joy's Vegetable Sarsaparilla, D-115 variant, labeled, 8³/₄", amber......... $60–$95
JT Hawk's Masury's Sarsaparilla, D-142-2, 11¹/₄", aqua .... $150–$200
Kelley & Co Sarsaparilla, D-117, OP, 7³/₄", aqua.................... $70–$110
Kennedy's Sarsaparilla, D-119 variant, double collar, 9¹/₂", aqua .... $90–$145
Kennedy's Sarsaparilla, D-119, 9⁵/₈", amber....................... $40–$60
Kennedy's Sarsaparilla, D-119, labeled, 9⁵/₈"...................... $90–$135
Langley's, D-126-2, aqua... $150–$225
Langley's, D-126-2, green .... $400–$600
Leon's Sarsaparilla, D-128, 9", aqua .... $50–$70

Leving's & Co, D-129, 7³/₄", blue green . . . . $250–$375
Log Cabin Sarsaparilla Rochester NY, 8⁷/₈", amber . . . . $125–$175
Manner's Double Extract, D-140, 7³/₄", aqua . . . . $60–$85
Masury's Sarsaparilla Cathartic, 11³/₈", aqua . . . . $300–$350
Masury's Sarsaparilla Cathartic, OP, 6⁵/₈", aqua . . . . $350–$425
Masury's Sarsaparilla Cathartic, OP, 8¹/₄", aqua . . . . $150–$240
McLean's Sarsaparilla, D-148, 9¹/₄", light green . . . . $60–$90
Myer's Vegetable Extract, D-158, IP, 8¹/₈" . . . . $200–$300
Myer's Vegetable Extract, D-158, lip chip, 8¹/₈", aqua . . . . $75–$115
Old Dr Jacob Townsend's Sarsaparilla, 10", aqua . . . . $35–$45
Old Dr Jacob Townsend's Sarsaparilla, 7¹/₂", aqua . . . . $30–$45
Primley's Sarsaparilla, D-172-2, 9¹/₂", aqua . . . . $40–$55
Radway's Sarsaparilla Resolvent, D-187, 7¹/₂", aqua . . . . $10–$16
Riker's, D-180, clear . . . . $40–$60
Rush's Sarsaparilla, New York, D-184, 8³/₄", aqua . . . . $25–$35
Sand's Genuine Sarsaparilla, D-188, OP, aqua . . . . $75–$110
Sand's Genuine Sarsaparilla, New York, rect., 10", aqua . . . . $70–$100
Sand's Sarsaparilla, New York, OP, aqua . . . . $25–$35
Sarsaparilla and Rose Willow, 7³/₄", aqua . . . . $400–$500
Shaker, labeled, D-123, aqua . . . . $60–$90
Steven's Sarsaparilla, D-198, 8¹/₄", aqua . . . . $30–$50
Turner's Sarsaparilla, SB, 12¹/₂", aqua . . . . $200–$325
Turner's Sarsaparilla, SB, 12", deep aqua . . . . $225–$325
Walker's, D-211, aqua . . . . $125–$175
West's Sarsaparilla, D-215, 8³/₄", aqua . . . . $75–$100
Wetherell's Sarsaparilla, D-216, 9³/₈", aqua . . . . $80–$120
WG Kidder Comp Tinct Sarsaparilla, D-121, 7³/₄", aqua . . . . $80–$120
Whipple's Sarsaparilla, D-217, 9¹/₈", aqua . . . . $60–$90
WS Green Compound Sarsaparilla Beer, D-88, pottery, pint, reddish brown . . . .
. . . . $200–$300
Wynkoop's Katharismic Sarsaparilla New York, IP, 10", sapphire . . . $5000–$6000
Yager's Sarsaparilla, D-233, 8³/₄", amber . . . . $55–$75

SCENT AND SMELLING BOTTLES

Scent and smelling bottles were important luxuries of colonial America, made
to help those of a feminine persuasion deal with some of the disagreeable
aspects of colonial life. With tight corsets and mammoth hoop skirts and gar-
ments the fashion rage of the day, smelling bottles were necessary to help
women overcome the fainting and dizzy spells which often accompanied such

tight and cumbersome clothing. Scent bottles, which were often filled with aromatic scents, were used to help the fairer sex overcome odiferous nuances associated with such things as the lack of bathing and sanitary facilities, and animals. Scent and smelling bottles were generally very small in size, and were often made in beautiful shapes and colors. The reader is referred to *American Bottles and Flasks and Their Ancestry* by McKearin and Wilson, pgs. 378–408.

Acorn Form, polished lip, 2¹/₄", light amethyst . . . . $150–$225
Concentric Ring, four rings, corrugated edge, clear, blue tint, OP . . . . $250–$300
Concentric Ring, four rings, corrugated edge, OP, 2¹/₄", amethyst . . . . $600–$900
Grape Cluster Form, polished lip, 2¹/₄", turquoise . . . . $150–$200
Hourglass Form, four vertical rigaree bands, long neck, clear, OP, 3" . . . . $250–$350
Hourglass Form, four vertical rigaree bands, long neck, OP, 3", aqua. . . . . $450–$600
Peace & Plenty, Sunburst, OP, 3¹/₄", emerald green . . . . $1750–$2500
Peace & Plenty, Sunburst, OP, sapphire blue . . . . $1750–$2500

Scent/smelling, two seahorse shaped.
PHOTO COURTESY OF SKINNER'S, INC.

Seahorse, ribbed, OP, 4", deep amethyst . . . . $400–$500
Seashell Form, 12 edges, 2³/₈", medium cobalt . . . . $200–$300
Sunburst, 12 rays, beaded edge, OP, 3", deep amethyst . . . . $350–$500
Sunburst, 12 rays, beaded edge, OP, 3", deep cobalt . . . . $250–$300
Sunburst, 12 rays, beads/waffle pattern, clear, OP, 2⁵/₈". . . . . $200–$300
Sunburst, 12 rays, beads/waffle pattern, OP, 2¹/₂", grass green . . . . $750–$1200
Sunburst, 12 rays, beads/waffle pattern, OP, 2³/₄", deep teal . . . . $400–$600
Sunburst, 12 rays, clear, corrugated edges, OP, 1³/₄" . . . . $150–$250
Sunburst, 14 cut rays, 1¹/₂", ice blue . . . . $250–$350
Sunburst, 14 cut rays, 1¹/₂", opaque powder blue . . . . $350–$550
Sunburst, 14 pinwheel rays, OP, 2¹/₈", deep aqua. $550–$750
Sunburst, 18 rays, corrugated edges, bead center, OP, 2", amethyst . . . . . . $750–$950
Sunburst, fleur de lis pattern, clear, corrugated edges, OP, 2¹/₄" . . . . $125–$175
Sunburst, oval, 12 rays/9 waffle design and scroll, OP, 2³/₄", cobalt . . . . . . $375–$500
Sunburst, oval, 12 rays/9 waffle design and scroll, OP, 2⁵/₈", amethyst . . . $750–$1150
Sunburst, ovoid, 12 rays, beaded border, OP, 3", peacock blue . . . . $750–$1000
Sunburst, ovoid, 12 rays, rope borders, OP, 2⁵/₈", amethyst. . . . . $600–$900

Sunburst, ovoid, MW105-14, OP, 3", emerald green . . . . $400–$500
Sunburst, petal form, 16 rounded rays, daisy center, OP, 2^1/$_4$", cobalt . . . . . $500–$750
Sunburst, petal form, 16 rounded rays, domed center, OP, 2^1/$_2$", cobalt. . . . $450–$650
Sunburst, petal form, 16 rounded rays, domed center, OP, amethyst . . . . . . $500–$750
Sunburst, petal form, MW105-8, OP, 1^7/$_8$", cobalt . . . . $300–$400
Sunburst, Prince of Wales Feather Pattern, 2", blue . . . . $150–$200
Sunburst, round, 24 rays, OP, 1^3/$_4$", opaque blue . . . . $350–$550
Sunburst, round, OP, 24 rays, sapphire blue . . . . $400–$600
Sunburst, shield form, 12 rays, beaded edge, clear, narrow body, OP, 3" . . $250–$300
Sunburst, shield form, 12 rays, beaded edge, clear, OP, 2^5/$_8$". . . . . $400–$600
Sunburst, shield form, 12 rays, beaded edge, OP, 2^3/$_4$", yellow green . . . . . $600–$850
Sunburst, shield form, 12 rays, MW105-4, short neck, OP, 2^5/$_8$", cobalt . . . $300–$400
Sunburst, shield form, 12 rays/waffle design, 3", emerald green . . . . $1000–$1500
Sunburst, shield form, beaded edge, clear, gray tint, 3" . . . . $300–$400
Sunburst, shield form, beaded edge, OP, 3", sapphire blue . . . . $350–$500
Swirled Rib, round, 20 ribs, flattened chestnut form, OP, 2", peacock blue . . . .
. . . . $150–$250
Tear Drop Form, 22 swirled ribs, OP, 3^1/$_2$", light amethyst. . . . . $100–$150
Tear Drop Form, flattened sides, 15 broken swirl ribs, OP, 3" . . . . $600–$800
Tear Drop Form, flattened sides, 16 swirled ribs, OP, 3", yellow olive. . . . $400–$550
Tear Drop Form, flattened sides, 2^1/$_2$", olive yellow . . . .
Tear Drop Form, flattened sides, tooled neck, edge rigaree, OP, 3^3/$_4$", amethyst . . . . .
. . . . $350–$500
Vertically Ribbed, round, 20 ribs, short neck, OP, 1^7/$_8$". . . . . $350–$500

SEAL BOTTLES

Seal bottles are those which have an applied glass seal on the shoulder or side of the bottle. The seal itself was a molten blob of glass placed on the side of the finished bottle; it was then stamped with a metal die upon which some pertinent information had been engraved.

Early seal bottles, which were ordinarily used by nobility and wealthy people, carried with them great prestige and were usually symbols of rank, position, and wealth. The seals often contained a date, name, initials, coat of arms or other symbol of significance. In the 17th and 18th centuries, the use of seals became widespread among tavern owners. It is unclear when the first seal bottles were manufactured in the United States, but it is possible that some may have been made in New Jersey around 1750.

Seal bottles are valuable not only because of their beauty and rarity, but because of their historical significance as well. Bottle researchers have been able to very specifically identify bottle forms and changes in forms which corresponded with the dates on the seals. Seals are found on a wide variety of bottles ranging from the early shaft-and-globe-type wine bottles through the squat wine bottles, case gin bottles, and handled chestnut bottles of the mid 19th century, and even thereafter.

Collectors should be aware that the date on a sealed bottle may not always correspond with the year of manufacture, though a thorough understanding of the evolution of wine bottle form should help to confirm the age of a given bottle. Interested collectors are well advised to read *Understanding Antique Wine Bottles* by Roger Dunbrell, as well as *American Bottles and Flasks and Their Ancestry* by McKearin and Wilson.

1791, OP, 7¼", dark olive amber................................. $350–$500
A Kelly, OP, early 19th century, 10½", dark olive .... $150–$190
AS / CR, OP, late 18th/early 19th century, 11", dark olive amber........ $100–$150
Brynker, SB, ¼" ring chip, 11¾", deep yellowish olive .... $100–$125
C, straight sided cylinder, OP, early 19th century, 11", olive amber......... $75–$95
Chestnut Form, flattened (rare form when sealed), late 18th century, "Wilt's Holt Mineral Water," OP, 9", olive amber .... $3000+
Class of 1846, Dyottville Glass Works Phila (on base), sloping collar, IP, 11", olive amber... $400–$600
Crown, ca. 1700, with greyhound's head, onion form, OP, minor chipping, 6½", olive amber.. $1800–$2500
Crown, ca. 1800 form, over C, OP, 8¾", dark olive amber .... $150–$200
Crown, ca. 1880, with letter P, SB, 11⅜", deep yellow olive.............. $45–$65
D Sears 4, Ricketts Glass Works (on base), OP, 11", yellowish green ...... $90–$120
Donerale House, HH Rickett & Co (on base), OP, 11", olive green ..... $150–$200
Emmanuel College, ca. 1810, OP, 11", deep yellow olive .... $100–$150
Erven L Bols Net Lootsje Amsterdam, late 19th century, squat form, 8⅜", olive amber.. $150–$190
HC, OP, late 18th century form, 10¾", olive amber .... $300–$400

Left: *Early seal bottle.* Right: *Close up of seal.* PHOTOS COURTESY OF GLASS WORKS AUCTIONS.

Seal, a late 18th-century bottle. PHOTO COURTESY OF SKINNER'S, INC.

HH Rickett & Co Glass Works Bristol (on base), ca. 1830-1840, these are English bottles, some have seals and average value is $150/$275, without seals . . . . . $65–$125
Inner Temple, straight sided cylinder, OP, 10", deep green . . . . $125–$175
Ino Walley Budleigh 1763, OP, 9", deep olive amber . . . . $800–$1200
Lancyck, "Ricketts Glass Works" (on base), OP, 11", deep yellow olive. . . . $90–$125
Mallet Form Bottle, "John Key 1726", 7¹/₂", olive green. . . . . $2500+
Mallet Form, ca. 1740, slightly more straight sided (later), "TB," 7", olive. . . . .
. . . . $500–$700
MJ, straight sided cylinder, OP, 10¹/₂", deep olive amber . . . . $200–$300
MW, ca. 1770, OP, 10¹/₄", olive amber . . . . $175–$275
Onion Form Bottle, ca. 1720, crown on seal, OP, 7³/₈", yellowish olive . . . . . . $1000+
Patent (on shoulder), Rickett's Glass Works Bristol (on base), OP, 11", olive amber .
. . . . $80–$120
PF Hearing (on ribbon seal), SB, late 19th century form, 8¹/₂", orange amber . . . .
. . . . $60–$90
RHC 1815, OP, 11¹/₈", deep yellow olive . . . . $150–$200
Shaft and Globe, ca. 1665, coat of arms on seal, very good, olive green . . . . . . $2500+
Shaft and Globe, ca. 1670, falcon on seal, very good condition, olive amber . . $2750+
Straight Sided Cylinder, slightly flaring out at base, "IT 1787", 10¹/₂", deep green . . .
. . . . $600–$900
Straight Sided Cylinder, wide body, "I Hennefsy 1774", 13", olive . . . . $1000–$1500
TC / CR, ca. 1830, OP, ¹/₄" lip chip, 10⁵/₈", deep yellow olive . . . . $100–$150
Three Piece Mold Seal Bottles, made ca. 1840-1860 usually valued. . . . . . $100–$200
Trelaske (on seal), OP, early 19th century, 10", olive amber . . . . $75–$125
W Leman Chard 1771, OP, 11¹/₈", deep olive green . . . . $150–$200
W Stannus 1722, OP, numerous lip/string ring chips, 7¹/₂", dark olive green . . . .
. . . . $1250–$1750
WA (on seal), OP, late 18th century form, 10⁷/₈", olive amber . . . . $175–$225
William Mustard Kincardine 1846, OP, 8", dark olive amber . . . . $250–$350

SNUFF BOTTLES

Snuff was introduced into Europe in the 16th century. It was a tobacco preparation which had been treated with a mixture of common salt and aromatic substances for scent and flavor such as cinnamon, nutmeg, and lavender. Snuff, which was generally inhaled via a powder form, was originally more popular than smoking tobacco and was used in both a recreational and sinus-clearing capacity. In the mid 18th century, snuff began to be advertised as a cure for headaches, catarrh, and other disorders.

Exactly when the first snuff bottles were blown in America is unclear, but it is certain that bottles were used in the 18th century, many of which were doubtless imported from England and Europe. Most of the 18th and early 19th century snuff bottles were unembossed and generally straight sided, either square or rectangular with beveled edges which were blown in clay molds. The bottles were made with both narrow and wide mouths.

Early embossed snuff bottles are very rare and the first one made in America was blown in the 1820's. In the 19th century, snuff began to appear in rectangular and cylindrical aqua and colorless bottles, occassionally embossed with the maker's name or labeled. The reader is referred to *American Bottles and Flasks and Their Ancestry* by McKearin and Wilson, pgs. 259–262.

A Delpit, IP, 4¹/₂", olive amber . . . . $750–$1000
A Delpit, SB, rect., 4¹/₂", olive green. . . . . $300–$450

Snuff, early.

American Gentleman, OP, 4½", olive yellow .... $300–$500
Bulbous, free blown, flaring lip, OP, 6½", amber .... $400–$600
Cylindrical, flaring lip, OP, unembossed, 7", olive amber .... $225–$325
Cylindrical, unembossed, blown from bottle mold, mold seams, OP, flared lip, 9" ....
.... $700–$950
Cylindrical, unembossed, crude applied lip, OP, 4½", amber .... $250–$375
Cylindrical, unembossed, flaring lip, OP, 4½", olive green .... $175–$250
Cylindrical, unembossed, straight sided, wide flaring lip, OP, 10", olive green.......
.... $275–$400
Cylindrical, unembossed, wide mouth, no lip flare, OP, 6½", olive amber ....
.... $350–$475
Cylindrical, unembossed, wide mouth, OP, 4", olive amber............. $200–$275

Left: *Tall cylindrical master snuff.* Right: *E. Roome, Troy, New York.*
PHOTOS COURTESY OF GLASS WORKS AUCTIONS.

Doct Marshall's Snuff, OP, 3¼", aqua.............................. $60–$80
E Roome Troy New York, OP, 4½", olive green..................... $150–$225
E Roome Troy New York, OP, 4½", pale blue green .... $600–$850
E Roome Troy New York, OP, full label, 4½", olive amber............ $225–$350
E Roome Troy New York, rect., OP, 4½", yellowish olive............. $150–$225
JJ Mapes No 61 Front St N York, OP, 4½", olive green .... $700–$900
JJ Mapes No 61 Front St N York, rect., OP, 4½", olive amber .... $700–$900
Labeled Snuff With Standing Indian, unembossed rect. bottle, OP, 4", green.......
.... $200–$300
Labeled Snuff, plain label, no figures, rect., OP, 4", olive amber........ $125–$175
Leonard Applyby Railroad Mills, OP, yellow amber .... $1200–$1500
Levi Garrett & Sons, labeled, square, beveled edges, OP, 4½", olive amber ....
.... $190–$250
Macoboy Snuff (on label), square, ABM, 3½", amber .... $5–$10
Otto Landsburg & Co Celebrated Snuff, 5", cobalt.................... $20–$28
Rectangular, beveled edges, "F" on base, OP, 4½", olive green .... $40–$60
Rectangular, beveled edges, unembossed, applied lip, OP, 6¾", olive amber........
.... $275–$350

Rectangular, beveled edges, unembossed, flaring lip, OP, 5¹/₂", olive amber . . . .
. . . . $305–$450
Rectangular, beveled edges, unembossed, offset mouth, OP, 5¹/₂", olive green . . . . . .
. . . . $325–$425
Rectangular, beveled edges, unembossed, OP, 4¹/₂", olive green . . . . $40–$55
Rectangular, beveled edges, unembossed, SB, 4¹/₂", amber . . . . $15–$20

Left: *Rectangular snuff with beveled edges.* Right: *Square snuff.* PHOTOS
COURTESY OF GLASS WORKS AUCTIONS.

Square, beveled edges, unembossed, flaring lip, 4¹/₂", olive amber . . . . $350–$450
Square, beveled edges, unembossed, OP, 4¹/₂", olive green . . . . $150–$250
Square, beveled edges, unembossed, OP, 5¹/₂", olive amber. . . . . $275–$375
Square, beveled edges, unembossed, SB, 3¹/₂", amber . . . . $10–$15
Square, unembossed, OP, flaring lip, 4¹/₂", olive amber . . . . $150–$200
Square, unembossed, OP, wide flaring lip, case gin form, 10", olive green . . . .
. . . . $700–$850
Square, unembossed, wide flaring lip, OP, 6¹/₂", light olive yellow . . . . $500–$750
True Cephalic Snuff by the King's Patent, OP, 3¹/₂", deep aqua. . . . . $175–$250
True Cephalic Snuff by the King's Patent, OP, 3³/₄", aqua . . . . $175–$225
Wyman's Copenhagen Snuff, quart, amber . . . . $60–$90

SODA BOTTLES

It was the popularity of mineral water which eventually led to the invention of soda. Basically, soda was artificially carbonated water, and it was being made in America in the first quarter of the 19th century. Then, in the 1830s, an English immigrant named John Matthews introduced the use of marble chips, which were broken down to form carbonic acid, into making soda water. In fact, by purchasing all the scrap marble which had been left over from the building of St. Patrick's Cathedral in New York City, Mr. Matthews had enough marble to make 25 million gallons of soda water! In the 1830s, various flavors also began to be added to the soda water.

As to the forms used for these early soda bottles, they were often similar to the types used for mineral waters. Because carbonated water was being used, however, a sturdier vessel had to be invented, which soon led to the use of the thick-walled blob top-type of soda bottle, which continued to be used into the 20th century. Also, because of the dangers of the corks popping out from the high pressure, several innovative solutions were developed, such as the Hutchinson-type wire stoppers, lightning-type wire stoppers, Cod stopper bottles, and the so-called "torpedo"-style bottles which lay on their sides, thus allowing the soda to keep the cork moist and prevent the cork from drying and popping out of the bottle.

One of the hottest areas of soda collecting today is the Applied Color Label (ACL) bottles, which are pyroglazed colors and designs added to the bottles, similar to milk bottles. What drives the value of ACL bottles is the number of pyroglaze colors used, with higher value corresponding to the number of different colors used; the scene or logo, with more value attached to an Indian head, for example; and the color of the bottle.

A Ritter Mineral Water Cincinnati R, ten sided, IP, 7$^{1}/_{4}$", light green . . . $150–$200
A Treat, man and woman, ACL, clear bottle, 12 ounces, red and white . . . . $3–$5
Adna H Southwick & GO Tupper New York, ten sided, IP, 7$^{1}/_{2}$", cobalt . . . .
. . . . $300–$400
Aetna Bottling Co, Concord NH, full label with Indian, stopper, 8$^{3}/_{8}$", aqua . . . .
. . . . $1500–$200
Aircraft, airplane on face and neck, ACL, clear bottle, 28 ounce, red and white . . . . . .
. . . . $20–$30
Ale 81, ACL, green bottle, 12 ounce, red and white . . . . $6–$9
Always Avery's Beverages, ACL, clear, 32 ounce, white and blue . . . . $5–$8
American Club Beverages, decorative frame, ACL, clear bottle, 12 ounces, red and white . . . . $6–$9
American Club Beverages, large eagle, PL, clear bottle, 28 ounce, red and white . . . .
. . . . $6–$9

American Desiccating Co of New York, SB, 7¹/₄", golden amber . . . . $150–$200
Atomic Cola, ACL, blue bottle, red and white . . . . $10–$14
B Bick & Co Mineral Water Cincinnati, IP, 7³/₈", deep aqua . . . . $150–$200
B Bick & Co Mineral Water Cincinnati, ten sided, IP, 7¹/₄", cobalt . . . . . $500–$700
B Bick Cincinnati This Bottle Is Never Sold, IP, cleaned, 7¹/₂", cobalt . . . $225–$275
Barq's Beverages Genuine Beverages, ACL, clear, 12 ounce, red and white. . . $3–$5
Bay City Soda Water C SF, SB, 7¹/₄", sapphire blue. . . . . $100–$145
Ben Hur, eagle, ACL, clear bottle, 26 ounce, red and white . . . . $12–$15
Berkeley Club Ginger Ale, ACL, green bottle, 7 ounce, red and white. . . . . $3–$5
Big Chief, Indian, ACL, clear, 7 ounce, white, cream and maroon . . . . $10–$16
Bimbo, Elephant, ACL, 10 ounce, blue and white . . . . $12–$18
Birmingham Bottling House, AN & Co, SB, 7¹/₂", aqua. . . . . $25–$35
Blue Ridge Ginger Ale, Marion, Va, ACL, green bottle, 7 ounce, red and white. . . . .
. . . . $3–$5
Boardman, IP, 7", medium sapphire . . . . $80–$110
Bob's Club, band, instruments, ACL, green bottle, 32 ounce, red and white . . . .
. . . . $35–$40
Boone Rock, Daniel Boone and Dog, ACL, clear, 12 ounce, green and white . . . .
. . . . $7–$10
Brownie, brownie elf on front and neck, ACL, clear bottle, 10 ounce, brown and white
. . . . $3–$5
Buffman's Sarsaparilla & Lemon Mineral Water Pittsburgh, ten sided, IP, cleaned,
base edge flake, 7⁵/₈", cobalt. . . . . $300–$425
Buffman's Sarsaparilla & Lemon Mineral Water Pittsburgh, ten sided, IP,
sparkling mint, not dug, 7⁵/₈", cobalt . . . . $1500–$2000
Bull's Eye, target and arrow, ACL, amber bottle, 10 ounce, yellow and red . . . . $6–$9
C Whittemore New York, IP, cleaned, 8¹/₈", medium emerald green . . . . . $150–$200
California Soda Works, (eagle), Hutchinson-type, aqua . . . . $25–$35
Canada Dry Ginger Ale (on base), carnival glass, marigold. . . . . $15–$18
Canada Dry Ginger Ale, New York, ACL, green bottle, 7 ounce, white and red. . . . .
. . . . : . . . . $3–$5
Canada Dry, crown and shield, ACL, green bottle, 6 ounce, white and red. . . . . $2–$3
Canada Dry, on shoulder, ACL, green bottle, 12 ounce, white, green and red. . . $2–$4
Castle, castle, ACL, clear bottle, 7 ounce, red and white. . . . . $6–$8
CB Owen & Co Bottlers Cincinnati CBO & Co, IP, lightly cleaned and potstone base
bruise, 7¹/₂", sapphire. . . . . $125–$165
CB Owen & Co Bottlers Cincinnati CBO & Co, IP, lightly cleaned, sparkling mint,
7¹/₂", cobalt . . . . $125–$175
CB Owen & Co Bottlers Cincinnati CBO & Co, IP, sparkling mint, lightly cleaned,
7¹/₂", medium sapphire . . . . $140–$175
CB Owen & Co Bottlers Cincinnati CBO & Co, IP, sparkling mint, lightly cleaned,
slight whittling to glass, 7¹/₂", deep cobalt . . . . $140–$180
CB Owen & Co Bottlers Cincinnati CBO & Co, IP, sparkling mint, not cleaned,
7¹/₂", deep sapphire. . . . . $250–$300
Chester Club, golfer, ACL, clear bottle, 8 ounce, red and white . . . . $6–$9
Chief, Indian Head, ACL, clear bottle, 7 ounce, white . . . . $14–$18
Chocolate Cow, running cow, ACL, clear, 8 ounce, red and white . . . . $3–$5
Cleo Cola, sitting queen, ACL, clear, 12 ounce, white and red. . . . . $10–$15
Cliquot Club Ginger Ale, Millis, Ma, eskimo, PL, green bottle, 7 ounce, white and red
. . . . $4–$6
Coca Cola (block letters), Hutchinson-type, various cities $400

Coca Cola (in script), Hutchinson-type, various cities $600

Coca Cola, hobbleskirt, raised letters, value varies by location, though most are $.25, light green . . . .

Coca Cola, hobbleskirt, white painted lettering, value depending on location, light green . . . .

Coca Cola, Lexington, Ky, straight sided, amber . . . . $20–$30

Cock & Bull Ginger Beer, rooster, ACL, clear bottle, red and green . . . . $7–$9

Colonial Beverages, woman in wide skirt, ACL, clear bottle, 8 ounce, red and white . . . . $6–$9

Commander, drum major, ACL, clear bottle, 28 ounce, red and white . . . . . . $35–$40

Country Club, woman golfer, ACL, clear bottle, 7 ounce, blue and white . . . . . $6–$9

Cowboy, cowboy on horse, ACL, clear, 6 ounce, red and white . . . . $7–$9

Craven-Union Glass Works / Phila, IP, exterior stain, 7", sapphire blue . . . . $80–$120

Crystal Palace Premium Soda Water W Eagle, IP, 7¹/₄", deep teal blue . . . . $800–$1200

Dad's Root Beer, man's head, ACL, amber, 10 ounce, yellow, blue and red . . . . $6–$8

Diamond Ginger Ale, Waterbury, Ct, diamonds, ACL, green bottle, 6 ounce, red and yellow . . . . $3–$4

Diamond Ginger Ale, Waterbury, Ct, diamonds, ACL, green bottles, 12 ounce, red and yellow . . . . $3–$5

Diehl's Mineral Water Patent, OP, exterior stained, 6¹/₂", medium green . . . . $150–$200

Dixon & Carson, 41 Walker St, NY, SB, 7", medium emerald green . . . . $30–$50

Domino Beverages, domino, ACL, clear bottle, 28 ounce, red and yellow . . . $12–$15

Donald Duck Lime Cola, Donald Duck head, ACL, light green, white and blue . . . . $15–$20

Double Dry Ginger Ale, Chattanooga, Tn, ACL, green bottle, 12 ounce, red and white . . . . $3–$4

Down East, sailing ship, ACL, clear bottle, 6 ounce, blue and white . . . . $6–$9

Dr Swett's, profile, ACL, clear, 10 ounce, yellow and red . . . . $6–$7

E Lester, St Louis, OP, 7¹/₂", aqua . . . . $40–$65

E Roussell Mineral Water Phila Patent, OP, 6⁷/₈", medium emerald green . . . . $400–$500

E Roussell Philada, IP, 7³/₈", emerald green . . . . $60–$90

E Smith Elmira NY, SB, 7³/₈", deep cobalt . . . . $100–$150

Eagle Figure, embossed, SB, 6⁷/₈", light green . . . . $50–$70

Eagle Works, Philada, IP, 7¹/₄", medium emerald green . . . . $50–$80

Eight Ball, ACL, 7 ounce, black on amber . . . . $10–$12

Elk Club Beverages, elk head, ACL, green bottle, 7 ounce, red and white . . . . . $6–$9

Frost King, snowman, ACL, clear, 7 ounce, blue and white . . . . $5–$8

G Ebberwein Savannah Geo Mineral Water, SB, 7", aqua . . . . $30–$45

Garrison Hill, lighthouse, ACL, clear, 8 ounce, red and white . . . . $18–$24

Gossman & Verhage Mineral Water Cincinnati, ten sided, IP, lightly cleaned, 7¹/₄", bluish aqua . . . . $150–$200

GP Fey & Co, ten sided, OP, small crack, 7³/₈", greenish aqua . . . . $125–$175

GW Felix Harrisburg, IP, 7¹/₄", cobalt . . . . $375–$475

H Nash & Co Root Beet Cincinnati, IP, 12 sided, 8⁷/₈", cobalt . . . . $800–$1200

H Verhage Cincinnati Ohio, lightly cleaned, 7³/₈", light cobalt . . . . $125–$175

Harris Springs, Waterloo, SC, ACL, clear bottle, 7 ounce, red and white . . . . . $2–$4

Hermann, clown, ACL, clear, 10 ounce, red and white . . . . $10–$15

Home Beverages, scene with house, ACL, green bottle, 28 ounce, red and white . . . . .
. . . . $12–$15
Home Beverages, scene with house, ACL, green bottle, 7 ounce, red and white . . . . . .
. . . . $12–$15
Home Beverages, scene with house, clear bottle, 7 ounce, red and white . . . . $12–$15
Hosmer Mountain, deer, house and mountain, ACL, clear bottle, 28 ounce, red and
white . . . . $12–$16
Howel's Beverages, man with tray, ACL, clear bottle, 7 ounce, blue and white . . . . . .
. . . . $6–$9
Hulshizer & Co Premium Mineral Water, eight sided, IP, 7^{1}/$_{2}$", emerald green . . . . .
. . . . $600–$850
I Browmell New Bedford This Bottle Never Sold, IP, 7^{1}/$_{2}$", medium cobalt . . . .
. . . . $125–$195
I Suttonh Cincinnati, lightly cleaned, IP, 7^{1}/$_{2}$", medium cobalt . . . . $400–$500
IA Lindestram, Madison, Wis, IP, 7^{1}/$_{4}$", aqua . . . . $80–$120
J & A Dearborn New York Mineral Water, eight sided, IP, lip bruise, 7", cobalt . . .
. . . . $200–$250
J Boardman & Co New York Mineral Water This Bottle Is Never Sold, eight sided,
IP, cleaned, 7^{3}/$_{4}$", cobalt . . . . $150–$250
J Boardman & Co New York Mineral Water This Bottle Is Never Sold, eight sided,
IP, cleaned, 7^{3}/$_{4}$", emerald green . . . . $400–$500
J Lamppin's Mineral Water Utica, IP, cylinder, half pint, sapphire blue . . . .
. . . . $400–$550
J Steel Easton Pa Mineral Waters, IP, lightly cleaned, 7^{1}/$_{4}$", cobalt blue. . . $90–$120
Jackson Napa Soda Spring, blob top, aqua . . . . $10–$15
James Ray Savannah Geo Ginger Ale, Hutchinson, stained, 8", cobalt . . . $150–$200
Jet Up, rocket, stars, planet, ACL, 7ounce, white on green . . . . $20–$25
Jno Postell Mineral Water Cincinnati P, ten sided, IP, lightly cleaned, 7^{1}/$_{2}$", greenish
aqua . . . . $150–$195
John Ogden's Mineral Water, Pittsburgh O, OP, 7^{1}/$_{2}$", aqua . . . . $60–$90
John Ryan 1866 Excelsior Soda Works Savannah Geo, SB, 7", cobalt . . . $75–$125
John Ryan 1866 Excelsior Sodaworks, Savannah, Geo, SB, 6^{3}/$_{4}$", medium cobalt . .
. . . . $60–$90
John S Baker Soda Water This Bottle Is Never Sold, eight sided, IP, cleaned, 7^{1}/$_{4}$",
emerald green . . . . $130–$190
Johnston & Co Philada Mineral Water, IP, 7^{1}/$_{4}$", emerald green . . . . $40–$60
Keach Balt, lip crack, 9", yellowish topaz torpedo . . . . $700–$900
Korker Lemon, Virginia Dare, ACL, green, 7 ounce, white and yellow . . . . . . $3–$5
Leonard's Ginger Ale, Rochester, NY, PL, green bottle, 28 ounce, red and white . . .
. . . . $15–$20
Liberty, Statue of Liberty, ACL, clear, 12 ounce, blue and white . . . . $6–$8
Lifter, hot air balloon, ACL, green, 7 ounce, red and white . . . . $12–$15
Light Rock Beverages, lighthouse, ACL, clear bottle, 7 ounce, blue and white . . . . . .
. . . . $20–$25
Like, flower, ACL, green bottle, 10 ounce, white and yellow . . . . $3–$5
Lucky Strike Ginger Ale, Nashua, NH, ACL, green bottle, 28 ounce, red and white .
. . . . $8–$10
Lucky Strike Ginger Ale, Nashua, NH, ACL, green bottle, 7 ounce, red and white . . .
. . . . $8–$10
Luke Beard, ten pin form, SB, 7^{1}/$_{4}$", medium emerald green . . . . $200–$240
M Altenbaugh Pittsburgh, IP, wear, 7^{7}/$_{8}$", medium blue green . . . . $100–$175

Left: *Eight-sided soda.*
Center: *Torpedo shaped
soda.* Right: *Mug based
soda.* PHOTOS COURTESY
OF GLASS WORKS
AUCTIONS.

M McCormick, This Bottle Never Sold, WMcC & Co, SB, 7", root beer amber . . . .
. . . . $35–$50
Ma's, Old Fashioned, woman's head, ACL, clear, 7 ounce, red and white . . . . . $5–$7
Mahaska, Indian with headdress, ACL, clear, 10 ounce, red and white $20
Manhattan Beverages, city skyline, ACL, clear bottle, 7 ounce, maroon and white . . .
. . . . $6–$9
Mason's Root Beer, ACL, amber, 8 ounce, yellow and white . . . . $2–$3
McKeon Washington DC, torpedo, 8⅝", medium emerald green . . . . . . $2500–$3500
Mohawk Ginger Ale, Pittsfield, Ma, ACL, green bottle, 7 ounce, white . . . . . . $3–$4
Mount Kineo Ginger Ale, Dexter, Me, Pale Dry, ACL, green bottle, 7 ounce, blue
and white . . . . $3–$4
Mount Zircon Beverages, mountains, ACL, red and white on clear, 7 ounce . . . $6–$8
Mountain Dew, white and orange on green, ACL, 7 ounce . . . . $2–$3
Moxie, New, Sparkling Beverages, ACL, red and white on clear, 7 ounce . . . . . $5–$7
Nehi, ACL, red and white on clear, 9 ounce . . . . $2–$3
Nemo, sea captain, ACL, white on clear, 7 ounce $20
Nu Grape Soda, yellow and red on clear, ACL, 6 ounce . . . . $2–$4
Ohio Bottling Clvd O Works, ten pin, SB, 7⅜", aqua. . . . . $75–$90
Old Newbury Beverages, Indian, ACL, blue and white on clear, 7 ounce . . . . $10–$15
Orange Crush, ACL, white and green on amber bottle, 12 ounce . . . . $3–$5
Owen Casey Eagle Soda Works Sac City, SB, 7", cobalt . . . . $75–$100
P Latterner Mineral Water Cincinnati, 12 sided, OP, polished base edge chip, 7½",
light blue green . . . . $100–$125
Paulsboro, knight on horse, ACL, orange and white on clear bottle, 30 ounce . . . .
. . . . $12–$16
Pepsi Cola, ACL, red and white on clear bottle, 16 ounce . . . . $2–$3
Pepsi Cola, in circle in rectangle on shoulder, red, white and blue on clear bottle,
32 ounce . . . . $6–$8
Pepsi Cola, Sparkling, ACL, red, white and blue on clear bottle, 12 ounce . . $10–$15
Pepsi Free, ACL, red, white and blue on clear bottle, 16 ounce . . . . $2–$3

Pequot Spring Beverages, Indian front and back, ACL, white on clear bottle, 8 ounce
.... $15–$20
Pequot Spring Water Beverages, two Indians, ACL, yellow, green, white on clear, 8 ounce .... $15–$20
Pequot, Indian character, ACL, black, green and white on clear bottle, 7 ounce ......
.... $18–$20
Philada Glassworks Burgin & Sons, IP, lightly cleaned, 7¼", deep blue green .....
.... $90–$125
Phoenix Glass Works Brooklyn, IP, cleaned, 7⅛", pale green .... $150–$200
Phoenix Glass Works Brooklyn, IP, cleaned, aqua .... $125–$175
Pine Spring, pine tree, ACL, green and white on green bottle, 7 ounce .... $6–$9
Pocahontas, Indian princess, ACL, white on clear bottle, 10 ounce .... $6–$8
Polar Club Ginger Ale, Worcester, Ma, ACL, bear on ice floe, three bears on neck, 7 ounce .... $3–$6
Popular Club Ginger Ale, Baltimore, ACL, red and white on green bottle, 6.5 ounce
.... $3–$4
Queen O, queens face, ACL, red and white on clear bottle, 7 ounce .... $6–$7
Quinan & Studer 1888 Savannah Ga, IP, sapphire blue................ $80–$110
RC & T New York XX, IP, 7½", deep puce....................... $800–$1200
RC, Royal Crown Cola, in painted circle, ACL, red and white on blue, 10 ounce ....
.... $2–$3
Red Fox, fox on neck, ACL, red and white on clear bottle, 7 ounce .... $3–$5
Red Rock Beverages, ACL, white and red on clear, 7 ounce .... $3–$4
Richardson's Root Beer, man with tray, ACL, orange and white on clear, 7 ounce ...
.... $5–$7
Richter's Bottling Works, Fresno, Cal, Hutchinson-type, aqua .... $40–$60
Robertson & Co, Philada, California Pop Beer, SB, 7¼", yellow amber..........
.... $70–$100
Robinson Wilson & Legallie 102 Sudbury St Boston, IP, 7", deep green ....
.... $150–$250
Rock Bridge Virginia Alum Water, SB, 9⅝", blue green .... $250–$300
Rock Creek Beverages, ACL, white, yellow and red on clear bottle, 12 ounce.......
.... $2–$4
Royal Crown Cola, crown on diamond, ACL, white and red on blue bottle, 6 ounce ..
.... $2–$4
Rutherford's Premium Mineral Water Cincinnati, IP, 7⅜", sapphire... $450–$600
Rutherford's Premium Mineral Water Cincinnati, ten sided, IP, 7¼", cobalt .....
.... $400–$600
Ryan Dry Ginger Ale, Niagara Falls, NY, ACL, red and white on green bottle, 7 ounce .... $3–$4
S Erven & Co Bottlers Philada Brown Stout, IP, wear, 6⅞", medium blue green ...
.... $60–$90
S Grossman Soda Mineral Water Philada Registered, Hutchinson, 7½", medium green .... $250–$300
S Martinelli, Watsonville, Hutchinson-type, aqua .... $15–$20
Saratoga Club, tree and spring, ACL, red and yellow on clear bottle, 32 ounce ......
.... $5–$7
Schweppes Ginger Ale, ACL, white and red on green bottle, 7 ounce......... $2–$3
Seal's, seal and glacier, ACL, black and white on clear bottle, 7 ounce ...... $12–$15
Seitz & Bro Easton Pa Premium Mineral Waters, eight sided, IP, 7¼", cobalt.....
.... $250–$350

Seps, dog in tuxedo, ACL, black and white on clear, 7 ounce . . . . $6–$9
Seven Up (vertical), ACL, white and orange on green bottle, 16 ounce . . . . $3–$4
Seven Up, bubble girl, ACL, white and orange on amber . . . . $10–$16
Seven Up, bubble girl, orange and white on green. . . . . $6–$8
Seven Up, in double square, also on shoulder, ACL, white and orange on green bottle, 16 ounce . . . . $3–$5
Seven Up, in double square, also on shoulder, ACL, white and orange on green bottle, 32 ounce . . . . $5–$6
Seymour & Co Buffalo NY, IP, 3/4" pontil crack, 7¹/₈", cobalt. . . . . $60–$80
Shasta, mountains and trees, ACL, blue and white on clear bottle, 7 ounce . . . . . $7–$8
Singer's, large musical note, ACL, green and white on clear bottle, 7 ounce . . . . $6–$9
Southwick & Tupper New York, ten sided, IP, sparkling mint, 7³/₈", cobalt . . . . $500–$700
Sprite, angled name, ACL, white on green bottle, 10 ounce . . . . $2–$3
Sprite, in shield on shoulder, ACL, white on green bottle, 28 ounce . . . . $4–$5
Squirt, ACL, red and yellow on green bottle, 12 ounce . . . . $2–$3
Sun Crest, sunrise, ACL, white and blue on clear bottle, 10 ounce . . . . $2–$4
Sun Drop Golden Cola, ACL, white, orange on green bottle, 7 ounce . . . . $2–$4
Superior Mineral Waters, eight sided, IP, 7¹/₄", cobalt. . . . . $200–$235
T Maher Savannah Geo, SB, 7", emerald green . . . . $35–$45
Tab, ACL, clear bottle, 10 ounce, yellow . . . . $2–$3
Texas Punch, cowboy, ACL, red, white, yellow on green bottle, 7 ounce . . . . . $6–$9
TH Muller's Mineral Water Cincinnati, IP, lightly cleaned, 7", deep cobalt . . . . $600–$800
Tiny Tim, bellhop, ACL, clear bottle, 7 ounce, red and white . . . . $5–$7
Tom Collins Jr, ACL, green bottle, red and white . . . . $4–$6
Top Beverages, top, ACL, clear bottle, 12 ounce, white. . . . . $5–$7
Tupper & Beebe, New York, eight sided, IP, cleaned, exterior wear, 7", emerald green . . . . $40–$60
Tweedle's Celebrated Soda & Mineral Waters, IP, 7¹/₄", medium cobalt. . . . . $250–$350
Twin Lights, two lighthouses in scene, ACL, clear bottle, 7 ounce, red and white . . . . $12–$15
Unembossed, round bottom, 6¹/₈", med yellowish olive amber. . . . . $400–$500
Variety Club Ginger Ale, Toledo, Ohio, ACL, clear bottle, 8.5 ounce, white and blue . . . . $3–$4
Variety Club, lion's crest, ACL, clear bottle, yellow, blue and cream . . . . $6–$8
Vernor's Ginger Ale, Detroit, Mi, ACL, clear bottle, 10 ounce, yellow and green . . . . $3–$5
Vernor's Ginger Ale, Detroit, Mi, ACL, clear bottle, 8 ounce, yellow and green . . . . $3–$5
Vernor's, winking man, ACL, clear bottle, 8 ounce, blue and green . . . . $9–$14
Vess, Billion Bubble, ACL, clear bottle, 7 ounce, orange and white . . . . $2–$3
W Wilke & Co Cin O, 12 sided, IP, lightly cleaned, 7¹/₂", medium green. . $300–$400
W Wilke & Co Cin O, 12 sided, IP, lightly cleaned, deep aqua. . . . . $100–$125
Walsh's Ginger Ale, Albany, NY, ACL, green bottle, 7 ounce, yellow and red . . . . $3–$5
Waring Webster & Co 192 West St NY, eight sided, IP, half pint, cobalt . . . . $400–$600
Warwick Club Ginger Ale, West Warwick, RI, ACL, clear bottle, 7 ounce, white and red . . . . $3–$5

Whistle, ACL, clear bottle, 7 ounce, blue and white . . . . $2–$3
White Lightning, moonshine still, ACL, amber bottle, 10 ounce, orange and white . . .
. . . . $5–$7
White Rock Ginger Ale, New York, ACL, green bottle, 7 ounce, red and white . . . . .
. . . . $3–$5
Wm Betz & Co Pittsbg Mineral Water, OP, ten sided, cleaned, 8", deep aqua . . . . . .
. . . . $120–$145
Wm Cook, ten sided, IP, lightly cleaned, 7", light emerald green . . . . $900–$1250
Wm P Davis & Co Excelsior Mineral Water Brooklyn, eight sided, IP, cleaned with
ground imperfections, 7$1/2$", cobalt . . . . $150–$190
Wm Russell, Balt, round bottom, 9", medium yellowish green . . . . $325–$450
Wm W Lappeus Premium Soda or Mineral Waters, Albany, ten sided, IP, cobalt . .
. . . . $275–$325
Worley's Root Beer, globe, ACL, amber bottle, 10 ounce, orange and white . . . $5–$7
Yankee Doodle, whistling boy, ACL, clear bottle, 7 ounce, red and white . . . . . . $5–$8
Zip, ACL, green bottle, 7 ounce, red and white . . . . $4–$6

TARGET BALLS

Target balls are small round bottles which were used much as clay pigeons are used today for target practice. Target balls were filled with smoke, confetti, silk ribbon or feathers to clearly mark when they were shot in midair. Although the bottles were introduced to America in the 1850s, they did not gain wide popularity until the 1860s and 1870s when Buffalo Bill Cody and Annie Oakley used them in their Wild West shooting shows. In the early days, the target balls were thrown by hand into the air, but in the 1880s a mechanical device was invented to throw the balls. By 1900, target balls had all but become obsolete, due to the invention of the clay pigeon. They are rare today since they were made to be broken, and they come in a variety of colors. Target balls have also become extremely collectible and costly in recent years.

Boer's & CP Delft Flesschenfabriek, diamond pattern, 2$3/4$", light green . . . .
. . . . $1200–$1600
Bogardus Glass Ball Patd April 10 1877, diamond pattern, 2$1/2$", amber . . . .
. . . . $140–$190
Bogardus Glass Ball Patd April 10 1877, diamond pattern, 2$1/2$", cobalt blue . . . .
. . . . $450–$575
Bogardus Glass Ball Patd April 10 1877, diamond pattern, 2$1/2$", medium olive green
. . . . $375–$575
Bogardus Glass Ball Patd April 10 1877, diamond pattern, 2$1/2$", olive amber . . . . . .
. . . . $375–$550

Target ball, Bogardus. PHOTO COURTESY OF
SKINNER'S, INC.

Bogardus Glass Ball Patd April 10 1877, diamond pattern, $2^1/_2$"., deep yellow olive .
. . . . $400–$600
Bogardus Glass Ball Patd April 10 1877, diamond pattern, $2^3/_4$", yellow olive . . . . . .
. . . . $350–$500
Bogardus Glass Ball Patd April 10 1877, diamond pattern, backward 6, $2^5/_8$", gold
amber. . . . . $400–$550
Bogardus Glass Ball Patd April 10 1877, hobnail pattern, $2^3/_4$", yellow amber . . . . . .
. . . . $2000
C Newman, $2^1/_2$", amber . . . . $750–$1100
Charlottenburg Glashutten FW Otte Jun, $2^5/_8$", clear . . . . $1000–$1500
EE Eaton Guns & C 53 State St Chicago, $2^5/_8$", golden yellow amber . . . .
. . . . $2500–$3500
Flesschenfabriek Boers & CP Delft, $2^5/_8$", light olive green . . . . $500–$700
For Hockeys Patent Trap, almost clear, $2^5/_8$", pale green . . . . $300–$400
Glasshuttenwotte Un Charlottenburg, $2^5/_8$", medium yellow olive . . . . $1500–$2000
Gurd & Son 185 Dundas Street London Ont, $2^3/_4$", root beer amber . . . . $400–$600
Gurd & Son 185 Dundas Street London Ont, yellowish root beer amber . . . .
. . . . $300–$450
Hockey Patent, $2^1/_2$", light green . . . . $600–$900
Ira Paine's Filled Ball Pat Oct 23 1877, $2^5/_8$", light yellow . . . . $275–$375
Ira Paine's Filled Ball Pat Oct 23 1877, $2^5/_8$", yellow, amber tone . . . . $175–$250
Ira Paine's Filled Ball Pat Oct 23, 1877, olive tone, $2^5/_8$", yellow amber . . . .
. . . . $200–$250
L Jones Gunmaker Blackburn Lancashire, diamond pattern, $2^3/_4$", light cobalt blue.
. . . . $175–$235
L Jones Gunmaker Blackburn Lancashire, diamond pattern, $2^3/_4$", light sapphire . . .
. . . . $250–$350
L Jones Gunmaker Blackburn Lancashire, diamond pattern, $2^5/_8$", cobalt . . . .
. . . . $200–$250
Man Shooting (in circle), diamond pattern, $2^1/_2$", light pinkish amethyst . . . .
. . . . $250–$300
Man Shooting (in circle), diamond pattern, $2^5/_8$", clear . . . . $150–$250
Man Shooting (in circle), diamond pattern, $2^5/_8$", deep amethyst. . . . . $200–$300
Man Shooting (in circle), diamond pattern, $2^1/_2$", medium pinkish amethyst . . . .
. . . . $350–$450
Man Shooting (in circle), diamond pattern, $2^5/_8$", medium emerald green. . . . .
. . . . $400–$500
NB Glass Works, $2^5/_8$", aqua. . . . . $90–$125
NB Glass Works, backwards "s," $2^5/_8$", medium cobalt . . . . $150–$200

NB Glass Works, backwards "s," upside down "p," 2⁵/₈", medium sapphirre . . . .
. . . . $150–$225
NB Glass Works, clear, diamond pattern, 2¹/₂" . . . . $250–$350
NB Glass Works, Perth, backwards "s," upside down "p," 2³/₄", light sapphire . . . . . .
. . . . $150–$200
Patd Sept 25th 1877 (on shoulder), grainy surface, 2⁵/₈", light olive green . . . .
. . . . $1800–$2300
Sophienhutte In Ilmenau (Thur), 2⁵/₈", amber . . . . $400–$600
Star Pattern, eight pointed star on both sides, 1¹/₂", medium sapphire . . . . $125–$175

Unembossed target ball, diamond patterned.
PHOTO COURTESY OF GLASS WORKS AUCTIONS.

Unembossed, diamond pattern top and bottom, central band with vertical lines, 2⁵/₈",
cobalt . . . . $325–$450
Unembossed, diamond pattern with central label band, 2³/₄", copper . . . . . . $150–$200
Unembossed, diamond pattern with central label band, 2⁵/₈", cobalt . . . . . . $300–$400
Unembossed, diamond pattern, no label panel, 2³/₄", cobalt . . . . $500–$700
Unembossed, large squares pattern, central label band, 2⁵/₈", medium cobalt . . . .
. . . . $150–$200
Unembossed, seven horizontal bands, 2⁵/₈", yellow amber . . . . $325–$475
Unembossed, small squares pattern, central label band, 2⁵/₈", sapphire . . . . $200–$300
Unembossed, three piece mold, no design, 2¹/₄", light cobalt blue . . . . $125–$185
Unembossed, three piece mold, no design, 2³/₄", light sapphire . . . . $175–$235
Unembossed, three piece mold, no design, 2⁵/₈", yellow amber . . . . $80–$120
Van Gutsem A St Quentin (in central band), full diamond pattern, 2³/₄", cobalt . . . .
. . . . $125–$175
Van Gutsem A St Quentin (on central band), diamond pattern on top portion only,
2⁵/₈", cobalt . . . . $400–$500
WW Greener St Mary's Works Birmm & Haymarket London, 2⁵/₈", cobalt . . . . . .
. . . . $90–$125
WW Greener St Mary's Works Birmm & Haymarket London, 2⁵/₈", pink amethyst
. . . . $275–$375
WW Greener St Mary's Works Birmm & Haymarket London, filled with feathers,
sealed with red wax, 2⁵/₈", medium cobalt . . . . $250–$350

TOBACCO JARS

Most of the tobacco jars covered here were made in the late 19th to early 20th century. The jars come in a range of colors, although amber is the most common. A jar lacking its tin lid or bail handle is greatly reduced in value.

Air Tight, original screw on metal lid, 5", deep amber . . . . $80–$120
American Eagle Tobacco (eagle) Detroit Mich, square, metal cap, 6$^{1}/_{2}$", amber . . . . .
. . . . $300–$425
American Eagle Tobacco Co Detroit Mich, square, metal lid, 6$^{3}/_{4}$", amber . . . .
. . . . $100–$150
Aristocratic Cigar, The, A 10¢ Cigar . . . , round, with lid, 5$^{1}/_{4}$", yellow amber . . . . .
. . . . $40–$55
Belfast Cigars United (in shield) Cut Plug, eight sided, 6$^{3}/_{4}$", yellow amber . . . .
. . . . $80–$120
Carl the Great A 10¢ Cigar for 5¢ . . . , metal lid, 5$^{1}/_{8}$", yellow amber . . . $125–$175
Globe Tobacco Co Detroit Mich (on base), round sided, 6$^{3}/_{4}$", amber . . . . . . $30–$40
Globe Tobacco Company Detroit & Windsor, amber tone, lid and handle, 2$^{3}/_{8}$",
yellow . . . . $325–$475
Globe Tobacco Company Detroit & Windsor, amber tone, lid and handle, 6$^{7}/_{8}$",
yellow . . . . $100–$150
Globe Tobacco Company Detroit Michigan, olive tone, lid and handle, 7$^{1}/_{8}$", yellow
. . . . $250–$300
Havana Cigars Est 1857 M Stachelberg & Co World's Fair 1893, lid, 6", yellow
amber . . . . $200–$300
Hays Hair Health, N-399, OP, 6$^{1}/_{2}$", light amber . . . . $25–$35
La Palina The Quality Cigar, clear jar, Congress Cigar Co on base, 7$^{1}/_{4}$" . . . $60–$90

Melon ribbed tobacco jar. PHOTO COURTESY OF
GLASS WORKS AUCTIONS.

Los Equalitos Factory No 63 . . . , amber tone, round, lid, 5¹/₄", golden yellow . . . . . .
. . . . $50–$65
Melon Ribbed Jar, with tin lid and bail, "UST" (on base), 5³/₄", sapphire blue . . . . . .
. . . . $150–$200
Melon Ribbed, UST Co (on base), no lid, 5¹/₂", golden yellow amber. . . . . . $50–$75
Melon Ribbed, UST Co (on base), with lid, 6³/₈", deep turquoise blue . . . . $250–$350
Mercantile Air Tight Havana Cigars, metal screw on lid, 5", amber. . . . . . $90–$135
Mercantile Air Tight Havana Cigars . . . , metal screw lid, 5¹/₄", amber . . . .
. . . . $100–$150
Peerless Food Cigar Manufactured . . . , six sided, amber tone, 6⁵/₈", golden yellow .
. . . . $200–$300
Temple Hummel Ellis Co Manufacturers . . . , amber tone, metal lid, 5", yellow. . . .
. . . . $300–$400
Wm S Kimball & Co Rochester NY, round, eight sided, with metal lid, 6³/₄", amber .
. . . . $40–$55
Wm S Kimball & Co Rochester NY, round, eight sided, with metal lid, 6³/₄", aqua . .
. . . . $30–$45
Wm S Kimball & Co Rochester NY, square, embossed metal lid, 6", yellowish amber
. . . . $125–$175

WARNER BOTTLES

The H.H. Warner Company of Rochester, New York, produced over 20 different varieties of proprietary medicines beginning in 1879. Warner, who previously had been a safe salesman, sold a variety of remedies developed by a
Doctor Craig, one of which had allegedly ridded Warner of Bright's disease.
Warner's products were extensively sold and well marketed, and branch
offices were opened in London, Melbourne, Frankfurt, Prague, and other foreign cities. Warner bottles are frequently found with their original colorful
labels and boxes. Additionally, Warner Almanacs were issued during the
1880s which are also popular with collectors.

Warner's Safe Cure Frankfurt, 9", amber . . . . $400–$475
Warner's Safe Cure Frankfurt, olive green . . . . $425–$600
Warner's Safe Cure Frankfurt, with contents, green . . . . $425–$625
Warner's Safe Cure London, Eng, Toronto, Canada, Rochester, NY, 11", amber. .
. . . . $325–$450
Warner's Safe Cure, London, 4⁵/₈", yellow amber . . . . $325–$425
Warner's Safe Cure, London, 7¹/₄", yellow. . . . . $80–$95
Warner's Safe Cure, London, 9¹/₂", dark amber . . . . $55–$75
Warner's Safe Cure, London, 9¹/₂", olive green . . . . $80–$100

Warner's Safe Cure, London, medium amber. . . . . $35–$45
Warner's Safe Cure, London, olive green. . . . . $100–$135
Warner's Safe Cure, Melbourne, 9¹/₂", amber . . . . $100–$135
Warner's Safe Cure, Melbourne, Aus, London, Eng, Toronto, . . . NY, USA, 9". . .
. . . . $110–$145
Warner's Safe Cure, Rochester NY, London England, Toronto Canada, 9¹/₂",
amber. . . . . $40–$55
Warner's Safe Cure, Rochester NY, with amber tint, 7¹/₄", yellow . . . . . . $90–$125
Warner's Safe Cure, Schutz Marke Pressburg, 9", red amber . . . . $700–$875
Warner's Safe Cure, Schutz Marke Pressburg, aqua . . . . $1000–$1500
Warner's Safe Diabetes Cure, amber tone, 9³/₈", yellow . . . . $120–$165
Warner's Safe Diabetes Cure, Frankfurt, 9³/₈", red amber . . . . $800–$1200
Warner's Safe Diabetes Cure, London, 9¹/₄", yellowish olive green . . . . . $200–$260
Warner's Safe Diabetes Cure, Melbourne, 9¹/₂", golden amber . . . . $300–$390
Warner's Safe Diabetes Cure, Rochester, NY, 9¹/₂", amber . . . . $90–$120
Warner's Safe Diabetes Remedy, Rochester, NY, 16ounce, 9¹/₂", amber . . . $40–$50

Warner's, Kidney & Liver Cure. PHOTO COURTESY OF NEIL GROSSMAN.

Warner's Safe Kidney & Liver Cure, Rochester, NY, 9¹/₂", amber . . . . $15–$20
Warner's Safe Kidney & Liver Cure, Rochester, NY, amber tone, 9¹/₂", yellow. . . .
. . . . $60–$85
Warner's Safe Kidney & Liver Cure, Rochester, NY, labels, 9¹/₄", yellow ambers. .
. . . . : $175–$275
Warner's Safe Kidney & Liver Cure, Rochester, NY, orange . . . . $40–$50
Warner's Safe Kidney & Liver Remedy, Rochester, NY, 16 fl. ounce, 9", amber . . .
. . . . $40–$50
Warner's Safe Log Cabin Liver Pills, with original wrapper . . . . $20–$30
Warner's Safe Nervine, Rochester NY, 7¹/₂", medium amber . . . . $30–$40
Warner's Safe Remedies Co, Rochester NY, 6 fl. ounce, ABM, label, 7¹/₈", medium
amber. . . . . $45–$65
Warner's Safe Remedies Co, Rochester NY, aqua. . . . . $40–$60
Warner's Safe Remedy, Rochester NY, 7¹/₂", medium amber . . . . $30–$45
Warner's Safe Remedy, Rochester NY, 8 fl. ounce, 7¹/₂", amber. . . . . $40–$50
Warner's Safe Rheumatic Cure, Melbourne (slug plate), 9¹/₂", amber . . . .
. . . . $225–$325

Warner's Safe Rheumatic Cure, Rochester, 9¹/₂", amber . . . . $45–$60
Warner's Safe Rheumatic Cure, Rochester, 9⁵/₈", chocolate amber . . . . $75–$90
Warner's Safe Rheumatic Cure, Rochester, full label, 9¹/₂", amber . . . . . $125–$200
Warner's Safe Rheumatic Cure, Rochester, USA, 9¹/₂", amber . . . . $35–$45
Warner's Safe Tonic, Rochester NY, 9¹/₂", medium amber . . . . $200–$250

WHIMSEYS

Whimseys are decorative nonfunctional items often fashioned by glass blowers for their friends and families as gifts. In addition, mass quantities of whimseys were imported from England and elsewhere, such as glass rolling pins and bellows bottles. Collectors should be ever vigilant for any free-hand pieces that have been made out of ordinary bottles, such as the glass mug listed below which was made from a Harrison's ink bottle. Also watch for bottles which have been converted into handled jugs, as well as bottles that were formed into fruit jars or snuff jars and any bottles or containers which have any applied figures or handles.

Several years ago, an unscrupulous dealer hired a glass factory to make "ready-made whimseys" by providing the factory with bottles, flasks, soda, snuffs, etc., which were then reheated and formed into whimsey hats, mugs, jars, etc. Always be cautious of whimseys made from bottles, and ask what collection they came from. Look for consistent wear both on the bottom and on the sides and lip area, since the reheating will fire polish areas of the bottle giving it that shiny, slippery feel of new glass, free of any wear.

Bellows Bottle, footed with rigaree, clear foot, red body, rigaree chips, 16¹/₂" . . . .
. . . . $90–$120
Cane, colorless with red, white and blue spirals, 41" . . . . $125–$175
Cannon Shaped Powder Horn, OP, colorless with blue and red looping, 14" . . . .
. . . . $200–$275
Flask, red and white looping . . . . $125–$175
Hat Made From Pint-Size Ball Fruit Jar, OP, 3³/₄", aqua $450
Hat, Miniature, OP, 1¹/₂", cobalt blue. . . . . $125–$175
Hat, Mrs M Gardners Indian Balsam, OP, 1¹/₈"x2³/₈", aqua $700
Miniature Bellows, colorless cased red with opaque white stripes, OP, 4" . . . .
. . . . $150–$200
Mug, Made From Blown Three Mold Ink, aqua . . . . $7000+
Mug, Made From Harrisons Ink Bottle, OP, 2¹/₁₆", cobalt blue . . . . $7500+
Pipe, free blown, OP, 17", yellow olive. . . . . $200–$300

Flask, tear drop shaped, red and white looping. PHOTO
COURTESY OF GLASS WORKS AUCTIONS.

Pipe, opaque white with pink loopings, 13$^1/_2$".............................$300+
Rolling Pin (possibly fishing float), 6", aqua ....$10–$30

Rolling pin whimsy. PHOTO COURTESY OF GLASS WORKS AUCTIONS.

Rolling Pin, 14", amethyst..$90–$110
Rolling Pin, free blown, OP, 14$^1/_2$", greenish aqua ....$60–$90
Rolling Pin, OP, 12$^3/_4$", cobalt blue..................................$90–$125
Rolling Pin, with opaque white loopings, 16$^3/_4$", aqua ....$200–$275
Rolling Pin, with white specks, OP, 14", dark olive amber.............$100–$140
Snuff, from Sunburst flask, wide mouth, pint, olive green ....$8000+
Turtle Doorstop, 6$^3/_4$"x4$^3/_4$", amber ....$50–$100
Turtle Doorstop, with cobalt shell, solid glass, 7$^1/_2$", aqua..............$200–$300
Witch Ball, 5$^3/_4$", deep amethyst ....$150–$250
Witch Ball, colorless with white loopings, 6$^1/_2$" ....$150–$200

Whimsey, witch balls. PHOTO COURTESY OF
SKINNER'S, INC.

Witch Ball, white milk glass with orange and brown loopings, 5" . . . . $250–$375
Witch Balls, Pair, opaque white with pink loopings, 3" . . . . $500–$700

WHISKEY BOTTLES

Man has enjoyed alcoholic beverages for thousands of years, and whiskey is a relative newcomer to the spirits field. Embossed whiskey bottles became widely available in the 19th century and come in a wide variety of shapes, sizes, and colors.

Acorn Distillery Tipperary Co Irish Whiskey, stoneware jug, 8" . . . . $125–$175
Adams Booth Co, clear, 12" . . . . $100–$150
Altona JT Gayen, SB, gin case, 9¼", olive amber . . . . $100–$145
AM Bininger & Co 19 Broad St New York, cannon, full labels, 12", medium amber .
. . . . $1400–$1800
AM Bininger & Co 19 Broad St NY, Old Kentucky 1849 Reserve, barrel, double collar, 9½", yellow amber . . . . $225–$275
AM Bininger & Co 338 Broadway NY, barrel, OP, 9½", amber . . . .
AM Bininger & Co 338 Broadway NY, Old Kentucky 1849 Reserve, barrel, double collar, 9½", amber . . . . $175–$250
AM Bininger & Co 338 Broadway NY, Old Kentucky 1849 Reserve, barrel, rare applied lip, 9½", amber . . . . $350–$475
AM Bininger & Co Heidelberg Branntwein, SB, 9⅝", yellow olive. . . . . $700–$950
AM Bininger & Co New York, square, 9⅞", amber . . . . $75–$110
AM Bininger & Co No 19 Broad St New York, handled, urn, 9", medium amber . . .
. . . . $1800–$2500
AM Bininger & Co No 19 Broad St New York, urn, 10", yellow amber . . . .
. . . . $1250–$1650
AM Bininger & Co No 375 Broadway NY, square, 9⅝", medium pink puce . . . .
. . . . $400–$550
AM Bininger & Co, No 338 Broad St NY Old London Dry Dock Gin, square, strong olive coloration, 9½", medium yellow. . . . . $150–$200
AM Bininger & Co, Old London Dock Gin, No 19 Broad St, square, 9⅝", yellow olive amber . . . . $125–$175
AM Bininger & Co, Old London Dock Gin, square, 8", medium amber . . $175–$225
AM Bininger & Co, Old London Dock Gin, square, 9½", deep orange amber . . . . . .
. . . . $150–$200
AM Bininger & Co, Old London Dock Gin, square, 9¾", emerald green . . . .
. . . . $200–$260
AM Bininger, No 338 Broadway NY, full labels, 9¾", olive green . . . . . $750–$1000
AM Biningers No 19 Broad St New York, handled, 7¾", medium amber . . . .
. . . . $250–$350

AM Biningers No 19 Broad St New York, handled, 7³/₄", olive green . . . .
. . . . $1200–$1600
Ambrosial, BM & EAW & Co, handled, OP, 8⁷/₈", golden amber chestnut . . . .
. . . . $125–$175
Bartlett's Glass Ware (on base), 11³/₄", yellow olive . . . . $150–$200
Bear Grass Kentucky Bourbon, 12", medium yellowish amber . . . . $3250–$4000
Bennett & Carroll No 120 Wood St Pitts Pa, barrel, IP, 9⁵/₈", amber . . . . $450–$650
Bennett & Carroll No 120 Wood St Pitts Pa, IP, 8¹/₂", amber . . . . $450–$650
Bennett & Carroll No 120 Wood St Pitts Pa, IP, 8³/₈", yellow amber . . . . $750–$950
BF & Co NY, handled stoneware whiskey flask, 7¹/₈" . . . . $250–$300
Bininger New York (grapes), on seal, Ricketts (on base), IP, OP, 11¹/₄", deep olive
amber. . . . . $1250–$1750
Bininger New York, flower (on seal), OP, 11¹/₄", olive amber . . . . $1000–$1250
Bininger's Night Cap No 19 Broad St NY, flask, inner screw threads, 8", amber . . . .
. . . . $350–$450
Bininger's Old Kentucky Bourbon 1849 Reserve No 19 Broad St NY, 9⁵/₈", medium
amber. . . . . $85–$110
Bininger's Old Times Family Rye No 338 Broadway AM Bininger & Co, square,
9³/₄", olive green . . . . $250–$350
Bininger's Peep O Day No 19 Broad St NY, flask, 7³/₄", medium amber. . . . .
. . . . $325–$450
Bininger's Regulator, clock form, OP, 6", amber . . . . $350–$425
Bininger's Regulator, clock form, OP, 6", aqua. . . . . $700–$950
Bininger's Traveler's Guide, tear drop, 6⁵/₈", yellow amber. . . . . $250–$325
Biningers Knickerbocker, handled, OP, 6¹/₂", medium golden amber . . $1200–$1500
Biningers Knickerbocker, OP, handle attachment crack, 6¹/₂", yellow amber . . . .
. . . . $400–$600
Biningers Old Dominion Wheat Tonic, No 19 Broad Street, NY, 10", deep olive
green . . . . $200–$250
BM & EA Whitlock & Co New York, barrel, OP, 8", aqua . . . . $400–$525
Booth & Sedgwick's London Cordial Gin, IP, 8¹/₄", medium emerald green . . . .
. . . . $100–$120
Booth & Sedgwick's London Cordial Gin, OP, square, 7¹/₂", olive green . . . .
. . . . $140–$180
Buchanan Extract of Sugar Corn, cannon, 8³/₄", gold amber. . . . . $1100–$1500
CA Richard's 99 Washington St Boston, 9¹/₂", red amber . . . . $200–$300
CA Richard's 99 Washington St Boston, body bruise, 9¹/₂". . . . . $100–$150
CA Richardson & Co 99 Washington St Boston, flask, 7¹/₂", aqua . . . . $30–$40
CA Richardson & Co 99 Washington St Boston, flask, 7", yellow amber. . . . .
. . . . $175–$250
Cabin Figural (See Log Cabin Figural, this listing)
Campus Gossler Bros Prop's, double handled, 9¹/₂", amber. . . . . $275–$375
Campus Gossler Bros Prop's, handled, 9³/₄", amber. . . . . $85–$125
Casper's Whiskey, 12", cobalt blue . . . . $375–$475
Chesley's Jockey Club Whiskey (race horse), clear, 12" . . . . $200–$240
Chestnut Grove Whiskey CW (on seal), handled chestnut, OP, 8⁵/₈", amber. . . . .
. . . . $150–$190
Chestnut Grove Whiskey CW (on seal), handled chestnut, OP, 8", medium amber . .
. . . . $175–$250
Chestnut Grove Whiskey CW (on seal), handled chestnut, OP, inner stain, 8⁷/₈", yellowish amber. . . . . $100–$145

Chestnut grove handled chestnut bottle. PHOTO
COURTESY OF GLASS WORKS AUCTIONS.

Chicken Cock Bourbon, enameled rooster, clear bar bottle, 6³/₄" . . . . $900–$1350
Coates & Co Original Plymouth Gin, enameled monk, clear bar bottle, 8¹/₂" . . . .
. . . . $150–$225
Cognac W & Co (on seal), handled, OP, 5³/₄", medium amber . . . . $300–$400
Continental Hotel 20th St & Broadway, strap flask, metal screw cap, 7¹/₄", yellow
amber. . . . . $100–$140
Cream of Old Scotch Whiskey Bonnie Castle, The, stoneware jug, 9" . . . . . $60–$90
Cutter OK Whiskey JH Cutter Old Bourbon, 12", yellowish amber . . . . . $75–$100
Davy Crockett Hey Grauerholtz & Co, 12³/₈", amber . . . . $700–$950
Don Rex Whiskey, with reclining and standing dogs, clear, 11" . . . . $800–$1000
Duffy Crescent Saloon 204 Jefferson St Louisville Ky, pig, 7⁵/₈", aqua . . . .
. . . . $700–$1000
Eagle Glass Works (on base), cylinder, 11¹/₄", deep red amber. . . . . $90–$135
Eagle Glen Whiskey (flying eagle), clear, 11" . . . . $100–$150
Ear of Corn Figural Decanter, with stopper, handled, 8³/₄", green. . . . . . . $140–$180
Edgewood Whiskey, enameled fat man, clear bar bottle, 7". . . . . $275–$375
Egg Nog Patented 1859, full label, 9", medium yellow amber. . . . . $500–$700
Elk's Heart Whiskey, with enameled Elk, clear bar bottle, 11" . . . . $900–$1200
Emerald Meehan's Superior Irish Whiskey, stoneware jug, 7". . . . . $100–$125
EN Cooke & Co Distillers Buffalo NY, case gin, 9³/₄", amber . . . . $225–$275
Ewbank's Topaz Cinchona Cordial, 9³/₈", amber. . . . . $125–$150
F (in diamond), 131 Bourbon, handled jug, 9¹/₂", amber. . . . . $300–$500
Fleckenstein & Mayer Portland Or, clear coffin flask, 5" . . . . $75–$100
Forest Lawn JVH, IP, 7¹/₂", olive green . . . . $350–$500
From the Casper Co Inc, 12", cobalt . . . . $700–$900
Good Samaritan Brandy, IP, olive amber . . . . $800–$1200
Grant's Liquer, pottery handled jug, with stopper, 8" . . . . $125–$175
Gray Thur, Erin Go Bragh Dew Thom . . ., stoneware jug, 7¹/₂" . . . . $90–$120
Griffith Hyatt & Co Baltimore, handled, OP, ¹/₂" lip chip, 7¹/₄", medium yellow
amber. . . . . $200–$225
Griffith Hyatt & Co Baltimore, handled, OP, 7¹/₄", golden amber . . . . $250–$375
Griffith Hyatt & Co Baltimore, handled, OP, 7¹/₄", yellow root beer amber . . . .
. . . . $400–$650

Griffith Hyatt & Co Baltimore, handled, OP, 7³/₈", medium olive green . . . .
. . . . $1600–$2200
Gromes & Ullrich Chicago (on seal), clear, 12¹/₂" . . . . $25–$30
H Pharazyn Phila Right Secured, Indian queen, 12", yellow amber . . . . $950–$1200
HA Graef's Son NY Canteen, double handled, SB, 6⁵/₈", olive green. . . . . $500–$625
Hall Luhr's & Co Sacramento, clear, 12" . . . . $75–$100
Hayner's Whiskey, clear, quart. . . . . $12–$16
Hayner's Whiskey, combination lock stopper, clear, quart . . . . $35–$45
Henry Chapman & Co Sole Agents Montreal, tear drop, inner screw thread with
stopper, 5¹/₂", amber . . . . $200–$250
Henry Koch Los Angeles Cal, 6¹/₂", clear pumpkinseed . . . . $150–$200
HG & Co Phila, flask, 6¹/₂", sapphire blue . . . . $225–$325
I Nelson's Old Bourbon Maysville Ky, barrel, 7³/₈", gold amber . . . . . . $2500–$3000
Imperial Levee J Noyes Hollywood Miss, IP, 9³/₈", yellowish amber. . . $1600–$2200
IXL Valley Whiskey E&B Bevan Pittston Pa, eight panels, OP, 7", red amber . . . . .
. . . . $800–$1200
J & R Dunster London, square, 9¹/₂", amber . . . . $35–$40
James Kerr Gibson Old Rye A Specialty, flask, 8", medium amber . . . . . $140–$180
JD Heise & Co Groceries Wines & Liquors, flask, 7", amber . . . . $2000–$2500
JFT & Co, Philad (on seal), handled, OP, 7", golden yellow amber . . . . . . $500–$750
JH & CF Miller, coffin form, 7¹/₂", medium amber . . . . $125–$175
JN Kline & Co Aromatic Digestive Cordial, 70% label, stopper, 5¹/₂", cobalt . . . . . .
. . . . $375–$475
JN Kline & Co Aromatic Digestive Cordial, tear drop, 5¹/₂", amber . . . . . $275–$350
JN Kline & Co Aromatic Digestive Cordial, tear drop, 5¹/₂", cobalt . . . . . $350–$450
Jos Melczer & Co Wholesale Liquor Dealers, clear, 11³/₄" . . . . $70–$95
KB Daly 118 Wall St New York, 8⁷/₈", deep amber. . . . . $75–$125
Kolberg & Cavagnaro Wholesale Liquors, clear, 11¹/₂" . . . . $200–$300
L Lyon's Pure Ohio Catawba Brandy, 13³/₈", deep amber . . . . $200–$275
Lancaster Glass Works Lancaster NY (on base), barrel, 9", puce amber . . . .
. . . . $200–$285
Laurel Crown Old Bourbon (crown over barrel), 11³/₄", amber. . . . . . $5000–$7000
Lediard's Morning Call, 10¹/₈", medium olive green . . . . $150–$200
LM & Co New York (on seal), handled, OP, 9⁵/₈", deep root beer amber . . . .
. . . . $1250–$1750
Log Cabin Figural Whiskey, unembossed, ABM, 9⁷/₈", amber. . . . . $80–$120
London Jockey Club House Gin, 9¹/₈", medium blue green . . . . $125–$175
LQC Wishart's Pine Tree Cordial Phila Patent, 9¹/₂", medium emerald green . . . . .
. . . . $150–$200
Mette & Kanne Distilling Co St Louis Mo, square, 9¹/₂", amber . . . . $30–$45
Meyer Bros & Co, square, 9¹/₂", amber . . . . $30–$45
Miller's Extra Trade Mark E Martin & Co Old Bourbon, flask, 7", amber . . . .
. . . . $2000–$3000
Mist of the Morning, barrel, 9⁷/₈", golden amber . . . . $250–$300
Mohawk Whiskey, Indian figural, 12³/₈", yellow amber. . . . . $1400–$1750
O'Donnel's Old Irish Whiskey, stoneware jug, 8". $70–$95
Ohio Cider, 1825 & 1827 S 7th St, cylinder, 11¹/₂", amber. . . . . $50–$75
Old Bourbon Castle Whiskey F Chevalier & Co, 12", medium yellow amber . . . . . .
. . . . $300–$400
Old Mill, The, Whitlock & Co (on medal around neck), pour spout, OP, handle, tail
missing, 8¹/₈", medium amber. . . . . $200–$250

Old Overholt Pure Rye, enameled old man's bust, clear bar bottle, 11" . . . $400–$525
Old Wheat Whiskey SM & Co, three piece mold, 11", amber . . . . $225–$275
Old Wheat Whiskey SM & Co, three piece mold, OP, 11", amber . . . . $350–$500
Osceola Exchange Tavaras Fla, strap flask, half pint, yellow amber . . . . . $300–$450
Our Choice Old Bourbon, 11⅞", medium orange amber . . . . $3000–$4000
Patented (around shoulder), 11¼", olive green . . . . $30–$45
Patented (around shoulder), Whitney Glassworks (on base), 11¼", aqua . . . $60–$95
Pepper Distillery Hand Made Sour Mash, 12", medium yellowish amber . . . .
. . . . $150–$225
Pure Malt Whiskey, Bourbon Co, Kentucky, handled, 8⅝", amber . . . . . $500–$750
RB Cutter Louisville Ky, handled, mint, 8½", golden amber . . . . $250–$350
RB Cutter Louisville Ky, handled, OP, 8½", medium yellow amber . . . . $300–$375
RB Cutter Louisville Ky, handled, OP, 8⅜", deep amber . . . . $200–$275
RB Cutter Louisville Ky, handled, OP, 8⅝", root beer amber . . . . $225–$275
RB Cutter Louisville Ky, handled, scratches, 8½", golden amber . . . . $200–$260
RB Cutter Pure Bourbon, handled, IP, 8¾", strawberry puce . . . . $300–$400
RB Cutter Pure Bourbon, handled, IP, 8⅜", medium smoky pinkish puce . . . .
. . . . $500–$750
RB Cutter Pure Bourbon, handled, OP, 8½", medium yellow amber . . . . $350–$475
Red Top Rye, cylinder, 12", olive green . . . . $140–$185
Relda Pure Rye, with enameled eagle, clear bar bottle, 11" . . . . $600–$800
Ribbed, 24 ribs swirled, flattened chestnut, handled, OP, golden amber . . . . $350–$450
Russ's Aromatic Schnapps New York, IP, 9⅞", deep aqua . . . . $300–$475
Simmond's Nabob Trade Mark Pure Ky Bourbon Whiskey, 11", amber . . . .
. . . . $600–$900
SM & Co NY (on seal), handled, OP, 7½", yellow amber . . . . $500–$700
SS Smith, Jr & Co Cincinnati O, cabin form, 9⅝", cobalt . . . . $2000–$3000
Star Whiskey New York WB Crowell Jr, handled, handle tail missing, OP, 8¼",
yellow amber. . . . . $250–$300
Star Whiskey New York WB Crowell Jr, handled, labeled, OP, 8⅛", yellow amber .
. . . . $500–$750
Star Whiskey New York WB Crowell Jr, handled, OP, 8", gold yellow amber . . . . .
. . . . $350–$500
Theodore Netter, Greeting, 1232 Market St, Philada, Pa, barrel, 6", cobalt . . . .
. . . . $200–$245
Theodore Netter, Greeting, 1232 Market St, Philada, Pa, clear barrel, 6" . . . .
. . . . $100–$125
TJ Dunbar & Co (on base), IP, 9⅜", olive amber . . . . $110–$160
Turner Brothers New York, barrel, 9¾", medium olive green . . . . $800–$1200
Turner Brothers New York, barrel, 9¾", pure olive green . . . . $200–$260
Turner Brothers New York, barrel, 9⅞", yellow olive . . . . $400–$525
Udolpho Wolfe's Schiedam Aromatic Schnapps, IP, 8", olive green . . . . . $90–$125
Udolpho Wolfe's Schiedam Aromatic Schnapps, SB, full label, 9¾", olive green . . .
. . . . $80–$120
Unembossed Flattened Chestnut, handled, OP, 8", yellow amber . . . . $40–$60
Unembossed Handled Chestnut, flattened, smooth base, 7", amber . . . . $25–$40
Unembossed Handled Ewer Form, 10", golden amber . . . . $100–$150
Unembossed Handled Globular Bottle, OP, 7", medium gold apricot puce . . . .
. . . . $150–$225
Unembossed Handled Jug, IP, sloping collar, 6⅛", deep puce . . . . $125–$175
Unembossed Inverted Cone Form, OP, double collar, 9", gold amber . . . . $150–$240

Whiskey, Turner Brothers, barrel. PHOTO COURTESY OF NEIL GROSSMAN.

Wharton's handled jug. PHOTO COURTESY OF GLASS WORKS AUCTIONS.

US Mail, mail box form, clear, 6⁷/₈" . . . . $75–$125
Van Dunck's Genever Trade Mark Ware & Schmitz, coachman, 8⁵/₈", amber . . . . .
. . . . $60–$90
Vidvard & Sheehan, handled, 9³/₄", yellow olive. . . . . $1400–$1800
Weeks & Gilson So Stoddard NH (on base), 11⁷/₈", olive amber. . . . . $350–$450
Weeks Glass Works (on base), cylinder, 11¹/₄", reddish amber. . . . . $75–$100
Wharton's Whiskey 1850 Chestnut Grove, handled, "Whitney Glassworks Glassboro
NJ" (on base), pour spout, 10", amber . . . . $300–$450
Wharton's Whiskey Chestnut Grove, tear drop, 5", cobalt blue . . . . $350–$400
Wharton's Whiskey Chestnut Grove, tear drop, 5", medium amber . . . . . $250–$300
Wharton's Whiskey Chestnut Grove, tear drop, lip flake, 5¹/₂", cobalt blue . . . .
. . . . $300–$375
White (seal) Whiskey, enameled, clear bar bottle, 11". . . . . $550–$750
Whitney Glassworks (on base), handled ewer form, SB, 9⁷/₈", yellow amber . . . .
. . . . $150–$200
Whitney Glassworks (on base), Patented on shoulder, 11", aqua . . . . $60–$95
Whitney Glassworks (on base), Patented on shoulder, 11", olive amber . . . . $40–$65
Wicklow Distiller Old Irish Whiskey, stoneware jug, 7¹/₂" . . . . $200–$260

Wickman & Lutchen Old Gilt Edge, clear flask, $5^7/_8$" . . . . $50–$75
Wisher's Club House, IP, case gin shaped, $9^5/_8$", deep red puce . . . . $450–$600
Wm H Daly Sole Importer New York, OP, $9^1/_4$", olive green . . . . $750–$1000
Wm H Spears & Co Old Pioneer Braunschweiger, clear, 12". . . . . $300–$360
Wm H Spears & Co Old Pioneer Whiskey A Fenkhausen, clear, 12" . . . $500–$700
WSC Club House Gin, case gin, SB, $9^1/_4$", olive green . . . . $190–$235
Young & Holmes Cincinnati O, cabin, $9^3/_8$", deep amber . . . . $300–$400

NEW BOTTLES

AVON BOTTLES

Avon has been calling for more than 50 years, and the call from collectors for imaginative, decorative toiletries and cosmetic bottles has brought a stampede upon the antique shops. As the modern leader in the nonliquor bottle field, Avon's vast range of bottles offers almost unlimited opportunities for the collector. Since none of their figurals are extremely rare, a complete collection of them is possible, though it would contain hundreds of specimens.

Today, the Avon figurals—shaped as animals, people, cars, and numerous other objects—are the most popular of the company's bottles, but not always the most valuable. Some of the early nonfigurals of the pre-World War II era sell for high prices because of their scarcity. Since there were virtually no Avon collectors in those days, very few specimens were preserved.

Avon collecting has become such a science that all of its bottles, and even the boxes that they came in, have been carefully catalogued. In fact, everything relating to Avon is now regarded as collectible, including brochures, magazine ads, and anything bearing the Avon name. Of course, the older material is more sought after than items of recent vintage.

Avon bottles are readily obtainable through specialized dealers and numerous other sources. Since some people who sell Avon are unaware of their value, the collector can often find bargain prices at garage sales or flea markets.

Although it seems that every possible subject has been exhausted, Avon continues to bring out original bottles in a variety of sizes, colors, and decorative designs. The new figurals in its line are issued in limited editions, with editions being rather large in order to accommodate the collector as well as the general public. Collectors of new Avons should purchase the new issues as soon as they reach the market since they often sell out quickly. When an Avon product has sold out, its price begins rising and can double in less than a year depending on its popularity. Even though this does not always happen, the original retail price will be lower than can be expected later on in the collector's market. Although Avon is the oldest toiletry company issuing decorative bottles, collecting interest in its products did not become widespread until stimulated by the 1965 release of an after-shave lotion in a stein decanter and a men's cologne in an amber boot. The interest created by those toiletries led many people to investigate the earlier Avon products, partly for collecting and partly for use as decorations. At that time they could be purchased inexpensively from secondhand shops and thrift bazaars. Unfortunately, by then many of the older ones had perished and were just not to be found.

By the late sixties, Avons were plentiful in antique shops with prices on the rise. Some collecting clubs were established. The early seventies saw further increases in collecting activity. The company, well aware of what was happening, expanded its line of figurals to meet public demand.

Many collectors doubt that modern Avon figurals can ever become really valuable because of the large quantities made. But with natural loss, passage of time, and increasing collector demand, Avon figurals may well reach respectable prices in five or ten years, making the 1984 prices look like great bargains.

Just as with many other collectibles, the Avons that prove least popular when issued sometimes end up being the scarcest and costliest. This is why collectors automatically buy each one as they come out. Avon began as the California Perfume Company, founded by DH McConnell, a door-to-door salesman who gave away perfume samples to prevent doors from being slammed in his face. Eventually he started selling perfume and abandoned book selling. Although it was located in New York, the name "Avon" was initially used in 1929 in conjunction with the California Perfume Company or CPC. After 1939 it was known exclusively as Avon. The C.P.C. bottles are naturally very desirable, having been used in relatively small quantities and not having been well preserved. These bottles are impossible to date accurately because many designs were used with various preparations. In most cases, sales do not occur frequently enough to establish firm price levels.

Therefore, the prices listed in this book should be regarded only as being approximate. There are numerous possible approaches to Avon collecting. The most popular is to amass as many figurals as one's budget, time, and energy (not to mention luck) allow. They can also be collected by subject matter, or according to the type of product they originally contained-such as perfume or after shave. Another favorite specialty is Avons with figural stoppers.

Abraham Lincoln, 1970-72, Wild Country After Shave . . . . $4–$7
After Shave On Tap, 1974-75, Wild Country. . . . . $3–$5
American Belle, 1976-78, Sonnet Cologne . . . . $4.75–$5.5
American Eagle, 1971-72, Windjammer After Shave . . . . $4–$6
American Schooner, 1972-73, Oland After Shave . . . . $3.50–$4.50
Angler, 1970, Windjammer After Shave . . . . $5–$7
Apothecary, 1973, Breath Fresh . . . . $3–$4
Apothecary, 1973-76, Lemon Velvet Moist Lotion . . . . $3–$4
Apothecary, Spicy After Shave, 1973-74 . . . . $3–$4

Aristocrat Kittens Soap, 1971 .... $4.75–$5.75
Armoire Decanter, 1972-75, Charisma Bath Oil .... $3–$5
Armoire Decanter, 1972-75, Elusive Bath Oil .... $3–$5
Armoire Decanter, 1972-75, Fields And Flowers Bath Oil .... $3–$4
Auto, Big Mack Truck, 1973-75, Windjammer After Shave .... $3–$5
Auto, Cord, 1937 Model, 1974-75, Wild Country Afte Shave .... $5–$8
Auto, Country Vendor, 1973, Wild Country After Shave .... $5–$6
Auto, Dune Buggy, 1971-73, Sports Rally Bracing Lotion .... $4.50–$5
Auto, Dusenberg, Silver, 1970-72, Wild Country After Shave .... $7.50–$8.75
Auto, Electric Charger, 1970-72, Avon Leather Cologne .... $4–$6
Auto, Electric Charger, 1970-72, Spicy After Shave. .... $4–$6
Auto, Hayes Apperson, 1973-74, 1902 Model, Avon Blend 7After Shave ..... $4–$6
Auto, Maxwell 23, 1972-74, Deep Woods After Shave .... $4–$6
Auto, MG, 1936, 1974-75, Wild Country After Shave .... $3–$5
Auto, Model A, 1972-74, Wild Country After Shave .... $4–$6
Auto, Red Depot Wagon, 1972-73, Oland After Shave .... $4–$6
Auto, Rolls Royce, 1972-75, Deep Woods After Shave .... $5–$8
Auto, Stanley Steamer, 1971-72, Windjammer After Shave .... $4–$6
Auto, Station Wagon, 1971-73, Tai Winds After Shave .... $4–$7
Auto, Sterling 6, 1968-70, Spicy After Shave. .... $3–$5
Auto, Sterling Six II, 1973-74, Wild Country After Shave .... $3–$4
Auto, Stutz Bearcat, 1974-77, 1914 Model, Avon Blend 7After Shave .. $4.75–$5.50
Auto, Touring T, 1969-70, Tribute After Shave. .... $4–$5
Auto, Volkswagen, 1972, Red, Oland After Shave. .... $2–$4
Avon Baby Soap, 1969-75. .... $1–$2
Avon Open, 1969-70, Windjammer After Shave .... $4–$6
Avon Open, 1972-75, Wild Country After Shave .... $4–$5
Avonshire Blue Soaps, 1971-74 .... $3–$5
Baby Grand Piano, 1971-72, Perfume Glace .... $5–$8
Bath Urn, 1971-73, Lemon Velvet Bath Oil .... $2–$3
Beautiful Awakening, 1973-74, Roses Roses. .... $3–$5
Benjamin Franklin, 1974-76, Wild Country After Shave .... $3–$4
Big Berry Strawberry, 1973-74, Bath Foam. .... $2–$2.50
Big Game Rhino, 1972-73, Tai Winds After Shave .... $3–$4
Bird House Powder Bubble Bath, 1969. .... $3–$5
Bird Of Paradise Cologne Decanter, 1972-74, Skin So Soft Bath Oil .... $3–$5
Blacksmiths Anvil, 1972-73, Deep Woods After Shave. .... $3–$4
Bloodhound Pipe, 1976, Deep Woods After Shave .... $4–$5
Blue Moo Soap On A Rope, 1972 .... $4–$6
Bon Bon Black, 1973, Field & Flowers Cologne .... $2–$3
Bon Bon White, 1972-73, Occur Cologne. .... $2–$3
Bon Bon White, 1972-73, Topaze Cologne. .... $2–$3
Boot Gold Top, 1966-71, Avon Leather After Shave .... $3–$4
Buffalo Nickle, 1971-72, Liquid Hair Lotion .... $3.50–$4.50
Bulldog Pipe, 1972-73, Oland After Shave. .... $3.50–$4.50
Bunny Puff & Talc, 1969-72, Her Prettiness Perfume Talc .... $1–$2
Buttercup Candlestick, 1974, Sonnet Cologne .... $3–$6
Buttercup Salt Shaker, 1974, Sonnet Cologne. .... $1–$2
Butterfly, 1972-73, Occur Cologne .... $2–$4
Butterfly, 1972-73, Somewhere Cologne .... $2–$4
Butterfly, 1972-73, Unforgettable Cologne. .... $2–$4

Butterfly, 1974-76, Unforgettable Cologne............................$2–$4
Camper, 1972-74, Deep Woods After Shave ....$4–$6
Canada Goose, 1973-74, Deep Woods Cologne.......................$4–$6
Candlestick Cologne, 1970-71, Elusive ....$3–$5
Candlestick Cologne, 1972-75, Moonwind ....$3–$5
Candlestick Cologne, 1972-75, Roses Wind.........................$3–$5
Capital Decanter, 1970-71, Tribute After Shave ....$3–$5
Caseys Lantern, 1966-67, Island Lime After Shave..................$30–$40
Catch A Fish, 1976-78, Field Flowers Cologne ....$4–$5
Chimney Lamp, 1973-74, Moonwind................................$2–$3
Christmas Ornament, 1970-71, Green Or Red ....$3–$4
Christmas Ornament, 1970-71, Orange, Bubble Bath.................$3–$5
Classic Beauty, 1972-76, Field Flowers Body Lotion.................$1–$2
Classic Decanter, 1969-70, Skin So Soft Bath Oil ....$3–$5
Classic Lion, 1973-75, Deep Woods After Shave....................$3–$5
Clean Shot, 1970-72 ....$2–$4
Club Bottle, 1972, 1st Annual ....$150–$200
Club Bottle, 1973, 2nd Annual ....$30–$50
Club Bottle, 1974, Bud Hastin....................................$70–$95
Club Bottle, 1974, CPC Factory ....$30–$40
Club Bottle, 1976, 5th Annual....................................$25–$30
Club Bottle, 1977, 1906 Avon Lady ....$25–$28
Cockatoo Powder, 1972-73, Floral Medley ....$4–$6
Collector's Pipe, 1973-74, Windjammer After Shave................$2–$4
Cologne Classic, 1967-68, Unforgettable ....$2–$3
Cologne Mist, 1966-67, Somewhere ....$0.50–$0.75
Cologne Royal, 1972-74, Field Flowers ....$1–$2
Cologne, Roses, 1972-74, Roses ....$2–$3
Compote Decanter, 1972-75, Moonwind ....$2–$4
Cornucopia, 1971-76, Skin So Soft.................................$2–$4
Country Kitchen, 1973-75, Moisture Hand Lotion ....$2–$4
Country Store Coffee Mill, 1972-74, Field Flowers ....$1–$3
Courting Carriage, 1973-74, Flower Talk Cologne..................$2–$3
Covered Wagon, 1970-71, Wild Country After Shave................$2–$4
Creamery Decanter, 1973-75, Roses Roses Body Lotion ....$2–$3
Crystalline Cologne, 1970-71, Somewhere ....$2–$3
Dolphin Soap Dish And Hostess Soaps, 1970-71 ....$7–$9
Dutch Girl Figurine, 1973-74, Somewhere ....$4–$5
Dutch Treat Demi Cup, 1971, Hawaiian White Ginger...............$2–$4
Eight Ball Decanter, 1973, Spicy After Shave ....$1–$2
Electric Guitar, 1974-75, Wild Country After Shave.................$4–$7
Elizabethan Fashion Figure, 1972, Field Flowers Cologne ....$10–$15
Emerald Bud Vase, 1971, Occuri Cologne...........................$1–$2
Emollient Freshener, 1972-74, Moonwind...........................$1–$2
Enchanted Frog Cream Sachet, 1973-76, Sonnet.....................$2–$3
English Provincial, 1972-74, any series............................$0.75–$1
Excalibur Cologne, 1969-73, Excalibur ....$2.50–$3.25
Fashion Boot, 1972-76, Moonwind Cologne.........................$3–$5
Fashion Boot, 1972-76, Sonnet Cologne............................$3–$5
Fashion Figurine, 1971-72, Bird Of Paradise.......................$6–$9
Fashion Figurine, 1971-72, Brocade...............................$6–$9

Fashion Figurine, 1971-72, Field Flowers .... $6–$9
Fashion Figurine, 1972-74, Roaring '20s, Unforgettable .... $6–$9
First Class Male, 1970-71, Wild Country After Shave .... $3–$5
First Down, 1970, Wild Country After Shave .... $3–$4
First Down, 1970-71, Soap On A Rope. .... $3–$5
First Volunteer, 1971-72, Tai Winds Cologne .... $6–$9
Floral Duet Hawaiian White Ginger, 1972-73 .... $2–$3
Flower Basket Soap Dish And Hostess Soaps, 1972-74 .... $4–$6
Flower Maiden, 1973-74, Cotillion .... $4–$5
Fragrance & Frills, 1972-75, Soap .... $5–$8
French Telephone, 1971, Moonwind Foaming Bath Oil .... $15–$25
Garden Girl, 1978-79, Sweet Honesty Cologne .... $2–$4
Garnet Bud Vase, 1973-76, To A Wild Rose Cologne .... $1–$2
Gavel, 1967-68, Island Lime After Shave .... $6–$9
George Washington, 1970-72, Spicy After Shave .... $2–$2.50
George Washington, 1970-72, Tribute After Shave .... $2–$2.50
Gift Cologne, 1969, Topaze .... $3.25–$3.75
Gift Of The Sea, 1987, Soaps And Baskets .... $3–$6
Grade Avon Hostess Soap, 1971-72 .... $3–$6
Grecian Pitcher, 1972-76, Skin So Soft Bath Oil .... $3–$4
Hearth Lamp, 1973-76, Roses .... $4–$7
Hobnail Bud Vase, 1973-74, Roses Cologne .... $2–$3
Hobnail Decanter, 1972-74, Moonwind Bath Oil .... $2–$4
Honeysuckle Floral Duet Set, 1972-73 .... $3–$4
Indian Chieftan, 1972-75, Protein Hair Lotion .... $2–$4
Indian Head Penny, 1970-72, Bravo After Shave .... $3–$6
Inkwell, 1969-70, Windjammer After Shave .... $4–$6
Iron Horse Shaving Mug, 1974-76, Avon Blend 7After Shave .... $1–$3
King, 1972-73, Tai Winds After Shave .... $4.50–$5.75
Kitten Petite, 1973-74, Moonwind Cologne .... $2–$4
Koffee Klatch, 1971-74, Honeysuckle Foam Bath Oil .... $2–$5
Koffee Klatch, 1971-74, Lilac Foaming Bath Oil .... $2–$5
Leisure Hours, 1970-72, Charisma Bath Oil .... $3–$5
Leisure Hours, 1970-72, Regence Bath Oil .... $3–$5
Liberty Bell, 1971-72, Tribute After Shave .... $2–$5
Liberty Dollar, 1970-72, Oland After Shave, silver .... $3–$5
Lip Pop Colas, 1973-74, Cherry .... $1–$2
Lip Pop Colas, 1973-74, Cola .... $1–$2
Lip Pop Colas, 1973-74, Strawberry .... $1–$2
Little Girl Blue, 1972-73, Brocade .... $4–$6
Little Girl Blue, 1972-73, Cotillion .... $4–$6
Long Drive, 1973-75, Electric Pre-Shave .... $2–$4
Looking Glass, 1970-72, Brocade Cologne .... $5–$8
Looking Glass, 1970-72, Elusive Cologne .... $5–$8
Looking Glass, 1970-72, Regence Cologne .... $5–$8
Love Bird Perfume, 1969-70, Elusive .... $3–$4.50
Lovely Touch Decanter, 1971, Rich Moisture Body Lotion .... $1–$2
Mandolin, 1971-72, Perfume Glace .... $6–$9
Mighty Mitt Soap On A Rope, 1969-72 .... $6–$9
Ming Cat, 1971, Bird Of Paradise Cologne .... $5–$7
Mini Bike, 1972-73, Sure Winner Bracing Lotion .... $3–$5

Moonwind Perfumed Soaps, 1972-73 .... $5.25–$6.25
Nile Blue Bath Urn, 1972-74, Skin So Soft Bath Oil .... $2–$3
Nile Blue Bath Urn, 1972-74, Skin So Soft .... $2–$3
Old Faithful, 1972-73, Wild Country After Shave .... $3–$6
Opening Play, 1968-69, Dull Golden, Spicy After Shave .... $8–$9.50
Opening Play, 1968-69, Shiny Golden, Spicy After Shave............... $15–$19
Oriental Egg Peach Orchard, 1974-75, Moonwind Perfume .... $5–$9
Oriental Figurine, 1972, Pomander...................................... $6–$7.50
Owl Fancy, 1974-76, Roses, Roses .... $1–$2
Owl Soap Dish And Soaps, 1970-71 .... $6–$9
Parlor Lamp Set, 1971-72, Moonwind Cologne And Talc .... $5–$9
Partridge & Pear Gift Soaps, 1974-75................................. $5–$8
Partridge, 1973-75, Occur... $1–$2
Peanuts Gang Soaps, 1970-72 .... $7–$11
Peep-A-Boo Soap On A Rope, 1970...................................... $5–$8
Peggy Pelican Soap On A Rope, 1972-73 .... $3–$5
Pennsylvania Dutch Cologne, 1973-74, Patchwork...................... $2–$4
Pennsylvania Dutch Sachet, 1973-75, Sonnet .... $2–$4
Period Piece, Moonwind, 1972-73 .... $2–$4
Piano Decanter, 1972, Tai Winds After Shave........................... $2–$5
Picture Frame, 1970-71, Elusive .... $8–$12
Picture Frame, 1970-71, Regence....................................... $8–$12
Pineapple Petite, 1972-74, Roses, Roses Cologne .... $1–$2
Pineapple, 1973-74, Moisturized Hand Lotion .... $1–$2
Pipe, 1971-72, Full, Decanter, Spicy After Shave, brown................ $2–$3
Pipe, 1972-74, Full, Decanter, Spicy After Shave, green................ $1–$3
Pitcher And Bowl, 1972-74, Delft Blue .... $5–$8
Pony Decanter, 1968-69, Short, Wild Country After Shave.............. $2–$3
Pony Express, 1971-72, Avon Leather After Shave .... $3–$4
Precious Owl, 1972-74, Charisma....................................... $1–$3
Precious Owl, 1972-74, Field Flowers .... $1–$3
President Lincoln, 1973, Tai Winds After Shave......................... $4–$7
President Washington, 1974-76, Deep Woods After Shave .... $2–$4
Purse Petite, 1971, Filed Flowers Cologne .... $2–$4
Queen Of Scotts, 1973-76, Sweet Honesty Cologne...................... $1–$3
Queen, 1973-74, Tai Winds After Shave................................. $2–$3
Rainbow Trout, 1973-74, Deep Woods After Shave .... $3–$5
Regal Peacock, 1973-74, Sonnet Cologne............................... $3–$5
Remember When School Desk, 1972-74, Cotillion Cologne............. $2–$4
Rook, 1973-74, Spicy After Shave....................................... $2–$3
Royal Apple, 1972-73, Bird Of Paradise Cologne........................ $2–$3
Royal Coach, 1972-73, Bird Of Paradise Bath Oil .... $2–$3
Royal Swan, 1971-72, Bird Of Paradise .... $2–$3
Scent Of Roses Decanter, 1972-73, Cologne Jelly....................... $1–$2
Scent With Love, 1971-72, Elusive Perfume .... $3–$4
Scent With Love, 1971-72, Field Flowers Perfume .... $3–$4
Scent With Love, 1971-72, Moonwind Perfume.......................... $3–$4
Sea Horse Miniature, 1973-76, Here's My Heart Cologne .... $2–$3
Sea Maiden, 1971-72, Skin So Soft Bath Oil .... $3–$4
Sea Sprite, 1973-76, Elusive .... $2–$3
Sea Treasure, 1971-72, Field Flowers................................... $3–$5

Sea Trophy, 1972, Windjammer After Shave . . . . $4–$6
Secretaire, 1972-75, Moonwind Foaming Bath Oil . . . . $3–$5
Shampoo Shower Soap, 1972-73, For Men . . . . $3–$4
Side-Wheeler, 1970-71, Tribute After Shave . . . . $2–$4
Side-Wheeler, 1971-72, Wild Country After Shave . . . . $2–$3
Sitting Pretty, 1971-73, Cotillion Cologne . . . . $3–$4
Skin So Soft Softener, 1972-74, Delft Blue . . . . $3–$4
Slipper Soap And Perfume Charisma, 1970-71 . . . . $6–$9
Small World Perfume Glace, 1971-72, Small World . . . . $2–$3
Smart Move, 1973-74, Oland Cologne . . . . $2–$4
Snail Perfume, 1968-69, Brocade . . . . $6–$9
Snoopy Soap Dish Refills, 1968-76. . . . . $2–$4
Snoopys Bubble Tub, 1971-72 . . . . $3–$5
Snoopys Surprise, 1969-71, Sports Rally Bracing Lotion . . . . $2–$4
Snowbird, 1973-74, Sonnet Cream Sachet . . . . $1–$3
Soap Boat, 1973-74, Floating Dish And Soap. . . . . $1–$3
Soap For All Seasons, 1973 . . . . $2–$4
Song Bird, 1971-72, Cotillion Cologne . . . . $2–$5
Song Bird, 1971-72, Unforgettable Cologne . . . . $2–$4
Spirit Of St Louis, 1970-72, Excalibur After Shave . . . . $5–$8
Spring Tulips Soaps, 1970-73. . . . . $10–$15
Stage Coach, 1970-77, Wild Country After Shave . . . . $2–$4
Strawberries & Cream, 1970, Bath Foam . . . . $1–$2
Strawberry Bath Foam, 1971-72, Bath Foam . . . . $1–$2
Strawberry Bath Gelee, 1971-72, Bath Gelee . . . . $1–$3
Super Cycle, 1971-72, Wild Country After Shave . . . . $3–$5
Super Cycle, 1971-73, Island Lime After Shave. . . . . $3–$5
Sure Winner Shower Soap, 1972-73 . . . . $3–$5
Swan Lake, 1972-76, Bird Of Paradise . . . . $2–$4
Sweet Shoppe Pin Cushion, 1972-74, Moonwind . . . . $3–$4
Swinger Golf Bag, 1969-71, Wild Country After Shave. . . . . $2–$4
Tee Off, 1973-75, Electric Pre-Shave . . . . $2–$3
Tee Off, 1973-75, Hair Lotion . . . . $2–$3
Ten Point Buck, 1973-74, Wild Country After Shave . . . . $3–$4
Thomas Jefferson, 1977-78, Wild Country After Shave . . . . $2–$3
Tiffany Lamp, 1972-74, Sonnet . . . . $5–$7
Town Pump, 1968-69, Windjammer After Shave. . . . . $5–$8
Treasure Turtle, 1971-73, Field Flowers Cologne . . . . $1–$2
Tub Racers, 1969, Three Cars. . . . . $6–$9
Twenty-Dollar Gold Piece, 1971-72, Windjammer After Shave . . . . $2–$4
Uncle Sam Pipe, 1975-76, Deep Woods After Shave . . . . $2–$3
Venetian Pitcher Col Mist, 1973-75, Patchwork . . . . $1–$3
Victorian Fashion Figurine, 1973-74, Field Flowers Cologne . . . . $22–$27
Victorian Pitcher, 1971-72, Skin So Soft Bath Oil. . . . . $3–$5
Victorian Washstand, 1973-74, Charisma Foam Bath Oil. . . . . $2–$3
Victoriana Pitcher And Bowl, 1971-72, Field Flowers Bath Oil. . . . . $6–$9
Victoriana Pitcher And Bowl, 1971-72, Skin So Soft . . . . $6–$9
Victoriana Powder Sachet, 1971-72, Field Flowers . . . . $2–$3
Western Boot, 1973-75, Wild Country After Shave . . . . $1–$3
Wise Choice, 1969-70, Excalibur After Shave . . . . $3–$5

BALLANTINE BOTTLES

Ballantine figural bottles are made to contain Ballantine imported Scotch whiskey. These ceramic bottles are brightly colored, generally reading "Blended Scotch Whiskey, 14 Years Old." When the bottle represents an animal or human figure, the head is the cap. Most of the Ballantine figurals are on sporting themes, such as Fisherman, Duck, and Golf Bag. Also collectible are the older Ballantine bottles which are nonfigurals but are often very decorative, such as a three-inch pottery jug in which the company's product was marketed around 1930.

Duck . . . . $5–$8
Fisherman . . . . $4–$9
Golf Bag . . . . $3–$7
Mallard Duck . . . . $4–$6
Old Crow Chessman . . . . $4–$7
Scottish Knight . . . . $5–$8
Seated Fisherman . . . . $7–$9
Silver Knight . . . . $10–$11
Zebra . . . . $9–$12

BARSOTTINI BOTTLES

The Barsottini bottle manufacturers from Italy, unlike other foreign companies, do not use American or nongeographic themes for the avid U.S. market. Barsottini bottles mostly represent European subjects, such as architectural bottles of the Arc de Triomphe, the Eiffel Tower, and the Florentine Steeple. Subjects from European history included an antique Florentine cannon from the early days of gunpowder. Most Barsottini bottles are large ceramics, often in gray and white to represent the brickwork of buildings. Prices very depending on quantities imported to this country and the extent of their distribution.

Alpine Pipe, ceramic, 10" . . . . $7–$11
Antique Automobile, ceramic, coupe . . . . $5–$8

Antique Automobile, open car .... $5–$8
Clock, with cherub .... $30–$40
Clowns, ceramic, 12" each .... $8–$11
Eiffel Tower, 15", gray and white .... $7–$11
Florentine Cannon, 15" L .... $13–$19
Florentine Steeple, gray and white .... $6–$9
Monastery Cask, ceramic, 12" .... $13–$19
Paris Arc De Triomphe, 7¹/₂" .... $7–$10
Pisa's Leaning Tower, gray and white .... $9–$12
Roman Coliseum, ceramic .... $5–$6
Tivoli Clock, ceramic, 15" .... $12–$15

JIM BEAM BOTTLES

AUTOMOBILES AND TRANSPORTATION SERIES

CHEVROLET
1957, black .... $50–$75
1957 Convertible, black, new .... $60–$80
1957, dark blue, PA .... $55–$70
1957, red .... $55–$70
1957, red, new .... $65–$85
1957, sierra gold .... $100–$130
1957, turqouise .... $40–$60
1957, yellow hot rod .... $40–$60
Camaro, 1969, blue .... $55–$65
Camaro, 1969, burgundy .... $90–$120
Camaro, 1969, green .... $90–$120
Camaro, 1969, pace car .... $50–$65
Camaro, 1969, silver .... $70–$95
Corvette, 1953, white, new .... $90–$135
Corvette, 1955, black, new .... $90–$115
Corvette, 1955, copper, new .... $55–$70
Corvette, 1955, red, new .... $90–$115
Corvette, 1963, black, PA .... $55–$65
Corvette, 1963, blue, NY .... $75–$95
Corvette, 1963, red .... $45–$65
Corvette, 1963, silver .... $40–$55
Corvette, 1978, black .... $110–$145

Corvette, 1978, pace car .... $140+
Corvette, 1978, red. .... $40–$50
Corvette, 1978, white. .... $40–$55
Corvette, 1978, yellow. .... $40–$55
Corvette, 1984, black. .... $60–$80
Corvette, 1984, bronze. .... $70–$95
Corvette, 1984, gold. .... $70–$95
Corvette, 1984, red. .... $60–$80
Corvette, 1984, white. .... $40–$50
Corvette, 1986, pace car, yellow, new. .... $65–$80
Corvette, blue, new .... $60–$80

DUSENBURG
Convertible Coupe, gray .... $150–$200
Convertible, cream. .... $100–$120
Convertible, dark blue .... $90–$120
Convertible, light blue .... $75–$100

FORD
Fire Chief, 1928. .... $85–$105
Fire Chief, 1934. .... $40–$50
Fire Pumper Truck, 1935. .... $30–$40
International Delivery Wagon, black. .... $70–$90
International Delivery Wagon, green .... $70–$90
Model A, 1903, black. .... $20–$30
Model A, 1903, red. .... $20–$30
Model A, 1928 .... $50–$70
Model A Fire Truck, 1930 .... $90–$125
Model A, Angelos Liquor .... $100–$150
Model A, Parkwood Supply .... $100–$145
Model T, 1913, black. .... $30–$45
Model T, 1913, green. .... $30–$45
Mustang, 1964, black. .... $80–$100
Mustang, 1964, red .... $30–$45
Mustang, 1964, white. .... $30–$50
Paddy Wagon, 1930 .... $80–$100
Phaeton, 1929. .... $40–$50
Pickup Truck, 1935. .... $30–$40
Police Car, 1929, blue .... $50–$70
Police Car, 1929, yellow .... $250+
Police Patrol Car, 1934. .... $40–$50
Police Tow Truck, 1935 .... $15–$20
Roadster, 1934, cream, PA, new .... $50–$75
Thunderbird, 1956, black .... $50–$60
Thunderbird, 1956, blue, PA .... $50–$75
Thunderbird, 1956, gray. .... $50–$60
Thunderbird, 1956, green. .... $50–$65
Thunderbird, 1956, yellow. .... $40–$50
Woodie Wagon, 1929 .... $45–$65

Jim Beam, bass boat. PHOTO COURTESY OF DAVE SMITH.

Jim Beam, fire truck. PHOTO COURTESY OF DAVE SMITH.

Oldsmobile, 1903 . . . . $18–$22
Olsonite Eagle Racer . . . . $40–$55
Police Patrol Car, 1934, yellow . . . . $90–$125
Space Shuttle . . . . $20–$30
Stutz, 1914, gray . . . . $40–$55
Stutz, 1914, yellow . . . . $40–$50
Thomas Flyer, 1909, blue . . . . $50–$60
Thomas Flyer, 1909, ivory . . . . $50–$60
Vendome Wagon . . . . $50–$60
Volkswagon, blue . . . . $35–$45
Volkswagon, red . . . . $35–$45

OTHER SERIES

The Executive series, which consists of 22K-gold decorated bottles, was issued to mark the corporation's 160th anniversary which distinguished the Beam Distilling Co. as one of the oldest American business enterprises.

In the same year, Beam started its Regal China series, one of the most popular series of Beam bottles. The Regal China bottles, issued annually at

MERCEDES
1974, 1974, blue ....
1974, 1974, gold ....
1974, 1974, green ....
1974, 1974, mocha ....
1974, 1974, red ....
1974, 1974, sand beige, PA ....
1974, 1974, silver, Australia..............................
1974, 1974, white ....

TRAINS
Baggage Car ....
Box Car, brown ....
Box Car, yellow ....
Bumper..
Caboose, gray.. $3
Caboose, red... $4
Caboose, yellow $40
Casey Jones Accessory Set $40
Casey Jones Caboose $20
Casey Jones with Tender $20
Coal Tender, no bottle.................................. $15
Combination Car .... $15–$
Dining Car.. $65–$
Flat Car .... $15–$
General Locomotive .... $50–$5
Grant Locomotive....................................... $50–$7
Log Car .... $40–$5
Lumber Car... $20–$25
Observation Car .... $15–$23
Passenger Car .... $30–$35
Tank Car .... $15–$20
Track .... $4–$6
Turner Locomotive...................................... $40–$60
Watertower .... $20–$30
Wood Tender.. $40–$45
Wood Tender, no bottle................................. $20–$25

OTHER
Ambulance.. $18–$22
Army Jeep .... $18–$20
Bass Boat .... $15–$20
Cable Car, 1983.. $25–$35
Circus Wagon .... $18–$22
Ernie's Flower Cart .... $18–$22
Golf Cart .... $18–$22
HC Covered Wagon, 1929 .... $9–$11
Jewel Tea.. $30–$48
Mack Fire Truck, 1917.................................. $90–$120
Mississippi Pumper Firetruck, 1867 .... $80–$110

intervals, honor significant people, places or events, concentrating on subjects based on Americana and the contemporary scene. The sporty figurals, frequent subject for Beam Regal Chinas, are handsome, striking, and very decorative. The first Regal China bottle, the Ivory Ashtray, still sells in a modest price range.

The following year, in 1956, the Beam Political Figures series started off with the traditional elephant and donkey, representing the Republican and Democratic parties, and has been issued with variations every four years for the presidential election.

Customer Specialties, bottles made on commission for customers who are usually liquor dealers or distributors, had its inception with a bottle created for Foremost Liquor Stores of Chicago.

In 1958 and 1959, the State series commemorated the admittance of Alaska and Hawaii into the Union during the 1950s. The Beam Distilling Co. continues to issue bottles in honor of other states with the intention of making bottles for each of the 50 states.

Over 500 types of Beam bottles have been issued since 1953. Beam's ceramic bottles, produced by the Wheaton Glass Co. of Millville, New Jersey are considerably more poplar than the glass bottles, probably because of their pleasing coloration.

Note: In the following listings, it should be noted that similar grouped items are arranged chronologically by date.

AC Spark Plug, 1977, replica of a spark plug in white, green, and gold . . . . . $22–$26
AHEPA 50th Anniversary, this striking Regal China bottle was designed in honor of AHEPA's (American Hellenic Education Progressive Association) 50th anniversary. The Order's anniversary logo is reproduced on the front. Current officers listed on the back. The "Greek Key" design appears on both the bottle and the stopper, which is a hollow vase. The bottle's neck is a traditional Greek Column., 12" . . . . $4–$6
Aida, figurine of character from the opera of the same name. Woman is dressed in blue and yellow with black cone-shaped hat. The first in the Opera series, this bottle comes with a music box which plays a selection from the Egyptian March. Bottle and base make up two-piece set. . . . . $80–$125
Akron Rubber Capital, 1973, a unique Regal China creation honoring Akron, Ohio, the rubber producing capital of the world. This creation is in the shape of an automobile tire and features a mag wheel. In the center of the wheel is the inscription Rubber Capital Jim Beam Bottle Club. . . . . $12–$15
Alaska, 1958, star shaped bottle in turquoise blue and gold. Symbols of Alaskan industry in corners of star, gold "49" in center. Regal China, 9¹/₂" . . . . $40–$50
Alaska, 1964-65, re-issued as above . . . . $30–$35
Alaska Purchase, 1966, blue and gold bottle with star shaped stopper. Mt. McKinley pictured with state flag on top. Regal China, 9¹/₂" . . . . $4–$6
American Samoa, 1973, the enchantment of one of America's outside territorial possessions is captured in this genuine Regal China bottle. The seal of Samoa signifies friendship, the whip and staff signify authority and power held by the great chiefs. . . . . .
. . . . $5–$7

American Veterans . . . . $4–$7
Antioch, 1967, the Regal China Company is located in Antioch, Illinois. This decanter commemorates the Diamond Jubilee of Regal. Large Indian head ("Sequoit") on one side. Blue and gold diamond on reverse. Regal China, 10" . . . . $5–$7
Antioch, 1967, same as above with arrow package . . . . $6–$8
Antique Clock . . . . $30–$32
Antique Coffee Grinder, replica of a box coffee mill used in the mid-19th century. Brown with black top and crank which moves, gold lettering . . . . $6–$9
Antique Globe, represents the Martin Behaim globe of 1492. The globe is blue and rotates on the wooden cradle stand. . . . . $6–$8
Antique Telephone, gold base with black speaker and ear phone. Replica of an 1897 desk phone. The second in the series of antique telephones. . . . . $40–$48
Antique Trader . . . . $4–$6
Antique Trader, 1968, the widely read Antique Trader weekly newspaper forms this bottle with the front page clearly shown in black and red, alongside the 1968 National Directory of Antique Dealers. Both are on a black base. Regal China, 10^1/$_2$" . . . . $4–$6
Appaloosa, 1974, the appaloosa was the favorite horse of the Old West and is shown on this bottle trotting along above an embossed horseshoe marked "Appaloosa." His body is brown and white while his tail and mane are black. The stopper is formed by his head. Regal China, 10" . . . . $7–$10
Arizona, 1968, embossed scene of canyon, river, and cactus in blue, yellow, and brown, "The Grand Canyon State, Arizona" in gold. Map embossed on stopper. Reverse has scenes of Arizona life. Regal China, 12" . . . . $2–$4
Armadillo . . . . $8–$12
Armanetti Award Winner, 1969, a pale blue bottle in the shape of the number 1, to honor Armanetti, Inc. of Chicago as "Liquor Retailer of the Year" in 1969. In shield, gold and blue lettering proclaims "Armanetti Liquors 1969 Award Winner." Heavily embossed gold scrolls decorate the bottle. . . . . $4–$6
Armanetti Shopper, 1971, the front of the bottle has a man pushing a shopping cart and the slogan "It's Fun to Shop Armanetti—Self Service Liquor Store." On the back of the bottle, there is an embossed view of the store with other Illinois locations of Armanetti stores, 11^3/$_4$" . . . . $2–$4
Armanetti Vase, 1968, yellow-toned decanter embossed with many flowers and a large letter A for Armanetti. . . . . $2–$4
Bacchus, 1970, this bottle was issued by the Armanetti Liquor Stores of Chicago, Illinois. The body of the bottle is made of a circular medallion showing Bacchus. The medallion is topped by grapes. The stopper is circular and bears the symbol of Armanetti Liquors. Regal China, 11^3/$_4$" . . . . $5–$6
Barney's Slot Machine, 1978, replica of the world's largest slot machine which is located in Barney's Casino on the South Shore at Lake Tahoe, Nevada. Red with small black stopper at the top. . . . . $15–$18
Barry Berish, 1985, Executive series . . . . $70–$85
Barry Berish, 1986, Executive series, bowl . . . . $70–$85
Bartender's Guild, 1973, a commemorative Regal China bottle honoring the International Bartenders' Association on the first International Cocktail Competition in the United States. . . . . $4–$7
Baseball, 1969, this baseball shaped bottle was issued to commemorate the 100th anniversary of the professional sport. "Professional Baseball's 100th Anniversary—1869-1969" is gold and black on the front. Decal of player in action on top. Reverse has history of growth of baseball. . . . . $18–$20
Beam Pot, 1980, shaped like a New England bean pot, a colonial scene is depicted on

the front. On the back, there is a large map of the New England states. The stopper is a large gold dome. This is the club bottle for the New England Beam Bottle and Specialties club. . . . . $8–$9

Beaver Valley Club, 1977, figurine of a beaver sitting on a stump wearing blue pants, white shirt, red jacket, black bow, and hat. The beaver is saluting. A club bottle to honor the Beaver Valley Jim Beam Club of Rochester. . . . . $8–$12

Bell Scotch, 1970, tan center, gold base, brown top with coat of arms of Arthur Bell & Sons on front. Bottle is in the shape of a large handbell. Regal China, 10¹/₂" . . . . $2–$3

Beverage Association, NLBA . . . . $2–$3

Bing Crosby 36th, 1976, same as the Floro de Oro except for the medallion below the neck. Urn shaped bottle with pastel wide band and flowers around the middle. Remainder of bottle is shiny gold with fluting and designs. . . . . $12–$19

Bing's 31st Clam Bake Bottle, an inspired Regal China bottle heavily decorated in gold. The front features a three-dimensional reproduction of the famous Pebble Beach, California, wind swept tree overlooking the Pacific Ocean. The back commemorates the 31st Bing Crosby National Pro-Am Golf Tournament at the world famous Pebble Beach course, January 1972. The stopper is the official seal of the tourney 10³/₄" . . . . $18–$22

Bing Crosby National Pro-Am, 1970. . . . . $3–$4
Bing Crosby National Pro-Am, 1971. . . . . $3–$4
Bing Crosby National Pro-Am, 1972. . . . . $15–$20

Bing Crosby National Pro-Am, 1973, the fourth in its series honoring the Bing Crosby Golf Tournament, genuine Regal China bottle in luxurious fired 22K gold with a white stopper, featuring replicas of the famous Crosby hat, pipe, and golf club. . . . . $15–$20
Bing Crosby National Pro-Am, 1974. . . . . $15–$20
Bing Crosby National Pro-Am, 1975. . . . . $45–$65
Bing Crosby National Pro-Am, 1977. . . . . $12–$18
Bing Crosby National Pro-Am, 1978. . . . . $10–$16

Black Katz, 1968, same kitty, different color, black cat, green eyes, red tongue, white base. Both Katz are Regal China, 14¹/₂" . . . . $7–$12

Blue Cherub Executive, 1960, blue and white decanter with heavily embossed figures of cherubs with bow and arrow gold details. Scrolls and chain holding Beam label around neck. Regal China, 12¹/₂" . . . . $50–$65

Blue Daisy, 1967, also known as Zimmerman Blue Daisy. Light Blue with embossed daisies and leaves around bottle. Background resembles flower basket. . . . . $3–$4

Blue Gill, Fish . . . . $8–$4

Blue Goose Order . . . . $3–$4

Blue Goose, replica of a blue goose with its characteristic grayish-blue coloring. Authenticated by Dr. Lester Fisher, director of Lincoln Park Zoological Gardens in Chicago. . . . . $7–$9

Blue Hen Club . . . . $12–$15

Blue Jay, 1969, tones of sky blue on the bird's body with black and white markings. Black claws grip "oak tree stump" with acorns and leaves embossed. . . . . $4–$7

Blue Slot Machine, 1967 . . . . $6–$9

Bob Devaney . . . . $8–$12

Bob Hope Desert Classic, 1973, the first genuine Regal China bottle created in honor of the Bob Hope Desert Classic, an annual charity fund-raising golf tournament. A profile of Bob Hope is shown on the front side, with a golf ball and tee perched at the tip of his nose. . . . . $8–$9

Bob Hope Desert Classic, 1974, this Regal China creation honors the famous Bob Hope Desert Classic. Bob Hope silhouette and the sport of golf is a color feature of the bottle. . . . . $8–$12

Bobby Unser Olsonite Eagle, 1975, replica of racing car used by Bobby Unser. White with black accessories and colored decals. . . . . $30–$40

Bohemian Girl, 1974, this bottle was issued for the Bohemian Cafe in Omaha, Nebraska, to honor the Czech and Slovak immigrants in the United States. She is wearing a white skirt decorated with flowers; also a white skirt and blue vest. Her white cap is the stopper. Regal China, 14^1/$_2$" . . . . $10–$15

Bonded Gold . . . . $2–$4

Bonded Mystic, 1979, urn shaped bottle with fluting on sides and lid. Small scroll handles, open work handle on lid. Burgandy-colored. . . . . $4–$7

Bonded Silver . . . . $2–$4

Boot Hill (See Dodge City) . . . .

Boris Godinov, with Base, 1978, 2nd in the Opera series. . . . . $150–$200

Bourbon Barrel . . . . $15–$20

Bowl, 1986 . . . . $15–$19

Bowling Proprietors . . . . $2–$3

Boys Town of Italy, 1973, a handsome genuine Regal China bottle created in honor of the Boys town of Italy. This home for Italian orphans began after World War II. The bottle features a map of Italy, showing the various provinces of that country. . . $7–$10

Broadmoor Hotel, 1968, to celebrate the 50th anniversary of this famous hotel in Colorado Springs, Colorado, Beam issued this bottle replica complete with details of windows, doors, roof tiles, and tower capped with a "roof" stopper. The base bears the legend "1918—The Broadmoor—1968" in white ovals on a black background. . $3–$5

Buffalo Bill, 1971, the front side of this bottle shows a bust of Buffalo Bill with his name above. The back illustrates his adventure as an Indian fighter and Pony Express rider. The stopper is a small figure of a buffalo. The bottle is beige and gold. Regal China, 10^1/$_2$" . . . . $4–$7

Bull Dog, 1979, bull dog with yellow infantry helmet with "Devil Dogs" embossed on front. Real leather collar with metal studding around his neck. The mascot of the United States Marine Corps, this bottle honors their 204th anniversary. . . . . $15–$20

Cable Car, 1968, a gray-green bottle in the form of a San Francisco cable car, complete with doors, windows, and wheels. A gold label with "Van Ness Ave., California & Market Streets" in black on one end, " Powell & Mason Streets" on the side. The stopper is the front light. Regal China, 4^1/$_2$" (h), 7" (l). . . . . $2–$4

Caboose, 1980, red caboose with black trim. Sign on side reads "New Jersey Central . . . . $35–$50

Cal-Neva, 1969, this is a standard square bottle, green toned with "Reno 100 Years" deeply embossed and "Cal-Neva, Casino—Hotel, Reno—Lake Tahoe" in the oval-shaped emblem. Regal China, 9^1/$_2$" . . . . $5–$7

California Mission, 1970, this bottle was issued for the Jim Beam Bottle Club of Southern California in honor of the 200th anniversary of the California Missions. A priest is shown leaning with one hand on his staff and the other around an Indian boy. Above them is a doorway and the steeple of the mission. The stopper is the very top of the mission. Regal China, 14". . . . . $10–$15

California Retail Liquor Dealers Association, 1973, made of genuine Regal China, this bottle was designed to commemorate the 20th anniversary of the California Retail Liquor Dealers Association. The bottle depicts the emblem of the association showing a liquor store superimposed on the state of California. . . . . $4–$6

Camellia City Club, 1979, replica of the cupola of the State Capitol building in Sacramento surrounded within camelias, since the capitol is known as "The Camelia Capitol of the World." . . . . $15–$20

Cameo Blue, 1965, also known as the Shepherd Bottle. Scenes of shepherd and dog in white on the sky blue square-shaped bottle. White glass stopper, 12³/₄" . . . . $3–$5

Cannon, with chain, 1970, this bottle was issued to commemorate the 175th anniversary of the Jim Beam Co. The bottle is octagonal with the muzzle of the cannon at a 45-degree angle with the base. The stopper is the end of the muzzle. Some of these bottles have a small chain shown on the cannon and some do not. Those without the chain are harder to find and more valuable 8" . . . . $1–$2

Cannon, no chain, 1970, same as above . . . . $6–$9

Canteen, 1979, replica of the exact canteen used by the armed forces with simulated canvas covering which has snap flaps and chained cap . . . . $8–$12

Captain and Mate, 1980, a sea-faring captain with blue jacket, white cap, and yellow duffel bag over his shoulder. The captain has his other arm around the shoulder of a small boy dressed in a red jacket and blue pants. He holds a toy boat. . . . . $6–$9

Cardinal (Kentucky Cardinal), 1968, a bright red bird with a black mask, tail, and markings, perched on a dark tree-stump-shaded base. . . . . $20–$24

Carmen, 1978, figurine of Carmen from the character in the opera of the same name. The third issue in the Opera series, it is a woman dressed in Spanish clothes of white, blue, gold, and red. She wears a small black cone-shaped hat. Music box plays Habanera, which is from the opera. Part of the three-piece set which includes base and paperweight. . . . . $40–$60

Carolier Bull, 1984, Executive series . . . . $14–$18

Cathedral Radio, 1979, replica of one of the earlier dome-shaped radios. Brown with gold trim and a large dome-shaped lid. . . . . $6–$9

Cats, 1967, trio of cats—Siamese, Burmese, and tabby. Colors are gray with blue eyes, dark brown and white with yellow eyes, and white and tan with blue eyes. Regal China, 11¹/₂" (h) . . . . $6–$9

Cedars of Lebanon, 1971, this bottle shows a green tree rising above a background of a gray- and gold-colored building. This bottle was issued in honor of the Jerry Lewis Muscular Dystrophy Telethon held in 1971. Near the base of the bottle, the words "Tall Cedars of Lebanon" appear. The stopper is the upper half of the tree. Regal China, 9³/₄" . . . . $2–$4

Charisma (1970), Executive series . . . . $5–$8

Charlie McCarthy (1976), replica of Edgar Bergen's puppet from the 1930s. A black ribbon is attached to his monocle. . . . . $16–$19

Cherry Hill Country Club, 1973 . . . . $3–$5

Cherry Hills Country Club, 1973, a very handsome genuine Regal China bottle, commemorating the 50th anniversary of the famous Cherry Hills Country Club. Located in Denver, Colorado, Cherry Hills has hosted some of the top professional golf tournaments. The front of the bottle illustrates the many activities available at Cherry Hills, while the name of the club circles the bottom in luxurious 22K gold. . . . . $3–$5

Cheyenne, Wyoming (1977), circular decanter in shape of a wheel. Spokes separate scenes of Cheyenne history. Regal China. . . . . $6–$9

Chicago Cubs, Sports series . . . . $25–$30

Chicago Show Bottle, 1977, stopper is a gold loving cup standing on a black pedestal. Commemorates the 6th Annual Chicago Jim Beam Bottle Show. . . . . $6–$9

Christmas Tree . . . . $90–$120

Churchill Downs—Pink Roses, 1969, same as below, pink embossed roses. . . . . . $3–$4

Churchill Downs—Red Roses, 1969, "Churchill Downs—Home of the 95th Kentucky Derby" is embossed in gold on the front, around the main paddock building. The shell-shaped bottle comes with red roses framing the scene. Reverse: "Aristedes," first Derby winner in 1875, on a decal. Regal China . . . . $3–$4

Circus Wagon, 1979, replica of a circus wagon from the late 19th century. Blue with gold embossing, white wheels, which are movable, with red trim. . . . . $18–$22

Civil War North, 1961, blue and gray bottle depicting Civil War battle scenes. Stopper has Lee's face on one side, Grant's on the other. Regal China, 10³/₄". . . . . $12–$18

Civil War South, 1961, one side portrays the meeting of southern Generals. Regal China. . . . . $15–$25

Clear Crystal Bourbon, 1967, patterned embossed with "swirl" stopper. Starburst design on base of the bottle. Clear glass, 11¹/₂" . . . . $5–$7

Clear Crystal Scotch, 1966, the original patterned embossed bottle. Glass stopper ("Doorknob"). Bottom is unpatterned and has number and date of issue, 11¹/₂". . $6–$9

Clear Crystal Vodka, 1967, same as above . . . . $5–$8

Cleopatra Rust, 1962, same as Cleopatra Yellow. Scene with Mark Antony and Cleopatra in white on rust-red background. . . . . $3–$5

Cleopatra Yellow, 1962, black and purple, two-handled, amphora decanter. Yellow figures of Mark Antony in armor and Cleopatra beside the Nile. Pyramid and sphinx background. Egyptian border design circles bottle, white stopper. Rarer than Cleopatra Rust. Glass, 13¹/₄". . . . . $8–$12

Clint Eastwood, 1973, a handsome genuine Regal China bottle, commemorating the Clint Eastwood Invitational Celebrity Tennis Tournament held in Pebble Beach. The bottle features an exact likeness of Clint Eastwood. Two ribbons adorn the front of the bottle: one with stars on a field of blue, the other in red with the name of the tournament emblazoned in 22K gold. . . . . $8–$11

Cobalt, 1981, Executive series. . . . . $12–$18

Cocktail Shaker, 1953, glass, Fancy Diz. Bottle, 9¹/₄". . . . . $2–$5

Coffee Grinder . . . . $8–$12

Coffee Warmers, 1954, four types are known in red, black, gold, and white necks; plastic cord over cork. The Corning Glass Co. made the Pyrex bottles. Round stoppers are made of wood. Pyrex glass, 9" . . . . $6–$9

Coffee Warmers, 1956, two types with metal necks and handles: black and gold stripes on one, gold neck with black handle on the other. White star design on sides of Pyrex glass on both. Round black plastic tops. Some have holder-type candle warmers. Pyrex glass, 10". . . . . $2–$5

Coho Salmon, 1976, gray with black speckles. Official seal of the National Fresh Water Fishing Hall of Fame is on the back. . . . . $10–$13

Colin Mead . . . . $110–$145

Jim Beam, Collector series. PHOTO COURTESY OF DAVE SMITH.

Collector's Edition, 1966, set of six, glass, famous paintings: The Blue Boy, On the Terrace, Mardi Gras, Austide Bruant, The Artist Before His Easel, and Laughing Cavalier, each . . . . $1–$2

Collector's Edition Volume II, 1967, a set of six flask-type bottles painted gold with pictures from the Renaissance period: George Gisze, Soldier and Girl, Night Watch, The Jester, Nurse and Child, and Man on Horse, each . . . . $1–$2

Collector's Edition Volume III, 1968, a set of eight bottles covered with a blue velvet finish and picturing a famous American painting on each: On the Trail, Indian Maiden, Buffalo, Whistler's Mother, American Gothic, The Kentuckian, The Scout, and Hauling in the Gill Net, each . . . . $1–$2

Collector's Edition Volume IV, 1969, a set of eight bottles with a brown leatherlike finish and setting on an angle. Each has a picture of a painting by a famous French artist. They are Balcony, The Judge, Fruit Basket, Boy with Cherries, Emile Zola, The Guitarist Zouave, and Sunflowers, each . . . . $1–$2

Collector's Edition Volume V, 1970, a set of six bottles finished in a gold flecked red paint with more French paintings featured. These include Au Cafe, Old Peasant, Boaring Party, Gare Saint Lazare, The Jewish Bride, and Titus at Writing Desk, each . . . . $1–$3

Collector's Edition Volume VI, 1971, this set of three bottles look like green picture frames around three more art masterpieces. They are Charles I by Van Dyck, The Merry Lute Player and Boy Holding Flute by Frans Hals, each . . . . $1–$3

Collector's Edition Volume VII, 1972, this set of three bottles is three different-colored, framed oval pictures of famous European paintings. These are The Bag Piper, Prince Baltasor, and Maidservant Pouring Milk, each . . . . $1–$3

Collector's Edition Volume VIII, 1973, this selection of three bottles features contemporary American artist Edward H. Weiss' portraits of Ludwig van Beethoven, Wolfgang Mozart, and Frederic Francois Chopin, each . . . . $1–$3

Collector's Edition Volume IX, 1974, this set of three bottles has a woodtone finish and features scenes of bird life designed and painted by James Lockhart, one of the finest wildlife artists in America today. The birds include the Cardinal, Ring-Neck Pheasant, and the Woodcock, each . . . . $1–$3

Collector's Edition Volume X, 1975, a set of three different-colored bottles featuring diamond-shaped pictures of the Sailfish, Rainbow Trout, and Largemouth Bass as painted by the esteemed naturalist Jim Lockhart, each . . . . $1–$3

Collector's Edition Volume XI, 1976, each of this set of three bottles features one of three reproductions of Jim Lockhart's paintings of the Chipmunk, Bighorn Sheep, and Pronghorn Antelope. . . . . $1–$3

Collector's Edition Volume XII, 1977, a set of four bottles of painted glass, each painted a different color and having a different reproduction of James Lockhart's on the front. Each picture is framed with a gold border. German Shorthaired Pointer is black with gold matting and black stopper, Labrador Retriever is dark purple. . . . . $1–$3

Collector's Edition Volume XIV, 1978, a set of four flask-type bottles. Glass made to appear like brown leather with framed wildlife scenes on the front which are reproductions of paintings by James Lockhart. Each picture has embossed details. The names and themes of the bottles are: Raccoon, Mule Deer, Red Fox, and Cottontail Rabbit, each . . . . . $1–$3

Collector's Edition Volume XV, 1979, a set of three flasks, each with a different reproduction of Frederic Remington's paintings titled: The Cowboy 1902, The Indian Trapper 1902, and Lieutenant S.C. Robertson 1890, each . . . . $1–$3

Collector's Edition Volume XVI, 1980, set of three flasks, each depicting scenes of ducks in flight on the front with an oval background and a bamboo style frame. Large domed lids. The Mallard, The Redhead, The Canvasback, Artwork by James Lockhart, one of the best wildlife artists in America. . . . . $1–$3

Collector's Edition Volume XVII, 1981, three flask bottles with ball-type lids featuring three more paintings by Jim Lockhart. These triangular pictures are of the Great Elk, Pintail Duck, and the Horned Owl (also known as the car owl), each . . . . . . $1–$3
Colorado, 1959, light turquoise showing pioneers crossing the rugged mountains with snow-capped peaks . . . . $20–$25
Colorado Centennial, 1976, replica of Pike's Peak with a miner and his mule in front with the word "Colorado" above the base. . . . . $8–$12
Colorado Springs . . . . $5–$8
Computer, Democrat, 1984 . . . . $10–$13
Computer, Republican, 1984 . . . . $10–$13
Convention Bottle, 1971, created to commemorate the occasion of the first national convention of the National Association of Jim Beam Bottle and Specialty Clubs hosted by the Rocky Mountain Club, Denver, Colorado, June 1971, 10" . . . . $5–$8
Convention Number 10—Norfolk, 1980, the sailing ship USS Beam passing between the spokes of ship's helm, with a gold flag atop the mast. The USS Beam is located at the Norfolk Naval base where the tenth convention was held . . . . $12–$18
Convention Number 10—Norfolk, 1980, Waterman, pewter . . . . $20–$30
Convention Number 10—Norfolk, 1980, Waterman, yellow . . . . $20–$30
Convention Number 11—Las Vegas, 1981, a Las Vegas dealer fox stands behind a barrel marked "Jim Beam Since 1795" dealing poker to two players while the chips are stacked by their hands. On the dealer's back is the logo of the International Association of Jim Beam Bottle and Specialty Clubs 10" . . . . $20–$22
Convention Number 11—Las Vegas, 1981, Showgirl, blonde . . . . $30–$40
Convention Number 11—Las Vegas, 1981, Showgirl, brunette . . . . $30–$40
Convention Number 12—New Orleans, 1982, an unusual bottle that represents a Mardi Gras float with Rex, the King of Mardi Gras, waving to the crowd. This is a green bottle, embellished with gold and "1982 Mardi Gras Rex" on the front. The bottle is open through the center around Rex 9$^1/_4$". . . . . $20–$28
Convention Number 12—New Orleans, 1982, Buccaneer, gold . . . . $20–$23
Convention Number 12—New Orleans, 1982, Buccaneer, in color . . . . $20–$30
Convention Number 13—St. Louis, 1983 . . . . $55–$70
Convention Number 13—St. Louis, 1983, Gibson girl, blue . . . . $65–$80
Convention Number 13—St. Louis, 1983, Gibson girl, yellow . . . . $65–$80
Convention Number 14—Florida, King Neptune, 1984 . . . . $15–$20
Convention Number 14—Florida, King Neptune, 1984, Mermaid, blonde . $18–$25
Convention Number 14—Florida, King Neptune, 1984, Mermaid, brunette $18–$25
Convention Number 15—Las Vegas, 1985 . . . . $30–$40
Convention Number 16—Pilgrim Woman, Boston, 1986 . . . . $35–$45
Convention Number 16—Pilgrim Woman, Boston, 1986, Minuteman, color . . . $60–$90
Convention Number 16—Pilgrim Woman, Boston, 1986, Minuteman, pewter . $65–$95
Convention Number 17—Louisville, 1987 . . . . $55–$75
Convention Number 17—Louisville, 1987, Kentucky Colonel, blue . . . . $60–$90
Convention Number 17—Louisville, 1987, Kentucky Colonel, gray . . . . $60–$90
Convention Number 18—Bucky Beaver, 1988. . . . . $20–$30
Convention Number 18—Bucky Beaver, 1988, Portland rose, red . . . . $20–$30
Convention Number 18—Bucky Beaver, 1988, Portland rose, yellow. . . . . . $20–$30
Convention Number 19—Kansas City, 1989 . . . . $35–$40
Convention Number 2, 1972, this beautiful Regal China creation honors the second annual convention of the National Association of Jim Beam Bottle and Specialty Clubs, held June 19-25 in Anaheim, California. Stopper features the national symbol of the Beam Bottle Club, 10 . . . . $20–$30

Convention Number 3—Detroit, 1973, round blue bottle designed like the world with a green U.S. outstanding and a large numeral 3. The stopper is a bust of a golden fox. Commemorates the third annual convention of Beam Bottle Collectors held in Detroit, 14"..$10–$12

Convention Number 4—Pennsylvania, 1974, a black and gold Amish wagon commemorating the annual convention of the Jim Beam Bottle Clubs held in Lancaster, Pennsylvania. On the back is listed in gold all the member clubs. A green fox is in the driver's seat 7½"..$15–$20

Convention Number 5—Sacramento, 1975, the famous gold pan frames an embossed scene of Sutter's Fort in Sacramento, California. Gold nuggets gleam in the miner's pan and in the transparent stopper of the bottle. On the back: "Hosted by Camellia City Jim Beam Bottle Club 1975" 10¾"..$6–$9

Convention Number 6—Hartford, 1976, Charter oak and gold lettering on the front. A map of the United States is on the back. Commemorates the annual convention of the Jim Beam Bottle Club held in Hartford, Connecticut.........................$3–$5

Convention Number 7—Louisville, 1978 ....$3–$5

Convention Number 8—Chicago, 1978, embossed scene with the Sears Tower, Hancock Building, Marina City, and Water Tower with Lake Michigan at the base. Commemorates the eighth Beam convention held in Chicago....................$3–$5

Convention Number 9—Houston, 1979, same as above, Cowboy, beige.... $35–$45

Convention Number 9—Houston, 1979, same as above, Cowboy, in color.. $35–$45

Convention Number 9—Houston, 1979, the mascot of the Beam clubs, a gray poodle named Tiffany, sits on the side of a space capsule. Commemorates the ninth Beam convention, which was held in Houston...............................$20–$30

Cowboy, 1979, either antique tan or multicolored. Cowboy leaning on a fence with one hand on his belt buckle and the other holding a rifle. His cowboy hat is the stopper. Awarded to collectors who attended the 1979 convention for the International Association of Beam Clubs..$25–$40

CPO Open ....$7–$10

Crappie, 1979, figure of a silver- and black-speckled crappie commemorates the National Fresh Water Fishing Hall of Fame...........................$10–$14

D-Day...$10–$13

Dark Eyes Brown Jug, 1978, beige, both flecked with color; the brown jug has red flecks, the beige jug has brown flecks. Regular jug shape with small handle at neck with black stopper..$4–$6

Del Webb Mint, 1970, a large gold "400" and "Del Webb's Las Vegas" embossed under crossed checkered flags. Stopper is gold dune buggy. Checkered flagson edge of bottle. Regal China, china or metal stopper. Metal stopper, 13" ....$7–$9

Del Webb Mint, 1970, same as above, China stopper......................$35–$45

Delaware Blue Hen Bottle, 1972, this diamond-shaped bottle, fashioned of genuine handcrafted Regal China, commemorates the state of Delaware, "the first state of the Union." The front of the bottle depicts the act of ratification of the Federal Constitution on December 7, 1787. The back shows the Delaware State House, a state map, and the famous Twin Bridges..$3–$5

Delco Freedom Battery, 1978, replica of a Delco battery. Entire plastic top is removable. ....$18–$22

Delft Blue, 1963, "Windmill Bottles"; a reverse has scene of embossed Dutch windmills on gray-white bottle. Dutch fishing boats under sail on front in "Delft" in dark blue handle and stopper, 13"....................................$3–$5

Delft Rose, 1963, rarer than Delft Blue; same as above; sailing scene in paleblue and pink. Windmill scene embossed on reverse. Glass, 13".................$4–$6

Devil Dog . . . . $10–$12
Dial Telephone, 1980, black reproduction of a 1919 desk model telephone with a movable dial. The fourth in a series of Beam telephone designs. . . . . $30–$40
Dodge City, 1972, this bottle was issued to honor the centennial of Dodge City. The bottle is roughly triangular and depicts the city as it must have looked a century ago. Above the town, the famous cemetery Boot Hill appears. A circular plaque on the bottle acknowledges the centennial. The stopper is a six pointed sheriff's badge. Regal China, 10" . . . . $3–$5
Doe, 1963, pure white neck markings, natural brown body. "Rocky" base. Regal China, 13¹/₂" . . . . $14–$19
Doe—Re-issued, 1967, as above . . . . $12–$16
Dog, 1959, long-eared Setter dog, soft broken eyes, black and white coat. Regal China, 15¹/₄" . . . . $15–$20
Don Giovanni, 1980, figurine of Don Giovanni from the Mozart opera of the same name. The fifth in the Operatic series, this bottle has a music box which plays the duet *La ci darem la mano.* . . . . $125–$145
Donkey and Elephant Ashtrays, 1956, they were made to be used as either ashtrays with coasters or book ends. The stylized elephant and donkey heads are in lustrous gray china. The Beam label fits the round coaster section of the bottle. Regal China, pair, 10" . . . . $8–$12
Donkey and Elephant Boxers, 1964, the G.O.P. elephant has blue trunks with red stripes, white shirt, and black top hat with stars on the band. His gloves are brown. The donkey has red trunks with a blue stripe, black shoes, and top hat. The hat band is white with red and blue stars, pair . . . . $9–$13
Donkey and Elephant Campaigners, 1960, elephant is dressed in a brown coat and blue vest with a gold chain. He carries a placard stating "Republicans—1960" and the state where the bottle is sold. Donkey is dressed in black coat, tan vest, and gray pants. His placard reads "Democrats—1960" and state where sold. Regal China, pair, 12" . . $8–$12
Donkey and Elephant Clowns, 1968, both are dressed in polka dot clown costumes. Elephant has red ruffles and cuffs with blue dots. Donkey has blue with red dots. Yellow styrofoam straw hat and clown shoes on both elephant and donkey. Their heads are the stoppers. Regal China, pair, 12" . . . . $2–$4
Donkey and Elephant Football Election Bottles, 1972, "Pick the winning team." The Democratic donkey and the G.O.P. elephant are depicted in football costumes atop genuine Regal China footballs in this 1972 version of Beam's famous election bottle series. Pair, 9¹/₂" . . . . $3–$5
Donkey New York City, 1976. . . . . $8–$10
Duck, 1957 . . . . $15–$20
Ducks and Geese, 1975 . . . . $5–$8
Ducks Unlimited 40th Mallard Hen, 1977 . . . . $40–$50
Ducks Unlimited American Widg Pr, 1983 . . . . $30–$40
Ducks Unlimited Black Duck, 1989. . . . . $50–$75
Ducks Unlimited Blue Bill, 1987 . . . . $35–$50
Ducks Unlimited Blue-Winged Teal, 1980 . . . . $40–$45
Ducks Unlimited Canvasback Drake, 1979 . . . . $30–$40
Ducks Unlimited Green-Winged Teal, 1981. . . . . $35–$45
Ducks Unlimited Mallard, 1974. . . . . $40–$50
Ducks Unlimited Mallard, 1978. . . . . $30–$40
Ducks Unlimited Mallard, 1984. . . . . $55–$65
Ducks Unlimited Pintail PR, 1985. . . . . $25–$30
Ducks Unlimited Redhead, 1986 . . . . $15–$25
Ducks Unlimited Wood Duck, 1975 . . . . $30–$40

Ducks Unlimited Wood Ducks, 1982............................. $35–$45
Eagle, 1966... $8–$12
Eldorado, 1978 .... $5–$8
Election, Democrat, 1988 .... $20–$30
Election, Republican, 1988........................... $20–$30
Elephant and Donkey Supermen, 1980.................... $8–$10
Elephant Kansas City, 1976........................... $6–$9
Elks... $3–$5
Elks National Foundation .... $7–$10
Emerald Crystal Bourbon, 1968 .... $4–$7
Emmet Kelly, 1973 .... $18–$22
Emmet Kelly, Native Son .... $50–$60
Ernie's Flower Cart, 1976 .... $18–$24
Evergreen.. $7–$10
Expo 74, 1974, this bottle was issued on the occasion of the World's Fair held at Spokane, Washington, in 1974. A very unusual bottle; six-sided panels form the bottle's sides. The top of the bottle is a clock tower. The stopper is the roof of the tower. Regal China, 7¼"... $5–$7
Falstaff, 1979, replica of Sir John Falstaff with blue and yellow outfit holding a gold goblet. Second in the Australian Opera series. Music box which plays *Va, vecchio, John*. Limited edition of 1000 bottles, comes with base................. $90–$120
Fantasia bottle, 1971, this tall, delicately handcrafted Regal China decanter is embellished with 22K gold and comes packaged in a handsome midnight blue and gold presentation case lined with red velvet., 16¼" .... $3–$4
Father's Day card .... $12–$18
Female Cardinal, 1973, the body of the bird is mostly brown with a red beak and some red on the tail feathers. The stopper is the upper part of the bird. Regal China, 13½" ... $8–$12
Fiesta Bowl, 1973, the second bottle created for the Fiesta Bowl. This bottle is made of genuine Regal China, featuring a football player on the front side., 13¼" ..... $9–$11
Fiesta Bowl, glass.................................. $8–$12
Figaro, 1977, figurine of the character Figaro from the opera *The Barber of Seville*. Spanish costume in beige, rose, yellow. Holds a brown guitar on the ground in front of him. Music box plays an aria from the opera........................ $140–$170
Fighting Bull .... $10–$14
First National Bank of Chicago, 1964, Note: Beware of reproductions. Issued to commemorate the 100th anniversary of the First National Bank of Chicago. About 130 were issued: 117 were given as mementoes to the bank directors, none for public distribution. This is the most valuable Beam bottle known. Sky blue color, circular shape, gold embossed design around banner lettered "The First National Bank of Chicago." Center oval was ornate bank logo "1st," and "100th Anniversary" in gold. Gold embossed "1st" on stopper. Bottom marked "Cr............................ $1200–$2000
Fish, 1957, sky blue sailfish, pink underside, black dorsal fin and side markings on "ocean waves" base. Regal China, 14"............................. $10–$15
Fish Hall of Fame .... $20–$30
Five Seasons, 1980, the club bottle for the Five Seasons Club of Cedar Rapids honors their home state, Iowa. The bottle is shaped like Iowa with a large ear of corn. The top of the corn is the lid .... $6–$9
Fleet Reserve Association, 1974, this bottle was issued by the Fleet Reserve Association to honor the Career Sea Service on their 50th anniversary. The bottle is roughly triangular with the words "Loyalty Protection Service" embossed on the front. The stopper is plain. Regal China, 9"................................... $4–$6

Florida Shell, 1968, shell-shaped bottles made in two colors—mother-of-pearl and iridescent bronze—for a shimmering luminescent effect. Reverse has map of Florida and "Sea Shell Headquarters of the World." Regal China, 9³/₄" . . . . $2–$4

Floro De Oro, 1976, urn-shaped bottle with pastel band around middle and yellow and blue flowers; remainder of the bottle is gold with fluting and designs, gold handle, 12" . . . . $6–$8

Flower Basket, 1962, blue basket filled with embossed pastel flowers and green leaves resting on gold base; gold details and stopper. Regal China, 12¹/₄" . . . . $20–$30

Football Hall of Fame, 1972, This bottle is a reproduction of the striking new Professional Football Hall of Fame Building, executed in genuine Regal China. The stopper is in the shape of half a football, 9³/₄" . . . . $9–$13

Foremost—Black and Gold, 1956, Pylon-shaped decanter with a deep black body embossed with gold nuggets. The square white stopper doubles as a jigger. This is the first Beam bottle issued for a liquor retailer, Foremost Liquor Store of Chicago; many others have followed. Regal China. . . . . $65–$95

Foremost—Gray and Gold, 1956, same as above. Tapered decanter with gray body and gold nuggets. Both decanters are 15¹/₂" (h) and are Regal China. . . . . $65–$95

Foremost—Speckled Beauty, 1956, the most valuable of the Foremost bottles. Also known as the Pink Speckled Beauty, was created in the shape of a Chinese Vase and spattered in various colors of pink, gold, black, and gray. The spattered colors may vary from bottle to bottle since it was hand-applied. Regal China, 14¹/₂" . . . . $75–$100

Fox, 1967, blue coat . . . . $60–$75

Fox, 1971, gold coat . . . . $30–$40

Fox, green coat . . . . $12–$18

Fox, Kansas City, blue, miniature . . . . $15–$25

Fox, on a dolphin . . . . $14–$15

Fox, Red Distillery . . . . $750–$950

Fox, Uncle Sam . . . . $5–$6

Fox, white coat . . . . $20–$30

Franklin Mint . . . . $4–$6

French Cradle Telephone, 1979, replica of a French cradle telephone. The third in the Telephone Pioneers of America Series, 7¹/₄" . . . . $15–$20

Fuji Islands . . . . $3–$4

Galah Bird, 1979, rose-colored Galah bird which is part of the cockatoo family from South Australia. It has a white plume on its head and touches of gray and white feathers. . . . . $10–$13

Gem City, club bottle. . . . . $25–$34

George Washington Commemorative Plate, 1976, plate-shaped bottle with a painting of George Washington in the center bordered by a band of gold. The bottle is blue with lettering around the outside rim. Commemorates the U.S. Bicentennial, 9¹/₂" . $12–$15

German Bottle—Weisbaden, 1973, This bottle, of genuine Regal China, depicts a map of the famous Rhine wine-growing regions of Germany. Special attention is given to the heart of this wine country at Weisbaden, 11". . . . . $3–$6

German Stein. . . . . $15–$25

Germany, 1970, this bottle was issued to honor the American Armed Forces in Germany. The body of the bottle is made up of a plaque on both sides showing rustic German scenes. The stopper is plain. Regal China, 10". . . . . $2–$4

Glen Campbell 51st, 1976, guitar-shaped bottle with a bust of Glen Campbell sculptured at top of guitar. Lid is the ends of gold clubs. Honors the 51st Los Angeles Open, a golf tournament held at the Riviera Country Club between February 16-20, 12³/₄" . . . . $7–$10

Golden Chalice, chalice with gray-blue body, gold accents. Band of embossed pastel flowers on the neck. Gold scrolled neck and base. Regal China, 12¼"...... $30–$40
Golden Gate, 1969, this almond-shaped bottle has "Las Vegas" embossed in bright gold in a banner on the front. Mountains, a helicopter, a golfer, and gambling montage, with "Golden Gate Casino" in gold on a shield are featured. Regal China, 12½"... $35–$42

Jim Beam, Executive series, 1969, urn. PHOTO COURTESY OF DAVE SMITH.

Golden Jubilee, 1977, Executive Series .... $8–$12
Golden Nugget, 1969, same as above; "Golden Nugget" in gold on shield in front. Regal China, 12½"... $35–$42
Golden Rose, 1978, three versions of this urn-shaped bottle; yellow embossed rose with a blue background framed in gold band, remainder of bottle goldmottled with two handles. Yellow Rose of Texas version has the name of this bottle beneath the rose, the Harolds Club VIP version has its title lettered under the rose also, 11½"..... $12–$18
Grand Canyon, 1969, "Grand Canyon National Park 50th Anniversary" in a circle around a scene of the Canyon in black with "1919-1969" in earth-red. A round bottle (same as Arizona) with a "stick up" spout and round stopper embossed with map of Arizona. Regal China, 12½".. $3–$6
Grant Locomotive, 1979, replica of Grant Locomotive, black engine with gold trim and bells, red wheels that move, 9" .... $40–$55
Gray Cherub, 1958, Checkered design, bordered with scroll work, accented with 22K gold. Three embossed cherubs on neck. Regal China, 12".......................
Great Chicago Fire Bottle, 1971, this historical decanter was created to commemorate the great Chicago fire of 1871, and to salute Mercy Hospital which rendered service to the fire victims. The first hospital of Chicago was started in 1852 by the Sisters of Mercy. The new Mercy hospital and Medical Center opened in 1968, is depicted on the reverse side. The front of the bottle shows towering flames engulfing Chicago's waterfront as it appeared on the evening of October 8, 1871. The look of actual flames has been realistically captured, 7½".................................. $10–$15
Great Dane, 1976, white with black markings and gold collar.............. $7–$9
Green China Jug, 1965, deep mottled green China jug, with embossed branches and buds on side. Solid handle. Regal Glass, 12½"..............................
Hank Williams, Jr... $30–$40

Hannah Dustin, 1973, a beautiful Regal China creation designed after the granite monument erected in her memory on Contoocook Island, in the Merrimack River north of Concord. This was where, in 1697, Hannah Dustin, her nurse, and young boy made their famous frantic escape from Indians, who held them captive for two weeks, 14$^{1}/_{2}$". . . . . $10–$12

Hansel and Gretel Bottle, 1971, the forlorn, lost waifs from the Brothers Grimm beloved fable and Hansel and Gretel are depicted on the front of this charming and beautiful Regal China bottle. Above them, the words, "Germany. . . Land of Hansel and Gretel" stand out in gold, 10$^{1}/_{4}$" . . . . $4–$6

Harley Davidson 85th Anniversary Decanter . . . . $110–$150
Harley Davidson 85th Anniversary Stein . . . . $180–$220
Harolds Club, 1970 . . . . $40–$60
Harolds Club, 1971 . . . .
Harolds Club, 1972 . . . . $15–$19
Harolds Club, 1973 . . . . $18–$24
Harolds Club, 1974 . . . . $12–$16
Harolds Club, 1975 . . . . $12–$18
Harolds Club, 1977 . . . . $15–$20
Harolds Club, 1978 . . . . $15–$20
Harolds Club, 1980 . . . . $20–$30
Harolds Club, 1982 . . . . $70–$90

Harolds Club VIP, 1976, same as Floro de Oro except for the Harolds Club patch on the base. Urn-shaped bottles with pastel band of blue and yellow flowers around the middle. Remainder of the bottle has very shiny gold with fluting and designs, 12" . . . .

Harolds Club VIP, 1979, double-urn-shaped bottle with wide alternating bands of gold and mother-of-pearl with double scroll handles on large screw lid, 11$^{1}/_{2}$" . . . . $20–$30

Harolds Club—Blue Slot Machine, 1967, a blue-toned "One Armed Bandit" with two gold bells showing in the window, and a gold-colored handle; the money slot is the stopper. "Harolds Club Reno" and a large H on a pinwheel emblem are on the front. Regal China, 10$^{3}/_{8}$" . . . . $7–$9

Harolds Club—Covered Wagon, 1969-70, a Conestoga wagon with "Harolds Club" embossed on the side pulled by a galloping ox, driven by a cowboy. This bottle is "arch" shaped, framing Nevada's mountains and the wagon. Regal China, 10" . . $4–$6

Harolds Club—Gray Slot Machine, 1968, same as "Covered Wagon" but with an overall gray tone. Regal China, 10$^{3}/_{8}$" . . . . $4–$6

Harolds Club—Man-In-A-Barrel, 1957, this was the first in a series made for the famous Harolds Club in Reno, Nevada. The man-in-a-barrel was an advertising logo used by the club. In 1957, Jim Beam issued a bottle using the figure of "Percy" in a barrel with "Harolds Club" embossed on the front. "Percy" has a top hat, a monocle, a mustache, a white collar, and a bright red tie and spats. He stands on a base of "Bad News" dice cubes. Regal China, 14" . . . . $350–$390

Harolds Club—Man-In-A-Barrel-2, 1958, twin brother of Percy No. 1. No mustache, "Harolds Club" inscribed on base of the bottle. Regal China, 14" . . . . $125–$145

Harolds Club—Nevada (Gray), 1963, "Harolds Club of Reno" inscribed on base of bottle created for the "Nevada Centennial—1864-1964" as a state bottle. Embossed picture of miner and mule on the "Harolds" side, crossed shovel and pick are on the stopper. Embossed lettering on base is gray-toned and not bold. This is a rare and valuable bottle. . . . . $80–$95

Harolds Club—Nevada (Silver), 1964, same as above. Base lettering now reads "Harolds Club Reno." Then letters are bolder and are bright silver. . . . . $90–$110

Hawaii—Re-issued, 1967, as above .... $30–$40
Hawaiian Open Bottle, 1972, cleverly decorated to simulate a pineapple with famous "Friendly Skies" logo in gold. This genuine Regal China bottle honors the 1972 Hawaiian Open Golf Tournament. The reverse side commemorates United Air Lines' 25th year (1972) of air service to Hawaii. The stopper is designed to look like pineapple leaves, 10". .... $4–$6
Hawaiian Open, 1973, the second bottle created in honor of the United Hawaiian Open Golf Classic. Of genuine Regal China designed in the shape of a golf ball featuring a pineapple and airplane on front, 11". .... $5–$6
Hawaiian Open, 1974, genuine Regal China bottle commemorating the famous 1974 Hawaiian Open Golf Classic, 15". .... $5–$8
Hawaiian Open Outrigger, 1975, a very unusual bottle. Two native girls are paddling an outrigger canoe on a wave beautifully colored in different shades of blue. The bottle is shaped like the wave. The stopper is the very top of the wave. Regal China, 8½". .... $9–$11
Hemisfair, 1968, the Lone Star of Texas crowns the tall gray and blue "Tower of the Americas." "The Lone Star State" is lettered in gold over a rustic Texas scene. The half map of Texas has "Hemisfair 68—San Antonio." Regal China, 13". .... $6–$8
Herre Brothers .... $25–$35
Hobo, Australia .... $10–$14
Hoffman, 1969, the bottle is in the shape of the Harry Hoffman Liquor Store with the Rocky Mountains in the background. Beam bottles and "Ski Country—USA" are in the windows. Reverse: embossed mountain and ski slopes with skier. Regal China, 9" .... $3–$5
Holiday—Caroliers .... $30–$40
Holiday—Nutcracker .... $30–$40
Home Builders, 1978, replica of a Rockford Builders bungalow, brown with touches of black. Oval medallion on the roof reads "Your Best Bet—A Home of Your Own." This bottle commemorates the 1979 convention of the Home Builders. .... $18–$22
Hone Heke .... $165–$195
Honga Hika, 1980, Honga Hika is the most famous warchief of the Ngapuki tribe. This is the first in a series of authentic Maori warrior bottles. .... $165–$195
Horse (Appaloosa). .... $8–$12
Horse (Black), 1962, black horse with white on blaze nose, white hooves, and black tail. Regal China, 13½" .... $18–$22
Horse (Black)—Re-issued, 1967, as above. .... $10–$12
Horse (Brown), 1962, brown horse with white blaze on nose, black hooves and tail. Regal China, 13½" H .... $15–$18
Horse (Brown)—Re-issued, 1967, as above. .... $10–$12
Horse (Mare and Foal) .... $20–$26
Horse (Oh Kentucky) .... $50–$60
Horse (Pewter). .... $12–$17
Horse (White), 1962, white mustang with white flowing mane and tail. Regal China, 13½". .... $12–$16
Horse (White)—Re-issued, 1967, as in previous entry .... $8–$11
Horseshoe Club, 1969, same as Reno and Cal-Neva bottles with "Reno's Horseshoe Club" and a horseshoe in yellow and black on the emblem, 9¼" .... $4–$6
Hula Bowl, 1975, brown football resting on a stand with a red helmet on the top. Medallion-type plaque on the front, football player in the center .... $8–$10
Hyatt House—Chicago. .... $7–$10
Hyatt House—New Orleans. .... $8–$11

Jim Beam, globe. PHOTO COURTESY OF DAVE SMITH.

Harolds Club—Pinwheel, 1965, a round bottle supporting a design of a spinning pinwheel of gold and blue, with gold dots on the edge. "Harolds Club Reno" embossed in gold in the center, "For Fun" on the stopper. Regal China, 10¹/₂" . . . . $30–$40

Harolds Club—Silver Opal, 1957, issued to commemorate the 25th anniversary of Harolds Club; bright silver color with a snowflake design center and a red label. Glass, 11¹/₈" . . . . $15–$20

Harolds Club—VIP Executive, 1967, an Aladdin's lamp-shaped decanter. "Harolds Club Reno" embossed gold label on bottle. Overall gold and green color on bottle. Limited quantity issued. Regal China, 12¹/₂" . . . . $35–$40

Harolds Club—VIP Executive, 1969, an oval-shaped decanter with an overall motif of roses. "Harolds Club Reno" is embossed in gold on the yellow-toned bottle. The bottle was used as a Christmas gift to the casino's executives. Regal China, 12¹/₂" . . . . . . $200–$250

Harolds Club-VIP Executive, 1968, an overall bubble pattern in cobalt blue with silver trim and handle distinguishes this bottle. "Harolds Club Reno" in silver, on an embossed oval emblem, is in the center of the bottle. Regal China, 12³/₄" . . . . $40–$50

Harp Seal . . . . $10–$15

Harrahs Club Nevada—Gray, 1963, this is the same round bottle used for the Nevada Centennial and Harolds Club with the miner, mule, and lettered "Nevada Centennial." The base has "Harrah's Reno and Lake Tahoe." embossed on the gray-tone base. Regal China, 11¹/₂" . . . . $500–$550

Harrahs Club Nevada—Silver, 1963, same as above. Nevada Centennial bottle, "Harrah's Reno and Lake Tahoe" embossed on base in silver. Regal China, 11¹/₂" . . . . $400–$500

Harry Hoffman . . . . $4–$7

Harveys Resort Hotel at Lake Tahoe, glass, 11¹/₂" . . . . $6–$10

Hatfield, 1973, the character of Hatfield from the famous story of the Hatfield and McCoy feud. Hatfield is shown standing holding a rifle at his side. He is dressed all in black. On the base of the bottle he is referred to as "Devil Anse Hatfield." His hat is the stopper. Regal China, 14" . . . . $15–$16

Hawaii, 1959, tribute to 50th state. Panorama and Hawaiian scenes, palm trees, the blue Pacific, outriggers, and surfboarders. Gold 50 in star. Regal China, 8¹/₂" . . . . . $25–$30

Hawaii, 1971 . . . . $6–$8

Hawaii Aloha, 1971, pear-shaped bottle with picture of Hawaiian king on the front and a scene of mountain and palm tree on reverse, 11" . . . . $6–$8

Hawaii Paradise, 1978, commemorates the 200th anniversary of the landing of Captain Cook. Embossed scene of a Hawaiian resort framed by a pink garland of flowers. Black stopper, 8³/₄" . . . . $12–$14

Idaho, 1963, bottle in the shape of Idaho. Skier on slope on one side and farmer on other side. Pick and shovel on stopper. Regal China, 12¼"................ $30–$45

Illinois, 1968, the log cabin birthplace of "Abe Lincoln" embossed on front; oak tree and banner with 21 stars (21st state) and "Land of Lincoln." Made to honor the Sesquicentennial 1818-1968 of Illinois, home of the James B. Beam Distilling Co. Regal China, 12¾"... $3–$4

Indian Chief, 1979, seated Indian chief with a peace pipe across his arm. Tan colored with touches of brown, green, and red.................................. $7–$9

Indianapolis 500 .... $6–$9

Indianapolis Sesquicentennial .... $3–$4

International Chili Society, 1976, upper body of a chef with recipe of C.V. Wood's World Championship Chili. .... $7–$9

Italian Marble Urn, 1985, Executive series .... $9–$13

Ivory Ashtray, 1955, designed for a dual purpose: as a bottle and as an ashtray. Bottle lies flat with cigarette grooves and round coaster seat. Ivory color. Regal China, 12¾"... $5–$7

Jackalope, 1971, the fabulous Wyoming Jackalope, a rare cross between a jackrabbit and antelope. It has the body and ears of the western jackrabbit and the head and antlers of an antelope. Golden brown body on prairie grass base. Regal China, 14"..... $5–$8

Jaguar.. $18–$23

Jewel T Man—50th Anniversary .... $35–$45

John Henry, 1972, this bottle commemorates the legendary Steel Drivin' Man. He is black and is shown barechested. In each hand he holds a steel hammer. Embossed on the base is "Big Bend Tunnel West Virginia." Regal China, 12¾"......... $10–$14

Joliet Legion Band, 1978, shield-shaped bottle with embossed details resembling a coat of arms in blue, green, and gold. Commemorates the 26 national championships won by the band, 12¼"...................................... $10–$14

Kaiser International Open Bottle, 1971, this handsome Regal China creation commemorates the fifth Annual Kaiser International Open Golf Tournament played that year at Silverado in California's beautiful Napa Valley. The stopper is a golf ball decorated with the Kaiser International Open logo suspended over a red tee. The logo is repeated, in gold against a blue field, in the center of the front panel and is surrounded by a ring of decorated golf balls. Listed on the back are the particulars of the tournament, 11¼"... $2–$3

Kangaroo, 1977, kangaroo with its baby in its pouch on a green pedestal. The head is the stopper, 11¾"... $9–$12

Kansas, 1960, round yellow-toned bottle shows harvesting of wheat on one side and "Kansas 1861–1961 Centennial" embossed in gold. On the other side, symbols of the modern age with aircraft, factories, oil wells, and dairies. Leather thong. Regal China, 11¾".. $30–$36

Kentucky Black Head, 1967, the stopper is a horse's head; some are made in brown, some black. State map on bottle shows products of Kentucky—tobacco, distilling, farming, coal, oil, and industries. Regal China, 11½"..................... $9–$11

Kentucky Brown Head, 1967, same as above, 11½"................. $15–$25

Kentucky Derby 95th, 1969, pink, red roses .... $4–$7

Kentucky Derby 96th, 1970, double rose........................... $15–$25

Kentucky Derby 97th, 1971 .... $4–$7

Kentucky Derby 98th, 1972, designed to commemorate the 98th Run for the Roses at Churchill Downs showing Canonero II, 1971 winner, garlanded with the traditional American Beauty roses. The reverse side depicts famous Churchill Downs clubhouse in relief and etched in gold. The stopper is a replica of an American Beauty rose, 11" . $4–$6

Kentucky White Head, 1967, same as above, 11½" .... $20–$25
Kentucky Derby 100th, 1974, this bottle commemorates the 100th anniversary of the running of the Kentucky Derby. The number "100" is embossed very large on the bottle and the interior of the numbers is decorated with pink flowers with green leaves and stems. Also on the front of the bottle are embossings of the first Derby winner, Aristides, and the 100th winner, Cannonade. Both horses' portraits are framed by horseshoes, 7½" .... $7–$10
Key West, 1972, This bottle was issued to honor the 150th anniversary of Key West, Florida. It is roughly triangular with embossed details such as palm trees and surf. Regal China, 9¾" .... $4–$7
King Kamehameha, 1972, a replica of the famous King Kamehameha statue, this genuine Regal China bottle has been designed to commemorate the 100th anniversary of King Kamehameha Day. A hero of the Hawaiian people, King Kamehameha is credited for uniting the Hawaiian islands..................................... $4–$7
King Kong, 1976, three-quarter body of King Kong. Commemorates Paramount's movie release in December 1976, 9¾". .... $4–$7

Jim Beam, King Kong. PHOTO COURTESY OF DAVE SMITH.

Kiwi, 1974, the kiwi bird is shown protecting its egg near a tree stump. The kiwi's feathers are brown and the egg is white. The stopper is plain. Regal China, 8½" .. $4–$7
Koala Bear, 1973, the koala bear, the native animal of Australia. A genuine Regal China creation. The bottle features two koala bears on a tree stump. The top of the stump is its pourer, with the name Australia across the front of the bottle, 9" .... $10–$13
Laramie, 1968, "Centennial Jubilee Laramie Wyo. 1868–1968" embossed around cowboy on bucking bronco. Locomotive of 1860s on reverse, 10½" .... $2–$4
Largemouth Bass Trophy Bottle, 1973, created in honor of the National Fresh Water Fishing Hall of Fame, located in Hayward, Wisconsin, completed in 1974. A genuine Regal China creation designed after the largemouth bass. Its stopper features the official seal of the Hall of Fame... $10–$14
Las Vegas, 1969, this bottle was also used for Customer Specials, Casino series. Almond-shaped with gold embossed "Las Vegas" in a banner, scenes of Nevada, and a gambling montage. Reverse: Hoover Dam and Lake Mead. Regal China, 12½" .... $2–$4
Light Bulb, 1979, regular bottle shape with replica of a light bulb for the stopper, picture of Thomas Edison in an oval, letter of tribute to Edison on the back, 11¼" .... $10–$12
Lombard, 1969, a pear-shaped decanter, embossed with lilacs and leaves around a circular motto "Village of Lombard, Illinois—1869 Centennial 1969"; lilac-shaped stopper. Reverse has an embossed outline of Illinois. Colors are lavender and green, 12¼". . $2–$4
London Bridge. .... $2–$4

Louisiana Superdome . . . . $7–$9
Louisville Downs Racing Derby, 1978, short oblong-shaped bottle. Scene with horse, buggy, and rider on front framed by wide white band with gold lettering. Medallion-type stopper, 9¹/₂" . . . . $4–$7
LVNH Owl. . . . . $15–$20
Madame Butterfly, 1977, figurine of Madame Butterfly character from the opera of the same name. Female dressed in blue and black kimono holding a realistic fan made of paper and wood. Music box plays *One Fine Day* from the opera; includes base and paperweight, 16¹/₂" . . . . $150–$200
Maine, 1970, a green triangular bottle with the outline of the state on the front and wording "The Pine Tree State," 12" . . . . $3–$4
Majestic, 1966, royal blue decanter with handle, on a base of golden leaves. Gold scrolled stopper and lip. Regal China, 14¹/₂" . . . . $15–$20
Male Cardinal . . . . $10–$16
Marbled Fantasy, 1965, decanter on a blue marbled base, set in a cup of gold with a heavy gold ring around the center. Gold lip and handle, blue and gold stopper. Regal China, 15" . . . . $28–$34
Marina City, 1962, commemorating modern apartment complex in Chicago. Light blue with "Marina City" in gold on the sides. Regal China, 10³/₄" . . . . $10–$15
Marine Corps . . . . $25–$35
Mark Antony, 1962, same as Cleo bottles, amphora decanter, two handles, white stopper. Mark Antony alone before Nile scene, white on rust background. Bottle color is black-purple. Glass, 13¹/₄" . . . . $15–$19
Martha Washington, 1976, designed like a collector's plate, with a portrait of Martha Washington encircled by a band of white with the outside rim in light blue and gold embossed lettering, 9¹/₂" . . . . $5–$8
McCoy, 1973, the character of McCoy from the famous story of the Hatfield and McCoy feud. McCoy is shown seated holding a rifle. On the base of the bottle he is referred to as "Randolph McCoy." The stopper is his hat. Regal China, 12". . . $10–$14
McShane—Cobalt, 1981, Executive Series . . . . $70–$90
McShane—Green Bell, 1983, Executive series . . . . $60–$70
McShane—Green Pitcher, 1982, Executive Series . . . . $60–$70
McShane—Mother-of-Pearl, 1979, Executive Series . . . . $60–$80
McShane-Titans, 1980 . . . . $60–$80
Mephistopheles, 1979, part of the Opera series, this figurine depicts Mephistopheles from the opera *Faust*. The music box plays Soldier's Chorus; bottle and base make up two-piece set, 14¹/₂" . . . . $100–$145
Michigan Bottle, 1972, the map of the Great Lakes State adorns the front of this striking commemorative Regal China bottle. The state flower and the major cities are shown with an insert plaque of an antique automobile, one of Michigan's traditional symbols. A capsule description of the state, a drawing of the magnificent Mackinac Bridge, and the state motto of the "Wolverine State" appear on a scroll on the back. The stopper depicts an antique wooden wheel on one side and a modern automobile wheel on the other, 11⁷/₈" . . . . $3–$4
Milwaukee Stein . . . . $20–$27
Minnesota Viking, 1973, A strikingly hadsome Regal China creation designed after the famous Viking statue in Alexandria, Minnesota, known as the Largest Viking in the World. The bottle features a helmet as its stopper. The back depicts a replica of the Kensington Runestone, 14". . . . . $9–$12
Mint 400, 1970, China stopper. . . . . $70–$90
Mint 400, 1971, Same as above. . . . . $5–$6

Mint 400, 1972, this bottle commemorates the fifth annual Greatest Off-Road Race held by Del Webb and Mint 400. A black and white checkered flag has the name in large gold letters across the flag, 11¼" .... $5–$7

Mint 400, 1973, an all-gold bottle honors the sixth annual Mint 400 Sahara Desert Rally, the world's greatest off-road race. An embossed scene is on the back, 13" $6–$8

Mint 400, 1974, metal stopper .... $4–$7

Mint 400 7th Annual, 1975, the checkerboard finish flag serves as a background for the emblem of the Mint 400 Desert Race. This $100,000 purse event includes both auto and cycle contests and they are shown on the gold-embossed back of the bottle, 8¼" .... $5–$6

Mint 400 8th Annual, 1976, medallion-shaped bottle. White bottle with gold lettering and gold center with black lettering. Commemorates the Mint 400, a road race spon-sored by Del Webb's Hotel and Casino in Las Vegas, 10" .... $9–$12

Mississippi Fire Engine, 1978, replica of the 1867 fire engine; red and black with brass simulated fittings. Bells, lanterns, water pump, and engine mountings are authentic, 11¾" .... $90–$110

Model A Ford 1903, 1978, replica of Henry Ford's Model A Ford in red with black trim or black with red trim. Simulated brass and trim. Stopper at the rear of the car, 8" .... $40–$50

Model A Ford 1928, 1980, beige Model A with black accessories; authentic details for the headlights, trim, and interior. Stopper underneath the rear trunk and spare tire, 6½" .... $55–$68

Montana, 1963, tribute to gold miners. Names of "Alder Gulch," "Last Chance Gulch," Bannack," and "Montana, 1864 Golden Years Centennial 1964" are embossed on bottle. Regal China, 11½" .... $50–$60

Monterey Bay Club, 1977, based on the bandstand in Watsonville city park, honors the Monterey Bay Beam Bottle and Specialty Club, 7½" .... $7–$8

Mortimer Snerd, 1976, country boy with buck teeth, straw hat, and bow tie; replica of famous character created by Edgar Bergen, 12" .... $18–$22

Mother-Of-Pearl, 1979, double-urn-shaped bottle with wide alternating bands of gold and mother-of-pearl with double scroll handles on large screw lid. Identical to the Harolds Club VIP bottle except no lettering on the front, 11½" .... $6–$8

Mount St. Helens, 1980, depicts the eruption of Mount St. Helens on May 18, 1980. A small vial of ash from the explosion is attached on the back, 9¼" .... $20–$22

Mr. Goodwrench, 1978, half-figure of Mr. Goodwrench based on the General Motors advertisement. The figure is the stopper which sits on a rectangular base. Blue and white, 13½" .... $24–$28

Musicians On A Wine Cask, 1964, old-time tavern scene: musicians, guitar, and accordian, embossed on cask-shaped embossed bottle. Wooden barrel effect and wood base. Gray china color. Regal China, 9¾" .... $2–$4

Muskie, 1971, the muskie is the state fish of Wisconsin. The bottle is a figure of the fish, the stopper is the head, the fish rests on a platform of water. Also on the bottle is a plaque indicating the muskie as the Wisconsin state fish. The bottle was issued in honor of the National Fresh Water Fishing Hall of Fame. Regal China, 14½" ...... $14–$18

National Tobacco Festival, 1973, Regal China bottle commemorating the 25th an-niversary of the National Tobacco Festival. The festival was held in Richmond, Vir-ginia, on October 6–13. On the base of the special bottle, historic data of the growth and development of the tobacco industry is featured. The unique closure is the bust of an American Indian... $3–$5

Nebraska, 1967, round bottle bears the words, "Where the West Begins" with a picture of a covered wagon drawn by oxen. Regal China, 12¼" .... $3–$5

Jim Beam, political. PHOTO
COURTESY OF DAVE SMITH.

Nebraska Football, 1972, this strikingly handsome genuine Regal China creation commemorates the University of Nebraska's national championship football team of 1970-71 season. The stopper features an exact likeness of Bob Devaney, The Cornhuskers' head coach, 8³/₄" .... $3–$5
Nevada, 1963, circular silver and gray bottle, with silver "Nevada," bearing outline of state with embossed mountain peaks, forests, and a factory. Reverse is a miner and donkey. Same bottle used by Harolds Club and Harrah's Regal China., 11¹/₂". $28–$33
New Hampshire, 1967, blue-tone bottle in the shape of the state. Decal of state motto, seal, flower, and bird. Stopper in the shape of the Old Man of the Mountain. Regal China, 13¹/₂" .... $3–$4
New Hampshire Eagle Bottle, 1971, under the New Hampshire banner on this beautiful Regal China bottle, a solid gold eagle against a blue field stands as a proud reminder of the original symbol, a great carved wooden bird, which was placed atop the New Hampshire State House when it was built in 1818. On the back of the bottle, beneath the slogan "Granite State," a decal recounts the history of the first New Hampshire eagle, 12¹/₂" .... $14–$18
New Jersey, 1963, gray map of state filled with embossed colorful fruits, vegetables, and flowers, set on a pyramid-shaped bottle. "New Jersey—The Garden State, Farm & Industry" in gold. Regal China, 13¹/₂" .... $35–$45
New Jersey Yellow, 1963, same as previous entry, yellow-toned map of New Jersey., 13¹/₂" .... $40–$50
New Mexico Bicentennial, 1976, square-shaped bottle with blue center. White lettering and gold eagle embossed on front. The governor's home is on the back, 10¹/₂" .... $6–$9
New Mexico Statehood, 1972, commemorating New Mexico's 60 years of statehood, this dramatic genuine Regal China bottle has been designed to represent the historical Indian ceremonial wedding vase which was used through the centuries by the New Mexico Indians in tribal wedding ceremonies, 9¹/₂". .... $2–$3
New York World's Fair, 1964, the emblem of New York World's Fair of 1964, the Unisphere, forms the shape of this bottle. Blue-tone oceans, gray continents crossed by space flight routes. Emblem embossed in gold "1964 World's Fair—1965." Stopper has Unisphere. Regal China, 11¹/₂". .... $5–$6
North Dakota, 1964, embossed memorial picture of a pioneer family in North Dakota—75" embossed in gold in banner. Yellows, greens, and browns. Regal China, 11³/₄" $45–$55
Northern Pike, 1977, Replica of the Northern Pike. Green and yellow with pointed head. The sixth in a series of bottles designed for the National Fresh Water Fishing Hall of Fame, 9" .... $10–$15

Nutcracker Toy Soldier, 1978, figurine based on the toy soldier character in the ballet *The Nutcracker*. This is not part of the Opera series. Small man dressed in red and white uniform with blue suspenders and gold trim. The music box plays a selection from The Parade of the Toy Soldiers, $12\frac{1}{2}$". . . . . $75–$95

Ohio, 1966, bottle in shape of state. One side bears state seal, other side has pictures of state industries. Regal China, 10". . . . . $3–$4

Ohio State Fair, 1973, A handsome bottle made of genuine Regal China, created in honor of the 120th Ohio State Fair, $10\frac{3}{4}$". . . . . $3–$4

Olympian, 1960, green urn decanter. Chariot, horses, and warriors design in white on light blue bottle. White glass stopper, embossed base. Glass, 14". . . . . $1–$2

One Hundred First Airborne Division, 1977, honors the division known during World War II as the Screaming Eagles. A gold flying eagle atop a white pedestal, 14". . . . . $4–$7

Opaline Crystal (1969), 1969, milk glass bottle; same pattern and embossing, and stopper. Milk glass, $11\frac{1}{2}$". . . . . $6–$7

Oregon, 1959, green-tone bottle to honor centennial of the state. Depicting famous scenery on both sides. Two beavers on bottle neck. Regal China, $8\frac{3}{4}$". . . . . $15–$20

Oregon Liquor Commission. . . . . $25–$30

Osco Drugs. . . . . $25–$30

Panda, 1980, adult panda on the ground with two cubs climbing the stump of a tree. Authenticated by Dr. Lester Fisher, Director of the Lincoln Park Zoological Gardens in Chicago. . . . . $15–$20

Paul Bunyan. . . . . $4–$7

Pearl Harbor Memorial, 1972, honoring the Pearl Harbor Survivors Association, this handsome genuine Regal China bottle is emblazoned with the motto: "Remember Pearl Harbor—Keep America Alert." The stopper features the official seal of the armed services that were present December 7, 1941—the Army, Navy, Marine Corps, and Coast Guard. The stopper is set off by an American eagle, $11\frac{1}{2}$". . . . . $14–$18

Pearl Harbor Survivors Association, 1976, medallion-shaped bottle with flying eagle in the center with a blue background and white lettering around the border. On the back, a scene of the island Oahu, with three battleships, $9\frac{3}{4}$". . . . . $5–$8

Pennsylvania, 1967, keystone-shaped bottle in blue tones. Decal of state seal "Historic Pennsylvania—The Keystone State" on front. Reverse: scenes of history and industry. Keystone stopper with gold "1776." Regal China, $11\frac{1}{2}$". $3–$4

Pennsylvania Dutch, club bottle. . . . . $7–$9

Permian Basin Oil Show, 1972, this dramatic genuine Regal China bottle is fashioned after an oil derrick and its attendant buildings. Commemorates the Permian Basin Oil Show in Odessa, Texas, October 18-21, 1972. The building is inscribed: "The E.E. 'Pop' Harrison No. 1 Well." The back of the flag says: "The oil industry provides energy, enterprise, employment for the nation." The stopper is fashioned in the shape of the logo for the Oil Field Workers Show with their motto "Let's Go," 13". . . . . $2–$4

Petroleum Man. . . . . $2–$3

Pheasant, 1960, ring-necked pheasant with red-circled eyes, green and blue head, and soft brown plumage perched on a fence base. Regal China, 13". . . . . $9–$13

Pheasant, 1961, re-issued also: '63, '66, '67, '68. As above. . . . . $7–$9

Phi Sigma Kappa (Centennial Series), 1973, a Regal China creation commemorating the 100th anniversary of this national fraternity dedicated to the promotion of brotherhood, the stimulation of scholarship, and the development of character. The fraternity insignia is in silver on a magenta background outlined in white and lavender. . . . . $3–$4

Phoenician, 1973, an elegantly handcrafted genuine Regal China, heavily embellished with 22K gold and featuring a floral design on the front. Each bottle comes in its own handsome presentation case lined with velvet . . . . $6–$9

Pied Piper of Hamlin, 1974, this charming bottle of genuine Regal China was especially produced for the United States Armed Forces in Europe as a commemorative of the famous German legend, the Pied Piper of Hamlin, 10^1/$_4$" . . . . $2–$4

Ponderosa, 1969, the home of the Cartwrights of "Bonanza" TV fame. A replica of the Ponderosa Ranch log cabin in brown tones. Reverse: Lake Tahoe. Bottles in green-lined box are worth more. Regal China, 7^1/$_2$" (h),10" (w). . . . . $4–$6

Ponderosa Ranch tourist, 1972, commemorating the one millionth tourist to the Ponderosa Ranch. This horseshoe-shaped bottle of genuine Regal China features the Ponderosa Pine and "P" symbol that has made the ranch famous. The stopper is traditional ten-gallon hat made famous by Dan Blocker, 11" . . . . $9–$11

Pony Express, 1968, clearly embossed figure of horse and Pony Express rider with "Sacramento, Calif.—October 1861" and "St. Joseph, Mo.—April 1860" and stars around figure. Reverse: map of the Pony Express route. Yellow and brown tones, 11" . . . . . $4–$7

Poodles—Gray and White, 1970, both poodles sit up with one paw on a ball. The gray has a green-banded ball embossed "Penny," the white has a blue-banded ball. Black eyes and nose with a gold color on each. Regal China, 12" . . . . $5–$6

Portland Rose Festival, 1972, to commemorate the 64th Portland (Oregon) Rose Festival which began in 1889. The Regal China bottle is encompassed in a garland of red roses which is commemorative of the oldest and largest rose show in America. On the reverse side there is a brief description of the festival with the very poignant line, "For You a Rose in Portland Grows," 10^1/$_4$" . . . . $2–$3

Portola Trek, 1969, this gold glass bottle has a painting of the Portola Trek reproduction in full color on the front. This bottle was issued to celebrate the 200th anniversary of San Diego, 11" . . . . $2–$4

Poulan Chain Saw, 1979, replica of the Poulan chainsaw with a plastic handle and blade. Green body with silver blade and black trim, 7" . . . . $20–$24

Powell Expedition, 1969, gold glass bottle with a full-color painting depicting John Wesley Powell's survey of the Colorado River and his traversing the Grand Canyon, 11". . . . $2–$4

Preakness, 1970, this bottle was issued to honor the 100th anniversary of the running of the Preakness. The body of the bottle is made up of a horseshoe surrounding the trophy awarded the Preakness winner, the Woodlawn Vase. In lettering on the horseshoe is "Pimlico Race Course." A wreath of daisies tops the horseshoe. The stopper is plain. Regal China, 11". . . . . $5–$6

Jim Beam, Preakness and Las Vegas conventions. PHOTO COURTESY OF DAVE SMITH.

Preakness Pimlico, 1975 . . . . $4–$7
Presidential, 1968, Executive series . . . . $4–$7
Prestige, 1967, Executive series. . . . . $4–$7
Pretty Perch, 1980, spiny-finned fish with dark bands, touches of orange on the fins.
The eighth in a series, this fish is used as the official seal of the National Fresh Water
Fishing Hall of Fame, 9" . . . . $10–$13
Prima-Donna, 1969, same as Cal-Neva with Prima-Donna Casino and show girls on
the emblem, 9¼" . . . . $4–$6
Professional Golf Association. . . . . $3–$6
Queensland, 1978, in the shape of the province Queensland, the Sunshine State of Australia. Embossed lettering and details, gold star on the back, medallion-type stopper
with "Australia" in center, 8½" . . . . $15–$20
Rabbit. . . . . $4–$7
Rainbow Trout, 1975, rainbow trout mounted on an oval plaque made to look like
wood. Produced for the National Fresh Water Fishing Hall of Fame. Their official seal
is on the back, 7½" . . . . $10–$15
Ralph Centennial, 1973, made of genuine Regal China, this bottle was designed to
commemorate the 100th anniversary of the Ralph Grocery Co. in California. The bottle
depicts two sides of a coin struck especially for the occassion and an early version of a
Ralph's delivery wagon, 7¾" . . . . $10–$13
Ralphs Market. . . . . $8–$12
Ram, 1958, stylized ram in soft tans and browns. Calender mounted on green base and
a round thermometer in the curve of the horn (without thermometer, value is less).
Regal China, 12½" . . . . $50–$70
Ramada Inn, 1976, a Ramada Inn attendant is shown as a sentinel at the door to a small
narrow building of red, white, and blue. Gold shingles with a black lid on the chimney,
11" . . . . $6–$9
Red Mile Racetrack . . . . $8–$12
Redwood, 1967, pyramid-shaped bottle, "Coast Redwoods" embossed on front in tones
of brown and green. "Redwood Empire of California" lettered below tree. Reverse:
scenes of Redwood country. Regal China, 12¾" . . . . $3–$4
Reflections, 1975, Executive series . . . . $8–$12
Regency, 1972, this elegantly handcrafted Regal China bottle is heavily embellished
with fired 22K gold and features a bouquet of tiny flowers about its mid-section. Each
bottle comes in its own handsome dark red presentation case lined with velvet. . . $6–$7
Reidsville, 1973, this bottle was issued to honor the city of Reidsville, North Carolina,
on the occasion of its centennial. The bottle is circular with leaves surrounding a central
plaque bearing the slogan "Yesterday Today Tomorrow." The bottle is blue and the
stopper is circular and bears the date "1973." Regal China, 12" . . . . $2–$4
Renee The Fox, 1974, this interesting Regal China bottle represents the companion for
the International Association of Jim Beam Bottle and Specialties Club's mascot. Renee
the fox is the life-long companion of Rennie the fox, 12½" . . . . $8–$12
Rennie The Runner, 1974, Rennie the fox is shown running in his brown running suit,
white running shoes, and black top hat. On a string around his neck is the seal of the
International Association of Beam Clubs, 12½" . . . . $8–$12
Rennie The Surfer, 1975, Rennie the fox dressed in an old-fashioned bathing suit and
a black top hat rides a small surfboard. He holds a bottle of Beam behind him with one
hand, 12½" . . . . $8–$12
Reno, 1968, "100 Years—Reno" embossed over skyline of downtown Reno. "The
Biggest Little City in the World" lettered over skyline. Reverse: "Reno 100 years" and
scenes of Reno, Regal China, 9¼" . . . . $3–$4

Republican Convention, 1972, gold, with plate . . . . $400–$475
Republic of Texas, 1980, star-shaped bottle with gold spout, handle, and top. White with a red border; symbols of the state are represented on the front. The stopper is a gold star, 12³/₄" . . . . $10–$13
Republican Football, 1972, GOLD . . . . $300+
Richard Hadlee . . . . $75–$100
Richards—New Mexico, 1967, created for Richards Distributing Co. of Albuquerque, New Mexico. Lettered "New Mexico" and "Richard Says Discover New Mexico" in blue. Embossed scene of Taos pueblo. Picture of Richard on stopper and front. Regal China, 11" . . . . $4–$6
Robin, 1969, an olive gray bird with a soft red breast, dark-toned head and tail. The robin has a yellow beak and stands on a tree trunk with an embossed branch and leaves. Regal China, 13¹/₂" . . . . $5–$6
Rocky Marciano, 1973, a handsome genuine Regal China bottle in honor of Rocky Marciano, the world's only undefeated boxing champion. The bottle takes the shape of a rock, with a likeness of Rocky Marciano on the front. The back of the bottle features Marciano's complete professional record of 49 fights, all victories (43 knockouts and 6 decisions) . . . . $15–$23
Rocky Mountain, club bottle. . . . . $7–$9
Royal Crystal, 1959, starburst design embossed on both sides on this clear flint glass decanter. Gold label on neck and flat black stopper. Starburst theme appears on label and stopper. Glass, 11¹/₂" . . . . $2–$3
Royal Di Monte, 1957, mottled design, black and white bottle. Handpainted with 22K gold and bordered in gold. Gold and black stopper. Regal China, 15¹/₂". . . . . . $30–$45
Royal Emperor, 1958, made in the shape of a classic Greek urn. Warrior figure with spear, helmet, and fret design in white on purple-black glass. White glass stopper. Glass, 14" . . . . $2–$3
Royal Gold Diamond, 1964, diamond-shaped decanter set on a flaring base, all in mottled gold. Gold chain holds label. Regal China, 12". . . . . $20–$28
Royal Gold Round, 1956, mottled with 22K gold, in classic round shape with graceful pouring spout and curved handle. Gold neck chain holds label. Regal China, 12" . . . . $60–$75
Royal Opal, 1957, a round handled bottle of opal glass. Embossed geometric design on one side. White glass stopper. Bottle made by Wheaton Glass of Millville, New Jersey. Same bottle in silver was used for Harolds Club, 25th anniversary. Glass, 10³/₄". $2–$3
Royal Porcelain, 1955, gleaming black decanter, tapered with a large flared pouring lip, white stopper, gold cord and tassel. Regal China, 14¹/₂" . . . . $300+
Royal Rose, 1963, decanter, gold embossed with handpainted roses on a background of soft blue; gold spout, stopper, base, and handle. Regal China, 17" . . . . $30–$34
Ruby Crystal, 1967, amethyst-colored, patterned embossed bottle. Swirl glass stopper. When bottle is filled with bourbon it's ruby red. Sunburst pattern on bottom. Amethyst glass, 11¹/₂" . . . . $6–$9
Ruidoso Downs with flat ears, 1968, same as above . . . . $4–$6
Ruidoso Downs with pointed ears, 1968, a round decanter with a unique "horsehead" stopper. Embossed silver horseshoe, branding iron, and cowboy hat; "Ruidoso Downs—New Mexico, World's Richest Horse Race" on front. Reverse: red, white, and blue emblem. The bottle is known in pointed and flat ears. Regal China, 12³/₄" $20–$25
Sahara Invitational Bottle, 1971, introduced in honor of the Del Webb 1971 Sahara Invitational Pro-Am Golf Tournament. The prominent feature of this Regal China bottle is a large "Del Webb Pro-Am 1971" golf ball atop a red tee on the face. Listed on the back are the winners of this annual contest from 1958-1970, 12" . . . . $5–$7

Jim Beam, slot machine. PHOTO
COURTESY OF DAVE SMITH.

Sam Bear—Donkey, 1973, Political series............................. $1000+
Samoa... $3–$5
San Diego, 1968, issued by the Beam Co. for the 200th anniversary of its founding in
1769. Honoring Junipero Serra, Franciscan missionary. "Serra" and "Conquistador"
embossed on gold front. Regal China, 10"............................... $3–$5
San Diego—Elephant, 1972....................................... $15–$20
Santa Fe, 1960, Governor's Palace, blue-toned sky, date 1610–1960 (350th anniversary).
Navaho woman with Indian basket on reverse. Gold lettering. Regal China, 10" ... $100–$130
SCCA, etched... $10–$14
SCCA, smooth.. $10–$13
Screech Owl, 1979, either red or gray shading. Birds are bisque replicas of screech
owls, authenticated by Dr. Lester Fisher, director of the Lincoln Zoological Gardens in
Chicago, 9³/₄"... $18–$22
Seafair Trophy Race, 1972, this dramatic genuine Regal China creation commemo-
rates the Seattle Seafair Trophy Race, August 6, 1972, and features an unlimited
hydroplane at speed with picturesque Mt. Rainier in the background, 11¹/₂" .. $15–$25
Seattle World's Fair, 1962, the Space Needle, as this bottle is known, is embossed in
gold on one side, "Century 21" on the other. Pylon-shaped with color scenes of fruit,
airplanes over mountains, salmon, etc. Stopper is the Fair's revolving restaurant. Regal
China, 13¹/₂".. $7–$9
Seoul—Korea, 1988.. $30–$40
Sheraton Inn .... $4–$6
Short Dancing Scot, 1963, a short barrel-shaped bottle with the dancing Scot and
music box in the base. Square-shaped stopper; a rare bottle. Glass, 11" ...... $40–$50
Short-Timer, 1975, brown army shoes with army helmet sitting on top. Produced for
all who have served in the armed forces, 8"........................... $15–$20
Shriners, 1975, embossed camel on front of bottle in blue, green, and brown with
bright red blanket flowing from the camel's saddle. A gold scimitar and star centered
with a fake ruby is on the back, 10¹/₂"................................ $10–$12
Shriners Pyramid, 1975, this bottle was issued by the El Kahir Temple of Cedar
Rapids, Iowa. It is shaped like a pyramid with embossing on the sides of the various
insignia of the Shriners. The bottle is white and brown and made to look as if it were
made of brick. The stopper is the very top of the pyramid. Regal China, 5" ... $10–$12

Shriners Temple, 1972, this beautiful Regal China bottle features the traditional symbols of Moila Templei, the scimitar, star and crescent, fez, and the pyramid with the stopper as the head of the sphinx. This bottle is unique in that it features three simulated precious stones, two of them in the handle of the sword and the third in the center point of the star, $11^1/_2$" .... $20–$25
Shriners Western Association .... $12–$16
Shriners—Indiana .... $4–$7
Sierra Eagle .... $11–$16
Sigma Nu Fraternity, 1977, rectangular bottle with badge and coat of arms of the Sigma Nu Fraternity embossed on the front. White and gold lettering and designs. Medallion-type stopper. .... $6–$9
Sigma Nu Fraternity—Kentucky .... $6–$9
Sigma Nu Fraternity—Michigan. .... $7–$9
Smiths North Shore Club, 1972, commemorating Smith's North Shore Club, at Crystal Bay, Lake Tahoe. This striking genuine Regal China bottle features the anchor, symbol of the club, and is topped by a giant golden golf ball, 12". .... $10–$12
Smoked Crystal, 1964, dark green in tone and resembling a genie's magic bottle, this tall bottle has a bulbous embossed base and a slender tapering shape, topped by an embossed glass topper. Glass, 14" .... $6–$9
Snow Goose, 1970, replica of a white goose with black wingtips. Authenticated by Dr. Lester Fisher, director of Lincoln Park Zoological Gardens in Chicago, $11^1/_2$".. $15–$25
Snowman .... $70–$95
South Carolina, 1970, the Palmetto State celebrated its tricentennial, 1670–1970. Palmetto trees are embossed on the outline map of the state which is outlined in gold. The South Carolina Dispensary is on the back, $9^1/_4$". .... $4–$6
South Dakota—Mount Rushmore, 1969, the faces of Washington, Jefferson, T. Roosevelt, and Lincoln are shown in relief in white with blue sky and green forest. This landmark is the Mount Rushmore National Memorial. Reverse: scroll with information about Memorial. Regal China, $10^1/_2$" .... $3–$4
South Florida—Fox On Dolphin, 1980, a fox dressed in hunting garb rides a dolphin. This bottle was sponsored by the South Florida Beam Bottle and Specialties Club which is located in Miami, $14^1/_2$" .... $14–$16
Sovereign, 1969, Executive series .... $4–$7
Spengers Fish Grotto, 1977, designed as a small boat with the captain at the helm. Brown, yellow, and blue, made in conjunction with Spenger's Fish Grotto Restaurant in Berkeley, California. .... $15–$19
Sports Car Club Of America, 1976, six-sided front with a Ridge-Whetworth wire wheel in the center on pedestal foot. Brief history of the club on the back, 11" . $8–$11
St. Bernard, 1979, replica of a St. Bernard with a small cask of Beam around his neck held by a real leather collar, $6^1/_2$" .... $20–$30
St. Louis Arch, 1964, The silhouette of St. Louis with the Mississippi River flowing past. The famous stainless steel arch frames the bottle; "St. Louis, gateway to the West" and "200 Years" embossed in gold. The ferry boat "Admiral" is on the back. Regal China, 11" .... $6–$9
St. Louis Arch—Re-issue, 1967, same as above .... $8–$11
St. Louis, club bottle .... $7–$9
St. Louis Statue, 1972, this handsome Regal China bottle features the famous statue of St. Louis on horseback atop its pedestal base. The entire statue is fired gold. The back bears the inscription, "Greater St. Louis Area Beam and Specialties Club," $13^1/_4$" .... $6–$8
Statue of Liberty, 1975, figural bottle with gold-embossed Statue of Liberty on the front with light blue background. Green base with plaque, $12^1/_2$" .... $6–$9

Statue of Liberty, 1985 . . . . $8–$13
Sturgeon, 1980, Exclusive issue for a group that advocates the preservation of sturgeon. Long brown colored fish, 6¼" . . . . $14–$17
Stutz Bearcat 1914, 1977, either yellow and black or gray and black. Replica of the 1914 four-cylinder Stutz Bearcat. Authentic details with movable windshield. Stopper is under plastic trunk and spare wheel, 7" . . . . $45–$55
Submarine Redfin, 1970, embossed submarine on ocean blue background. "Manitowoc Submarine Memorial Association" in black. Round stopper with map of Wisconsin, Regal China, 11½" . . . . $4–$5
Submarine—Diamond Jubilee. . . . . $25–$34
Superdome, 1975, replica of Louisiana Superdome which opened in August 1975. White and gold with black lettering around the top, 6½" . . . . $2–$4
Swagman, 1979, replica of an Australian hobo called a swagman who roamed that country looking for work during the Depression. He wears a grayish outfit with red kerchief around his neck. A brown dog and a sheep are curled around his feet, 14" . . . . $10–$12
Sydney Opera House, 1977, replica of the building housing the Sydney Opera in Sydney, Australia. Music box is in the base, 8½" . . . . $12–$17
Tall Dancing Scot, 1964, a small Scotsman encased in a glass bubble in the base dances to the music of the base. A tall pylon-shaped glass bottle with a tall stopper. No dates on these bottles. Glass, 17" . . . . $12–$19
Tavern Scene, 1959, two "beer stein" tavern scenes are embossed on sides, framed in wide gold band on this round decanter. Regal China, 11½" . . . . $30–$45
Telephone No. 1, 1975, replica of a 1907 phone of the Magneto wall type which was used from 1890 until the 1930s, 9½" . . . . $25–$35
Telephone No. 2, 1976, replica of an 1897 desk set . . . . $25–$30
Telephone No. 3, 1977, replica of a 1920 cradle phone . . . . $15–$20
Telephone No. 4, 1978, replica of a 1919 dial phone . . . . $40–$50
Telephone No. 5, 1979, pay phone . . . . $14–$18
Telephone No. 6, 1980, battery phone. . . . . $30–$40
Telephone No. 7, 1981, digital dial phone. . . . . $20–$30
Ten-Pin, 1980, designed as a bowling pin with two red bands around the shoulder and the neck. Remainder of the pin is white, screw lid, 12" . . . . $8–$11
Texas Hemisfair . . . . $6–$8
Texas Rose, 1978, Executive series. . . . . $10–$12
Thailand, 1969, embossed elephant in the jungle and "Thailand—A Nation of Wonders on the front. Reverse: a map of Thailand and a dancer. Regal China, 12½" . $2–$4
The Big Apple, 1979, apple-shaped bottle with embossed Statue of Liberty on the front with New York City in the background and the lettering "The Big Apple" over the top . . . . $7–$9
The Magpies, 1977, black magpie sitting on tip of a football with the name "The Magpies" on the front, honors an Australian football team, 10½" . . . . $12–$17
The Tigers, 1977, tiger head on top of football which reads "The Tigers." Honors an Australian football team, 7¾" . . . . $20–$24
Thomas Flyer 1907, 1976, replica of the 1907 Thomas Flyer, 6-70 Model K Flyabout which was a luxury car of its day. Comes in blue or white. Plastic rear trunk covers the lid to the bottle. . . . . $50–$60
Tiffany Poodle, 1973, genuine Regal China bottle created in honor of Tiffaney, the poodle mascot of the National Association of the Jim Beam Bottle and Specialty Clubs, 8½". . . . . $12–$16
Tiger—Australian. . . . . $10–$13
Titian, 1980, urn-shaped bottle, reproduces the designs created by the Venetian artist Titian in his oil paintings. Long fluted neck, with double-scrolled handle, 12½" . . . . $9–$12

Tobacco Festival . . . . $8–$12
Tombstone . . . . $3–$4
Travelodge Bear . . . . $3–$4
Treasure Chest, 1979, partially open treasure chest with gold coins, pearls, and jewelry. The lid is a screw top, 6" . . . . $6–$9
Trout Unlimited, 1977, large traditionally shaped bottle with a large yellow trout placed across the front of the bottle at the shoulder. Stopper reads "Limit Your Kill, Don't Kill Your Limit." To honor the Trout Unlimited Conservation Organization, 12" . . . . $10–$13
Truth or Consequences Fiesta, 1974, a ruggedly handsome Regal China bottle in honor of Ralph Edward's famous radio and television show and the city of Truth or Consequences, New Mexico, 10" . . . . $5–$6
Turquoise China Jug, 1966, alternating bands of scrolled designs spiral up the turquoise decanter. Regal China, 13$1/4$" . . . . $4–$6
Twin Bridges Bottle, 1971, designed to commemorate the largest twin bridge complex of its kind in the world. The twin bridges connect Delaware and New Jersey and serve as major links between key East Coast cities. Handsomely accented in gold and bearing the shield of the Twin Bridges Beam Bottle and Specialties Club, this Regal China bottle portrays the twin spans on the front and provides a descriptive story on the back. The stopper is a replica of the bridge toll house, 10$1/2$" . . . .
. . . . $20–$25
Twin Cherubs, 1974, Executive series . . . . $6–$9
Twin Doves, 1987, Executive series . . . . $14–$18
US Open, 1972, whimsically depicts Uncle Sam's traditional hat holding a full set of golf clubs. This charming Regal China creation honors the US Open Golf Tourney at the famous Pebble Beach course in California, 10$1/2$" . . . . $6–$9
Vendome Drummers Wagon, 1975, replica of a delivery wagon; green and cream wood with yellow wheels, which are plastic. Honored the Vendomes of Beverly Hills, California, a food-chain store which was first established in 1937, 8$1/2$" . . . . . . $40–$50
VFW Bottle, 1971, a handsome Regal China creation designed to commemorate the 50th anniversary of the Department of Indiana VFW. This proclamation is made on the neck of the bottle, in a plaque in the shape of the state of Indiana, over a striking reproduction of the medal insignia of the VFW, 9$3/4$" . . . . $5–$6
Viking, 1973, the Viking is holding a shield and sword and is leaning against a stone. The words "Minnesota, Land of the Vikings" appear on the shield. On the stone is recorded the Viking exploration of 1362. The stopper is his helmet. Regal China, 14" . . . . $9–$12
Volkswagen Commemorative Bottle—Two Colors, 1977, commemorating the Volkswagen Beetle, the largest selling single production model vehicle in automotive history. Handcrafted of genuine Regal China, this unique and exciting bottle will long remain a memento for bottle collectors the world over, 14$1/2$" . . . . $30–$38
Vons Market . . . . $20–$27
Walleye Pike, 1977, tall blue bottle with a large figurine of a yellow pike at the base. Designed for the National Fresh Water Fishing Hall of Fame in Hayward, Wisconsin. . . . . $12–$15
Walleye Pike, 1987 . . . . $17–$23
Washington, 1975, a state series bottle to commemorate the Evergreen State, which was honored with this green bottle featuring an apple and a fir tree in bas relief, 10" . . . . $5–$6
Washington State Bicentennial, 1976, patriot dressed in black and orange holding drum. Liberty bell and plaque in front of drummer, 10" . . . . $6–$8

Waterman, 1980, in pewter or glazed. Boatman at helm of his boat wearing rain gear. Glazed version in yellow and brown, 13^1/$_2$". . . . . $40–$50

West Virginia, 1963, waterfall scene in blue and green with gold embossed "Blackwater Falls—West Virginia—1863 Centennial 1963" surrounded by scrolled picture frame bottle. Reverse: state bird, red cardinal, and gold "35" in a star. Bear's head and maple leaf on each side of stopper, 10^1/$_4$". . . . . $90–$125

Western Shrine Association, 1980, designed to commemorate the Shriners' convention in 1980 which was held in Phoenix, Arizona. Rounded surface with a desert scene; red stopper designed as a fez with a tassel . . . . $18–$20

White Fox, 1969, this bottle was issued for the second anniversary of the Jim Beam Bottles and Specialties Club, Berkeley California. It shows a standing fox with his arms folded behind him. He is wearing a white jacket and a gold medallion and chain. The medallion displays a happy birthday message to the Berkeley Club, 12^1/$_2$" . . . . $30–$45

Wisconsin Muskie Bottle, 1971, this striking Regal China sculpture pays tribute to the state fish of Wisconsin, as the mighty muskellunge dances on his powerful tail in a burst of gold-flecked blue water, 14". . . . . $10–$14

Woodpecker, 1969, bright glazed red head, white breast and markings, black beak, and dark wings and tail. Woody grips a tree trunk base. Regal China, 13^1/$_2$". . . . . $4–$6

Wyoming, 1965, an embossed bucking bronco with a cowboy hanging on with mountains in the background and "Wyoming—The Equality State" in gold on tones of blue and tan. A rectangle shape of a pyramid, with a gold buffalo on the stopper. Reverse: state bird, flower, and Old Faithful. . . . .

Yellow Katz, 1967, the emblem of the Katz Department Stores (Missouri), green-eyed meowing cat, is the head (and stopper) of this bottle. The pylon-shaped, orange color body has a curved tail. The Katz commemorates the 50th birthday of the store. . . $4–$6

Yellow Rose, 1978, Executive series, 14^1/$_2$" . . . . $7–$10

Yellowstone Park Centennial. . . . . $2–$4

Yosemite, 1967, oval-shaped bottle with scenes from the park and trees embossed on the front. "Yosemite California" lettered on front. Gold pine tree on stopper, 11" $2–$4

Yuma Rifle Club . . . . $18–$23

Zimmerman Bell, 1976, bell-shaped bottle in cobalt blue with flowers and foliage embossed in blue and gold. Designed for Zimmerman Liquor Store of Chicago, 12^1/$_2$" . . . . $3–$4

Zimmerman Bell, 1976, bell-shaped bottle in light blue with lavender lid. Floral and foliage designs embossed on the front, 12^1/$_2$". . . . . $3–$4

Zimmerman Cherubs, 1968, winged cherubs and leaves and vines are embossed over the surface of these slender round pink and lavender bottles. They were issued for the Zimmerman Liquor Stores of Chicago. Regal China, 11^1/$_2$" . . . . $2–$3

Zimmerman Oatmeal Jug . . . . $30–$35

Zimmerman Two-Handled Jug, 1965, shaped and colored like an avocado, this dark green bottle has embossed grapes and grape leaves on the front, and two side handles. Regal China, 10^1/$_4$". . . . . $45–$60

Zimmerman Vase, brown . . . . $3–$5

Zimmerman Vase, green. . . . . $3–$5

Zimmerman—50th Anniversary. . . . . $30–$45

Zimmerman—Art Institute . . . . $5–$8

Zimmerman—Blue Beauty, 1969, the name "Zimmerman's Liquors" is embossed in bright gold on a sky blue bottle decorated with flowers and scrolls. Reverse has Chicago skyline embossed on blue-toned bottle. Arrow with "Zimmerman's" points to store. Regal China, 10". . . . . $4–$7

Zimmerman—Blue Daisy. . . . . $3–$4

Zimmerman—Chicago... $2–$3
Zimmerman—Eldorado... $2–$3
Zimmerman—Glass, 1969, a white outline of the Chicago skyline with "Zimmerman's" store on front of this glass bottle. White stopper has Max Zimmerman's portrait. Glass, 11¹/₄" .... $3–$5
Zimmerman—The Peddler Bottle, 1971, this unusual bottle in genuine Regal China was made in honor of Zimmerman's, the world's largest liquor store in Chicago, Illinois. Max Zimmerman, The Peddler himself, who specializes in personal service and works the counters of the store himself, is famous for his Stetson hat and cowboy boots. He is affectionately known in the trade as Max the Hat. Zimmerman's has always been active in merchandising Beam's collector's bottles, 12" .... $5–$7

BISCHOFF BOTTLES

Founded at Trieste, Italy, in 1777, Bischoff's was issuing decorative figurals in the 18th century long before the establishment of most companies who presently issue figural bottles. The early specimens are extremely rare because of limited production and loss over the years. Since sales do not occur often enough for firm values to be established, they are not included in this listing. Imported into the United States in 1949, the modern Bischoff's attracted little notice at first due to lack of American interest in bottle collecting at that time. Most sales were made for gift giving. The bottles are produced by the foremost glass, pottery, and porcelain companies in Bohemia, Czechoslovakia, Murano, Italy, Austria, and Germany.

KORD BOHEMIAN DECANTERS

Handblown, handpainted glass bottles were created in Czechoslovakia by the Kord Co., based on a long tradition of Bohemian cut, engraved, etched, and flashed glass. Typical Bohemia themes were used to decorate the decanters. Complete bottles with stoppers and labels are very difficult to find today. Cut glass and ruby-etched decanters, traditional forms of Bohemian glass, were imported into the United States in the early 1950s. Cut glass specimens are of lead crystal with hand cutting. The ruby-etched decanters are executed in the usual two-layer manner with the exterior ruby glass etched through to show the clear glass beneath. Designs are quite elaborate including leaping deer, castles, scrolls, foliage, wild birds, grapes, and latticework. The overall color can be amber or topaz with ruby the most common. When the underlayer of glass is opaque, the cut designs show very distinctly. Several of the etched decanters, made in Austria and Germany, should have labels indicating the place of origin. Most Bischoff Kord Bohemian decanters had matching sets of glasses. The Double Dolphin, Hunter and Lady, and Horse's Head decanters are thick handblown glass made in Czechoslovakia. Not as rare as the ruby-etched decanter since importation continues, they have value only when complete with stoppers.

Amber Flowers, 1952, a two-toned glass decanter. Amber flowers, stems, and leaves on a pale amber background. The long tapering neck is etched in panels and circles. The stopper is dark amber and handground to fit, $15^1/2$", amber . . . . $30–$40

Amber Leaves, 1952, multi-toned bottle with dark amber leaves and flowers on pale amber etched background. Stopper neck and base are cut in circles and panels. Round bottle with long neck, $13^1/2$" . . . . $30–$40

Anisette, 1948–51, clear glass bottle with two handles and a ground glass stopper. Clear glass ribbing on sides of bottle, 11" . . . . $20–$30

Bohemian Ruby-Etched, 1949–51, etched design in typical Bohemian style; castel, birds, deer, and scrolls and curlecues in clear glass, ruby red color flashed on bottle, except for etching and cut neck. Ground glass, etched stoppers on this tall, round decanter, tapered neck, $15^1/2$" . . . . $25–$35

Coronet Crystal, 1952, a broad band of flowers, leaves, and scrolls circle this multi-toned bottle. The designs are cut in dark amber glass revealing the opaque pale amber background. Stopper neck and base are cut in circles and panels. A round tall bottle, 14" . . . . $25–$35

Cut Glass Decanter (Blackberry), 1951, a geometric design handcut overall on this lead glass decanter. The stopper is cut and ground to fit the bottle, $10^1/2$" . . . . . $25–$30

Czech Hunter, 1958, round thick clear glass body with green collar and green buttons and heavy round glass base. The stopper head is of glass with a jaunty green Bohemian hat with feather crowning, pop-eyes, white mustache, and red button nose, $8^1/2$" . . . . $18–$26

Czech Hunter's Lady, 1958, "Mae West"-shaped decanter of cracked clear glass. Green collar at neck of bottle with amber glass stopper head. Brown hair, glasses, and yellow earrings make up the lady's head. She's taller than the hunter, 10" . . . . $18–$26

Dancing-Country Scene, 1950, clear glass handblown decanter with handpainted and signed colorful scene of peasant boy and girl doing a country dance beside a tree, Bohemian village background. Spider bold white lines painted on bottle and stopper, $12^1/4$" . . . . $20–$25

Dancing-Peasant Scene, 1950, colorful peasants in costume, dancing to music of bagpipes, handpainted and signed. The decanter is of pale amber glass, fine black lines painted on bottle. Stopper is ground to fit and fine-line painted, 12" . . . . $20–$25

Double-Dolphin, 1949–69, fish-shaped twin bottles joined at the bellies. They are made of handblown glass and have fins and "fish tail" ground glass stoppers; each has fish eyes and mouth. . . . . $20–$25

Flying Geese Pitcher, 1952, green glass handled pitcher. Handpainted and signed; colorful scene of wild geese flying over Czech marshes. Gold neck, pouring lip, and green stopper. This pitcher has a glass base . . . . $15–$18

Flying Geese Pitcher, 1957, clear crystal handled pitcher. Handpainted and signed; colorful scene of wild geese flying over Czech marshes. Gold neck, pouring lip, and stopper, $9^1/2$" . . . . $15–$18

Horse Head, 1947-69, pale amber-colored bottle in the shape of a horse's head. Embossed details of horse's features are impressed on this handblown bottle. Round pouring spout on top, 8" . . . . $12–$16

Jungle Parrot-Amber Glass, 1952, same as next entry, except bottle is flashed a yellow amber color, 15¹/₂" . . . . $25–$30

Jungle Parrot-Ruby Glass, 1952, profusely hand-etched jungle scene with parrot, monkeys, insects, flowers, leaves, cut through the ruby-flashed body. A tall round decanter with tapering etched neck, 15¹/₂" . . . . $20–$25

Old Coach Bottle, 1948, old-time coach and white horses handpainted on a handblown Bohemian glass bottle, pale amber color Round ground glass stopper. Bottle and stopper are both numbered, 10" . . . . $20–$25

Old Sleigh Bottle, 1949, handpainted, signed, Czech winter old-time sleigh scene. Driver sits on lead horse and blows trumpet, passengers on top of coach are pouring drinks. Glass decanter has fine white trace lines. Glass stopper is clear and painted, 10" . . . . $15–$20

Wild Geese-Amber Glass, 1952, same as below except bottle is a yellow amber color. (Matching glasses were made for both the ruby and amber), 15¹/₂". . . . . $20–$30

Wild Geese-Ruby Glass, 1952, etched design of wild geese rising above the marshes. A tall round decanter with tapering etched neck, and etched handground stopper. Ruby-red color "flashed" on bottle. (Matching glasses were made for both the ruby and amber), 15¹/₂" . . . . $20–$30

VENETIAN GLASS FIGURALS

Bischoff's Venetian glass figurals are made in limited editions by the Serguso Glass Co. in Murano, Italy, a town historically famous for its artistic glass. The Bischoff figurals, originally containing the firm's liquors, are quite unique in design and color. Chief themes depict natural subjects such as birds, mammals, and fish.

Black Cat, 1969, glass cat with curled tail, 12" L, black. . . . . $20–$30

Dog-Alabaster, 1969, seated alabaster glass dog, 13". $30–$50

Dog-Dachshund, 1966, alabaster long dog with brown tones, 19" L . . . . $40–$60

Duck, 1964, alabaster glass tinted pink and green, long neck, upraised wings, 11" L . . . . $40–$60

Fish-Multicolor, 1964, round fat fish, alabaster glass, green, rose, yellow. . . . $20–$30

Fish-Ruby, 1969, long, flat, ruby glass fish, 12" L . . . . $25–$40

CERAMIC DECANTERS AND FIGURALS

Many of the most interesting, attractive, and valuable Bischoff bottles are made of ceramic, stoneware or pottery. They have a "rougher" surface appearance than the glass or porcelain bottles. Values quoted are for complete bottles with handles, spouts, and stoppers in mint condition.

African Head, 1962. . . . . $15–$18

Bell House, 1960 . . . . $30–$40

Bell Tower, 1960 . . . . $15–$25
Boy (Chinese) Figural, 1962 . . . . $25–$30
Boy (Spanish) Figural, 1961 . . . . $20–$30
Clown with Black Hair, 1963 . . . . $25–$30
Clown with Red Hair, 1963 . . . . $15–$20
Egyptian Dancing Figural, 1961 . . . . $10–$15
Egyptian Pitcher - 2 Musicians, 1969 . . . . $10–$16
Egyptian Pitcher - 3 Musicians, 1959 . . . . $15–$21
Floral Canteen, 1969 . . . . $15–$19
Fruit Canteen, 1969 . . . . $15–$20
Girl in Chinese Costume, 1962 . . . . $20–$35
Girl in Spanish Costume, 1961 . . . . $20–$35
Greek Vase Decanter, 1969 . . . . $10–$16
Mask-Gray Face, 1963 . . . . $15–$20
Oil and Vinegar Cruets-Black And White, 1959 . . . . $15–$20
Vase-Black and Gold, 1959 . . . . $12–$18
Watchtower, 1960 . . . . $10–$14

BORGHINI BOTTLES

Borghini bottles, exported from Pisa, Italy, are ceramics of modernistic style,
dealing mostly with historical themes. Their sizes vary more than bottles from
other manufacturers. Easily obtainable in the United States, as is often the case
with imported bottles, their prices vary greatly in different parts of the country.
The lowest values tend to be in areas either closest to the points of distribution
or heaviest in retail sale. Most of the recent Borghini bottles are stamped
"Borghini Collection Made in Italy."

Cats, with red ties, 6", black . . . . $11–$15
Female Head, ceramic, 9$1/2$" . . . . $11–$15
Penguin, 1969, 12", black and white . . . . $12–$16
Penguin, 6", black and white . . . . $8–$11

MARIE BRIZARD
BOTTLES

The Marie Brizard bottles are ceramics, usually deep brown in color, with distinctive modeling. New editions are issued only occasionally. The Chessman series, which consists of bottles representing figures from the chessboard, are their most popular products. Among the more valuable of the Brizard bottles is a large model of a Parisian kiosk or newsstand, standing 11 ½" (h).

Bishop, ceramic chessman, dark brown . . . . $15–$20
Castle, ceramic chessman, dark brown . . . . $15–$20
Kiosk, colorful Parisian signpost, 11½" . . . . $5–$8
Knight, ceramic chessman, dark brown . . . . $15–$20
Lady In Ermine Cape, 7" . . . . $18–$22
Pawn, ceramic chessman, dark brown . . . . $15–$19

EZRA BROOKS BOTTLES

Ezra Brooks rivals Jim Beam as one of the chief whiskey companies in America manufacturing figural bottles. First issuing figurals in 1964, Brooks started a decade later than Beam, but became competitive because of effective promotion and a heavy production schedule. Due to creative design, imaginative choice of subjects, and an efficient distribution network, the Ezra Brooks bottles are collected throughout the country.

Some of the Brooks figurals deal with traditional themes for bottles such as sports and transportation. But Brooks has designed bottles based on subjects that are both suprising and striking. The very realistic Maine Lobster is among its masterpieces—a bottle that looks good enough to eat. One of the most popular series of their bottles represents various antiques, a subject neglected by most manufacturers. These include an Edison phonograph, a grandfather clock, and a Spanish cannon.

While the number of bottles produced fluctuates each year, Brooks usually adds new editions annually, often highlighting an American historical event or anniversary.

The Ezra Brooks Distilling Co., located in Frankfort, Kentucky, manufactures bottles containing Kentucky bourbon. Before 1968 their most brisk sales occurred around the Christmas/New Year season as the majority were bought for gift giving. When interest grew in the United States for figural bottles, most sales went to collectors.

Alabama Bicentennial, 1976. . . . . $12–$14
American Legion, 1971, distinguished embossed star emblem born out of WW I struggle. On blue base, combination blue and gold . . . . $20–$30
American Legion, 1972, Ezra Brooks salutes the American Legion, its Illinois Department, and Land of Lincoln and the city of Chicago, host of the Legion's 54th national convention. . . . . $40–$50
American Legion, 1973, Hawaii, our 50th state, hosted the American Legion's 1973 annual convention. It was the largest airlift of a mass group ever to hit the islands. Over 15,000 Legionnaires visited the beautiful city of Honolulu to celebrate the Legion's 54th anniversary . . . . $2–$9
American Legion, 1973, Miami Beach. . . . . $6–$9
American Legion, 1977, Denver. . . . . $15–$20
Amvets, 1973, Polish Legion . . . . $8–$12
Amvets, 1974, dolphin . . . . $8–$10
Antique Cannon, 1969 . . . . $6–$9
Antique Phonograph, 1970, Edison's early contribution to home entertainment. White, black, morning glory horn. Richly detailed in 24K gold . . . . $15–$20
Arizona, 1969, man with burro in search of Lost Dutchman Mine; golden brown mesa, green cactus, with 22K-gold base; "Arizona" imprinted . . . . $6–$9
Auburn 1932, 1978, classic car . . . . $18–$20
Badger No. 1, 1973, boxer. . . . . $9–$11
Badger No. 2, 1974, football . . . . $10–$14
Badger No. 3, 1974, hockey. . . . . $9–$12
Baltimore Oriole Wildlife, 1979. . . . . $20–$30
Bare Knucklefighter, 1971 . . . . $6–$9
Baseball Hall of Fame, 1973, baseball fans everywhere will enjoy this genuine Heritage China ceramic of a familiar slugger of years gone by. . . . . $15–$20
Basketball Player, 1974 . . . . $14–$16
Bear, 1968 . . . . $5–$9
Bengal Tiger Wildlife, 1979 . . . . $20–$30
Betsy Ross, 1975 . . . . $8–$12
Big Bertha, Nugget Casino's very own elephant with a raised trunk; yellow and gold trim, blanket and stand, gray, red, white, black . . . . $10–$13
Big Daddy Lounge, 1969, salute to South Florida's state liquor chain and Big Daddy Lounges, white, green, red . . . . $4–$6
Bighorn Ram, 1973. . . . . $14–$18
Bighorn Ram, 1973. . . . . $14–$18
Bird Dog, 1971. . . . . $12–$14
Bordertown, Borderline Club where California and Nevada meet for a drink. Brown, red, white. Club building, with vulture on roof stopper, and outhouse . . . . $5–$10
Bowler, 1973 . . . . $7–$9

Bowling Ten-Pins, 1973, in colonial days, Massachusetts and Connecticut banned bowling at nine-pins along with dice and cards. But bowlers avoided the law by simply adding the tenth pin. Thus ten-pin bowling was born. Today the sport of bowling is enjoyed by more than 30,000,000 Americans. . . . . $9–$12
Brahma Bull, 1972 . . . . $10–$15
Buck Badger, 1975, hockey. . . . . $18–$24
Bucket of Blood, 1970, fabled Virginia City, Nevada, saloon. Bucket-shaped bottle. Brown, red with gold lettering on reverse side . . . . $5–$7
Bucking Bronco, 1973, Rough Rider . . . . $7–$9
Bucky Badger, 1973, No. 1, boxer . . . . $9–$12
Bucky Badger, football . . . . $20–$25
Buffalo Hunt, 1971 . . . . $6–$9
Bull Moose, 1973. . . . . $12–$15
Bulldog, 1972, might canine mascot and football symbol. Red, white . . . . $10–$14
Busy Beaver, this genuine Heritage China ceramic is a salute to the beaver . . . . $4–$7
Cabin Still, hillbilly, papers from company, gallon. . . . . $20–$35
Cable Car, 1968, San Francisco's great trolley-car ride in bottle form. Made in three different colors: green, gray, and blue with red, black, and gold trim. Open cable car with passengers clinging to sides. . . . . $5–$6
California Quail, 1970, widely admired game bird-shape bottle. Crested head stopper. Unglazed finish. Green, brown, white, black, gray. . . . . $8–$10
Canadian Loon Wildlife, 1979. . . . . $25–$35
Candian Honker, 1975 . . . . $9–$12
Cardinal, 1972. . . . . $20–$25
Casey At Bat, 1973 . . . . $15–$20
CB Convoy Radio, 1976 . . . . $5–$9
Ceremonial Indian, 1970 . . . . $15–$18
Charolais Beef, 1973, the Charolais have played an important role in raising the standards of quality in today's cattle. . . . . $10–$14
Cheyenne Shootout, 1970, honoring the Wild West and its Cheyenne Frontier Days. Sheriff and outlaw shoot-out over mirrored bar. Brown tone with multicolors . . . .
. . . . $6–$10
Chicago Fire, 1974 . . . . $20–$30
Chicago Water Tower, 1969. . . . . $8–$12
Christmas Decanter, 1966 . . . . $5–$8
Christmas Tree, 1979 . . . . $13–$17
Churchill, 1970, commemorating "Iron Curtain" speech at Westminster College; Churchill at lectern with hand raised in V sign. Fulton, Missouri, gold color . . . . $5–$9
Cigar Store Indian, 1968, sidewalk statue in bottle form. The original Wooden Indian first appeared in 1770. Dark tan . . . . $5–$8
Classic Firearms, 1969, embossed gun set consisting of Deringer, Colt 45, Peacemaker, Over and Under Flintlock, Pepper box, Green, blue violet, red . . . . $15–$19
Clown, 1978, Imperial Shrine . . . . $9–$11
Clown Bust No. 1, 1979, Smiley. . . . . $22–$28
Clown Bust No. 2, 1979, cowboy . . . . $20–$25
Clown Bust No. 3, 1979, Pagliacci . . . . $15–$22
Clown Bust No. 4, Keystone cop. . . . . $30–$40
Clown Bust No. 5, Cuddles . . . . $20–$30
Clown Bust No. 6, tramp . . . . $20–$30
Clown With Accordian, 1971. . . . . $15–$25
Clown With Balloon, 1973 . . . . $15–$25

Club Bottle, 1973, the third commemorative Ezra Brooks Collectors Club bottle is created in the shape of America. Each gold star on the new club bottle represents the location of an Ezra Brooks Collectors Club .... $14–$18
Club Bottle, birthday cake .... $9–$12
Club Bottle, distillery .... $9–$12
Clydesdale Horse, 1973, in the early days of distilling, Clydesdales carted the bottles of whiskey from the distillery to towns all across America .... $10–$15
Colt Peacemaker, 1969, flask .... $4–$8
Conquistadors Drum and Bugle, 1972 .... $12–$15
Conquistadors, tribute to a great drum and bugle corps. Silver-colored trumpet attached to drum .... $6–$9
Corvette, 1976, 1957 classic .... $100–$120
Corvette Indy Pace Car, 1978 .... $45–$55
Court Jester, a common sight in the throne rooms of Europe. Yellow and blue suit, pointed cap .... $6–$9
Dakota Cowboy, 1975 .... $20–$30
Dakota Cowgirl, 1976 .... $20–$26
Dakota Grain Elevator, 1978 .... $20–$30
Dakota Shotgun Express, 1977 .... $15–$20
Dead Wagon, 1970, to carry gunfight losers to Boot Hill, old-time hearse with tombstones on side. Vulture adornment on stopper. White, with black details .... $5–$7
Delta Belle, 1969, proud paddlewheel boat on the New Orleans to Louisville passage; steamboat shape with embossed details. White, brown, red with 22K gold trim. . $6–$7
Democratic Convention, 1976 .... $10–$16
Derringer, 1969, flask .... $5–$8
Distillery, 1970, club bottle, reproduction of the Ezra Brooks Distillery in Kentucky, complete with smokestack. Beige, black, brown with 22K gold color .... $9–$11
Duesenberg, jaunty vintage convertible. Famous SJ model reproduction complete with superchargers and white sidewalls. Blue and gold, or solid gold color .... $24–$33
1804 Silver Dollar, 1970, commemorates the famous and very valuable 1804 silver dollar. Embossed replica of the Liberty Head dollar. Platinum-covered round dollar-shaped bottle on black or white base .... $5–$8
Elephant, 1973, based on an Asian elephant which has small ears and tusks .... $7–$9
Elk, 1973, while the elk herd is still relatively scarce in the United States, the elk name flourishes as a symbol for many worthwhile organizations, especially those whose primary object is the practice of benevolence and charity in its broadest sense. ....
.... $20–$28
English Setter-Bird Dog, 1971, happy hunting dog retrieving red pheasant. White-flecked with black, yellow base .... $10–$13
Equestrienne, 1974 .... $7–$10
Esquire, ceremonial dancer .... $10–$16
Farthington Bike, 1972 .... $6–$8
Fire Engine, 1971 .... $14–$18
Fireman, 1975 .... $15–$20
Fisherman, 1974 .... $8–$12
Flintlock, 1969, dueling pistol rich in detail. Japanese version has wooden rack; "Made in Japan" on handle .... $7–$9
Flintlock, 1969, Heritage China gun has plastic rack, less detail. Gun-metal gray and brown, silver and gold trim .... $8–$12
Florida "Gators," 1973, tribute to the University of Florida Gators football team ....
.... $9–$11

FOE Eagle, 1978 . . . . $10–$15
FOE Eagle, 1980 . . . . $25–$40
FOE Eagle, 1981 . . . . $18–$28
FOE Flying Eagle, 1979 . . . . $15–$22
Football Player, 1974 . . . . $10–$14
Ford Mustang . . . . $20–$30
Ford Thunderbird-1956, 1976 . . . . $70–$80
Foremost Astronaut, 1970, tribute to major liquor supermart, Foremost Liquor Store. Smiling "Mr. Bottle-Face" clinging to space rocket on white base. . . . . $6–$9
Fresno Decanter, map of famed California grape center. Stopper and inscription has gold finish. Blue, white. . . . . $5–$12
Fresno Grape With Gold . . . . $48–$60
Fresno Grape, 1970. . . . . $6–$11
Gamecock, 1970, all feathers and fury against rival birds. Red with yellow base. . . . . .
. . . . $9–$13
Go Big Red No. 1, 1970, football-shaped bottle with white bands and laces on base embossed "Go Big Red." Brown, white, gold detail. . . . . $20–$28
Go Big Red No. 2, 1971, with hat . . . . $18–$22
Go Big Red No. 3, 1972, with rooster . . . . $10–$14
Go Tiger Go, 1973. . . . . $10–$14
Gold Prospector, 1969, rugged miner with white beard panning for gold. . . . . . $5–$9
Gold Seal, 1972 . . . . $12–$14
Gold Turkey . . . . $35–$45
Golden Antique Cannon, 1969, symbol of Spanish power. Embossed details on barrel, wheels, and carriage. Dark brown, with lavish 22K-gold trim. Brown, gold. . . . . $5–$7
Golden Eagle, 1971, rich plumage, sitting on a branch. Gold color. . . . . $18–$22
Golden Grizzly Bear, 1970, a bear-shaped bottle, on haunches. Brown with golden highlights . . . . $4–$6
Golden Horseshoe, 1970, salute to Reno's Horseshoe Club. Good luck symbol on horseshoe. 24K-gold covered, in a blue base. . . . . $7–$9
Golden Rooster No.1, a replica of the famous solid gold rooster on display at Nugget Casino in Reno, Nevada. Glowing rooster in 22K-gold on black base. . . . . $35–$50
Grandfather Clock, 1970, brown with gold highlights, embossed detail. Brown, gold
. . . . $5–$7
Great Stone Face-Old Man Of The Mountain, 1970, famous profile found in mountain of New Hampshire. Stopper has seal of New Hampshire. . . . . $10–$14
Great White Shark, 1977 . . . . $8–$14
Greater Greensboro Open, 1972, green, gold . . . . $15–$20
Greater Greensboro Open, 1972, to commemorate this event, Ezra Brooks has designed this genuine Heritage Ceramic bottle . . . . $20–$30
Greater Greensboro Open, 1973, golfer . . . . $17–$24
Greater Greensboro Open, 1974, map.. . . . . $29–$36
Greater Greensboro Open, 1975, cup . . . . $20–$25
Greater Greensboro Open, 1977, club and ball. . . . . \. . . . . $15–$20
Hambletonian, 1971, harness racer honors the NY town and race track that sired harness racing and trotting; horse pulling driver and sulky, yellow, blue, green, brown, white . . . . $13–$16
Happy Goose, 1975 . . . . $12–$15
Harolds Club Dice, 1968, Lucky 7 dice combination topped wth H-cube stopper, on round white base. Red and white with gold trim. . . . . $8–$12
Hereford, 1971. . . . . $12–$15

Hereford, 1972, brown, white face .... $12–$15
Historical Flask, 1970, Old Ironsides, green........................... $3–$5
Historical Flask, 1970, eagle, blue .... $3–$5
Historical Flask, 1970, flagship, purple .... $3–$5
Historical Flask, 1970, Liberty, amber .... $3–$5
Historical Flask, 1970, set of four.................................. $3–$5
Hollywood Cops, 1972 .... $12–$18
Hopi Indian, 1970, "Kachina Doll." Creative tribe doing ritual song and dance. White, red ornamental trim.. $15–$20
Hopi Kachina, 1973, genuine Heritage China ceramic reproduction of a Hummingbird Kachina doll .... $50–$75
Idaho-Ski The Potato, 1973, Ezra Brooks salutes the beautiful state of Idaho, its ski resorts, and famous Idaho potatoes, with this genuine Heritage China ceramic bottle... .... $8–$10
Indian Ceremonial, colorful tribal dancer from New Mexico reservation. Multicolored, gold trim.. $13–$18
Indian Hunter, 1970, traditional buffalo hunt. Indian on horseback shooting buffalo with bow and arrow. White horse, brown buffalo, yellow base. .... $12–$15
Indianapolis 500, sleek, dual-exhaust racer. White, blue, black, silver trim. .. $30–$35
Iowa Farmer, 1977 .... $25–$35
Iowa Grain Elevator, 1978....................................... $20–$25
Iron Horse Locomotive, replica of old-time locomotive, complete with funnel, cow-catcher, and oil-burning headlamp. Black and red with 22K-gold trim. .... $8–$14
Jack O' Diamonds, 1969, the symbol of good luck, a bottle in the shape of the "Jack" right off the card. A royal flush decorates the front. White, red, blue, and black. . $4–$6
Jay Hawk, 1969, funny bird with a large head perched on a "tree trunk" base. Symbol of Kansas during and after the Civil War. .... $6–$8
Jester, 1971 .... $6–$8
John L. Sullivan, 1970, the great John L., last of the bare knuckle fighters in fighting stance. Mustached with red tights, gold belt cord, white gym shirt. John stands on a gold base. .... $15–$20
Jug, Old-Time, 1.75 Liter .... $9–$13
Kachina Doll No. 1, 1971 .... $70–$80
Kachina Doll No. 2, 1973, hummingbird .... $50–$65
Kachina Doll No. 3, 1974 .... $55–$70
Kachina Doll No. 4, 1975 .... $20–$25
Kachina Doll No. 5, 1976 .... $30–$40
Kachina Doll No. 6, 1977, white buffalo........................... $25–$35
Kachina Doll No. 7, 1978, mud head .... $35–$45
Kachina Doll No. 8, 1979 .... $50–$60
Kansas Jayhawk, 1969 .... $4–$7
Katz Cats Philharmonic, 1970, commemorating its 27th annual Star Night, devoted to classical and pop music. Black tuxedo, brown face, pair. .... $6–$10
Katz Cats, 1969, seal point and blue point. Siamese cats are symbolic of Katz Drug Co. of Kansas City, Kansas. Gray and blue, tan and brown .... $7–$9
Keystone Cop, 1980.. $32–$40
Keystone Cops, 1971.. $25–$35

Killer Whale, 1972 . . . . $15–$20
King Of Clubs, 1969, figure of card symbol. Sword and orb symbolize wisdom and justice. Royal flush in clubs in front. Yellow, red, blue, black and white with gold trim.
. . . . \ . . . . . $4–$6
King Salmon, 1971, bottle in shape of leaping salmon, natural red . . . . $18–$24
Liberty Bell, 1970, replica of the famous bell complete with wooden support. Dark copper color, embossed details. . . . . $5–$6
Lincoln Continental Mark I, 1941. . . . . $20–$25
Lion On The Rock, 1971. . . . . $5–$7
Liquor Square, 1972. . . . . $5–$7
Little Giant, 1971, replica of the first horse-drawn steam engine to arrive at the Chicago fire in 1871. Red, black with gold trim. . . . . $11–$16
M & M Brown Jug, 1975 . . . . $12–$16
Maine Lighthouse, 1971 . . . . $18–$24
Maine Lobster, 1970, bottle in lobster shape, complete with claws. Pinkish-red color. Bottle is sold only in Maine. . . . . $15–$18
Man-O-War, 1969, Big Red captured just about every major horseracing prize in turfdom. Replica of famous horse in brown and green, 22K-gold base. Embossed "Man-O-War," brown, green, gold . . . . $10–$16
Map, 1972, USA club bottle. . . . . $7–$9
Masonic Fez, 1976. . . . . $6–$9
Max, 1976, The Hat Zimmerman. . . . . $20–$25
Military Tank, 1971 . . . . $15–$22
Minnesota Hockey Player, 1975. . . . . $18–$22
Minuteman, 1975. . . . . $10–$15
Missouri Mule, 1972, brown . . . . $7–$9
Moose, 1973 . . . . $20–$28
Motorcycle, motorcycle rider and machine. Rider dressed in blue pants, red jacket, with stars and stripes helmet. Black motorcycle with red tank on silver base. . . $10–$14
Mountaineer, 1971, figure dressed in buckskin, holding rifle. "Mountaineers Are Always Free" embossed on base. Bottle is handtrimmed in platinum. One of the most valuable Ezra Brooks figural bottles. . . . . $40–$55
Mr. Foremost, 1969, an authentic reproduction of the famous bottle-shaped symbol of Foremost Liquor stores, Mr. Foremost, known for good wines and spirits. Red, white, and black. . . . . $7–$10
Mr. Maine Potato, 1973, from early beginnings the people of Maine have built the small potato into a giant industry. Today potatoes are the number one agricultural crop in the state. Over 36 billion pounds are grown every year. . . . . $6–$10
Mr. Merchant, 1970, Jumping Man; whimsical, checkered-vest caricature of amiable shopkeeper, leaping into the air, arms outstretched. Yellow, black. . . . . $6–$10
Mule . . . . $8–$12
Mustang Indy Pace Car, 1979 . . . . $20–$30
Nebraska-Go Big Red!, 1972, genuine Heritage China reproduction of a game ball and fan, trimmed in genuine 24K gold. . . . . $12–$15
New Hampshire State House, 1970, 150-year-old State House. Embossed doors, windows, steps. Eagle-topped stopper. Gray building with gold. . . . . $6–$9
North Carolina Bicentennial, 1975 . . . . $8–$12

Nugget Classic, replica of golf pin presented to golf tournament participants. Finished in 22K gold. . . . . $7–$12
Oil Gusher, bottle in shape of oil-drilling rig. A silver, jet-black stopper in shape of gushing oil. . . . . $6–$8
Old Capital, 1971, bottle in shape of Iowa's seat of government when the corn state was still frontier territory. Embossed windows, doors, pillars. "Old Capital Iowa 1840–1857" on base. Reddish color with gold dome stopper. . . . . $30–$40
Old EZ No. 1, 1977, barn owl . . . . $15–$20
Old EZ No. 2, 1978, eagle owl . . . . $40–$55
Old EZ No. 3, 1979, show owl . . . . $20–$25
Old Man Of The Mountain, 1970 . . . . $10–$14
Old Water Tower, 1969, famous landmark. Survived the Chicago fire of 1871. Embossed details, towers, doors, stones, windows. Gray and brown gold base. $12–$16
Oliver Hardy Bust. . . . . $12–$18
Ontario 500, 1970, California 500 is a speedway classic with an "Indy"-style racing oval. Red, white, blue, and black with silver trim. . . . . $18–$22
Over-Under Flintlock, 1969, flask. . . . . $6–$9
Overland Express, 1969, brown stagecoach bottle. $17–$20
Panda-Giant, 1972, giant panda ceramic bottle . . . . $12–$17
Penguin, 1972, Ezra Brooks salutes the penguin with genuine Heritage China ceramic figural bottle. . . . . $8–$10
Penny Farthington High-Wheeler, 1973, Ezra Brooks salutes the millions of cyclists everywhere and the new cycling boom with this genuine Heritage China ceramic of the Penny Farthington bicycle. . . . . $9–$12
Pepperbox, 1969, flask. . . . . $4–$6
Phoenix Bird, 1971, famous mythical bird reborn from its own ashes honoring Arizona. Blue bird with outstretched wings arising from gold flame, blue . . . . $15–$20
Phoenix Jaycees, 1973, Ezra Brooks is proud to honor the Phoenix Jaycees and the Rodeo of Rodeos with this Heritage China reproduction of a silver saddle. . . . $10–$14
Phonograph . . . . $15–$20
Piano, 1970, an old-time piano player and his upright piano. Player wears blue pants, striped shirt, red bow tie, black derby, and yellow vest. Piano is brown in gold trim. . . . . . $12–$13
Pirate, 1971, a swashbuckling sailor with beard, eye patch, and hook hand who flew the Jolly Roger (skull and crossbones) over the Seven Seas. Black hat, jacket, boots, yellow striped shirt, pistol, sword, and treasure chest on gold base. . . . . $6–$10
Polish Legion American Vets, 1978. . . . . $18–$26
Portland Head Lighthouse, it has guided ships safely into Maine Harbor since 1791. White, red trim, gold light stopper. "Maine" embossed on rock base. . . . . $18–$24
Pot-Bellied Stove, 1968, old-time, round coal-burning stove with ornate legs and fire in the grate. Black and red. . . . . $5–$6
Queen Of Hearts, 1969, playing card symbol with royal flush in hearts on front of bottle . . . . $4–$6
Raccoon Wildlife, 1978. . . . . $30–$40
Ram, 1973 . . . . $13–$18
Razorback Hog, 1969, bright red hog with white tusks and hooves running on green grass. . . . . $12–$18
Razorback Hog, 1979 . . . . $20–$30
Red Fox, 1979, wildlife . . . . $30–$40
Reno Arch, 1968, honoring the Biggest Little City in the World, Reno, Nevada. Arch shape with "Reno" embossed on yellow. Front of bottle multicolor decal of dice, rabbit's foot, roulette wheel, slot machine, etc. White and yellow, purple stopper. . . . . $4–$8

Sailfish, 1971, leaping deep-water sailfish with swordlike nose and large spread fin. Blue-green luminous tones on green waves base. .... $7–$11

Salmon, 1971, Washington King .... $20–$26

San Francisco Cable Car, 1968 .... $5–$8

San Francisco Cable Car, 1968 .... $4–$8

Sea Captain, 1971, salty old seadog, white hair and beard in blue captain's jacket with gold buttons and sleeve stripes, white cap, gold band. Holding pipe, on wooden stanchion base.. .... $10–$14

Sealion-Gold, 1972, Ezra Brooks commemorates the state of California and its world-famous marine showmen with the California Sealion ceramic bottle hand detailed in 24K gold.. .... $11–$14

Senator, 1971, cigar-chomping, whistle-stopping state senator, stumping on a platform of pure nostalgia. Black western hat and swallow-tail coat, red vest, string tie, gold, black, red, white.. .... $8–$10

Senators Of The US, 1972, Ezra Brooks honors the senators of the United States of America with this genuine Heritage ceramic old-time courtly senator.......... $6–$9

Setter, 1974 .... $10–$15

Shrine King Tut Guard, 1979 .... $15–$20

Silver Saddle, 1973 .... $15–$20

Silver Spur Boot, 1971, cowboy-boot-shaped bottle with silver spur buckled on. "Silver Spur-Carson City Nevada" embossed on side of boot. Brown boot with platinum trim.. .... $7–$11

Simba, 1971, beautifully detailed lion is reddish-brown color. Head of lion is stopper. Rock base is dark gray... $9–$12

Ski Boot, 1972, Ezra Brooks salutes the exciting sport of skiing with this genuine Heritage ceramic ski boot... $5–$7

Slot Machine, 1971, a tribute to the slots of Las Vegas, Nevada. A replica of the original nickle Liberty Bell slot machine invented by Charles Fey in 1895. The original is in Reno's Liberty Belle Salloon. Top window shows two horseshoes and a bell; bottom panel show .... $14–$18

Snowmobiles, 1972, a tribute to the chief means of transportation in Alaska and Canada. .... $8–$11

South Dakota Air National Guard, 1976 .... $15–$19

Spirit Of '76, 1974. .... $5–$7

Spirit Of St. Louis, 1977, 50th anniversary .... $6–$11

Sprint Car Racer, a decanter replica of the race car sponsored by Ezra Brooks. Supercharged racer with black Firestone racing tires, and silver and blue trim. Goggled driver in white and red jumpsuit at wheel. Cream-colored car with silver and blue trim. .....
.... $30–$40

Stagecoach, 1969 .... $10–$12

Stan Laurel Bust, 1976 .... $10–$16

Stock Market Ticker, 1970, a unique replica of a ticker-tape machine. Gold colored mechanism with white market tape under plastic dome. Black base with embossed plaque "Stock Market Quotations".................................... $8–$11

Stonewall Jackson, 1974.. $18–$24

Strongman, 1974... $14–$18

Sturgeon, 1975.. $20–$28

Syracuse-New York, 1973, Ezra Brooks salutes the great city of Syracuse, its past and its present.. $11–$16

Tank Patton, 1972, reproduction of a U.S. Army tank. Turret top with cannon is the stopper. Embossed details on tracks, tools, etc. Camouflage green and brown. .... $16–$20

Tecumseh, 1969, the figurehead of the U.S.S. Delaware, this decanter is an embossed replica of the statue of the United States Naval Academy in Annapolis, MD. Feathers in quiver-form stopper. Gold figure on brown wood base...................... $5–$6

Telephone, 1971, a replica of the old-time upright handset telephone, 24K-gold trimmed body, mouth piece, and base trim; black receiver, wires, base, and head. Mouthpiece and head form the stopper............................... $10–$14

Tennis Player, 1972, Ezra Brooks salutes tennis lovers everywhere with this genuine Heritage China ceramic tennis player bottle............................ $8–$12

Terrapin, 1974, Maryland .... $10–$15

Texas Longhorn, 1971, realistic longhorn on tall green Texas grass base. Longhorn head is stopper. Reddish brown body, white horns and mask, gold trimmed base...... .... $18–$22

Ticker Tape, 1970 .... $4–$6

Tiger On Stadium, 1973, to commemorate college teams who have chosen the tiger as their mascot.. $10–$15

Tom Turkey, replica of the American white feathered turkey. Tail spread, red head and wattles, yellow feet and beak. On a brown tree trunk base................. $18–$24

Tonopah, 1972... $10–$13

Totem Pole, 1972, Ezra Brooks commemorates the totem art of the American Indian with this genuine Heritage China reporduction of an ornate intricately designed Indian totem pole... $6–$9

Totem Pole, 1973, the Indians of North America have a proud history and in many instances that history is beautifully portrayed in totem pole art. It is a truly remarkable art form that will enrich the world for generations to come .... $8–$12

Tractor, 1971, a model of the 1917 Fordson made by Henry Ford. Embossed details of engine and hood seat and steering wheel. Red tractor wheels, gray body with silver trim. .... $10–$15

Trail-Bike Rider, 1972, Ezra Brooks salutes the trail-bike riders of America with this genuine Heritage China ceramic bottle.............................. $10–$12

Trojan Horse, 1974 .... $10–$16

Trojans-USC Football, 1973, a tribute to the Trojans who have given U.S.C. seven Pacific-Eight Conference titles, six Rose Bowl teams, 23 All-Americans, two Heisman Trophy winners (Mike Garrett and O.J. Simpson), three undefeated seasons, and three national championships.. $12–$18

Trout & Fly, 1970, the rainbow trout leaping and fighting the McGinty Fly. A lumines-cent replica of this angler's dream on a blue water base, complete with scales, fins, and flashing tail.. $7–$11

Truckin' & Vannin', 1977 .... $6–$9

Vermont Skier, 1972... $10–$12

VFW-Veterans Of Foreign Wars, 1973, Ezra Brooks salutes the Veterans of Foreign Wars of the United States and the 1.8 million fighting men of five wars who wear the Cross of Malta.. $6–$10

Virginia-Red Cardinal, 1973, a glorious bird, the cardinal represents this illustrious state.. $10–$15

Walgreen Drugs, 1974 .... $16–$24

Weirton Steel, 1973... $12–$16

West Virginia-Mountaineer Lady, 1972........................... $14–$20

West Virginia-Mountaineer, 1971................................. $50–$58

Western Rodeos, 1973, Ezra Brooks salutes the rodeo, from its early pioneers to its professional circuit riders, with this genuine Heritage China bottle......... $15–$19

Whale, 1972.. $14–$20

Wheat Shocker, 1971, the mascot of the Kansas football team in a fighting pose. Wheat yellow figure with black turtleneck sweater; "Wheat Shocker" embossed in yellow on front. Wheat stalk tops are the stopper, wheat plants are the base. . . . . $5–$7
Whiskey Flasks, 1970, reproductions of collectible American patriotic whiskey flasks of the 1800s: Old Ironsides, Miss Liberty, American Eagle, Civil War Commemorative. Embossed designs in gold on blue, amber, green and red. . . . . $12–$14
White Turkey, 1971 . . . . $20–$25
Whitetail Dear, 1947. . . . . $18–$24
Wichita. . . . . $4–$8
Wichita Centennial, 1970, replica of Wichita's center of culture and commerce, Century II, the round building with the square base. Blue roof with gold airliner atop symbol of "Air Capital of the World." Blue, brown, black and gold. . . . . $4–$6
Winston Churchill, 1969. . . . . $5–$8

J.W. DANT BOTTLES

The bottles of J.W. Dant Distilling Co. from Louisville, Kentucky, are not as numerous as those of Ezra Brooks and Jim Beam, the other major Kentucky distilleries, but their following is strong. Introduced in 1968, the Dant figurals carry American themes, including patriotic events, folklore, and animal species such as the mountain quail, woodcock, and prairie chicken. Dant's preoccupation with American history originates from the period of its establishment in 1863 during the Civil War.

Most Dant bottles are conventionally shaped with historical scenes in full color. The back of all rectangular bottles carries an embossed American eagle and shield with stars. Several of the Boston Tea Party bottles have an error: the eagle's head faces his left side instead of his right.

All Dant bottles are limited editions and the company assures customers that the molds will not be reused.

Alamo. . . . . $2–$4
American Legion. . . . . $2–$3
Atlantic City . . . . $2–$4
Bobwhite . . . . $3–$5
Boeing 747 . . . . $2–$4
Boston Tea Party, eagle to left . . . . $2–$3
Boston Tea Party, eagle to right . . . . $4–$6
Bourbon. . . . . $2–$3
California Quail . . . . $3–$5

Chukar Partridge	$3–$4
Clear Tip Pinch	$3–$4
Constitution And Guerriere	$2–$3
Duel Between Burr And Hamilton	$3–$6
Eagle	$2–$4
Eagle	$2–$4
Fort Sill Centennial, 1969	$4–$7
Indianapolis 500	$5–$7
Mountain Quail	$3–$4
Mt. Rushmore	$3–$4
Patrick Henry	$2–$3
Paul Bunyan	$2–$3
Prairie Chicken	$2–$3
Reverse Eagle	$3–$4
Ring-Necked Pheasant	$3–$5
Ruffed Grouse	$3–$4
San Diego	$2–$3
Speedway 500	$2–$4
Stove-Pot Belly	$5–$7
Washington Crossing Delaware	$2–$3
Woodcock	$2–$3
Wrong-Way Charlie	$8–$12

GARNIER BOTTLES

The prestigious figural bottles of the Garnier firm are among the oldest ones issued continuously since 1899 by a spirits company. But during the American prohibition and World War II, which eliminated the majority of the Garnier market, production ceased temporarily. *Garnet et Cie,* a French firm founded in 1858, is recognized as the pioneer of the modern "collector" bottle for liquor. Of course, figural and other decorative bottles for liquor existed before the Garnier products but these were not issued in the form of a series which encouraged the building up of a collection. Garnier actually had a line of figural bottles 50 years before Jim Beam. Some antique historians claim to have found a relationship between Garnier bottles and the later Hummel porcelain figurines, believing that the former inspired the latter. The two companies' figurals are similar.

    The older Garniers, produced prior to World War II, are scarce and valuable. They are not listed because their price levels are difficult to establish. Some of the better known "old Garniers" are the Cat (1930), Clown (1910), Country Jug (1937), Greyhound (1930), Penguin (1930), and Marquise (1931). Garnier released its new figurals gradually with only 52 available within a 31-year span. But since 1930, new figurals have been produced more frequently.

Aladdin's Lamp, 1963, $6^1/_2$", silver .... \$40–\$50
Alfa Romeo 1913, 1970, red body, yellow seats, black trim, 4" x $10^1/_2$" ..... \$19–\$27
Alfa Romeo 1929, 1969, pale blue body, red seat, black trim, 4" x $10^1/_2$" .... \$19–\$27
Alfa Romeo Racer, 1969, maroon body, black tires and trim, 4" x 10" ...... \$19–\$27
Antique Coach, 1970, multicolor, pastel tones, 8" x 12" .... \$25–\$30
Apollo, 1969, yellow quarter-moon, blue clouds, silver Apollo spaceship, $13^1/_2$" .....
.... \$17–\$22
Aztec Vase, 1965, stone tan, multicolor Aztec design, $11^3/_4$" .... \$12–\$15
Baby Foot-Soccer Shoe, 1963, black with white trim, $3^3/_4$" x $8^1/_2$" .... \$10–\$15
Baby Trio, 1963, clear glass, gold base, $6^1/_4$" .... \$7–\$10
Bahamas, black policeman, white jacket and hat, black pants, red stripe, gold details. .
.... \$14–\$18
Baltimore Oriole, 1970, multicolor, 11", green, yellow, blue............. \$10–\$16
Bandit Figural, 1958, pin-ball shape, multicolor, $11^1/_2$"................. \$10–\$14
Bedroom Candlestick, 1967, white with handpainted flowers, $11^1/_2$" ...... \$15–\$20
Bellows, 1969, 4" x $14^1/_2$", gold, red .... \$12–\$16
Bird Ashtray, 1958, clear glass, gold stopper, 3", gold................... \$3–\$4
Bluebird, 1970, two blue birds, multicolor green, brown, and yellow, approx. 11"....
.... \$12–\$18
Bouquet, 1966, white basket, multicolor flowers, $10^3/_4$".................. \$12–\$16
Bull (And Matador) Animal Figural, 1963, a rocking bottle, $12^1/_2$" x $12^1/_2$", bronze, gold.. \$12–\$18
Burmese Man Vase, 1965, stone gray, multicolor Eastern design, 12" ...... \$14–\$18
Canada, Mountie in red jacket, black jodphurs, brown boots .... \$6–\$9
Candlestick Glass, 1965, ornate leaves and fluting, 10".................. \$12–\$15
Candlestick, 1955, yellow candle, brown holder with gold ring, $10^3/_4$" ...... \$13–\$18
Cannon, 1964, with wheels and carriage, mottled yellow-brown, $7^1/_2$" x $13^1/_2$ \$40–\$48
Cardinal State Bird-Illinois, 1969, bright red bird, green and brown tree, $11^1/_2$" .....
.... \$10–\$12
Cat-Black, 1962, black cat with green eyes, $11^1/_2$" .... \$10–\$16
Cat-Gray, 1962, grayish-white cat with yellow eyes, $11^1/_2$"............... \$10–\$16
Chalet, 1955, white, red, green, and blue, 9".......................... \$30–\$40
Chimney, 1956, red bricks and fire, white mantel with picture, $9^3/_4$" .... \$40–\$50
Chinese Dog, 1965, Foo dogs, carved, embossed, ivory white on dark blue base, 11"..
.... \$12–\$16
Chinese Statuette-Man, 1970, yellow robe, dark skin, blue base, 12"....... \$12–\$18
Chinese Statuette-Woman, 1970, ebony skin tones, lavender robe, blue base, 12" ...
.... \$12–\$18
Christmas Tree, 1956, dark green tree, gold decorated, white candles, red flame, $11^1/_2$"
.... \$40–\$55
Citroen, 1922, 1970, yellow body, black trim wheels, 4" x $10^1/_2$" .... \$15–\$20
Classic Ashtray, 1958, clear glass, round with pouring spout, $2^1/_2$".......... \$3–\$4
Clock, 1958, clear glass, round on black base. Working clock in center, 9", black.....
.... \$15–\$19
Clown Holding Tuba, 1955, green clown with gold trim, $12^3/_4$" .... \$9–\$12

Coffee Mill, 1966, white with blue flowers . . . . $15–$25

Columbine Figural, 1968, female partner to harlequin, green and blue, black hair and mask, 13" . . . . $15–$19

Drunkard-Drunk On Lampost, figure in top hat and tails holding "wavy" lampost; black, red, blue, and white, 14³/₄". . . . . $15–$20

Duckling Figural, 1956, yellow duckling, white basket and red flowers, pink hat. . . . .
. . . . $18–$26

Duo, 1954, two clear glass bottles stacked, two pouring spouts, 7¹/₄" . . . . $12–$18

Egg Figural, 1956, white egg-shape house; pink, red, green, 8³/₄" . . . . $50–$65

Eiffel Tower, 1951, ivory with yellow tones, 12¹/₂" . . . . $9–$12

Eiffel Tower, 1951, ivory with yellow tones, 13¹/₂" . . . . $15–$19

Elephant Figural, 1961, Black with ivory white tusks, 6³/₄" . . . . $15–$20

Empire Vase, 1962, green and white, gold design and trim, 11¹/₂". . . . . $9–$13

Fiat Neuvo, 1913, 1970, open top, blue body and hub caps, yellow and black trim, 4" x 10³/₄". . . . . $19–$24

Flask Garnier, 1958, clear glass, embossed cherries, 3". . . . . $9–$12

Flying Horse Pegasus, 1958, black horse, gold mane and tail, red "marble" candle holder, 12". . . . . $38–$46

Ford, 1913, 1970, green open body and wheels, black trim, 4" x 10³/₄" . . . . . . $15–$20

Fountain, 1964, brown with gold lion head spout and embossing, 12¹/₂". . . . . $16–$20

Giraffe, 1961, yellow marble, modern animal figure, 18" . . . . $15–$25

Goldfinch, 1970, yellow bird, black wings and tail, green and brown leaves and limbs, 12". . . . . $10–$12

Goose, 1955, white with gold decoration, modern swirl-shaped goose, 9¹/₄" . . $11–$16

Grenadier, 1949, light blue soldier with sword in uniform of 1880s (faceless figure), 13³/₄". . . . . $40–$48

Harlequin Standing, 1968, columbine's mate, brown costume, blue cape, black cap and shoes, 13¹/₄" . . . . $13–$19

Harlequinn With Mandolin, 1958, seated comedy figure, mandolin and mask, white with multicolored circles, black buttons and shoes, 14¹/₂". . . . . $25–$30

Horse Pistol, 1964, embossed brown antique pistol, gold details, 18", brown . $14–$18

Hunting Vase, 1964, tan and gold with embossed hunting scene, 12¹/₄", gold, tan . . . .
. . . . $20–$26

Hussar, 1949, French Cavalry soldier of 1800s holding sword, maroon color, 13³/₄", maroon . . . . $19–$24

Indian, 1958, Big Chief with headdress, bowling-pin shape, bright Indian design colors, 11³/₄" . . . . $12–$16

India, turbaned figure, with white jacket, blue kilts, red sash . . . . $10–$14

Jockey, 1961, bronzed gold horse and jockey rocking bottle, 12¹/₂" x 12" . . . . $15–$24

Lancer, 1949, light green soldier, 13", green. . . . . $10–$14

Locomotive, 1949, tan, old-fashioned locomotive, 9" . . . . $11–$16

Log-Round, 1958, brown and tan log shape, silver handle and spout, 10", brown, tan, silver . . . . $15–$24

London-Bobby, dark blue uniform, silver helmet shield. . . . . $9–$13

Loon, 1970, sitting bird; white, brown, tan, blue base, 11" . . . . $9–$14

M.G. 1933, 1970, green body, orange trim, white wheels, 4" x 11" . . . . $10–$16

Maharajah, 1958, white and gold Indian ruler with turban, 11³/₄". . . . . $40–$54

Mockingbird, 1970, black and white bird on tree stump, 11", white . . . . $6–$8

Montmartre Jug, 1960, colorful Parisian Bohemian scene, 11", green . . . . $7–$11

Monuments, 1966, a cluster of Parisian monuents; Eiffel Tower spout, multicolor, 13"
. . . . $8–$11

Napoleon On Horseback, 1969, rearing white horse, Napoleon in red cloak, black hat, and uniform, 12" . . . . $12–$16
Nature Girl, 1959, native girl under palm tree, black with bronze, 13" . . . . $4–$7
New York Policeman, dark blue uniform with gold shield and buttons, blue . . . $5–$8
Packard, 1930, 1970, orange body, cream roof and wheels, black trim, 4" x 10" . . . . .
. . . . $15–$22
Painting, 1961, multicolor painting of girl in tan wood frame, 12", multicolor $19–$21
Paris Taxi, 1960, old-time cab; yellow body, red windows and headlights, black wire frame, 9" x 10¹/₂", yellow, red, black . . . . $12–$19
Paris, French policeman in black, white gloves, hat and garness . . . . $6–$8
Partridge, 1961, multicolor game bird, on leaf base, 10" . . . . $15–$20
Pheasant, 1969, multicolor game bird on rocking tree-trunk base, 12", multicolor . . . .
. . . . $15–$22
Pigeon-Clear Glass, 1958, bird-shaped bottle, gold stopper, 8" . . . . $8–$10
Pony, 1961, modern-shaped horse, wood grain tan, 8³/₄" . . . . $19–$24
Poodle, 1954, begging poodles in white or black with red trim, 8¹/₂" . . . . $6–$9
Renault, 1911, 1969, green body and hood, red hubs, black trim, 4" x 10³/₄" . $15–$20
Road Runner, 1969, multicolor bird, green cactus pouring sprout, 12" . . . . $7–$9
Robin, 1970, multicolor bird on tree stump with leaves, 12", multicolor . . . . $7–$9
Rocket, 1958, rocket-shaped bottle, wire holder, yellow nose, 10³/₄" . . . . $6–$11
Rolls Royce 1908, 1970, open touring car in yellow, red seats and hubs, black trim, 4" x
10¹/₂" . . . . $15–$25
Rooster, 1952, crowing rooster with handle, black or maroon with gold trim, 12" . . . .
. . . . $10–$18
S.S. France-Large, 1962, commemorative model of ocean liner, black hull, blue-green decks, red and black stacks, with gold labels, 5" x 19" . . . . $60–$90
S.S. France-Small, 1962, commemorative model of ocean liner, black hull, blue-green decks, red and black stacks, with gold labels, 4¹/₂" x 14". . . . . $40–$49
S.S. Queen Mary, 1970, black hull, green-blue decks, blue water, three red and black stacks, 4" x 16" . . . . $15–$24
Saint Tropez Jug, 1961, colorful French Riviera scene, tan jug, black handle $14–$18
Scarecrow, 1960, yellow straw body and hat, green jacket, red stripe face and tie, bird on shoulder, 12" . . . . $15–$25
Sheriff, 1958, two guns, badge and cowboy hat, pin-ball shape, white and gold, 12" . .
. . . . $10–$19
Snail, 1950, white and brown with spiral shell, 6¹/₂" x 10", white, brown . . . . $40–$50
Soccer Shoe, 1962, black shoe, white laces, 10" . . . . $20–$30
Stanley Steamer 1907, 1970, open blue car, yellow and black trim, 10¹/₂" . . . $11–$17
Teapot, 1935. . . . . $10–$16
Teapot, 1961, yellow and black striped body, black handle and spout, 8¹/₂" . . $12–$18
Trout, 1967, gray-blue speckled leaping trout, water base, 11" . . . . $12–$14
Valley Quail, 1969, black-marked bird on wood base, 11". . . . . $6–$9
Violin, 1966, white violin, handpainted flowers and details, 14". . . . . $19–$25
Watch-Antique, 1966, antique pocket watch, tan and gold, 10". . . . . $10–$15
Water Pitcher, 1965, glass body, silver base, handle, and top, 14" . . . . $7–$9
Watering Can, 1958, handpainted design, handle and pouring spout, 7" . . . . $7–$9
Young Deer Vase, 1964, embossed figures, tan color, 12" . . . . $15–$20

HOFFMAN BOTTLES

The Hoffman bottles are limited edition ceramics. Each issue is restricted in the number of bottles made and when this designated number is reached the mold is destroyed to prevent reproductions in the future. Consequently, the "out of production" designs quickly become collectors' items achieving high prices on the market. Hoffmans have sometimes been called the Hummels of the bottle world because they often depict figures in European dress at various kinds of occupations. These include shoemaker, a doctor, and a bartender. However, the firm also focused upon American themes, such as its 1976 centennial bottles with Pioneer of 1876 and Hippie of 1976.

OCCUPATION SERIES

Harpist With Music Box, Do-Re-Mi . . . . $10–$15
Lucky With Music Box, When Irish Eyes Are Smiling . . . . $14–$18

Hoffman, Mr. Lucky. PHOTO COURTESY OF DAVE SMITH.

Mr. Bartender With Music Box, He's a Jolly Good Fellow . . . . $25–$30
Mr. Charmer With Music Box, Glow Little Glow Worm. . . . . $10–$13
Mr. Dancer With Music Box, The Irish Washerwoman . . . . $15–$19
Mr. Doctor With Music Box, As Long as He Needs Me . . . . $20–$25
Mr. Fiddler With Music Box, Hearts and Flowers . . . . $20–$22
Mr. Guitarist With Music Box, Johnny Guitar . . . . $15–$20
Mr. Shoe Cobbler With Music Box, Danny Boy. . . . . $12–$16
Policeman With Music Box, Don't Blame Me. . . . . $20–$35
Sandman With Music Box, Mr. Sandman . . . . $10–$20
Saxophonist With Music Box, Tiger Rag. . . . . $15–$20

BICENTENNIAL SERIES, 4/5-QT. SIZE

Betsy Ross With Music Box, Star Spangle Banner.................... $30–$40
Generation Gap, depicting "100 Years of Progress" .... $30–$38
Majestic Eagle With Music Box, America the Beautiful................ $40–$60

C.M. RUSSELL SERIES, 4/5-QT. SIZE

Buffalo Man... $18–$23
Flathead Squaw.. $15–$18
Last Of Five Thousand.. $14–$18
Red River Breed .... $23–$28
The Scout.. $25–$34
The Stage Drive... $15–$22
Trapper .... $18–$26

JAPANESE BOTTLES

Bottlemaking in Japan is an ancient art. Although the collectible bottles presently produced in Japan are mainly for exportation, they still reflect native designing in their characteristic shapes and handsome enameling. Japanese bottles are increasing in numbers on the American market but prices remain modest. Japan produces figural bottles also. The popular Kamotsuru bottles picture characters from Japanese mythology.

Daughter .... $10–$15
Faithful Retainer... $20–$25
Golden Pagoda .... $10–$12
"Kiku" Geisha, 13¹/₄", blue.................................... $12–$16
Maiden... $9–$12
Noh Mask... $9–$12
Okame Mask .... $40–$55
Playboy... $7–$9
Princess.. $7–$12
Princess.. $7–$12
Red Lion Man .... $30–$45
Sake God, colorful robe, poreclain, 10".......................... $15–$22
Sake God, white, bone china, 10" .... $9–$12
White Lion Man .... $25–$35
White Pagoda .... $7–$15
"Yuri" Geisha, pink, red sash, 13¹/₄" .... $22–$33

KENTUCKY GENTLEMEN BOTTLES

Kentucky Gentlemen, another Kentucky whiskey distiller, issues figural bottles. Their figurals are released less frequently than those of Beam or Brooks. To date, they have concentrated on ceramics, picturing costumes worn at various times in American history, especially from the Civil War period. Large-sized, more than a foot high, they are impressively modeled and colored. Each stands on a rectangular base, the front of which reads "Kentucky Gentlemen. "

Confederate Infantry, 1969, in gray uniform, with sword, 13½" . . . . $7–$9
Kentucky Gentlemen, 1969, figual bottle; frock coat, top hat, and cane; "Old Colonel," gray ceramic, 14" . . . . $7–$9
Pink Lady, 1969, long bustle skirt, feathered hat, parasol, pink, 13¾" . . . . . . $15–$20
Revolutionary War Officer, in dress uniform and boots, holding sword, 14" . . . .
. . . . $9–$11
Union Army Sergeant, in dress blue uniform, with sword, 14" . . . . $6–$8

LIONSTONE BOTTLES

Lionstone Distillery, a relative newcomer into the ranks of figural bottle makers, has already garnered a substantial reputation. Their bottles stress realism in design with a great variety of subjects. Lionstone combines the better elements of classical porcelain-making with the traditional art of bottle manufacturing in their creations. Prices of the more popular issues have increased rapidly. Lionstone produced the most ambitious of all collector bottles in terms of components and detail. Their Shoot-out at O.K. Corral, based upon an authentic incident in the Old West history, consists of three bottles with nine human figures and two horses.

Lionstone issues all their bottles in series form, including the Oriental Worker series, Dog series, Sports series, Circus series, and Bicentennial series, with new ones added periodically. The most popular with collectors are the Western Figurals, a lengthy series depicting various characters from western

American history such as Jesse James, Sod Buster, Mountain Man, Highway Robber, and Gentleman Gambler. Lionstone's Annie Oakley bottle comes complete with guns and sharpshooter medals.

Since prices of Lionstones on the collector market continue to be firm, buyers should investigate the possibility of spirits dealers still having some old unsold stock on hand.

Bar Scene No. 1	$125–$140
Bartender	$18–$22
Belly Robber	$12–$16
Blacksmith	$20–$30
Buffalo Hunter	$20–$24
Calamity Jane	$18–$23
Camp Cook	$13–$17
Camp Follower	$9–$12
Canadian Goose	$45–$55
Molly Brown	$18–$25

LUXARDO BOTTLES

Made in Torreglia, Italy, the Girolamo Luxardo bottles boast a long and distinctive history. Imported into the United States in 1930, the bottles gradually acquired an impressive following among American collectors. Chiefly a manufacturer of wine, Luxardo also sells liquors.

The Luxardo line, extremely well modeled and meticulously colored, captures the spirit of Renaissance glass. Varying hues of color are blended on most specimens which radiate brilliantly when light shines through the bottles. The effective coloring techniques of the Luxardo bottles compare to those of ancient Egypt where color was the most important consideration. While Egyptian bottles were often colored garishly, the Luxardos carefully balance splashiness and restraint—the dominant colors never obscure the pastel shades.

Many of Luxardo's bottles, both glass and majolica, are figural. Natural history subjects as well as classical themes predominate. Most of the majolica decanters can be reused as vases, jars, lamp bases or ashtrays.

The firm maintains a regular schedule for its bottle production. Between three to six new designs are chosen each January for that year's production. The most popular, such as the Cellini bottle introduced in the early 1950s, continue to be used. Occasionally a design is discontinued after just one year. The Chess Set, produced in 1959, was discontinued because of manufacturing difficulty.

Unfortunately, the names and dates of production of the earlier Luxardo decanters are mostly unknown, due to many owners removing the paper identification labels.

The rare Zara decanters, made before World War II, are expected to increase further in value and scarcity. The First Born of the Murano Venetian glass, if ever located, will command a very strong price. Eventually, all the Naponelli "signed" decanters should rise markedly in value because of the small quantities issued.

Although the knowledgeable dealers are aware of the Luxardo prices, remarkable bargains are sometimes obtainable by shopping at garage sales, thrift stores, and charity outlets.

Specimens in mint condition with the original manufacturer's label always command the highest sums. All prices listed are for empty bottles in fine to mint condition.

If current or recent Luxardo bottles are not available at your local spirits dealer, the dealer can order them from the American distributor, Hans Schonewalk, American Beverage Brokers, 420 Market Street, San Francisco, California 94111.

Alabaster Fish Figural, 1960–68 . . . . $20–$30
Alabaster Goose Figural, 1960–68, green and white, wings, etc. . . . . $15–$20
Ampulla Flask, 1958–59 . . . . : . . . . $15–$20
Apothecary Jar, 1960, handpainted multicolor, green, and black . . . . $15–$20
Assyrian Ashtray Decanter, 1961, gray, tan, black . . . . $9–$12
Autumn Leaves Decanter, 1952, handpainted, two handles . . . . $20–$28
Autumn Wine Pitcher, 1958, handpainted country scene, handled pitcher . . . $18–$24
Babylon Decanter, 1960, dark green, gold . . . . $12–$15
Bizantina, 1959, gold embossed design, white body, gold, white . . . . $20–$25
Blue and Gold Amphora, 1968, blue and gold with pastoral scene in white oval . . . . .
. . . . $15–$19
Blue Fiammetta or Vermillian, 1957, decanter . . . . $12–$19
Brocca Pitcher, 1958, white background pitcher with handle, multicolor flowers, green leaves . . . . $15–$25
Buddha Goddess Figural, 1961, Goddess head in green gray stone . . . . $9–$12
Buddha Goddess Figural, 1961, Goddess head in green gray stone, miniature . . . .
. . . . $7–$9
Burma Ashtray Specialty, 1960, embossed with white dancing figure, dark green background . . . . $14–$19
Calypso Girl Figural, 1962, black West Indian girl, flower headdress in bright color . . . . $12–$15
Candlestick Alabaster, 1961 . . . . $15–$22
Cellini Vase, 1957, glass and silver handled decanter, fancy with serpent handle . . . . .
. . . . $8–$11
Cellini Vase, 1958–68, glass and silver decanter, fancy . . . . $7–$9
Ceramic Barrel, 1968, barrel shape, barrel color, painted flowers, embosed scroll with cameo head on decorative stand . . . . $8–$11
Cherry Basket Figural, 1960, white basket, red cherries . . . . $8–$11

Classical Fragment Specialty, 1961, embossed classic Roman female figure and vase
.... $14–$19
Cocktail Shaker, 1957, glass and silver decanter, silver-plated top .... $7–$9
Coffee Carafe Specialty, 1962, old-time coffee pot with handle and spout, white with
blue flowers.. $8–$11
Curva Vaso Vase, 1961, green, green and white, ruby red............... $12–$15
Deruta Amphora, 1956, colorful floral design on white, two-handled decanter ......
.... $7–$9
Deruta Cameo Amphora, 1959, colorful floral scrolls and cameo head on eggshell
white, two-handled vase .... $12–$20
Deruta Pitcher, 1953, multicolor flowers on base perugia, white single handled pitcher
.... $8–$11
Diana Decanter, 1956, white figure of Diana with deer on black, single handled
decanter... $8–$11
Dogal Silver And Green Decanter, 1952–56, handpainted gondola .... $7–$9
Dogal Silver Ruby Decanter, 1956, handpainted Venetian scene and flowers ....
.... $7–$12
Dogal Silver Ruby, 1952–56, handpainted gondola, silver band neck .... $7–$9
Dogal Silver Smoke Decanter, 1952–55, handpainted gondola............. $8–$11
Dogal Silver Smoke Decanter, 1953–54, handpainted gondola............. $8–$10
Dogal Silver Smoke Decanter, 1956, handpainted gondola, buildings, flowers, neck
bands... $7–$11
Dogal Silver Smoke Decanter, 1956, handpainted silver clouds and gondola... $7–$9
Dolphin Figural, 1959, yellow, green, blue .... $30–$40
"Doughnut" Bottle, 1960 Clock Bottle, 1959, cherry Este working clock in doughnut-
shaped bottle .... $12–$16
Dragon Amphora, 1953, two-handled white decanter with colorful dragon and flowers
.... $8–$11
Dragon Pitcher, 1958, one handle, white pitcher, color dragon, and scroll work......
.... $7–$9
Duck-Green Glass Figural, 1960, green and amber duck, clear glass base... $25–$30
Eagle, 1970... $40–$48
Egyptian Specialty, 1960, two-handled amphora, Egyptian design on tan and gold
background .... $10–$13
Etruscan Decanter, 1959, single-handled black Greek design on tan background ....
.... $10–$14
Euganean Bronze, 1952–55 .... $9–$12
Euganean Coppered, 1952–55, Mojolica............................. $9–$1
Fighting Cocks, 1962, combination decanter and ashtray, black and red fighting birds.
.... $10–$13
Fish-Green And Gold Glass Figural, 1960, green, silver and gold, clear glass base ..
.... $20–$24
Fish-Ruby Murano Glass Figural, 1961, ruby red tones of glass .... $20–$24
Florentine Majolica, 1956, round-handled decanter, painted pitcher, yellow, dragon,
blue wings... $12–$18
Frenza Decanter, 1952–56, colorful country scene on white single-handled decanter .
.... $14–$17
Gambia, 1961, black princess, kneeling holding tray, gold trim, 10³/₄" .... $6–$9
Golden Fakir, 1960, seated snake charmer, with flute and snakes, black and gray ....
.... $15–$24
Golden Fakir, 1961, seated snake charmer, with flute and snakes, gold...... $15–$25

Gondola, 1959, highly glazed abstract gondola and gondolier in black, orange and yellow, stopper on upper prow, 12³/₄", black, orange, yellow . . . . $10–$14
Gondola, 1960, same as 1959, stopper moved from prow to stern . . . . $8–$11
Grapes, Pear Figural . . . . $12–$18
Mayan, 1960, a Mayan temple god head mask; brown, yellow, black, white, 11" . . . . .
. . . . $12–$15
Mosaic Ashtray, 1959, combination decanter ashtray; mosaic pattern of rearing horse, 11¹/₂", black, yellow, green. . . . . $12–$18
Mosaic Ashtray, 1959, combination decanter ashtray; mosaic pattern of rearing horse, miniature, 6", black, green . . . . $7–$9
Nubian, kneeling black figure, gold dress and headdress, 9¹/₂". . . . . $8–$12
Nubian, kneeling black figure, gold dress and headdress, miniature, 4³/₄" . . . . . . $2–$4
Opal Majolica, 1957, two gold handles, translucent opal top, pink base; also used as lamp base, 10". . . . . $7–$9
Penguine Murano Glass Figural, 1968, black and white penguin, crystal base . . . . . .
. . . . $20–$24
Pheasant Murano Glass Figural, 1960, red and clear glass on a crystal base, red, gold
. . . . $22–$27
Pheasant Red And Gold Figural, 1960, red and gold glass bird on crystal base . . . . .
. . . . $25–$32
Primavera Amphora, 1958, two-handled vase shape, with floral design in yellow, green, and blue, 9³/₄". . . . . $8–$12
Puppy Cucciolo Glass Figural, 1961, amber and green glass,. . . . .
. . . . $14–$23
Puppy Murano Glass Figural, 1960, amber glass, crystal base. . . . . $12–$18
Silver Blue Decanter, 1952–55, handpainted silver flowers and leaves . . . . . . $10–$12
Silver Brown Decanter, 1952–55, handpainted silver flowers and leaves, silver. . . . . .
. . . . $10–$16
Silver Brown Decanter, 1952–55, handpainted silver flowers and leaves . . . . $10–$16
Sir Lancelot, 1962, figure of English knight in full armor with embossed shield, tan gray with gold, 12" . . . . $7–$9
Springbox Amphora, 1952, vase with handle; leaping African deer with floral and lattice background; black, brown, 9³/₄". . . . . $7–$9
Squirrel Glass Figural, 1968, amethyst-colored squirrel on crystal base, amethyst . . .
. . . . $30–$40
Sudan, 1960, two-handled classic vase, incised figures, African motif in browns, blue, yellow and gray, 13¹/₂" . . . . $7–$9
Torre Rosa, 1962, rose-tinted tower of fruit, 10¹/₄" . . . . $8–$12
Torre Tinta, 1962, multicolor tower of fruit, natural shades . . . . $10–$15
Tower Of Fruit, 1968, various fruits, in natural colors, 22¹/₄" . . . . $9–$14
Tower Of Fruit Majolicas Torre Bianca, 1962, white, and gray tower of fruit, 10¹/₄"
. . . . $9–$13

MCCORMICK BOTTLES

The McCormick bottles are made for retailing McCormick Irish Whiskey. There are four different series: Cars, Famous Americans, Frontiersman Decanters, and Gunfighters. The category for cars includes various forms of transportation. The lengthiest series has been the Famous American, encompassing celebrities from colonial times to the 20th century. Released in limited numbers, the prices on all of the McCormicks are automatically higher than most figurals.

BARREL SERIES

Barrel, 1968, with stand and gold hoops . . . . $8–$11
Barrel, 1968, with stand and plain hoops. . . . . $6–$9
Barrel, 1968, with stand and shot glasses . . . . $14–$19

BIRD SERIES

Blue Jay (1971) . . . . $9–$16
Canadian Goose, miniature . . . . $10–$15
Gambel's Quail (1982) . . . . $35–$45
Ring Neck Pheasant . . . . $30–$38
Wood Duck (1980). . . . . $20–$25

CAR SERIES

Packard (1937) . . . . $30–$40
The Pony Express . . . . $40–$45
The Sand Buggy Commemorative Decanter . . . . $20–$30

CONFEDERATE SERIES

Jeb Stuart. . . . . $25–$35
Jefferson Davis . . . . $25–$30
Robert E. Lee. . . . . $25–$35
Stonewall Jackson. . . . . $25–$35

COUNTRY AND WESTERN SERIES

Hank Williams, Sr. (1980) . . . . $55–$75
Hank Williams, Jr. (1980) . . . . $55–$70
Tom T. Hall (1980) . . . . $30–$50

FAMOUS AMERICAN PORTRAIT SERIES

Abe Lincoln, with law book in hand .... $20–$30
Alexander Graham Bell, with apron .... $3–$6
Captain John Smith .... $6–$9
Charles Lindbergh .... $12–$18
Eleanor Roosevelt .... $8–$10
George Washington Carver .... $14–$22
Henry Ford .... $20–$25
Lewis Meriwether .... $10–$15
Pocahontas .... $30–$42
Robert E. Perry .... $15–$20
Thomas Edison .... $33–$44
Ulysses S. Grant, with coffee pot and cup....................... $12–$15
William Clark .... $7–$10

FOOTBALL MASCOTS

Alabama Bamas .... $20–$25
Arizona Sun Devils .... $30–$34
Arizona Wildcats... $12–$16
Arkansas Hogs (1972)... $10–$12
Auburn War Eagles .... $10–$12
Baylor Bears (1972).. $20–$26
California Bears .... $15–$22
Drake Bulldogs (1974), blue helmet and jersey .... $7–$9
Georgia Bulldogs, black helmet and red jersey.................
Georgia Tech Yellowjackets..................................... $15–$25
Houston Cougars (1972)... $14–$24
Indiana Hoosiers (1974) ....
Iowa Cyclones (1974) .... $45–$55
Iowa Hawkeyes (1974) .... $60–$70
Iowa Purple Panthers.. $25–$28
Louisiana State Tigers (1974) .... $11–$13
Michigan State Spartans .... $7–$12
Michigan Wolverines (1974) .... $15–$20
Minnesota Gophers (1974)....................................... $15–$25
Mississippi Rebels (1974) .... $15–$22
Mississippi State Bulldogs (1974), red helmet and jersey ...... $12–$18
Nebraska Cornhuskers (1974).................................... $12–$18
Nebraska Football Player....................................... $20–$30
Nebraska, Johnny Rogers, No. 1 .... $160+
New Mexico Lobo .... $32–$40
Oklahoma Sooners Wagon (1974).................................. $15–$22
Oklahoma Souther Cowboy (1974)................................. $7–$9
Oregon Beavers (1974).. $15–$25
Oregon Ducks (1974) .... $10–$20
Purdue Boilermaker (1974) .... $15–$25
Rice Owls (1972) .... $14–$18
SMU Mustangs (1972) .... $8–$12
TCU Horned Frogs (1972) .... $20–$26

Tennessee Volunteers (1974) .... $8–$12
Texas A & M Aggies (1972) .... $18–$20
Texas Horns (1972) .... $20–$25
Texas Tech Raiders (1972) .... $12–$17

FRONTIERSMEN COMMEMORATIVE DECANTERS, 1972

Daniel Boone .... $15–$22
Davy Crockett .... $17–$25
Jim Bowie .... $12–$15
Kit Carson .... $14–$18

GENERAL

A & P Wagon .... $40–$48
Airplane (1969), Spirit of St. Louis .... $60–$80
American Bald Eagle (1982) .... $30–$40
American Legion Cincinnati (1986) .... $15–$20
Buffalo Bill (1979) .... $50–$65
Cable Car .... $15–$20
Car (1980), Packard 1937, black or cream; first in a series of classic cars, rolling wheels, and vinyl seats .... $30–$40
Chair, Queen Anne .... $25–$35
Ciao Baby (1978) .... $20–$25
Clock (1971), cuckoo .... $20–$30
De Witt Clinton Engine (1970) .... $35–$40
French Telephone (1969) .... $15–$25
Globe (1971), Angelica .... $19–$24
Henry Ford (1977) .... $18–$22
Hutchinson Kansas Centennial (1972) .... $15–$25
Jester (1972) .... $20–$28
Jimmy Durante (1981), with music box, plays Inka Dinka Do .... $31–$40
Joplin Miner (1972) .... $15–$20
JR Ewing (1980), with music box, plays theme song from Dallas ... $12–$15
JR Ewing, gold colored .... $25–$40
Julia Bulette (1974) .... $70–$90
Lamp, hurricane .... $13–$18
Largemouth Bass (1982) .... $20–$28
Lobsterman (1979) .... $15–$20
Louis Armstrong .... $45–$55
Mark Twain (1977) .... $12–$15
Mark Twain, mini .... $10–$12
McCormick Centennial (1956) .... $60–$80
Mikado (1980) .... $45–$65
Missouri Sesquicentennial China (1970) .... $6–$9
Missouri Sesquicentennial Glass (1971) .... $3–$7
Ozark Ike (1979) .... $22–$27
Paul Bunyan (1979) .... $25–$30
Pioneer Theatre (1972) .... $8–$12
Pony Express (1978) .... $40–$50

Renault Racer (1969) . . . . $30–$40
Sam Houston (1977) . . . . $18–$24
Stephen F. Austin (1977) . . . . $12–$15
Telephone Operator . . . . $45–$55
Thelma Lu (1982) . . . . $20–$25
US Marshal (1979) . . . . $25–$35
Will Rogers (1977). . . . . $12–$15
Yacht Americana (1971). . . . . $20–$30

KING ARTHUR SERIES

King Arthur On Throne. . . . . $30–$40
Merlin The Wizard with his Wise Old Magical Robe (c.1979). . . . . $25–$35
Queen Guinevere, The Gem of Royal Court . . . . $15–$20
Sir Lancelot of the Lake in Armor, A Knight of Roundtable . . . . $15–$20

THE LITERARY SERIES

Huck Finn (1980), sits fishing, leaning on a tree trunk, and smoking a pipe . . $15–$20
Tom Sawyer (1980), stands in front of a fence scratching his head . . . . $18–$24

SPORTS SERIES

Air Race Propeller (1971). . . . . $12–$18
Air Race Pylon (1970). . . . . $10–$15
Johnny Rodgers No. 1 (1972). . . . . $150–$175
Johnny Rodgers No. 2 (1973). . . . . $55–$65
KC Chiefs (1969). . . . . $18–$25
KC Royals (1971) . . . . $9–$12
Muhammud Ali (1980) . . . . $40–$50
Nebraska Football Player (1972). . . . . $25–$32
Skibob (1971). . . . . $10–$11

TRAIN SERIES

Jupiter Engine (1969) . . . . $14–$18
Mail Car (1970). . . . . $18–$22
Passenger Car (1970) . . . . $20–$30
Wood Tender (1969). . . . . $9–$13

OLD COMMONWEALTH BOTTLES

The brand name Old Commonwealth is produced by J.P. Van Winkle and Son. Opening in 1974, it was one of the newer companies involved in producing collector decanters with high quality whiskey. The company presently bottles its products at the Hoffman Distilling Co., located in Lawrenceburg, Kentucky. Their ceramic decanters are manufactured in the Orient, but they brew their own 80-proof Kentucky bourbon whiskey, which is distributed nationally.

Their decanters are easily identified because the titles of most pieces appear on front plaques. The first Old Commonwealth mini piece was made in 1980 when a small version of Coal Miner No. 1 was offered. Today, the majority of the decanters are produced in regular and miniature sizes.

Alabama Crimson Tide, 1981, University of Alabama symbol; front of elephant thrusting through a large red A, elephant's foot propped on top of a football, "Crimson Tide" printed on the front . . . . $12–$15
Bulldogs, 1982, the mascot of the Georgia Bulldogs; front portion of a bulldog stands in the center of a large G with one front paw propped on a football . . . . $15–$20
Chief Illini No. 1, 1979, the mascot for the University of Illinois; warrior stands with arms up and spread wide, dressed in beige buckskin and ceremonial warbonnet . . . . . .
. . . . $70–$85
Chief Illini No. 2, 1981, the mascot of the University of Illinois; warrior running with arms flung back to the sides, dressed in beige buckskins and orange feathered head-dress; a large letter I in orange and blue stands behind him . . . . $45–$57
Chief Illini No. 3, 1979 . . . . $50–$60
Coal Miner No. 1, 1975, man stands holding shovel in one hand and other hand on jacket; bucket of coal at his feet . . . . $60–$80
Coal Miner No. 1, 1980, man stands holding shovel in one hand and other hand on jacket; bucket of coat at his feet, Mini . . . . $15–$20
Coal Miner No. 2, 1976, man stands with pick in one hand and a latern in the other; wears blue mining outfit with red kerchief; plaque reads "Old Time Coal Miner" . . . . .
. . . . $20–$30
Coal Miner No. 2, 1982, Man stands with pick in one hand and a lantern in the other; wears blue mining outfit with red kerchief; plaque reads "Old Time Coal Miner," Mini
. . . . $19–$23
Coal Miner No. 3, 1977, miner kneels on one leg, holding shovel in one hand and coal in the other hand; bucket of coal at his feet . . . . $28–$36
Coal Miner No. 3, 1981, miner kneels on one leg, holding a shovel in one hand and coal in the other hand; bucket of coal at his feet, Mini . . . . $20–$25
Coal Miner-Lunch Time No. 4, 1980, miner sits eating lunch, red apple in one hand; wears blue overalls and red miner's hat . . . . $30–$35

Coal Miner-Lunch Time No. 4, 1980, miner sits eating lunch, red apple in one hand; wears blue overalls and red miner's hat, Mini .... $12–$15

Cottontail, 1981, jumping rabbit lands on front feet with hind feet extended in the air; short stump .... $25–$35

Elusive Leprechaun, 1980, leprechaun sits on top of a pot of gold with arms wrapped around bent knees; wears dark green hat and boots, and red jacket. .... $24–$30

Fisherman, "A Keeper," 1980, old man sits holding fish in both hands, his pole tucked in one arm; fishing tackle sits on the ground .... $25–$35

Golden Retriever, 1979, dog sits with game lying between front feet .... $25–$32

Kentucky Thoroughbreds, 1976, red mare and colt with dark manes and tails, prancing on blue grass .... $30–$40

Kentucky Wildcat .... $20–$28

LSU Tiger, 1979, the mascot for Louisiana State University; ferocious tiger stands with front legs resting on stone structure, a football under one paw, "LSU" in yellow on structure .... $35–$45

Lumberjack .... $15–$25

Missouri Tiger .... $30–$40

Old Rip Van Winkle No. 1, 1974, old man sits on stump with legs crossed and musket held across his lap; wears green hat and jacket, and red pants .... $30–$40

Old Rip Van Winkle No. 2, 1975, old man sprawled with his back resting against a stump, sleeping, musket held between crossed hand .... $30–$35

Old Rip Van Winkle No. 3, 1977, old man stands stroking his long white beard, musket propped on ground, held in crook of arm; wears tattered clothes ..... $25–$30

Pointing Setter Decanter, 1965, dog on point; brown, tan, and white; glass, 12" .... $12–$18

Quail On The Wing Decanter, 1968, round glass bottle, three-color design, 12" .. $5–$8

Rebel Yell Rider, 1970, figurine, Confederate cavalryman bottle in six colors, sold only in the South, $9^3/_4$" .... $16–$19

Rip Van Winkle Figurine, 1970, famous Catskill character with blunderbuss and elf, $9^1/_4$", multicolor .... $25–$28

Songs Of Ireland, 1972, porcelain .... $15–$20

Sons of Erin, 1969, porcelain .... $6–$9

South Carolina Tricentennial, 1970 .... $10–$14

South Carolina Tricentennial, 1970 .... $10–$14

Tennessee Walking Horse, 1977, black prancing horse, red and yellow bridle, stands on aqua green grass .... $20–$28

USC Trojan, 1980, the mascot for the University of Southern California; a warrior stands at base of pillar with sword, shield, and Trojan helmet, Mini .... $9–$12

USC Trojan, 1980, the mascot for the University of Southern California; a warrior stands at base of pillar with sword, shield, and Trojan helmet .... $35–$45

Weller Masterpiece, 1963, white porcelain apothecary bottle, rebus design, gold bands, $10^5/_8$" .... $15–$25

Western Boot Decanter, 1982, replica of a brown leather boot with exact shading, $10^1/_2$" .... $15–$19

Western Boot Decanter, 1982, replica of a brown leather boot with exact shading, Mini, 4" .... $6–$9

Western Logger, 1980, man stands on log, holding a logger's tool in one hand and an axe in the other hand .... $25–$34

Wildcats, 1982, the mascot for Kansas State; front portion of figure thrusts through a large Letter K with front paw propped on a football .... $30–$40

Wings Across The Continent, 1972, porcelain, duck finial .... $8–$15

Yankee Doodle, Yankee figure wearing blue pants, white shirt, yellow vest, and black hat rides brown pony, on large stand with brick fence, plaque on front with part of the song, music box plays *Yankee Doodle*, 11" .... $14–$17

MODERN FIREFIGHTERS SERIES

Note: The following are listed consecutively by number.

Modern Hero No. 1, (1982), stands clutching an axe and oxygen mask, wears black firefighting outfit with yellow stripes, number "1" on helmet. 12". .... $40–$60
Mini. .... $10–$18
The Nozzleman No. 2, (1982), firefighter kneels on rubble of bricks, holding fire hose; wears oxygen mask over face and yellow tank on his back; number "2" on helmet. 9¹/₂"
.... $45–$65
Mini. 5". .... $20–$29
On Call No. 3, (1982), pair of black firefighting boots with yellow toes, red helmet rests on top of boots, number "3" on helmet. 8¹/₂" .... $45–$55
Mini. .... $15–$25
Fallen Comrade No. 4, (1982), pair of firefighters with one unconscious on his back, the other kneels next to him while placing an oxygen mask over the victim's face; kneeling firefighter wears helmet with the number "4." 7" .... $35–$50
Mini. 3¹/₂" .... $20–$30

WATERFOWLER

Good Boy No. 3, 1981, hunter kneels beside tree stump with shotgun in one hand and the other hand cradling a retrieved duck hanging from the mouth of a black bird dog ..
.... $32–$42

OLD FITZGERALD BOTTLES

———

Old Fitzgerald bottles are made by the Old Fitzgerald Distilling Co. to contain their whiskey and bourbon. Old Fitzgeralds are sometimes called Old Cabin Still bottles after one of the brand names under which they are sold. The company issues both decanter-style and figural bottles. The decanters are ceramics in various styles and colors. Its figurals portray many different Irish and American subjects. New figurals are added to the line irregularly. The number of bottles issued by this firm is small.

Americas Cup Commemorative, 1970 .... $10–$15
Blarney Castle, 1970, porcelain .... $6–$9
Browsing Deer Decanter, 1967, deer and woods scene; brown, tan, and white; amber stopper.. $6–$9
California Bicentennial, 1970....................................... $10–$12
Candlelite Decanter, 1955, removable gold candle holder mounted on flint glass, pair .... $10–$15
Colonial Decanter, 1969, glass .... $3–$5
Crown Decanter .... $2–$4
Gold Coaster Decanter, 1954, flint glass decanter, gold metal coaster ...... $10–$15
Gold Web Decanter, 1953, flint glass, gold web and frame fused onto decanter. $6–$9
"Golden Bough" Decanter, 1971, glass .... $3–$5
Hillbilly Bottle, 1954, pint, hillbilly on barrel with rifle; in brown, tan, black and green, $9^1/_8$" .... $8–$11
Hillbilly Bottle, 1954, gallon, same as above, very rare .... $40–$50
Hillbilly Bottle, 1954, quart, same as above, $11^3/_8$"................... $8–$11
Hillbilly, 1969, same bottle as 1954 Hillbilly; more detail and color, $11^1/_2$".... $8–$11
Jewel Decanter, 1951-52, flint glass, beveled neck....................... $6–$9
Leaping Trout Decanter, 1969....................................... $7–$9
Leprechaun Bottle, 1968, porcelain bottle; gold band, green shamrocks, Irish verse, $10^1/_8$".. $20–$25
LSU Alumni Decanter, 1970 .... $20–$25
Man O' War Decanter, 1969, glass .... $2–$4
Memphis Commemorative, 1969, porcelain .... $8–$12
Nebraska, 1971 .... $20–$25
Nebraska, 1972 .... $12–$17
Ohio State Centennial, 1970.. $8–$12
Old Cabin Still Decanter, 1958, gold letters "Old Cabin Still" infused on flint glass bottle; solid faceted stopper .... $12–$19
Pilgrim Landing Commemorative, 1970.............................. $12–$16

SKI COUNTRY BOTTLES

Ski Country bottles produces limited edition bottles in two sizes——regular and miniature. The company offers many different bottle series including Indians, owls, game birds, and Christmas and customer specialties. The bottles manufactured by Ski Country are exquisitely detailed and highly sought after by collectors.

ANIMALS

Badger Family.. $20–$30
Badger Family, Mini... $10–$14

Bobcat Family . . . . $45–$60
Bobcat Family, Mini . . . . $16–$25
Coyote Family . . . . $30–$38
Coyote Family, Mini . . . . $15–$20
Kangaroo . . . . $15–$25
Kangaroo, Mini . . . . $14–$19
Koala . . . . $16–$22
Raccoon . . . . $30–$38
Raccoon, Mini . . . . $20–$26
Skunk Family . . . . $25–$35
Skunk Family, Mini . . . . $20–$25
Snow Leopard . . . . $25–$32
Snow Leopard, Mini . . . . $20–$28

BIRDS

Blackbird . . . . $34–$40
Blackbird, Mini . . . . $29–$30
Black Swan . . . . $20–$28
Black Swan, Mini . . . . $18–$24
Blue Jay . . . . $35–$45
Blue Jay, Mini . . . . $42–$49
Cardinal . . . . $40–$50
Cardinal, Mini . . . . $35–$45
Case gin, square, slightly tapering sides, applied lip, OP, 16½", olive amber . . . .
. . . . $375–$550
Condor . . . . $45–$55
Condor, Mini . . . . $25–$30
Gamecocks . . . . $100–$115
Gamecocks, Mini . . . . $40–$46
Gila Woodpecker . . . . $35–$45
Gila Woodpecker, Mini . . . . $20–$25
Peace Dove . . . . $30–$38
Peace Dove, Mini . . . . $15–$20
Peacock . . . . $60–$80
Peacock, Mini . . . . $35–$40
Penguin Family . . . . $30–$45
Penguin Family, Mini . . . . $12–$15
Wood Duck . . . . $110–$150
Wood Duck, Mini . . . . $70–$95

CHRISTMAS

Bob Cratchit . . . . $30–$40
Bob Cratchit, Mini . . . . $15–$20
Mrs. Cratchit . . . . $30–$40
Mrs. Cratchit, Mini . . . . $15–$25
Scrooge . . . . $30–$38
Scrooge, Mini . . . . $12–$18

CIRCUS

Clown . . . . $22–$36
Clown, Mini . . . . $19–$23
Elephant On Drum . . . . $20–$30
Elephant On Drum, Mini . . . . $20–$28
Jenny Lind, blue dress . . . . $40–$55
Jenny Lind, blue dress, Mini . . . . $30–$45
Lion On Drum . . . . $20–$25
Lion On Drum, Mini . . . . $18–$21
P.T. Barnum . . . . $32–$40
P.T. Barnum, Mini . . . . $20–$25
Palomino Horse . . . . $26–$32
Palomino Horse, Mini . . . . $15–$20
Ringmaster . . . . $15–$20

Ski Country, Ringmaster, P.T. Barnum.
PHOTO COURTESY OF DAVE SMITH.

Ringmaster, Mini . . . . $7–$9
Tiger On Ball . . . . $25–$30
Tiger On Ball, Mini . . . . $18–$24
Tom Thumb . . . . $20–$25
Tom Thumb, Mini . . . . $16–$21

CUSTOMER SPECIALITIES

Ahrens-Fox Fire Engine . . . . $140–$180
Bonnie And Clyde, pair, Mini . . . . $55–$62
Bonnie And Clyde, pair . . . . $60–$70
Caveman . . . . $16–$23
Caveman, Mini . . . . $18–$22
Caveman, Mini . . . . $18–$22
Mill River Country Club . . . . $25–$30
Olympic Skier, blue . . . . $20–$30
Olympic Skier, blue, Mini . . . . $20–$25
Olympic Skier, gold . . . . $50–$65
Olympic Skier, Mini, red . . . . $20–$25

Olympic Skier, red.. $15–$22
Political Donkey and Elephant .... $40–$50

DOMESTIC ANIMALS

Basset Hound.. $35–$40
Basset Hound, Mini.. $15–$24
Holstein Cow .... $30–$40

EAGLES, FALCONS, AND HAWKS

Birth Of Freedom, 1976 .... $85–$95
Birth Of Freedom, 1976, Mini .... $65–$75
Eagle On The Water.. $90–$110
Eagle On The Water, Mini.. $38–$45
Easter Seals Eagle.. $40–$50
Easter Seals Eagle, mini .... $15–$24
Falcon Gallon $275
Gyrfalcon... $40–$50
Gyrfalcon, Mini .... $20–$26
Harpy Eagle... $60–$75
Harpy Eagle, Mini... $55–$70
Mountain Eagle.. $75–$95
Mountain Eagle, Mini.. $60–$80
Osprey Hawk... $100–$120
Osprey Hawk, Mini... $70–$90
Peregrine Falcon.. $60–$70
Peregrine Falcon, Mini.. $10–$14
Prairie Falcon .... $40–$60
Prairie Falcon, Mini .... $25–$35
Red Shoulder Hawk .... $40–$60
Red Shoulder Hawk, Mini .... $20–$30
Redtail Hawk.. $55–$65
Redtail Hawk, Mini.. $25–$30
White Falcon.. $45–$60
White Falcon, Mini .... $15–$22

FISH

Muskellunge... $25–$30
Muskellunge, Mini... $15–$18
Rainbow Trout .... $40–$50
Rainbow Trout, Mini .... $24–$30
Salmon .... $30–$35
Salmon, Mini .... $18–$22
Trout, mini, brown.. $20–$25

Ski Country, trout. PHOTO COURTESY OF DAVE SMITH.

GAME BIRDS

Banded Mallard	$40–$50
Chukar Partridge	$20–$25
Chukar Partridge, Mini	$8–$11
King Eider Duck	$35–$45
Mallard, 1973.	$35–$45
Pheasant In The Corn.	$50–$75
Pheasant In The Corn, Mini.	$35–$45
Pheasant, golden	$35–$40
Pheasant, golden, Mini	$20–$25
Pheasant, standing, Mini	$40–$48
Pheasants Fighting	$70–$80
Pheasants Fighting, half gallon.	$145–$165
Pheasants Fighting, Mini	$35–$45
Pintail.	$50–$75
Prairie Chicken	$40–$48
Ruffed Grouse	$40–$50
Ruffed Grouse, Mini	$22–$28
Turkey	$80–$100
Turkey, Mini	$100–$120

GRAND SLAM

Desert Sheep	$75–$90
Desert Sheep, Mini	$25–$30
Mountain Sheep	$50–$60
Mountain Sheep, Mini.	$24–$30
Stone Sheep	$50–$65
Stone Sheep, Mini	$27–$34

HORNED AND ANTLERED ANIMALS

Antelope.	$35–$45
Big-Horn Ram.	$40–$60
Big-Horn Ram, Mini.	$20–$25

Mountain Goat . . . .$40–$56
Mountain Goat, gallon . . . . $450+
Mountain Goat, Mini . . . . $40–$50
White Tail Deer . . . . $75–$100
White Tail Deer, Mini . . . . $75–$100

INDIANS

Ceremonial Antelope Dancer . . . . $52–$62
Ceremonial Antelope Dancer, Mini . . . . $36–$45
Ceremonial Buffalo Dancer . . . . $80–$105
Ceremonial Buffalo Dancer, Mini . . . . $30–$35
Ceremonial Deer Dancer . . . . $70–$90
Ceremonial Deer Dancer, Mini . . . . $30–$40
Ceremonial Eagle Dancer . . . . $90–$125
Ceremonial Eagle Dancer, Mini . . . . $20–$30
Ceremonial Falcon Dancer . . . . $85–$100
Ceremonial Falcon Dancer, Mini . . . . $35–$45
Ceremonial Wolf Dancer . . . . $30–$45
Ceremonial Wolf Dancer, Mini . . . . $30–$35
Chief No. 1 . . . . $60–$80
Chief No. 1, Mini . . . . $14–$22
Chief No. 2 . . . . $60–$80
Chief No. 2, Mini . . . . $14–$20
Cigar Store Indian . . . . $32–$40
Dancers Of The Southwest, set . . . . $150+
Dancers Of The Southwest, set, Mini . . . . $100+

OWLS

Barn Owl . . . . $60–$70
Barn Owl, Mini . . . . $30–$35
Great Gray Owl . . . . $48–$55
Great Gray Owl, Mini . . . . $20–$25
Horned Owl . . . . $30–$38
Horned Owl, gallon . . . . $900+
Horned Owl, Mini . . . . $30–$40
Saw Whet Owl . . . . $40–$50
Saw Whet Owl, Mini . . . . $30–$35
Screech Owl Family . . . . $80–$90
Screech Owl Family, Mini . . . . $68–$75
Spectacled Owl . . . . $60–$70
Spectacled Owl, Mini . . . . $40–$60

RODEO

Barrel Racer . . . . $40–$55
Barrel Racer, Mini . . . . $20–$25
Bull Rider . . . . $30–$35

Bull Rider, Mini..$15–$20
Wyoming Bronco ....$30–$40
Wyoming Bronco, Mini..$15–$25

APPENDIXES

APPENDIX A: TRADEMARKS

FOREIGN

A in a circle: Alembic Glass Industries, Bangalore, India.

A (big) in center of italic GM: Australian Glass Mfg. Co., Kilkenny, So. Australia.

A.B.C.: Albion Bottle Co. Ltd., Oldbury, Nr. Birmingham, England.

A G B Co: Albion Glass Bottle Co., England; trademark is found under Lea & Perrins, ca. 1880–1900.

A.G.W.: Alloa Glass Limited, Alloa, Scotland.

AVH–A.: Van Hoboken & Co, Rotterdam, The Netherlands, 1800–1898.

B & Co. L: Bagley & Co., Ltd., est. 1832, still operating (England).

Beaver: Beaver Flint Glass Co., Toronto, Ontario, Canada, ca. 1897–1920.

Bottle in frame: Veb Glasvoerk Drebkau, Drebkau, N.L. Germany.

Crown with figure of a crown: Excelsior Glass Co., St. Johns, Quebec, and later Diamond Glass Co., Montreal, Quebec, Canada, ca. 1879–1913.

Crown with three dots: Crown Glass, Waterloo, N.S. Wales.

CS & Co.: Cannington, Shaw & Co., St. Helens, England, ca. 1872–1916.

D in center of a diamond: Dominion Glass Co., Montreal, Quebec, Canada.

D.B.: In a book frame, Dale Brown & Co., Ltd., Mesborough, Yorks, England.

Excelsior: Excelsior Glass Co., St. John, Quebec, Canada, 1878–1883.

Fish: Veb Glasvoerk Stralau, Berlin.

Hamilton: Hamilton Glass Works, Hamilton, Ontario, Canada, 1865–1872.

Hat: Brougba, Bulgaria.

HH: Werk Hermannshutte, Czechoslovakia.

Hunyadi Janos: Andreas Saxlehner, Buda-Pesht, Austria-Hungary, ca. 1863–1900.

IYGE all in a circle: The Irish Glass Bottle, Ltd., Dublin.

KH: Kastrupog Holmeqaads, Copenhagen.

L on a bell: Lambert S.A., Belgium.

LIP: Lea & Perrins, London, England, 1880–1900.

LS in a circle: Lax & Shaw, Ltd., Leeds, York, England.

M in a circle: Cristales Mexicanos, Monterey, Mexico.

N in a diamond: Tippon Glass Co., Ltd., Tokyo, Japan.

NAGC: North American Glass Co., Montreal, Quebec, Canada, 1883–1890.

PG: Verreries De Puy De Dome, S.A. Paris.

R: Louis Freres & Co., France, ca. 1870–1890.

S in a circle: Vetreria Savonese. A. Voglienzone, S.A. Milano, Italy.

S.A.V.A. all in a circle: Asmara, Ethiopia.

S & M: Sykes & Macvey, Castleford, England, 1860–1888.

T in a circle: Tokyo Seibin Co., Ltd., Tokyo, Japan.

vFo: Vidreria Ind. Figuerras Oliveiras, Brazil.

VT: Ve-Tri S.p.a., Vetrerie Triventa, Vicenza, Italy.

VX: Usine de Vauxrot, France.

WECK in a frame: Weck Glaswerk G.mb.H, ofligen, Bonn.

Y in a circle: Etairia Lipasmaton, Athens, Greece.

UNITED STATES

The words and letters in italic are only a representation or brief description of the trademark as it appeared on a bottle. This is followed by the complete name and location of the company and the approximate period of time in which the trademark was in use.

A: John Agnew & Son, Pittsburgh, PA, 1854–1866.

A in a circle: American Glass Works, Richmond, VA, and Paden City, WV, ca. 1909–1936.

A in a circle: Armstrong Cork Co., Glass Division, Lancaster, PA, 1938–1968.

A & B together (AB): Adolphus Busch Glass Mfg. Co., Bellville, IL, and St. Louis, MO, ca. 1904–1907.

A & Co.: John Agnew & Co., Pittsburgh, PA; Indian Queen, Ear of Corn, and other flasks, ca. 1854–1892.

A B Co.: American Bottle Co., Chicago, IL, 1905–1930.

A B G M Co.: Adolphus Busch Glass Mfg. Co., Bellville, IL, and St. Louis, MO, ca. 1886–1928.

A C M E: Acme Glass Co., Olean, NY, ca. 1920–1930.

A & D H C: A. & D.H. Chambers, Pittsburgh, PA; Union flasks, ca. 1842–1886.

AGEE and Agee in script: Hazel Atlas Glass Co., Wheeling, WV, ca. 1921–1925.

A.G.W. Co.: American Glass Works, Ltd., 1880–1905.

AGW: American Glass Works, ca. 1880.

Anchor figure with H in center: Anchor Hocking Glass Corp., Lancaster, OH, ca. 1955.

A.R.S.: A.R. Samuels Glass Co., Philadelphia, PA, ca. 1855–1872.

A S F W W Va.: A.S. Frank Glass Co., Wellsburg, WV, ca. 1859.

ATLAS: Atlas Glass Co., Washington, PA, and later Hazel Atlas Glass Co., 1896–1965.

AVH: A. Van Hoboken & Co., Rotterdam, The Netherlands, 1800–1898.

Ball and Ball in script: Ball Bros. Glass Mfg. Co., Muncie, IN, and later Ball Corp., 1887–1973.

Bernardin in script: W. J. Latchford Glass Co., Los Angeles, CA, ca. 1932–1938.

The Best: Gillender & Sons, Philadelphia, PA, ca. 1867–1870.

B F B Co.: Bell Fruit Bottle Co., Fairmount, IN, ca. 1910.

B.G. Co.: Belleville Glass Co., IL, ca. 1882.

Bishop's: Bishop & Co., San Diego and Los Angeles, CA, 1890–1920.

B K: Benedict Kimber, Bridgeport and Brownsville, PA, ca. 1822–1840.

Boyds in script: Illinois Glass Co., Alton, IL, ca. 1900–1930.

Brelle (in script) Jar: Brelle Fruit Jar Mfg. Co., San Jose, CA, ca. 1912–1916.

Brilliantine: Jefferis Glass Co., Fairton, NJ, and Rochester, PA, ca. 1900–1905.

C in a circle: Chattanooga Bottle & Glass Co. and later Chattanooga Glass Co., since 1927.

C in a square: Crystal Glass Co., Los Angeles, CA, ca. 1921–1929.

C in a star: Star City Glass Co., Star City, WV, since 1949.

Canton Domestic Fruit Jar: Canton Glass Co., Canton, OH, ca. 1890–1904.

C & Co. or C Co.: Cunninghams & Co., Pittsburgh, PA, 1880–1907.

CCCo: C. Conrad & Co. (Beer), 1878–1883.

C C Co.: Carl Conrad & Co., St. Louis, MO, 1876–1883.

C C G Co.: Cream City Glass Co., Milwaukee, WI, 1888–1893.

C.F.C.A.: California Fruit Canners Association, Sacramento, CA, ca. 1899–1916.

C G M Co.: Campbell Glass Mfg. Co., West Berkeley, CA, 1885.

C G W: Campbell Glass Works, West Berkeley, CA, 1884–1885.

C & H: Coffin & Hay, Winslow, NJ, ca. 1838–1842.

C L G Co.: Carr–Lowrey Glass Co., Baltimore, MD, ca. 1889–1920.

Clyde, N.Y.: Clyde Glass Works, Clyde, NY, ca. 1870–1882.

The Clyde in script: Clyde Glass Works, Clyde, NY, ca. 1895.

C. Milw: Chase Valley Glass Co., Milwaukee, WI, ca. 1880.

Cohansey: Cohansey Glass Mfg. Co., Philadelphia, PA, 1870–1900.

CS & Co.: Cannington, Shaw & Co., St. Helens, England, ca. 1872–1916.

C.V. Co. No. 1 & No. 2: Milwaukee, WI, 1880–1881.

DB: Du Bois Brewing Co., Pittsburgh, PA, ca. 1918.

Dexter: Franklin Flint Glass Works, Philadelphia, PA, ca. 1861–1880.

Diamond (plain): Diamond Glass Co., since 1924.

The Dictator: William McCully & Co., Pittsburgh, PA, ca. 1855–1869.

Dictator: Same as previous entry, only ca. 1869–1885.

D & O: Cumberland Glass Mfg. Co., Bridgeton, NJ, ca. 1890–1900.

D O C: D.O. Cunningham Glass Co., Pittsburgh, PA, ca. 1883–1937.

D S G Co.: De Steiger Glass Co., LaSalle, IL, ca. 1867–1896.

Duffield: Duffield, Parke & Co., Detroit, MI, 1866–1875.

Dyottsville: Dyottsville Glass Works, Philadelphia, PA, 1833–1923.

Economy (in script) Trade Mark: Kerr Glass Mfg. Co., Portland, OR, 1903–1912.

Electric Trade Mark in script: Gayner Glass Works, Salem, NJ, ca. 1910.

Electric Trade Mark: Same as above, only ca. 1900–1910.

Erd & Co., E R Durkee: E.R. Durkee & Co., New York, NY, post-1874.

E R Durkee & Co: Same as above, only ca. 1850–1860.

Eureka 17: Eureka Jar Co., Dunbar, WV, ca. 1864.

Eureka in script: Same as above, only ca. 1900–1910.

Everlasting (in script) Jar: Illinois Pacific Glass Co., San Francisco, CA, ca. 1904.

Excelsior: Excelsior Glass Co., St. John, Quebec, Canada, 1878–1883.

F inside of a jar outline: C.L. Flaccus Glass Co., Pittsburgh, PA, ca. 1900–1928.

F & A: Fahnstock & Albree, Pittsburgh, PA, 1860–1862.

FL or FL & Co.: Frederick Lorenz & Co., Pittsburgh, PA, ca. 1819–1841.

G E M: Hero Glass Works, Philadelphia, PA, ca. 1884–1909.

G & H: Gray & Hemingray, Cincinnati, OH, ca. 1848–1864.

Gilberds: Gilberds Butter Tub Co., Jamestown, NY, ca. 1883–1890.

Greenfield: Greenfield Fruit Jar & Bottle Co., Greenfield, IN, ca. 1888–1912.

H (with varying numbers): Holt Glass Works, West Berkeley, CA, ca. 1893–1906.

Hamilton: Hamilton Glass Works, Hamilton, Ontario, Canada, 1865–1872.

Hazel: Hazel Glass Co., Wellsburg, WV, 1886–1902.

Heinz & Noble: Same as above, only ca. 1869–1872.

Helme: Geo. W. Helme Co., Jersey City, NJ, ca. 1870–1895.

Hemingray: Hemingray Brothers & Co. and later Hemingray Glass Co., Covington, KY, since 1864.

F. & J. Heinz: Same as above, only ca. 1876–1888.

H. J. Heinz: H. J. Heinz Co., Pittsburgh, PA, ca. 1860–1869.

H. J. Heinz Co.: Same as above, only since 1888.

HS in a circle: Twitchell & Schoolcraft, Keene, NH, 1815–1816.

Hunyadi Janos: Andreas Saxlehner, Buda–Pesth, Austria–Hungary, ca. 1863–1900.

I G: Illinois Glass, F inside of a jar outline, C.L. Flaccus, Pittsburgh, PA, ca. 1900–1928.

I G: Illinois Glass Co., Alton, IL, before 1890.

I G Co.: Ihmsen Glass Co., Pittsburgh, PA, ca. 1870–1898.

I.G. Co.: Same as previous entry, only ca. 1895.

I.G. Co. (monogram): Illinois Glass Co. on fruit jar, 1914.

IG Co in a diamond: Same as above, only ca. 1900–1916.

Ill. Glass Co.: 1916–1929.

Improved G E M: Hero Glass Works, Philadelphia, PA, ca. 1868.

I.P.G. (in diamond): Illinois Pacific Glass Corp., San Francisco, CA, 1925–1930.

I P G: Same as above, only 1902–1932.

JAF & Co., Pioneer and Folger: J.A. Folger & Co., San Francisco, CA, since 1850.

J D 26 S: John Duncan & Sons, New York, NY, ca. 1880–1900.

J R: Stourbridge Flint Glass Works, Pittsburgh, PA, ca. 1823–1828.

JSB (monogram): Joseph Schlitz Brewing Co., Milwaukee, WI, ca. 1900.

J T: Mantua Glass Works and later Mantua Glass Co., Mantua, OH, ca. 1824.

J T & Co.: Brownsville Glass Works, Brownsville, PA, ca. 1824–1828.

Kensington Glass Works: Kensington Glass Works, Philadelphia, PA, ca. 1822–1932.

Kerr in script: Kerr Glass Mfg. Co. and later Alexander H. Kerr Glass Co., Portland, OR; Sand Spring, OK; Chicago, IL; Los Angeles, CA, since 1912.

K H & G: Kearns, Herdman & Gorsuch, Zanesville, OH, 1876–1884.

K & M: Konz & McKee, Wheeling, WV, 1824–1829.

K Y G W and KYGW Co.: Kentucky Glass Works Co., Louisville, KY, 1849–1855.

Lamb: Lamb Glass Co., Mt. Vernon, OH, 1855–1964.

L G Co: Louisville Glass Works, Louisville, KY, ca. 1880.

Lightning: Henry W. Putnam, Bennington, VT, 1875–1890.

L I P: Lea & Perrins, London, England, 1880–1900.

L K Y G W: Louisville Kentucky Glass Works, Louisville, KY, ca. 1873–1890.

L & W: Lorenz & Wightman, PA, 1862–1871.

"Mascot," "Mason," and M F G Co: Mason Fruit Jar Co., Philadelphia, PA, all ca. 1885–1900.

Mastadon: Thomas A. Evans Mastadon Works and later Wm. McCully & Co., Pittsburgh, PA 1855–1887.

MG (slant letters): Maywood Glass, Maywood, CA, 1930–1950.

M.G. Co.: Missouri Glass Co., 1900.

M.G. Co: Modes Glass Co., IN, 1895–1904.

M. G. W.: Middletown Glass Co., NY, ca. 1889.

Moore Bros.: Moore Bros., Clayton, NJ, 1864–1880.

N B B G Co: North Baltimore Bottle Glass Co., North Baltimore, OH, 1885–1930.

O: Owen Bottle Co.

O–D–1 0 & diamond & I: Owens Ill. Pacific Coast Co., CA, 1932–1943. Mark of Owen–Ill. Glass Co. merger in 1930.

P G W: Pacific Glass Works, San Francisco, CA, 1862–1876.

Premium: Premium Glass Co., Coffeyville, KS, ca. 1908–1914.

Putnam Glass Works in a circle: Putnam Flint Glass Works, Putnam, OH, ca. 1852–1871.

P & W: Perry & Wood and later Perry & Wheeler, Keene, NH, ca. 1822–1830.

Queen (in script) Trade Mark (all in a shield): Smalley, Kivlan & Onthank, Boston, MA, 1906–1919.

R: Louis Freres & Co., France, ca. 1870–1890.

R & C Co: Roth & Co., San Francisco, CA, 1879–1888.

Rau's: Fairmount Glass Works, Fairmount, IN, ca. 1898–1908.

Red with a key through it: Safe Glass Co., Upland, IN, ca. 1892–1898.

R G Co: Renton Glass Co., Renton, WA, 1911.

Root: Root Glass Co., Terre Haute, IN, 1901–1932.

S in a side of a star: Southern Glass Co., LA, 1920–1929.

S.B. & G. Co.: Streator Bottle & Glass Co., IL, 1881–1905.

S & C: Stebbins & Chamberlain or Coventry Glass Works, Coventry, CT, ca. 1825–1830.

S F G W: San Francisco Glass Works, San Francisco, CA, 1869–1876.

S & M: Sykes & Macvey, Castleford, England, 1860–1888.

S.F. & P.G.W.: John Wieland's extra pale Cac. Bottling Works S.F., CA.

Squibb: E.R. Squibb, M.D., Brooklyn, NY, 1858–1895.

Standard (in script) Mason: Standard Corp. Glass Co. and later Standard Glass Co., Marion, IN, ca. 1894–1932.

Star Glass Co.: Star Glass Co., New Albany, IN, ca. 1860–1900.

Swayzee: Swayzee Glass Co., Swayzee, IN, 1894–1906.

T C W: T.C. Wheaton Co., Millville, NJ, since 1888.

TS: Coventry Glass Works, Coventry, CT, 1820–1824.

W & CO: Thomas Wightman & Co., Pittsburgh, PA, ca. 1880–1889.

W C G Co: West Coast Glass Co., Los Angeles, CA, 1908–1930.

WF & S MILW: William Franzen & Son, Milwaukee, WI, 1900–1929.

W G W: Woodbury Glass Works, Woodbury, NJ, 1882–1900.

WT & Co: Whitall-Tatum & Co., Millville, NJ, 1857–1935.

APPENDIX B: BOTTLE CLUBS

UNITED STATES

ALABAMA

Alabama Bottle Collectors Society—2768 Hanover Circle, Birmingham, AL 35205, (205) 933-7902.

Azalea City Beamers Bottle & Spec. Club—100 Bienville Avenue, Mobile, AL 36606, (205) 473-4251.

Bama Beamers Bottle & Spec. Club—Rt. 1, P.O. Box 72, Sheffield, AL 35660, (205) 383-6884.

Choctaw Jim Beam Bottle & Spec. Club—218 S. Hamburg Street, Butler, AL 36904, (205) 459-3140.

Heart of Dixie Beam Bottle & Spec. Club—2136 Rexford Road, Montgomery, AL 36116.

Mobile Bottle Collectors Club—8844 Lee Circle, Irvington, AL 36544, (205) 951-6725.

Mobile Bottle Collectors Club—Rt. 4, P.O. Box 28, Theodore, AL 36582.

Montgomery, Alabama, Bottle Club—1940A Norman Bridge Court, Montgomery, AL 36104.

Montgomery Bottle & Insulator Club—2021 Merrily Drive, Montgomery, AL 36111, (205) 288-7937.

North Alabama Bottle & Glass Club—P.O. Box 109, Decatur, AL 35601.

Tuscaloosa Antique Bottle Club—1617 11th Street, Tuscaloosa, AL 35401.

Southern Beamers Bottle & Spec. Club—1400 Greenbrier Road, Apt. G-3, Anniston, AL 36201, (205) 831-5151.

Vulcan Beamers Bottle & Spec. Club—5817 Avenue Q, Birmingham, AL 35228, (205) 831-5151.

ALASKA

Alaska Bottle Club (formerly The Anchorage Beam Club)—8510 E. 10th, Anchorage, AK 99504.

ARIZONA

Avon Collectors Club—P.O. Box 1406, Mesa, AZ 86201.

Fort Smith Area Bottle Collectors Association—4618 S. "Q," Fort Smith, AZ 72901.

Kachina Ezra Brooks Bottle Club—3818 W. Cactus Wren Drive, Phoenix, AZ 85021.

Phoenix A.B.C. Club—1939 West Waltann Lane, Phoenix, AZ 85023, (602) 933-9757.

Pick & Shovel A.B.C. of Arizona, Inc.—P.O. Box 7020, Phoenix, AZ 85011.

Southern AZ Historical Collector's Association, Ltd.—6211 Piedra Seca, Tucson, AZ 85718.

Tri-City Jim Beam Bottle Club—2701 E. Utopia Road, Sp. #91, Phoenix, AZ 85024, (602) 867-1375.

Valley of the Sun Bottle & Specialty Club—212 E. Minton, Tempe, AZ 85281.

White Mountain Antique Bottle Collectors Association—P.O. Box 503, Eager, AZ 85925.

Wildcat Country Beam Bottle & Spec. Club—2601 S. Blackmoon Drive, Tucson, AZ 85730, (602) 298-5943.

ARKANSAS

Fort Smith Area Bottle Collectors Assn.—2201 S. 73rd Street, Ft. Smith, AR 72903.

Hempsted County Bottle Club—710 S. Hervey, Hope, AR 71801.

Little Rock Antique Bottle Collectors Club—12 Martin Drive, North Little Rock, AR 72118, (501) 753-2623.

Madison County Bottle Collectors Club—Rt. 2, Box 304, Huntsville, AR 72740.

Razorback Jim Beam Bottle & Spec. Club—2609 S. Taylor, Little Rock, AR 72204, (501) 664-1335.

Southwest Arkansas Bottle Club—Star Route, Delight, AR 71940.

CALIFORNIA

Amethyst Bottle Club—3245 Military Avenue, Los Angeles, CA 90034.

Antique Bottle Club Association of Fresno—P.O. Box 1932, Fresno, CA 93718.

Antique Bottle Collectors of Orange County—223 E. Pomona, Santa Ana, CA 92707.

A-OK Beamers—7650 Balboa Boulevard, Van Nuys, CA 91406, (213) 787-2674.

Argonaut Jim Beam Bottle Club—8253 Citadel Way, Sacramento, CA 95826, (916) 383-0206.

Avon Bottle & Specialties Collectors—Southern California Division, 9233 Mills Avenue, Montclair, CA 91763.

Bay Area Vagabonds Jim Beam Club—224 Castleton Way, San Bruno, CA 94066, (415) 355-4356.

Beach Cities Beamers—3111 Highland Avenue, Manhattan Beach, CA 90266.

Beam Bottle Club of Southern California—3221 N. Jackson, Rosemead, CA 91770.

Beaming Beamers Jim Beam Bottle & Spec. Club—3734 Lynhurst Way, North Highlands, CA 95660, (916) 482-0359.

Beam's Orange County Bottle & Spec. Club—1516 E. Harmony Lane, Fullerton, CA 92631, (714) 526-5137.

Bidwell Bottle Club—Box 546, Chico, CA 95926.

Bishop Belles & Beaux Bottle Club—P.O. Box 1475, Bishop, CA 93514.

Blossom Valley Jim Beam Bottle & Spec. Club—431 Grey Ghost Avenue, San Jose, CA 95111, (408) 227-2759.

Bodfish Beamers Jim Beam Bottle Club—19 Dow Drive, P.O. Box 864-A, Bodfish, CA 93205, (714) 379-3280.

California Ski Country Bottle Club—212 South El Molino Street, Alhambra, CA 91801.

Camellia City Jim Beam Bottle Club—3734 Lynhurst Way, North Highlands, CA 95660.

Central Calif. Avon Bottle & Collectible Club—P.O. Box 232, Amador City, CA 95601.

Cherry Valley Beam Bottle & Specialty Club—6851 Hood Drive, Westminster, CA 92683.

Chief Solano Bottle Club—4-D Boynton Avenue, Sulsun, CA 94585.

Curiosity Bottle Association—Box 103, Napa, CA 94558.

Fiesta City Beamers—329 Mountain Drive, Santa Barbara, CA 93103.

First Double Springs Collectors Club—13311 Illinois Street, Westminster, CA 92683.

Five Cities Beamers—756 Mesa View Drive, Sp. 57, Arroyo Grande, CA 93420.

Fresno Raisin Beamers—3850 E. Ashian #A, Fresno, CA 93726, (209) 224-3086.

Glass Belles of San Gabriel—518 W. Neuby Avenue, San Gabriel, CA 91776.

Glasshopper Figural Bottle Association—P.O. Box 6642, Torrance, CA 90504.

Golden Bear Ezra Brooks Bottle Club—8808 Capricorn Way, San Diego, CA 92126.

Golden Bear Jim Beam Bottle & Specialty Club—8808 Capricorn Way, San Diego, CA 92126.

Golden Gate Beam Club—35113 Clover Street, Union City, CA 94587, (415) 487-4479.

Greater Cal. Antique Bottle Collectors—P.O. Box 55, Sacramento, CA 95801.

Grizzly Guzzlers Jim Beam Bottle Club—40080 Francis Way, P.O. Box 3725, Big Bear Lake, CA 92351.

High Desert Bottle Hunters—P.O. Box 581, Ridgecrest, CA 93558.

Highland Toasters Beam Bottle & Spec. Club—1570 E. Marshall, San Bernardino, CA 92404, (714) 883-2000.

Hoffman's Mr. Lucky Bottle Club—2104 Rhoda Street, Simi Valley, CA 93065.

Hollywood Stars Ezra Brooks Bottle Club—2200 N. Beachwood Drive, Hollywood, CA 90028.

Humboldt Antique Bottle Club—P.O. Box 6012, Eureka, CA 95501.

Jewels of Avon—2297 Maple Avenue, Oroville, CA 95965.

Jim Beam Bottle Club—139 Arlington, Berkeley, CA 94707.

Jim Beam Bottle Club of So. Calif.—1114 Coronado Terrace, Los Angeles, CA 90066.

Juniper Hills Bottle Club—Rt. 1, Box 18, Valyerma, CA 93563.

Kern County Antique Bottle Club—P.O. Box 6724, Bakersfield, CA 93306.

Lilliputian Bottle Club—13271 Clinton St., Garden Grove, CA 92643.

Lionstone Bottle Collectors of America—P.O. Box 75924, Los Angeles, CA 90075.

Livermore Avon Club—6385 Claremont Avenue, Richmond, CA 94805.

Lodi Jim Beam Bottle Club—429 E. Lodi Avenue, Lodi, CA 95240.

Los Angeles Historical Bottle Club—P.O. Box 60762, Terminal Annex, Los Angeles, CA 90060, (213) 332-6751.

Mission Bells (Beams)—1114 Coronada Terrace, Los Angeles, CA 90026.

Mission Tesore Jim Beam Bottle & Spec. Club—7701 E. Zayante Road, Felton, CA 95018, (408) 335-4317.

Mission Trail Historical Bottle Club—P.O. Box 721, Seaside, CA 93955, (408) 394-3257.

Mission Trails Ezra Brooks Bottles & Specialties Club, Inc.—4923 Bel Canto Drive, San Jose, CA 95124.

Modesto Beamers—1429 Glenwood Drive, Modesto, CA 95350, (209) 523-3440.

Modesto Old Bottle Club (MOBC)—P.O. Box 1791, Modesto, CA 95354.

Monterey Bay Beam Bottle & Specialty Club—P.O. Box 258, Freedom, CA 95019.

Motherlode Bottle Club—P.O. Box 337, Angels Camp, CA 95222.

M. T. Bottle Club—P.O. Box 608, Solana Beach, CA 92075.

Mt. Bottle Club—422 Orpheus, Encinitas, CA 92024.

Mt. Diablo Bottle Club—4166 Sandra Circle, Pittsburg, CA 94565.

Mt. Diablo Bottle Society—1699 Laguna #110, Concord, CA 94520.

Mt. Whitney Bottle Club—P.O. Box 688, Lone Pine, CA 93545.

Napa-Solano Bottle Club—1409 Delwood, Vallejo, CA 94590.

National Jim Beam Bottle & Spec. Club—5005 Cochrane Avenue, Oakland, CA 94618, (415) 655-5005.

Northern California Jim Beam Bottle & Specialty Club—P.O. Box 186, Montgomery Creek, CA 96065.

Northwestern Bottle Club—P.O. Box 1121, Santa Rosa, CA 95402.

Northwestern Bottle Collectors Association—1 Keeler Street, Petaluma, CA 94952.

Ocean Breeze Beamers—4841 Tacayme Drive, Oceanside, CA 92054, (714) 757-9081.

Original Sippin Cousins Ezra Brooks Specialties Club—12206 Malone Street, Los Angeles, CA 90066.

Palomar Jim Beam Club—246 S. Las Posas, P.O. Box 125, San Marcos, CA 92069, (714) 744-2924.

Pebble Beach Jim Beam Bottle Club—419 Alvarado Street, Monterey, CA 93940, (408) 373-5320.

Peninsula Bottle Club—P.O. Box 886, Belmont, CA 94002.

Petaluma Bottle & Antique Club—P.O. Box 1035, Petaluma, CA 94952.

Quail Country Jim Beam Bottle & Spec. Club—625 Pleasant, Coalinga, CA 93210.

Queen Mary Beam & Specialty Club—P.O. Box 2054, Anaheim, CA 92804.

Relic Accumulators—P.O. Box 3513, Eureka, CA 95501.

Santa Barbara Beam Bottle Club—5307 University Drive, Santa Barbara, CA 93111.

Santa Barbara Bottle Club—P.O. Box 30171, Santa Barbara, CA 93105.

San Bernardino County Historical Bottle and Collectible Club—P.O. Box 127, Bloomington, CA 92316.

San Diego Antique Bottle Club—P.O. Box 536, San Diego, CA 92112.

San Diego Jim Beam Bottle Club—2620 Mission Village Drive, San Diego, CA 92112.

San Francisco Bay Area Miniature Bottle Club—160 Lower Via Casitas #8, Kentfield, CA 94904.

San Joaquin Valley Jim Beam Bottle & Specialties Club—4085 N. Wilson Avenue, Fresno, CA 93704.

San Jose Antique Bottle Collectors' Assn.—P.O. Box 5432, San Jose, CA 95159.

San Luis Obispo Antique Bottle Club—124-21 Street, Paso Robles, CA 93446.

Santa Maria Beam & Spec. Club—528 E. Harding, Santa Maria, CA 93454, (805) 922-1238.

Sequoia Antique Bottle Society—P.O. Box 3695, Visalia, CA 93278, (209) 686-1873.

Shasta Antique Bottle Collectors Association—Rt. 1, Box 3147-A, Anderson, CA 96007.

Sierra Gold Ski Country Bottle Club—5081 Rio Vista Avenue, San Jose, CA 95129.

Ski-Country Bottle Club of Southern California—3148 N. Walnut Grove, Rosemead, CA 91770.

Solar Country Beamers—940 Kelly Drive, Barstow, CA 92311, (714) 256-1485.

South Bay Antique Bottle Club—2589½ Valley Drive, Manhattan Beach, CA 90266.

Southern California Miniature Bottle Club—5626 Corning Avenue, Los Angeles, CA 90056.

Southwestern Wyoming Avon Bottle Club—301 Canyon Highlands Drive, Oroville, CA 95965.

Stockton Historical Bottle Society, Inc.—P.O. Box 8584, Stockton, CA 95204.

Sunnyvale Antique Bottle Collectors Association—613 Torrington, Sunnyvale, CA 94087.

Superior California Bottle Club—P.O. Box 555, Anderson, CA 96007.

Taft Antique Bottle Club—P.O. Box 334, Taft, CA 93268.

Teen Bottle Club—Rt. 1, Box 60-TE, Eureka, CA 95501.

Tehama County Antique Bottle Club—Rt. 1, Box 775, Red Bluff, CA 96080, (916) 527-1680.

Tinseltown Beam Club—4117 E. Gage Avenue, Bell, CA 90201, (213) 699-8787.

Western World Collectors Assn.—P.O. Box 409, Ontario, CA 91761, (714) 984-0614.

Wildwind Jim Beam Bottle & Specialties Club—905 Eaton Way, Sunnyvale, CA 94087, (408) 739-1558.

World Wide Avon Collectors Club—44021 Seventh Street, E. Lancaster, CA 93534, (805) 948-8849.

COLORADO

Alamosa Bottle Collectors—Rt. 2, Box 170, Alamosa, CO 81101.

Avon Club of Colorado Springs, CO—707 N. Farragut, Colorado Springs, CO 80909.

Colorado Mile-High Ezra Brooks Bottle Club—7401 Decatur Street, Westminster, CO 80030.

Foot-Hills Jim Beam Bottle & Spec. Club—1303 Kilkenny Street, Boulder, CO 80303, (303) 665-3957.

Four Corners Bottle & Glass Club—P.O. Box 45, Cortez, CO 81321.

Horsetooth Antique Bottle Collectors, Inc.—P.O. Box 944, Ft. Collins, CO 80521.

Lionstone Western Figural Club—P.O. Box 2275, Colorado Springs, CO 80901.

Mile-Hi Jim Beam Bottle & Spec. Club—13196 W. Green Mountain Drive, Lakewood, CO 80228, (303) 986-6828.

National Ski Country Bottle Club—1224 Washington Avenue, Golden, CO 80401, (303) 279-3373, (800) 792-6452.

Northeastern Colorado Antique Bottle Club—P.O. Box 634, Ft. Morgan, CO 80701.

Northern Colorado Antique Bottle Club—227 W. Beaver Avenue, Ft. Morgan, CO 80701.

Northern Colorado Beam Bottle & Spec. Club—3272 Gunnison Drive, Ft. Collins, CO 80526, (303) 226-2301.

Ole Foxie Jim Beam Club—P.O. Box 560, Westminster, CO 80020.

Peaks & Plains Antique Bottle Club—P.O. Box 814, Colorado Springs, CO 80901.

Rocky Mountain Jim Beam Bottle & Specialty Club—Alcott Station, P.O. Box 12162, Denver, CO 80212.

Telluride Antique Bottle Collectors—P.O. Box 344, Telluride, CO.

Western Figural & Jim Beam Specialty Club—P.O. Box 4331, Colorado Springs, CO 80930.

CONNECTICUT

Connecticut Specialty Bottle Club, Inc.—P.O. Box 624, Stratford, CT.

The Milk Route—4 Ox Bow Road, Westport, CT 06880.

Somers Antique Bottle Club—P.O. Box 373, Somers, CT 06071, (203) 487-1071.

Southern Connecticut Antique Bottle Collectors Association, Inc.—Ole Severson, 34 Dartmouth Drive, Huntington, CT 06484, (203) 929-5197.

Western Connecticut Jim Beam Bottle & Spec. Club—Rt. 1, Box 442, Old Hawleyville Road, Bethel, CT 06801, (203) 744-6118.

DELAWARE

Blue Hen Jim Beam Bottle & Spec. Club—303 Potomac Drive, Wilmington, DE 19803, (302) 652-6378.

Mason-Dixon Bottle Collectors Association—P.O. Box 505, Lewes, DE 19958.

Tri-State Bottle Collectors and Diggers Club—730 Paper Mill Road, Newark, DE 19711.

FLORIDA

Antique Bottle Collectors Assn. of Florida—5901 S.W. 16th Street, Miami, FL 33144, (305) 266-4854.

Antique Bottle Collectors of Florida, Inc.—2512 Davie Boulevard, Ft. Lauderdale, FL 33312.

Antique Bottle Collectors of North Florida—P.O. Box 380022, Jacksonville, FL 32205-9266, (904) 284-1499.

Bay Area Historical Bottle Collectors—P.O. Box 3454, Apollo Beach, FL 33570.

Central Florida Insulator Collectors Club—3557 Nicklaus Drive, Titusville, FL 32780, (305) 267-9170.

Central Florida Jim Beam Bottle Club—1060 W. French Avenue, Orange City, FL 32763, (904) 775-7392.

Crossarms Collectors Club—1756 N.W. 58th Avenue, Lauderhill, FL 33313.

Deep South Jim Beam Bottle & Spec. Club—16100 S.W. 278th Street, Homestead, FL 33031, (305) 248-7301.

Everglades A.B.C.—6981 S.W. 19th Street, Pompano, FL 33068.

Everglades Antique Bottle & Collectors Club—400 S. 57 Terrace, Hollywood, FL 33023, (305) 962-3434.

Florida Association of Antique Bottle Collectors—P.O. Box 3105, Sarasota, FL 33579, (941-6550).

Florida Panhandle Jim Beam Bottle & Spec. Club—706 James Court, Ft. Walton Beach, FL 32548, (904) 862-3469.

Gateway of the Palms Beam Bottle & Spec. Club—6621 Katherine Road, West Palm Beach, FL 33406, (305) 683-3900.

Gold Coast Collectors Club—Joseph I. Frakes, P.O. Box 10183, Wilton Manors, FL 33305.

Halifax Historical Society—224$^1/_2$ S. Beach Street, Daytona Beach, FL 32018.

Harbor City Bottle Collectors Club—1232 Causeway, Eau, FL 32935.

Longwood Bottle Club—P.O. Box 437, Longwood, FL 32750.

Mid-State Antique Bottle Collectors—88 Sweetbriar Branch, Longwood, FL 32750, (407) 834-8914.

M. T. Bottle Collectors Assn., Inc.—P.O. Box 581, Deland, FL 32721.

Northwest Florida Regional Bottle Club—P.O. Box 282, Port St. Joe, FL 32456.

Original Florida Keys Collectors Club—P.O. Box 212, Islamorada, FL 33036.

Pensacola Bottle & Relic Collectors Association—1004 Freemont Avenue, Pensacola, FL 32505.

Ridge Area Antique Bottle Collectors—1219 Carlton, Lake Wales, FL 33853.

Sanford Antique A.B.C.—2656 Grandview Avenue, Sanford, FL 33853, (305) 322-7181.

Sarasota-Manatee A.B.C. Assn.—P.O. Box 3105, Sarasota, FL 34230, (941) 923-6550.

South Florida Jim Beam Bottle & Specialty Club—7741 N.W. 35th Street, West Hollywood, FL 33024.

Suncoast Antique Bottle Club—P.O. Box 12712, St. Petersburg, FL 33733.

Suncoast Jim Beam Bottle & Spec. Club—P.O. Box 5067, Sarasota, FL 33579.

Tampa Antique Bottle Collectors—P.O. Box 4232, Tampa, FL 33607.

West Coast Florida Ezra Brooks Bottle Club—1360 Harbor Drive, Sarasota, FL 33579.

GEORGIA

Bulldog Double Springs Bottle Collector Club of Augusta, Georgia—1916 Melrose Drive, Augusta, GA 30906.

Coastal Empire Bottle Club—P.O. Box 3714, Station B, Savannah, GA 31404.

The Desoto Trail Bottle Collectors Club—406 Randolph Street, Cuthbert, GA 31740.

Flint Antique Bottle & Coin Club—c/o Cordele-Crisp Co., Recreation Department, 204 2nd Street North, Cordele, GA 31015.

Flint River Jim Beam Bottle Club—Rt. 3, P.O. Box 6, Camilla, GA 31730, (912) 336-7034.

Georgia Bottle Club—2996 Pangborn Road, Decatur, GA 30033.

Georgia-Carolina Empty Bottle Club—P.O. Box 1184, Augusta, GA 30903.

Macon Antique Bottle Club—P.O. Box 5395, Macon, GA 31208.

Macon Antique Bottle Club—c/o 5532 Jane Run Circle, Macon, GA 31206.

The Middle Georgia Antique Bottle Club—2746 Alden Street, Macon, GA 31206.

Peachstate Bottle & Specialty Club—5040 Vallo Vista Court, Atlanta, GA 30342.

Peachtree Jim Beam Bottlers Club—224 Lakeshore Drive, Daluth, GA 30136, (404) 448-9013.

Peanut State Jim Beam Bottle & Spec. Club—767 Timberland Street, Smyrna, GA 30080, (404) 432-8482.

Southeastern Antique Bottle Club—P.O. Box 657, Decatur, GA 30033.

HAWAII

Hauoli Beam Bottle Collectors Club of Hawaii—45-027 Ka-Hanahou Place, Kaneohe, HI 96744.

Hawaii Bottle Collectors Club—6770 Hawaii Kai Drive, Apt. 708, Hawaii Kai, HI 96825.

IDAHO

Buhl Antique Bottle Club—500 12th, N. Buhl, ID 83316.

Eagle Rock Beam & Spec. Club—3665 Upland Avenue, Idaho Falls, ID 83401, (208) 522-7819.

Em Tee Bottle Club—P.O. Box 62, Jerome, ID 83338.

Fabulous Valley Antique Bottle Club—P.O. Box 769, Osburn, ID 83849.

Gem Antique Bottle Collectors Assn., Inc.—P.O. Box 8051, Boise, ID 83707.

Idaho Beam & Spec. Club—2312 Burrell Avenue, Lewiston, ID 83501, (208) 743-5997.

Idaho Bottle Collectors Association—4530 S. 5th Street, Pocatello, ID 83201.

Inland Empire Jim Beam Bottle & Collectors' Club—1117 10th Street, Lewiston, ID 83501.

Rock & Bottle Club—Rt. 1, Fruitland, ID 83619.

Treasure Valley Beam Bottle & Spec. Club—2324 Norcrest Drive, Boise, ID 83705, (208) 343-6207.

ILLINOIS

A.B.C. of Northern Illinois—P.O. Box 571, Lake Geneva, WI 53147.

Alton Area Bottle Club—2448 Alby Street, Alton, IL, (618) 462-4285.

Blackhawk Jim Beam Bottle & Specialties Club—2003 Kishwaukee Street, Rockford, IL 61101.

Central Illinois Jim Beam Bottle & Spec. Club—3725 S. Sand Creek Road, Decatur, IL 62521.

Central & Midwestern States Beam & Specialties Club—44 S. Westmore, Lombard, IL 60148.

Chicago Ezra Brooks Bottle & Specialty Club—3635 W. 82nd Street, Chicago, IL 60652.

Chicago Jim Beam Bottle & Specialty Club—1305 W. Marion Street, Joliet, IL 60436.

Dreamer Beamers—5721 Vial Parkway, LaGrange, IL 60525, (312) 246-4838.

Eagle Jim Beam Bottle & Spec. Club—1015 Hollycrest, P.O. Box 2084 CFS, Champaign, IL 61820, (217) 352-4035.

1st Chicago A.B.C.—P.O. Box A-3382, Chicago, IL 60690, (708) 945-5493.

Heart of Illinois Antique Bottle Club—2010 Bloomington Road, East Peoria, IL 61611.

Illini Jim Beam Bottle & Specialty Club—P.O. Box 13, Champaign, IL 61820.

Illinois Bottle Club—P.O. Box 181, Rushville, IL 62681.

International Association of Jim Beam—4338 Saratoga Avenue, Down Grove, IL 60515.

Kelly Club—147 North Brainard Avenue, La Grange, IL 60525.

Land of Lincoln Bottle Club—2515 Illinois Circle, Decatur, IL 62526.

Lewis & Clark Jim Beam Bottle & Specialty Club—P.O. Box 451, Wood River, IL 62095.

Lionstone Bottle Collectors of America—P.O. Box 2418, Chicago, IL 60690.

Little Egypt Jim Beam Bottle & Spec. Club—Rt. 2, Flat Rock, IL 62427, (618) 584-3338.

Louis Joliet Bottle Club—12 Kenmore, Joliet, IL 60433.

Metro East Bottle & Jar Association—309 Bellevue Drive, Belleville, IL 62223, (618) 233-8841.

Metro East Bottle & Jar Association—1702 North Keesler, Collinsville, IL 62234.

Metro East Bottle & Jar Association—P.O. Box 185, Mascoutah, IL 62234.

National Ezra Brooks Club—645 N. Michigan Avenue, Chicago, IL 69611.

North Shore Jim Beam Bottle & Spec. Club—542 Glendale Road, Glenview, IL 60025.

Pekin Bottle Collectors Assn.—P.O. Box 372, Pekin, IL 61554, (309) 347-4441.

Rock River Valley Jim Beam Bottle & Spec. Club—1107 Avenue A., Rock Falls, IL 61071, (815) 625-7075.

Starved Rock Jim Beam Bottle & Spec. Club—P.O. Box 177, Ottawa, IL 61350, (815) 433-3269.

Sweet Corn Capital Bottle Club—1015 W. Orange, Hoopeston, IL 60942.

Tri-County Jim Beam Bottle Club—3702 W. Lancer Road, Peoria, IL 61615, (309) 691-8784.

INDIANA

City of Bridges Jim Beam Bottle & Spec. Club—1017 N. 6th Street, Logansport, IN 46947, (219) 722-3197.

Crossroads of America Jim Beam Bottle Club—114 S. Green Street, Brownsburg, IN 46112, (317) 852-5168.

Fort Wayne Historical Bottle Club—5124 Roberta Drive, Fort Wayne, IN 46306.

Hoosier Jim Beam Bottle & Specialties Club—P.O. Box 24234, Indianapolis, IN 46224.

Indiana Ezra Brooks Bottle Club—P.O. Box 24344, Indianapolis, IN 46224.

Lafayette Antique Bottle Club—3664 Redondo Drive, Lafayette, IN 47905.

Michiana Jim Beam Bottle & Specialty Club—58955 Locust Road, South Bend, IN 46614.

Mid-West Antique Fruit Jar & Bottle Club—P.O. Box 38, Flat Rock, IN 47234, (812) 587-5560.

The Ohio Valley Antique Bottle and Jar Club—214 John Street, Aurora, IN 47001.

Steel City Ezra Brooks Bottle Club—Rt. 2, Box 32A, Valparaiso, IN 46383.

Three Rivers Jim Beam Bottle & Spec. Club—Rt. 4, Winchester Road, Ft. Wayne, IN 46819, (219) 639-3041.

We Found 'Em Bottle & Insulator Club—P.O. Box 578, Bunker Hill, IN 46914.

IOWA

Five Seasons Beam & Spec. Club of Iowa—609 32nd Street, NE, Cedar Rapids, IA 52402, (319) 365-6089.

Gold Dome Jim Beam Bottle & Spec. Club—2616 Hull, Des Moines, IA 50317, (515) 262-8728.

Hawkeye Jim Beam Bottle Club—658 Kern Street, Waterloo, IA 60703, (319) 233-9168.

Iowa Antique Bottlers—1506 Albia Road, Ottumwa, IA 52501, (319) 377-6041.

Iowa Great Lakes Jim Beam Bottle & Spec. Club—Green Acres Mobile Park, Lot 88, Estherville, IA 51334, (712) 362-2759.

Larkin Bottle Club—107 W. Grimes, Red Oak, IA 51566.

Midlands Jim Beam Bottle & Spec. Club—Rt. 4, Harlan, IA 51537, (712) 744-3686.

Quad Cities Jim Beam Bottle & Spec. Club—2425 W. 46th Street, Davenport, IA 52806, (319) 391-4319.

Shot Tower Beam Club—284 N. Booth Street, Dubuque, IA 52001, (319) 583-6343.

KANSAS

Air Capital City Jim Beam Bottle & Spec. Club—3256 Euclid, Wichita, KS 67217, (316) 942-3162.

Bud Hastin's National Avon Collector's Club—P.O. Box 12088, Overland Park, KS 66212.

Cherokee Strip Ezra Brooks Bottle & Specialty Club—P.O. Box 63, Arkansas City, KS 67005.

Flint Hills Beam & Specialty Club—201 W. Pine, El Dorado, KS 67042.

Jayhawk Bottle Club—7919 Grant, Overland Park, KS 66212.

Kansas City Antique Bottle Collectors—5528 Aberdeen, Shawnee Mission, KS 66205, (816) 433-1398.

Southeast Kansas Bottle & Relics Club—115 N. Lafayette, Chanute, KS 66720, (316) 431-1643.

Walnut Valley Jim Beam Bottle & Spec. Club—P.O. Box 631, Arkansas City, KS 67005, (316) 442-0509.

Wichita Ezra Brooks Bottle & Specialties Club—8045 Peachtree Street, Wichita, KS 67207.

KENTUCKY

Derby City Jim Beam Bottle Club—4105 Spring Hill Road, Louisville, KY 40207.

Gold City Jim Beam Bottle Club—286 Metts Court, Apt. 4, Elizabethtown, KY 42701, (502) 737-9297.

Kentuckiana A.B. & Outhouse Society—5801 River Knolls Drive, Louisville, KY 40222.

Kentucky Bluegrass Ezra Brooks Bottle Club—6202 Tabor Drive, Louisville, KY 40218.

Kentucky Cardinal Beam Bottle Club—428 Templin, Bardstown, KY 41104.

Land by the Lakes Beam Club—Rt. 6, Box 320, Cadiz, KY 42211, (502) 522-8445.

Louisville Bottle Collectors—11819 Garrs Avenue, Anchorage, KY 40223.

Pegasus Jim Beam Bottle & Spec. Club—9405 Cornflower Road, Valley Station, KY 40272, (502) 937-4376.

LOUISIANA

Ark-La-Tex Jim Beam Bottle & Spec. Club—1902 Carol Street, Bossier City, LA 71112, (318) 742-3550.

Bayou Bottle Bugs—216 Dahlia, New Iberia, LA 70560.

"Cajun Country Cousins" Ezra Brooks Bottle & Specialties Club—1000 Chevis Street, Abbeville, LA 70510.

Cenia Bottle Club—c/o Pam Tullos, Rt. 1, Box 463, Dry Prong, LA 71423.

Crescent City Jim Beam Bottle & Spec. Club—733 Wright Avenue, Gretna, LA 70053, (504) 367-2182.

Dixie Diggers Bottle Club—P.O. Box 626, Empire, LA 70050.

Historical Bottle Association of Baton Rouge—1843 Tudor Drive, Baton Rouge, LA 70815.

Ken Tally Jim Beam Bottle Club—110 Ken Tally Estates, Hammond, LA 70401, (504) 345-6186.

New Albany Glass Works Bottle Club—732 N. Clark Boulevard, Parksville, LA 47130.

New Orleans Antique Bottle Club—c/o Ralph J. Luther, Jr., 4336 Palmyra Street, New Orleans, LA 70119.

North East Louisiana A.B.C.—P.O. Box 4192, Monroe, LA 71291, (318) 322-8359.

Red Stick Jim Beam Bottle Club—2127 Beaumont, Suite 4, Baton Rouge, LA 70806.

Sanford's Night Owl Beamers—Rt. 2, Box 102, Greenwell Springs, LA 70739, (504) 261-3658.

Shreveport Antique Bottle Club—1157 Arncliffe Drive, Shreveport, LA 71107, (504) 221-0089.

MAINE

Dirigo Bottle Collectors Club—R.F.D. 3, Dexter, ME, 04473, (207) 924-3443.

Dover Foxcroft Bottle Club—50 Church Street, Dover Foxcroft, ME 04426.

The Glass Bubble Bottle Club—P.O. Box 91, Cape Neddick, ME 03902.

Jim Beam Collectors Club—10 Lunt Road, Falmouth, ME 04105.

Kennebec Valley Bottle Club—9 Glenwood Street, Augusta, ME 04330.

Mid-Coast Bottle Club—c/o Miriam Winchenbach, Waldoboro, ME 04572.

New England Bottle Club—45 Bolt Hill Road, Eliot, ME 03903.

Paul Bunyan Bottle Club—237 14th Street, Bangor, ME 04401.

Pine Tree Antique Bottle Club—Buxton Road, Saco, ME 04072.

Pine Tree State Beamers—15 Woodside Avenue, Saco, ME 04072, (207) 284-8756.

Tri-County Bottle Collectors Association—R.F.D. 3, Dexter, ME 04930.

Waldo County Bottlenecks Club—Head-of-the-Tide, Belfast, ME 04915.

MARYLAND

Antique Bottle Club of Baltimore—c/o Fred Parks, 10 S. Linwood Avenue, Baltimore, MD 21224, (301) 732-2404.

Blue & Gray Ezra Brooks Bottle Club—2106 Sunnybrook Drive, Frederick, MD 21201.

Catoctin Jim Beam Bottle Club—c/o Ron Danner, 1 North Chatham Road, Ellicott City, MD 21063, (410) 465-5773.

Mason Dixon Bottle Collectors Association—601 Market Street, Denton, MD 21629.

Mid-Atlantic Miniature Whiskey Bottle Club—208 Gloucester Drive, Glen Burnie, MD 21061, (410) 766-8421.

South County Bottle Collector's Club—Bast Lane, Shady Side, MD 20867.

MASSACHUSETTS

Baystate Beamers Bottle & Spec. Club—27 Brookhaven Drive, Ludlow, MA 01056, (413) 589-0446.

Berkshire Antique Bottle Assoc.—R.D. 1, West Stockbridge, MA 01266.

The Cape Cod Antique Bottle Club—c/o Mrs. John Swanson, 262 Setucket Road, Yarmouth, MA 02675.

Merrimack Valley Antique Bottle Club—c/o M. E. Tarleton, Hillside Road, Boxford, MA 02675.

New England Beam & Specialty Club—1104 Northampton Street, Holyoke, MA 01040.

Scituate Bottle Club—54 Cedarwood Road, Scituate, MA 02066.

Yankee Pole Cat Insulator Club—105 Richards Avenue, North Attleboro, MA 02760.

MICHIGAN

Central Michigan Krazy Korkers Bottle Club—Mid-Michigan Community College, Clare Avenue, Harrison, MI 48625.

Chief Pontiac Antique Bottle Club—13880 Neal Road, Davisburg, MI 48019, c/o Larry Blascyk, (313) 634-8469.

Dickinson County Bottle Club—717 Henford Avenue, Iron Mountain, MI 49801.

Flint Antique Bottle Collectors Association—450 Leta Avenue, Flint, MI 48507.

Flint Eagles Ezra Brooks Club—1117 W. Remington Avenue, Flint, MI 48507.

Grand Valley Bottle Club—31 Dickinson S.W., Grand Rapids, MI 49507.

Great Lakes Jim Beam Bottle Club of Michigan—1010 South Harvey, Plymouth, MI 48170, (313) 453-0579.

Great Lakes Miniature Bottle Club—P.O. Box 245, Fairhaven, MI 48023.

Huron Valley Bottle Club—2475 West Walton Blvd., Waterford, MI 48329-4435, (810) 673-1650.

Lionstone Collectors Bottle & Specialties Club of Michigan—3089 Grand Blanc Road, Swartz Creek, MI 48473.

Manistee Coin & Bottle Club—207 E. Piney Road, Manistee, MI 49660.

Metro & East Bottle and Jar Assn.—309 Bellevue Park Drive, Fairview Heights, MI 49660.

Michigan Bottle Collectors Association—144 W. Clark Street, Jackson, MI 49203.

Michigan's Vehicle City Beam Bottles & Specialties Club—907 Root Street, Flint, MI 48503.

Mid-Michee Pine Beam Club—609 Webb Drive, Bay City, MI 48706.

Northern Michigan Bottle Club—P.O. Box 421, Petoskey, MI 49770.

Old Corkers Bottle Club—Rt. 1, Iron River, MI 49935.

Red Run Jim Beam Bottle & Spec. Club—172 Jones Street, Mt. Clemens, MI 48043, (313) 465-4883.

Traverse Area Bottle & Insulator Club—P.O. Box 205, Acme, MI 49610.

West Michigan Avon Collectors—331 Bellevue S.W., Wyoming, MI 49508.

W.M.R.A.C.C.—331 Bellevue S.W., Grand Rapids, MI 49508.

Wolverine Beam Bottle & Specialty Club of Michigan—36009 Larchwood, Mt. Clemens, MI 48043.

World Wide Avon Bottle Collectors Club—22708 Wick Road, Taylor, MI 48180.

Ye Old Corkers—c/o Janet Gallup, Box 7, Gastr, MI 49927.

MINNESOTA

Arnfalt Collectors Beam Club—New Richard, MN 56072.

Dump Diggers—P.O. Box 24, Dover, MN 55929.

Gopher State Jim Beam Bottle & Spec. Club—1216 Sheridan Avenue N., Minneapolis, MN 55411, (612) 521-4150.

Heartland Jim Beam Bottle & Spec. Club—Box 633, 245 Elm Drive, Foley, MN 56329, (612) 968-6767.

Hey! Rube Jim Beam Bottle Club—1506 6th Avenue N.E., Austin, MN 55912, (507) 433-6939.

Lake Superior Antique Bottle Club—P.O. Box 67, Knife River, MN 55609.

Minnesota's First Antique B.C.—5001 Queen Avenue, N. Minneapolis, MN 55430.

Paul Bunyan Jim Beam Bottle & Spec. Club—Rt. 8, Box 656, Bemidji, MN 56601, (218) 751-6635.

Truman, Minnesota Jim Beam Bottle & Spec. Club—Truman, MN 56088, (507) 776-3487.

Viking Jim Beam Bottle & Spec. Club—8224 Oxborough Avenue S., Bloomington, MN 55437, (612) 831-2303.

MISSISSIPPI

Gum Tree Beam Bottle Club—104 Ford Circle, Tupelo, MS 38801.

Magnolia Beam Bottle & Spec. Club—2918 Larchmont, Jackson, MS 39209, (601) 354-1350.

Middle Mississippi Antique Bottle Club—P.O. Box 233, Jackson, MS 39205.

Oxford Antique Bottlers—128 Vivian Street, Oxford, MS 38633.

South Mississippi Antique Bottle Club—203 S. 4th Avenue, Laurel, MS 39440.

South Mississippi Historical Bottle Club—165 Belvedere Drive, Biloxi, MS, 388-6472.

MISSOURI

A.B.C. of Central Missouri—726 W. Monroe, Mexico, MO 65265, (314) 581-1391.

Antique Bottle & Relic Club of Central Missouri—c/o Ann Downing, Rt. 10, Columbia, MO 65210.

Arnold, Missouri Jim Beam Bottle & Spec. Club—1861 Jean Drive, Arnold, MO 63010, (314) 296-0813.

Barnhart, Missouri Jim Beam Bottle & Spec. Club—2150 Cathlin Court, Barnhart, MO 63012.

Bud Hastin's National Avon Club—P.O. Box 9868, Kansas City, MO 64134.

Chesterfield Jim Beam Bottle & Spec. Club—2066 Honey Ridge, Chesterfield, MO 63017.

"Down in the Valley" Jim Beam Bottle Club—528 St. Louis Avenue, Valley Park, MO 63088.

The Federation of Historical Bottle Clubs—10118 Schuessler, St. Louis, MO 63128, (314) 843-7573.

Festus, Missouri Jim Beam Bottle & Spec. Club—Rt. 3, Box 117H, Frederick Road, Festus, MO 63028.

First Capital Jim Beam Bottle & Spec. Club—731 McDonough, St. Charles, MO 63301.

Florissant Valley Jim Beam Bottles & Spec. Club—25 Cortez, Florissant, MO 63031.

Greater Kansas City Jim Beam Bottle & Speciality Club—P.O. Box 6703, Kansas City, MO 64123.

Kansas City Antique Bottle Collectors Association—1131 E. 77 Street, Kansas City, MO 64131.

Maryland Heights Jim Beam Bottle & Spec. Club—2365 Wesford, Maryland Heights, MO 63043.

Mineral Area Bottle Club—Knob Lick, MO 63651.

Missouri Arch Jim Beam Bottle & Spec. Club—2900 N. Lindbergh, St. Ann, MO 63074, (314) 739-0803.

Mound City Jim Beam Decanter Collectors—42 Webster Acres, Webster Groves, MO 63119.

North-East County Jim Beam Bottle & Spec. Club—10150 Baron Drive, St. Louis, MO 63136.

Northwest Missouri Bottle & Relic Club—3006 S. 28th Street, St. Joseph, MO 64503.

Rock Hill Jim Beam Bottle & Spec. Club—9731 Graystone Terrace, St. Louis, MO 63119, (314) 962-8125.

Sho Me Jim Beam Bottle & Spec. Club—Rt. 7, Box 314-D, Springfield, MO 65802, (417) 831-8093.

St. Charles, Mo. Jim Beam Bottle & Spec. Club—122 S. Cardinal, St. Charles, MO 63301.

St. Louis Ezra Books Ceramics Club—Webster Acres, Webster Grove, MO 63119.

St. Louis Jim Beam Bottle & Spec. Club—2900 Lindbergh St. Ann, MO 63074, (314) 291-3256.

Troy, Missouri Jim Beam Bottle & Spec. Club—121 E. Pershing, Troy, MO 63379, (314) 528-6287.

Valley Bank Park Jim Beam Bottle & Spec. Club—614 Benton Street, Valley Park, MO 63088.

Walnut Park Jim Beam Bottle & Spec. Club—5458 N. Euclid, St. Louis, MO 63114.

West County Jim Beam Bottle & Spec. Club—11707 Momarte Lane, St. Louis, MO 63141.

MONTANA

Hellgate Antique Bottle Club—P.O. Box 411, Missoula, MT 59801.

NEBRASKA

Cornhusker Jim Beam Bottle & Spec. Club—5204 S. 81st Street, Ralston, NE 68127, (402) 331-4646.

Mini-Seekers—"A" Acres, Rt. 8, Lincoln, NE 68506.

Nebraska Antique Bottle and Collectors Club—P.O. Box 37021, Omaha, NE 68137.

Nebraska Big Red Bottle & Specialty Club—N Street Drive-in, 200 S. 18th Street, Lincoln, NE 68508.

NEVADA

Jim Beam Bottle Club of Las Vegas—212 N. Orland Street, Las Vegas, NV 89107.

Las Vegas Bottle Club—3115 Las Vegas Boulevard N., Space 56, North Las Vegas, NV 89030, (702) 643-1101.

Las Vegas Bottle Club—884 Lulu Avenue, Las Vegas, NV 89119.

Lincoln County A.B.C.—P.O. Box 191, Calente, NV 89008, (702) 726-3655.

Nevada Beam Club—P.O. Box 426, Fallon, NV 89406.

Reno/Sparks A.B.C.—P.O. Box 1061, Verdi, NV 89439.

Southern Nevada Antique Bottle Club—431 N. Spruce Street, Las Vegas, NV 89101.

Virginia & Truckee Jim Beam Bottle & Specialties Club—P.O. Box 1596, Carson City, NV 89701.

Wee Bottle Club International—P.O. Box 1195, Las Vegas, NV 89101.

NEW HAMPSHIRE

Bottlers of New Hampshire—125A Central Street, Farmington, NH 03835.

Granite State Bottle Club—R.F.D. 1, Belmont, NH 03220.

Yankee Bottle Club—P.O. Box 702, Keene, NH 03431, (603) 352-2959.

NEW JERSEY

Antique Bottle Collectors Club of Burlington County—18 Willow Road, Bordentown, NJ 08505.

Artifact Hunters Association, Inc.—c/o 29 Lake Road, Wayne, NJ 07470.

The Jersey Devil Bottle Diggers Club—14 Church Street, Mt. Holly, NJ 08060.

Jersey Jackpot Jim Beam Bottle & Spec. Club—197 Farley Avenue, Fanwood, NJ 07023, (201) 322-7287.

The Jersey Shore Bottle Club—P.O. Box 995, Toms River, NJ 08753.

Jersey Shore Bottle Collectors—Box 95, Toms River, NJ 08753.

Lakeland A.B.C.—18 Alan Lane, Mine Hill, Dover, NJ 07801, (201) 366-7482.

Lionstone Collectors Club of Delaware Valley—R.D. 3, Box 93, Sewell, NJ 08080.

Meadowland Beamers—413 24th Street, Union City, NJ 07087, (201) 865-3684.

New Jersey Ezra Brooks Bottle Club—S. Main Street, Cedarville, NJ 08311.

South Jersey Heritage Bottle & Glass Club, Inc.—P.O. Box 122, Glassboro, NJ 08028, (609) 423-5038.

Sussex County Antique Bottle Collectors—Division of Sussex County Historical Society, 82 Main Street, Newton, NJ 07860.

Trenton Jim Beam Bottle Club, Inc.—17 Easy Street, Freehold, NJ 07728.

Twin Bridges Beam Bottle & Specialty Club—P.O. Box 347, Pennsville, NJ 08070.

West Essex Bottle Club—76 Beaufort Avenue, Livingston, NJ 07039.

NEW MEXICO

Cave City Antique Bottle Club—Rt. 1, Box 155, Carlsbad, NM 88220.

Roadrunner Bottle Club of New Mexico—2341 Gay Road S.W., Albuquerque, NM 87105.

NEW YORK

Auburn Bottle Club—297 S. Street Road, Auburn, NY 13021.

Big Apple Beamers Bottle & Spec. Club—2901 Long Branch Road, Oceanside, NY 11572, (516) 678-3414.

Catskill Mountains Jim Beam Bottle Club—6 Gardner Avenue, Middletown, NY 10940.

Chautauqua County Bottle Collectors Club—Morse Motel, Main Street, Sherman, NY 14781.

Eastern Monroe County Bottle Club—c/o Bethlehem Lutheran Church, 1767 Plank Road, Webster, NY 14580.

Empire State Bottle Collectors Association—c/o Bob Dicker, 22 Paris Rd., New Hartford, NY 13413.

Empire State Jim Beam Bottle Club—P.O. Box 561, Main Street, Farmingdale, NY 11735.

Finger Lakes Bottle Club Association—P.O. Box 815, Ithaca, NY 14850.

Genessee Valley Bottle Collectors Assn.—P.O. Box 7528, West Ridge Station, Rochester, NY 14615, (716) 872-4015.

Greater Catskill Antique Bottle Club—P.O. Box 411, Liberty, NY 12754.

Hudson River Jim Beam Bottle and Specialties Club—48 College Road, Monsey, NY 10952.

Long Island Antique Bottle Assoc.—P.O. Box 147, Bayport, NY 11705.

National Bottle Museum—c/o Marilyn Stephenson, Pres., 45 West High Street, Ballston Spa, NY 12020.

Niagra Frontier Beam Bottle & Spec. Club—17 Ravensbrook Court, Getzville, NY 14066, (716) 688-6624.

North Country Bottle Collectors Association—Rt. 1, Canton, NY 13617.

Rensselaer County Antique Bottle Club—P.O. Box 792, Troy, NY 12180.

Rochester New York Bottle Club—7908 West Henrietta Road, Rush, NY 14543.

Southern Tier Bottle & Insulator Collectors Association—47 Dickinson Avenue, Port Dickinson, NY 13901.

Suffolk County Antique Bottle Association of Coney Island, Inc.—P.O. Box 943, Melville, NY 11746.

Tryon Bottle Badgers—P.O. Box 146, Tribes Hill, NY 12177.

Twin Counties Old Bottle Club—Don McBride, Star Route, Box 242, Palenville, NY 12463, (518) 943-5399.

Upper Susquehanna Bottle Club—P.O. Box 183, Milford, NY 13807.

Warwick Valley Bottle Club—Box 393, Warwick, NY 10990.

West Valley Bottleique Club—Box 204, Killbuck, NY 14748, (716) 945-5769.

Western New York, B.C.A.—c/o 62 Adams Street, Jamestown, NY 14701, (716) 487-9645.

Western New York Bottle Collectors—87 S. Bristol Avenue, Lockport, NY 14094.

NORTH CAROLINA

Blue Ridge Bottle and Jar Club—Dogwood Lane, Black Mountain, NC 28711.

Carolina Bottle Club—c/o Industrial Piping Co., Anonwood, Charlotte, NC 28210.

Carolina Jim Bean Bottle Club—1014 N. Main Street, Burlington, NC 27215.

Catawba Valley Jim Beam Bottle & Spec. Club—265 5th Avenue, N.E., Hickory, NC 28601, (704) 322-5268.

Goldsboro Bottle Club—2406 E. Ash Street, Goldsboro, NC 27530.

Greater Greensboro Moose Ezra Brooks Bottle Club—217 S. Elm Street, Greensboro, NC 27401.

Kinston Collectors Club, Inc.—325 E. Lenoir, Kinston, NC 28501.

Pelican Sand Dunners Jim Beam Bottle & Spec. Club—Lot 17-J, Paradise Bay Mobile Home Park, P.O. Box 344, Salter Path, NC 28575, (919) 247-3290.

Tar Heel Jim Beam Bottle & Spec. Club—6615 Wake Forest Road, Fayetteville, NC 28301, (919) 488-4849.

Wilmington Bottle & Artifact Club—183 Arlington Drive, Wilmington, NC 28401, (919) 763-3701.

Wilson Antique Bottle & Artifact Club—Rt. 5, Box 414, Wilson, NC 27893.

Yadkin Valley Bottle Club—General Delivery, Gold Hill, NC 28071.

OHIO

Beam on the Lake Bottle & Spec. Club—9151 Mentor Avenue, F 15, Mentor, OH 44060, (216) 255-0320.

Buckeye Bottle Club—229 Oakwood Street, Elyria, OH 44035.

Buckeye Bottle Diggers—Rt. 2, P.O. Box 77, Thornville, OH 44035.

Buckeye Jim Beam Bottle Club—1211 Ashland Avenue, Columbus, OH 43212.

Carnation City Jim Beam Bottle Club—135 W. Virginia, Sebring, OH 44672, (216) 938-6817.

Central Ohio Bottle Club—931 Minerva Avenue, Columbus, OH 43229.

Diamond Pin Winners Avon Club—5281 Fredonia Avenue, Dayton, OH 45431.

The Federation of Historical Bottle Clubs—c/o Gary Beatty, Treasurer, 9326 Court Road 3C, Galion, OH 44833.

Findlay Antique Bottle Club—P.O. Box 1329, Findlay, OH 45840, (419) 422-3183.

First Capital B.C.—c/o Maxie Harper, Rt. 1, Box 94, Laurelville, OH 43135.

Gem City Beam Bottle Club—1463 E. Stroop Road, Dayton, OH 45429.

Greater Cleveland Jim Beam Club—5398 W. 147th Street, Brook Park, OH 44142, (216) 267-7665.

Heart of Ohio Bottle Club—P.O. Box 353, New Washington, OH 44854, (419) 492-2829.

Jeep City Beamers—531A Durango, Toledo, OH 43609, (419) 382-2515.

Jefferson County A.B.S.—1223 Oakgrove Avenue, Steubenville, OH 43952.

Lakeshore Beamers—2681 Douglas Road, Ashtabula, OH 44004, (216) 964-3457.

Maple Leaf Beamers—8200 Yorkshire Road, Mentor, OH 44060, (216) 255-9118.

Northeastern Ohio Bottle Club—P.O. Box 57, Madison, OH 44057, (614) 282-8918.

Northern Ohio Jim Bottle Club—43152 Hastings Road, Oberlin, OH 44074, (216) 775-2177.

Northwest Ohio Bottle Club—104 W. Main, Norwalk, OH 44857.

Ohio Ezra Brooks Bottle Club—8741 Kirtland Chardon Road, Kirtland Hills, OH 44094.

Pioneer Beamers—38912 Butternut Ridge, Elyria, OH 44035, (216) 458-6621.

Queen City Jim Beam Bottle Club—4327 Greenlee Avenue, Cincinnati, OH 45217, (513) 641-3362.

Rubber Capital Jim Beam Club—151 Stephens Road, Akron, OH 44312.

Sara Lee Bottle Club—27621 Chagrin Boulevard, Cleveland, OH 44122.

OKLAHOMA

Bar-Dew Antique Bottle Club—817 E. 7th Street, Dewey, OK 74029.

Frontier Jim Beam Bottle & Spec. Club—P.O. Box 52, Meadowbrook Trailer Village, Lot 101, Ponca City, OK 74601, (405) 765-2174.

Green Country Jim Beam Bottle & Spec. Club—Rt. 2, P.O. Box 233, Chouteau, OK 74337, (918) 266-3512.

McDonnel Douglas Antique Club—5752 E. 25th Place, Tulsa, OK 74114.

Ponca City Old Bottle Club—2408 Juanito, Ponca City, OK 74601.

Sooner Jim Beam Bottle & Spec. Club—5913 S.E. 10th, Midwest City, OK 73110, (405) 737-5786.

Southwest Oklahoma Antique Bottle Club—35 S. 49th Street, Lawton, OK 73501.

Tri-State Historical Bottle Club—817 E. 7th Street, Dewey, OK 74029.

Tulsa Antique Bottle & Relic Club—P.O. Box 4278, Tulsa, OK 74104.

OREGON

Central Oregon Bottle & Relic Club—671 N.E. Seward, Bend, OR 97701.

Central Oregon Bottle & Relic Club—1545 Kalama Avenue, Redmond, OR 97756.

Central South Oregon Antique Bottle Club—708 S. F. Street, Lakeview, OR 97630.

Emerald Empire Bottle Club—P.O. Box 292, Eugene, OR 97401.

Frontier Collectors—504 N.W. Bailey, Pendleton, OR 97801.

Gold Diggers Antique Bottle Club—1958 S. Stage Road, Medford, OR 97501.

Lewis & Clark Historical Bottle & Collectors Soc.—8018 S.E. Hawthorne Boulevard, Portland, OR 97501.

Lewis & Clark Historical Bottle Society—4828 N.E. 33rd, Portland, OR 97501.

Molalla Bottle Club—Rt. 1, Box 205, Mulino, OR 97042.

Oregon Antique Bottle Club—Rt. 3, Box 23, Molalla, OR 97038.

Oregon B.C.A.—3661 S.E. Nehalem Street, Portland, OR 97202.

Oregon Beamer Beam Bottle & Specialties—P.O. Box 7, Sheridan, OR 97378.

Pioneer Fruit Jar Collectors Association—P.O. Box 175, Grand Ronde, OR 97347.

Siskiyou Antique Bottle Collectors Assn.—P.O. Box 1335, Medford, OR 97501.

PENNSYLVANIA

Anthracite Jim Beam Bottle Club—406 Country Club Apartments, Dallas, PA 18612.

Antique Bottle Club of Burlington County—8445 Walker Street, Philadelphia, PA 19136.

Beaver Valley Jim Beam Club—1335 Indiana Avenue, Monaca, PA 15061.

Bedford County Antique Bottle Club—107 Seifert Street, Bedford, PA 15522.

Camoset Bottle Club—P.O. Box 252, Johnstown, PA 15901.

Christmas Valley Beamers—150 Second Street, Richlandtown, PA 18955, (215) 536-4636.

Classic Glass Bottle Collectors—R.D. 2, Cogan Station, PA 17728.

Cumberland Valley Jim Beam Club—P.O. Box 132, Middletown, PA 17057, (717) 944-5376.

Delaware Valley Bottle Club—12 Belmar Road, Hatboro, PA 19040.

Del-Val Bottle Club—Rt. 152 & Hilltown Pike, Hilltown, PA.

East Coast Double Springs Specialty Bottle Club—P.O. Box 419, Carlisle, PA 17013.

East Coast Ezra Brooks Bottle Club—2815 Fiddler Green, Lancaster, PA 17601.

Endless Mountain Antique Bottle Club—P.O. Box 75, Granville Summit, PA 16926.

Erie Bottle Club—P.O. Box 373, Erie, PA 16512.

Flood City Jim Beam Bottle Club—231 Market Street, Johnston, PA 15901.

Forks of the Delaware Bottle Collectors, Inc.—Box 693, Easton, PA 18042.

Friendly Jim's Beam Club—508 Benjamin Franklin H.W. East, Douglasville, PA 19518.

Indiana Bottle Club—240 Oak Street, Indiana, PA 15701.

Keystone Flyers Jim Beam Bottle Club—288 Hogan Boulevard, Box 42, Lock Haven, PA 17745, (717) 748-6741.

Kiski Mini Beam and Spec. Club—816 Cranberry Drive, Monroeville, PA 15146.

Middletown Area B.C.A.—P.O. Box 1, Middletown, PA 17057, (717) 939-0288.

Pagoda City Beamers—735 Florida Avenue, Riverview Park, Reading, PA 19605, (215) 929-8924.

Penn Beamers' 14th—15 Gregory Place, Richboro, PA 18954.

The Pennsylvania Bottle Collectors Association—251 Eastland Ave., York, PA 17402.

Pennsylvania Dutch Jim Beam Bottle Club—812 Pointview Avenue, Ephrate, PA 17522.

Philadelphia Bottle Club—8203 Elberon Avenue, Philadelphia, PA 19111.

Philadelphia Coll. Club—8445 Walker Street, Philadelphia, PA 19111.

Pittsburgh Bottle Club—P.O. Box 401, Ingomar, PA 15127.

Pittsburgh Bottle Club—1528 Railroad Street, Sewickley, PA 15143.

Susquehanna Valley Jim Beam Bottle & Spec. Club—64 E. Park Street, Elizabethtown, PA 17022, (717) 367-4256.

Tri-County Antique Bottle & Treasure Club—R.D. 2, P.O. Box 30, Reynoldsville, PA 15851.

Valley Forge Jim Beam Bottle Club—1219 Ridgeview Drive, Phoenixville, PA 19460, (215) 933-5789.

Washington County Bottle & Insulator Club—R.D. 2, P.O. Box 342, Carmichaels, PA 15320, (412) 966-7996.

Whitetail Deer Jim Beam Bottle Club—94 Lakepoint Drive, Harrisburg, PA 17111, (717) 561-2517.

RHODE ISLAND

Little Rhody Bottle Club—c/o Ted Baldwin, 3161 West Shore Road, Warwick, RI 02886.

Seaview Jim Beam Bottle & Spec. Club—362 Bayview Avenue, Cranston, RI 02905, (401) 461-4952.

SOUTH CAROLINA

Greer Bottle Collectors Club—P.O. Box 142, Greer, SC 29651.

Lexington County Antique Bottle Club—201 Roberts Street, Lexington, SC 29072.

Palmetto State Beamers—908 Alton Circle, Florence, SC 29501, (803) 669-6515.

Piedmont Bottle Collectors—c/o R.W. Leizear, Rt. 3, Woodruff, SC 29388.

South Carolina Bottle Club—1119 Greenbridge Lane, Columbia, SC 29210.

Union Bottle Club—107 Pineneedle Road, Union, SC 29379.

TENNESSEE

Cotton Carnival Beam Club—P.O. Box 17951, Memphis, TN 38117.

Music City Beam Bottle Club—2008 June Drive, Nashville, TN 37214, (615) 883-1893.

TEXAS

Alamo Chapter Antique Bottle Club Association—701 Castano Avenue, San Antonio, TX 78209.

Alamo City Jim Beam Bottle & Spec. Club—5785 FM 1346, P.O. Box 20442, San Antonio, TX 78220.

Austin Bottle & Insulator Collectors Club—1614 Ashberry Drive, Austin, TX 78723.

Cowtown Jim Beam Bottle Club—2608 Roseland, Ft. Worth, TX 76103, (817) 536-4335.

El Paso Insulator Club—Martha Stevens, Chairman, 4556 Bobolink, El Paso, TX 79922.

The Exploration Society—603 9th Street NAS, Corpus Christie, TX 78419, (210) 922-2902.

Foard C. Hobby Club—P.O. Box 625, Crowell, TX 79227.

Fort Concho Bottle Club—1703 W. Avenue, N. San Angelo, TX 76901.

Foursome (Jim Beam)—1208 Azalea Drive, Longview, TX 75601.

Golden Spread Jim Beam Bottle & Spec. Club—1104 S. Maddox, Dumas, TX 79029, (806) 935-3690.

Gulf Coast Beam Club—128 W. Bayshore Drive, Baytown, TX 77520.

Gulf Coast Bottle & Jar Club—P.O. Box 1754, Pasadena, TX 77501, (713) 592-3078.

Oil Patch Beamers—1300 Fairmont 112, Longview, TX 75604, (214) 758-1905.

Republic of Texas Jim Beam Bottle & Specialty Club—616 Donley Drive, Euless, TX 76039.

San Antonio Antique Bottle Club—c/o 3801 Broadway, Witte Museum Auditorium, San Antonio, TX 78209.

UTAH

Utah Antique Bottle Club—P.O. Box 15, Ogden, UT 84402.

VIRGINIA

Apple Valley Bottle Collectors Club—P.O. Box 2201, Winchester, VA 22601.

Bottle Club of the Virginia Peninsula—P.O. Box 5456, Newport News, VA 23605.

Buffalo Beam Bottle Club—P.O. Box 434, Buffalo Junction, VA 24529, (804) 374-2041.

Chesapeake Bay Beam Bottle & Spec. Club—515 Briar Hill Road, Norfolk, VA 23502, (804) 461-3763.

Country Cousins Beam Bottle & Spec. Club—Rt. 2, Box 18C, Dinwiddle, VA 23841, (804) 469-7414.

Dixie Beam Bottle Club—Rt. 4, Box 94-4, Glen Allen, VA 23060.

Hampton Roads Area Bottle Collector's Assn.—Virginia Beach Federal Savings & Loan, 4848 Virginia Beach Boulevard, Virginia Beach, VA 23462.

Merrimac Beam Bottle & Spec. Club—433 Tory Road, Virginia Beach, VA 23462, (804) 497-0969.

Metropolitan Antique Bottle Club—109 Howard Street, Dumfries, VA 22026, (804) 221-8055.

Old Dominion Beam Bottle & Spec. Club—624 Brandy Creek Drive, Mechanicsville, VA 23111, (804) 746-7144.

Shenandoah Valley Beam Bottle & Spec. Club—11 Bradford Drive, Front Royal, VA 22630, (703) 743-6316.

Tidewater Beam Bottle & Specialty Club—P.O. Box 14012, Norfolk, VA 23518.

Ye Old Bottle Club—General Delivery, Clarksville, VA 23927.

WASHINGTON

Antique Bottle and Glass Collectors—P.O. Box 163, Snohomish, WA 98290.

Apple Capital Beam Bottle & Spec. Club—300 Rock Island Road, E. Wenatchee, WA 98801, (509) 884-6895.

Blue Mountain Jim Beam Bottle & Spec. Club—P.O. Box 147, Russet Road, Walla Walla, WA 99362, (509) 525-1208.

Capitol Collectors & Bottle—P.O. Box 202, Olympia, WA 98507.

Cascade Treasure Club—254 N.E. 45th, Seattle, WA 98105.

Chinook Ezra Brooks Bottle Club—233 Kelso Drive, Kelso, WA 98626.

Evergreen State Beam Bottle & Specialty Club—P.O. Box 99244, Seattle, WA 98199.

Inland Empire Bottle & Collectors Club—7703 E. Trent Avenue, Spokane, WA 99206.

Klickital Bottle Club Association—Goldendale, WA 98620.

Mt. Rainer Ezra Brooks Bottle Club—P.O. Box 1201, Lynwood, WA 98178.

Northwest Jim Beam Bottle Collectors Association—P.O. Box 7401, Spokane, WA 99207.

Northwest Treasure Hunter's Club—E. 107 Astor Drive, Spokane, WA 99208.

Pacific Northwest Avon Bottle Club—25425 68th St., Kent, WA 98031.

Seattle Jim Beam Bottle Collectors Club—8015 15th Avenue, N.W., Seattle, WA 98107.

Skagit Bottle & Glass Collectors—1314 Virginia, Mt. Vernon, WA 98273.

South Whedley Bottle Club—c/o Juanita Clyde, Langley, WA 98260.

Washington Bottle Collectors Association—P.O. Box 80045, Seattle, WA 98108.

WEST VIRGINIA

Blennerhassett Jim Beam Club—Rt. 1, 26 Popular Street, Davisville, WV 26142, (304) 428-3184.

Wild Wonderful W. VA. Jim Beam Bottle & Spec. Club—3922 Hanlin Way, Weirton, WV 26062, (304) 748-2675.

WISCONSIN

Badger Bottle Diggers—1420 McKinley Road, Eau Claire, WI 54701.

Badger Jim Beam Club of Madison—P.O. Box 5612, Madison, WI 53705.

Belle City Jim Beam Bottle Club—8008 104th Avenue, Kenosha, WI 53140, (414) 694-3341.

Bucken Beamers Bottle Club of Milw. WI.—N. 95th Street, W. 16548 Richmond Drive, Menomonee Falls, WI 53051, (414) 251-1772.

Cameron Bottle Diggers—P.O. Box 276, 314 South 1st Street, Cameron, WI 54822.

Central Wisconsin Bottle Collectors—1608 Main Street, Stevens Point, WI 54481.

Heart of the North Beam Bottle and Bottle Club—1323 Eagle Street, Rhinelander, WI 54501, (715) 362-6045.

Hooten Beamers—2511 Needles Lane, Wisconsin Rapids, WI 54494, (715) 423-7116.

Indianhead Jim Beam Club—5112 Berry Street, Rt. 7, Menomonee, WI 54751, (715) 235-5627.

Lumberjack Beamers—414 N. 5th Avenue, Wausau, WI 54401, (715) 842-3793.

Milwaukee Antique Bottle Club—N. 88 Street W., 15211 Cleveland Avenue, Menomonee Falls, WI 53051.

Milwaukee Antique Bottle Club, Inc.—2343 Met-To-Wee Lane, Wauwatosa, WI 53226, (414) 257-0158.

Milwaukee Jim Beam Bottle and Specialties Club, Ltd.—N. 95th Street W., 16548 Richmond Drive, Menomonee Falls, WI 53051.

Packerland Beam Bottle & Spec. Club—1366 Avondale Drive, Green Bay, WI 54303, (414) 494-4631.

Shot Tower Jim Beam Club—818 Pleasant Street, Mineral Point, WI 53565.

South Central Wisconsin Bottle Club—c/o Dr. T.M. Schwartz, Rt. 1, Arlington, WI 53911.

Sportsman's Jim Beam Bottle Club—6821 Sunset Strip, Wisconsin Rapids, WI 54494, (715) 325-5285.

Sugar River Beamers—Rt. 1, Box 424, Brodhead, WI 53520, (608) 897-2681.

WYOMING

Cheyenne Antique Bottle Club—4417 E. 8th Street, Cheyenne, WY 82001.
Insubott Bottle Club—P.O. Box 34, Lander, WY 82520.

CANADA

Bytown Bottle Seekers—P.O. Box 375, Richmond, Ontario, Canada K0A 2Z0,
   (613) 838-5802.
St. John B.C.—25 Orange Street, St. John N.B. E2L 1L9.

APPENDIX C: BOTTLE DEALERS

UNITED STATES

ALABAMA

BIRMINGHAM—Steve Holland, 1740 Serene Dr., Birmingham, AL 35215, (205) 853-7929. Bottles dug around Alabama.

BIRMINGHAM—Walker's Antique Bottles, 2768 Hanover Circle, Birmingham, AL 35205, (205) 933-7902. Medicines, crown sodas.

FORT PAYNE—Terry & Katie Gillis, 115 Mountain Dr., Fort Payne, AL 35967, (205) 845-4541.

FORT PAYNE—C.B. and Barbara Meares, Rt. 3, Box 161, Fort Payne, AL 35967, (205) 638-6225.

MOBILE—Bottles and Stuff, Clinton P. King, 4075 Moffatt Rd., Mobile, AL 36618, (205) 344-2959. Pontiled medicines, local bottles, black glass, pottery.

MOBILE—Loretta and Mack Wimmer, 3012 Cedar Cresent Dr., Mobile, AL 36605.

OZARK—Old Time Bottle House and Museum, 306 Parker Hills Dr., Ozark, AL 36360. Old bottles, stone jugs, fruit jars.

SPANISH FORT—Elroy and Latrelle Webb, 203 Spanish Main, Spanish Fort, AL 36527, (205) 626-1067.

THEODORE—Ed's Lapidary Shop, 7927 Historic Mobile Parkway, US Hwy. 90, Theodore, AL 36582, (205) 653-0713. Locally dug bottles.

ARIZONA

PHOENIX—The Brewery, 1605 N. 7th Ave., Phoenix, AZ 85007, (602) 252-1415. Brewery items.

PHOENIX—Tom and Kay Papa, 3821 E. Mercer Lane, Phoenix, AZ 85028, (602) 996-3240.

PINETOP—Ray and Dyla Lawton, Box 374, Pinetop, AZ 85935, (602) 366-4449.

ARKANSAS

ASHDOWN—Buddy's Bottles, 610 Park Ave., Ashdown, AR 71822, (501) 898-5877. Hutchinson sodas, medicines, Arkansas bottles always wanted.

JACKSONVILLE—Charles and Mary Garner, 620 Carpenter Dr., Jacksonville, AR 72076, (501) 982-8381.

RISON—Rufus Buie, P.O. Box 226, Rison, AR 71665, (501) 325-6816.

CALIFORNIA

AROMAS—Bobbie's Country Store, in the Big Red Barn, 1000 El Camino Real, Hwy. 101, P.O. Box 1761, Carmel, CA 93921, (408) 394-3257.

BEVERLY HILLS—Alex Kerr, 9584 Wilshire Blvd., Beverly Hills, CA 90212, (213) 762-6320.

BUENA PARK—Walter Yeargain, 6222 San Lorenzo Dr., Buena Park, CA 90620, (714) 826-5264.

BUTLER—Wayne Hortman, P.O. Box 183, Butler, CA, 31006, (912) 862-3699.

CHICO—Randy Taylor, 566 E. 12th St., Chico, CA, (916) 342-4928.

CITRUS HEIGHTS—Duke Jones, P.O. Box 642, Citrus Heights, CA 95610, (916) 725-1989. California embossed beers.

CONCORD—Stoney and Myrt Stone, 1925 Natoma Dr., Concord, CA 94519, (415) 685-6326.

CORONA—Russell Brown, P.O. Box 441, Corona, CA 91720, (714) 737-7164.

CYPRESS—Gary and Harriet Miller, 5034 Oxford Dr., Cypress, CA 90630, (714) 828-4778.

FILLMORE—Mike and Joyce Amey, 625 Clay St., Fillmore, CA 93015, (805) 524-3364.

HESPERIA—Gene and Phyllis Kemble, 14733 Poplar St., Hesperia, CA 92345, (714) 244-5863.

HUNTINGTON BEACH—Larry Caddell, 15881 Malm Circle, Huntington Beach, CA 92647, (714) 897-8133.

LOS ALTOS—Louis and Cindy Pellegrini, 1231 Thurston, Los Altos, CA 94022, (415) 965-9060

MARIETTA—John and Estelle Hewitt, 366 Church St., Marietta, CA, 30060, (404) 422-5525.

REDDING—Byrl and Grace Rittenhouse, 3055 Birch Way, Redding CA 96002, (916) 243-0320.

REDDING—Ralph Hollibaugh, 2087 Gelnyose Dr., Redding, CA 96001, (916) 243-4672.

SACRAMENTO—George and Rose Reidenbach, 2816 "P" St., Sacramento, CA 95816, (916) 451-0063.

SACTO—Peck and Audie Markota, 4627 Oakhallow Dr., Sacto, CA 95842, (916) 334-3260.

SAN FRANCISCO—Bill Groves, 2620 Sutter St., San Francisco, CA 94115, (415) 922-6248.

SAN JOSE—Terry and Peggy Wright, 6249 Lean Ave., San Jose, CA 95123, (408) 578-5580.

SOLANA BEACH—T.R. Schweighart, 1123 Santa Luisa Dr., Solana Beach, CA 92075.

STOCKTON—Frank and Judy Brockman, 104 W. Park, Stockton, CA 95202, (209) 948-0746.

SUTTER CREEK—The Glass Bottle, 22 Main St., Sutter Creek, Hwy. 49. Mailing address: P.O. Box 374, Sutter Creek, CA 95685, (209) 267-0122. Old figurals, perfumes, whiskey, milks.

WESTWOOD—Whitman's Bookkeeping Service, 219 Fir St., P.O. Drawer KK, Westwood, CA 96147, (916) 256-3437. Soda.

WINDSOR—Betty and Ernest Zumwalt, 5519 Kay Dr., Windsor, CA 95492, (707) 545-8670.

YREKA—Sleep's Siskiyou Specialties, 217 W. Miner, P.O. Box 689, Yreka, CA 96097.

COLORADO

SNOWMASS VILLAGE—Jim Bishop, Box 5554, Snowmass Village, CO 81615, (303) 923-2348. Miniature liquors.

CONNECTICUT

ASHFORD—Woodlawn Antiques, P.O. Box 277, Mansfield Center, Ashford, CT 06250, (203) 429-2983. Flasks, bitters, inks.

FAIRFIELD—Stephen Link, 953 Post Rd., Fairfield, CT 06430.

HARTFORD—B'Thea's Cellar, 31 Kensington St., Hartford, CT 06112, (203) 249-4686.

LIME ROCK—Mary's Old Bottles, White Hollow Rd., Lakeville, CT 06039, (203) 435-2961.

MYSTIC—Bob's Old Bottles, 656 Noank Rd., Rt. 215, Mystic, CT 06355, (203) 536-8542.

NEW HAVEN—Gerald "J." Jaffee and Lori Waldeck, P.O. Box 1741, New Haven, CT 06507, (203) 787-4232. Poisons (bottles), insulators.

NEWTOWN—Time In A Bottle, Gail Quick, Rt. 25, Hawleyville, CT 06440, (203) 426-0031.

NIANTIC—Albert Corey, 153 W. Main St., Niantic, CT 06357, (203) 739-7493. No. Eastern bottles, jars, stoneware.

SAYBROOK—Bill Stankard, 61 Old Post Rd., Saybrook, CT 06475, (203) 388-4235.

WATERTOWN—George E. Johnson, 2339 Litchfield Rd., Watertown, CT 06795, (203) 274-1785.

WOODSTOCK—Norman and Elizabeth Heckler, Woodstock Valley, CT 06282, (203) 974-1634.

FLORIDA

BROOKSVILLE—E.S. and Romie Mackenzie, Box 57, Brooksville, FL 33512, (904) 796-3400.

FORT MEADE—M and S Bottles and Antiques, Marlaine and Steve, 421 Wilson St., Mailing address: Rt. 2, Box 84B3, Fort Meade, FL 33841, (904) 285-9421.

FT. PIERCE—Gore's Shoe Repair, 410 Orange Ave., Ft. Pierce, FL 33450. Old bottles, Florida bottles, black glass.

HOLLISTER—This-N-That Shop (Albert B. Coleman), P.O. Box 185, Hollister, FL 32047, (904) 328-3658.

HOLLYWOOD—Hickory Stick Antiques, 400 So. 57 Terr., Hollywood, FL 33023, (904) 962-3434. Canning jars, black glass, household.

JACKSONVILLE—The Browns, 6512 Mitford Rd., Jacksonville, FL 32210, (904) 771-2091. Sodas, mineral waters, milk, glass, black glass.

KEY LARGO—Dwight Pettit, 33 Sea Side Dr., Key Largo, FL 33037, (305) 852-8338.

NEW PORT RICHEY—Gerae and Lynn McLarty, 6705 Dogwood Ct., New Port Richey, FL 33552, (813) 849-7166.

ORMOND BEACH—Mike Kollar, 50 Sylvania Pl., Ormond Beach, FL 32074.

PALMETTO—Jon Vander Schouw, P.O. Box 1151, Palmetto, FL 33561, (813) 722-1375.

SANFORD—Hidden Bottle Shop, 2656 Grandview, Sanford, FL 32771, (813) 322-7181.

TALLAHASSEE—Harry O. Thomas, 2721 Parson's Rest., Tallahassee, FL 32308, (904) 893-3834.

TITUSVILLE—Insulators-L.L. Linscott, 3557 Nicklaus Dr., Titusville, FL 32780, (305) 267-9170. Fruit jars, porcelain insulators.

GEORGIA

BUTLER—Wayne's Bottles, Box 183, Butler, GA 31006, (912) 862-3699. Odd colors, odd shapes.

DUNWOODY—Carlo and Dot Sellari, Box 888553, Dunwoody, GA 30338, (404) 451-2483.

EATONTON—James T. Hicks, Rt. 4, Box 265, Eatonton, GA 31024, (404) 485-9280.

LAURENCEVILLE—Dave and Tia Janousek, 2293 Mulligan Circle, Laurenceville, GA 30245.

MACON—Schmitt House Bottle Diggers, 5532 Jane Rue Circle, Macon, GA 31206, (912) 781-6130. Indiana, Kentucky bottles.

NEWNAN—Bob and Barbara Simmons, 152 Greenville St., Newnan, GA 30263, (404) 251-2471.

HAWAII

HONOLULU—The Hawaiian Antique Bottle Shop, Kahuku Sugar Mill, P.O. Box 495, Honolulu, HI 96731, (808) 293-5581. Hawaiian soda, whiskeys, medicines, milks.

HONOLULU—The Hawaii Bottle Museum, 1044 Kalapaki St., P.O. Box 25153, Honolulu, HI 96825, (808) 395-4671. Hawaiian bottles, Oriental bottles, and pottery.

IDAHO

BUHL—John Cothern, Rt. 1, Buhl, ID 83316, (208) 543-6713.

SILVER CITY—Idaho Hotel, Jordan St., Box 75, Murphy, ID 83650, (208) 495-2520.

ILLINOIS

ADDISON—Ronald Selcke, 4N236 8th Ave., Addison, IL 60101, (312) 543-4848.

ALTON—Sean Mullikin, 5014 Alicia Dr., Alton, IL 62002, (312) 466-7506.

ALTON—Mike Spiiroff, 1229 Alton St., Alton, IL 62002, (618) 462-2283.

BELLEVILLE—Wayne and Jacqueline Brammer, 309 Bellevue Dr., Belleville, IL 62223, (618) 233-8841.

CERRO GORDO—Marvin and Carol Ridgeway, 450 W. Cart, Cerro Gordo, IL 61818, (217) 763-3271.

CHAMPAIGN—Casad's Antiques, 610 South State St., Champaign, IL 61820, (217) 356-8455. Milk bottles.

CHICAGO—Tom and Gladys Bartels, 5315 W. Warwick, Chicago, IL 60641, (312) 725-2433.

CHICAGO—Ernest Brooks, 9023 S. East End, Chicago, IL 60617, (312) 375-9233.

CHICAGO—1st Chicago Bottle Club, P.O. Box A3382, Chicago, IL 60690.

CHICAGO—Joe Healy, 3421 W. 76th St., Chicago, IL 60652.

CHICAGO—William Kiggans, 7747 South Kedzle, Chicago, IL 60652, (312) 925-6148.

CHICAGO—Carl Malik, 8655 S. Keeler, Chicago, IL 60652, (312) 767-8568.

CHICAGO—Jerry and Aryliss McCann, 5003 W. Berwyn, Chicago, IL 60630, (312) 777-0443.

CHICAGO—Louis Metzinger, 4140 N. Mozart, Chicago, IL 60618, (312) 478-9034.

CHICAGO—L.D. and Barbara Robinson, 1933 So. Homan, Chicago, IL 60623, (312) 762-6096.

CHICAGO—Paul R. Welko, 5727 S. Natoma Ave., Chicago, IL 60638, (312) 582-3564. Blob top and Hutchinson sodas.

CHICAGO HTS.—Al and Sue Verley, 486 Longwood Ct., Chicago Hts., IL 60411, (312) 754-4132.

DEERFIELD—Jim Hall, 445 Partridge Lane, Deerfield, IL 60014, (312) 541-5788.

DEERFIELD—John and Claudia Panek, 816 Holmes, Deerfield, IL 60015, (312) 945-5493.

DIETERICH—Ray's and Betty's Antiques, Dieterich, IL 62424, (217) 925-5449. Bitters.

ELMWOOD PARK—Keith and Ellen Leeders, 1728 N. 76th Ave., Elmwood Park, IL 60635, (312) 453-2085.

GODFREY—Jeff Cress, 3403 Morkel Dr., Godfrey, IL 62035, (618) 466-3513.

HICKORY HILLS—Doug and Eileen Wagner, 9225 S. 88th Ave., Hickory Hills, IL 60457, (312) 598-4570.

HILLSBORO—Jim and Penny Lang, 628 Mechanic, Hillsboro, IL 62049, (217) 532-2915.

INGELSIDE—Art and Pat Besinger, 611 Oakwood, Ingelside, IL 60041, (312) 546-2367.

LaGRANGE—John Murray, 301 Hillgrove, LaGrange, IL 60525, (312) 352-2199.

LAKE VILLA—Lloyd Bindscheattle, P.O. Box 11, Lake Villa, IL 60046.

LEMONT—Russ and Lynn Sineni, 1372 Hillcrest Rd., Lemont, IL 60439, (312) 257-2648.

MOKENA—Neal and Marianne Vander Zande, 18830 Sara Rd., Mokena, IL 60448, (312) 479-5566.

MORRISON—Emma's Bottle Shop, Emma Rosenow, Rt. 3, Morrison, IL 61270, (815) 778-4596. Beers, inks, bitters, sodas.

O'FALLON—Tom and Ann Feltman, 425 North Oak St., O'Fallon, IL 62269, (618) 632-3327.

PARK FOREST—Vern and Gloria Nitchie, 300 Indiana St., Park Forest, IL 60466, (312) 748-7198.

PARK RIDGE—Ken's Old Bottles, 119 East Lahon, Park Ridge, IL 60068, (312) 823-1267. Milks, inks, sodas, and whiskeys.

PEKIN—Harry's Bottle Shop, 612 Hillyer St., Pekin, IL 61555, (309) 346-3476. Pottery, beer, sodas, and medicines.

PEKIN—Oertel's Bottle House, Box 682, Pekin, IL 61555, (309) 347-4441. Peoria pottery, embossed picnic beer bottles, fruit jars.

QUINCY—Bob Rhinberger, Rt. 7, Quincy, IL 62301, (217) 223-0191.

RIVERDALE—Bob and Barbara Harms, 14521 Atlantic, Riverdale, IL 60627, (312) 841-4068.

SAUK VILLAGE—Ed McDonald, 3002 23rd St., Sauk Village, IL 60511, (312) 758-0373.

TRENTON—Jon and Char Granada, 631 S. Main, Trenton, IL 62293, (618) 224-7308.

WHEATON—Ben Crane, 1700 Thompson Dr., Wheaton, IL 60187, (312) 665-5662.

WHEATON—Scott Garrow, 2 S. 338 Orchard Rd., Wheaton, IL 60187.

WHEELING—Hall, 940 E. Old Willow Rd., Wheeling, IL 60090, (312) 541-5788. Sodas, inks, medicines, etc.

WHEELING—Steve Miller, 623 Ivy Ct., Wheeling, IL 60090, (312) 398-1445.

WOODSTOCK—Michael Davis, 1652 Tappan, Woodstock, IL 66098, (815) 338-5147.

WOODSTOCK—Mike Henrich, 402 McHenry Ave., Woodstock, IL 60098, (815) 338-5008.

INDIANA

BOGGSTOWN—Ed and Margaret Shaw, Rt. 1, Box 23, Boggstown, IN 46110, (317) 835-7121.

CLINTON—Tony and Dick Stringfellow, 714 Vine, Clinton, IN 47842, (317) 832-2355.

FLORA—Bob and Morris Wise, 409 E. Main, Flora, IN 46929, (219) 967-3713.

FORT WAYNE—Annett's Antiques, 6910 Lincoln Hwy. E., Fort Wayne, IN 46803, (219) 749-2745.

GOSHEN—Gene Rice, 61935 CR37, Rt. 1, Goshen, IN 46526.

GOSHEN—Wayne Wagner, 23558 Creek Park Dr., Goshen, IN 46526.

GREENFIELD—George and Nancy Reilly, Rt. 10, Box 67, Greenfield, IN 46140, (317) 462-2441.

INDIANAPOLIS—John and Dianna Atkins, 3168 Beeler Ave., Indianapolis, IN 46224, (317) 299-2720.

NOBELSVILLE—Rick and Becky Norton, Rt. G, Box 166, Nobelsville, IN 46060, (317) 844-1772.

PERU—Herrell's Collectibles, 265 E. Canal St., Peru, IN 46970, (317) 473-7770.

SCOTTSBURG—Fort Harrod Glass Works, 160 N. Gardner St., Scottsburg, IN 47170, (812) 752-5170.

TERRE HAUTE—Harry and Dorothy Frey, 5210 Clinton Rd., Terre Haute, IN 47805, (812) 466-4642.

WESTFIELD—Doug Moore, 9 Northbrook Circle, Westfield, IN 46074, (317) 896-3015.

IOWA

ELKADER—The Bottle Shop, 206 Chestnut, S.E. Mailing address: Box 188, Max Hunt, Elkader, IA 52043, (319) 245-2359. Sarsaparillas and bitters.

STORM LAKE—Ralph and Helen Welch, 804 Colonial Circle, Storm Lake, IA 50588, (712) 732-4124.

KANSAS

HALSTEAD—Doanald Haury, Rt. 2, Halstead, KS 67056, (316) 283-5876.

LAWRENCE—Mike Elwell, Rt. 2, Box 30, Lawrence, KS 66044, (913) 842-2102.

MERRIAM—Dale Young, 9909 West 55th St., Merriam, KS 66203, (913) 677-0175.

PAOLA—Stewart and Sons Old Bottle Shop, 610 E. Kaskaskia, Paola, KS 66071, (913) 294-3434. Drugstore bottles, blob-top beers.

TOPEKA—Joe and Alyce Smith, 4706 West Hills Dr., Topeka, KS 66606, (913) 272-1892.

KENTUCKY

ALEXANDRIA—Michael and Kathy Kolb, 6 S. Jefferson, Alexandria, KY 41001, (606) 635-7121.

JEFFERSONTOWN—Paul Van Vactor, 10004 Cardigan Dr., Jeffersontown, KY 40299.

LOUISVILLE—Gene Blasi, 5801 River Knolls Dr., Louisville, KY 40222, (502) 425-6995.

LOUISVILLE—Jerry and Joyce Phelps, 6013 Innes Trace Rd., Louisville, KY 40222.

LOUISVILLE—Paul and Paulette Van Vactor, 300 Stilz Ave., Louisville, KY 40299, (502) 895-3655.

PADUCAH—Earl and Ruth Cron, 808 N. 25th St., Paducah, KY 42001, (502) 443-5005.

LOUISIANA

BATON ROUGE—Sidney and Eulalle Genius, 1843 Tudor Dr., Baton Rouge, LA 70815, (504) 925-5774.

BATON ROUGE—Bobby and Ellen Kirkpatrick, 7313 Meadowbrook Ave., Baton Rouge, LA 70808.

BATON ROUGE—Sheldon L. Ray, Jr., Summer address: 2316 Amalie, Monroe, LA 71201. Mailing address: P.O. Box 17238, LSU, Baton Rouge, LA 70893, (504) 388-3814.

JENNINGS—Cajun Pop Factory, P.O. Box 1113, Jennings, LA 70546, (318) 824-7078. Hutchinsons, blob-tops, and pontil sodas.

MONROE—Everett L. Smith, 100 Everett Dr., Monroe, LA 71202, (318) 325-3534. Embossed whiskeys.

NATCHITOCHES—Ralph and Cheryl Green, 515 Elizabeth St., Natchitoches, LA 71457.

NEW ORLEANS—Dr. Charles and Jane Aprill, 484 Chestnut, New Orleans, LA 70118, (504) 899-7441.

NEW ORLEANS—Bep's Antiques, 3923 Magazine St., New Orleans, LA 70115, (504) 891-3468. Antique bottles, import bottles.

RUSTON—The Dirty Digger, 1804 Church St., Ruston, LA 71270, (318) 255-6112.

RUSTON—Bob and Vernell Willett, 1804 Church St., Ruston, LA 71270, (318) 255-6112.

MAINE

BETHEL—F. Barrie Freeman, Antiques, Paradise Hill Rd., Bethel, ME 04217, (207) 824-3300.

BRYANT POND—John and Althea Hathaway, Bryant Pond, ME 04219.

EAST WILTON—Don McKeen Bottles, McKeen Way, P.O. Box 5A, E. Wilton, ME 04234.

MILFORD—Spruce's Antiques, Main St., P.O. Box 295, Milford, ME 04461, (207) 827-4756.

SEARSPORT—Morse and Applebee Antiques, US Rt. 1, Box 164, Searsport, ME 04974, (207) 548-6314. Early American glass.

WALDOBORO—Daniel R. Winchenbaugh, RFD 4, Box 21, Waldoboro, ME 04572, (207) 832-7702.

WALDOBORO—Wink's Bottle Shop, Rt. 235, Waldoboro, ME 04572, (207) 832-4603.

MARYLAND

NORTH EAST—Pete's Diggins, Rt. 40 West, RR 3, Box 301, North East, MD 21901, (301) 287-9245.

SUDLERSVILLE—Fran and Bill Lafferty, Box 142, Sudlersville, MD 21668.

MASSACHUSETTS

DUXBURY—Joe and Kathy Wood, 49 Surplus St., Duxbury, MA 02332, (617) 934-2221.

LEVERETT—Metamorphosis, 46 Teewaddle Rd., RFD 3, Leverett, MA 01002. Hairs, medicines.

LITTLETON—The Thrift & Gift Shop, Littleton Common, Box 21, Littleton, MA (617) 486-4464.

MANSFIELD—Shop in My Home, 211 East St., Mansfield, MA 02048, (617) 339-6086. Historic flasks.

NORTH EASTON—The Applied Lip Place, 26 Linden St., North Easton, MA 02356, (617) 238-1432. Medicines, whiskeys.

WELLESLEY—Carlyn Ring, 59 Livermore Road, Wellesley, MA 02181, (617) 235-5675.

WEST SPRINGFIELD—Leo A. Bedard, 62 Craig Dr., Apt. 7A, West Springfield, MA 01089. Bitters, whiskeys, medicines.

YARMOUTH—Gloria Swanson Antiques, 262 Setucket Rd., Yarmouth, MA 02675, (617) 398-8848. Inks.

MICHIGAN

ANN ARBOR—John Wolfe, 1622 E. Stadium Blvd., Ann Arbor, MI 48104, (313) 665-6106.

BLOOMFIELD HILLS—Jim and Robin Meehan, 25 Valley Way, Bloomfield Hills, MI 48013, (313) 642-0176.

BUCHANAN—Old Chicago, 316 Ross Dr., Buchanan, MI 49107, (616) 695-5896. Hutchinson sodas, blob beers.

CLARKLAKE—Fred and Shirley Weck, 8274 S. Jackson Rd., Clarklake, MI 49234, (517) 529-9631.

DAVIDSBURG—Chief Pontiac Antique Bottle Shop, 13880 Neal Rd., Davidsburg, MI 48019, (313) 634-8469.

DETROIT—Michael and Christina Garrett, 19400 Stout, Detroit, MI 48219, (313) 534-6067.

DUNDEE—Ray and Hillaine Hoste, 366 Main St., Dundee, MI 48131, (313) 529-2193.

GAINES—E & E Antiques, 9441 Grand Blanc Road, Gaines, MI 48436, (517) 271-9063. Fruit jars, beer bottles, milks.

GRAND RAPIDS—Dewey and Marilyn Heetderks, 21 Michigan N.E., Grand Rapids, MI 49503, (616) 774-9333.

IRON RIVER—Sarge's, 111 E. Hemlock, Iron River, MI 49935, (906) 265-4223. Old mining town bottles, Hutchinsons.

KALAMAZOO—Mark and Marty McNee, 1009 Vassar Dr., Kalamazoo, MI 49001, (616) 343-9393.

KALAMAZOO—Lew and Leon Wisser, 2837 Parchmount, Kalamazoo, MI 49004, (616) 343-7479.

LATHRUP VILLAGE—The Jar Emporium, Ralph Finch, 19420 Saratoga Lathrup Village, MI 48076, (313) 569-6749. Fruit jars.

MANISTEE—Chris and Becky Batdorff, 516 Maple St., Manistee, MI 49660, (616) 723-7917.

MONROE—Don and Glennie Burkett, 3942 West Dunbar Rd., Monroe, MI 48161, (313) 241-6740.

STAMBAUGH—Copper Corner Rock & Bottle Shop, 4th and Lincoln, Stambaugh, MI 49964, (906) 265-3510. Beer, Hutchs, medicines.

ST. JOSEPH—Anvil Antiques, two blocks so. of exit 27, I-94, 3439 Hollywood Rd., St. Joseph, MI 49085, (616) 429-5132. Bottles, insulators.

STUGIS—John and Kay Petruska, 21960 Marathon Rd., Stugis, MI 49091, (616) 651-6400.

WUCHANAN—James Clengenpeel, 316 Ross Dr., Wuchanan, MI 49107, (616) 695-5896.

MINNESOTA

EXCELSIOR—Jim Conley, P.O. Box 351, Excelsior, MN 55331, (612) 935-0964.

MINNEAPOLIS—Steve Ketcham, P.O. Box 24114, Minneapolis, MN 55424, (612) 920-4205.

MINNEAPOLIS—Neal and Pat Sorensen, 132 Peninsula Rd., Minneapolis, MN 55441, (612) 545-2698.

RICHFIELD—Ron and Vernie Feldhaus, 6904 Upton Ave., S. Richfield, MN 55423, (612) 866-6013.

ST. PAUL—J & E, 1000 Arcade St., St. Paul, MN 55106, (612) 771-9654.

MISSISSIPPI

BILOXI—Vieux Biloxie Bottlery Factory Restaurant, US 90 E., Biloxi, MS 39530, (601) 374-0688. Mississippi bottles.

COLUMBIA—Robert A. Knight, 516 Dale St., Columbia, MS 39429, (601) 736-4249. Mississippi bottles and jugs.

McCOMB—Robert Smith, 623 Pearl River Ave., McComb, MS 39642, (601) 684-1843.

STARKVILLE—Jerry Drott, 710 Persimmon Dr., P.O. Box 714, Starkville, MS 39759, (601) 323-8796. Liniments, drug stores.

VICKSBURG—Ted and Linda Kost, 107 Columbia Ave., Vicksburg, MS 39180, (601) 638-8780.

MISSOURI

ELSBERRY—Dave Hausgen, Rt. 1, Box 164, Elsberry, MO 63343, (314) 898-2500.

GLENCOE—Sam and Eloise Taylor, 3002 Woodlands Terrace, Glencoe, MO 63038, (314) 273-6244.

HANNIBAL—Bob and Debbi Overfield, 2318 Chestnut St., Hannibal, MO 63401, (314) 248-9521.

INDEPENDENCE—Mike and Carol Robison, 1405 N. River, Independence, MO 64050, (816) 836-2337.

KANSAS CITY—Donald Kimrey, 1023 W. 17th St., Kansas City, MO 64108, (816) 741-2745.

KANSAS CITY—Robert Stevens, 1131 E. 77th, Kansas City, MO 64131, (816) 333-1398.

LINN CREEK—The Bottle House, 1 mile north of Linn Creek on Hwy. 54, Rt. 1, Box 111, Linn Creek, MO 65052, (314) 346-5890.

ST. LOUIS—Gene and Alberta Kelley, 1960 Cherokee, St. Louis, MO 63126, (314) 664-7203.

ST. LOUIS—Jerry Mueller, 4520 Langtree, St. Louis, MO 63128, (314) 843-8357.

ST. LOUIS—Terry and Luann Phillips, 1014 Camelot Gardens, St. Louis, MO 63125, (314) 892-6864.

ST. LOUIS—Hal and Vern Wagner, 10118 Schuessler, St. Louis, MO 63128, (314) 843-7573. Historical flasks, colognes, early glass.

TAYLOR—Barkely Museum, one mile south on U.S. 61 (service road), Taylor, MO (314) 393-2408. 10,000 old bottles for sale, plus thousands of other collector items.

TIPTON—Joseph and Jean Reed, 237 E. Morgan, Tipton, MO 65081, (816) 433-5937.

WESTPHALIA—Randy and Jan Haviland, American Systems Antiques, Westphalia, MO 65085, (314) 455-2525.

NEBRASKA

OMAHA—Born Again Antiques, 1402 Williams St., Omaha, NE 68108, (402) 341-5177.

OMAHA—Karl Person, 10210 "W" St., Omaha, NE 68127, (402) 331-2666.

OMAHA—Fred Williams, 5712 N. 33rd St., Omaha, NE 68111, (402) 453-4317.

NEVADA

FALLON—Don and Opal Wellman, P.O. Box 521, Fallon, NV 89406, (702) 423-3490.

SPARKS—Don and Bonnie McLane, 1846 F. St., Sparks, NV 89431, (702) 359-2171.

NEW HAMPSHIRE

AMHERST—Dave and Carol Waris, Boston Post Rd., Amherst, NH 03031, (603) 882-4409.

DOVER—Bob and Betty Morin, RD 3, Box 280, Dover, NH 03820.

EXETER—Lucille Stanley, 9 Oak St., Exeter, NH 03833, (603) 772-2296.

HAMPSTEAD—Murray's Lakeside Bottle Shop, Benson Shores, P.O. Box 57, Hampstead, NH 03841, (603) 329-6969. All types: pontils, bitters, sarsaparillas, balsams, hairs, labeled, medicines, general line. Open 7 days, mail order too.

MANCHESTER—Jim and Joyce Rogers, Harvey Rd., Rt. 10, Manchester, NH 03103, (603) 623-4101.

TROY—House of Glass, 25 High St., Troy, NH 03465, (603) 242-7947.

NEW JERSEY

BRANCHVILLE—Richard and Lesley Harris, Box 400, Branchville, NJ 07826, (201) 948-3935.

CALIFON—Phil and Flo Alvarez, P.O. Box 107, Califon, NJ 07830, (201) 832-7438.

ENGLEWOOD—Ed and Carole Clemens, 81 Chester Pl., Apt. D-2, Englewood, NJ 07631, (201) 569-4429.

FLEMINGTON—John Orashen, RD 6, Box 345-A, Flemington, NJ 08822, (201) 782-3391.

HOPEWELL—Tom and Marion McCandless, 62 Lafayette St., Hopewell, NJ 08525, (609) 466-0619.

HOWELL—Howell Township, Bruce and Pat Egeland, 3 Rustic Drive, Howell, NJ 07731, (201) 363-0556. Second shop open 7 days a week at shop 106, building 3, Red Bank Antique Center, West Front St., and Bridge Ave., Red Bank, NJ.

MICKLETON—Sam Fuss, Harmony Rd., Mickleton, NJ 08056, (609) 423-5038.

SALEM—Old Bottle Museum, 4 Friendship Dr., Salem, NJ 08079, (609) 935-5631. 10,000 old bottles for sale, plus thousands of other collector items.

NEW MEXICO

ALBUQUERQUE—Irv and Ruth Swalwell, 8826 Fairbanks NE, Albuquerque, NM 87112, (505) 299-2977.

DEMING—Krol's Rock City & Mobile Park, 5 miles east of Deming on State Hwy. 26, Star Rt. 2, Box 15A, Deming, NM 88030. Hutchinson sodas, inks, Avons.

NEW YORK

AUBURN—Brewster Bottle Shop, 297 South St. Rd., Auburn, NY 13021, (315) 252-3246. Milk bottles.

BALLSTON LAKE—Tom and Alice Moulton, 88 Blue Spruce Lane, RD 5, Ballston Lake, NY 12019.

BINGHAMTON—Jim Chamberlain, RD 8, 607 Nowland Rd., Binghamton, NY 13904, (607) 772-1135.

BINGHAMTON—Jo Ann's Old Bottles, RD 2, Box 638, Port Crane, NY 13833, (607) 648-4605.

BLODGETT MILLS—Edward Pettet, P.O. Box 1, Blodgett Mills, NY 13738, (607) 756-7891. Inks.

BLOOMING GROVE—Old Bottle Shop, Horton Rd., P.O. Box 105, Blooming Grove, NY, 10914, (914) 496-6841.

CENTRAL VALLEY—J.J.'s Pontil Place, 1001 Dunderberg Rd., Central Valley, NY, (914) 928-9144.

CLIFTON PARK—John Kovacik, 11 Juniper Dr., Clifton Park, NY 12065, (518) 371-4118.

CLIFTON PARK—Richard Strunk, RD 4, Grooms Rd., Clifton Park, NY 12065. Bottles, flasks, bitters, Saratogas.

CRANBERRY LAKE—The Bottle Shop Antiques, P.O. Box 503, Cranberry Lake, NY (315) 848-2648.

ELMIRA—Leonard and Joyce Blake, 1220 Stolle Rd., Elmira, NY 14059, (716) 652-7752.

LEROY—Kenneth Cornell, 78 Main, Leroy, NY 14482, (716) 768-8919.

LOCH SHELDRAKE—The Bottle Shop, P.O. Box 24, Loch Sheldrake, NY 12759, (914) 434-4757.

MONTICELLO—Manor House Collectibles, Rt. 42, South Forestburgh, RD 1, Box 67, Monticello, NY 12701, (914) 794-3967. Whiskeys, beers, sodas.

NEW WINDSOR—David Byrd, 43 E. Kenwood Dr., New Windsor, NY 12550, (914) 561-7257.

NEW YORK CITY—Bottles Unlimited, 245 East 78th St., N.Y.C., NY 10021, (212) 628-8769. 18th and 19th century.

NEW YORK CITY—Chuck Moore, 3 East 57th St., N.Y.C., NY 10022.

ROCHESTER—Burton Spiller, 169 Greystone Lane, Apt. 31, Rochester, NY 14618, (716) 244-2229.

ROCHESTER—Robert Zorn, 23 Knickerbocker Ave., Rochester, NY 14615, (716) 254-7470.

WEBSTER—Dick and Evelyn Bowman, 1253 LaBaron Circle, Webster, NY 14580, (716) 872-4015.

NORTH CAROLINA

BLOWING ROCK—Vieve and Luke Yarbrough, P.O. Box 1023, Blowing Rock, NC 28605, (704) 963-4961.

CHARLOTTE—Bob Morgan, P.O. Box 3163, Charlotte, NC 28203, (704) 527-4841.

DURHAM—Clement's Bottles, 5234 Willowhaven Dr., Durham, NC 27712, (919) 383-2493. Commemorative soft drink bottles.

GOLD HILL—Howard Crowe, P.O. Box 133, Gold Hill, NC 28071, (704) 279-3736.

GOLDSBORO—Vernon Capps, Rt. 5, Box 529, Goldsboro, NC 27530, (919) 734-8964.

RALEIGH—Rex D. McMillan, 4101 Glen Laurel Dr., Raleigh, NC 27612. (919) 787-0007. N.C. blobs, saloon bottles, colored drug store.

NORTH DAKOTA

MANDAN—Robert Barr, 102 N. 9th Ave. N.W., Mandan, ND 58554.

OHIO

AKRON—Don and Barb Dzuro, 5113 W. Bath Rd., Akron, OH 44313, (216) 666-8170.

AKRON—Jim Salzwimmer, 3391 Tisen Rd., Akron, OH 44312, (216) 699-3990.

BEACHWOOD—Allan Hodges, 25125 Shaker Blvd., Beachwood, OH 44122, (216) 464-8381.

BLUFFTON—Schroll's Country Shop, 3 miles east of county line on Co. Rd. 33, (419) 358-6121.

BYESVILLE—Albert and Sylvia Campbell, RD 1, Box 194, Byesville, OH 43723, (614) 439-1105.

CINCINNATI—Kenneth and Dudie Roat, 7755 Kennedy Lane, Cincinnati, OH 45242, (513) 791-1168.

CLEVELAND—Joe and Mary Miller, 2590 N. Moreland Blvd., Cleveland, OH 44120, (216) 721-9919.

DAYTON—Don and Paula Spangler, 2554 Loris Dr., Dayton, OH 45449, (513) 435-7155.

DUBLIN—Roy and Barbara Brown, 8649 Dunsinane Dr., Dublin, OH 43017, (614) 889-0818.

FRANKFORT—Roger Durflinger, P.O. Box 2006, Frankfort, OH 45628, (614) 998-4849.

HANNIBAL—Gilbert Nething, P.O. Box 96, Hannibal, OH 43931. Hutchinson sodas.

LANCASTER—R. J. and Freda Brown, 125 S. High St., Lancaster, OH 43130, (614) 687-2899.

LEWISTOWN—Sonny Mallory, P.O. Box 134, Lewistown, OH 43333, (513) 686-2185.

NORTH HAMPTON—John and Margie Bartley; 160 South Main, North Hampton, OH 45319, (513) 964-1080.

POWHATAN POINT—Bob and Dawn Jackson, 107 Pine St., Powhatan Point, OH 43942, (614) 795-5567.

REYNOLDSBURG—Bob and Phyllis Christ, 1218 Creekside Place, Reynolds-burg, OH 43068, (614) 866-2156.

SPRINGFIELD—Ballentine's Bottles, 710 W. First St., Springfield, OH 45504, (513) 399-8359. Antique bottles.

SPRINGFIELD—Larry R. Henschen, 3222 Delrey Rd., Springfield, OH 45504, (513) 399-1891.

STEUBENVILLE—Tom and Deena Caniff, 1223 Oak Grove Ave., Steubenville, OH 43952, (614) 282-8918.

STEUBENVILLE—Bob and Mary Ann Willamagna, 711 Kendall Ave., Steubenville, OH 43952, (614) 282-9029.

STOW—Doug and Joann Bedore, 1483 Ritchie Rd., Stow, OH 44224, (216) 688-4934.

TORONTO—Bob Villamagna, 1518 Madison Ave., P.O. Box 56, Toronto, OH 43964, (614) 537-4503. Tri-state area bottles, stoneware.

WARREN—Michael Cetina, 3272 Northwest Blvd., Warren, OH 44485, (216) 898-1845.

WASHINGTONVILLE—Al and Beth Bignon, 480 High St., Washingtonville, OH 44490, (216), 427-6848.

WAYNESVILLE—The Bottleworks, 70 N. Main St., P.O. Box 446, Way-nesville, OH 45068, (513) 897-3861.

WELLINGTON—Elvin and Cherie Moody, Trails End, Wellington, OH 44090, (216) 647-4917.

XENIA—Bill and Wanda Dudley, 393 Franklin Ave., Xenia, OH 45385, (513) 372-8567.

OKLAHOMA

ENID—Ronald and Carol Ashby, 831 E. Pine, Enid, OK 73701. Rare and scarce fruit jars.

OKLAHOMA CITY—Joe and Hazel Nagy, 3540 NW 23, Oklahoma, City, OK 73107, (405) 942-0882.

SANDSPRINGS—Larry and Linda Shope, 310 W. 44th, Sandsprings, OK 74063, (918) 363-8481.

OREGON

HILLSBORO—Robert and Marguerite Ornduff, Rt. 4, Box 236-A, Hillsboro, OR 97123, (503) 538-2359.

PORTLAND—Alan Amerman, 2311 S.E. 147th, Portland, OR 97233, (503) 761-1661. Fruit jars.

PORTLAND—The Glass House, 4620 S.E. 104th, Portland, OR 97266, (503) 760-3346. Fruit jars.

PENNSYLVANIA

ALBURTIS—R.S. Riovo, 686 Franklin St., Alburtis, PA 18011, (215) 965-2706. Milk bottles, dairy go-withs.

BRADFORD—Ernest Hurd, 5 High St., Bradford, PA 16701, (814) 362-9915.

BRADFORD—Dick and Patti Mansour, 458 Lambert Dr., Bradford, PA 16701, (814) 368-8820.

CANONSBURG—John and Mary Schultz, RD 1, Box 118, Canonsburg, PA 15317, (412) 745-6632.

COUDERSPORT—The Old Bottle Corner, 508 South Main St., Mailing address: 102 West Maple St., Coudersport, PA 16915, (814) 274-7017. Fruit jars, blob tops.

EAST GREENVILLE—James A. Hagenbach, 102 Jefferson St., East Greenville, PA 18041, (215) 679-5849.

EAST PETERSBURG—Jere and Betty Hambleton, 5940 Main St., East Petersburg, PA 17520, (717) 569-0130.

HATBORO—Al and Maggie Duffield, 12 Belmar Rd., Hatboro, PA 19040, (215) 675-5175. Hutchinsons and inks.

LANCASTER—Barry and Mary Hogan, 3 Park Lane, Lancaster, PA 17603.

LEVITTOWN—Ed Lasky, 43 Nightingale Ln., Levittown, PA 19054, (215) 945-1555.

MARIENVILLE—Harold Bauer Antique Bottles, 136 Cherry St., Marienville, PA 16239.

McKEES ROCKS—Chuck Henigin, 3024 Pitch Fork Lane, McKees Rocks, PA 15136, (412) 331-6159.

MUNCY—Harold Hill, 161 E. Water St., Muncy, PA 17756, (717) 546-3388.

PIPERSVILLE—Allen Holtz, RD 1, Pipersville, PA 18947, (215) 847-5728.

PITTSBURGH—Carl and Gail Onufer, 210 Newport Rd., Pittsburgh, PA 15221, (412) 371-7725. Milk bottles.

ROULETTE—R.A. and Esther Heimer, P.O. Box 153, Roulette, PA 16746, (814) 544-7713.

STRONGSTOWN—Butch and Gloria Kim, RD 2, Box 35, Strongstown, PA 15957.

RHODE ISLAND

KENYON—Wes and Diane Seemann, Box 49, Kenyon, RI 02836, (203) 599-1626.

SOUTH CAROLINA

EASHEY—Bob Durham, 704 W. Main St., Eashey, SC 29640.

MARION—Tony and Marie Shank, P.O. Box 778, Marion, SC 29571, (803) 423-5803.

TENNESSEE

KNOXVILLE—Ronnie Adams, 7005 Charlotte Dr., Knoxville, TN 37914, (615) 524-8958.

McMINNVILLE—Terry Pennington, 415 N. Spring St., McMinnville, TN 37110. Jack Daniels, amber Coca-Cola.

MEMPHIS—Bluff City Bottlers, 4630 Crystal Springs Dr., Memphis, TN 38123, (901) 353-0541. Common American bottles.

MEMPHIS—Larry and Nancy McCage, 3772 Hanna Dr., Memphis, TN 38128, (901) 388-9329.

MEMPHIS—Tom Phillips, 2088 Fox Run Cove, Memphis, TN 38138, (901) 754-0097.

TEXAS

AMARILLO—Robert Snyder, 4235 W. 13th St., Amarillo, TX 79106.

EULESS—Mack and Alliene Landers, P.O. Box 5, Euless, TX 76039, (817) 267-2710.

HOUSTON—Bennie and Harper Leiper, 2800 W. Dallas, Houston, TX 77019, (713) 526-2101.

PASADENA—Gerald Welch, 4809 Gardenia Trail, Pasadena, TX 77505, (713) 487-3057.

PORT ISABEL—Jimmy and Peggy Galloway, P.O. Drawer A, Port Isabel, TX 78578, (512) 943-2437.

RICHARDSON—Chuck and Reta Bukin, 1325 Cypress Dr., Richardson, TX 75080, (214) 235-4889.

SAN ANTONIO—Sam Greer, 707 Nix Professional Bldg., San Antonio, TX 78205, (512) 227-0253.

VERMONT

BRATTLEBORO—Kit Barry, 88 High St., Brattleboro, VT 05301, (802) 254-2195.

VIRGINIA

ALEXANDRIA—A. E. Steidel, 6167 Cobbs Rd., Alexandria, VA 22310.

ARLINGTON—Dick and Margie Stockton, 2331 N. Tuckahoe St., Arlington, VA 22205, (703) 534-5619.

CHESTERFIELD—Tom Morgan, 3501 Slate Ct., Chesterfield, VA 23832.

FREDERICKSBURG—White's Trading Post, Boutchyards Olde Stable, Falmouth, VA. 1903 Charles St., Fredericksburg, VA 22401, (703) 371-6252. Fruit jars, new and old bottles.

HINTON—Vic and Betty Landis, Rt. 1, Box 8A, Hinton, VA 22801, (703) 867-5959.

HUNTLY—Early American Workshop, Star Route, Huntly, VA 22640, (703) 635-8252. Milk bottles.

MARSHALL—John Tutton, Rt. 1, Box 261, Marshall, VA 22115, (703) 347-0148.

RICHMOND—Lloyd and Carrie Hamish, 2936 Woodworth Rd., Richmond, VA 23234, (804) 275-7106.

RICHMOND—Jim and Connie Mitchell, 5106 Glen Alden Dr., Richmond, VA 23234.

WASHINGTON

BELLEVUE—Don and Dorothy Finch, 13339 Newport Way, Bellevue, WA 98006, (206) 746-5640.

BREMERTON—Ron Flannery, 423 N.E. Conifer Dr., Bremerton, WA 98310, (206) 692-2619.

SEATTLE—John W. Cooper, 605 N.E. 170th St., Seattle, WA 96155, (206) 364-0858.

WISCONSIN

ARLINGTON—Mike and Carole Schwartz, Rt. 1, Arlington, WI 53911, (608) 846-5229.

MEQUON—Jeff Burkhardt, 12637 N. River Forest Cir., Mequon, WI 53092, (414) 243-5643.

MEQUON—Bor Markiewicz, 11715 W. Bonniwell Rd., Mequon, WI 53092, (414) 242-3968.

OSKOSH—Richard Schwab, 65-5 Lareen Rd., Oskosh, WI 54901, (414) 235-9962.

STEVENS POINT—Bill and Kathy Mitchell, 703 Linwood Ave., Stevens Point, WI 55431, (715) 341-1471.

WAUTOMA—George and Ruth Hansen, Rt. 2, Box 26, Wautoma, WI 54962, (414) 787-4893.

FOREIGN

CANADA

BADEN, ONTARIO—John and Sara Moore, Rt. 2, Baden, Ontario.

DOLLARD-DES-ORMEAUX, P.Q.—Richard Davis, 39 Brunswick #115, Dollard-Des-Ormeaux, P.Q., (314) 683-8522.

OTTAWA, ONTARIO—Paul Hanrahan, 292 Byron Ave. #2, Ottawa, Ontario, (613) 929-5675.

CENTRAL AMERICA

BELIZE CITY, BELIZE—Paul Hunt, Managing Director, Fort George Hotel, Belize Hotels Limited, Belize City, Belize.

BELIZE CITY, BELIZE—Emory King, 9 Regent Street, Belize City, Belize.

ENGLAND

TRENT—David Geduhon, Box 85, Cayuga Ind. & Burton-on-Trent, England.

YORKSHIRE—John Morrison, 33 Ash Grove, Leeds G., Yorkshire, England.

GLOSSARY

Amber-colored glass: Nickel was added in glass production to obtain this common bottle color. The theory was that the dark color would prevent the sun from spoiling the contents of the bottle.

Amethyst-colored glass: This is clear glass that has been exposed to the sun or a very bright light for a period of time, and has turned a light purple color. *Note*: Only glass containing manganese will turn purple. This glass has remained in production since 1800.

Applied lip: On older bottles (pre-1880), the neck was applied after removal from the blowpipe; the seams, therefore, ended below the top of the lip. This helps distinguish old bottles from new—if the seam ends below the top of the lip it is usually a handblown applied top; if it runs to the very top of the lip, the bottle was probably machine-made.

Aqua-colored glass: This is the natural color of glass. The shades of aqua depend on the iron oxide contained in the sand used in glass production. This type of glass was produced until the 1930s.

Black glass: Carbon was added in glass production to obtain this dark olive green color. This type of glass was produced between 1700–1880.

Blob seal: A popular way of identifying an unembossed bottle was to apply a molten coin-shaped blob of glass to the shoulder of the bottle, into which a seal with the logo or name of the distiller, date, or product name was impressed.

Blob top: A large thick blob of glass was placed around the lip of soda or mineral water bottles. The wire that held the stopper was seated below the blob and anchored the wire when the stopper was closed, to prevent carbonation from escaping.

Blowpipe: This is a long tube used by the blower to pick up the molten glass which is then either blown in mold or free blown outside a mold to create unlimited varieties of shapes.

Cobalt-colored glass: This color was used in the days of patented medicines and poisons to distinguish them from the rest of the bottles.

Ground pontil: This is the pontil scar that has been ground off.

Imperfections: Bubbles of all sizes and shapes, bent shapes and necks, imperfect seams, errors in spelling, and embossing increase rather than decrease the value of old bottles, providing these imperfections were formed as a part of the natural production of the bottle. The more imperfections, the greater the value.

Kick-up bottom: An indented bottom of any bottle is known as a "kick-up." This can vary from deep indentations to a very slight impression. Wine bottles as a group are usually indented.

Lady's leg: These were called by the manufacturers "long bulbous neck." The shape of the neck earned this type of bottle its nickname.

Milk glass: Tin is added in glass production to obtain this color, primarily used for cosmetic bottles.

Mold, full-height three-piece: The entire bottle was formed in the mold, and the two seams run the height of the bottle to below the lip on both sides.

Mold, three-piece dip: In this mold the bottom part of the bottle mold was one piece, and the top, from the shoulder up, was two separate pieces. Mold seams appear circling the bottle at the shoulder and on each side of the neck. These bottles date from 1806 to 1889.

Opalization: This is seen on the frosty bottle or variated color bottle that has been buried in the earth in mud or silt, and minerals in these substances have interacted with the glass of the bottle to create these effects. Many collectors place a high value on bottles of this type.

Pontil marks: To remove the newly blown bottle from the blowpipe, an iron rod with a small amount of molten glass was applied to the bottom of the bottle after the neck and lip were finished. A sharp tap removed the bottle from the pontil, leaving a jagged glass scar. This "pontil scar" can be either round, solid or ring-shaped. On better bottles, the jagged edges were ground down. These marks date from 1618 to 1866; also, some modern handblown bottles have them.

Pumpkinseed: A small round flat flask, often found in the western areas. Generally made of clear glass, the shape resembled nothing more than the seed of the grown pumpkin. These bottles are also known as "Mickies," "saddle flasks," or "two-bit ponies."

Round bottoms: Many soda bottles containing carbonated beverages were made of heavy glass, designed in the shape of a torpedo. This enabled the bottle to lie on its side, keeping the liquid in contact with the cork, and preventing the cork from drying and popping out of the bottle.

Sheared lip: In the early years of bottle making, after the bottle was blown, a pair of scissorlike shears clipped the hot glass from the blowpipe. Frequently no top was applied, and sometimes a slight flange was created. The sheared top is a usual feature of old patriotic flasks. These bottles were produced from 1800 to 1830.

Snap: A more effective way of detaching the blown bottle from the blowpipe was the "snap." This device, which made its appearance in the 1860s, was used to grip the blown bottle in a spring cradle in which a cup held the bottom of the bottle. The bottles, held in a snap during manufacture, have no pontil scars or marks but may have grip marks on the side.

Turn-mold bottles: These are bottles which were turned in forming in a mold containing a special solvent. The action of turning and the solvent erased all seams and mold marks, and imparted a higher luster to the finished bottle. As a group, most old wine bottles were made this way.

White mold, or whittle marks: Many molds used in the 1800s and earlier were carved of wood. Bottles formed in these molds have genuine "whittle marks." The same effect was also caused by forming hot glass in cold early morning molds; this combination caused "goose pimples" on the surface of these bottles. As the mold warmed, the later bottles were smooth. "Whittle mold" and "whittle mark" bottles are in demand and command high prices.

BIBLIOGRAPHY

Bangert, Albrecht, *Antiquitaten Glas,* Wilhelm Heyne Verlag Munchen, 1977.

Beck, Doreen, *The Book of Bottle Collecting,* Hamlin Publishing Group, Ltd., 1973.

Creswick, Alice M., *Redbook Number 5: The Collectors Guide to Old Fruit Jars,* 1986.

DeGrafft, John, *American Sarsaparilla Bottles,* 1980.

Drumbrell, Roger, *Understanding Antique Wine Bottles,* Antique Collectors Club, 1983.

Eikelberner, George and Serge Agadjanian, *The Compleat American Glass Candy Containers Handbook,* Adele Bowden, 1986.

Gardner, Paul Vickens, *Glass,* Smithsonian Illustrated Library of Antiques, 1979.

Garths Auctions, Inc., *Bottle Sale Catalogs,* 2690 Stratford Road, Delaware, OH 43015.

Glass Works Auctions, *Bottle Sale Catalogs,* P.O. Box 187, East Greenille, PA 18041.

Heckler, Norman, *Bottle Sale Catalogs,* Bradford Corner Road, Woodstock Valley, CT 06282.

———, *American Bottles in the Charles B. Gardener Collection,* Robert W. Skinner, Inc., 1975.

Holiner, Richard, *Collecting Barber Bottles,* Collector Books.

Hunter, Frederick William, *Stiegel Glass,* Dover Publications, New York, 1950.

Innes, Lowell, *Pittsburgh Glass 1797–1891,* Houghton Mifflin Company, Boston, 1976.

Ketchum, William C. Jr., *A Treasury of American Bottles,* Rutledge Books, 1975.

Klesse, Brigitt and Hans Mayr, *European Glass from 1500 to 1800, the Ernesto Wolf Collection,* Kremayr and Scheriau, 1987.

Knittle, Rhea Mansfield, *Early American Glass,* Garden City Publishing Company, 1948.

Kovill, William E. Jr., *Ink Bottles and Ink Wells,* William L. Sullwold, 1971.

Lee, Ruth Webb, *Antique Fakes and Reproductions,* Ruth Webb Lee, 1950.

McKearin, Helen and George S., *American Glass,* Crown Publishers, New York, 1956.

————, *Two Hundred Years of American Blown Glass,* Crown Publishers, 1950.

McKearin, Helen and Kenneth M. Wilson, *American Bottles and Flasks and Their Ancestry,* Crown Publishers, New York, 1978.

Namiat, Robert, *Barber Bottles with Prices,* Wallace Homestead Book Company, 1977.

Nielsen, Frederick, *Great American Pontiled Medicines,* The Cortech Corporation, Cherry Hill, NJ, 1978.

Northend, Mary Harrod, *American Glass,* Tudor Publishing Company, New York, 1940.

Pepper, Adeline, *The Glass Gaffers of New Jersey,* Charles Scribners Sons, New York, 1971.

Ring, Carlyn, *For Bitters Only,* The Nimrod Press, Inc., 1980.

Schwartz, Marvin D., "American Glass," from the pages of *Antiques* magazine, Volume 1; *Blown and Molded,* Pyne Press, Princeton, 1974.

Skinner's, Inc., *Bottle Sale Catalogs,* Route 117, Boston, MA 01740.

Sloan, Gene, *Perfume and Scent Bottle Collecting,* Wallace Homestead Book Company, 1986.

Spiegel, Walter Von, *Glas,* Battenberg Verlag, Munchen, 1979.

Spillman, Jane Shadel, *Glass Bottles, Lamps and Other Objects,* Alfred A. Knopf, New York, 1983.

Toulouse, Julian Harrison, *Bottle Makers and Their Marks,* Thomas Nelson Incorporated, 1971.

Tucker, Donald, *Collectors Guide to the Saratoga Type Mineral Water Bottles,* privately printed, 1986.

Tuckhaber, Bernard C., *Saratogas,* Bernard C. Tuckhaber.

Tutton, John, *Udderly Delightful,* John Tutton.

Umberger, Joe and Arthur L., *Collectible Character Bottles,* Corker Book Company, Tyler, TX, 1969.

Watson, Richard, *Bitters Bottles,* Thomas Nelson & Sons, 1965.

Webster, Donald Blake, *Decorated Stoneware Pottery of North America,* Charles E. Tuttle Company, Rutland, VT, 1985.

Wilson, Kenneth M., *New England Glass and Glass Making,* Thomas Y. Crowell Company, 1972.

Zumwalt, Betty, *Ketchup, Pickles, Sauces,* Mark West Publishers, 1980.

Index

About the Author

JIM MEGURA was an early glass and bottle consultant for Skinner, Inc., the fifth largest auction house in the United States and one of the top glass auction houses.

His interest in antiques began at an early age, and he has been a bottle collector and a member of a Connecticut bottle club for nearly thirty years. For several years he operated his own glass-blowing studio.

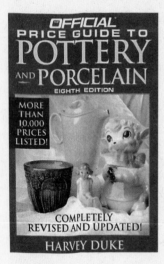